Implementing and Administering
Microsoft Project Server 2010

Gary L. Chefetz

Dale A. Howard

Tony Zink

D1294968

Implementing and Administering
Microsoft Project Server 2010

Copyright © 2010 Chefetz LLC dba MSProjectExperts

Publisher: Chefetz LLC dba MSProjectExperts
Authors: Gary L. Chefetz, Dale A. Howard and Tony Zink
Cover Design: Emily Baker
Copy Editor: Tim Clark
Cover Photo: Peter Hurley

ISBN: 978-1-934240-09-0

Library of Congress Control Number: 2010927826

Published and distributed by Chefetz LLC dba MSProjectExperts, 90 John Street, Suite 404, New York, NY 10038. (646) 736-1688 http://www.msprojectexperts.com

We provide the information contained in this book on an "as is" basis, without warranty. Although we make every effort to ensure the accuracy of information provided herein, neither the authors nor the publisher shall have any liability to any person or entity with respect to any loss or damage caused or allegedly caused directly or indirectly by the information contained in this work.

MSProjectExperts publishes a complete series of role-based training/reference manuals for Microsoft's Enterprise Project Management software including Microsoft Project and Microsoft Project Server. Use our books for self-study or for classroom learning delivered by professional trainers and corporate training programs. To learn more about our books and courseware series for Administrators, Implementers, Project Managers, Resource Managers, Executives, Team Members, and Developers, or to obtain instructor companion products and materials, contact MSProjectExperts by phone (646) 736-1688 or by email info@msprojectexperts.com.

Contents

Download the Extra Files xiv

Module 01 Introduction and Project Server Overview 1

Welcome 3

What's New for Project Server 2010 3

Introducing the Microsoft 2010 EPM Platform 6

    Applying EPM Terminology to Project Server 7

Understanding Project Server Terminology 7

    Enterprise Project 7

    Enterprise Resource 7

    Check In and Check Out 8

    Portfolio Analyses 8

    Portfolio Analysis 8

Enterprise Resource Pool Overview 8

Enterprise Global Overview 9

Understanding the EPM Platform Technology Stack 9

Project Server Installation Types 11

    Understanding Project Server Physical Environments 11

Understanding Databases in the Enterprise 13

Understanding the Project Communications Lifecycle 13

    Collaboration and Management Tools Overview 17

Module 02 Understanding the Human Challenge 19

Thinking Outside the Project 21

    Confronting the "PM" Challenge 22

    Why Do EPM Initiatives Fail? 23

Understanding the Formulas for Disaster 24

    Boiling the Ocean 25

    Managing One Big Project 25

    Suffering from Methodology Overload 26

    Serving the Technology Buffet 26

Preparing Strategies for EPM Deployment Success 27

    Understanding Your Stakeholders 28

    Understanding Your Organization's Culture 29

    Understanding and Making Management Commitments 31

    Understanding Your Process 34

    Acquiring or Improving Scheduling Competencies 35

Marketing Your Solution 35

Module 03 Applying a Deployment Process **37**

Understanding the Deployment Process 39

Defining Your Deployment and Deployment Team 40

Understanding the Analyst Role 43

Understanding Technical Roles 44

Rounding Out the Team 45

Managing the Discovery Phase 46

Discovery Phase Summary 46

Discovery Key Ingredients 47

Other Valuable Discovery Inputs 47

Discovery Next Steps 49

Determining your Implementation Archetype 49

Building Your Straw Man Requirements 51

Introducing the Requirements and Definition Template 52

Applying the Template to the Straw Man 53

Summarizing the Discovery Phase 53

Managing the Definition Phase 53

Definition Phase Summary 54

Core Requirements 54

Defining the Portfolio Organization 55

Defining the Project Organization 56

Defining the Task Organization 59

Defining the Resource Organization 59

Defining Working Times and Calendars 60

Defining Company Holidays 61

Defining Security Requirements 61

Defining Training Requirements 61

Determining System Notifications 62

Managing the Design Phase 62

Design Phase Summary 63

Determining System Design Information 63

Managing the Deployment Phase 67

Deploy Phase Summary 67

Managing the Pilot Phase 68

Pilot Phase Summary 69

Managing the Rollout Phase 69

Rollout Phase Summary 69

Contents

Module 04 Installing Project Server 2010 ....**71**

Installing Project Server 2010 Overview...73

Preparing to Install SharePoint Server and Project Server 2010 73

  Meet or Exceed Minimum Hardware Requirements...74

  Meet or Exceed Minimum Software Requirements..74

  Prepare the Security Environment...75

  Prepare SQL Server for SharePoint Server and Project Server 77

  Prepare SQL Server Analysis Services for Project Server 86

  Prepare Your Server for Project Server Installation 89

Installing SharePoint Server 2010 and Project Server 2010 90

  Install Software Prerequisites..90

  Install SharePoint Server 2010 Software 94

  Install Project Server 2010...97

  Run SharePoint Products Configuration Wizard 100

  Configure Your SharePoint Farm 106

Create a Project Server 2010 Web App 112

Creating a Service Application Manually 117

Module 05 Post-Installation Configuration **121**

Configuring SharePoint Service Applications 123

  Preparing to Configure Excel Services...123

  Configuring Excel Services 125

  Harvesting URLs for Trusted Data Connection Libraries and Report Libraries........................127

  Configuring Excel Services Global Settings...129

  Configuring Trusted Data Connection Libraries 131

  Configuring Trusted File Locations 132

  Configuring the Secure Store Service Application 136

Configuring the Cube Building Service..141

  Obtaining the Necessary Software Files..141

  Installing the SQL Server Native Client..142

  Installing the SQL Server Management Objects Collection 146

  Creating a SQL Login for the Service Account Running Analysis Services 149

Setting Optional SQL Server Performance Enhancements 151

  Creating Additional TempDB Files...152

Verifying Project Server Functionality...153

  Verifying Project Web App Connectivity..153

  Creating a Login Account in Project Professional 2010 154

  Performing Basic Functional Tests 158

  Verifying Cube Building Capability...165

Verifying Reporting Capability in the BI Center *168*

Creating Additional Project Server Instances 171

Configuring Your New Project Server Instance *173*

Creating a New Excel Services Application Instance *174*

Pointing Data Connections to the New Secure Store Target Application *176*

Module 06 Understanding the Project Web App Interface **181**

Tools for Configuration 183

Using the Project Web App User Interface 183

Logging into Project Web App from another Workstation *186*

Using the Quick Launch Menu *186*

Using the Ribbon Menus *188*

Manipulating the Data Grid *197*

Printing the Data Grid *200*

Exporting the Data Grid to Excel *201*

Using the Project Web App Administration Interface 202

Module 07 Creating System Metadata and Calendars **209**

Understanding Significant Changes to Project Server 2010 Metadata Architecture 211

Introducing Departments *211*

Introducing Project Types *213*

Introducing Business Drivers *214*

Working with Enterprise Custom Fields and Lookup Tables 214

Understanding Enterprise Field Types *215*

Understanding Built-In Fields and Lookup Tables *215*

Modifying Built-In Lookup Tables 218

Modifying the Cost Type Lookup Table *222*

Modifying the Health Lookup Table *223*

Modifying the RBS Lookup Table *224*

Creating the Team Names Lookup Table *226*

Creating and Modifying Custom Lookup Tables 228

Creating a New Lookup Table *229*

Modifying a Custom Lookup Table *233*

Creating Custom Fields 233

Creating Free Entry Custom Fields 234

Making Fields Required *236*

Creating a Custom Field with a Lookup Table 237

Modifying Built-In Project and Resource Department Fields *240*

Creating a Custom Field with a Formula 243

Understanding Field Types with Formulas *243*

Contents

Creating a Formula Using Project Web App 246

Creating a Formula Using Project Professional 2010 250

Importing a Local Field as a Custom Enterprise Field 257

Displaying Graphical Indicators in Custom Fields 259

Creating Graphical Indicators Using Project Web App 259

Creating Graphical Indicators Using Project Professional 2010 263

Understanding the Connection between Formulas and Graphical Indicators 266

Deleting a Custom Field or Lookup Table 267

Planning for Matching Generic Resources 268

Creating Enterprise Calendars 270

Setting Company Holidays 271

Setting the Daily Working Schedule 274

Creating a New Base Calendar 278

Importing a Base Calendar from a Project 280

Module 08 Configuring Lifecycle Management **283**

Understanding Lifecycle Management 285

Understanding Demand Management 285

Understanding Decision Management 285

Understanding Project Types and Lifecycle Management 286

Understanding Phases and Stages 287

Understanding Project Detail Pages 288

Understanding the Lifecycle Management Configuration Process 288

Creating Lifecycle Management Elements 289

Creating and Editing Project Detail Pages 296

Sample Project Detail Pages in Action 300

Creating Business Drivers 304

Configuring Workflow Phases 306

Configuring Workflow Stages 307

Creating Enterprise Project Templates 312

Creating an Enterprise Project Template Manually 312

Creating and Modifying Enterprise Project Types 314

Editing an Enterprise Project Type 319

Working with the Sample Workflow 319

Adapting the Sample Workflow for Your Needs 327

Configuring Project Workflow Settings 328

Working with the Dynamic Workflow Solution Starter 329

Deploying the Dynamic Workflow Solution Starter 330

Creating and Configuring a Dynamic Workflow Instance 331

Considerations for Working with the Dynamic Workflow Tool..334

Module 09 Building and Managing the Enterprise Resource Pool **337**

Enterprise Resource Pool Overview 339

    Understanding Enterprise vs. Local Resources...339

Understanding Enterprise Resource Types...340

Working with the Resource Center Data Grid..341

    Creating an Ad Hoc Filter..342

    Using AutoFilter 344

    Sorting the Data in the Grid 344

    Configuring Columns 345

    Applying Views 346

Creating Resources Using Project Professional 2010 346

    Entering General Information..350

    Changing Working Time..352

    Using the Custom Fields Page 361

    Creating Non-Work Resources 362

Editing Enterprise Resources Using Project Professional 2010 367

    Checking Out Enterprise Resources for Editing 368

Using Project Web App to Create an Enterprise Resource 369

    Setting Type Options 371

    Setting Identification Information Options...371

    Setting User Authentication Options 372

    Setting Assignment Attributes Options 372

    Setting Exchange Server Details Options 373

    Setting Departments Options 373

    Setting Resource Custom Fields Options..374

    Setting Security Options...374

    Setting Group Fields Options 375

    Setting Team Details Options 376

Mass Editing Enterprise Resources 376

    Bulk Editing Enterprise Resources 377

    Individually Editing Enterprise Resources by Batch 379

Adding Resources Using Active Directory Synchronization...382

Preparing to Import Enterprise Resources 384

    Importing Resources from Active Directory 386

    Importing Resources from Your Address Book 390

    Verifying a Windows Account for a Resource 392

    Preparing Custom Field Data 394

Importing Enterprise Resources 398

Contents

Deactivating an Enterprise Resource 400

Module 10 Initial Project Server Configuration **403**

Configuring Project Server 2010 405

Setting High-Level Enterprise Functionality 405

    Changing the Project 2007 Compatibility Mode 407

    Specifying Project Professional Versions 407

    Specifying Enterprise Settings Options 408

    Specifying Currency Settings Options 409

    Specifying Resource Capacity Settings 410

    Specifying the Resource Plan Work Day Option 410

    Specifying the Exchange Server Details Option 411

    Specifying Task Mode Settings 411

Configuring Exchange Server Synchronization 412

    Determine the Account running the Queue Service for Project Server 412

    Configure Exchange Server 412

    Create a Project Web App Account for each Exchange Client Access Server ... 413

    Configure Exchange Users 414

    Configure a Project Web App User for Exchange Server Synchronization .. 415

    Special Considerations for Test Environments 416

    Understanding How Exchange Synchronization Works 417

Configuring Alerts and Reminders 418

Setting Options for the OLAP Cube 420

    Configuring the OLAP Database 423

    Deleting an Existing OLAP Database 427

Configuring Event Handlers 428

Configuring the Quick Launch Menu 431

Module 11 Configuring Time and Task Tracking **437**

Understanding Tracking 439

Defining Financial Periods 439

Defining Time Reporting Periods 442

Configuring Timesheet Options 446

    Creating Line Classifications 446

    Setting Timesheet Options 447

Configuring Administrative Time 450

Disabling the Timesheet Functionality 452

Setting the Task Tracking Method 454

    Specifying the Tracking Method 456

    Locking Down the Tracking Method 460

Setting the Reporting Display..461

Protecting User Updates..461

Defining the Near Future Planning Window.................................462

Setting Up the Timesheet Page..463

Customizing the Tasks Page...466

Using Percent of Work Complete..466

Using Actual Work Done and Work Remaining............................470

Using Hours of Work Done per Period..471

Tips for Using Tracking Methods..472

Using Percent of Work Complete..472

Using Actual Work Done and Work Remaining............................473

Summary..473

Module 12 Configuring Project Server Security..............................**475**

Project Server Security Overview..477

Setting Organizational Permissions..477

Understanding Users vs. Resources..491

Users and Resources Can Be the Same Person..............................491

Managing User Accounts...492

Creating a New User Account...493

Editing User Information...498

Deactivating a User Account...499

Controlling Security with Groups and Categories..............................499

Associating Multiple Groups and Categories................................505

Understanding Built-in Groups..506

Understanding Built-in Categories..506

Understanding Permissions..509

Understanding Global Permissions and Category Permissions......509

Understanding Denied, Allowed and Not Allowed......................509

Understanding Permissions Cumulative Behavior.......................510

Managing Permissions through Groups..511

Creating a New Group...516

Deleting a Group..517

Managing Permissions through Categories..518

Creating a New Category...527

Deleting a Category..530

Using and Managing Security Templates..530

Creating a New Security Template...531

Deleting a Security Template..534

Contents

Managing AD Synchronization for Groups 534

Resolving Common Security Requirements 538

Module 13 Building the Project Environment **543**

Building the Project Environment 545

Importing Existing Projects and Templates 545

Publishing an Imported Project 555

Changing the Project Owner and Status Manager 556

Building the OLAP Cube 562

Module 14 Creating and Managing Views **565**

Understanding Views 567

Creating Gantt Chart Formats 568

Creating Grouping Formats 572

Managing Project Web App Views 575

Copying and Modifying Views 577

Deleting Views 578

Creating Custom Views in Project Web App 579

Creating a Custom Project View 580

Creating a Custom Project Center View 585

Creating a Custom Resource Assignments View 588

Creating a Custom Resource Center View 592

Modifying My Work Views 596

Creating a Custom Resource Plan View 600

Modifying a Team Tasks View 602

Creating a Custom Team Builder View 604

Modifying the Timesheet View 608

Creating a Portfolio Analyses View 609

Creating a Portfolio Analysis Project Selection View 613

Understanding Enterprise Views in Project Professional 2010 614

Working with the Enterprise Global File 615

Adding Custom Views to the Enterprise Global 616

Removing Pollution from the Enterprise Global 617

Using the 4-Step Method to Create a New View 619

Select or Create a Table 620

Select or Create a Filter 620

Select or Create a Group 620

Create the New Custom View 620

Creating Useful Enterprise Views 621

Creating an Enterprise Duration Variance View 621

xii

Creating an Enterprise Publishing View *631*

Creating an Enterprise Resource Sheet View *634*

Module 15 Managing Project Sites **641**

Introducing SharePoint 643

Understanding the SharePoint Model *644*

Managing the SharePoint/Project Server Connection 650

Managing Project Site Provisioning *650*

Managing Project Sites *653*

Bulk Updating Project Sites *656*

Modifying Project Sites 656

Managing List and Library Metadata *657*

Managing Views of List and Library Items *674*

Managing List and Library Settings *692*

Creating New Lists and Libraries *720*

Creating and Editing Pages *734*

Managing Project Site Settings *744*

Module 16 Configuring Business Intelligence and Reporting **763**

Reporting and Business Intelligence Overview 765

Reporting Architecture Overview 768

Relational Database Overview *768*

OLAP Database Overview *769*

Business Intelligence Center Overview 774

Understanding the Business Intelligence Center Site *774*

Built-In Microsoft Excel Reports Overview *779*

Business Intelligence Center Security Overview *779*

Microsoft SharePoint Excel Services Overview 780

Working With the Built-In Microsoft Excel Reports 782

Excel Sample Reports Overview *782*

Excel Report Templates Overview *784*

Excel Data Connection Files Overview *785*

Viewing the Sample Excel Reports in Your Web Browser *789*

Opening the Sample Excel Reports with Microsoft Excel *794*

Creating a Custom Excel Report by Modifying a Sample Report *796*

Creating a Custom Excel Report Based on a Template *798*

Common Methods of Modifying an Excel Pivot Report *800*

Creating a Custom Excel Report Using a Data Connection File *813*

Working with SharePoint Dashboards 821

Creating a Dashboard Page *821*

Embedding Excel Data into a Dashboard Page *823*

Adding Non-Project Server Users as Report Viewers 827

Module 17 Managing Project Server Day to Day **829**

Supporting Project Server 831

Performing Database Management through PWA 831

Checking in Enterprise Objects 831

Deleting Enterprise Objects 833

Deleting Enterprise Projects *834*

Deleting Resources and Users *837*

Deleting Status Report Responses *841*

Deleting Timesheets *842*

Deleting User Delegates *843*

Working with Administrative Backups 844

Setting an Automatic Daily Backup Schedule *845*

Backing Up Enterprise Objects Manually *846*

Restoring Backed-up Objects *847*

Changing or Restarting Workflows 850

Configuring and Managing the Queue 853

Understanding the Queue Process *854*

Understanding Job States *855*

Working with the Manage Queue Jobs Page *857*

Troubleshooting the Queue *861*

Configuring the Queue *862*

Monitoring Project Server Licenses 865

Monitoring and Troubleshooting Project Server 866

Working with Unified Logging Service (ULS) files *867*

Using the Reliability and Performance Monitor *872*

Configuring a SQL Server 2008 Maintenance Plan 873

Index **881**

Download the Extra Files

You can download the extras for this book from the following URL:

http://www.msprojectexperts.com/admin2010

Module 01

Introduction and Project Server Overview

Learning Objectives

After completing this module, you will be able to:

- Be familiar with the components in the Microsoft EPM platform

- Understand Project Server's enterprise project management terminology

- Be familiar with the Enterprise Resource Pool and the Enterprise Global file

- Describe the new features in Project Server 2010

- Understand the EPM platform technology stack

- Understand the Project Server 2010 installation types

- Name the databases used by Project Server 2010 and Windows SharePoint Services

- Describe the project communications life cycle used in Project Server

- Be familiar with Project Server team collaboration tools

- Understand the concept of publishing with Project Server

- Acquire an overview understanding of OLAP cubes and Data Analysis views

Inside Module 01

Welcome 3

What's New for Project Server 2010 3

Introducing the Microsoft 2010 EPM Platform...6

Applying EPM Terminology to Project Server 7

Understanding Project Server Terminology 7

Enterprise Project...7

Enterprise Resource...7

Check In and Check Out..8

Portfolio Analyses 8

Portfolio Analysis 8

Enterprise Resource Pool Overview **8**

Enterprise Global Overview **9**

Understanding the EPM Platform Technology Stack **9**

Project Server Installation Types **11**

Understanding Project Server Physical Environments 11

Understanding Databases in the Enterprise **13**

Understanding the Project Communications Lifecycle **13**

Collaboration and Management Tools Overview 17

Welcome

I have been waiting for this Project Server release for ten years. Project Server 2010 epitomizes the potential I saw for this new web-based project management information system when I first started using Project Central in 2000 after discovering it tucked away on my Microsoft Project 2000 installation CD (Installation CD, how quaint). Imagine that, a hidden goody shipped almost as an afterthought, becoming the defining industry-standard application in its space in under a decade. Working as a PMO Director for a major retailer at the time, little did I know then how much this application would change my life, and little did any of us, including Microsoft, know in the year 2000 how impactful this technology would become.

To appreciate Microsoft Project 2010 and Microsoft Project Server 2010 fully, you must also appreciate Microsoft SharePoint Server 2010 Enterprise Edition. Project Server 2010 is completely dependent on SharePoint Server 2010. Simply put, Project Server is now a SharePoint application. Project Server and SharePoint started dating in 2003. By the time Microsoft released the 2007 versions of these products, they were living together. With the introduction of Microsoft's 2010 Office computing platform, Project Server and SharePoint are married.

This is remarkable because SharePoint 2010 is revolutionary in what it brings to the office computing market. Never before have we seen the depth and breadth of capabilities SharePoint Server Enterprise provides in one centrally managed bundle. From records management, to document management, to collaboration and social networking technologies, there is no precedent for an office-computing platform with SharePoint's capacities; never has there been one completely prewired for business intelligence.

Despite the fact that the SharePoint Enterprise requirement has raised the price point for Microsoft EPM, it more than makes up for that with the benefits it provides. To understand the value that Microsoft EPM brings to the enterprise, you must also understand and appreciate the value that the SharePoint platform provides. It is important to understand this while evaluating the strategic investment, as well as understanding how to take advantage of these capabilities at a tactical level. More than ever, it is important for both technologists and non-technologists to know SharePoint in order to leverage and manage Project Server.

While I give you brief introductions to the various SharePoint Server technologies as you encounter them during the installation process in Module 4 and Module 5, you should endeavor to learn more about SharePoint's capabilities if you are evaluating Project Server for your organization. If you are a Project Server administrator, you simply have no choice but to dive in. Now is the time to improve your SharePoint knowledge.

What's New for Project Server 2010

This is a big topic, probably enough for a book a quarter of the size of this one. You learn all about every new feature as you work your way through this book. Perhaps the most important thing to know first about what's new in Project Server is what is not new. The Project Server 2010 back-end processing engine is not new for 2010, the way it was for 2007. Rather, it is an improved and extended version of its 2007 predecessor. This is actually good news, because back-end rewrites tend to cause all kinds of bug fall-out and resulting instability of early releases. This is not a problem for 2010. Moreover, Microsoft employed a new customer-forward strategy by moving early builds of Project Server 2010, along with SharePoint and the entire Office product family, into the hands of community users and customers for early feedback. As a result, the entire 2010 product wave from Microsoft is of equal quality or better than the quality precedent Microsoft set with the release of Windows 7. Like Windows 7, this is a first release build that you can trust before the first service pack. It is about time, Microsoft!

To a large degree, Project Server 2010 is a front-end rewrite. Microsoft framed its investments in this version by casting eight vision areas (investment areas), as follows:

- **Demand Management**: Provide the ability to capture and manage project proposals in a central place and manage the requests through a defined governance lifecycle through user-manageable workflows.

- **Portfolio Analysis**: Provide the ability to analyze project proposals against definable business measures, including strategic alignment, cost constraints, resource constraints and custom user-definable attributes in order to drive intelligent business decisions in prioritizing and selecting projects for execution. The significant outcome of this vision area was the integration of Portfolio Server capabilities into Project Server as a single platform.

- **Enterprise Development Management and Improved Developer Experience**: Focused on improving the developer experience by making it easier to develop and deploy workflow driven processes, removing active-X dependencies, providing a read/write API for Portfolio Management services, and retraining backwards compatibility with existing applications. Part of this was developing and standardizing on the new AJAX grid control.

- **Enterprise Metadata and Business Intelligence**: Provide an accessible approach to reporting in Project Server, traditionally a weak spot for the application. The result of this vision area is the new integration with Excel Services and the BI Center in SharePoint Server, which also leverages Performance Point Services for KPI management. Power users can now easily attach Excel workbooks to data connections to the reporting database and OLAP cubes in Project Server to build rich reports and graphs using a familiar tool.

- **Time and Task Progressing**: An effort to make time and task tracking more flexible and more robust using both the Tasks page and Timesheet capabilities in Project Web App. These improvements include a new *Single Entry* mode that provides users a one-click option for submitting time and task progress, as well as the flexibility to run the system using a *Freeform* tracking method that allows users to decide what to report and can even provide complete flexibility with reporting periods.

- **Server Administration**: This investment area included ease of deployment and upgrade, as well as the integration into the SharePoint Service Application architecture. Further, Microsoft added *Department* fields for system-wide data filtering. Project Server 2010 also provides a more robust mechanism for allowing users to take actions in the system on behalf of other users called *Delegates*.

- **Enhanced Project Management**: Includes providing the ability for light-weight project management tasks without the requirement for the Project client, providing the ability to publish projects to SharePoint sites rather than Project Server, and enabling better project schedule collaboration.

- **Project Management in Enterprise**: Making it easier for users to create, save and publish a project by providing a server-based method to complement the client tool and by enhancing resource management capabilities.

My summary of these investment areas may have left out a nugget or two in Microsoft's vision, but it should be enough to give you a good idea how of Microsoft approached the 2010 release. In the end, I give Microsoft high marks for both the focus with which it approached the investment areas and for the success it achieved in execution. The following sums up my take on these:

To me, **Demand Management** understates the achievement the product team accomplished, even if it does not understate the original goal. Yes, Microsoft gives us a great way to collect demand for project work, and follows this accomplishment nicely with the *Portfolio Analysis* vision area with the integration of former Portfolio Server capabilities into Project Server; but the usability of the toolset goes way beyond *Demand Management*, providing full *Lifecycle* management capabilities. Workflow-driven project proposal development is the headline actor in this vision area. It allows Project Server administrators to implement process-driven steps to gathering proposal data, requiring or not requiring approval steps through the process per an organization's requirements. A spectacular rewrite to PWA that allows you to display multiple pages containing proposal and project information called *Project Detail Pages*, which you display at specific stages for a project governed by workflow, enhances this capability. These tools do not stop working at the end of the proposal selection process. In fact, you can use these tools to maintain workflow control of the project through an entire user-definable project lifecycle, including a post-mortem and archiving activities. The ability to create and manage an entire project lifecycle is a very important new feature in Project Server 2010.

The ***Portfolio Analysis*** vision area was a "no-brainer" in the sense that the Portfolio Server capabilities had to be integrated into Project Server, at least for me to take seriously the value proposition that *Project Server is a complete Portfolio and Project management system*. As a stand-alone product, Portfolio Server impressed me the first time I saw it as a third-party solution, but it did not get very far past a "third-party feel" until Project Server 2010. Now you have fully integrated capabilities in a common interface.

Inasmuch as I am not a developer, it is difficult for me to offer opinions on the success of the ***Enterprise Development Management and Improved Developer Experience*** vision area, but my colleagues seem pleased, particularly with improvements to Visual Studio 2010 that make developing for SharePoint and Project Server much easier. You can learn more about these improvements in Stephen Sanderlin's book, *Developer's Guide to Project Server 2007 and 2010*, ISBN # 978-1-934240-08-3.

Enterprise Metadata and Business Intelligence represents an area of big changes for Project Server. I used to dread when potential new customers asked me about reporting in Project Server. Clearly, this was not one of Project Server's strengths in prior editions, as getting at data required significant database and development skills. By leveraging SharePoint's commitment to business intelligence and reporting, Project Server now has a virtually unlimited reporting capability. The big story here is that you now build reports using Excel workbooks connected to reporting database or to OLAP cubes. Further, Project Server now supports multiple OLAP cubes containing different subsets of enterprise data. A big improvement in the metadata story for Project Server 2010 is the implementation of a master content filtering system based on *Department* fields that allow you to segregate data based on the audience. All of these combine to make your Project Server reporting possibilities vast and extensible for 2010. If you leverage some of SharePoint's other BI tools, such as Business Connectivity Services, your users will be building reports that not only contain beautifully presented EPM data, but also pull in data from LOB systems.

Time and Task Progressing is another area with big changes for Project Server 2010. While I appreciate the flexibility that *Free Form* task tracking and user-definable time periods introduce to Project Server, I still shudder at the thought of implementing these. While my rational mind tells me that these settings enable more business cases, the thought takes some getting used to! A very big change to Project Server 2010 includes the ability to run the timesheet system in single-entry mode so that a single submission of a timesheet feeds both the timekeeping system and project tracking all at once. What required the implementation of an additional solution in 2007 is as easy as selecting a check box in 2010.

I am not convinced that ***Server Administration*** gets much easier for Project Server 2010. Firstly, there is so much more to configure and administer, it is difficult to imagine how things get easier when the system is expanding in many directions. For example, the first part of the server installation is easier in that SharePoint now provides a prerequisites tool that locates, downloads and installs the server prerequisites for you, a tedious job eliminated from the 2007 implementation experience. While this makes installing the software bits much faster and friendlier, you have a lot more to do to configure all the SharePoint service applications you now use in 2010. This is a matter of trade-offs, I suppose. While some things get easier, you have more to manage when you deploy Project Server 2010 than you did when you deployed 2007.

Enhanced Project Management is a very big area of improvement for Project 2010 and Project Server 2010. This investment area includes some of the most dramatic changes to the Project client ever included in a single release. The most dramatic of these is *Manually Scheduled* tasks. Microsoft Project now supports manually controlled scheduling, a 180-degree paradigm shift from all previous versions. This new capability provides an easier on-ramp to project management for users who currently choose Microsoft Excel as their primary project management tool. It also provides the ability to support top-down planning in Microsoft Project and to better accommodate less-structured scheduling practices and methodologies such as SCRUM and other agile methods. Other enhancements in this area include the *Team Planner* view in Project that allows you to drag unassigned tasks to available resources, rather than the traditional Microsoft Project model of assigning resources to tasks.

Finally, the **Project Management in Enterprise** investment area contains major changes for Project Server. When you drill down into a project from the Project Center in Project Server 2010, you can now open and edit your projects through Internet Explorer. This change is to Project Server what manually scheduled tasks are to Project, a complete paradigm shift. Your ability to edit projects through the web is surprisingly rich, with many fewer restrictions than I first imagined. This facility is perfect for creating powerful collaborative scheduling scenarios. The ability to edit projects on the web is just so convenient! How did we live without this for so many years?

There are many small subtle changes in the system, and you learn about these in each of the following modules in this book. The above discussion highlights only the major changes and improvements in the system.

Introducing the Microsoft 2010 EPM Platform

Microsoft uses the term EPM to refer to its offering of tools for coordinating and standardizing project management functionality in the Enterprise. The EPM platform facilitates project collaboration between project managers, team members, executives, and other stakeholders. This toolset includes:

- Microsoft Project Professional 2010
- Microsoft Project Server 2010
- Project Web App 2010 (Part of Project Server)
- Microsoft Windows SharePoint Foundation 4.0
- Microsoft SQL Server
- Microsoft SQL Server Analysis Services
- Microsoft SQL Reporting Services
- Microsoft SharePoint Server 2010 Enterprise

When you implement Microsoft EPM, you employ all of these technologies across a Windows server farm consisting of one or more servers. The number of servers you use depends on the scale of your deployment, determined in part by the number of system users, the number of projects to support, and the amount of associated content you plan to store in your EPM environment.

This book does not extensively cover Microsoft SharePoint Server Enterprise, but the extent to which you intend to use it is an important consideration for almost everyone evaluating Microsoft EPM. Microsoft SharePoint Server (MSS) is an approachable platform for building enterprise content management solutions, including portals, communities, document management sites, and much too much to describe in a sentence.

Applying EPM Terminology to Project Server

In the world of enterprise project management, you hear terms like project, program, and portfolio. How do these terms apply to your organization's project management environment? Unless I otherwise note, this book accepts the Project Management Institute (PMI) definition of a **project**: "a temporary endeavor undertaken to create a unique product or service." A project is temporary, meaning that it has a beginning and an end. A project is unique, meaning that it is something that your organization has not done before.

For the purposes of this book, a **program** is "a collection of related projects" and a **portfolio** is "a collection of programs and/or projects within a business unit or across an entire enterprise." Many companies have their own interpretation of these terms, reflecting their approach to project management. Sometimes the sheer size of the organization drives these definitions.

The concept of a portfolio is flexible, depending on the size of the company. A smaller organization may have a single portfolio of projects, whereas a larger business may conceive of an enterprise portfolio made up of numerous departmental or line-of-business portfolios, each containing its own set of programs and projects. Regardless of how a business conceives these terms, you can model them in Project Server.

Understanding Project Server Terminology

Two terms that you must understand in the context of the Project Server 2010 environment are **enterprise project** and **enterprise resource**. Very specific criteria determine whether a project is an enterprise or non-enterprise project, and whether a resource is an enterprise or local resource. In addition, you must also understand how to **check in** and **check out** a project.

Enterprise Project

A project is an **enterprise project** when one of the following two conditions is true:

- You create the project using the Project Professional 2010 client while connected to Project Server 2010 and save the project in the Project Server database.

- You import the project to the enterprise using the *Import Project Wizard* in Project Professional 2010.

It is not possible to create an enterprise project in any other manual way, because all enterprise projects are stored in the Project Server database. Any project not stored in the Project Server database, such as a project saved as an .mpp file, is termed a non-enterprise project or a local project.

Enterprise Resource

A resource is an **enterprise resource** when one of the following two conditions is true:

- You create the resource in the Enterprise Resource Pool using the Project Professional 2010 client while connected to Project Server 2010, or you create the resource using Project Web App.

- You import the resource into the Enterprise Resource Pool using the *Import Resources Wizard* in Project Professional 2010.

If a resource exists in an enterprise project but does not exist in the Enterprise Resource Pool, then this resource is termed a **local resource**, meaning that it is local to the particular project only.

Check In and Check Out

The terms **check in** and **check out** apply to enterprise projects, enterprise resources, the Enterprise Global file and other objects in the Project Server system. A user must check out any of these before editing, so that others have read-only access until the user checks them in.

Portfolio Analyses

When you encounter this term in Project Server it refers to the collection of individual analysis studies performed by various users in the system to determine the viability of proposed project investments in the system.

Portfolio Analysis

The term **portfolio analysis** refers to an analysis of a batch or group of projects in the system for the purposes of selecting projects for execution by best matching the strategic objectives of the organization and fit within resource and cost constraints set by management consensus. Project Server 2007 uses this term to identify a type of view built against an OLAP cube but it is not used in that context in Project Server 2010.

Enterprise Resource Pool Overview

A centralized Enterprise Resource Pool is the centerpiece of advanced resource management functionality in Project Server. This resource pool contains resources and resource attribution that drives functionality to match people to tasks using skills comparisons or other attributes based on department, location or other criteria that you configure in the system. You must define these resource attributes in enterprise custom fields using the facilities provided in Project Web App administration. Typical resource attribution can contain all manners of details, such as practice groups, location, department, or any other company-specific information that project and resource managers use to assign resources to task assignments. You can use these same management tools to drive reporting and analysis. After defining custom fields for your organization, your Project Server administrator assigns values to these fields to each resource in the enterprise resource pool.

After you complete the task planning process in Project Professional 2010, you begin the resource management process by building a team for your project using resources from the Enterprise Resource Pool. Initial resource management activities include assembling the project team and making specific task assignments. Using team-building tools such as the *Build Team from Enterprise* dialog and the *Assign Resources* dialog, Project Server 2010 allows you to locate resources by both skill and availability, even if you are using a large resource pool. This simplifies the project staffing process not only by leveraging the custom attributes in the pool, but also by providing instant access to availability data enhanced with graphical representations of current and future workload and availability.

In addition to manual staffing tools, Project Server also offers you an automated staffing tool; the *Resource Substitution Wizard*. This wizard rapidly analyzes the resources in the Enterprise Resource Pool to identify skills and availability for staffing a single project or a group of projects. You can save the resulting staffing results as a recommendation for input into manual team building or directly update the results into the working plan.

Enterprise Global Overview

Every time a project manager launches Project Professional 2010 and connects to Project Server, the system opens a copy of two global files in the background. One is the Global.mpt file and the other is the Enterprise Global file. Both Global files contain a library of project objects including views, tables, filters, groups, reports, etc.

The Global.mpt file contains the standard set of project objects shipped with the Project Professional 2010 client, as well as any custom objects created by the individual user to whom the profile belongs. The Enterprise Global file is your organization's "library" of custom enterprise objects. This gives your project managers access to all custom objects stored for enterprise-wide use, including custom enterprise views. The Enterprise Global file is the vehicle through which an organization can standardize objects across a user population.

Understanding the EPM Platform Technology Stack

Previous versions of Project Server leveraged Windows SharePoint Services (WSS) to provide management of issues and risks, to provide collaborative tools native to WSS, and to integrate content stored in document libraries. The integration between the two applications was rough but functional. With the release of the 2010 version, Project Server is now a service running under the SharePoint umbrella, and its web interface is now a Windows SharePoint application.

Because Project Server 2010 Web App is a Windows SharePoint application, you can no longer implement Project Server without first installing Windows SharePoint Server Enterprise. If you do not have WSS Enterprise preinstalled on your server, it installs with your Project Server installation. You can now manage many system functions such as IIS and server event logging directly through SharePoint Central Administration.

You must procure a copy of Microsoft Project 2010 Professional for each user who manages projects in the EPM system and requires the advanced scheduling capabilities found only in the Microsoft Project client; for each application administrator; and possibly for other managers depending upon the responsibilities you define for their role. The most common extended use requirement is for Resource Managers to take on resource management responsibilities that require the Project client. Understand that there are two available editions of Microsoft Project 2010, just as there were for 2003. Along with some feature differentiators, the primary difference between the two editions is that the Standard edition cannot connect to Project Server whereas the Professional edition can. If you do not intend to implement Project Server, you may not need to purchase the more expensive professional edition unless you want features such as the Team Planner and the ability to publish projects to SharePoint without third-party tools.

 You must use Project 2010 Professional to connect to Project Server 2010. You can also use Project Professional 2007 to connect to Project Server 2010, but only in *Backward Compatibility* mode, which is available only when you upgrade a Project Server 2007 implementation. Project Professional 2010 is **not compatible** with any earlier version of Project Server.

One of the most compelling technologies you must acquire with the EPM mix is Microsoft Office SharePoint Server 2010 (MSS), previously called Portal Server. MSS provides a rich set of content management tools, including rich document versioning and a new workflow engine that allows you to bake best-practice process into the content store. The new MSS capabilities open the door to building solutions that control workflow at the deliverable level, reducing the need to capture these individual steps in the work breakdown structure and providing the capability of gathering progress data without relying upon resources to report it. You should evaluate the inclusion of MSS early in your deployment planning, as it is a feature-rich and powerful tool.

Microsoft's Office technologies suite, including MSS combined with Project Server and Microsoft Office desktop tools, as well as other data integration technologies, provide the tools necessary to build complete Enterprise Content Management (ECM) solutions. As is typical for Microsoft, the price points for these technologies make them accessible to a much broader audience by removing the cost barriers set by other vendors whose products are unapproachable for all but large companies that can entertain seven-figure technology investments. For this reason, you should carefully consider how to leverage other benefits by deploying the 2010 Office desktop technologies, which feature tighter integration to the latest SharePoint technologies. This is particularly an important consideration if you plan to make heavy use of SharePoint collaboration tools.

When you deploy the Microsoft 2010 EPM platform, you commit yourself to a number of supporting Microsoft technologies at the most basic level, and you have options to deploy an extended set of closely related and generally related Microsoft technologies as well. For instance, a basic Project Server implementation includes Windows Server, SQL Server, SQL Analysis Server, Windows SharePoint Server, Internet Information Services, and the Dot Net Framework 3.5. In addition to this base configuration, you can elect to add SQL Reporting Services, additional service applications that are part of Microsoft SharePoint Server, and other 2010 Office components. Figure 1 - 1 shows the technology stack with the core technologies in the darker shaded boxes. Note that I include Analysis Services and SQL Reporting Services in the SQL Server layer. These are not required, but you can implement them at no extra charge if you maintain them on a single SQL Server box.

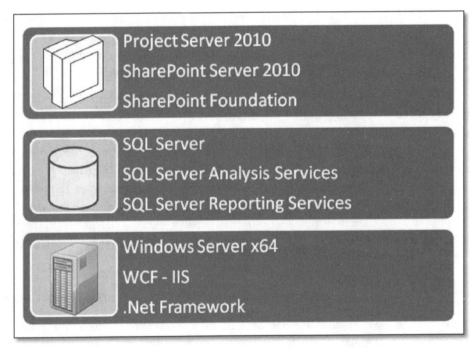

Figure 1 - 1: Technology Stack

Yes, it is a lot of software! However, the breadth and the strength of the Microsoft SharePoint Server collaboration platform give the Microsoft EPM platform its greatest competitive advantage. No other EPM product supports the range of solutions that the Microsoft 2010 EPM platform can support. In fact, it is difficult even to refer to any of the competing products as a "platform," while there is no question that Microsoft provides a customizable solution platform. This is an important distinction to remember when comparison-shopping.

For your consideration, a number of Microsoft partners provide connector solutions for integrating Microsoft EPM to various popular ERP systems including the Microsoft Dynamics solutions.

Project Server Installation Types

When you install Microsoft Project Server 2010, you have two primary implementation choices: Stand-Alone and Server Farm. The important distinction between these two types is functionality, as the stand-alone implementation is limited. Server Farm implementations are scalable from small to large, and you can deploy a server farm on a single server, but the ideal scenario is to at least provide separation between your application (web) server and your database server.

Stand-Alone – This type of implementation installs Project Server onto a single server using default settings and SQL Server 2008 Express. It does not activate all of the enterprise capability that a server farm implementation does and is appropriate for very small organizations. For instance, SQL Express does not support Analysis services, so you lose your most interesting reporting source by going this route. I do not specifically cover Stand-Alone implementations, because the subject matter of this book focuses on enterprise solutions. Understand that stand-alone implementations are limited in functionally and scalability.

Server Farm – Server Farm implementations include all of Project Server's enterprise features, requiring that you use a full version of SQL Server such as SQL Server 2005 or SQL Server 2008. Project Server is specifically dependent on Microsoft database technologies. You cannot use other branded database applications such as Oracle or IBM DB2. You can implement a server farm on one or more servers and expand the farm as your needs grow. I recommend that you always use at least two servers for production implementations, including a dedicated server for SQL Server and a separate dedicated machine to host your SharePoint/Project Server applications.

Understanding Project Server Physical Environments

Because Project Server and SharePoint are inseparable, and because of the compelling value-add that including MSS in the technology mix brings to the table, it is very likely that you will consider the benefits of SharePoint in your requirements when designing and building your physical environment. While it is possible to implement Project Server 2010 on a single box, Microsoft does not recommend a single-box deployment, and you may experience performance problems or service synchronization issues when taking this approach.

If you do install an enterprise configuration on a single box, be sure to implement the special instructions I include in Module 05 to ensure that your environment is stable. In my experience, you can deploy this way for evaluation implementations, but you should strongly consider using one box for SQL Server and a second box for your application services, as illustrated in Figure 1 - 2. This configuration gives you separation between the application and data environments, providing greater stability and serviceability.

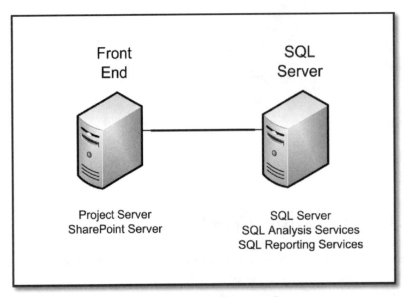

Figure 1 - 2: Two-server implementation

Your next option is to consider a higher-availability solution, which requires twice as many servers. Figure 1 - 3 shows a four-box implementation where the application servers are Network Load Balanced (NLB) and include failover clustered SQL Servers. This configuration provides inherent failover capability, whereby if one frontend server fails the other remains available, with the same for the SQL backend. I strongly recommend a high-availability solution if you plan to implement with MSS. While you might be able to absorb downtime on your EPM platform, if you also use MSS to manage other content, your platform uptime becomes more critical.

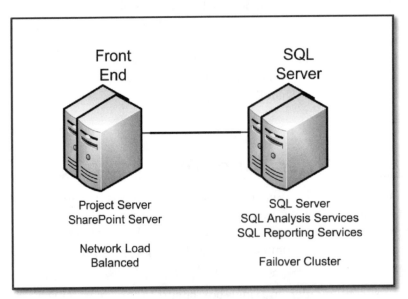

Figure 1 - 3: High Availability Configuration

This is by no means an exhaustive exploration of potential architecture configurations. When you deploy Windows SharePoint Server enterprise edition, you have numerous architectural decisions to consider. The more feature you deploy, and the more users you deploy to, will ultimately determine your server size, count and configuration.

Understanding Databases in the Enterprise

The database structure in Project Server 2010 is the same as it was for 2007. Project Server uses four distinct databases to represent and manage project data. This arrangement provides data management granularity through a well-defined data flow. Each database serves a specific purpose. Because Microsoft now provides a distinct database for reporting purposes and a much more functional Advanced Programming Interface (API) called the Project Services Interface (PSI), it provides documentation for the reporting database only. Microsoft recommends that consumers never directly use the other three databases for reporting or building additional system functionality, and doing so can disqualify Microsoft supportability. The four databases used by Project Server 2010 are as follows:

- **Draft** – When Project Managers first save a project plan, the system saves it to the draft database, where it is not visible to users through Project Web App until the manager publishes the plan. The copy of the plan in the Draft database is always the working version. When project managers modify their project plans, the system saves the changes only to the Draft database until the project manager explicitly publishes the changes.

- **Published** – When project managers publish project data, the system writes the information to the Published database, which contains all published projects viewable in PWA. It also contains enterprise resources, the enterprise global records and project templates. The system also stores Project-Web-Access-specific tables, such as security and timesheet information, in the Published database

- **Archive** – The Archive database contains backup project plans and other server objects that the system allows you to back up, as well as prior versions of project plans.

- **Reporting** – When project managers publish project data, the system writes the information to the Reporting database. The Reporting database contains a de-normalized set of tables designed to make project data reporting easier for end users who mine and retrieve data in the system. It provides near real-time information for reporting purposes. This is the only Project Server database Microsoft documents in its Software Developer's Kit (SDK).

In addition to the four databases used by Project Server 2010, the system also includes two Windows SharePoint Services Databases:

- **WSS Configuration** – Required for SharePoint Server and Project Server 2010, this database defines the WSS farm.

- **WSS Content** – Required for Project Server 2010, this database contains the SharePoint content data for the Project Server instance, including documents, risks, issues, deliverables and other content that users create or upload to the SharePoint sites created for each project published in the Project Server system.

Understanding the Project Communications Lifecycle

Project Server's core functionality provides a cyclical assignment and update process between project managers and team members. This cycle is the heart of Project Server's work and resource management system. Work assignments flow from the plan to resources performing the work, and resources report progress data back to the plan. This project communication cycle flows through the following steps:

1. The project manager saves the project plan in the Project Server database, as illustrated in Figure 1 - 4. This action saves the project in the Draft database only. Project information is not visible in the Project Center and assignments are not visible to Team Members.

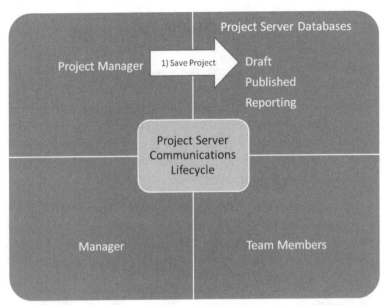

Figure 1 - 4: Save the project in Project Server Draft database

2. When the project manager publishes a project, as illustrated in Figure 1 - 5, the system writes the project data to the Published and Reporting databases. If you enable Project Server's notification feature, Project Server optionally activates a messaging service and sends an email to each resource notifying them of their new task assignments. Using an embedded link in the email message, team members can quickly click to view their task assignments in the project through Project Web App or through Outlook. Publishing makes project data visible in the *Project Center* and *Project Detail* views, and the project data is included in the next cube build.

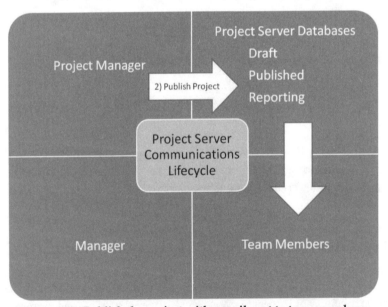

Figure 1 - 5: Publish the project with e-mail sent to team members

3. At the end of each reporting period, team members optionally update their timesheets, if you enable time-sheets in your configuration. They then update their actual progress on the project and send the updates to the Project Manager via the Project Web App interface as illustrated in Figure 1 - 6. Actual progress includes completion percentages and/or hours worked on each task, based on the organization's reporting method.

The updates are visible to the project manager, but the updates do not flow into the plan until the project manager accepts the updates in the next step or unless the project manager uses automation rules.

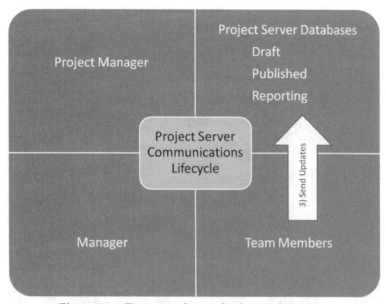

Figure 1 - 6: Team members submit actual progress

4. The project manager receives and reviews each set of task updates from project team members as illustrated in Figure 1 - 7. The project manager can individually accept or reject each task update or process them in total or in batches using automation tools.

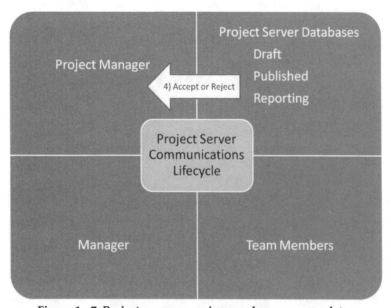

Figure 1 - 7: Project manager reviews and processes updates

5. After accepting or rejecting each task update, the project manager saves the latest schedule changes in the Draft database. After saving the project, the project manager publishes the latest project schedule changes to the Published and Reporting databases, as illustrated in Figure 1 - 8. This makes the schedule changes visible

in the *Project Center*, the Reporting database, the OLAP cubes, and the *Timesheet* and *Tasks* pages for team members.

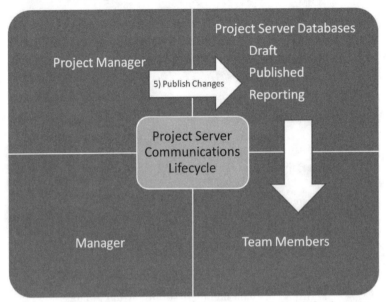

Figure 1 - 8: Project manager publishes the latest schedule changes

6. At any time throughout the life of the project, executives within the organization can view all projects or individual projects in the organization's portfolio, as illustrated in Figure 1 - 9. Project Server provides numerous view entry points, including the *Project Center*, which is also the gateway to detailed project views, and the *Resource Center*, which provides resource data and a gateway to resource details. In addition, Project Server provides a rich data analysis theater leveraging SQL Analysis Services.

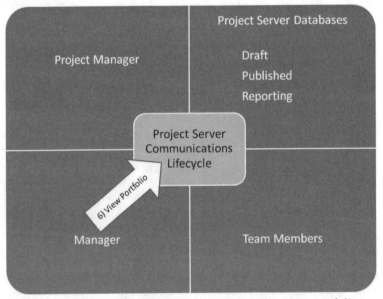

Figure 1 - 9: Executives view the organization's project portfolio

Project Managers can create automation rules to process updates from resources automatically. Project Managers can use a combination of rules and manual actions to maintain their projects by accepting updates from resources.

Collaboration and Management Tools Overview

Beyond the core communication between project managers and project team members, Project Server provides additional features for project team collaboration. Some of these features are native to Project Server, whereas others leverage integration with Windows SharePoint Server (WSS) and Windows SharePoint Foundation. The features that are native to Project Server include:

- **Status Reports** – Status Reports allow project managers, resource managers, and executives to establish single or periodic status reports to which team members must respond. Team members may also create their own unrequested reports and submit them at any time. The status report feature can save a manager time, as it automatically compiles a team report from individual responses.

- **Automated Alerts and Reminders** – Project Server features an automated reminder system that generates email notices for a variety of situations, including reminding team members of upcoming and overdue task work, and of status reports that are due. In addition to reminders, alerts provide instant notification when certain events occur, such as a new task assignment. All users have the ability to set their own alerts and reminders, and managers have the added ability to set reminders for their resources.

- **Exchange Integration** – This feature allows users to display Project Web App tasks on the Outlook task list and status the tasks using the percent complete method.

- **Task Reassignment** – The system supports a team lead structure where functional leaders participate in the work distribution and management process. If the project manager enables task reassignment for team members in a project, team members can transfer work to each other, subject to the project manager's approval.

- **Ad hoc Reporting** – You can quickly print information from data grids in Project Web App, selecting and ordering fields and formatting the results. You can also export grid data and analysis cube data to Excel for additional manipulation and reporting.

- **Issues** – Team members log and track project issues from creation to resolution using the Project Server Issues list created as part of each project's Project Workspace. You can link issues to risks, tasks, documents, and other issues. The links create indicators that appear in the Project Center views, where the system flags a project with an icon indicating it contains issues. Similarly, the system flags tasks in Project views when they have issues linked to them.

- **Risks** – Team members can identify, prioritize, and track project risks using the Issues List created as part of each project's workspace. Risks use a different field array than issues, but each function the same when it comes to linking and the flagging that the system performs in response.

- **Documents** – Project Web App provides a general public document library available to all system users. The public document library is an excellent place to make common process documentation available as part of a standardized environment. Each project has its own document library within the Project Workspace into which users can load documents and link them to tasks, issues, risks and other documents in the system.

- **Project Proposals** – System users can create and submit project proposals for consideration and approval. This feature enables the enterprise to build a demand-management system for new projects in the enterprise. You can tailor the approval process to meet your organization's workflow.

- **Resource Plans** – Used in conjunction with project proposals and projects, resource plans provide a means to estimate and measure future resource loads.

- **Time Sheets** – Timesheets provide enterprise users with fully functional time reporting capabilities that can collect time at any reporting level. Most importantly, the timesheet feature includes the ability to create a full audit trail, allowing system implementers to create regulatory-compliant solutions. You can use timesheet data to drive task progress or maintain this data without using it to drive task updates. You can also use the *Tasks* page to collect task progress as in previous versions of Project Server.

- **Deliverables** – Project managers can define deliverables linked to tasks that other project managers can consume in their projects, thereby creating a new of way cross-linking projects. With the addition of Microsoft Office SharePoint Server (MSS) to the server farm, previously known as Microsoft Office Portal Server, managers can apply SharePoint workflows to the deliverables. Workflows are new in the 2010 version of MSS.

The modules that follow walk you through the deployment process in a logical systematic workflow. Each module builds upon the learning of the previous module to increase your understanding of the toolset and provides you with the learning necessary for each step of the deployment process. Now that you have a high-level overview of how the Microsoft EPM technologies work together to provide a complete solution, you must understand the non-technical challenges, the human side of the equation. By far the most challenging aspect of an EPM deployment is user acceptance and adoption. The next module provides you insight into these challenges.

Module 02

Understanding the Human Challenge

Learning Objectives

After completing this module, you will be able to:

- Understand organizational challenges to implementing EPM
- Understand necessary change management commitments
- Understand how EPM deployments can psychologically influence your user audience

Inside Module 02

Thinking Outside the Project **21**

Confronting the "PM" Challenge 22

Why Do EPM Initiatives Fail? 23

Understanding the Formulas for Disaster **24**

Boiling the Ocean 25

Managing One Big Project 25

Suffering from Methodology Overload 26

Serving the Technology Buffet 26

Preparing Strategies for EPM Deployment Success **27**

Understanding Your Stakeholders 28

Understanding Your Organization's Culture 29

Understanding and Making Management Commitments 31

Understanding Your Process 34

Acquiring or Improving Scheduling Competencies 35

Marketing Your Solution 35

Thinking Outside the Project

For many of you reading this book, EPM simply means Enterprise Project Management and the difference between Project Management and Enterprise Project Management is scope. The "E" for enterprise suggests a broader concept, something happening enterprise-wide. While most people would probably endorse this simple definition, my work with Project Server, and Project Central before it, has forced me to reconsider how these preconceptions fail to describe the growing and changing face of Project Management.

A simpler translation of "E" is to think of EPM as "Everyone's Project Management." Everyone is a critical concept to effective EPM, which assumes participation across a group of resources working on the same or related activities that contribute to a single goal or defined set of goals. EPM introduces the concept that everyone on the team is responsible for and contributes to healthy project tracking and collaboration. This is the essential difference between EPM and stand-alone project management performed by that person in the office down the hall, the one with Gantt charts covering all the available wall space.

Project Management is a process. More specifically, project management is a process used to control other processes, as shown in Figure 2 - 1. According to the Project Management Institute (PMI), a project is a temporary and unique endeavor with a finite beginning and end, or a unique process that occurs once and never repeats itself. This definition traditionally separates so-called normal everyday business operations from the extraordinary one-time endeavors that require a higher level of soft skills and controls outlined in the PMI Guide to the Project Management Body of Knowledge, or PMBOK.

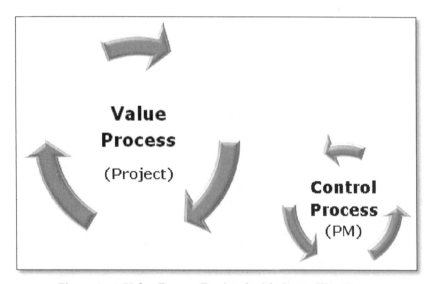

Figure 2 - 1: Value Process Depicted with Controlling Process

The combination of global economics, social evolution and technology advancements are now challenging the very fundamental description of the project management milieu, by pushing project management practices further into the organization and applying project management disciplines to processes that do not conform to the traditional concept of "occurs once and never repeats." Between economic pressure to improve efficiency and the availability of new collaborative technologies such as Microsoft SharePoint and Microsoft Project Server, more and more organizations are turning to enterprise project management and enterprise collaboration tools as agents of change.

Without collaborative tools, project management is a back-room science. Operating in typical isolation, project managers tend to produce lots of strong planning but often fail to track the progress of the projects for which they are responsible. Project managers are not nearly as empowered as they need to be to demand the feedback level they require for accurate progress tracking. So tracking very often goes undone. The plan comes out of the bottom left hand drawer and is hastily updated when an executive requests a status report.

By applying simple collaborative tools, organizations are able to improve performance substantially. Nothing speaks to this more amply than the user testimonials I run across for less-sophisticated collaborative or project management offerings from other vendors, or the success stories I hear from people who have improved project management performance simply by deploying SharePoint sites or E-rooms for project collaboration. More than anything, these testimonials speak to the value that transparency brings to the endeavor. Transparency is the first benefit that you realize when you implement enterprise project management tools and collaborative platforms.

Organizations, particularly those that implement sophisticated project management tools like Microsoft Project Server 2010, want and expect much more from their EPM system than simple transparency. Some organizations will settle for the benefits of transparency, and others are happy to achieve a "managed state" where they are able to track project execution, the middle ground of achievement in a structured project management environment. Overwhelmingly, though, the company managers I speak with on a day-to-day basis are struggling with resource management. They want to go beyond the incremental benefits that transparency provides and claim the grand prize for a successful deployment effort, the ability to manage resources across a department or entire enterprise.

To achieve this goal, you must represent and capture the entire work of the organization or organizational unit that the system serves. This, alone, obviates the "occurs once and never repeats" mantra because it means that you must also capture the mundane work streams in the organization to begin to understand what portion of your available resources are available for project work, and what portion of that portion's time is available for project work. Once upon time in a world where big projects roamed the landscape with dedicated project teams and budgets, drawing a line in the sand at "occurs once and never repeats" worked, but in today's fast-paced integrated environments, applied project management practice must evolve well beyond that limitation.

Confronting the "PM" Challenge

If we are willing to concede that the definition of "project" is getting fuzzier, then the first conundrum we face is sorting out what we mean by "PM." Which PM is your concern? Is it project management, program management, or portfolio management? According to most current taxonomies, programs are comprised of one or more related projects while portfolios may comprise one or more related or unrelated programs or projects. Defining each of these more specifically depends heavily on your organization's corporate vocabulary. While many organizations might struggle to define any of these constructs, in other organizations these are each highly differentiated and require very special skill sets.

Next, consider people management and process management. Are these skills fundamental to Project Management? If managing projects is applying a process to control other processes, then are we not simply engaging in process management when performing project, program or portfolio management? Boiling these down to their lowest common denominators, I consistently conclude that there are only two primary elements to business control: people management and process management. This may come as bad news for software and professional services firms who market using the notion that it's all about people, process and technology. Technology is simply another tool, albeit somewhat more mysterious and awe inspiring in today's world than a hammer--but let us not forget how fundamental the hammer remains in today's world.

The point is if you have a rigid notion of what Project Management is, you may limit both your perspective and your opportunity to capitalize on a marvelous toolset that has many interchangeable elements and configurations. You also run the risk of over-applying your methodology. You do not need to leverage all the knowledge, tools and techniques that comprise the PMI Project Management Body of Knowledge (PMBOK) to manage projects successfully. Likewise, you can apply PMBOK knowledge to manage business processes that do not necessarily fit the classic "Project" definition. In our consulting practice, many of the implementations we work on are for controlling business processes that as little as five years ago would not be considered candidates for Project Management tools. With the help of accessible technology like Project and Project Server, it is now possible to use project management methodologies with fewer entry barriers. More importantly, today's technologies give us the opportunity to embed controls into our processes if we have the fortitude to apply them.

For instance, it used to be that people working in accounts payable and accounts receivable needed to understand which general ledger account or accounts applied to a transaction to book it correctly. Now, our intelligent systems embed this knowledge in codified logic so that today's accounting workers need only concern themselves with single journal entries into a system that already knows how to generate the appropriate general ledger transactions. Similar to the way technology changed the face of accounting, tools like Microsoft Project and Project Server are changing the applicability of Project Management practices, allowing us to apply project management practices and techniques to a business process without having the special training that PMI certified Project Managers must prove to earn their certifications. In fact, by embedding this knowledge in intelligent systems, we can implement good project management practice and leverage its benefits without formally declaring it to our stakeholders, which very often bodes well for success.

Of course, when implementing Microsoft EPM technologies, the product name is a dead giveaway. This would not matter so much if it were not for the high number of failed attempts to implement Project Management practices in corporations and organizations since its benefits became evident and its practice more popular. In most organizations, it is not difficult to find people with horror stories to tell. These bad experiences, and the prejudices that develop in their wake, can doom an effort before it begins. Although these negative forces are powerful and sometimes pervasive, particularly when the horror story is internal to the organization and in recent memory, you can overcome them by recognizing these as challenges and managing them effectively.

Why Do EPM Initiatives Fail?

Paul Strebel wrote in the Harvard Business Review, May-June 1996, "Corporate reengineering success rates in Fortune 1,000 companies are well below 50%; some say they are as low as 20%." Although he was not citing established facts in this assessment, it certainly rings true in our own experience, and I have not found many people who would disagree with this statement. If you have been in the business world for more than 10 years, chances are you have lived through a "business improvement" disaster that ended with personnel changes and praise for the non-participants. As an organization ages and enough failure cycles occur, the incumbent staff and management becomes more and more wary of "business improvement" efforts, leading inevitably to an organization's inability to change. The status quo is always safer. Any change embodies a degree of risk.

From this, I conclude that the primary reason that Project Management initiatives fail is because they invoke change in an organization. People are naturally resistant to change. When you mix in a history of failed change initiatives with this natural resistance and an implementation effort that is blind to these challenges, you have the perfect recipe for disaster. Worse yet, our culture works against us in combating the root cause of these failures. Despite the fact that we can rationalize the difficulty people have with change in their environment, we do not confront the emotional genesis of failure because it is generally taboo to deal with emotions in the workplace. When we show up for work, our culture dictates the expectation to check our emotions at the door and reclaim them only when the workday is over. Oh what a happy delusion this is.

It is little wonder, then, that small start-ups, which are less likely to carry negative baggage, very often drive innovation. These tend to be organizations not yet jaded by repetitive failure cycles. It also explains why it is so difficult to implement change initiatives in companies with highly stable organization charts and a high rate of incumbent longevity, which is more likely to be a characteristic of old well-established companies than smaller and younger organizations. In steady-state organizations, people become much more firmly planted in their positions and are more likely to see change as a threat to their turf or incumbency. These are organizations where the terms "corporate policy" and "corporate politics" are interchangeable, and people perceive decision making as risky for fear of consequences that the wrong decision can bring.

Working in the field on EPM deployments, I will often ask a group of management stakeholders whether they think their organization needs changing, which is very likely to evoke a "no" response. When I ask whether their organization needs improvement, many of the same people will answer, "Yes." Naturally I then ask, "How does an organization improve without making changes?" Improvement, by definition, embodies change. The more interesting point is that the terms "change" and "improvement evoke a different mental model; the former with negative connotations and the latter with happy feelings. It illustrates the change-management challenge we face when we endeavor to improve our organizations and processes. If you disagree that this is the number one challenge in implementing an EPM practice, then put down the book and step away from the software; you're going nowhere with that misconception.

EPM initiatives, like other corporate reengineering efforts, succeed only when at least one of the following conditions is true:

1. People perceive that the pain caused by current business performance is greater than their perception of the pain caused by change.

2. The organization carefully and aggressively manages the change.

When things get bad enough, people become more responsive to change. Waiting for this condition to occur, or counting on it, is rather foolish and risky; yet desperation probably drives more successful corporate change efforts than careful management. It certainly provides an impetus to overcome organizational inertia, but it is much better to manage perception as part of your proactive human change management. This happens best when it begins at square one. Using effective change management to reshape an organization is much more fruitful than relying upon desperation because it is a reusable skill, a gift that keeps on giving.

Unfortunately, people involved in EPM implementations more typically become very enamored with methodologies and technologies and caught up in bells and whistles, bar charts, pie charts, workflow diagrams, and the marvelous tools they have acquired. They lose sight of the actual challenge; or, worse, they ignore it completely, living in a delusion that "if we build it, they will come." Nothing could be further from the truth. EPM is not a self-fulfilling practice. In order to add value it requires the full support and cooperation of the organization in which it is implemented. People make this work, not technology--although the technology is certainly the enabler.

Despite the fact that you probably purchased this book to learn about Microsoft EPM technologies, the most important takeaway here is that the technology, alone, is not the solution; it is but a mere part of it. If your organization has not already established successful process and change management practices, these must be your primary focus. The goal of this book is to elucidate the technology effectively enough to allow you to focus on helping your organization work with the technology and making the technology work for your organization; not just making it work in your data center. Implementing the technology is far easier than recognizing and implementing the management and organizational commitments that success requires.

Understanding the Formulas for Disaster

I have observed four classic impetuses for EPM implementations that lead to failure with such regularity that you should consider them avoidable, if only because they are so recognizable. Does your EPM implementation resemble any of the following four scenarios? If so, take steps now to correct your course.

Boiling the Ocean

While it is true that Microsoft produces great software, it also seems to produce lots of buzzwords, acronyms and expressions, almost creating a language of its own. One of the more catchy phrases I have heard circulating Microsoft's Redmond campus is "we can't boil the ocean," which paraphrases the simple wisdom that you should not bite off more than you chew. If any company could boil the ocean, one would think Microsoft would stand a chance, but Microsoft is smart enough not to attempt it most of the time, hence the catchy phrase!

For the rest of us, it is an appropriate reminder that one of the least successful approaches to EPM deployments is to go big and go fast. That approach rarely works. While it is quite all right to aspire to such heights for your EPM deployment, starting with the notion that you are going to launch with hundreds or thousands of users is, to put it mildly, ill advised.

Remembering that EPM technology changes the way people work, and has serious psychological impacts on the organization, it's always best to start with a proof of concept, or what we could call a pilot. Of course this is sound advice for any technology implementation but particularly poignant for technologies with any magnitude of organizational impact. Implementing EPM is much more akin to rolling out a new ERP system than it is to rolling out the latest version of Office. Although the 2010 Office applications have changed substantially, you're much more likely to succeed in rolling out the latest version of Microsoft Word to 100,000 users than you are in rolling out EPM to one hundred users. Once past the initial testing and compatibility checks the Word rollout might require a bit of floor support for your users, but implementing EPM requires building new competencies and ingraining new behaviors for both management and staff members alike.

In selecting your pilot group, stack the deck for success. Keep it contained to a group of people who are most likely to embrace the change and succeed. Look to engineer small wins and celebrate them when they occur. Market your solution to your organization by advertising your wins and encourage your pilot participants by giving them a voice in the system design from the very beginning and by recognizing them for their contributions. Do not launch your new EPM system with the largest project in your portfolio; rather select a smaller, more resource-contained initiative on which to cut your EPM teeth.

Managing One Big Project

Twenty weeks into your 40-million-dollar ERP initiative is not the time to decide that you need new Project Management controls for your project and that implementing Project Server is part of the answer. While your attempts here may end up succeeding under the auspices of desperation, one project, no matter how large or complex, does not justify an EPM tool implementation.

To begin with, if your project is already off to a chaotic start, it is rather unlikely that you can carve out the time necessary to take on EPM as a project as well. Rather than one failed control initiative, you will now have two. Further, if your organizational maturity has allowed you to progress this far down the road to disaster, chances are you will not be able to change that culture in time to realize EPM benefits on your current project. Instead, you run the risk of distracting your attention from your other full-time jobs.

If you want an EPM initiative to succeed, you should introduce it gently, not as a crisis management solution. The best you can hope to achieve applying the technology as an after-the-fact solution is to add a degree of transparency to your project, as you will not have the time or the organizational bandwidth to adopt the behaviors and management commitments necessary to benefit fully from an EPM initiative. Because your organization's underlying bad habits are not going to change with this approach, the benefits you can realize are not going to be significantly important to your stakeholders in the midst of the larger crisis at hand. Such is the way for companies that run their projects through crisis management. Your deployment will be useful only to a handful of users.

Suffering from Methodology Overload

"Methodology Overload" implementations are those that imagine that one can spread methodology adoption across an organization like cream cheese on a bagel. These typically fail in the earliest stages. The benefits of Project Management methodologies and controls are so obvious to the proponents that nobody among indoctrinates can imagine that there could ever be a hint of organizational resistance to them. Why plan for the impossible? Instead of organizational change, these initiatives focus on methodology and miss their marks in doing so.

Characteristic of these deployments, committees pore over drafts and rewrites of the company's new standards for project management, inevitably leading to a document release that I can only describe as the My Company PMBOK. In these situations, methodology proponents spend weeks or months rewriting PMI PMBOK guidance to fit their corporate vernacular, all the while thinking that they are achieving buy-in because they are working in committee. Ultimately, the work product ends up tossed aside because it is too technical and voluminous to interest or guide anyone except for the true believers who wrote it. For the authors, it becomes a prayer book and nothing more. Because the prescribed procedures are so cryptic in nature, many in the organization see this attempt at guidance as another furtive effort to undermine their status quo.

In my opinion, the greatest opportunity that EPM tools present to most companies is to introduce organizational controls that follow intelligent methodologies without the need to indoctrinate the organization at-large into a complex management science. The goal is to embed control intelligence into the process and process controls rather than providing a written prescription. This requires a primary focus on the controlled process and less focus on the controlling process. Unfortunately, most methodology-overload projects are lost in theory and tend to focus on the controlling process only. After many years of working with numerous organizations, I have yet to see such a document received with acclaim and excitement by a general audience. For some, this is the result of a shortsighted initiative, while for others it is the result of organizational constraints. In either case, it is not a promising way to launch an EPM effort.

Serving the Technology Buffet

When an IT department serves up EPM to its business units as part of a "technology buffet," willing diners will always line up for a free meal. In companies where this occurs, the buffet offering often accompanies an ill-defined internal push for project management. There might be a corporate improvement initiative underway that is giving lip service to process improvement, efficiency initiatives, or quality management solutions to bolster or encourage take-the-plunge approaches. Sudden executive interest might have an impact at budget time. For all the positive motivating factors one can identify, mostly this type of misguided deployment occurs because the technology is too accessible.

"The licenses came with our Enterprise Agreement so we might as well use them," is a typical rationale. This, too, smacks of the build-it-and-they-will-come mentality that so often characterizes the boil the ocean deployment, but its poison is much more insidious as the buffet attendee is ill prepared for what comes next. Ideally it should take a bit of wrangling for a business unit to get a new software application sanctioned for use, and this wrangling comes in the form of due diligence such as a cost benefit analysis, and other process and budget hurdles, which engenders a more solid footing to begin with. In the case where the application is pre-sanctioned, these obstacles and their natural sanity checkpoints do not exist. The lowered barriers typically include a much less rigorous challenge to the requesting organization, resulting in little or significantly lower due diligence overall, and a high rate of deployment failure.

The diligence due in this case is the organizational commitment and a process to follow for success. In many cases, EPM appears on the buffet table with little or no regard given to these critical elements. Very often, the IT team offering up the application does not understand it, and often has no intention of internalizing it as a standard for itself and therefore no intention of building the required competencies to support it in and out of the datacenter. Somebody needs to make a competency commitment, or deployments fail rather quickly, but in these cases, it is up to the implementers in the business unit to rudely discover this fact and attempt to quickly correct midstream. Sadly, this is a difficult miscalculation from which to recover.

Preparing Strategies for EPM Deployment Success

All EPM deployments have two things in common: a shared process and a shared pool of resources to manage can largely predict the nature and scope of your EPM deployment challenge by examining the number of organizational silos that your shared resource pool contains. The more silos your deployment must cross, the greater your challenge. Cross-departmental deployments are always more difficult to shepherd to success than a single-department deployment. Even within a single department, cultural factors and tolerance for detail varies from one subgroup to another. Using the IT example, developers in your applications development group are much more likely to function well with detailed task tracking than your infrastructure and networking resources that are constantly fighting fires. Similarly, the engineers in your product development group are more likely to tolerate detailed task tracking than are your marketing stakeholders. Like individuals, departments and departmental subgroups have their own personalities and tolerances, and you must identify and consider these in designing your EPM solution.

Typically, EPM deployments happen for specific organizational units, such as a department or business unit or around a value-chain process that transcends organizational units. A deployment for controlling IT projects in an organization is a good example of a portfolio-based deployment where the coalescing factor is an organizational unit. A deployment coalesced around a value-chain process, such as an end-to-end solution for bringing a product to market from concept through marketing, is an example of a process-centered deployment that typically involves multiple departments. The first scenario requires buy-in across a single department and stands its best chance with a management mandate. Getting all the directors in a unified IT department to agree and support such an initiative can be amazingly difficult despite the fact that one person has the ability to simply mandate it. It is surprising how few senior managers are willing to go that far. More importantly, the new generation of Microsoft SharePoint 2010 with Microsoft Project Server 2010 will likely drive much broader deployments in an effort to achieve portfolio management at the highest levels in the organization. The appeal and promise of this exciting new platform with its prewired "Business Intelligence" capabilities is certain to intoxicate senior management sufficiently to start this trend.

No matter how much organizational desire you bring to the table, your organization's ability to express its target process or projects as a cogent well-organized schedule is also fundamental to success. This naturally demands a commitment to a scheduling competency and the ability to rationalize the subject process. Executing on project progress tracking is typically a new skill for most organizations, and including end-users in that process is usually revolutionary unless an organization already has a time or task-tracking requirement in place for its resources. While the prior existence of a timekeeping system indicates a propensity for success, it may also present its own challenge for the organization in reconciling its desired level of tracking detail with its actual level of tracking detail. Existing timekeeping systems generally do not track work at a detail level sufficient to drive effort-based tracking for most project management needs. Even with the advantages of prior practice alignment with PM goals, your EPM deployment inevitably requires you to implement management process change across your subject resource pool.

Understanding Your Stakeholders

Repeatedly we consult with companies who have achieved more-or-less underwhelming or unsatisfactory system adoption. Often these deployments suffer from poor reporting compliance regardless of the selected tracking method. Although these less-than-thriving deployments characteristically feature a lukewarm management commitment, they often suffer a handicap from lack of end-user focus that originated at deployment conception. Very few of these implementations properly considered their most important stakeholders, the resources expected to maintain the data integrity in the system. Implementers simply forget to ask what is in it for the resources and what their needs are.

All too often, EPM deployment planning is limited to discussions with senior management and the Project Management Office (PMO) or the governing body responsible for the implementation. While it is relatively easy to get a group of managers to agree that implementing EPM holds the promise of great benefits for portfolio analysis and reporting, it is much more difficult to get the people doing the work to consistently report on their work. Without this reporting consistency, your EPM system data is not terribly interesting to management. While garnering management mandates for task tracking early in the game is a good strategy for success, by making your EPM deployment useful, compelling and valuable to your resources, you solidify a foundation for success. The ultimate measure of success is the degree to which you find that your organization cannot live without its EPM system. To that end, you must consider your end-user needs. In fact, if you focus on their needs first, and deliver value for them, you have an excellent chance at delivering amazing results for the organization. Keep in mind that you can only roll-up great information from a system that contains fundamentally sound data. When you succeed at tracking, you fulfill the EPM promise for your organization. Anything short of that success typically relegates your EPM system to the interests of the few.

Involve your end users, representing all of them, early in the process. How can you determine what your EPM system can do for your resources if you do not ask them? Simply asking your end users for their opinions and ideas during your requirements phase is often enough to begin the process of breaking down resistance to the change you are introducing. You must sell your EPM solution to everyone whom you expect to participate in its care and feeding, and there is no better way to sell a solution than to instill a sense of ownership in your stakeholders. You can achieve this by giving them a voice in the planning process and by keeping them involved in advisory roles. Inclusion sparks the collaborative spirit that an effective EPM solution requires. You must carefully nurture collaborative behaviors to grow them in an organization. You cannot simply expect them to materialize because you erected a computer platform that facilitates collaboration.

Treb Gatte, currently a Program Manager for the Microsoft Project product group, delivered a Keynote address at the Project Technical Briefing held June 1, 2004. In his presentation, he gave us powerful insight into the human challenge of EPM deployment in his "Market Opportunity" slide shown in Figure 2 - 2. At the time, Treb was working for Wachovia and managing Wachovia's corporate EPM deployment.

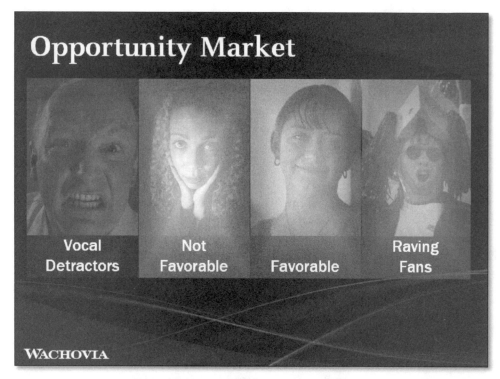

Figure 2 - 2: Opportunity Market

Figure 2 - 2 neatly categorizes the attitudes you typically encounter in a worker population when implementing an EPM solution. Essentially, in a Role Culture environment, 80% of your resources are likely to fall into the Favorable or Not Favorable categories. I discuss organizational culture types in the next section. Each of these groups, which hug the center of the bell curve, is mildly prone to their positive or negative attitudes. Most of the people falling into the Favorable category are positive about most things in life and it is their nature to cooperate in the team spirit. Most of the people in the Not Favorable category are simply resistant to change by nature, and you can gently influence them toward a favorable attitude through acknowledgement and techniques that give them a voice in the solution design and deployment process.

Your largest potential obstacle in the human equation is the Vocal Detractors group, which is typically comprised of people in positions of significant influence and seniority. Incumbency tends to breed this type of behavior or at least seems to facilitate it. One must possess a sense of tenure to feel comfortable enough to oppose an improvement initiative. These influences can be very poisonous unless you aggressively address them. Not surprisingly, people who become Raving Fans present an opportunity to counter the negative vibes coming from your detractors. You can enlist the "cheese heads" to help you sell your solution, dulling the effect of the Vocal Detractors. If you work hard at it, you can convert your Vocal Detractors into Raving Fans as these two groups are essentially riding the same sense of passion. Of course, your goal is to retune these passions to a positive wavelength.

Understanding Your Organization's Culture

One of the keys in defining your EPM challenge is to understand the culture or cultures you must facilitate in your target audience. Charles Handy, in his consummate work, *Understanding Organizations,* identifies four primary culture types: Person Culture, Power Culture, Role Culture, and Task Culture. EPM functions best when supported by a Task Culture or matrix organization. More importantly, implementing EPM forces a cultural shift toward a Task Culture whether the implementers recognize it or not. This cultural shift embodies the change you must manage on the human side of the equation.

The **Person Culture** is the rarest of organizational cultures. In this culture, the individual person is the focus. You expect to find a person culture in small law firms, literary agencies and other organizations where the organization is not the focus; rather the organization is one of convenience. This type of organization exists to share office space and resources among individuals who each "do their own thing." The culture does not seek to build value by following its own objectives. In Figure 2 - 3, a graphic representing a constellation of stars illustrates the Person Culture. Because EPM satisfies an organizational need, rather than individual need, it is usually inapplicable to organizations with a Person Culture.

Figure 2 - 3: Person Culture

The **Power Culture** is typical of the small entrepreneurial organization where a single power source rules. Like the Person Culture, the Power Culture emphasizes the individual, but unlike the Person Culture, it maintains organizational objectives as well. You may find a Power Culture in various parts of larger organizations such as the executive team, sometimes in marketing groups, and in other groups where a single individual may be the primary source of power. Figure 2 - 4 illustrates the Power Culture as a web, with bands of power emanating from the center. In organizations such as this, there is little bureaucracy and structure as it relies heavily on resource power. Organizations with Power Cultures are not likely to implement EPM and are candidates for it only when they are part of a larger organization with an EPM initiative.

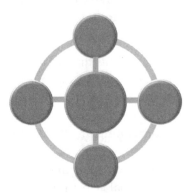

Figure 2 - 4: Power Culture

Bureaucracy characterizes the **Role Culture** organization. Thick with procedures, rules, and authorities, the Role Culture organization places emphasis on the job position rather than the individual. The Role Culture is characteristic of a steady-state organization and depends on stability. Role Culture organizations typically feature heavy departmental silos, which Figure 2 - 5 represents metaphorically as the pillars of a temple. Because Role Culture organizations tend to be rigid, they do not adapt well to EPM initiatives because they cause cultural shift in the organization. Role Culture organizations are extremely resistant to change, even when they need it most. Commercial Role Culture organizations are the most likely to engage in EPM initiatives in order to implement process improvements.

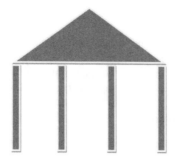

Figure 2 - 5: Role Culture

The **Task Culture** is job or project oriented. This is the culture of the "matrix organization" celebrated by modern business theorists and promoted by the Project Management Institute and other progressive business organizations. This is the favored culture where market competition is steep and the need for innovation is significant. Here the job or product is the common focus and the organization aligns itself to achieve its task. A "matrix" or "net" structure in Figure 1-6 represents the Task Culture.

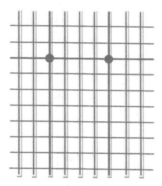

**Figure 2 - 6: Task Culture
or Matrix Organization**

Your primary purpose in identifying your subject culture is to define the organizational culture shift you must manage during your implementation process. In my opinion, failure to manage culture shift is the root cause of the majority of EPM implementation failures. Make sure your implementation team realistically evaluates the current culture state in your department, or culture states in your multi-department deployment, so that you have a go-forward strategy to manage this change proactively.

Understanding and Making Management Commitments

Perhaps the best way to describe the change process invoked in implementing an EPM solution is to view it as a maturation process. With the current popularity in developing and pursuing new and more elaborate maturity models, it's not surprising that Microsoft has included significant reference to Project Management Maturity in its EPM implementation guidance. While it is fundamentally sound to frame this discussion within a model for maturity, the recent flurry in maturity model promulgation and their increasing complexity, in my opinion, has diminished their usefulness and accessibility. Further, it seems as though much of the complexity baked into recent maturity model entrants targets building professional service revenue around the models rather than increasing their usability and applicability.

All of the current popular maturity models are process-focused and do not consider the organizational culture shifts they invoke or the cultural abrasion they might cause. Moreover, as far as Project Management Maturity models go, they focus on maturing the project management process, rather than the organization's value process or the organization itself. In this case, the focus is on the controlling process. Relying on such a tool alone can be dangerous if not fruitless. Your most concerted effort must remain on the organizational shifts, unless your organization is fully culturally ready.

What started with the Software Engineering Institute at Carnegie Mellon University offering a fairly simple and elegant approach to explaining the steps by which a company matures its software development process, the fundamental wisdom embodied in the original Capabilities Maturity Model (CMM), has become more obscure in the shadow of this special-interest bloat. The result is guidance that is confusing to practitioners and frightening to average stakeholders. Nonetheless, the fundamental wisdom recognized and captured in the original CMM model remains valid and can help us elaborate and understand the management commitments required for successful EPM deployments.

The original SEI model for CMM, developed in the early eighties, presents five levels of maturity. The University of California, Berkeley, offered a Project Management Maturity Model (PMM) a couple years after the advent of CMM that leveraged the CMM model and adapted it to maturing a Project Management process, as shown in Figure 2 - 7. Not surprisingly, the original PMM model maintained the taxonomy promulgated in CMM. Both of these describe the maturation of a process and to some extent the maturation of an organization around the process. A shift toward an organizational focus is more evident in recent offerings from PMI and others, but they have wandered away from the simplicity that makes them practical tools in all situations.

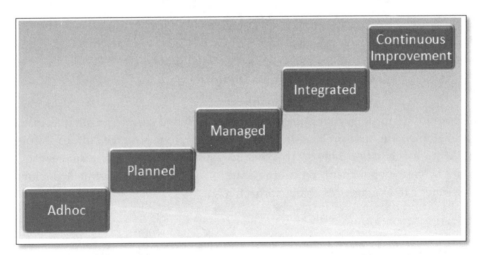

Figure 2 - 7: UC Berkeley Project Management Maturity Model

Notice in Figure 2 - 7 that the original CMM and PMM models used the term "Continuous Improvement" to describe level five. I believe that this is a flaw in the taxonomy and it would be more appropriate to call it "Sustained." Not only do the words seem taxonomically incorrect, in my observations, continuous improvement occurs at all levels of maturity if the organization is at all moving up the ladder. A lack of continuous improvement indicates at best a steady state in the organization or at worst stagnation or regression. The presence of continuous improvement does not itself indicate a level of achievement as much as it indicates a propensity toward growth and achievement. Essentially, I believe that the model over-reaches when it identifies a fifth level, which I might describe as an "ideal state" if I believed that it existed.

About twenty years prior to the SEI release of CMM, in 1963, Jean Piaget published his work on human cognitive development. Figure 2 - 8 shows the human maturity model represented in his work. This science has remained the benchmark in our understanding of cognitive development for more than 40 years.

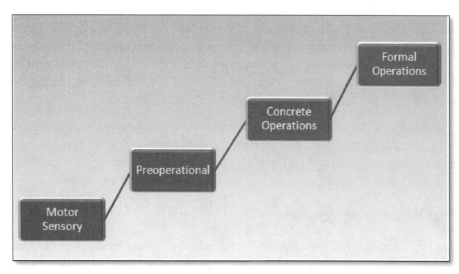

Figure 2 - 8: Jean Piaget's human cognitive development model

This model maps nicely to the first four levels identified in the original CMM/PMM models. Piaget describes the Motor Sensory stage as simple and non-conceptual. Operating in an ad-hoc state conceptually paraphrases this concept. Similarly, the preoperational phase of human development begins to invoke conceptual thought requirements whereby we begin to apply taxonomies to our world, which nicely aligns with the concept of being able to plan (although Piaget describes the stage as egocentric). In the Concrete Operations phase, we learn to apply logic and interpersonal skills, which aligns well with the ability to manage. Finally, Piaget concludes his model with Formal Operations and describes the application of logic to all classes of problems, corresponding nicely to the concept of an integrated approach to problem solving.

Our ability to align these models helps to validate the essential wisdom they contain. Our industry tends to focus only on process maturity itself without considering the cultural underpinnings that support higher-level process maturities. Therefore, to complete the picture, we must overlay process and human maturity with organizational maturity and culture.

Ultimately, both people and organizations reach their inevitable end. Organizations that have staying power have harnessed and embraced change and are therefore able to reinvent themselves. This simple reality disproves the notion that continuous improvement is a maturity end-state. Processes, like people, mature until they reach a steady state. Once at a steady state, they require an impetus to change. A steady-state organization tends to develop a Role Culture, which is highly resistant to change. The more time an organization spends in a steady state, the more engrained the culture becomes and the greater the challenge is to both providing the impetus to change and effecting it. General Motors struggled with its inability to change for 30 years before running out of equity to spend, underscoring the fact that either reinvention or demise is the ultimate last step in the maturity process.

Unless you are a member of the PM choir or a business theory junkie like me, this conversation may now have you reeling with either distaste for the subject matter or disdain for the proposition. This is reflective of the risk you run by over-doing your methodology push in your EPM deployment. Nonetheless, the maturity model insight is valuable input to your process. Understand that EPM solutions enable the progression of your organization from a level-two maturity to a level-three maturity. The progression between level 2 and level 3 maturities invokes a culture shift from your current culture state toward a Task Culture state. Even if your culture assessment reveals that your organization has a Task Culture, an EPM implementation forces a deeper plunge. Culture shift causes friction, friction causes discomfort and discomfort causes people to push back. EPM solutions can help you bridge the gap--if you understand where gap boundaries lie.

Understand that maturity and maturity achievement do not manifest themselves in neat little compartments as the models suggest. Organizational Maturity is something that is in continuous flux. Part of the organization may be at one level while another subset of the organization operates at another level. Even within what otherwise would seem homogeneous groups, for example a single department or organizational unit, maturity disparities occur. This is normal and expected. Just as we typically do not walk a set of stairs by placing both feet on one stair step before progressing to the next level, the process is gradual and natural.

Targeting maturity and appropriate organizational culture states is not a one-size-fits-all exercise. It is important that you align your expectations for cultural and maturity achievement with what best fits each subgroup in your organization. Forcing the proverbial square peg into a round hole is not a strategy for success. Rather, tailor your EPM implementation to accommodate the realities of your organization whenever possible.

Understanding Your Process

Every now and then I run across a frustrated consultant complaining that their client does not have a process. I chuckle at this, because every organization has a process. It may not be a formal process, it may not be well constructed, and it may not be something anyone in the organization can cogently express, but there is a process in play. An inability to express the process is characteristic of the Role Culture and less typical in a Task Culture. In a Role Culture organization, as the name might suggest, work that transcends departmental boundaries passes from one department to another rather than from one task to the next. In organizations like this, there may actually be barriers to transparency rooted in territorial behaviors that a Role Culture cultivates.

If you are undertaking an EPM initiative to control a process as far-reaching in an organization such as new product development, and your organization does not already have a complete process map, fulfilling your process understanding may very well become your critical path to deployment. I say this because it takes a significant amount of time to ferret out the details of a complicated process, let alone to identify all of its dependencies and estimate its work and document its expected durations. Adding to the challenge is a myriad of psychologies that come into play once you begin translating tribal knowledge to a formal process map.

First, you must contend with the pushback that your initiative is generating at the most basic level. This may make stakeholder scheduling more difficult, significantly increasing the time it should take to complete your work. Then you have the difficulty of prying this process information from your less-than-forthcoming stakeholders. Superseding these two problems, you may notice yet another phenomenon, which is the tendency of some to get overly granular in their process detail. This tendency naturally follows the realization that the system will add transparency to the process and your stakeholders suddenly want everyone to "see how much they do." Therefore, some of your stakeholders may overdo the detail for appearances only. Your next challenge is sifting through the work and eliminating the duplication of work paths, which may repeat for numerous departments. This is particularly true of Role Culture organizations where every deliverable represents a work path for each specific department with a review or approval stake in it. Sometimes different departments refer to the same work path or deliverable with different names, making this all the more difficult to sort out.

Once you gather the necessary input to construct a complete work breakdown structure (WBS) for your subject process, you must express it as an intelligent schedule with integrated workflows. Some of your stakeholders may have difficulty accepting an integrated workflow presentation. Because they are accustomed to seeing their work in its own departmental capsule, some will find your integrated representation difficult to understand, or even react to it as if it is just plain wrong. Your challenge is to help them understand that the representation does not change the fact that they perform the work and that they own the work and are responsible for the results. Some people will find this threatening to their perceived turf boundaries. To address these concerns, you can add attribution to your WBS at the task level to facilitate your ability to build views of your workflow that are more familiar to your stakeholders, helping them to build a comfort level with the new system. You learn about Project Server 2010's metadata architecture in Module 07.

Acquiring or Improving Scheduling Competencies

Just as failing to manage culture change is the single most common reason why EPM deployments fail at the strategic level, failing to understand the need for rigorously maintained schedules is the single most common reason that EPM deployments fail tactically. After 10 years of working on EPM deployments in all types of companies, the one thing I still struggle with on most of these engagements is convincing people how little they actually know about using Microsoft Project and, more importantly, how much skill is required to manage schedules in an EPM environment.

Your ability to build a well-structured schedule is not only a fundamental requirement for success, it is critical. Remember that your project and work schedules contain the data that eventually populates users' task pages, timesheets, and lights up all of the interesting business intelligence features and reporting in Project Web App. If your schedule is lacking, you simply amplify its deficiencies when you broadcast it through Project Server. Imagine that Project Server is a 50,000 watt amplifier. Do your schedules create music, or ear-crushing static?

In 2007, the Project Management Institute (PMI) College of Scheduling (COS) issued the *Practice Standard for Scheduling*, a must-have for EPM implementers. This important document defines practice standards for building schedule models. It should come as no surprise that if you follow the practice standards outlined in this groundbreaking document, you will produce schedules that work well in Microsoft Project Server. Regardless of the scheduling method you select, whether it is CPM, Critical Chain or Critical Event Chain methods, following the COS modeling standards immediately puts you in good stead for managing a schedule with an EPM tool. Providing tool training for your competent schedulers is also important.

For many reasons, including the fact that Project bore the "Office" label in recent years, managers who have no familiarity with Microsoft Project will assume that it is as easy to use as Word or Excel. Further, Microsoft Project users who have successfully used the tool to manage project schedules on the desktop frequently overestimate their own abilities, and almost everyone underestimates the rigor required to manage complex schedules. Time after time I have looked on while a manager decides that their admin should handle the schedule, or assigns a novice Microsoft Project user to model a 10-million-dollar supply chain initiative. In only a few weeks or months, everyone is pointing their fingers at the tool for the crappy data coming out of it.

Your ability to build a cogent and dynamic schedule is fundamental. If your scheduling skills are lacking or your basic Project skills are lacking, you are facing a severe handicap. Make sure that your organizational readiness assessment addresses this concern and that you take steps to correct any deficiencies that you identify. Extend your deployment duration if necessary. Always incorporate training into your deployment plan.

Marketing Your Solution

We live in a world that is marketing driven. Good marketers convince us to buy $2,500 handbags and $5.00 cups of coffee, and that one brand of toothpaste is superior to another containing the exact same ingredients. Why, then, do we overlook this powerful force when we bring change to our organizations? The most effective strategies for bringing change to an organization include selling the solution to its constituency.

The most successful deployments make solution-selling part of the equation. Recognizing this need early on sets the stage for success by orienting the deployment team to end-user needs and provides a foundation for the end-user focus I discussed previously under the topic of recognizing your stakeholders. Your taking a marketer's point of view can profoundly change your team's posture.

You should devise a marketing plan for your solution. How you position your approach depends entirely on what you determine to be your organization's motivators. Available resources certainly affect your ability here as well. One tactic that seems to appeal to most organizations is branding. Essentially, you give your project an action name that appeals to your organization's sensibilities and adds a little excitement and exclusivity. Something as simple as team shirts carrying the solution brand can help stir interest.

Mercedes Benz's American marketing organization, MBUSA, leveraged their digital media group to produce a stunning intranet video to convey the essence of their program improvement message for their EPM initiative around launching new vehicle models. The script, written by members of the deployment team, introduced the solution concepts in a way that spoke to the needs of everyone involved in the process. The dialog, which included splashes of inside humor, connected with the project's constituency by echoing their own concerns and by setting a congenial tone for the change effort involved with participation and strong endorsements from top management. Better examples of sound change management simply do not exist.

Another organization I worked with decided to have their stakeholders use Microsoft Project to manage their 90-day performance goals as a means toward achieving adoption. For this organization, it proved to be a strong motivator. Yet another organization I worked with opted to produce a series of high-profile lunch-and-learn events to introduce their solution and educate their stakeholders. At this company, nobody ever turns down a free lunch, and the deployment team made the events even more appealing by orchestrating top-level management participation. The resulting dialogs set the stage for better collaboration across the organization.

In the end, you always have the option for management to mandate the solution. Treat this as a fall back solution and make sure that you have a management commitment to do so up front, or understand that you have no operative plan "B" unless you prepare for this possibility. Understand, also, that any strategy and tactics you employ to make system compliance happen through selling your solution to your end users is far better than any mandate strategy.

Now that you have a sense of what you are signing up for from an organizational change perspective, you are ready to learn about and take command of the technology. Remember to give the human side of the equation constant nurturing attention to maintain your best chance for success.

Module 03

Applying a Deployment Process

Learning Objectives

After completing this module, you will be able to:

- Understand a best practice approach to deploying Microsoft EPM

- Follow a six-phase implementation model

- Use the template included with this book to organize your implementation information

Inside Module 03

Understanding the Deployment Process **39**

Defining Your Deployment and Deployment Team 40

Understanding the Analyst Role 43

Understanding Technical Roles 44

Rounding Out the Team 45

Managing the Discovery Phase **46**

Discovery Phase Summary 46

Discovery Key Ingredients 47

Other Valuable Discovery Inputs 47

Discovery Next Steps 49

Determining your Implementation Archetype 49

Building Your Straw Man Requirements 51

Introducing the Requirements and Definition Template 52

Applying the Template to the Straw Man 53

Summarizing the Discovery Phase 53

Managing the Definition Phase **53**

Definition Phase Summary 54

Core Requirements 54

Defining the Portfolio Organization 55

Defining the Project Organization...56

Defining the Task Organization..59

Defining the Resource Organization...59

Defining Working Times and Calendars..60

Defining Company Holidays...61

Defining Security Requirements..61

Defining Training Requirements...61

Determining System Notifications...62

Managing the Design Phase **62**

Design Phase Summary...63

Determining System Design Information 63

Managing the Deployment Phase...**67**

Deploy Phase Summary 67

Managing the Pilot Phase **68**

Pilot Phase Summary...69

Managing the Rollout Phase..**69**

Rollout Phase Summary 69

Understanding the Deployment Process

As with the introduction of any new technology, you should follow a best-practice lifecycle methodology already familiar to your organization, or other standard methodology to frame your Project Server 2010 deployment. In our consulting practice, we follow a simple methodology that provides a strong likelihood of success as well as a smooth exit strategy should circumstances dictate that course of action. Inasmuch as there is no known business productivity solution that can boast a 100% successful adoption track record, it's only sensible to imagine that your initiative might fail, and you should be prepared to gracefully deal with the consequences.

 Although I organize this book to describe the systematic process that you should follow during your deployment, you may not do your best job at requirements definition and system design without prior system knowledge. Consider reading this Module and the book in its entirety before you return to this Module for re-reading prior to an actual deployment. Substantial system knowledge greatly enhances your thought process during requirements definition.

The best way to reserve the possibility of a graceful exit is to describe your initial effort as a "pilot" or "proof of concept." Regardless of whether you differentiate between the meanings of those two terms, one is likely to be an appropriate choice for your organization. Even if your management team is hell-bent on making a project tracking system succeed, and is willing to mandate compliance, the entire experience for your organization improves when success is orchestrated rather than mandated. You always have the option to issue edicts, but try not to begin your deployment this way.

Our systematic approach to a smooth deployment includes each of the following phases:

- **Discover** – During this phase, you gather as many documents as possible to document the current process in place for managing and reporting on projects in your subject business unit or organization. Based on your discoveries, you produce a straw man version of your requirements document to help facilitate requirements interviews and discussions.

- **Define** – During this phase, you interview and conduct work sessions with your stakeholders to capture and document their system requirements. You continuously update your requirements document during this process, sharing iterations with your deployment team.

- **Design** – During this phase, you add technical specifications for configuration to your document deliverable based on the requirements you identified in the previous phase.

- **Deploy** – During this phase, you install and configure your hardware and software to conform to the design you specified in the previous phase.

- **Pilot** – During this phase, you train your first adopters and take the system through "N" weeks of tracking iterations to demonstrate the viability of your configuration to the organization and to surface any inadequacies in your system or organizational preparedness.

- **Rollout** – During this phase, you steadily expand system use to full deployment to its intended audience. Provided you did a good job identifying your requirements, expanding system use rarely requires additional work on the system; rather it requires organizational focus on education and tracking compliance.

Defining Your Deployment and Deployment Team

Most typically, EPM deployments happen across a bell-curve that occurs between 100 and 500 resources peaking in the range of 250 to 300 resources. While smaller and mega-deployments occur, this seems to be the functional organization sweet spot. It is a typical business pattern more than it is a system or methodological limit. Given Project Server 2010's new capabilities, I expect to see more enterprise-wide deployments than with previous versions.

As with most projects, one of your first steps is to define an organizational scope for your project and build a deployment team. The resource pool for your deployment is the most important and determinate attribute in understanding your organizational scope. The resource pool you have the authority to manage and track for the most part determines what process or processes you can manage.

For instance, if you want to manage the end-to-end process for bringing your products to market, but the design and marketing groups object to the perceived burden of this collaborative process, and you do not have the personal influence/authority or stakeholder influence/authority to overcome the objections, their lack of participation compromises your control system vision. The important takeaway is that if you do not have the authority to demand participation or you do not command the organizational influence to garner resource pool participation, you should consider aiming at a less ambitious portfolio. The quality of your tracking information is never going to be any better than your organization's commitment to producing it.

In typical EPM deployments, the lion's share of work falls upon one person. This is particularly true if the deployment is for a single business unit with a single pyramid in its management structure. The example shown in Figure 3 - 1 depicts a highly centralized Information Technology organization. In an organizational structure like this, one person, the CIO, has the authority to mandate resource compliance with your new tracking system. Even in a highly centralized organization such as this, it is a good idea to start with a deployment contained within one of the operating groups, such as Applications Development. In suggesting Applications Development, I am drawing upon my real-world experience. This experience tells me that application developers, who typically focus on a single development task at any given time, have a greater tolerance for detail than the network operations staff members that are pulled in every direction at once.

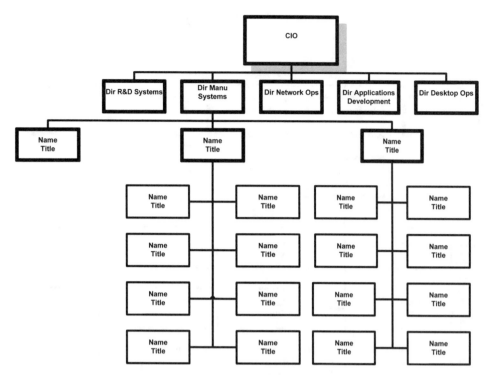

Figure 3 - 1: Information Technology Org Chart Example (Partial)

Any of the five directors in this organizational model can apply negative energy that could damage your deployment's opportunity for success. You therefore need a commitment from each of them to contemplate a successful deployment across all of these functional groups. Enlisting the CIO as your executive sponsor most certainly helps garner this commitment. This is the organizational-level commitment you need for a successful deployment. If your initiative is the work product of only one of these groups, such as Applications Development, you may be very successful with managing projects and parts of projects executed by this specific group, but fail to succeed in propagating that success across the other four silos. Without adequate executive sponsorship, your success outside the initiating silo will depend on how well you establish your EPM bandwagon as the one that everyone wants to jump on!

Working in your favor with this organizational structure is that everyone works in the same location. In fact, they may even work in the same building. Therefore, you are much more likely not to encounter cultural disparities that can create difficult-to-resolve disconnects between the silos.

In this case, it is very likely that one person will own both the deployment project and the application in production. Many organizations underestimate the amount of effort this requires from the deployment project owner, and then completely fail to recognize that the application requires care and feeding from a subject matter expert for the duration of its use. This is an important consideration for organizations using professional service companies for deployment assistance. You cannot ignore this internal competency requirement and expect smooth sailing later on. Therefore, you must work with a company that focuses on transferring this knowledge to your team, rather than helping you to build a dependency on professional support services.

Deployments that cover multiple top-level pyramid structures in the organization require representation from each of the power centers depicted in the underlying org chart included in your deployment boundaries. The org chart featured in Figure 3 - 2 depicts an example of a decentralized organization with multiple power centers. The more of these you must cover, the more challenging your deployment. For this type of deployment, your team must include representation from each of the top-level pyramid structures. Each power center needs its own subject matter expert and support structure.

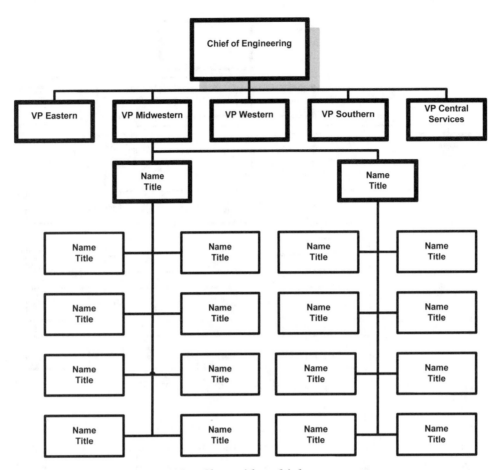

Figure 3 - 2: Org Chart with multiple power centers

In the example depicted above, the organization is much more likely to be culturally fragmented. Here we have an organization geographically divided. It crosses both blue states and red states, and all sorts of socio-economic boundaries. You cannot ignore the fact that this organization is more challenging by nature compared to the organization in the previous example, even if the number of resources in each of the two examples is identical. In an organization like this, you may work with a person for a year or more before you actually meet her face-to-face. Organizations like this are also more likely to be the product of acquisition rather than direct growth. The popular practice of growth through acquisition is very likely to leave cultural disparity in its wake through arbitrary organizational remodeling that slaps pieces of one organization together with pieces of other organizations.

For a deployment covering a regionally diverse organization, such as depicted in the above example, you ideally want the Chief at the top of the pyramid as your actively involved executive sponsor. Alternately, you want someone very close to the top of the food chain. Even if one of the silos is specifically tasked with process improvement, without up-front buy-in and high-level commitment, succeeding with an EPM deployment across all divisions is an uphill battle at best.

It is highly unlikely that one person can carry the torch for the entire extended group for this type of deployment. Each regional silo requires its own subject matter expert, not only to meet the physical support demands, but also to represent the culture and concerns particular to that part of the organization. This extends the time it takes to execute an EPM deployment. More voices and opinions simply take more time to satisfy. A popular do-it-yourself approach simply ignores end-user involvement in the process, but the price is greater in the end.

If possible, try to contain your initial pilot deployment to one power center within the organization. Using the example shown previously in Figure 3 - 2, limiting the initial deployment to one of the regional organizations allows you to test your assumptions in a smaller group first, before propagating them to the larger organization. For the initial pilot, try to select a project or projects that do not cross the regional boundaries, as it is much easier to achieve success within a power center rather than across two or more power centers. Once you have worked out the kinks in your approach, expand your system use gradually and in a controlled manner.

MSProjectExperts recommends that you assign a project manager to your Project Server 2010 deployment with the intention that this person becomes the application owner when the system rolls out to full production. If this person will not be available to serve as the application owner, the person designated to assume this role should be a team member from the very beginning.

Understanding the Analyst Role

The one role in an EPM deployment that is perhaps the most difficult to fill is the business analyst responsible for producing the requirements and configuration deliverables. While some would argue that the analyst role is typically the most difficult to fill, the challenge for your EPM deployment is amplified by the general lack of experience in the market. Project and Process management automation is relatively new to the open market. Before the introduction of Project Server, such implementations were the exclusive territory of larger organizations or those with highly specialized needs that could justify the significant cost. With Microsoft making this technology available to a broader audience, the need for people with these skills and experience continues to outpace the market's ability to create competent people.

More to the point, deploying EPM solutions in the year 2010 is much like financial system deployments 20-some years ago when accounting software and low-cost computers were making their market debuts, for the first time making them accessible to average businesses. Like early financial system deployments, EPM solutions require businesses to develop new taxonomies for classifying projects, resources, and work that typically the organization has not yet considered. Much the same way a computerized accounts payable system integrated with a general ledger suddenly opened the door to tracking expenses at a finer level of detail, an EPM solution opens the door to tracking work and scheduling that requires the business to develop a new "chart of accounts" for tracking these activities. When a business went from paper to computer, overnight it went from a few dozen general ledger accounts to fifty or a hundred.

The analyst, therefore, must be able to recognize patterns in existing business documentation and envision new organizational taxonomies, having both an understanding of the specific information uncovered during the discovery and definition process and specific knowledge of what the new technology capabilities support. Specifically, an analyst needs to combine the following competencies:

1. Possess a competency with the toolset to recognize opportunities for effective application.

2. Have a well-developed understanding of project management, process mapping, business management practices and related management disciplines.

3. Already possess specific knowledge of the organization or have a rapid ability to absorb and comprehend organizational structures and challenges across numerous industries.

Simply put, not that many people can adequately cover all three competencies without a significant need to develop at least one. If you can cover the second and third competencies in-house, to succeed with a do-it-yourself implementation your in-house analyst and subject matter expert need the time and means to develop the first competency. Consider extending the pilot process when this is the case. There is no reason that the analyst on your team cannot also be the project manager and application owner if you are lucky enough to have such a capable resource on staff. If you use an outside consultant, that person should instantly recognize the difference between the organizational challenges presented by each of the previous organizational examples. Experience and references remain your best tools in making your consultant decision.

 Warning: One of the most common misjudgments people make during do-it-yourself deployments is to underestimate the time it takes to fully learn and understand Microsoft's EPM technology. If you choose to take the proverbial plunge on your own, start small and seek training.

Understanding Technical Roles

Because a substantial number of EPM deployments occur in IT organizations, the first consideration in understanding how to define the roles for your deployment project and your production system for your organization is to understand where your deployment lives relative to your technology organization. When you deploy within the technology organization, chances are you will have an easier time getting the resources you need, although this certainly is not always the case. Remember that if you are trying to manage a portfolio across an IT organization as in the example given earlier in this module, and you do not have buy-in across the entire director level, you might even face outright hostility toward your solution. This is much more evident when a non-technology business unit drives the effort, making decisions in the process that are contrary to IT recommendations or preferences.

Your technical team size or the number of technical resources you require is largely a function of the size of your IT organization. The larger the technology organization is, the more specialized job descriptions become. Of course, this is true of all organizations. Because you are deploying a solution that lives on one or more servers, that uses multiple technologies, that you might expose through an extranet, and that requires the normal care and feeding a software application demands in an enterprise environment, you may need quite a few different resources from your technology organization. In a very large organization, you may need the following roles on your technical team:

- A Security Team member to create application service accounts

- A Network Administrator to add DNS entries

- A Datacenter Operations person to rack your servers and set up your backups

- A Network person to connect your solution to the corporate backbone

- A Data Management person to provision SQL services

- A Desktop Support team to deploy your client-side applications

- A Help Desk team to support your end-users

The list can go on, limited only by the degree of specialization in your organization. The only correct method to understanding your technical team requirements is to map the solution to your organization's support structure.

Confronting this right up front opens the door to more realistic expectations from the system and the technical people designated to support it. When a business unit introduces an EPM solution, it typically overestimates the level of support its technology department will provide or underestimates the amount of application support that falls onto the shoulders of business resources, and more specifically the subject matter experts within the business unit. Most technology organizations stop short of providing subject matter expertise for their supported applications and platforms. In other words, you can call your IT department to get your system updated to the latest version of Word, but you cannot ask them how to format a paragraph. A finance department, for instance, typically understands the functional application of the company's ERP system better than the technology organization. Unless your organization has a help desk organization willing or mandated to support your EPM solution, you must plan for and expect to provide this support for your organization.

While your initial deployment may require participation from many different resources in your technology organization, its daily care should not require more than the normal service level that your technology group provides for other applications running in your data center. This service-level-agreement (SLA) typically consists of guaranteeing connectivity and server health as well as handling backups for disaster recovery. Asking for more may not get you anywhere, and expecting more may damage your opportunity for success if you fail to plan for application support.

It is a good idea to consider bringing in a Project Server 2010 specialist to do your software installation and initial configuration while your in-house team learns to support it. For do-it-yourselfers, with a team that has substantial experience with the Microsoft web technologies platform and SharePoint technologies, and someone with the bandwidth to take on a learning curve, Microsoft provides a lot of good documentation on TechNet and MSDN as well as the knowledgebase and now through countless employee-authored BLOGS.

Rounding Out the Team

In addition to your deployment project manager, your executive sponsor, the people who provide Project Server skills (including your technical specialist and analyst), your key management stakeholders and your IT stakeholders, your team might also include any of the following:

- **Project Managers** – You must always have your project manager constituency amply represented on your team, because these people have the heaviest burden in maintaining the system and its data. Even if you do not refer to this role as "project manager" in your organization, we can simply generalize this to include all people responsible for managing schedules in the system. While you may find ways around resource non-compliance with system goals, if you are unable to get your schedulers to achieve a tracking competency and discipline, your system is likely to flounder.

- **Team Members** – Constituents of the target work organizations are, perhaps, the most overlooked participants in EPM deployments, but they are the people most affected by the EPM system decision and design process, the people who do the work that the system is intended to manage. Including team member resources in your entire implementation process often yields a better, more functional system design and leads to resource buy-in during rollout.

 MSProjectExperts recommends that you include team members during the definition process to examine how the system can serve their business needs. Achieving tracking compliance is easier when your resources see a tangible benefit from their participation.

- **Finance SME** – Finance is usually a provider of information for your definition process. The more your EPM deployment seeks to calculate, capture or present cost data, the more you need a finance stakeholder. Ask your finance representative for help with determining what rates to load for your resources, what financial system-related identifiers you should include in EPM metadata, and how to model other cost data in the system. Sometimes finance is an active partner in the implementation, in which case you will have a representative by virtue of natural stakeholder participation. In most other cases, you will likely find your Finance group very forthcoming if you ask for a resource, because they feel as though they are rarely asked.

- **Human Resources SME** – You may not require an HR representative to show up for weekly core team meetings, unless, of course, the deployment is for HR, but you are very likely to need facts about the resource hiring process so that you can consume data from it, or inject data into it. Depending on how highly you rate your resource pool management process, and to the degree that your organization stores resource data exclusively in HR systems, you may need an HR representative as well as an IT counterpart to provide HR systems expertise.

- **EPM Trainer** – The person in this role is very likely to be an outsourced contractor unless you are deploying for a very large organization with a training department that makes a significant commitment to supporting Microsoft Project 2007 and Microsoft Project Server 2010.

- **Internal Mentors** – Another typically overlooked role is that of peer mentors for floor support. Your best candidates for this role are among the raving fans described in the previous module. When you flip one of the verbal detractors into this role, you gain an opportunity to manage your opposition. Use this technique cautiously.

- **Executives** – It is particularly important to have executive participation if you intend on deploying the Portfolio management capabilities in Project Server 2010. The only way a portfolio decision-making tool makes any sense is with full support of the management team that uses it to govern their decision-making process. Partial buy-in is not an option. To implement a successful portfolio management practice you must capture all project demand through a controlled and unified workflow. In order for this to happen, you must have a management commitment.

The size and makeup of your deployment team should support the scope, goals and objectives that you define for your deployment. There is simply no one right way to do it; what works for your organization may not work for another.

Managing the Discovery Phase

During the Discovery Phase, you have three basic objectives:

- Select and schedule your stakeholder interviews.

- Obtain documentation and synthesize the available information into your Straw Man Requirements document.

- Determine your team's current ability to build workable schedules.

We always begin our deployment engagements by studying our client organizations through their artifacts, such as current schedules and reports. The goal is to get familiar with the organization enough to request access to stakeholders, and to provide a skeletal or "straw man" requirements document version with enough correct and semi-correct information to catalyze conversation. This is "homework" or "pre-work" for a good analyst and the method we recommend that you apply to your deployment even if you are starting with inside knowledge.

Discovery Phase Summary

The Discovery Phase includes each of the following elements:

- **Suppliers** – Management stakeholders from all areas of the organization included in the deployment

- **Inputs** – Existing project artifacts including schedules, plans, reports, lists, PowerPoint presentations, and other transferable documentation

- **Process** – Analyst gathers existing documentation, uses it to populate preliminary data into the requirements template, and modifies the template to meet organization specifics, while the project team produces a high-level plan

- **Output** – Straw Man or starter-version Requirements Deliverable and a high-level project plan

- **Consumers** – Analyst receives data from stakeholders, stakeholders receive deliverable output for review

Your goal during discovery is to get your hands on as much relevant information as possible. Making this more challenging is the fact that people will tend to dismiss the relevance of useful information simply because they do not know any better. To accomplish your objective, you need to play detective and ferret out project reports and sample reports that reveal the organization's process. Friendly persistence provides your best advantage. Collect as much documentation as possible. Electronic submissions are easier to work with, and therefore preferred, but do not ignore written documents if that is the only way they are available.

Secondary to your discovery work, but nonetheless essential, is the initial planning that you should begin immediately. During the Discovery Phase, you produce a high-level project plan to begin working toward a realistic timeline for your deployment. I am careful to frame this as a "realistic timeline" because, in our experience, most people have unrealistic expectations of the amount of work involved in implementing an EPM solution; they therefore have unrealistic expectations of the time it will take.

Discovery Key Ingredients

The two most important inputs on your discovery list are:

- The organization chart for the target organization and resource pool

- Samples of the schedules that contain the work you are planning to manage

By far, these are the two most important inputs, because the possibilities and limitations that these two inputs reveal largely determine everything else you do and the order in which you do it. In all cases, you must work through a certain amount of requirements exercises, but as I pointed out earlier in this module, the org chart, all by itself, can reveal your organization's cultural proclivities and challenges. Defining your organization's workflow into cogent schedules can often prove to be the most significant challenge for the internal team. Therefore, it is extremely important to get an early grip on how much your organization needs to invest in schedule development. It is better to recognize this investment rather than suffer a delay later on in the deployment process.

> **Warning:** Allowing time for both schedule development and scheduling skills development can often consume more resource time than the deployment team first realizes.

Other Valuable Discovery Inputs

Once you procure the key documentation inputs mentioned above, you should focus on obtaining additional documentation that reveals the organizations' working metadata. You examine these to uncover the proposed taxonomies you build for the Straw Man version of your requirements document. The types of discovery documents that you should seek include, but are not limited to, the following:

1. Existing Project Plans in all formats currently used

2. Documents and reports that you create from Project data including:

    2.1. Excel spreadsheets

    2.2. Word documents

    2.3. PowerPoint slides

    2.4. Existing Resource data in any existing formats

    2.5. MS Project Resource Pools

    2.6. Spreadsheets

    2.7. Other lists (electronic)

3. Resource Organization

    3.1. Resource reporting org charts

    3.2. Project reporting org charts

4. Project Initiation

    4.1. Project costing

    4.2. Project spending

    4.3. Project accounting

    4.4. Project request

    4.5. Project justification

5. Project Process documents including:

    5.1. Methodology guides and documentation

    5.2. Project Deliverable templates

    5.3. Standardized project documentation

    5.4. Document management standards

    5.5. Risk assessment forms and methodology docs

    5.6. Communications process and procedures

    5.7. Corp/Dept meeting standards

    5.8. Project procurement forms and procedures

    5.9. Project outsourcing materials – vendor management

    5.10. Progress reporting status reporting forms & schedules

    5.11. Quality program information

The preceding list provides you with ideas for the types of documents for which you should ask. Depending on the type of business and specific industry you are working in, the nomenclature may vary significantly. More is better. It is easier to recover from an overload of information than it is to spark the requirements gathering process with a paucity of reference material.

Discovery Next Steps

As Business Analyst, the first activity for which you use the org chart as input is identifying stakeholders for your requirements sessions. Selecting stakeholders can be a daunting experience in itself, particularly if the subject organization is large, politically charged, or both. You may need to consult with your core team and your executive sponsor in deciding whom to invite to which work sessions and in what groups. Even if your selection process is relatively easy, expect a larger challenge in scheduling your appointments. In our consulting practice our clients typically express much more aggressive implementation goals than their cultures support, mostly because they simply don't know what to expect, and also because they seriously overestimate the availability of resources to support the effort. This should come as no surprise, as over-estimating resource availability is likely a problem your organization expects your EPM implementation to solve. Once you determine which stakeholders you want to interview, and you create your appointment schedule, you can create a detailed schedule for your requirements phase, allowing time to author and cycle your deliverable through some stakeholder feedback.

The Requirements work sessions present an opportunity to explore how people are "feeling" about their work. In a way, this provides some therapeutic value for the participants and can provide some extraordinary insight for the analyst on how to meet end-user needs. Realizing this value is best accomplished using a third-party facilitator, rather than attempting it with in-house resources that may not be able to establish the resource trust or comfort necessary to spark this type of honest conversation.

Determining your Implementation Archetype

After gathering your discovery input, your job is to cull as much organizational and process insight from your document collection as possible. One of the ways to apply your discovery documents is to determine your implementation archetype, because you can determine a range of likely design decisions based on the organization's high-level system archetype. Implementation archetypes come in two primary flavors that have a natural alignment to "cost centers" and "profit centers" in the EPM deployment world. These unfortunate terms tend to pigeonhole organizational types, where a more enlightened view places each of these archetypes as member units of a value center. As such, we might also refer to these organization types as producer or server organizations. Even though the terms "cost center" and "profit center" are in many ways pejorative, they are nonetheless useful stereotypes for your consideration.

If you have not previously determined this fundamental leaning in your subject business unit or organization, you should have enough information to reach this conclusion after gathering your discovery documents. Understand that in defining archetypes or stereotypical characteristics, we must also acknowledge that there are exceptions to all rules, just as there are hybrid organizations that behave as both cost centers and profit centers, and there are specific requirements that can drive an organization to adopt non-stereotypical behaviors. Further, your implementation may cross these boundaries, although this is a less likely scenario. With all appropriate disclaimers in play, the characteristics of cost-center and profit-center stereotypes follow:

Cost Centers

A cost center organization is more likely to track time as part of its implementation, suggesting that cost centers are the most likely candidates for effort-based planning and effort-based tracking. Because management often casts cost center organizations in the "necessary evil" role, they struggle for budget and resources. Effort tracking is particularly attractive to cost center organizations, because it helps them justify head count and budget, and helps them fine-tune operations. Effort-based planning and tracking provides the most granular approach to cycling schedule data, and therefore provides the best feedback for process tuning. Typical examples of cost center organizations include most technology groups in most organizations, groups such as facilities maintenance, most human resource organizations, business services groups and other parts of the organization that are typically not viewed as directly connected to the company's primary value chain. The economic driver for cost center organizations is "cost to produce." Cost center organizations are under constant pressure to reduce costs and improve efficiencies.

Profit Centers

Profit center organizations are those that overlay the primary value chain. In a company that produces products, profit center participants may cover everyone involved in producing the company's products including, Product Management, Design and Innovation groups, engineering, field engineering, marketing and sales. Because "time-to-market" economic pressure most often drives the departments in organizations that bring new products to market, cost-to-produce considerations are less pressing for them. When a company relies on a product in its sales plan, it often faces more financial risk by being late to the market than by overrunning production budgets. The potential losses from production overruns are quantifiable and finite, while the potential losses related to a late market introduction are irrecoverable. The market waits for no one. Profit center organizations are under constant pressure to get more product or services to the market faster and faster.

Profit center organizations are less likely to care about tracking effort. In many cases, schedule transparency is the ultimate goal. The answer to the question, "Where are we in the process?" is often more important than the answer to the question, "How are we performing on budget?" For the typical profit center organization tracking duration, as well as actual start and finish, provides the right amount of feedback for the organization.

Hybrids, Exceptions and Challenges

Professional Services and service organizations, in general, tend toward more hybridization in their requirements. Any professional service business with a model that charges time and materials has an obvious need to track effort, but professional services organizations may or may not desire to drive their schedules using time. A major challenge that you will likely face in deploying an EPM solution to most professional service organizations and other organizations that already have a time tracking requirement is that they already have a time tracking system. When you introduce a project management system, you typically introduce a new level of granularity to the tracking detail. This creates an instant disconnect between the time detail you now collect and the time data you need to drive assignment and task tracking in your EPM system. Very few corporate timekeeping systems ever contemplated the level of detail that a work management system like Project Server 2010 can handle. This includes all of the well-known ERP systems that include so-called project management modules.

Most commercial timekeeping systems do not have the flexibility to track at the detail level possible with timesheets in Project Server 2010. If your subject organization has an existing timekeeping system, one of your team's first challenges, then, is to reconcile your assignment tracking requirements with the capabilities and the replaceability of your existing timekeeping system. Most often, replacing the existing system is not an option, leaving you with limited choices. You will not boost your popularity or your chances for success by suggesting that your resources enter time into two systems; we have seen this done, but I do not recommend it. Therefore, you are more likely not to use effort-based tracking in your EPM system when it means that you have to reconcile with an existing timekeeping system, regardless of whether this approach is the best long-term choice.

When you run across deeply embedded timekeeping solutions, the ideal solution is to modify or have modified the existing timekeeping system to accommodate the granularity requirements of EPM. The next best option is to replace it with an application that already integrates with your EPM solution. There are a number of these available from Independent Microsoft Solution Providers. The option most companies select is to accept the tracking disconnect, continuing to collect hours at a charge code level and opting to track duration. In these cases, you must rely upon duration variances and conversations with resources to lead you to logical conclusions about what caused a work variance when it occurs.

 MSProjectExperts recommends that you establish your EPM solution's viability through a pilot before contemplating the replacement of existing timekeeping systems. This should always be phase-next work.

Prior versions of Microsoft Project Server did not support separating time collection from assignment progress. In other words, once you turned on time collection by hours or by days worked, the system forced you to use that same data to drive your schedules. In fact, a workaround to implement this construct using previous Project Server versions requires you to create a detailed tracking plan and a separate timekeeping plan. Project Server 2010 dramatically changes this model, giving you the ability to track time using one methodology and track assignment progress using another. Of course, it also allows you to use the data you enter in the timesheet for both purposes. This plays well with the concept that you can keep your current timekeeping system and use simple assignment tracking in Project Web App to update your schedules. The negative is that you do not provide your users with one-stop shopping. In the 2007 version, even Project Web App presents time tracking and task updating in two separate screens.

Ultimately, any organization that charges back another part of the company for all or part of its work, particularly for part of its total work, is most likely to want to implement effort-based planning and tracking regardless of its cost center/profit center status. This is particularly true if no prior timekeeping system is in place. Typical manifestations of chargeback situations include regional organization charge-backs to headquarters, a commercial entity component of a company charge-backs to its foreign parent, charge-backs between sister operating companies related by ownership, and the like. Wherever companies use effort to justify FTE allowances and charge-backs between entities, your initial conclusion should be that your situation likely calls for effort-based planning and tracking.

Organizations that do not have critical cost justification pressures, do not have charge-back requirements or other get-paid motivators, are neither likely to want to implement effort-based tracking, nor likely to sustain such efforts. Professional services organizations that are highly productized, and work exclusively with fixed-price engagements, are not likely to want to engage in time tracking. Frankly, most businesses that do not currently track time are rarely motivated to implement timekeeping for project tracking alone, unless the organization is significantly mature in its management practice and this is part of the organization's natural progress to maturity.

Building Your Straw Man Requirements

Now that I have given you some direction to help you determine your organizational archetype and you've gathered a healthy portion of discovery input from your subject organization, it's time to get what you know, and what you think you might know, onto paper. Because our goal in building a Straw Man document is to help drive the requirements sessions, it is acceptable to be substantially more speculative than you might otherwise be in preparing the typical business document. Consider that your stakeholders will have stronger reactions to, and more to say about, incorrect or partially incorrect information in your document than they are likely to have to correct information. It is rather easy to read and accept correct data, although it is very difficult to ignore blatant mistakes. In this early part of the deployment cycle, seeding the document with "best guesses" drives conversation further than does a blank page. Apply this technique whenever you can construct something reasonable through speculation, rather than providing no starting point at all.

When you begin your requirements document from scratch, you have the tedious job of determining a structure for your deliverable and determining what the likely contents and subject matter should be. This is a slow process when you start with a blank page. If you regularly work on EPM deployments, you probably have a template to work from that you created during your previous work. If this is your first time working on a deployment, or you are leading a do-it-yourself effort, you do not have the advantage of using a template, except for the fact that you made the wise choice to purchase this book, since it includes a template.

Introducing the Requirements and Definition Template

In our consulting practice, we take an integrated approach to our system documentation. We prefer to update and evolve a single-source deliverable that begins its life as a Straw Man, develops into full-blown requirements, then gets layered with configuration specifications and finally completed with as-built system information. This keeps the reason with the rhyme in a one-stop reference. We recommend that you consider adopting this standard unless you anticipate producing document deliverables that are so large as to not be practical as an aggregate document. An implementation large enough to require separating these deliverables is rare.

Warning: Using a professional template **does not** improve or increase your ability to understand various aspects of EPM and the Microsoft solution, but it may give some end-users a false sense of confidence. Remember that none of us knows what we do not know!

It may help you to print a copy of the template to refer to while reading the following topics in this module.

At the insistence of some clients, I have had occasion to provide a sample of our template in advance of requirements work sessions. Every time I have done this, the client has invariably returned the document to me "so-called completed" prior to our first requirements work session with a declaration that the requirements are done and we are ready for our next step. Of course, most of the template entries end up as "N/A" or some other form of not applicable. How can you possibly do the requirements for an EPM deployment until you have done one? Even if you do stumble through it, how do you do it well? The problem is that you do not know what is possible and plausible until you have some experience with both the technology and the practice. Going at this without experience is likely to result in many missed opportunities and some bad decisions along the way. You can succeed if you persevere and give yourself the learning time.

You can find the **Requirements and Configuration Template.docx** in the download package for this book. For those of you who are familiar with Project Server history, our template for this book is very much inspired by the approach taken in the Enterprise Implementation Framework (EIF), although our tool is much simpler (just a boring Word document) and now very much more accessible. Understand that the value of the template is first to help you remember everything you need to cover and secondly to organize the information into a useful structure. You should also understand that this document is constantly evolving in our practice. You should change and improve it to meet your personal preferences as you complete additional deployments. Most importantly, understand that the template does not contain a silver bullet solution to your deployment woes, and it will not cover every deployment scenario. The template may make your life easier, but it does not do the work for you!

To keep things simple, the template contains seven primary sections that you work mostly in the order that they occur. Although the template generally integrates requirements, design and specification information throughout, you mostly complete the first section, Core Requirements, before you complete much of the System Design information, and you complete the last two sections as you build your solution. Naturally, any of your requirements can be subject to change before, during, and after you build your system. The primary template sections are:

- Core Requirements

- Portfolio Organization

- Project Organization

- Task Organization

- Resource Organization

- System Design Information

- Application Server Information

- Security Information

Applying the Template to the Straw Man

Because I cover the specifics of each template section in the requirements-gathering topics later in this module, I do not directly cover them in this section. Inasmuch as constructing your Straw Man is a "light" version of your requirements documentation, you should read the balance of this Module and the topics on requirements gathering and documentation before building your first document version from the template. The same strategies and techniques for modeling your Requirements and Configuration documentation apply to your Straw Man, because it is nothing more than a pre-version of your actual deliverable.

Summarizing the Discovery Phase

During the Discovery Phase, you complete the following deliverables and planning activities:

- Identify and enroll your deployment team.

- Identify your stakeholders.

- Create a high-level project schedule and plan for your deployment.

- Garner a good understanding of your organization's particular cultural challenges and a plan to market your solution to overcome cultural and organizational objections.

- Produce a Straw Man Requirements Document.

Managing the Definition Phase

During the Definition Phase, the quality of your requirements gathering work is a crucial determining factor in your ultimate success. Those of you familiar with the 1-10-100 rule understand that for each hour you invest in getting requirements correctly identified up front will likely save you 10 hours of effort in building your system and as many as

100 hours supporting it. Also referred to as "envisioning," effective requirements gathering focuses your deployment on organizational needs rather than technology bells and whistles. More importantly, it provides you with an avenue to gaining buy-in.

Definition Phase Summary

The Definition Phase includes each of the following elements:

- **Suppliers** – Stakeholders from all areas of the organization included in the deployment

- **Inputs** – Existing project artifacts including schedules, plans, reports, lists, PowerPoint presentations, and other transferable documentation that you did not capture during discovery, as well as your Straw Man document

- **Process** – Discussions between the Analyst and stakeholder groups and project team members to validate the known requirements and determine the full set of organizational needs

- **Output** – A completed Requirements Deliverable, a detailed project plan, schedule and adoption strategies

- **Consumers** – Business stakeholders and deployment resources

Goal one during the definition phase is to capture your system requirements and organizational requirements. Simply put, system requirements are your stakeholders' wants, needs, and results expectations, while your organizational requirements specify the commitments that the organization must make to achieve the system requirements. All too often, people overlook the latter requirement type. During the definition phase, you also develop your deployment strategies and tactics to bridge the gaps between your current organizational state and your organizational requirements.

For example, you identify a fundamental system requirement to manage very complex projects; one of the organizational requirements this system invokes is a well-developed scheduling competency including an in-depth understanding of Microsoft Project's scheduling engine and its programming bias. Undoubtedly, you must define a strategy to acquire, introduce or improve scheduling skills in your organization and then define tactics such as training and recruiting to realize your strategy. You can bet that this example applies to your deployment to some extent. That is why the EPM Requirements and Specifications deliverables I prepare always contain an organizational training requirement and I reserve an area for this requirement in the template.

Core Requirements

The first statement that I try to construct in this section is meant to capture the raison d'être for deploying the system. At the highest level possible, provide the answer to the question, "What is the number one problem that this system is expected to solve?" Typically you end up with a statement like, "The system must provide scheduling transparency across the engineering organization," or "The system must provide demand and capacity management for human resources across the IT portfolio of projects." Your project sponsor and key stakeholders must provide this vision focus. Some stakeholder groups can state this with great clarity, while others need your help to focus their thoughts.

Given that Project Server 2010 has vastly expanded capabilities that you may not want to implement, or for practical reasons are unable to implement, you must immediately decide what your goal is. For instance, not every deployment of Project Server is likely to include the portfolio decision-making tools in its scope. Many organizations deploy Project Server to manage a single process such as product launch. A deployment of this type is unlikely to require much in the way of Enterprise Project Type configuration and few unique workflows, if any.

Ultimately, your challenge is staying true to your primary objective. Along the way, you will encounter many detailed requirements that serve specific constituencies. As a good analyst, you must record these, whether or not you believe the system can or should include them. This type of information can be very useful to the deployment team later on when considering human needs and system adoption motivators. Eventually, you must classify all of these requirements as "must–haves" and "nice-to-haves." By determining a primary objective, you can quickly perform prioritization according to how well each requirement aligns with it.

In this section, you also capture any other business challenges that your EPM initiative is intended to solve and capture the business rules that apply to each challenge. If your deployment has many unique and custom requirements, this section of your deliverable may grow quite large. If your requirements are less specialized or custom, you may find very little material for this section. You must address three subsections to Core Requirements, including:

- **Process Improvement Requirements and Goals** – What you require from the tool usually, in turn, places demands on the organization. It is very important to note the organizational improvements and management commitments that the organization must make to its process and competencies to achieve success with the platform. The organization must meet these requirements to use the tool effectively. Including this in your document creates a contract with your stakeholders when they sign off on the requirements.

- **Deployment Scope** – This refers to defining the user group(s) to whom you will deploy the solution. This requirement statement could be as simple as "IT application development group" or as complex as "All of engineering covering two functional departments and five regional organizations across North America."

- **Project Definition** – This statement should fully describe the nature of the schedules intended to become system content. Once again, this could be a statement indicating a simple homogeneous portfolio of IT Development Projects or a very broad declaration of a heterogeneous portfolio such as "The entire end-to-end process for bringing new Whacky Widgets to market."

Understanding the three preceding core requirements is the key criterion for scaling your hardware and for constructing your rollout plans and strategies. Very often, achieving the process improvements and management commitments requires a greater effort and duration than simply building the system.

Defining the Portfolio Organization

The Portfolio Organization section contains both requirements and design information. Notice that this section contains a table in the main section followed by a number of sections containing either tables or blank space. This section captures high-level information required to implement lifecycle management, demand management, and portfolio decision-making tools for the organization.

- Portfolio Key Field Definitions

- Departments

- Project Types

- Workflows

- Business Drivers

The table in the first section contains primarily requirements information along with some design information. In fact, all the sections that follow contain mostly or only design information. You should not expect to address all of these during your requirements pass-through of the document. You certainly should capture design-specific information in your document if it becomes available to you during the Define Phase, but you should try to focus on requirements as much as possible. Frankly, it is sometimes difficult to distinguish requirements from design information when working with Customizable-off-the-Shelf-Software (COTSS) products, because so much is tool-specific and you must live within the boundaries the COTSS developers set for you.

Notice in the template Implement Portfolio Decision Making item that the first row of the Portfolio Organization table contains a question mark followed by "(Y/N)" indicating that this is a Boolean value field. Throughout the document, answering yes to any of these template questions obligates you to describe the requirement further. For instance, if you answered yes to the *"Project work spans multiple locations"* question, in the adjacent cell you should describe how; do not simply enter the character "Y." Simply entering "Y" does not give you enough information to design your system architecture or the metadata you need to meet the requirement. You need to know how many locations, where they are, how many resources work at each location, what type of work takes place at each location, to name just a few valuable details.

One of the main objectives of this section is to determine first whether you will implement portfolio analyses features, and then capture enough information to determine the scope of that effort. The questions in the grid help you determine whether you implement the portfolio analyses features, and then whether you implement one level of analysis for a single enterprise or department, or whether your goal is to provide the decision-making support to multiple departments.

 The Portfolio Key Fields section is a design specification that captures special custom fields specific to enabling Portfolio Analyses functionality in Project Server 2010. These are, essentially, the fields that you will likely control within a workflow envelope, although the workflow requirement is not necessary. You must define at least one custom enterprise project cost field in order to perform cost constraint analysis, and you must define at least one enterprise custom resource field to identify resource roles in order to perform resource constraint analysis. If you deploy decision-making tools to multiple departments, you may need to create different fields for unique process requirements for each department.

For each department that you intend to implement portfolio analyses capabilities, you undertake an exercise in standardization. To use the decision-making tools effectively, you must have all of the proposed projects available for the analysis. To do this, your management organization must make a commitment to capturing all demand in a standardized way. To enable this at the system-level, Project Server provides Department Filtering capabilities that allow you to segregate data by audience as a way of formally declaring project types for those audiences. You must identify and classify the type of projects for which you want to capture demand and determine their custom filed requirements, workflow requirements, and template requirements for both schedules and Project Sites.

Defining business drivers is an exercise you must conduct with the C-Level executives in your company that engage in portfolio decision making. An effective approach to this is to meet with each member of the executive team individually to define and prioritize business drivers. After working with each individual member of the executive team, you gather the team together to reach a consensus using the individual responses as inputs for this exercise. If you are deploying portfolio management for less than the entire organization, a single department for instance, then your team may consist of a department head and the senior managers in that department.

Defining the Project Organization

The Project Organization template section contains both requirements and design information. Notice that this section contains a table in the main section followed by a number of sections containing either tables or blank space.

- Project Tracking Methods and Options
- Custom Project Filters
- Custom Project Tables

- Custom Project Groupings
- Custom Project Views
- Custom Project Toolbars
- Custom Project Modules
- Custom Project Maps
- Custom Project Reports
- Project Templates
- Library Customizations
- Issues Customizations
- Risks Customizations
- PWA Menu Customizations
- Custom PWA Gantt Chart Formats
- Custom PWA Grouping Formats
- Project Web App Views

The tables in the first two sections contain primarily requirements information along with some design information. In fact, all the sections that follow contain mostly or only design information. You should not expect to address all of these during your requirements pass-through of the document. You certainly should capture design-specific information in your document if it becomes available to you during the Define Phase, but you should try to focus on requirements as much as possible.

Are you surprised that the first row in the table is for System Archetype? I put it right up front because, as you now know, you can predict a lot about your system requirements and configuration based on its archetype. Do your best to determine the content values for all of the line items in the two tables, knowing that you can revise these with your stakeholders as they learn more about the system and that some of the answers may not be clear early in the process.

Many of the rows in the first section seek to address users, projects, and resources by quantity. You use these measures, along with the facts captured in the table, to determine your platform capacity requirements and configuration. The last seven rows generally lead you to defining custom enterprise project fields. Answering yes to these requirements means that you must produce a corresponding taxonomy, defined as a flat or hierarchical lookup table used to classify your projects. If you are able to capture this information when you first encounter it, you may want to jump to the Custom Fields topic in the System Design Information section to record the specifics. You learn more about custom Enterprise fields and their importance to your configuration in Module 07.

Keep in mind as you work with the template that you may need to jump around the document quite a bit if you are attempting to populate it during your requirements work sessions and interviews. MSProjectExperts recommends that you consider a good paperless note taking system such as Microsoft Office OneNote to support your requirements efforts. This gives you free-style note taking capacity, and the notes you capture are easy to transfer to the deliverable document.

For all implementations, much of your quest during the Define Phase is determining the custom attribution metadata for your system, as this is essential to drive your business-specific reporting and analysis. This is particularly important at the project level, because your attribution largely determines the applicability of your system. Here your goal is to determine the classification of your projects. For instance, an IT organization might want to sort and roll-up data about projects by the system or type of system that they support, in which case you define the attribution as system and then capture the values for "system" according to evidence and stakeholder input. An IT organization for a retailer might create a system hierarchy as shown in the simplified example in Figure 3 - 3.

This classification construct applied as a portfolio attribute allows you to roll-up information through the hierarchy. If you applied a grouping in a Project Server view using this attribute, you would see such things as the planned and actual work effort as well as work variance at each node in the lookup table. Likewise, you can view costs and cost variance along these dimensions as well. Finding the key project attributes through your requirements activity is your most important job.

```
Store
    POS
    Inventory
    Signs
Finance
    ERP
    Payroll
    EDI
    Accounts Payable
Human Resources
    HR Management
    Skills Management
Logistics
    Freight Routing
    Freight Claims
Productivity
    Desktop
    Other
```

Figure 3 - 3: Project Attribute for System

Module 07 contains in-depth coverage of custom fields and lookup tables. It may help you to review this module to learn what is possible in the system.

Of all the remaining topical areas in the Project Organization section, you should attempt to populate the Project Templates table during the Define Phase. Very often, the project templates you identify do not exist, or if they do exist, their creators are likely to tell you that they "need work." The list you identify here may very well become your critical path to launching your system. This is particularly true if you are introducing formal scheduling for the first time. If you have complicated schedules and little prior experience developing schedules, the effort required to develop these may be significant and the "way there" may necessarily involve stakeholders who slow down the process. The remaining topic areas generally address customizations that you determine during Design, so I save discussion of these specifics for the Design Phase discussion in the next section. These custom elements may be in response to core or reporting requirements identified elsewhere in the document.

Defining the Task Organization

Defining the task organization is typically the lighter side of requirements gathering for most organizations. Where task requirements tend to get deep is for organizations that are tracking effort and want to classify it in numerous or complex ways when it comes to reporting and analysis. Although Job Number is a typical Project-level attribute, as most organizations will track one unique line item in their financial systems for each project, some organizations have tracking requirements or job codes that you can apply only at the task level. When an organization applies job codes at the task level, you need to apply the attribute at the task level.

Some organizations may classify and capture work by a charge code that differentiates between task base budget and contract line item accounts. Others want to differentiate between capital and expense. Again, these scenarios call for an attribute at the task level. Breaking down your organization's preference to see its work organized by silo in the overall plan often involves the promise of providing a project view of the data by this criterion. When you must provide your constituency with project views by department, you might simply add a Department attribute at the task level to provide for easy grouping and filtering of task data.

Defining the Resource Organization

Defining your resource organization and maintaining the attribution in your resource pool is extremely important for implementations with large resource pools. Good resource attribution also provides an opportunity to roll-up information in analysis and reports, much the way it does at the project level. If resource demand and capacity management is one of your system goals, then resource attribution is essential. Not only will your resource managers want to see capacity and demand by skill set or role type, they'll want to be able to evaluate this information by department and along other dimensions as well.

The built-in security groups in Project Server 2010 can help you narrow the field when selecting resources for your project, but they are rarely enough to help you determine which resource is best for the job. You accomplish this by defining your resources with more granular attribution. This provides the ability, once again, to roll-up information along the classification attributes you create. For instance, defining a skill set attribute for your IT department deployment might look something like the abbreviated example in Figure 3 - 4.

The hierarchical construct shown in the example allows managers in the system to view work and availability numbers for each first node roll-up and at the subordinate level. In other words, you can see how much total capacity you have in the Database group, as well as individual capacity, demand and costs at the Data Modeler, DBA and Data Steward level as well.

```
Network
    Engineer
    Planner
Applications Development
    Dot Net Developer
    SQL Developer
    Legacy Developer
Database
    Data Modeler
    DBA
    Data Steward
Support
    Help Desk
    Floor Support
```

Figure 3 - 4: Skill attribute snippet

More important than the dimensional roll-up that this attribute provides in views and the OLAP cube, Project Server 2010 can use this field to help your project and resource managers match people to tasks. Project Server 2010 provides this ability through a construct called Generic Resources that you create and attribute to represent resource types as defined by your Skill code. By applying the same attribute to the human resources, you give the system the information it needs to match generic resources you initially use to model your plan to a human resource in your pool that has both the skills and the availability that best suits your need. This is one of the very powerful benefits of building an EPM system.

Project Server 2010 adds additional potential complexity to the resource attribution challenge, as these requirements may vary widely between departments performing very different roles in the organization. Further, the system allows you to look at capacity by many dimensions in the OLAP cubes, and allows you to use a completely different construct when you use portfolio analyses tools. Project managers and resource managers are likely to want a more robust explosion of roles for detailed planning than is practical to use at the portfolio level. Then again, you may find that everyone is happy with a single approach in your organization. The point is that the system is flexible enough to accommodate multiple scenarios for analytics, and you must be prepared to design for these scenarios.

Defining Working Times and Calendars

Does everyone in your resource pool work the same set of standard hours, or does your organization provide for flexible scheduling? Working calendar information is an absolute requirement to accurate scheduling. In order for Project Server to schedule the work correctly in your projects, it must know what calendars govern resource and project work. Does all work happen during standard working times, or does your organization have additional shifts? Do you have a need for scheduling work that can occur only during non-standard work times, such as maintenance work that must occur over a weekend? You must ask yourself and your stakeholders these types of questions in defining the working times and determining the calendars for your EPM implementation.

Project Server uses calendars to determine task and assignment scheduling. When you first construct a schedule without adding resources, Project Server uses the standard calendar to determine when tasks can occur after considering all of the other task elements you build into your plan, such as task type or any duration you may specify. However, Project Server cannot calculate duration for you based on work until you apply a resource to the task, creating an assignment. Until you apply a resource assignment, any work you specify for a task is simply a notation. When you apply resources to a task, the system uses the work value you set for each resource to calculate the duration. In calculating duration, the system applies the project base calendar, the resource calendar, and a task calendar if you specify one. The system schedules each resource to work only during resource working times. For instance, you might schedule a task to occur the Tuesday through Friday after Labor Day, but when you apply the resource whose calendar contains vacation days the rest of that week, the assignment moves to the following week accordingly. You do not need to create calendars for each resource, as the system creates them for you when you add resources to the pool. However, you must enter the calendar exceptions for resources in order for the scheduling engine to do its work correctly. During the definition phase you should determine where this information is available in your organization and how, or most appropriately, who will be tasked with the job of maintaining it.

 Warning: Maintaining the Enterprise Resource Pool is generally a "hot potato" issue before, during, and after your system build. If you do not determine a method for updating calendar exception information in your resource pool, it will damage your system's perception as it renders useless or inaccurate scheduling results.

If your organization maintains time-away-from-work data in codified systems, then it is a very valid decision to explore automating the data from the foreign system into Project Server 2010. HR system integration for resource information, time-away-from-work data, departmental membership, and other resource attributes can be a significant enhancement to your system, as well as a significant labor saver. Otherwise, you face a tough decision of making this the responsibility of a designated person or the work of many by distributing it, perhaps, to all line managers. Although the distribution of this work seems logical, you should do this knowing that you must train your line managers and give them the tools to do it. If you choose this route, make sure to note this in your training requirements.

Defining Company Holidays

One could aptly say that this is a no-brainer, but you must gather your company holidays and enter them in the standard working calendar for your organization. You probably have this information on your Outlook calendar or easily available to you on the company Intranet. Consider this a rote step, but it is important information that you must have at your fingertips when you start to build your system.

Defining Security Requirements

Because security always ties to users and user classes, you tackle your security requirements while you define your resource organization. You must determine each resource's role in the system, and for each role you must define your data access requirements and limitations. In most organizations, a person's role largely determines what he or she can access in the system. Project Server 2010 has some built-in role classifications called Security Groups. These consist of Executives, Project Managers, Resource Managers, Team Leads, and Team Members. These groups map to specific permissions in the system. As you might imagine, by default an executive has access to almost all system data, while team members have much more limiting default permissions.

At this point, you use plain language terms to express what data the members of each standard system group can see and what functions they can perform on the data set. Ultimately, you must map these to standard groups and/or create your own groups or modify the existing ones. The system contains a special built-in custom resource attribute called the RBS, which stands for Resource Breakdown Structure. The RBS more or less reflects the Org Chart for the organization, but can be either much flatter in structure than the actual Org Chart or nearly as detailed. This depends solely on how you intend to use it. It is a built-in custom field because it plays a special role in crafting and applying security in the system. It is a "custom" field because you must provide its contents. The RBS establishes relationships between resources, defining subordination in the pool that you can leverage in designing your security matrix. You can use the reports-to relationships it defines to apply security rules, such as whether Resource Managers can see all data for resources they manage, or only for their direct reports. The RBS indicates these relationships in the system. To learn more about the RBS field, see *Modifying the RBS Lookup Table* in Module 7.

Defining Training Requirements

In completing your resource organization requirements, you must determine your training requirements. It is patently unfair to throw this tool on user desktops, even if it is only the web portion, and expect people to know how to use it. Expect to train all system users. You may be able to handle training your resources how to use the web interface to update their tasks and collaborate with other project team members as an in-house activity performed by your Project Managers and system mentors, but your Project Managers and system mentors will likely require two to four days of professional training to properly learn the system. Most people think they know more about using Microsoft Project than they actually do. Therefore, you can expect some contention around defining these requirements. Naturally, people who think they know it all are rarely up for training. The question is rarely whether your PMs know how to use Project Server 2010 (as they generally do not); but you can expect quite a bit of arguing over how well they know how to use the Project client.

 MSProjectExperts recommends that you use a litmus test for determining whether your project managers need additional training on the Project client application. Ask them, "Do you get frustrated by what Microsoft Project does to your dates?" Follow up with the question, "Do you manually type dates into your project schedule?" A "yes" answer to either of these questions is a strong indication that the project manager has a lot to gain from basic tool training.

Gaining consensus on training for your organization can be very contentious, not only because people assume they already have the necessary skills, but also because people have a lot of work on their plates and the training interruption becomes another reason not to like the system. You may also get a lot of resistance from managers who do not want to lose their workers for an hour, let alone days. Because you have little hope of succeeding without training, your solution-selling effort should frame the training as "career enhancing" to steer the focus to possible personal and organizational gains rather than on the time it takes to accomplish. Proper training is an important investment for success that you should not overlook.

The balance of the Requirements and Configuration template contains system design information that you can certainly capture and record during your requirements efforts, so it helps to be familiar with them. However, l cover these as part of the Design Phase where they are more in context with the work.

Determining System Notifications

Here your challenge is to determine whether the system natively supports what your organization wants in the way of notifications, or whether your notification requirements demand custom programming. During requirements gathering, consider this a wish list. Notice that the template contains two areas for notifications, one for each of the two Project Server instances that we recommend you create.

Managing the Design Phase

During the Design Phase, you flesh-out the specific system configurations that you use to build your system. Through this process, you must complete your taxonomy designs for your system metadata. To perform this function well, you must have in-depth knowledge of Project Server 2010 system features and design.

The design phase progresses rather quickly until you stumble over an unclear or missed requirement and you do not have the information you need to complete the design. The quickness of this effort is largely because you no longer have to work each topic with stakeholders. Going back to the well slows you down.

MSProjectExperts recommends the Design Phase as the perfect time to launch your training activities, particularly basic tool training for Project Managers. Because it is a good idea to allow a little "sink-in" time between basic tool training and Enterprise tool training, running your basic tool training concurrent with your system design and build activities is almost always ideal. You realize another benefit from this strategy if your base templates and ongoing project schedules need work, as they usually do. Project Managers can apply their new skills to getting these ready for prime time in your new system. Training concurrently while you build speeds up your launch. It is good to use the tool soon after training while the information is fresh in the student's mind.

Design Phase Summary

The Design Phase includes each of the following elements:

- **Suppliers** – The deployment team and stakeholders when necessary

- **Inputs** – The requirements version of your deliverable and knowledge for system design and capabilities

- **Process** –A configuration specification designed by the Analyst for the Project Server system

- **Output** – A completed Requirements and Configuration Deliverable, an updated project plan, training schedule, deployment schedule and adoption strategies

- **Consumers** – Business stakeholders and deployment resources

During the Design Phase, you transition all of the raw input you captured in your requirements version and convert it to near-final specifications. Note that I always assume that some things will change during the design process, and you likely will make changes during the pilot phase.

MSProjectExperts recommends that you always capture changes in the document so that you have an up-to-date as-built system record. This is important information for those who will maintain the system after your promotion to Vice President!

Determining System Design Information

As you design your system, the template helps make things easier for you by providing a space for almost everything that maps back to the system configuration. Therefore, it serves as both a placeholder and a reminder to do the design work. To facilitate this process you make your third pass through the document. The first time you filled in information from discovery; during the second pass you detailed the requirements with your stakeholders; now you must fill in the configuration information that maps to your requirements.

Returning to the Core requirements section, you now focus on the items that you did not specifically capture during the requirements pass. These items likely include all or most of the following:

- **Project Tracking Methods and Options** – Here you describe the tracking method or methods allowable in the system, such as tracking by effort or percent of completion. If you plan to use timesheets in Project Server 2010, you record the detail options here. The options for configuring timesheets in Project Server are complex.

Notice that you also capture certain financial elements in this section, such as system currency support for costing and fiscal year settings. If you do not plan to use timesheets, this section contains many rows of data that you can ignore.

- **Custom Project Filters** – In this section, you list and describe the new filters you must provide to your users to support their work with Project views in Project Professional 2010. The system includes numerous predefined filters, however none of them contains enterprise custom fields, so you must create or modify existing filters if you intend to filter on this data. Although you create these filters in the Project client, Project Server 2010 allows you to distribute these quickly and easily to your project managers through the enterprise environment. You use project filters to create new views or when working with existing views in Project Professional 2010.

- **Custom Project Tables** – This is where you specify the custom data tables you must create to support the views you intend to provide for your Project Professional 2010 users. Tables contain the data columns that display in Project views. As with filters, Project Professional 2010 ships with numerous data tables, but your use of enterprise fields may drive the need for you to create new tables.

- **Custom Project Groups** – In this section, you specify the groupings you must define to support the views you intend to provide for your Project client users. Once again, Project Professional 2010 ships with numerous predefined Groups, but none of them include enterprise custom fields.

- **Custom Project Views** – Here you list the views and the data fields the views must contain to meet your Project Manager's requirements. You may have noticed that views contain filters, tables and groupings, or at least the most interesting and useful views most often do. Creating well-thought-out Project Professional 2010 Views is a critical factor for success in leveraging the power of enterprise custom fields. When you add task level attribution, for example, you must think about what view creation or modifications support the use of that data. You will certainly need to create new views for your enterprise users. In addition to listing the basic view information in the table area in the template, you may want to include an appendix item for the view and, eventually, a screen shot of the as-built view.

- **Custom Project Modules** – Like other Microsoft Office applications, Project Professional 2010 supports Visual Basic for Applications (VBA). You can create code modules to execute useful functions that can relieve your team from tedious manual tasks. List your code modules here with a description, but you may want to add an appendix to the document to specify additional detail such as the code requirements and specifications, particularly if these are complex.

- **Custom Project Maps** – Project uses data maps to exchange information with other applications, such as Access, Outlook and other ODDBC compliant databases and applications. If you identify requirements that call for moving data between applications, specify your maps in this section.

- **Custom Project Reports** – In this section, specify the report customizations that map to your requirements. You may or may not be able to meet all of your requirements using the reporting capabilities built into Project Professional 2010 or Project Server 2010. Here you should specify modifications you want to make to built-in reports as well as specify reports that are better suited to SQL Server Reporting Services (SSRS), which is similar to the better-known application Crystal Reports. In addition to listing the basic report information in the table area in the template, you may want to include an appendix item for the report and, eventually, a screenshot of the as-built report.

- **Project Templates** – Project Server 2010 provides a means to standardize your projects through enterprise project templates. Enterprise project templates are perhaps the most important method of standardization in your system. More than any other object in this bulleted list, project templates provide more embedded logic because they contain the process maps for your organization. List all base project templates that you intend on loading into the system in this section.

Although this book contains topics about how you use these in the enterprise environment, its primary focus is Implementing and Configuring Project Server 2010. It assumes that you possess prior competency using the Microsoft Project objects listed above, as these features predate Microsoft's enterprise offering. Project Server 2010, of course, brings new value to these as enterprise objects that you can distribute widely and manage centrally.

For more in-depth learning about VBA Macros, consider MVP Rod Gill's *Developer's Guide to Microsoft Project 2010*. For an in-depth exploration in creating and managing the other objects on the list above, consider purchasing *Ultimate Study Guide Microsoft Project 2010 Foundations*.

In light of the workflows supported in MSS, I am reluctant to recommend using the Project Guide. Taking the SharePoint approach is a safer investment. Consider its inclusion in the template a supported legacy feature, an obligatory inclusion. If you currently use it, or believe you can leverage value from it, specify your customizations in this template section.

In the next four sections, you define changes that you want to make to the base Project Workspace. At your discretion, Project Server 2010 creates a team workspace for each project you publish to the system. The Project Workspace, itself, is an independent SharePoint Site customized for use with Project Server. In the Project Workspace Customizations section, you map your requirements to design specifics. The first title, alone, covers all of the customization under one heading, but I like to differentiate between unrestricted parts of the site and the ones that Project Server 2010 touches directly, and therefore require special consideration. If you or the deploying organization has limited prior experience and competency with SharePoint technologies, you should consider adding this skill acquisition to your training requirements, if you come to believe that you will heavily rely on it. Changes to the base Project Workspace can include:

- **Project Workspace Customizations** – You can address many collaborative requirements and less formal work scenarios in your Project Workspaces. You essentially have the entire SharePoint world of possibilities available to you, along with some extra goodies that the Project development team created.

- **Library Customizations** – Project Server 2010 allows users to link tasks in Project Server to documents in two ways. The first way is a general project library where you can put just about any type of document file or electronic project artifact that you can think of. The second way is a special type of document library for deliverables addressed in the next section. You can create custom attributions for your document libraries as well as custom views, to name only a few. Specify the customizations and any content you want to pre-populate into the Project Workspace base environment in this section.

- **Deliverables Customizations** – The Deliverables library is a special SharePoint document library that Project Server uses for connecting to deliverable documents maintained in SharePoint. The deliverables function allows other project managers to consume the dates in these fields as predecessors for work paths. Do not make changes to this library unless you fully understand the system functionality. If you have specific requirements that map to a solution design that includes Deliverables library modifications, include them in this section of the document.

- **Issues Customizations** – The Issues List is a SharePoint list modified to connect issues to tasks in the project. As with other SharePoint lists, you can add or modify the fields, filters and views. Project Web App relies on the consistency of certain fields and values for its connectivity, so exercise care in mapping your design. List your design customizations for the base issues list template in this section.

- **Risk Customizations** – The Risk List is essentially a variant of the Issues List. Treat this section the same as the previous list, being careful to avoid changing attributes that Project Server 2010 relies on containing specific values.

- **PWA Menu Customizations** – You can customize the Project Web App menu structure by adding, deleting, and moving menu items and menu hierarchies. In this section, record your menu and submenu items and their targets for the changes that you intend to apply to the standard Project Web App menus.

- **Custom PWA Gantt Chart Formats** – You can modify the Gantt chart formats that Project Web App uses to render web views. Capture your Gantt chart format settings for Gantt chart formats in this section. Keep in mind that the options here are not as rich as in the Project client.

- **Custom PWA Grouping Formats** – You can apply grouping to many views in Project Web App. Specify the colors, fonts and other style elements you need to support your views in this section.

- **Project Web App Views** – In this section, list your Project Web App custom views and standard view modifications. View and analysis are where you leverage your metadata most. None of the standard views contains your custom fields until you add them. Specify the fields appropriate to each view type. In addition to listing the basic view information in the table area in the template, you may want to include an appendix item for the view and, eventually, a screenshot of the as-built view.

Consider designing your Project Web Access views interactively with your users, after loading representative test data in the system. You can quickly get to yes with the help of instant feedback. Do not forget to record your changes in the document.

- **Notifications** – In this section, you record your standard system settings along with your custom requirements. Notice that I allow for two instances here, assuming that you will follow our best practice recommendations to create a training instance. The important thing to remember here is that you generally want to turn off notifications in the training instance so it does not annoy people with nonsense notifications.

- **Custom Enterprise Fields and Lookup tables** – Expect to spend a lot of time and effort fleshing out your custom field and lookup table designs, because these are pivotal to views and reporting in your system.

Some or many of the above sections may not apply to your configuration, or may not apply to your initial implementation, so it is perfectly fine to complete your design process with many of these sections blank. You may already have captured information for some of these during discovery or your definition phase. For example, perhaps you captured a requirement to theme the application with a color scheme that follows your organization's color scheme. This might have led you to design some grouping formats to comply with that requirement while it was fresh on your mind.

The remaining sections of the document capture physical implementation data. You may or may not be able to populate this information during the design phase, but you should record this information during or immediately after you perform your physical server farm build and install the Project Server 2010 software.

- **Windows SharePoint Services Configuration:** The template includes two sections for this information, one for your production instance and one for your training instance. The grid contains information documenting where services are located on your server farm as well as the database server and databases configured for each instance.

- **Homepage links and content additions:** Use this area to record changes you make to content links on the home page either by adding web parts or by adding menu items.

- **Web Site Information:** You record the port number, virtual directory and physical path information for each website your system uses in this section.

- **Project Server URLs:** Record the intranet and extranet URLs for each Project Server instance in this section.

- **Application Account Information:** In this section, record the service account information for the service accounts you used for application installation.

- **Server Configuration Requirements:** In this section, record the physical build configuration for your server farm. List each service running on each server.

> **Warning:** Some of these sections are sensitive in nature, such as the application account information. Therefore, you may want to redact these sections when you distribute the document to people who do not need access to this information.

Managing the Deployment Phase

During the Deployment Phase, you build out your Project Server 2010 system. This may begin with building a new SharePoint server farm or expanding an existing one, followed by installing the Project Server 2010 software and then configuring your system to the specifications that you determined during the Design Phase.

Deploy Phase Summary

The Deploy Phase includes each of the following elements:

- **Suppliers** – Technology procurement providers and other IT resources required to accomplish your server build

- **Inputs** – The completed Requirements and Configuration Specification deliverable

- **Process** – Deployment team builds a new, or expands an existing SharePoint server farm, installs the Project Server 2010 software and configures the system and tests it

- **Output** – Working production and training Project Server 2010 instances

- **Consumers** – All project stakeholders and EPM system users

The steps you follow during your build, by no coincidence, follow the ordering of the remaining modules in this book, which proceed through installation and post-installation configuration covered in modules 04 and 05, through the steps to configure your system for production in modules 06 through 13. Because these modules provide the detail you need, there is no need to discuss these steps here. Essentially, the bulk of this book's content teaches you the Deploy Phase.

At minimum, you should allow one week for building and testing your configuration if you have experience building Project Server systems and your initial build does not include significant custom coding work. If this is the first time you are configuring Project Server, you should allow two to three weeks to allow for your learning curve.

Assuming that you did a fine job defining your requirements and addressing them through your configuration design, the build and test process should proceed smoothly and quickly. Of course, the core team and others close to the project will be eager to take it for a test drive, and you might as well strike while the anvil is hot! For users to have a good experience using Microsoft Project Server, they must receive training. For most people, the application simply is not intuitive enough to learn on their own.

To shorten your deployment time, you can fast-track your implementation by scheduling your initial training to kick off shortly after you anticipate completing your build. For organizations with aggressive testing policies, you may need to extend these durations significantly. Make your scheduling commitments based on your own assessment of the risk involved in not providing for slack time.

MSProjectExperts recommends the following training time minimums by role:

• Project Managers who require better Project Client skills – Fundamentals training on the Project Professional 2010 desktop client followed by a Managing Enterprise Projects class

• Project Managers new to the EPM environment – Managing Enterprise Projects class

• Application Administrators –Managing Enterprise Projects class (to understand how the project managers actually use the system) followed by Administrator training

• Team Members –Project Web Access Training specifically for team members

If you are implementing other roles, such as Resource Manager, you need to train these users as well. The training requirements here may include most of what a project manager learns, or substantially less, according to how you define and implement the role. Because this can vary from one deployment to another, it is difficult to define a best practice similar to the roles in the Best Practice note above. Other users that you may need to train during the Deploy Phase are management users who mostly or exclusively require reporting usage. In many cases, you can introduce reporting users to the system after your deployment has progressed to the point that it contains interesting data. This type of user is motivated to use the system when it contains compelling data relevant to their job. There is no sense in training people far in advance of their actual system usage.

Managing the Pilot Phase

Piloting an application before rolling it out to many people simply makes too much sense not to do it. Because you are working with COTTS software, you can take a lighter approach to the formality you employ during your pilot, but the main point is to buy yourself and the deployment team some time to make corrections to the system. You may need to make corrections to the system, or your adoption approach, or both. While you were able to test the mechanics of your system using simple techniques, you first test your adoption approach when you add end-users to the equation.

Pilot Phase Summary

The Pilot Phase includes each of the following elements:

- **Suppliers** – Project Server build team and Project Server Trainers

- **Inputs** – A working Project Server 2010 platform and trained users

- **Process** – "Soft launch" the EPM system with a handful of carefully chosen users, monitor their usage, and make system and adoption approach corrections based on pilot user feedback

- **Output** – System tuned for rollout, and organization ready for wider adoption and rollout

- **Consumers** – Management and all EPM system users

If you use your pilot phase to prove your configuration only, you miss an important opportunity to spur system adoption. By choosing your pilot users and projects carefully, you should be able to engineer some early wins for your "pilot project" to stir up positive notice for it. Yes, I am talking "marketing" or "solution selling" if you prefer. Creating positive buzz for your effort is as important as the results themselves when you attempt to orchestrate organizational change. Therefore, your ultimate pilot phase goal is two-fold: 1) prove your configuration and stabilize your implementation, and 2) carefully orchestrate a marketing win for your initiative. Make people want it.

Your official pilot phase should last as long as necessary for you and your deployment team to feel comfortable and confident in bringing the application to a wider audience. Because your pilot limitation is self-imposed and your EPM build is ready for production, you can transition to full production at any pace comfortable for your organization.

Managing the Rollout Phase

During the Rollout Phase, you gradually expand Project Server 2010 system usage until you reach your full deployment goal. If you have executed well on your requirements and stacked your pilot for success, rolling out your system to additional users should not require much rework. During your pilot, you likely made necessary adjustments to views and templates to reflect the hands-on needs that you might have missed during your requirements and design phases. You continue this process as you add users and constituencies and respond to changing business conditions during the life of your system.

Rollout Phase Summary

The Rollout phase includes each of the following elements:

- **Suppliers** – Technology procurement providers and other IT resources required to accomplish your server build

- **Inputs** – The completed Requirements and Configuration Specification deliverable

- **Process** – The deployment team builds a new, or expands an existing SharePoint server farm, installs the Project Server 2010 software and configures the system and tests it

- **Output** – Working production and training Project Server 2010 instances

- **Consumers** – All project stakeholders and EPM system users

During your rollout activities, your team continues its system marketing efforts and continues to celebrate each "win" that the system delivers, thereby continuously building interest and commitment to the system. You should maintain these efforts until all users reliably adopt and comply with system usage rules. Your goal is to make this system "the way we work" in your organization. The true measure of your success is the degree to which your users would complain if you take it away.

Armed with a sound deployment plan, you are now ready to move on to the business of installing, testing and configuring your Project Server system. The following sections and modules walk you through that process.

Module 04

Installing Project Server 2010

Learning Objectives

After completing this module, you will be able to:

- Identify hardware and software requirements for a Project Server 2010 installation
- Understand service accounts required for installation and operation
- Configure SQL Server and Analysis Services for SharePoint Server and Project Server
- Install SharePoint Server and Project Server
- Create A Project Server Web App
- Create SharePoint Service Applications Manually

Inside Module 04

Installing Project Server 2010 Overview 73

Preparing to Install SharePoint Server and Project Server 2010 73

Meet or Exceed Minimum Hardware Requirements..74

Meet or Exceed Minimum Software Requirements 74

Prepare the Security Environment 75

Prepare SQL Server for SharePoint Server and Project Server 77

Prepare SQL Server Analysis Services for Project Server..86

Prepare Your Server for Project Server Installation 89

Installing SharePoint Server 2010 and Project Server 2010..90

Install Software Prerequisites 90

Install SharePoint Server 2010 Software 94

Install Project Server 2010..97

Run SharePoint Products Configuration Wizard 100

Configure Your SharePoint Farm..106

Create a Project Server 2010 Web App..112

Creating a Service Application Manually 117

Installing Project Server 2010 Overview

Installing Project Server and SharePoint Server has traditionally been a very tedious task with numerous prerequisite steps and downloads as well as server tweaks and configurations. With the introduction of 2010, Microsoft removed dozens of small manual steps from the process, providing a much more streamlined and automated installation experience. A Project Server implementer's life gets markedly better in 2010.

One major difference between installing Project Server 2007 and Project Server 2010 is that the automated installation routine now performs most of the server prerequisite configuration and component gathering and implementation for you. You heard that right: if you have an available Internet connection, the new *Microsoft SharePoint Products and Technologies 2010 Preparation Tool* not only configures the application server for you, it reaches out to Microsoft download sites to gather all of the additional software bits you previously needed to hunt down yourself, and then it installs them for you. Included are such things as the appropriate version of the *.NET Framework, PowerShell,* the new *Windows Identity Foundation* (Geneva Framework), *Office Communication Server* and *SQL Server* components from the *SQL Server Feature Pack,* to name only a few of the chores removed from your plate.

The second big change to the Project Server 2010 installation is that Project Server now slips into the SharePoint envelope as a service. This marks the completion of the SharePoint integration journey that began with the introduction of Project Server 2002. During the 2002/2003 product years, Project Server and SharePoint started dating. By the time 2007 rolled out, dating turned into living together, and with the 2010 release Project Server and SharePoint server are officially married. Once you run the SharePoint Products Configuration wizard for your Project Server/SharePoint Server installation, you now manage Project Server 2010 and Project Server 2010 Project sites just like you'd manage any other SharePoint application. You no longer need a shoehorn for the process, and gone are Shared Service Providers as a more streamlined management experience emerges as well!

One of the most significant impacts of this arrangement is that all Project Server reporting is now handled by Excel Services in SharePoint Server, leveraging PerformancePoint Services and the Business Intelligence Center. In fact, it seems likely that the desire to leverage this powerful facility, offered only with the SharePoint Server Enterprise SKU, is the driving factor behind the inter-SKU dependency. While the Project Server installation is now a relative cinch, Project Server implementers and administrators need to be much more conversant with managing SharePoint than ever before, and must now become very competent with the new version of Excel Services, which underlies all Project Server reporting capabilities. You still have to spend time configuring the SharePoint environment after you install the software.

Finally, one last major change for Project Server implementers and administrators is the new integration with Exchange Server to synchronize Project Server tasks with tasks in Outlook. By eliminating the Outlook add-in, Microsoft is removing a big pain for administrators who must keep it working out in desktop world. From the continuously annoying active-X installation failures to other strange behaviors in deployment, I doubt many will be sad to see this one go. Configuring the new integration with Exchange Server could best be described as similar to the chore of configuring Active Directory sync for the first time, and similar in its requirements for administrative attention as well.

Preparing to Install SharePoint Server and Project Server 2010

To install SharePoint Server 2010 and Project Server 2010 successfully, you must either be a Domain Administrator, or enlist the support of a Domain Administrator to create an AD account for the Farm Administrator as well as other service accounts and Active Directory groups for your implementation. You must be a SQL Server administrator in order to perform the SQL Server and SQL Analysis Services configuration tasks required for installation, and you must be a local administrator on your target installation Server(s). Finally, you must either be an Exchange Server administrator or enlist the support of your Exchange Server administrator to configure Exchange Server for Project Server integration.

Meet or Exceed Minimum Hardware Requirements

Because Project Server 2010 is built on SharePoint Server 2010, your system must meet the minimum requirements for SharePoint Server. The following guidelines are Microsoft's published minimum standard, but are not likely to provide optimal performance for implementations with many users. Assuming that you are planning on installing SQL Server on a separate server, your new Project Server machine must have a 64-bit, dual processors running at 3 GHz or above, 4 GB of RAM, and at least 80 GB of disk space. MSProjectExperts strongly recommends that you deploy a server with dual quad-core processors, 8 GB of RAM or more, and 200 GB of disk space at RAID 1.

Meet or Exceed Minimum Software Requirements

Like its hardware requirements, Project Server 2010 software requirements are also driven by its SharePoint Server host.

Application Server Requirements

Your server must have Windows Server 2008 installed with Service Pack 2 and all critical updates. You can use Windows Server 2008 Standard, Enterprise, or Datacenter editions. MSProjectExperts recommends that you use Windows Server 2008 R2 as your platform of choice for the production release of Project Server 2010. Keep in mind that you cannot install SharePoint Server to a Windows Server 2008 core installation. As in previous editions of Project Server, your host server must have the Application Server and Web Server roles enabled. Unlike previous editions, you do not have to configure these roles in advance, as the new *Microsoft SharePoint Products and Technologies 2010 Preparation Tool* configures these roles for you. You must install SharePoint Server Enterprise Edition prior to installing Project Server 2010. Project Server 2010 also requires that you install the *Microsoft SQL Server 2008 Native Client* and the *Microsoft SQL Server Analysis Services Analysis Management Objects (AMO) client software* on the server running Project Server 2010 to support reporting connectivity. The Preparation tool installs the *Microsoft SQL Server 2008 Native Client* component for you; however it does not install *Microsoft SQL Server Analysis Services Analysis Management Objects (AMO) client software.* You can install this after you install SharePoint Server and Project Server; however, you cannot build an OLAP cube until you do. Always install the *SQL Server 2008 Native Client* before installing the *Analysis Services Analysis Management Objects. The SharePoint Products and Technologies Preparation Tool* installs required server patches for you, including Service Pack 2 for Windows Server 2008, if you don't already have this installed. For a complete list of components handled by the tool, see *Installing Software Prerequisites* later in this module.

 Warning: If you install the Analysis Services Analysis Management Objects after you install Project Server, you must stop and restart the Project Application Service before Project Server will recognize their presence.

SQL Server Requirements

Project Server 2010 supports installations using SQL Server 2005 patched with Service Pack 3 and Service Pack 3 Cumulative Update 4 released on June 15, 2009. It also supports installations using SQL Server 2008 patched to RTM

Cumulative Update 5, released on May 18, 2009. Both Project Server and SharePoint Server connect only to the SQL Server database engine; tools from other manufacturers, such as Oracle, are not supported. Project Server is dependent on SQL Analysis Services, SQL Reporting Services, SQL Management tools, SQL Connectivity components and the SQL Server Agent Service. You must also install the SQL Server 2008 Native Client on the computer running SQL Analysis Services when you install SQL Analysis Services on a separate server.

Desktop Requirements

Project Web App requires Internet Explorer 7.0 or higher running on Windows XP Service Pack 2 or higher. You must have IE installed on your Project Server 2010 machine to complete the installation, and all client systems that connect to Project Web App must meet this requirement as well.

Prepare the Security Environment

Both SharePoint Server 2010 and Project Server 2010 require domain user accounts to run a variety of server-based services. You must prepare your service accounts before you begin your installation. Depending on the size of your implementation and your organization's security and account policies, you may choose to create one or more physical accounts for your deployment that fulfill one or more logical account roles.

Create Service Accounts

You must prepare your service accounts before you begin your installation. The account roles used in a SharePoint Server 2010 environment with Project Server 2010 deployed are potentially numerous. For secure farm environments and organizations that require compliance with Windows security best practices, following the principle of least privilege involves creating separate physical service accounts for each of the logical account roles for potentially all of the following account roles:

- **SQL Server Process Account Role:** The system uses the account assigned to this account role to run the various services that are part of Microsoft SQL Server. This includes SQL Server itself, the SQL Server Agent, Analysis Services, and Reporting Services. Depending on your organization's requirements, you may use multiple accounts to fulfill this role (e.g. DOMAIN\Sql_Svc for SQL, DOMAIN\SSAS_Svc for Analysis Services, and DOMAIN\SSRS_Svc for Reporting Services). This account must be a domain account and the physical account allocated to this account role should be unique within the deployment for security purposes. You can create separate accounts for SQL Server and Analysis Services. The Analysis Services service account will require db_datareader access to all Project Server reporting databases for which it builds cubes.

- **Server Farm Account Role:** The system uses the account assigned to this account role to access the SharePoint Configuration database and as the Application Pool identity for the SharePoint Central Administration site. This is also the account under which the Windows SharePoint Services Timer service runs. This account receives membership in the Logins, db_Creator, SecurityAdmin, and db_owner SQL Server security roles during the configuration of the SharePoint farm. Microsoft's documentation also refers to this account role as the Database Access Account.

 Warning: You cannot use a local Windows account for the Server Farm account role. You must install SharePoint Server 2010 into a domain environment.

If you want to build a Virtual machine environment for development or demo purposes, you must enable the Active Directory Role on your server.

- **Application Pool Process Account Role:** The system uses the account assigned to this account role as the Application Pool identity for a Web application and for accessing the content database associated with that particular Web application. The account must be a domain account, but it does not need to be a member of any particular security group. You should consider providing each Web application you plan to create with its own Application Pool Process Account Role.

Application pools are an Internet Information Services feature that enables you to run Web applications in an isolated process from other Web applications. This isolation construct prevents a crash in one application from affecting other applications running on the same server farm.

- **Site Collection Owner Account Role:** The account assigned to this account role has administrative rights over the Windows SharePoint Services site collection you create to host a SharePoint site. First, you create a Web application, which is essentially an extended Web site, to host the SharePoint site. Then, you create a new Windows SharePoint Services site collection. You enter this account when you specify a primary site collection owner. This account should be a domain user. In all likelihood, you will want to use either your personal account or the standardized administrator account provided by your organization for this purpose.

A site collection is a group of Microsoft Windows SharePoint Services sites that are sub-sites of a single top-level site.

- **Project Server Instance Administrator Role:** During the installation, you must specify the initial administrator for the instance of Microsoft Project Server 2010 that you are installing. This account must be a valid domain user. In all likelihood, you will want to use either your personal account or the standardized administrator account provided by your organization for this purpose.

- **SharePoint Search Service Account Role:** The SharePoint Search Service runs as the account assigned to this account role. The account also receives read/write access to the content databases for all Web applications, read access to the SharePoint Configuration database, and read/write access to the SharePoint Search database.

- **SharePoint Search Content Access Account Role:** The SharePoint Content Access Service uses the account assigned to this account role to access content within the SharePoint farm. The account should be a domain account, and you may use the same account used for the SharePoint Search Service Account Role for this account role. For security purposes, this account should not have permission to modify any content within the farm.

- **Excel Services Account Role:** The account under which Excel Services runs.

- **Project Server Application Account Role:** The application service account for the Project Server 2010 Service running on SharePoint Server.

- **Secure Store Service Account Role:** The account under which the Secure Store Service runs.

- **PerformancePoint Services Service Account Role:** The account under which PerformancePoint Services runs

- **Secure Store Target Application Role:** The account that the *Target Application* for the Secure Store instance for the Business Intelligence Center uses to access data for the *Report Viewers* group in the Business Intelligence Center.

- **State Services Account Role:** The account under which the State Services runs.

- **Other Service Account Roles:** These include an account for each additional SharePoint Service application that you choose to create.

 For single-front-end-server farm environments, MSProjectExperts recommends that you create a single Active Directory account to use for all account roles except the SQL Server Process Accounts and the Target Application for the Secure Store Service.

Create Domain Global Groups for Reporting

Project Server 2010 reporting requires two domain groups: one group that provides security privileges for Report Authors, users who have the right to create and edit reports in Project Server 2010; and one group for Report Viewers, users who can access the reports in the Project Server 2010 Report Center. You use these groups when configuring Excel Services.

Prepare SQL Server for SharePoint Server and Project Server

This procedure assumes that you previously installed Microsoft SQL Server 2005 or 2008 along with its respective version of Analysis Services. After installing the SQL engine, you must configure or verify a number of settings, and Microsoft recommends best-practice for performance settings that you should strongly consider adopting as well.

For Project Server 2010 to work correctly, SQL Server must be configured to allow remote connections using TCP/IP. This is the default configuration for SQL Server, but you should verify this configuration prior to installing Project Server.

Configure SQL Network Settings for SQL Server 2008 (SQL 2005 users skip to next section)

To configure the network settings for SQL Server 2008 complete the following steps:

1. From the computer console click the *Start* button ➤ All Programs ➤ Microsoft SQL Server 2008

2. Expand *Configuration Tools* and select *SQL Server Configuration Manager* from the menu as shown in Figure 4 - 1.

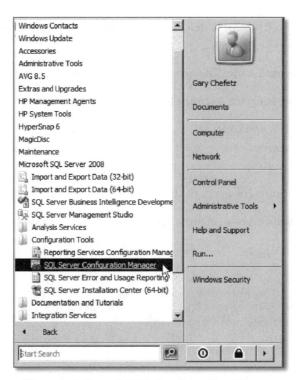

**Figure 4 - 1: Launch SQL Configuration Manager
from the *All Programs* menu**

The system displays the *SQL Server Configuration Manager*.

3. In the left pane, expand *SQL Server Network Configuration,* and then select the target SQL Server instance for your Project Server databases.

4. Verify that the *TCP/IP* option is enabled in the right frame.

Your *SQL Configuration Manager* should appear as shown in Figure 4 - 2.

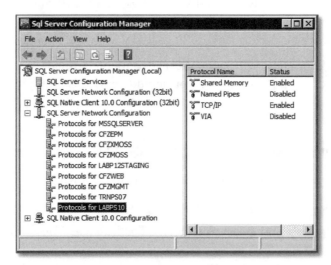

**Figure 4 - 2: SQL Server 2008 Configuration Manager
Showing TCP/IP Enabled**

Although the Named Pipes transport setting is not enabled in the example, you can enable this transport without affecting Project Server 2010

Configure SQL Network Settings for SQL Server 2005

To configure the network settings for SQL Server 2005 complete the following steps:

1. Click Start ➤ All Programs ➤ Microsoft SQL Server 2005 ➤ Configuration Tools ➤ SQL Server Surface Area Configuration. The system displays the *SQL Server 2005 Surface Area Configuration* dialog shown in Figure 4 - 3.

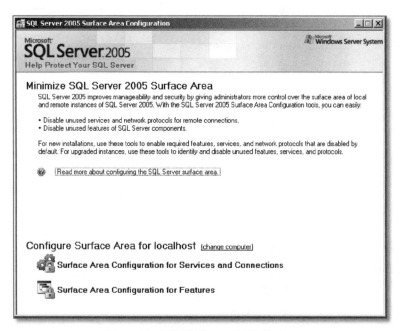

Figure 4 - 3: SQL Server 2005 Surface Area Configuration dialog

2. In the *SQL Server 2005 Surface Area Configuration* dialog, click the *Surface Area Configuration for Services and Connections* link. The system displays the *Surface Area Configuration for Services and Connections* dialog for the local machine as shown in Figure 4 - 4.

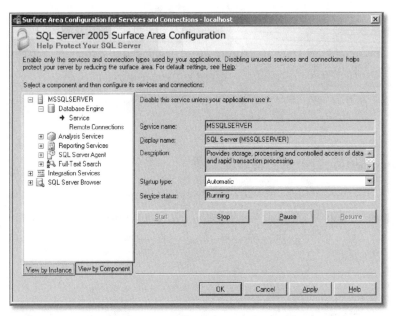

**Figure 4 - 4: SQL Server 2005 Surface
Area Configuration for Services and Connections dialog**

2.   In the tree view pane on the left, expand the node for your instance of SQL Server, expand the *Database Engine* node, and then click *Remote Connections*.

3.   The system changes the dialog display to reflect your selection as shown in Figure 4 - 5. Select the *Local and remote connections* option, then select the *Using both TCP/IP and named pipes* sub option, and then click the *OK* button.

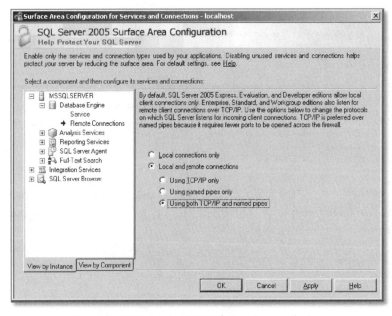

Figure 4 - 5: Using both TCP/IP and named pipes

The system displays the *Connection Settings Change Alert* dialog shown in Figure 4 - 6.

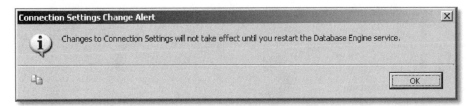

**Figure 4 - 6: Connection Settings
Change Alert dialog**

4. Click the *OK* button in the *Connection Settings Change Alert* dialog and close the *Surface Area Configuration for Services and Connections* window.

5. To respond to the alert dialog and restart your SQL Server instance, click Start ➤ All Programs ➤ Microsoft SQL Server 2005 ➤ SQL Server Management Server.

6. If the system prompts you to select a connection, select the appropriate server and click the *Connect* button in the *Connect to Server* dialog shown in Figure 4 - 7.

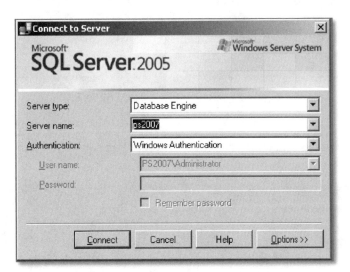

Figure 4 - 7: Connect to Server dialog

7. After you click the *Connect* button in the *Connect to Server* dialog, the system displays the *Microsoft SQL Server Management Studio* window shown in Figure 4 - 8. Right-click on the server name and select the *Restart* item on the shortcut menu.

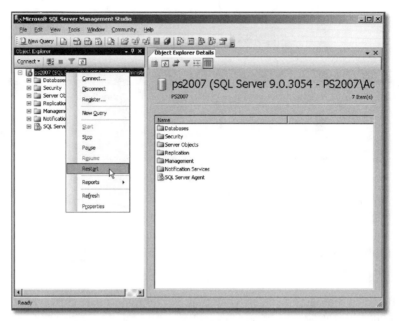

Figure 4 - 8: Restart the MSSQLSERVER service

8. When the system prompts for verification as shown in Figure 4 - 9, click the *Yes* button to restart the service.

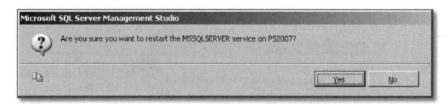

**Figure 4 - 9: Restart the MSSQLSERVER
service confirmation**

The system reports its progress displaying the Service Control dialog shown in Figure 4 - 10.

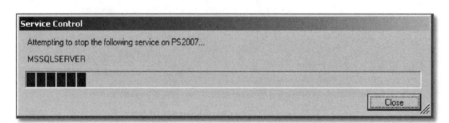

**Figure 4 - 10: Restart the MSSQLSERVER service
progress Service Control dialog**

Add a SQL Server Login for the Farm Administrator Account

Project Server 2010 requires that the Farm Administrator Role Account have a SQL Server login with *public*, *dbcerator*, *securityadmin* and *sysadmin* roles in SQL Server. To create a SQL Server login and add the roles for the login, complete the following steps:

1. Open SQL Server Management Studio.

2. Connect to the database engine for your Project Server 2010 target instance as shown in Figure 4 - 11.

The screen shot examples that follow are based on SQL Server Management Studio for SQL Server 2008.

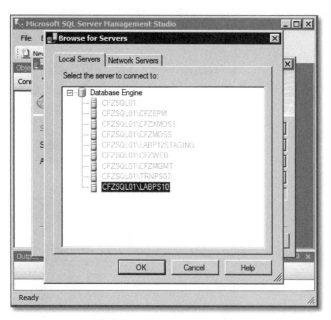

**Figure 4 - 11: Connect to SQL Server instance for
Project Server 2010 installation**

3. Expand the *Security* node, then right-click on *Logins* and select the *New Login* option as shown in Figure 4 - 12.

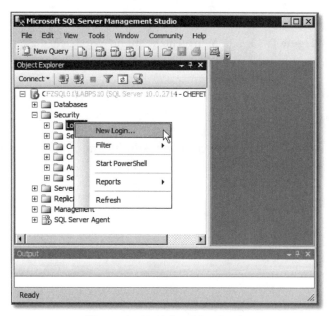

Figure 4 - 12: Select *New Login*

4. The system displays the *New Login* dialog shown in Figure 4 - 13.

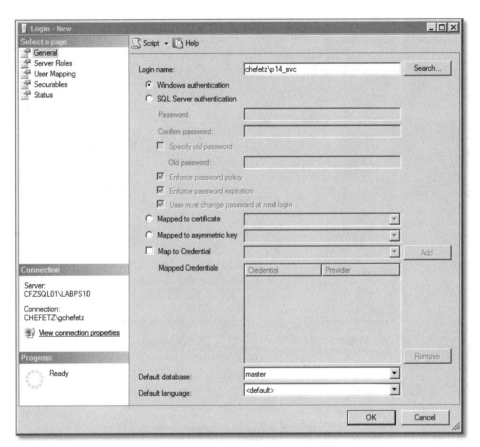

Figure 4 - 13: SQL Management Studio *New Login* dialog

5. Enter the domain account you created for the Farm Administrator in the *Login Name* field. From the *Select a page* list on the left, select *Server Roles*. The system displays the *Server Roles* page as shown in Figure 4 - 14.

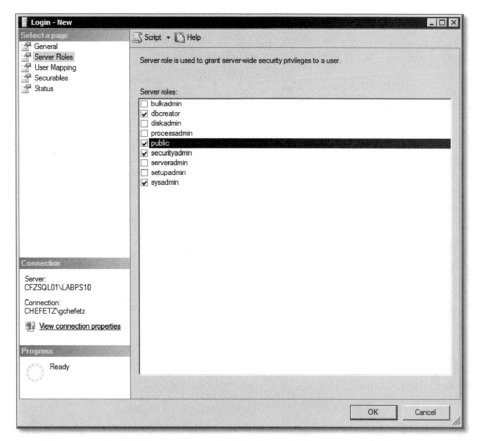

Figure 4 - 14: SQL Management Studio *Server Roles* page for the New Login

6. In the *Server roles* list, select the *dbcreator, securityadmin*, and *sysadmin* check boxes. The *public* roles checkbox is selected by default. Leave this setting selected.

7. Click the *OK* button to continue.

Enable the Common Language Runtime

Enabling the *Common Language Runtime* (CLR) for SQL Server improves Project Server 2010 performance by 30% on average, according to Microsoft. To enable the common language runtime, click on the *New Query* button in the *SQL Server Management Studio* window and copy the following query into the *SQL Query* pane as shown in Figure 4 - 15.

```
sp_configure 'clr enabled', 1;
go
reconfigure;
go
```

Figure 4 - 15: New Query Window to Enable CLR

Click the *Execute* button to execute the query and enable the CLR. After executing the query the output section should report a success message like the one shown in Code Sample below. Note that the Query includes the RECONFIGURE statement, and it is not necessary to run this again.

```
Configuration option 'clr enabled' changed from 0 to 1. Run the RECONFIGURE state-
ment to install.
```

Set SQL Server Database Collation

Your SQL Server collation must be configured for case-insensitive. In a default English language version, the default collation (SQL_Latin1_General_CP1_CI_AS) is compliant with this requirement. If you are not working with a default English SQL Server installation, you may need to change your SQL Server database collation to case-insensitive, accent-sensitive, Kana-sensitive, and width-sensitive.

Prepare SQL Server Analysis Services for Project Server

You must complete two simple configuration steps to prepare your instance of SQL Server Analysis Services for Project Server 2010: 1) Add the Farm Administrator Role account to the *OLAP Users Local Group* on the server, and 2) Configure the Farm Administrator Role account permissions in SQL Server Analysis services.

To add the Farm Administrator account to the *OLAP Users Local Group*, complete the following steps:

1. Log in to the computer running Analysis Services and select Administrative Tools from the *Start* menu and select *Computer Management* from the submenu.

2. On the *Computer Management* page, in the left pane under *System Tools*, expand the *Local Users and Groups* item. Click to expand the *Groups* folder and locate the *OLAP Users Local Group* for your Analysis Services instance as shown for SQL Analysis Services 2008 in Figure 4 - 16 .

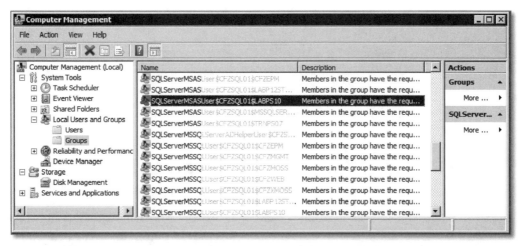

Figure 4 - 16: Located Local OLAP Users Group for SQL Analysis Services 2008

The group names are in the following possible formats:

SQLServer2005MSOLAPUser$<SERVERNAME>$MSSQLSERVERINSTANCE (SQL Server 2005) or
SQLServerMSASUser$<SERVERNAME>$MSSQLSERVERINSTANCE (SQL Server 2008).

3. Double-click on the group name to open the group *Properties* dialog shown in Figure 4 - 17.

**Figure 4 - 17: Local OLAP User Group
Properties dialog**

4. In the *Properties* dialog, click the *Add* button. The system displays the *Select Users, Computers, or Groups* dialog shown in Figure 4 - 18.

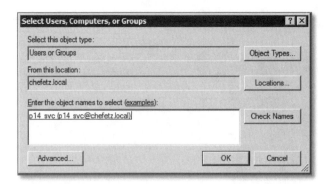

Figure 4 - 18: Select Users, Computers, or Groups dialog

5. In the *Select Users, Computers, or Groups* dialog, enter the name of your Farm Administrator account. You may click the *Check Names* button to verify your entry, or click the *OK* button to accept your entry. The account now appears in the *Members* section of the *Group Properties* dialog shown previously in Figure 4 - 17 above. Click the *OK* button to close the *Group Properties* dialog and then close the *Computer Management* page to continue.

To add the Farm Administrator as an Analysis Services server administrator complete the following steps:

1. Open SQL Server Management Studio. In the *Connect to Server* window, select or browse to connect to the SQL Server Analysis Services instance for your Project Sever 2010 deployment.

2. In *Microsoft SQL Server Management Studio Object Explorer*, right-click on your SQL Server 2005 Analysis Services instance name, and then click *Properties* from the pop-up menu. The system displays the *Analysis Services Properties* dialog. From the *Select a page* pane, click the *Security* item. Your *Analysis Server Properties* dialog should look like the one shown in Figure 4 - 19.

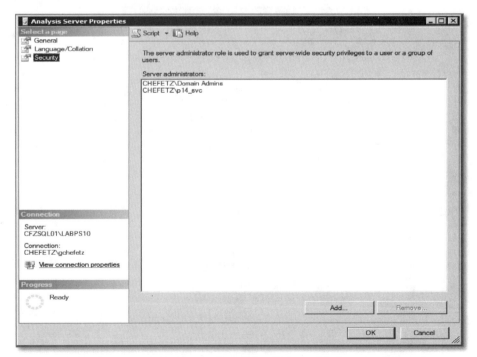

Figure 4 - 19: Analysis Server Properties dialog with Security Selected

3. Click the *Add* button. The system displays the *Select Users or Groups* dialog as shown in Figure 4 - 20.

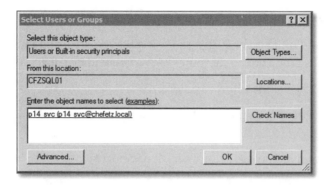

Figure 4 - 20: Select Users or Groups dialog

4. On the *Select Users or Groups* dialog, type the name of the Farm Administrator account.

5. Click the *OK* button to add the Farm Administrator account to *the Server Administrators* list.

6. Click the *OK* button on the *Analysis Server Properties* page to exit the operation.

Prepare Your Server for Project Server Installation

There are a couple of small tasks left to complete before you begin the actual SharePoint Server 2010 and Project Server 2010 software installation.

Configure Proxy Server Bypass

If you have a proxy server in your environment, it may be necessary for you to configure the proxy server settings on the server to bypass the proxy server for local addresses. To change these settings, follow these steps:

1. In Internet Explorer, click Tools ➢ Internet Options.

3. Select the *Connections* tab and in the *Local Area Network (LAN) Settings* area, click the *LAN Settings* button.

3. In the *Proxy Server* area, select the *Use a proxy server for your LAN* and *Bypass proxy server for local addresses* checkboxes.

4. Click the *OK* button to close the *Local Area Network (LAN) Settings* dialog.

5. Click the *OK* button again to close the Internet Options dialog.

Disable Internet Explorer Enhanced Security Settings

Use the following procedure to disable Internet Explorer Enhanced Security settings on your server:

1. Click Start ➢ Programs ➢ Administrative Tools ➢ Server Manager.

2. In the *Server Manager* window, expand the *Server Summary* in the navigation tree on the right.

3. In *Security Information* section, click the *Configure IE ESC* link. The system opens the *Internet Explorer Enhanced Security Configuration* dialog.

4. In the *Administrators* section, click the *Off* option to disable the Internet Explorer Enhanced Security settings.

5. Click the *OK* button to complete your configuration.

Add the Farm Administrator Role Account to the Local Admin Group

Before you begin installing SharePoint Server 2010 and Project Server 2010, you must add the Farm Administrator account to the *Local Administrators* group on the computer where you will install SharePoint Server and Project Server.

To add a local administrator, complete the following steps:

1. Log in to the computer where you will be installing SharePoint Server 2010 with local administrator credentials.

2. Click Start ➢ Administrative Tools ➢ Computer Management.

3. Expand the *Local Users and Groups* node and click on the *Groups* folder.

4. Double-click the *Administrators* group to open the *Administrators Properties* dialog.

5. Click the *Add* button in the *Administrators Properties* dialog to open the *Select Computers, Users or Groups* dialog.

6. Type the name of the Farm Administrator account in the *Enter the object names to select* window.

7. Click the *OK* button. The Farm Administrator account now appears in the *Members* list.

8. Click the *OK* button to close the *Administrators Properties* dialog.

Installing SharePoint Server 2010 and Project Server 2010

Now that you have added the Farm Administrator account to the local Administrators group, log off the server and log on again using the Farm Administrator account. Remain logged on using that account as you complete the rest of the installation and configuration. At this point of the installation process you had to gather and install a series of prerequisite software components manually. The SharePoint 2010 product series introduces the *SharePoint 2010 Preparation Tool* that you can launch from the SharePoint Server 2010 setup wizard to gather and install the prerequisites automatically. This is one of the big improvements to the installation experience that I mentioned in the introduction of this module. To use this feature, you must have an Internet connection available. The instructions in the rest of this section assume that you are using the *SharePoint 2010 Preparation Tool*. You can elect to install each of these manually.

Install Software Prerequisites

Installing SharePoint Server 2010 consists of two primary steps, installing the prerequisites and installing the server software. To install prerequisites using the *SharePoint Server 2010 Preparation Tool*, follow the steps below. The tool not only installs all necessary software components, it also configures the *Application Server* and *Web Server* server roles.

The SharePoint Server 2010 Preparation Tool installs the following components on your system if they are not already installed. You may choose to gather these and install them manually:

- Windows Server 2008 Service Pack 2
- Application Server Role, Web Server (IIS) Role
- Microsoft SQL Server 2008 Native Client
- Microsoft .NET Framework 3.5 SP1: was already installed (no action taken)
- Hotfix for Microsoft Windows (KB976394)

- Windows PowerShell 2.0 • Windows Identity Foundation (KB974405): was already installed (no action taken)

- Microsoft Sync Framework Runtime v1.0 (x64)

- Microsoft Chart Controls for Microsoft .NET Framework 3.5

- Microsoft Filter Pack 2.0

- Microsoft SQL Server 2008 Analysis Services ADOMD.NET

- Microsoft Server Speech Platform Runtime (x64)

- Microsoft Server Speech Recognition Language - TELE(en-US)

- SQL 2008 R2 Reporting Services SharePoint 2010 Add-in

When you are ready to begin your installation, launch the SharePoint Server 2010 executable package. The system momentarily displays an *Extracting files* dialog and then displays the *SharePoint Server 2010* installation launcher shown in Figure 4 - 21.

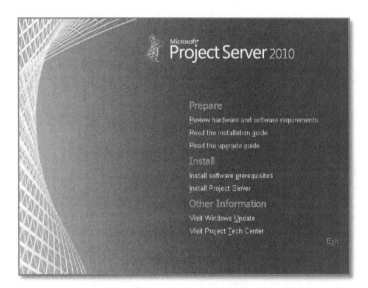

Figure 4 - 21: SharePoint Server 2010 Installation Launcher

Notice that the *Installation Launcher* contains links to documentation including a document outlining hardware and software requirements, and an installation guide and an upgrade guide accessible from the *Prepare* selections at the top. To install software prerequisites automatically, select *Install software prerequisites* from the *Install* section of the page. The system displays the *Welcome Page* for the *SharePoint Products and Technologies 2010 Preparation Tool* dialog as shown in Figure 4 - 22.

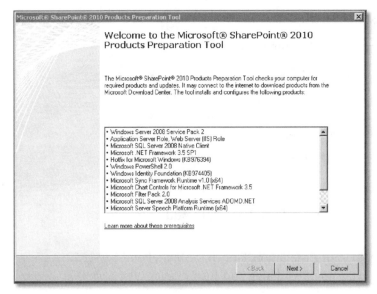

**Figure 4 - 22: SharePoint Products and
Technologies 2010 Preparation Tool Welcome Page**

The page lists the prerequisite software components to install. Click the *Next* button to begin the automatic prerequisite installation process. The system displays the *SharePoint Products and Technologies 2010 Preparation Tool* End User License Agreement (EULA) shown in Figure 4 - 23.

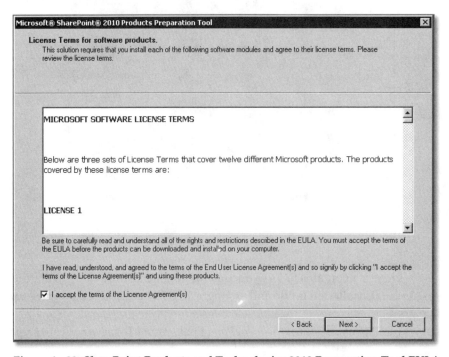

Figure 4 - 23: SharePoint Products and Technologies 2010 Preparation Tool EULA

On the *License Terms for software products* page, read the license agreement. In order to continue you must accept the terms. To accept the terms, select the *I accept the terms of the License Agreement(s)* check box. Click the *Next* button to continue. The system displays the progress page shown in Figure 4 - 24.

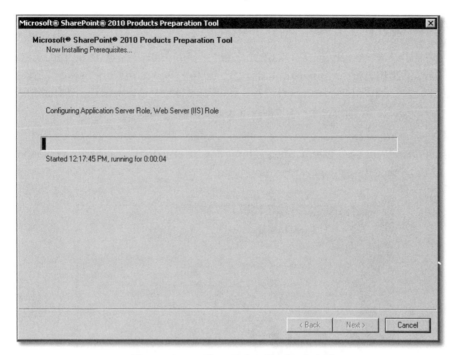

**Figure 4 - 24: SharePoint Products and
Technologies 2010 Preparation Tool Progress Page**

The system proceeds to download and install prerequisite software components. When the process completes, the system displays the *Installation Complete* page as shown in Figure 4 - 25.

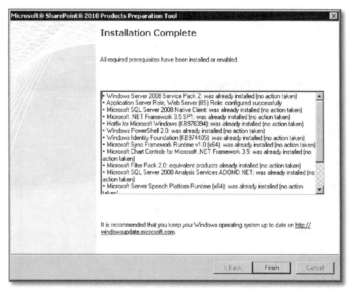

Figure 4 - 25: Installation Complete Confirmation Page

When the wizard finishes, click the *Finish* button. If the system prompts you, restart the computer. This will depend upon which prerequisites you installed during this process.

Install SharePoint Server 2010 Software

After you complete the software prerequisite installation either manually or by using the wizard, you are ready to start the SharePoint Server 2010 application installation. To install the SharePoint Server 2010 software, launch the installation package. If you are installing from a DVD, your system may auto-run the *SharePoint Server 2010* installation launcher shown previously in Figure 4 - 21. Complete the following steps:

1. Click the *Install SharePoint Server* item. The system may briefly display a loading splash page before displaying the *Enter Your Product Key* page shown in Figure 4 - 26.

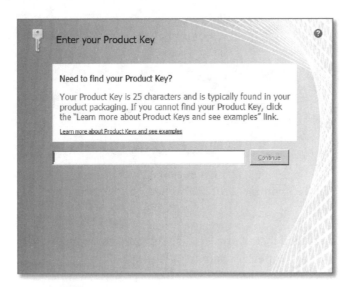

Figure 4 - 26: Enter Your Product Key Page

2. Enter your product key on the page and click the *Continue* button after the system validates your key. The system displays the *Read the Microsoft Software License Terms* page shown in Figure 4 - 27.

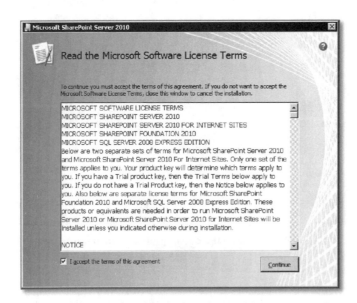

Figure 4 - 27: Read the Microsoft Software License Terms Page

3. Read the license terms. In order to continue you must accept the terms. To accept the terms, select the *I accept the terms of this agreement* check box, and then click the *Continue* button. The system displays the *Choose the installation you want* page shown in Figure 4 - 28.

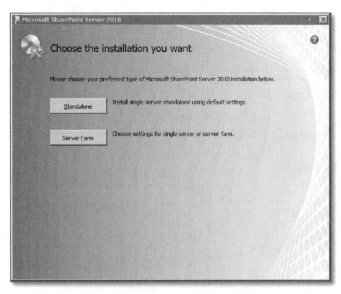

Figure 4 - 28: Choose the Installation You Want Page

4. On the *Choose the installation you want* page, click the *Server Farm* button. The system displays the *Server Type* page shown in Figure 4 - 29.

 Standalone installations of SharePoint Server 2010 and Project Server 2010 use SQL Express only, which limits you to a 4 gigabyte database, and does not support the use of Analysis Services for reporting . The functionality supported by this type of installation is limited. This book focuses on full enterprise installations and does not cover standalone installations. To learn more about this type of installation, visit http://technet.microsoft.com. Do not select this option on either page.

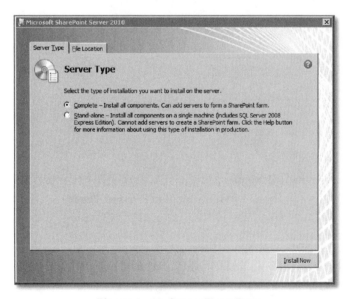

Figure 4 - 29: Server Type Page

95

5. On the *Server Type* page, select the *Complete* option and then click on the *File Location* tab. The system displays the *Choose a file location* page shown in Figure 4 - 30.

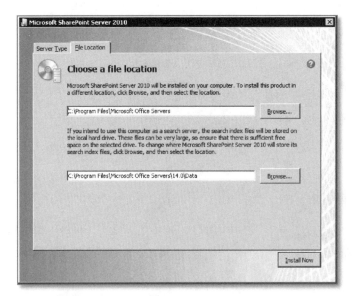

Figure 4 - 30: Choose a File Location Page

6. On the *Choose a file location* page you can accept the default file locations for programs and Search Server files or specify alternate file locations. When you complete these selections, click the *Install Now* button to continue. The system displays the *Installation Progress* page shown in Figure 4 - 31.

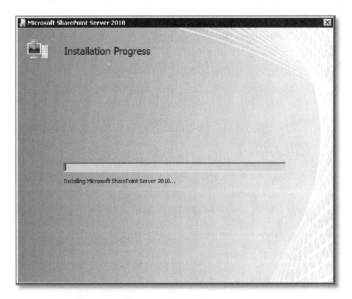

Figure 4 - 31: Installation Progress Page

7. When the wizard completes the SharePoint Server 2010 installation, the system displays the *Run Configuration Wizard* page to launch the *SharePoint Products and Technologies Configuration Wizard* as shown in Figure 4 - 32.

The SharePoint Server 2010 installation may take five to ten minutes to complete.

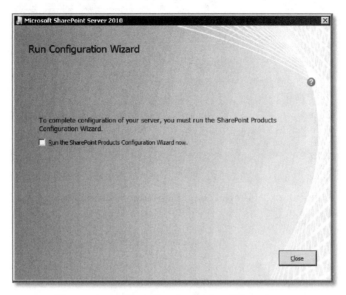

Figure 4 - 32: Run Configuration Wizard page

8. Deselect the *Run the SharePoint Products and Technologies Configuration Wizard now* check box and click the *Close* button to continue.

 Rather than running the *SharePoint Products and Technologies Configuration Wizard* twice, once after the base SharePoint Server installation and then again after installing the Project Server software, you will run the wizard only after completing the Project Server software installation.

9. Click the *Exit* link on the SharePoint Server 2010 installation page to Exit.

Install Project Server 2010

The next step is to install the Project Server 2010 application software. Use the following procedure to install the Project Server 2010 software:

1. On the Project Server 2010 DVD, run *default.hta*, which may launch automatically when you load the disc, or launch the installation executable from a file source to open the *Project Server 2010 Installation Launcher* shown in Figure 4 - 33.

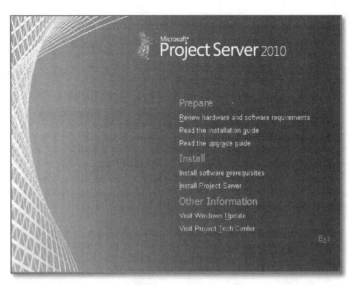

Figure 4 - 33: Project Server 2010 Installation Launcher

2.   Select the *Install Project Server* link from the *Install* section of the page. The system displays the *Enter your Product Key* page shown in Figure 4 - 34.

Figure 4 - 34: Project Server Enter your Product Key Page

3.   Enter your license key in the *Enter your Product Key* page and click the *Continue* button when the software validates you license entry. Click the *Continue* button to advance to the *Read the Microsoft Software License Terms* page shown in Figure 4 - 35.

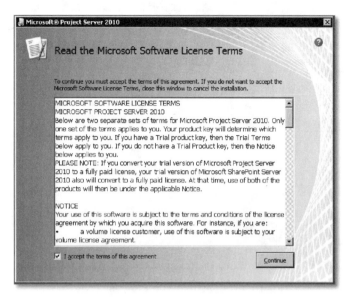

Figure 4 - 35: Project Server End User License Agreement

4. On the *Read the Microsoft Software License Terms* page, read the license terms. In order to continue you must accept the terms. To accept terms of the End User License Agreement, select the *I accept the terms of this agreement* check box. Then click the *Continue* button to proceed to the *Choose a file location* page shown in Figure 4 - 36.

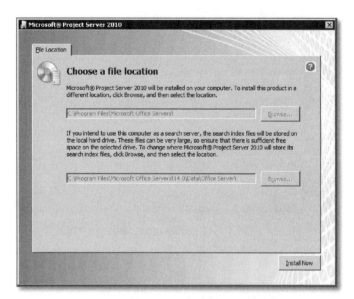

Figure 4 - 36: Choose a File Location Page

5. Note that the file locations on the *Choose a file location* page are grayed out. Your Project Server program files install to the same directory as SharePoint Server. Click the *Install Now* button to continue. The system displays the *Installation Progress* page shown in Figure 4 - 37.

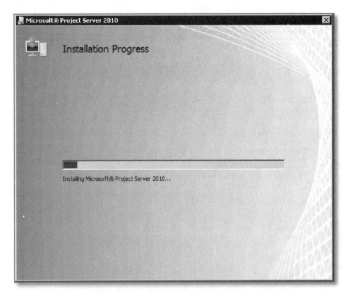

Figure 4 - 37: Installation Progress Page

6. When the system completes the installation in several minutes, the system displays the *Run Configuration Wizard* page as shown in Figure 4 - 38.

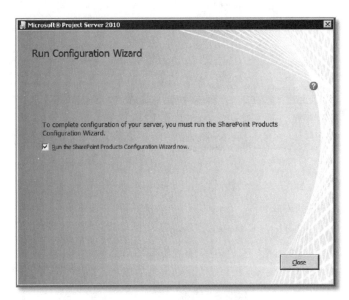

Figure 4 - 38: Run Configuration Wizard Page

Run SharePoint Products Configuration Wizard

From the *Run Configuration Wizard* page shown previously in Figure 4 - 38, select the *Run the SharePoint Products Configuration Wizard now* check box and click the *Close* button to continue. The system displays the *Welcome to SharePoint Products* page shown in Figure 4 - 39.

You can also run the *SharePoint Products Configuration Wizard* manually from the Windows *Start Menu* by selecting Start ➤ All Programs ➤ Microsoft SharePoint 2010 Products.

Figure 4 - 39: Welcome to SharePoint Products Page

Continue with the following steps:

1. On the *Welcome to SharePoint Products* page, click the *Next* button. The system displays a confirmation dialog showing a list of services that may need to be restarted as shown in Figure 4 - 40.

Figure 4 - 40: Service Restart Warning

2. Click the *Yes* button in the dialog to continue. The system displays the *Connect to a server farm* page shown in Figure 4 - 41.

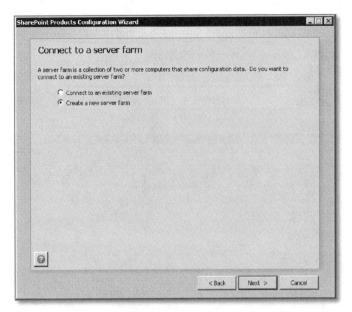

Figure 4 - 41: Connect to a Server Farm Page

3. On the *Connect to a server farm* page, select the *Create a new server farm* option, and then click the *Next* button to continue. The system displays the *Specify Configuration Database Settings* page shown in Figure 4 - 42.

Figure 4 - 42: Specify Configuration Database Settings Page

4. On the *Specify Configuration Database Settings* page enter your database server name in the *Database server* field. Accept or change the default name for the *SharePoint_Config* database in the *Database name* field. Type the user name and password for the Database access account role in the *Username* and *Password* fields. You can use the Farm Administrator account for this purpose. When you complete your entries, click the *Next* button to continue. The system displays the *Specify Farm Security Settings* page shown in Figure 4 - 43.

Figure 4 - 43: Specify Farm Security Settings Page

5. On the *Specify Farm Security Settings* page, enter and confirm a passphrase for the farm, and then click the *Next* button to proceed to the *Configure SharePoint Central Administration Web Application* page shown in Figure 4 - 44.

**Figure 4 - 44: Configure SharePoint Central Administration
Web Application Page**

6. On the *Configure SharePoint Central Administration Web Application* page, select the *Specify port number* checkbox to enter a port number for your new Central Administration site or accept the default randomly generated port number. Under *Configure Security Settings*, select *NTLM* or *Negotiate (Kerberos)*. Click the *Next* button to continue to the *Completing the SharePoint Products Configuration Wizard* page shown in Figure 4 - 45.

MSProjectExperts recommends that you use a standardized port number for your SharePoint Central Administration sites for easier human recall.

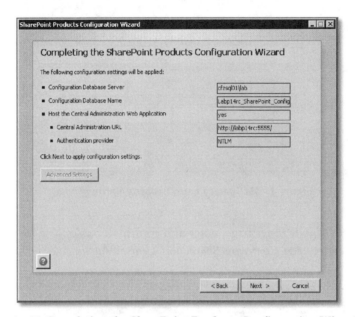

Figure 4 - 45: Completing the SharePoint Products Configuration Wizard Page

7. Confirm your entries on the *Completing the SharePoint Products Configuration Wizard* page. Correct any mistakes by using the *Back* button to navigate to the page that requires updating. Confirm the information displayed by clicking the *Next* button to continue. The system displays the *Configuring SharePoint Products* progress page shown in Figure 4 - 46.

Figure 4 - 46: Configuring SharePoint Products Progress Page

This process may run for five to ten minutes before reaching completion.

8. When the process completes, the system displays the *Configuration Successful* page as shown in Figure 4 - 47.

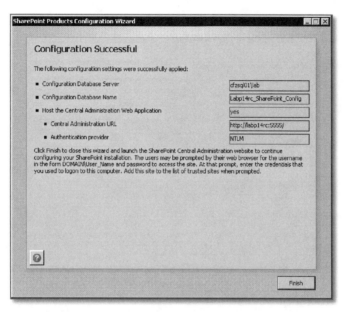

Figure 4 - 47: Configuration Successful Page

9. On the *Configuration Successful* page, click the *Finish* button to close the *SharePoint Products Configuration Wizard*. The system loads the new Central Administration site in a browser window with the *Help Make SharePoint Better* dialog shown in **Error! Reference source not found.**.

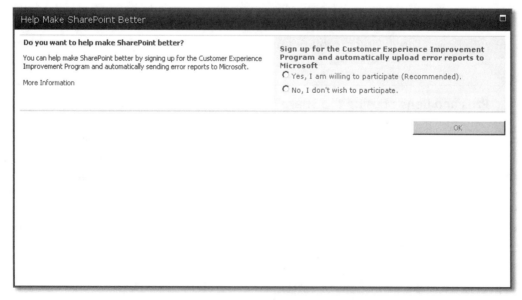

Figure 4 - 48: Help Make SharePoint Better

10. Select to participate or select to not participate and click the *OK* button to continue. The system displays the *Configure your SharePoint farm* page shown in Figure 4 - 49.

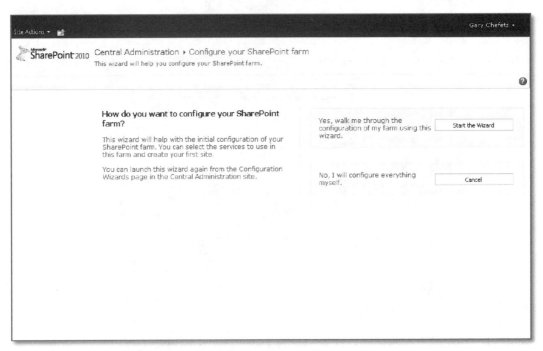

Figure 4 - 49: Configure your SharePoint farm page

You can run the SharePoint Farm Configuration wizard now or choose to cancel by clicking the *Cancel* button and run the wizard later by launching it from SharePoint Central Administration.

Configure Your SharePoint Farm

By completing all of the previous steps in this module, you now have an empty SharePoint Server farm with Project Server available as a service application on the farm. Most importantly, you now have a Central Administration site from which you can create new standard and custom SharePoint Server 2010 site collections, provisioning as many sites as you want with Project Server 2010 capabilities provided you stay within your practical system limits.

Pros and Cons of using the SharePoint Products Configuration Wizard

When you use the SharePoint Products Configuration Wizard, you lose control of numerous configuration options for each Service Application, such as the Service Application name, the service account that it uses and the application pool that it uses. Administrators following the principle of least privilege should create each instance of a service application separately to control these variables. When you use the wizard, all service applications are created under a new application pool that the system creates for you using a GUID for a name and runs the application pool under the Farm Administrator Account that you specified when creating your farm. You can change these later using the Application Server Snap-in for Windows 2008 Server Manager. I show you how to manually create a Service Application in the last topic of this module.

Select Services and Create a Site Collection

When the *SharePoint Products Configuration Wizard* completes, it is time to complete the SharePoint and server configurations required to start the project service and create your first Project Server application instance and site. You use the *SharePoint 2010 Farm Configuration Wizard* to perform the following tasks:

1. Select the *Configuration Wizards* link from the *Central Administration* menu of the *SharePoint 2010 Central Administration* screen shown in Figure 4 - 50 or click the *Start the Wizard* button shown in the previous figure.

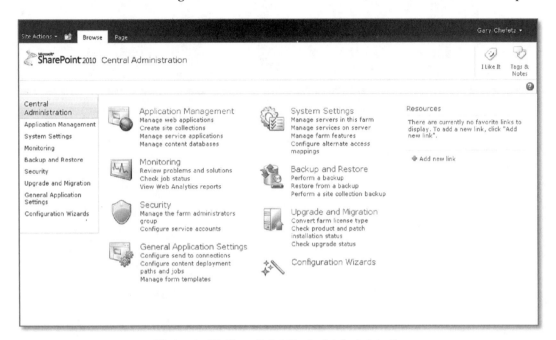

Figure 4 - 50: SharePoint Central Administration

2. The system displays the *Configurations Wizards* page shown in Figure 4 - 51.

Figure 4 - 51: Configuration Wizards Page

3. Click on the *Launch the Farm Configuration Wizard* link. The system displays the *Configure your SharePoint farm* page shown previously in Figure 4 - 49. Click the *Start the Wizard* button to advance to the *Select the services you want to run in your farm* page shown in Figure 4 - 52.

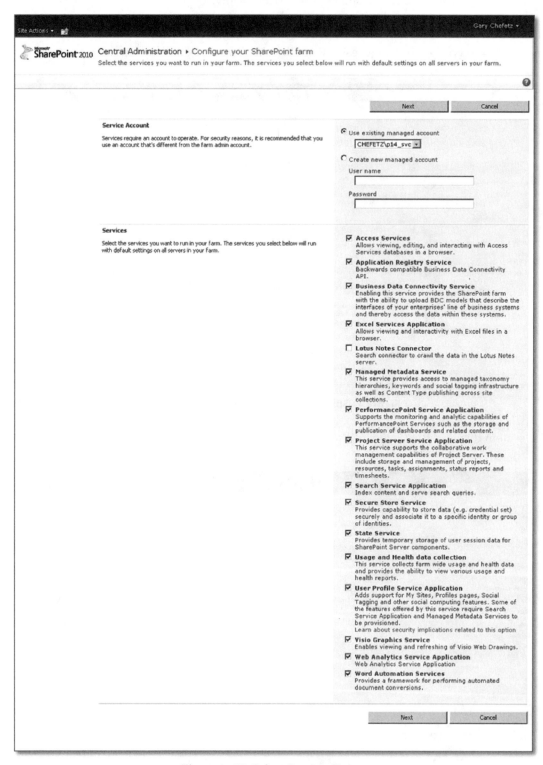

Figure 4 - 52: Select Services Page

4. In the *Service Account* section, select the *Use existing managed account* option, selecting the farm administrator account, unless you're using a more granular service account approach. In the *Services* section, select the services that you want to run for this instance. The services required for Project Server 2010 are Excel Services Application, PerformancePoint Service Application, Project Server Service Application, Secure Store Service, and State Service. You can choose to enable additional services based on the requirements you identified for your organization or server farm. Click the *Next* button to continue. The system displays a *Processing* page while it applies your selections. This process may take several minutes to complete. Upon completion, the system displays the *Create Site Collection* page shown in Figure 4 - 53.

You can deselect all or as many of the other services that you do not want. Remember that each additional service requires additional server resources. To optimize system performance , activate only those services that you will actually use.

When you select services to activate in the *Farm Configuration Wizard*, the wizard not only starts the service on your farm, for all built-in SharePoint services, and for Project Server, it also creates a service applicaiton for the service, or a running instance of the service. You can activate additional services later through SharePoint Central administration, but when you do this, you must take the separate step of creating the service application manually. Another method you can use to add services, along with a respective service applicaiton, is to re-run the Farm Configuration Wizard.

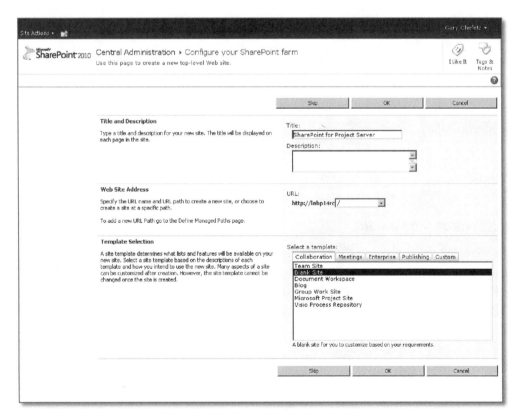

Figure 4 - 53: Create Site Collection Page

5. Next, you create a new top-level website for your Project Server site collection. Give your site a title and optionally a description. Determine your Web Site Address, select the *Blank Site* template in the template section and click the *OK* button to create the site collection top-level site. When the system completes the site creation, it displays the confirmation page shown in Figure 4 - 54.

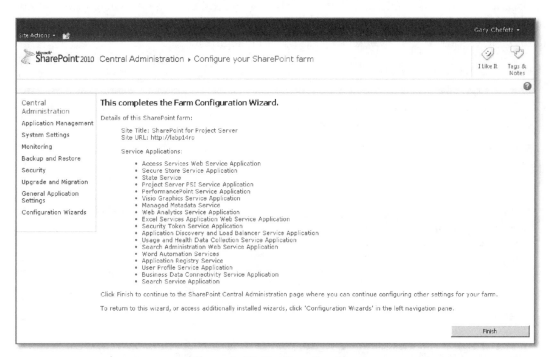

Figure 4 - 54: Confirmation Page

6. Click the *Finish* button to close the *Configure your SharePoint farm wizard*. The system returns to the *SharePoint Central Administration* homepage shown previously in Figure 4 - 50.

Set Read Permissions on the New Site

Now that you have created a new top-level site collection to contain your Project Server 2010 site instances, you must first give your users read permission to the new top level web site you created using the wizard. To accomplish this, you must navigate to the site. In the example above, I created the new top-level site at the server root. To navigate to the root site, enter "http://<servername>" in your browser. The system displays the homepage of your new site as shown in Figure 4 - 55.

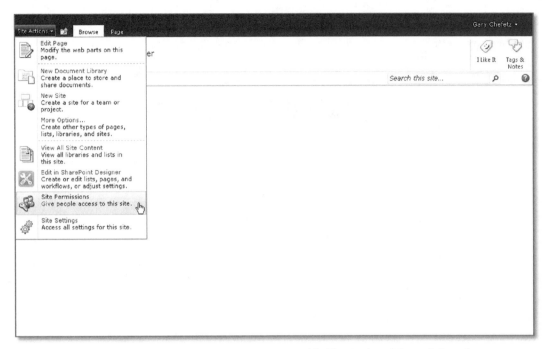

Figure 4 - 55: Top Level Site Homepage with Site Actions Menu Selected

7. On your root-site homepage, click on the *Site Actions* menu and select *Site Permissions*. The system displays the *Edit permissions* page shown in Figure 4 - 56.

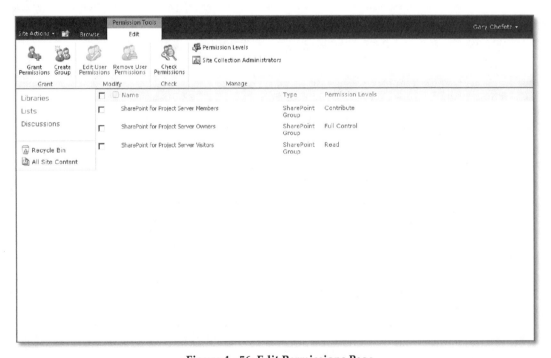

Figure 4 - 56: Edit Permissions Page

8. Click the *Grant Permissions* button on the ribbon menu. The system displays the *Grant Permissions* window shown in Figure 4 - 57.

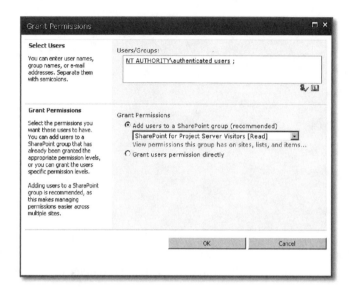

Figure 4 - 57: Grant Permissions Window

9. In the *Users/Groups* text box, type "NT AUTHORITY\authenticated users" without the quotes, and in the *Grant Permissions* selection list, select *Add users to a SharePoint group (recommended)*, choose the *SharePoint for Project Server Visitors (Read)* group for your top-level site, and click the *OK* button to continue. The system returns to the *Edit Permissions* page shown in the previous figure.

Create a Project Server 2010 Web App

Now that you have a top-level site collection prepared to house your Project Web App sites, it is time to create your first Project Web App instance. To create a new Project Web App site, select *Manage service applications* from the *Application Management* section of the SharePoint Central Administration homepage shown previously in Figure 4 - 50 **Error! Reference source not found.** The system displays the *Service Applications* page shown in Figure 4 - 58.

If you are new to SharePoint and Project Server, keep in mind that Project Server 2010 is a SharePoint Server 2010 service application and it derives all of its platform capability from SharePoint Server, and is managed as an application through SharePoint Server. Pay close attention to the following steps and spend some time on each screen to get familiar with using the SharePoint Central Administration user interface.

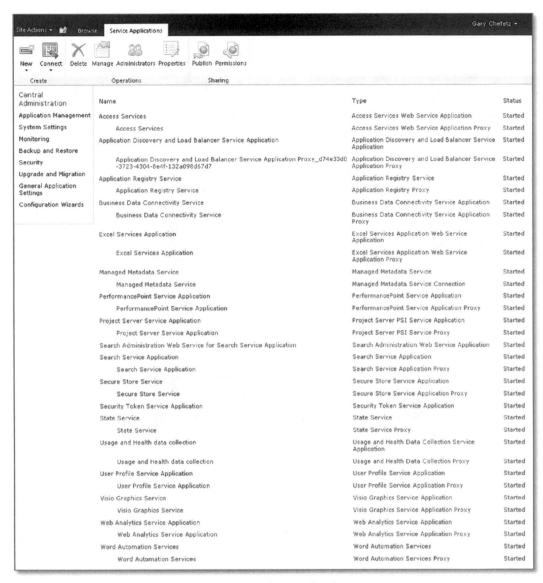

Figure 4 - 58: Service Applications Page

Continue with the following steps:

1. On the *Service Applications* page, select the *Project Server Service Application* link from the page or select the *Project Server Service Application* row to activate the *Operations* section icons on the ribbon and then click on the *Manage* button. The system displays the *Manage Project Web App Sites* page shown in Figure 4 - 59. Complete the steps that follow to provision your new Project Web App site.

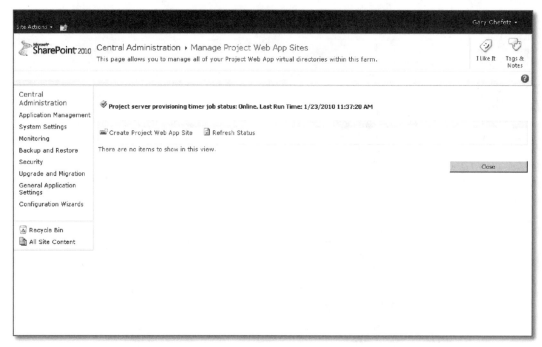

Figure 4 - 59: Manage Project Web App Sites Page

2. On the *Manage Project Web App Sites* page, click the *Create Project Web App Site* link. The system displays the *Create Project Web App Site* page shown in Figure 4 - 60.

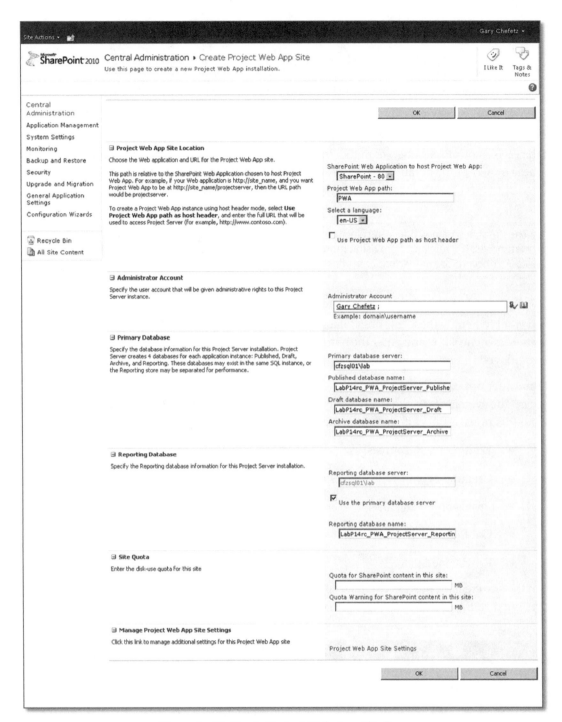

Figure 4 - 60: Create Project Web App Site Page

3.   Notice that in the *Project Web App Site Location* section, the page defaults to the location of the new top-level site collection you created at the root. To create a site at http://<servername>/pwa, leave the defaults as is. To create a Project Web App instance using WSS host header mode, select the *Use Project Web App path as host header* option, and enter the full URL that you want to use for Project Server in the *Project Web App Path* field (Example: http://www.mycompany.com). In the *Administrator Account* field, enter the user account that will be the first authorized Project Server administrator. This defaults to the account you used to logon.

Warning: The *Manage Project Web App Site Settings* link displayed is not yet active, and will not be accessible until you complete the process to create a new Project Server site. Ignore this link.

4. In the *Primary Database* section, specify the database server that will contain the Published, Draft, and Archive databases for your Project Server in the Primary database server field, and then enter your database names for these or accept the defaults in each respective database name field.

The database names that you select must be unique to the SQL Server instance that will house the databases. If you plan to provision more than one instance of Project Server 2010, adding a recognizable convention to the name that identifies the instance helps to identify the databases later.

5. If you want to deploy the Reporting database on a different instance of SQL Server, clear the *Use the primary database server* checkbox and enter the name of the SQL Server instance where you want the Reporting database deployed.

6. You may set optional site quotas in the *Site Quota* section. Click the *OK* button to start the site creation process. The system starts the PWA site creation process, which may take five to ten minutes to complete. During this process the system reports the following status:

    *   Waiting for Resources

    *   Creating Project Web App Site

    *   Provisioning Databases

    *   Configuring the new Project Web App site

    *   Provisioned

When the site creation process completes, the URL appears on the *Manage Project Web App Sites* page with a Provisioned status as shown in Figure 4 - 61.

Figure 4 - 61: Manage Project Web App Sites with One PWA Site Provisioned

You now have your first Project Server 2010 site; however you still have configuration work to do. The following module, Post-Installation Steps, walks you through the process of configuring various services necessary to support all of the features your Project Server installation has to offer, and takes you through some basic functional tests to make sure that your Project Server site is ready to configure for your organization.

Creating a Service Application Manually

Earlier in this module, I showed you how to run the *Farm Configuration Wizard* that allows you to select the service applications to create, and then it creates them for you. In the prior example, I allowed the system to create all of the available service applications by accepting the default selections on the *Select Services* page shown previously in Figure 4 - 52. By default, the system assumes that you want to create every possible service application available except for the *Lotus Notes Connector*. If you are installing on a single server machine, you should be cautious about enabling every service as each adds a significant load to the server.

In this example, I create a new PerformancePoint Service Application. To create a new service application, navigate to the SharePoint *Central Administration* home page and click the *Manage service applications* link in the *Application Management* section. The system displays the *Manage Service Applications* page shown in Figure 4 - 62.

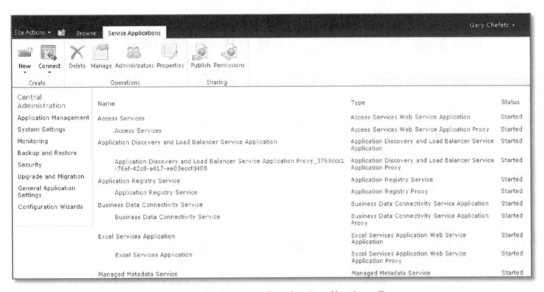

Figure 4 - 62: Manage Service Applications Page

On the *Manage Service Applications* page, click the *New* button in the *Create* section of the ribbon menu and select *PerformancePoint Service Application* from the drop-down menu as shown in Figure 4 - 63.

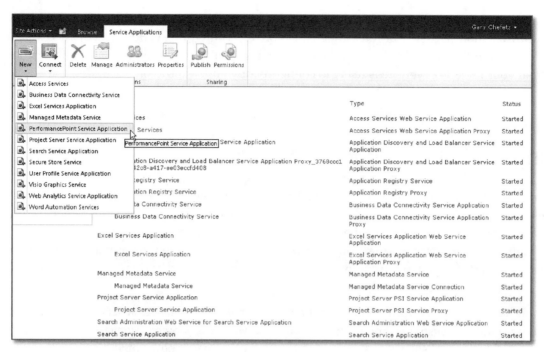

Figure 4 - 63: Select to Create New PerformancePoint Application

The system displays the *New PerformancePoint Service Application* page shown in Figure 4 - 64.

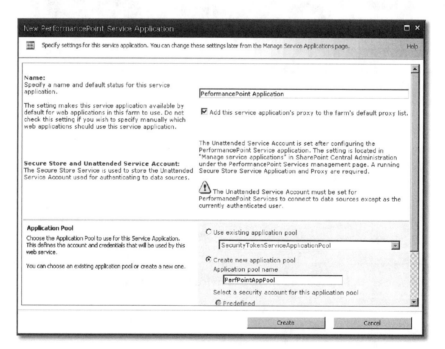

Figure 4 - 64: New PerformancePoint Service Application Page

Type a name for your new PerformancePoint application, select an application pool or create a new application pool for your new PerformancePoint application (Recommended) by selecting the *Create new application pool* option and entering a name for the new application pool in the *Application pool name* field. Scroll down the page and select the *Configurable* option in the *Select a security account for this application pool* section and select a registered account to run the application pool. Click the *Create* button to create your new PerformancePoint application. The system may take a couple minutes to create the application. When complete, the system displays the *New PerformancePoint Service Application* page with a confirmation as shown in Figure 4 - 65.

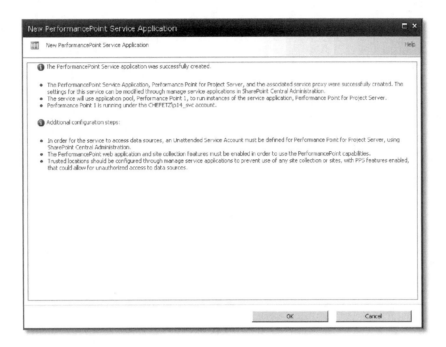

Figure 4 - 65: PerformancePoint application successfully created

Click the *OK* button to close the confirmation page. The system refreshes the SharePoint *Manage Service Applications* page with your new PerformancePoint application displayed and started.

Module 05

Post-Installation Configuration

Learning Objectives

After completing this module, you will be able to:

- Configure Excel Services and PerformancePoint Services for your new Project Server site
- Configure Secure Store Services for Reporting
- Install the SQL Server Native Client and Analysis Management Objects
- Tune SQL Server for best performance
- Verify Project Server Functionality

Inside Module 05

Configuring SharePoint Service Applications 123

    Preparing to Configure Excel Services...123

    Configuring Excel Services...125

    Harvesting URLs for Trusted Data Connection Libraries and Report Libraries...............................127

    Configuring Excel Services Global Settings 129

    Configuring Trusted Data Connection Libraries...131

    Configuring Trusted File Locations 132

    Configuring the Secure Store Service Application...136

Configuring the Cube Building Service 141

    Obtaining the Necessary Software Files 141

    Installing the SQL Server Native Client 142

    Installing the SQL Server Management Objects Collection 146

    Creating a SQL Login for the Service Account Running Analysis Services 149

Setting Optional SQL Server Performance Enhancements...151

    Creating Additional TempDB Files..152

Verifying Project Server Functionality 153

Verifying Project Web App Connectivity...153

Creating a Login Account in Project Professional 2010..154

Performing Basic Functional Tests..158

Verifying Cube Building Capability 165

Verifying Reporting Capability in the BI Center..168

Creating Additional Project Server Instances **171**

Configuring Your New Project Server Instance 173

Creating a New Excel Services Application Instance 174

Pointing Data Connections to the New Secure Store Target Application..176

Configuring SharePoint Service Applications

Now that you have completed the installation procedure in Module 04, you have all the software parts in place where you need them. The next step is to wire them all together so that they can interact with one another as a complete system. For instance, you created a Global Group for Report Authors during the server preparation steps in the previous module, but you now need to connect that global group to the *Reporting Database* in Project Server, something you couldn't do until you created a Project Server 2010 site on your system. Much of your work in this module involves making that type of connection between the various software components.

You now have a provisioned, but not completely configured, Project Server application and site. You can click the link on the *Manage Project Web App Sites* page and your new PWA site will launch. After you verify that your site exists, the next step is to configure your system for reporting. Project Server 2010 uses the *SharePoint Server 2010 Business Intelligence Center Web application* to provide a central point for hosting reports, dashboards, and report connections. You can modify the sample reports or manually author additional reports as your users require them. The *Business Intelligence Center* is driven by PerformancePoint Services and Excel Services in SharePoint Server 2010.

Preparing to Configure Excel Services

For report authors to access the Project Server 2010 Reporting database from Excel 2010, they must be a member of the domain global group you created for Report Authors at the beginning of Module 04, and the global group must have db_datareader rights on the reporting database. The login must allow explicit access to the Project Server 2010 Reporting database to get schema information and data. Follow these steps to create the login:

1. On the computer running SQL Server or another computer with SQL Server Management Studio installed, launch Microsoft SQL Server 2008 SQL Server Management Studio and select the instance of SQL Server containing your Project Server 2010 reporting database and click the *Connect* button. Expand the *Security* folder and right-click *Logins*, and then select *New Login* from the popup menu as shown in Figure 5 - 1.

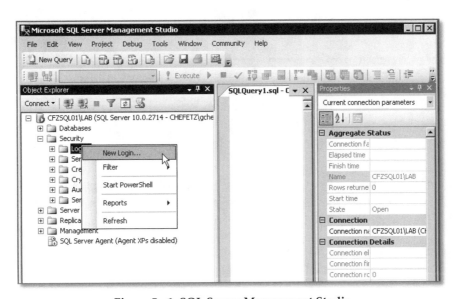

Figure 5 - 1: SQL Server Management Studio

2. The system displays the *Login - New* dialog shown in Figure 5 - 2. Enter the name of the global group as domainname\groupname in the *Login name* field and click the *OK* button. If you do not remember the name, you can search for it using the *Search* button. In the search window, click on the *Object Types* button and select groups in the resulting window. Type the name of the group in the *Enter the object name to select* field and click the *Check Names* button to search. Click the *OK* button to select the located group.

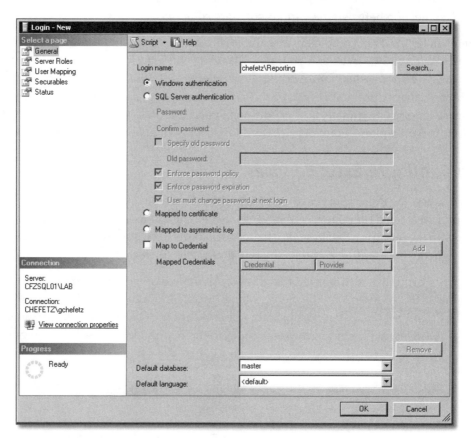

Figure 5 - 2: SQL Management Studio Login – New Window dialog

3. Select the *User Mapping* page. In the *Users mapped to this login* section, select the checkbox to map your Project Server Reporting database, and in the *Database role membership for:* section, select the checkbox for db_datareader and leave the db_public role selected as shown in Figure 5 - 3.

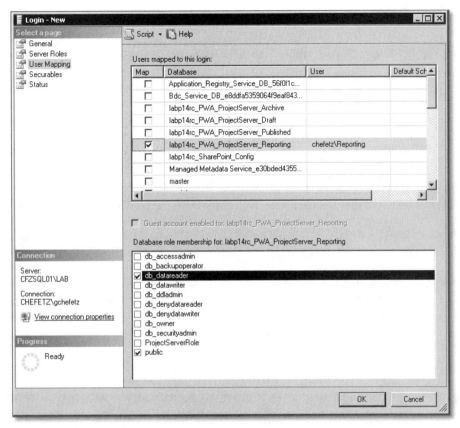

Figure 5 - 3: User Mapping page for SQL Server login

4. Click the *OK* button to complete the new login, and exit from SQL Management Studio if you like.

Configuring Excel Services

Excel Services for SharePoint Server 2010 provides the reporting foundation for Project Server. In a simple sense, Excel Services provides a platform for sharing spreadsheets on the web. Excel Services not only provides a fully interactive presentation layer for Excel Spreadsheets on the web with a similar experience to the Excel client, it also provides a rich security framework within which report authors and administrators can control user access. This functionality includes the ability to secure spreadsheet elements at a granular level; you can secure parts of a spreadsheet while exposing others. For instance, you can show certain users only Summary task information displayed on one sheet in the workbook while preventing them from seeing the detailed task information driving the summary tasks and contained in a different sheet in the workbook.

Microsoft Excel 2010 provides lush new data visualization features and conditional formatting capabilities that allow you to create visually stunning reports. You can then drop these into SharePoint web pages as web parts to create executive and team dashboards to drive decision making and collaboration. Users can interact with spreadsheets on the web using a familiar interface presented through the web using the new Microsoft Office Web Applications. By integrating Project Server with Excel Services, Microsoft has taken the Project Web App interface from offering a paucity of reporting capacity to now providing a limitless data mining experience.

Project Server 2010 is also compatible with Excel 2007.

Discussing Excel Services and focusing only on the way Project Server leverages Excel Services by default is barely scratching the surface of its capabilities within and way beyond your EPM implementation. To be effective as a Project Server administrator, you should learn as much as possible about Excel Services and the business intelligence capabilities that ship with Microsoft SharePoint Server Enterprise Edition.

You build Project Server reports by using Excel spreadsheets connected to data sources such as the Project Server Reporting database and the Project Server OLAP cubes. Excel connects to data sources by using trusted connections that are defined and stored in a SharePoint document library. To determine the URL for your connection library, launch your new Project Web App site and select *Business Intelligence* from the *Quick Launch menu* as shown in Figure 5 - 4.

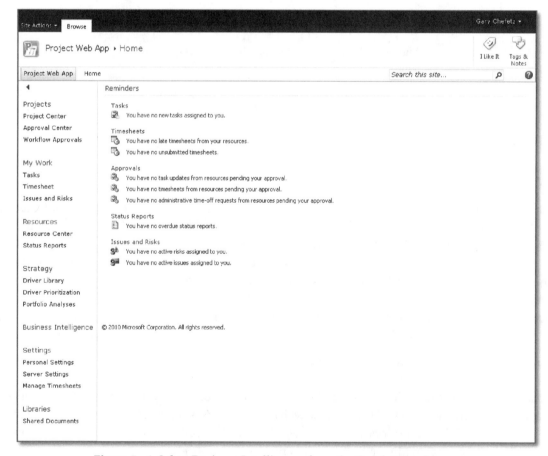

Figure 5 - 4: Select Business Intelligence from the Quick Launch menu

The system displays the *Business Intelligence Center* home page as shown in Figure 5 - 5.

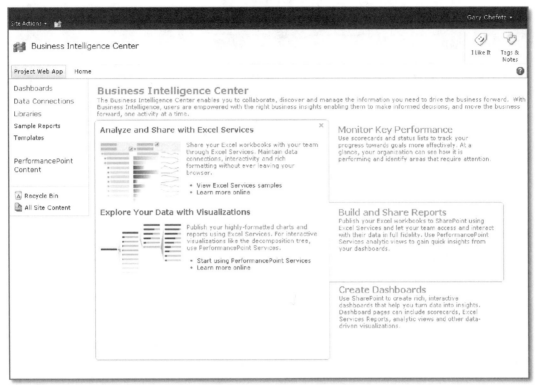

Figure 5 - 5: Business Intelligence Center Home Page

Welcome to your new Business Intelligence Center: you have arrived. By this I mean that the Business Intelligence Center is the most important value center Project Server 2010 inherits from the SharePoint Server Enterprise platform. It may take you a while to comprehend the enormity of the opportunity this provides for you to mine and analyze your Project Server data. The new platform allows you to mash-up your project and portfolio data with line of business systems and a vast array of disparate data sources, especially if you select to deploy the *Business Data Connectivity service*, also included with SharePoint Enterprise. The tool capabilities presented through combining Excel Services 2010 and PerformancePoint Services 2010, along with all of other conveniences of the SharePoint environment, make business intelligence more accessible to the average business user than ever before.

This becomes the single source of all serious reporting information for your Project Server 2010 environment. The only business analysis that has its own special home resides within the Portfolio Analysis area that supports project portfolio decision making. This specialized feature, previously provided by Microsoft Portfolio Server 2007, is generally not for the average business user. Project Server ships with sample reports and templates to form a basic reporting framework upon which you can build your own organization-specific content. You learn more about building Reports and Dashboards in Module 16.

Harvesting URLs for Trusted Data Connection Libraries and Report Libraries

To proceed with your implementation, you must harvest the URLs for your *Data Connections* library and your *Reports* library. To harvest the *Data Connections* library URL, select the *Data Connections* link from the Quick Launch menu. On the *Data Connections* page, select the *English (United States)* Project Server Data Connections check box. The system displays the *Data Connections* page shown in Figure 5 - 6. Hover your mouse pointer to the left of the folder icon for *English (United States)* or your specific locale and select the check box that appears. Selecting the checkbox automatically selects the *Library Tools* menu displaying the options on this menu.

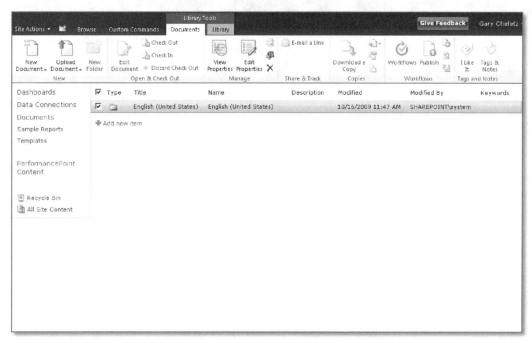

Figure 5 - 6: Data Connections Page

In the ribbon, click the *View Properties* button. The system displays the *Data Connections* dialog shown in Figure 5 - 7.

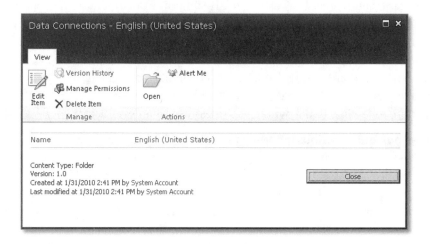

Figure 5 - 7: Data Connections Properties dialog

On the *Data Connections Properties* page, right-click the *English (United States)* Project Server Data Connections link, and then select *Properties*. The system displays the *Properties* dialog shown in Figure 5 - 8.

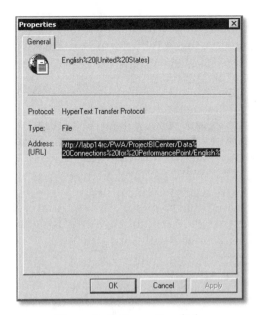

Figure 5 - 8: Properties dialog

Notice that the system displays the URL for your *Data Connections* library, which you need in order to set up a trusted data connection for the library in the steps that follow. On the *Properties* dialog box, select the *Address (URL)* value and press *Ctrl + C*, or right-click the selected text, and then click *Copy* to harvest the URL. Note that the entire URL is not displayed in the dialog window and you must capture all the text by scrolling if you are using a mouse or click into the URL and press *Ctrl + A* to select all. Click the *Cancel* button after you copy the URL to your clipboard. Save the URL to a handy place, such as a new Notepad document, for later use. Then click the *Close* button on the *Data Connections Properties* dialog. Repeat these steps to harvest the URL for your Sample Reports library, and save the URL in a handy place.

Configuring Excel Services Global Settings

Navigate to your SharePoint *Central Administration* site to set up the trusted connection for Excel Services. From the *Central Administration* home page, select the *Manage service applications* link from the *Application Management* section. The system displays the *Service Applications* page shown in Figure 5 - 9.

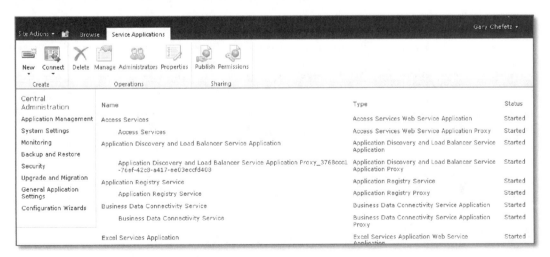

Figure 5 - 9: Service Applications Page

Select the *Excel Services* row by clicking on the non-hyperlink portion of the row. (Note that clicking on the *Excel Services* hyperlink navigates you off the current page.) With the row selected, click the *Manage* button on the menu or click the *Excel Services* link. The system displays the *Manage Excel Services Application* page shown in Figure 5 - 10.

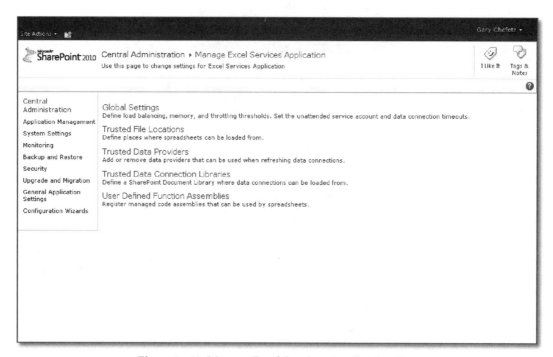

Figure 5 - 10: Manage Excel Services Application Page

On the *Manage Excel Services Application* page, click the *Global Settings* link. Scroll to the bottom of the page, and in the *External Data* section enter ProjectServerApplication in the *Application ID* text box as shown in Figure 5 - 11.

Warning: You must use "ProjectServerApplication" without the quotes and maintaining the case-sensitivity, as the SecureStore Service application expects this value, and it is embedded in your connection documents.

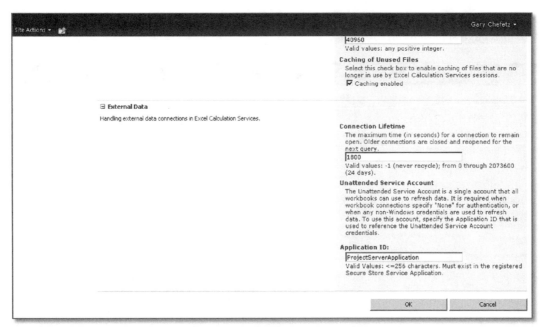

Figure 5 - 11: Enter Application ID

After completing your entry, click the *OK* button to save your data and return to the *Manage Excel Services Application* page shown previously in Figure 5 - 10. On the *Manage Excel Services Application* page, click the *Trusted File Locations* link. The system displays the *Excel Services Application Trusted File Locations* page shown in Figure 5 - 14.

Configuring Trusted Data Connection Libraries

From the SharePoint *Central Administration* home page, click on the *Manage service applications* link in the *Application Management* section. The system displays the *Manage service applications* page shown previously in Figure 5 - 9. Select the *Excel Services* row without clicking on a link portion of the row, and then click the *Manage* button on the menu. The system displays the *Manage Excel Services Application* page shown previously in Figure 5 - 10. Click the *Trusted Data Connection Libraries* link. The system displays the *Excel Services Application Trusted Data Connection Libraries* page shown in Figure 5 - 12.

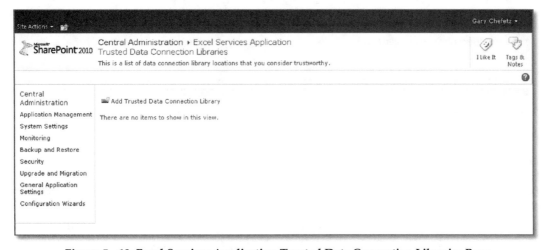

Figure 5 - 12: Excel Services Application Trusted Data Connection Libraries Page

Click the *Add Trusted Data Connection Library* link. The system displays the *Excel Services Application Add Trusted Data Connections Library* page shown in Figure 5 - 13.

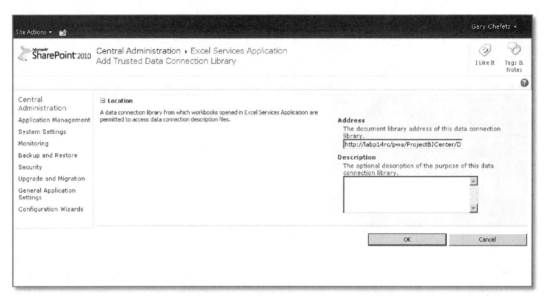

Figure 5 - 13: Excel Services Application Add Trusted Data Connection Library Page

In the *Address* field, type the URL for the data connection library that you harvested previously. It should be in the following format:

```
http://<ServerName>/<ProjectSiteName>/ProjectBICenter/
Data%20Connections%20for%20PerformancePoint/English%20(United%20States)
```

 Note that you do not have to use the complete URL that you harvested. Instead, you can set the trusted connection library at a higher level, such as at the "Data Connections for PerformancePoint" level of the library, as long as you set the library to trust children. This may work to your advantage, as this allows you to create additional directories in the library that are automatically trusted by the system when you create them. To follow the rule of least privelege in configuring your security, you can trust each connection library seperately.

Click the *OK* button to save your new trusted connection.

Configuring Trusted File Locations

From the SharePoint *Central Administration* home page, click on the *Manage service applications* link in the *Application Management* section. The system displays the *Manage service applications* page shown previously in Figure 5 - 9. Select the *Excel Services* row without clicking on a link portion of the row, and then click the *Manage* button on the menu. The system displays the *Manage Excel Services Application* page shown previously in Figure 5 - 10. Click the *Trusted File Locations* link. The system displays the *Excel Services Application Trusted File Locations* page shown in Figure 5 - 12.

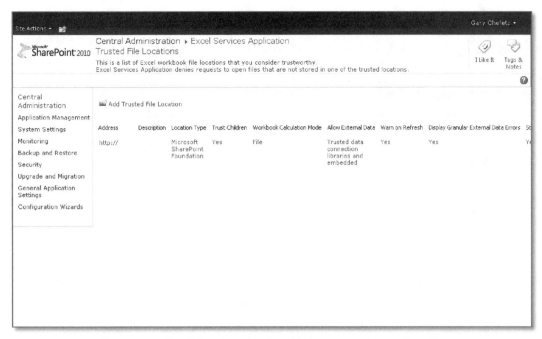

Figure 5 - 14: Excel Services Application Trusted File Locations Page

Click the *Add Trusted File Location* link. The system displays the *Excel Services Application Add Trusted File Location* page shown in Figure 5 - 15. Note that the figure below continues across two pages.

Figure 5 - 15: Excel Services Application Add Trusted File Location details page

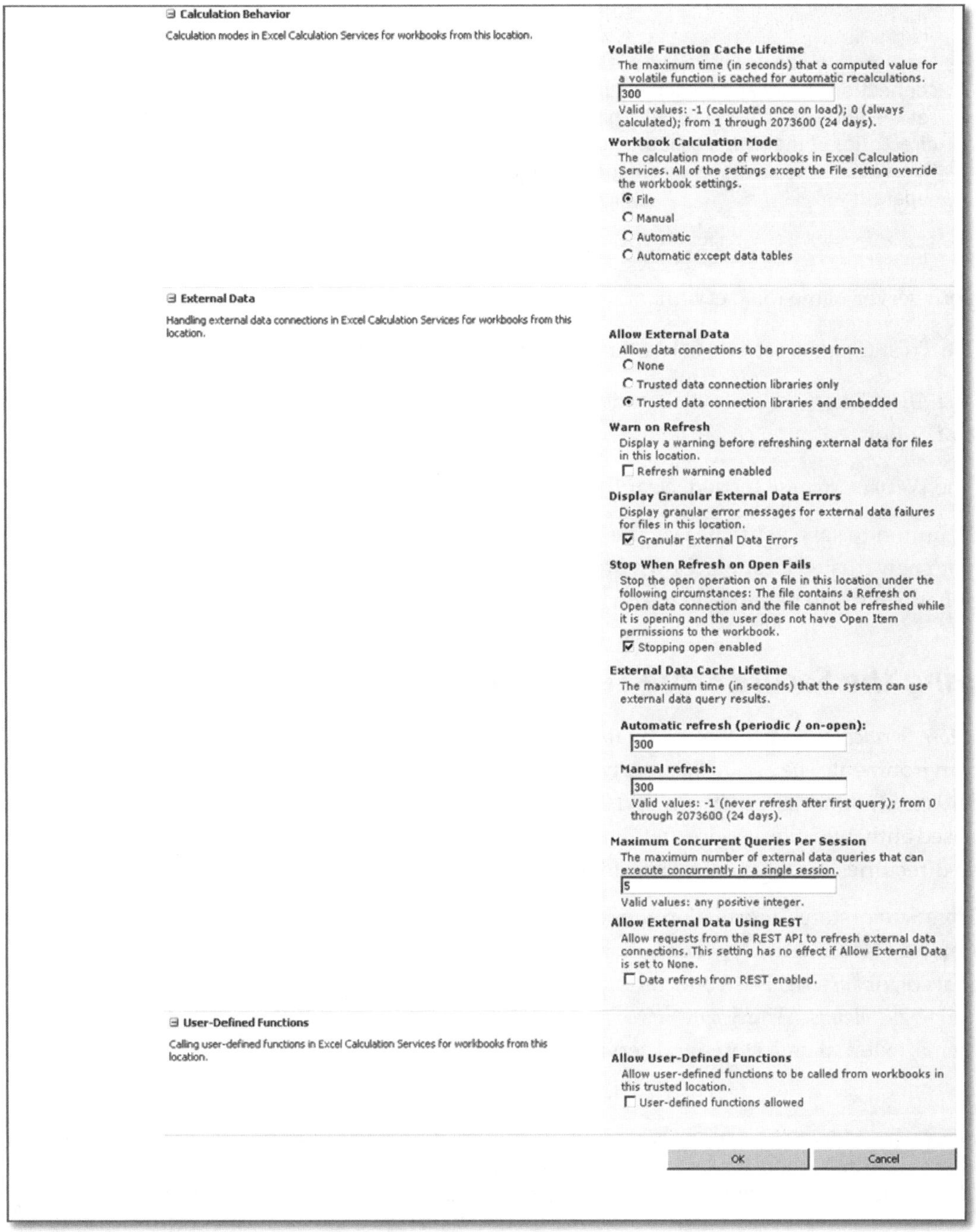

Figure 5 - 15: Excel Services Application Add Trusted File Location details page (continued)

In the *Address* field at the top of the page, enter the URL that you copied for your Business Intelligence Center *Sample Reports* library. It should look something like the following:

```
http://<servername>/<projectsitename>/ProjectBICenter/
Sample%20Reports/English%20(United%20States)
```

Note that you do not have to use the complete URL that you harvested. Instead, you can set the trusted connection library at a higher level, such as at the "Sample Reports" level of the library, as long as you set the library to trust children. This may work to your advantage, as this allows you to create additional directories in the library that are automatically trusted by the system when you create them. To follow the rule of least privilege in configuring your security, you should trust each connection library separately.

Substitute your server name for <servername> and your Project Web App site name for <projectsitename>.

- In the *Trust Children* section, select the *Children trusted* check box.

- In the *Allow External Data* section underneath *External Data*, select the *Trusted data connection libraries and embedded* option.

- In the *Warn on Refresh* section, clear the *Refresh warning enabled* check box.

Click the *OK* button to save your entries. The system redisplays the *Excel Services Application Trusted File Locations* page, with your new trusted location, shown previously in Figure 5 - 14. Click the *Central Administration* link at the top of the Quick Launch menu to return to the SharePoint *Central Administration* home page.

Configuring the Secure Store Service Application

The *Secure Store Service*, formerly known by its code name "Geneva," provides claims-based authentication to the SharePoint environment. The *Secure Store Service* is the marriage of three Microsoft technologies: 1) *Active Directory Federation Services*, 2) *Windows CardSpace*, and 3) *Windows Identity Foundation* working together to provide a flexible standards-based authentication service that can interact with any business identity system including Active Directory, LDAP-based directories, application-specific identity systems as well as user-centric systems like Microsoft's *LiveID*.

The *Secure Store Service* stores information about users connecting from various systems in its own metadata store. The system accepts and issues security tokens, more commonly referred to simply as "*tokens,*" that contain information about the rights of, or "*assertions*" about, various users to access system objects and data. These "*assertions*" are collectively referred to as "*claims.*" The *Secure Store Service* acts as a common security broker that provides a bridge between identity systems, external data stores and service applications running within the SharePoint envelope.

Microsoft's best-practice recommendation is to isolate your *Secure Store Service* deployment as much as possible. If you are deploying within a larger SharePoint farm, you probably planned your architecture by following Microsoft's best practices for deploying SharePoint Server farms. If you haven't already read this guidance, you should review the available SharePoint Server 2010 deployment documentation on TechNet. Microsoft's best-practice recommendations are as follows:

- Run the secure store service in its own isolated application pool.

- Run the secure store service on its own application server.

- Create the secure store database on a different SQL Server than the one hosting your SharePoint Server 2010 databases.

If you are building a small farm to house your Project Server environment on its own server island, then you may not be able to follow these best-practice guidelines, and you may not have the luxury of using multiple SQL Server boxes, but you can isolate these using SQL Server instances. Of course there are licensing impacts to extending your SharePoint Server farm and SQL Server deployments onto additional processors.

Generate a New Encryption Key

The next step is to generate an encryption key for the Secure Store. Because this is the key the system uses to encrypt and decrypt user credentials data housed in the secure store, it deserves careful handling. Be certain to read the following best-practice note before proceeding with this part of the configuration process.

Before generating a new encryption key, you should always back up the secure store database. In addition, you should back up the Secure Store database immediately after you create it in the previous steps. Now would be the time to do this.

After completing the initial setup of the Secure Store Service, back up your encryption key, and back it up each time you regenerate it.

Store the database backup and Encryption Key backup on separate physical backup media. A malicious user must have access to both to compromise the data store.

Warning: When you regenerate a key, the system re-encrypts the database with the new key. If the key refresh fails, you cannot return to the previous state without both a backup of both the Secure Store Service database and its corresponding key backup.

From the SharePoint *Central Administration* home page, select the *Manage service applications* link in the *Application Management* section. From the *Manage Service Applications* page, select either link for the *Secure Store Service* application. The system displays the *Secure Store Service Application: Secure Store Service* page shown in Figure 5 - 16.

Figure 5 - 16: Secure Store Service Page

137

Notice that the system alerts you that you must generate a key before you can create a new *Secure Store Target Application*. To generate a new key, click the *Generate New Key* button in the *Key Management* section of the menu. The system displays the *Generate New Key* page shown in Figure 5 - 17.

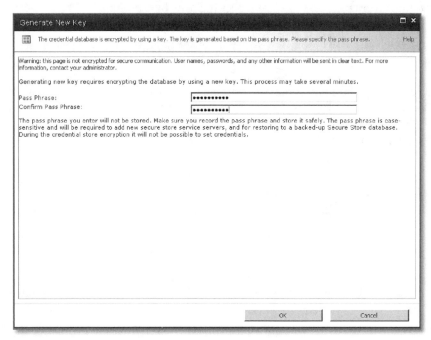

Figure 5 - 17: Generate New Key Page

Enter a pass phrase for the encryption key in the *Pass Phrase* field and confirm it in the *Confirm Pass Phrase* field. Your pass phrase should consist of upper case and lower case letters as well as one or more numbers and special characters. Click the *OK* button to submit your pass phrase. After processing momentarily, the system redisplays the *Secure Store Service Target Applications* page without the stop warning as shown previously in Figure 5 - 16. Remain on this page to complete the next procedure.

Create a Secure Store Target Application

In this step, create the *Secure Store Target Application*. Click the *New* button in the *Manage Target Applications* section of the menu. The system displays the *Create New Secure Store Target Application* page shown in Figure 5 - 18.

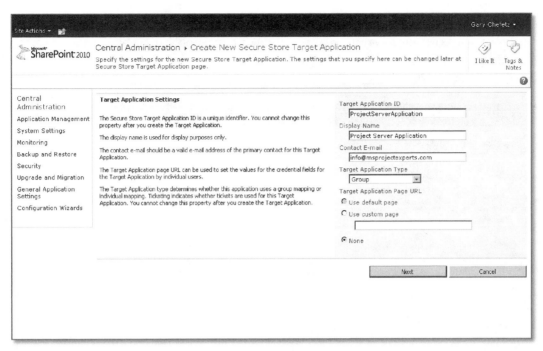

Figure 5 - 18: Create New Secure Store Target Application Page

In the *Target Application ID* box, type "ProjectServerApplication" and type a display name for your new *Target Application*. Enter a valid email address in the *Contact E-mail* field, and select *Group* from the *Target Application Type* pick list. The system automatically selects the *None* option in the *Target Application Page URL* section. Click the *Next* button to confirm your entries. The system displays the *Specify the credential fields for your Secure Store Target Application* page shown in Figure 5 - 19.

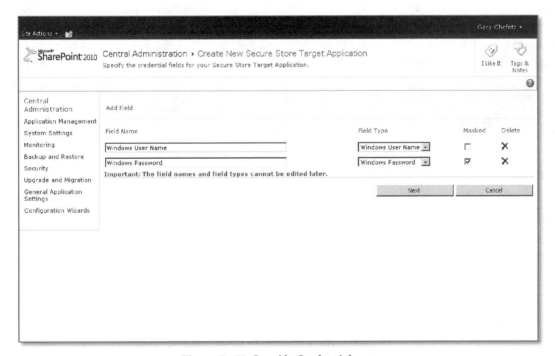

Figure 5 - 19: Specify Credentials page

The page defaults to the fields necessary to authenticate with Windows credentials, which include the *Windows User Name* and *Windows Password* fields. Notice that you can determine the display name for the fields that you can select from the *Field Type* pick lists and that you can select the *Masked* option or delete the default fields. You might use a different set of fields when creating a *Target Application* for a different application, but for the Project Server *Target Application*, you use the defaults. Click the *Next* button to continue. The system displays the *Specify the membership settings* page shown in Figure 5 - 20.

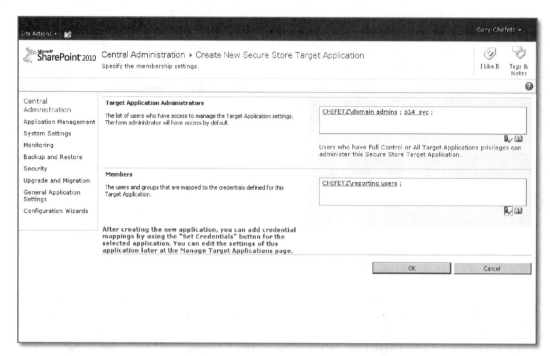

Figure 5 - 20: Specify the membership settings page

On the *Specify the membership settings* page, type the username for the Farm Administrator role in the *Target Application Administrators* field. In the *Members* field, enter the name of the domain group you created for report viewers. Verify that you entered the correct names by clicking the people icon with the check mark. Click the *OK* button to continue. The system proceeds to create the *Secure Store Target Application*. This may take several minutes. When the process completes, the system displays the *Target Application* page for the Secure Store Service shown in Figure 5 - 21.

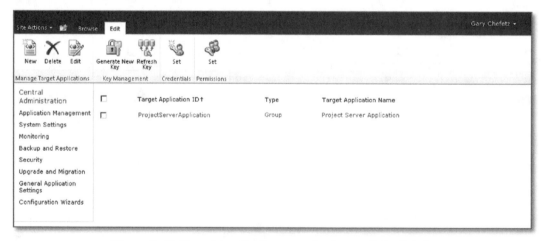

Figure 5 - 21: Target Application page for Secure Store Service

Select the Secure Store Target application that you just created and click the *Set: Credentials* button on the ribbon. The system displays the *Set Credentials for Secure Store Target Application (Group)* page shown in Figure 5 - 22.

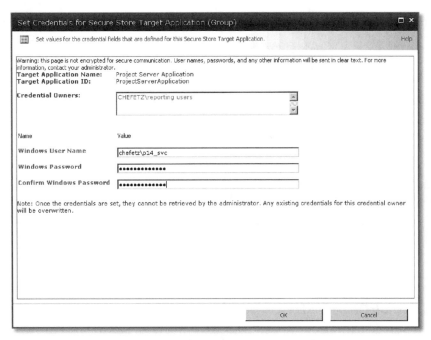

Figure 5 - 22: Set Credentials for Secure Store Target Application

Enter the service account identity you want to use for the Secure Store application as well as the password for the account in the appropriate entry fields. Click the *OK* button to set the credentials for your new target application.

Configuring the Cube Building Service

The first step in setting up Analysis services for Project Server is to verify that you have the necessary SQL components installed on each server in your configuration. If you installed to an environment with more than one server, you must install SQL client components on servers running the Project Server service application on your farm. If you installed to a single server or if you used the SharePoint Technologies preparation tool, you may already have these components installed on your system. You must install the *SQL Server 2008 Native Client* and the *SQL Server 2008 Analysis Management Objects* (AMO) on the server running Project Server 2010, regardless of whether you are using SQL Server 2005 or SQL Server 2008. Project Server 2010 uses the *Analysis Management Objects,* a departure from the Project Server 2007 approach which used the *SQL Server Analysis Services Decision Support Objects* (DSO). You must also install the *SQL Server 2008Native Client* on the computer running Analysis Services if this is located on a separate machine.

Obtaining the Necessary Software Files

Your first objective is to obtain the necessary components for Microsoft downloads. Go to the primary download site at http://www.microsoft.com/downloads and search for "SQL Server feature pack." As Microsoft download locations can change, it is always best to begin with a search, which also allows you to obtain the latest available version.

You can download the *SQL Server 2008 Native Client* here:

http://go.microsoft.com/fwlink/?LinkId=123718&clcid=0x409

You can download the *SQL Server 2008 Analysis Management Objects* (AMO) here:

http://go.microsoft.com/fwlink/?LinkId=130655&clcid=0x409

> If the above links do not work, remember that the Feature Pack for SQL is available for both standard 32-bit (X86) systems and for 64-bit systems (X64). Select the appropriate X64 files for your server.

Installing the SQL Server Native Client

To install the *SQL Server Native Client* components, follow the directions below:

1. Double-click the MSI Package that you downloaded for the Microsoft *SQL Server Native Client* (sqlnclix64.msi). The system displays the *SQL Server Native Client Setup* screen shown in Figure 5 - 23.

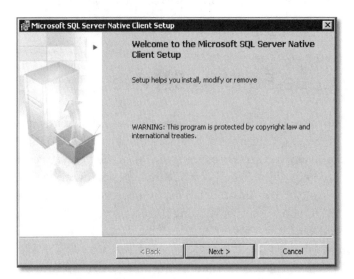

Figure 5 - 23: SQL Server Native Client

2. Click the *Next* button. The system displays the *SQL Server Native Client End User License Agreement* shown in Figure 5 - 24.

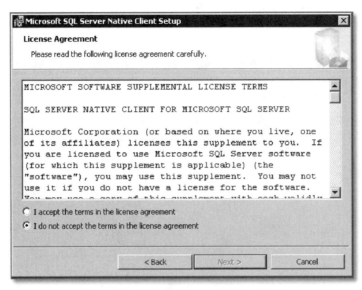

**Figure 5 - 24: SQL Server Native Client
EULA page**

3. Read the license agreement. In order to continue you must accept the terms; to accept the terms, select the *I accept the terms in the license agreement* radio button and click the *Next* button to continue the installation. The system displays the *Registration Information* page shown in Figure 5 - 25.

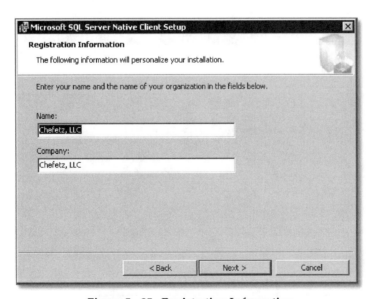

Figure 5 - 25: Registration Information

4. Complete the information on the *Registration Information* page and click the *Next* button to continue. The system displays the *Feature Selection* page shown in Figure 5 - 26.

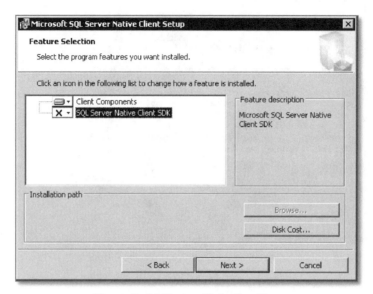

Figure 5 - 26: Feature Selection Page

5. Select the *Client Components* and, optionally, the *Microsoft SQL Server Native Client SDK (Software Developers Kit)* as well. Note that you can view the Disk space requirements for the selected components by clicking on the *Disk Cost* button. Click the *Next* button to continue and the system displays the *Ready to Install the Program* page shown in Figure 5 - 27.

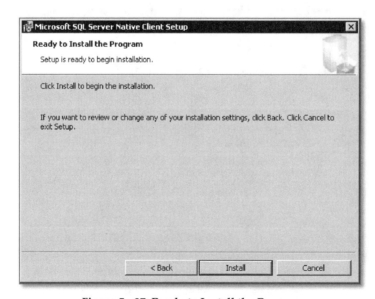

Figure 5 - 27: Ready to Install the Program

6. Click the *Install* button to continue with the installation. The system displays the *Installing Microsoft SQL Server Native Client* progress dialog shown in Figure 5 - 28.

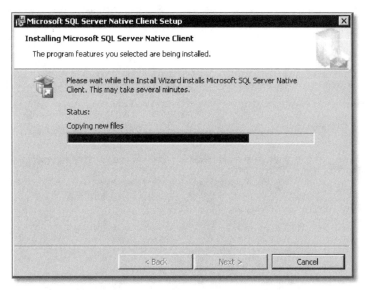

Figure 5 - 28: Installing Microsoft SQL Server Native Client

7. The system displays the progress dialog until the installation is complete. When it is complete, the system displays the *Completing the Microsoft SQL Server Native Client Setup* dialog shown in Figure 5 - 29.

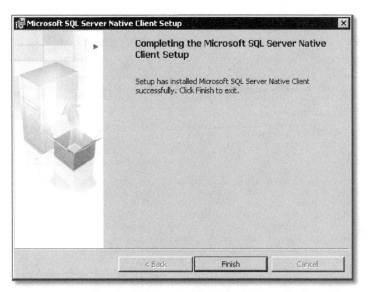

Figure 5 - 29: Completing the Microsoft SQL Server Native Client

8. Click the *Finish* button to close the installation window.

Installing the SQL Server Management Objects Collection

Complete the following steps to install the Microsoft SQL Server 2008 Management Objects Collection:

1. Double click on the MSI file that you downloaded to start the installation. After a brief loading period, the system displays the *Welcome to the Microsoft SQL Server Management Objects Collection Setup* page shown in Figure 5 - 30.

The screens and steps for installing SQL components may change slightly with each new release from Microsoft. Most steps remain the same from version to version.

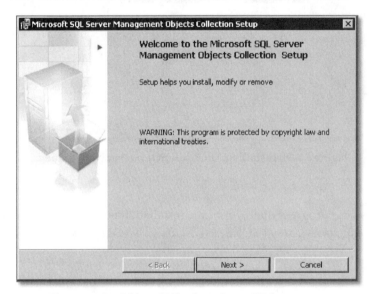

Figure 5 - 30: Object Collections Setup Welcome page

2. On the *Welcome to the Microsoft SQL Server Management Objects Collection Setup* page, click the *Next* button to continue the installation. The system displays the *License Agreement* page shown in Figure 5 - 31.

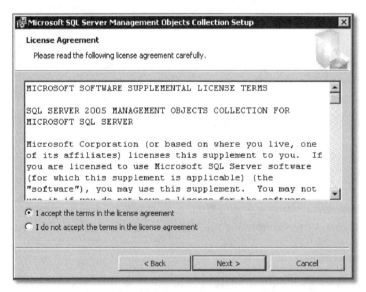

Figure 5 - 31: License Agreement Page

3. On the License Agreement page, read the license agreement. In order to continue you must accept the terms; to accept the terms, select the *I accept the terms of this license agreement* option and then click the *Next* button. The system displays the *Registration Information* page shown in Figure 5 - 32.

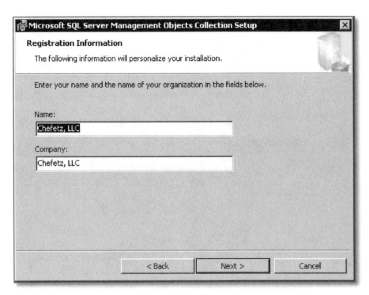

Figure 5 - 32: Registration Information Page

4. On the *Registration Information* page, enter your name and company. Click the *Next* button to continue. The system displays the *Ready to Install the Program* page shown in Figure 5 - 33.

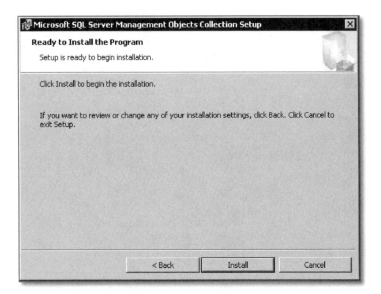

Figure 5 - 33: Ready to Install the Program Page

5. On the *Ready to Install the Program* page, click the *Install* button to continue the installation. The system displays the *Installing Microsoft SQL Server Management Objects Collection* installation progress page shown in Figure 5 - 34.

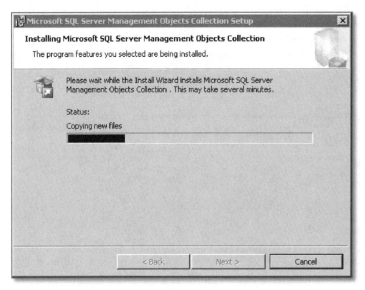

Figure 5 - 34: Installation Progress page

6. After the installation completes, the system displays the *Completing the Microsoft SQL Server Management Objects Collection Setup* page shown in Figure 5 - 35. Click the *Finish* button to complete the installation.

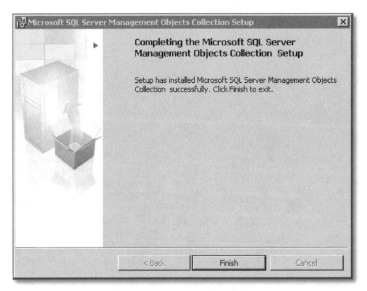

Figure 5 - 35: Completion page

Creating a SQL Login for the Service Account Running Analysis Services

The cube building service runs under the OLAP Services account. Therefore, the OLAP Services account also needs *datareader* rights on the Project Server 2010 reporting database. This process is similar to the steps you followed to create a login for the *Report Authors* global group earlier in this module. If you are using the Farm Administrator account for all services, this step in not necessary, as the Farm Administrator account is already the dbo for the databases. If you do need to create a login and assign the necessary rights, complete the following steps:

1. Using *SQL Server Management Studio*, connect to the SQL Server instance containing your Project Server reporting database. Expand the *Security* folder and right click on the *Logins* folder and select the *New Login* menu item as shown in Figure 5 - 36.

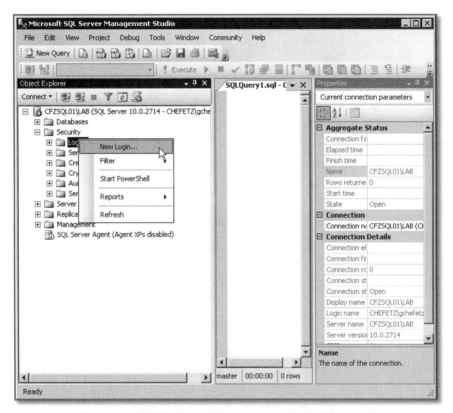

Figure 5 - 36: SQL Server Management Studio New Login

2. The system displays the *Login – New* page shown in Figure 5 - 37.

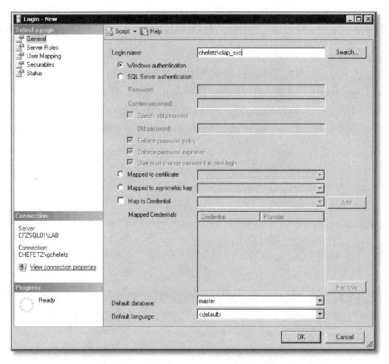

Figure 5 - 37: SQL Server Login – New Page

3. Enter the service OLAP service account information in the *Login name* field and then select the *User Mapping* page in the *Select a page* section of the window. The system displays the *User Mapping* page shown in Figure 5 - 38.

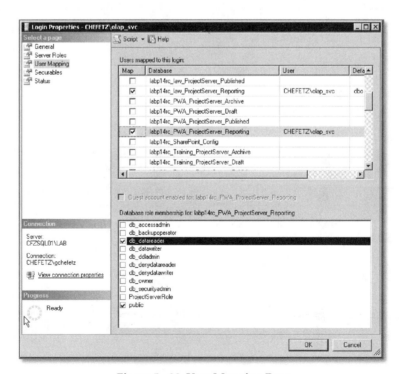

Figure 5 - 38: User Mapping Page

4. In the *Users mapped to this login* section of the upper window, select the checkbox for your Project Server Reporting database. In the *Database role membership for <databasename>* section of the lower window, select the checkbox for *db_datareader* and leave the *public* role selected. Click the *OK* button to complete your entry.

Setting Optional SQL Server Performance Enhancements

There are two SQL Server database settings that are set to OFF by default, but can cause performance issues in your environment if they are turned ON: 1) AUTO_CLOSE and 2) AUTO_SHRINK.

AUTO_CLOSE

This option is set to OFF by default for both SQL Server 2005 and SQL Server 2008, and in all likelihood you will not have to change it. With the AUTO_CLOSE option set to ON, the database engine closes and shuts down when all processes in the database complete and the last user exits the database. Project Server makes and breaks connections to SQL Server repeatedly, so using the AUTO_CLOSE option forces the system to use a lot of system overhead to repeatedly reopen the databases and should not be used for Project Server databases.

AUTO_SHRINK

This option is set to OFF by default for both SQL Server 2005 and SQL Server 2008. When this option is set to ON, the system marks all of the database's files for shrinking, which causes SQL Server to initiate a shrink process automatically when more than 25 percent of the file contains unused space. With the option set to ON your production system will suddenly suffer a performance decline when SQL Server decides it is shrink-time.

To verify the status of these settings for your databases, you can use the following queries respectively:

```
SELECT DATABASEPROPERTYEX('DatabaseName','IsAutoClose')
GO
SELECT DATABASEPROPERTYEX('DatabaseName','IsAutoShrink')
GO
```

The system returns a value of 0 for OFF or 1 for ON. To view these properties for all of your databases, use the following query:

```
SET NOCOUNT ON
SELECT [name] AS DatabaseName
  , CONVERT(varchar(10),DATABASEPROPERTYEX([Name] , 'IsAutoClose')) AS AutoClose
  , CONVERT(varchar(10),DATABASEPROPERTYEX([Name] , 'IsAutoShrink')) AS AutoShrink
FROM master.dbo.sysdatabases
Order By DatabaseName
```

AUTO UPDATE STATISTICS and AUTO_UPDATE_STATISTICS_ASYNC

By default, the system sets SQL Server databases to enable AUTO UPDATE STATISTICS. This command can run during core business hours when activity on the server is high, affecting performance. With the introduction of SQL Server 2005, Microsoft introduced a new database property, AUTO_UPDATE_STATISTICS_ASYNC, which configures a database to update statistics asynchronously vs. synchronously. Updating statistics synchronously is the default behavior in both SQL Server 2005 and 2008. In synchronous mode, if a query request triggers an AUTO UPDATE STATISTICS event, the query must wait for the system to update the statistics. Once the system completes updating the statistics, the system executes the query. However, if you enable the AUTO_UPDATE_STATISTICS_ASYNC property, the query executes immediately against the existing statistics. At the same time a background request tells the database engine to update the statistics automatically as soon as possible, without preventing any query requests. When the background operation completes, new query requests begin using the new statistics information. This option affects only AUTO UPDATE STATISTICS events, not manually requested statistic updates or statistic updates scheduled through a SQL maintenance plan. To set these property values using *SQL Query Manager* use the following queries respectively:

```
ALTER DATABASE DatabaseName SET AUTO_UPDATE_STATISTICS ON
GO
ALTER DATABASE DatabaseName SET AUTO_UPDATE_STATISTICS_ASYNC ON
GO
```

To change the status of these settings using *SQL Server Management Studio*, expand the tree in *Object Explorer*, locate your database, and right click on the database name and select *Properties* from the popup menu. The system displays the *Database Properties* page. In the *Select a Page* pane on the left, select *Options*. Your *Database Properties* window should appear similar to Figure 5 - 39.

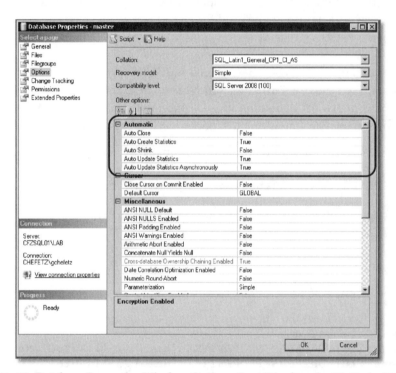

Figure 5 - 39: Database Properties Window Options Page Displayed with Default Settings

In the *Automatic* options section, set your desired values by clicking into the value column and selecting your value from the dropdown list.

Creating Additional TempDB Files

Both Project Server 2010 and Microsoft SharePoint Server 2010 make extensive use of TempDB during SQL transactions. To improve performance, create additional TempDB files. To optimize performance, create an additional TempDB file for each processor (core) in the computer running SQL Server. Create the files on a separate partition from other database files.

Verifying Project Server Functionality

Now that the installation and initial configuration process is complete, you should verify system functionality and connectivity. If you have not already done so, you must install the Project Professional 2010 client on at least one workstation to complete the work in this module. Make sure that you apply the same Service Pack level to both the client and the server.

Verifying Project Web App Connectivity

Log in to your workstation using the account that you designated as the Project Server Administrator, which is the only account that has access to your Project Web App site at this time. Enter the URL for your new Project Server installation in your browser to verify that your new Project Web App site loads from a system on your network other than the server where it is installed. The system displays your home page as shown in Figure 5 - 40. Note that the system welcomes you by login name at the top right of the page.

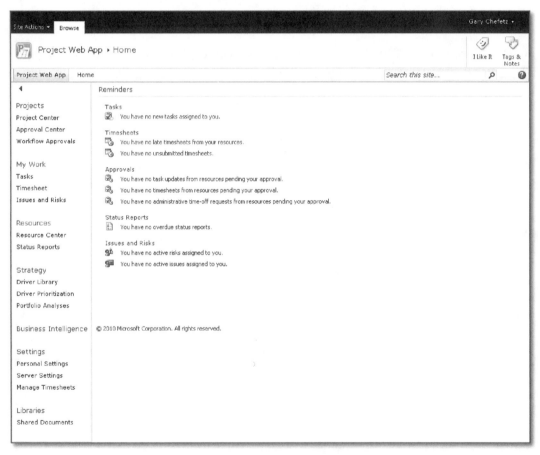

Figure 5 - 40: Project Web App
Home page for an administrator

You should see a page that has nothing to report in the *Reminders* section. Figure 5 - 40 reflects a first-time login to a Project Server instance without any data.

Creating a Login Account in Project Professional 2010

During the installation process, Project Server 2010 creates a single Project Server user, which is an administrator-level account. It uses the Windows account that you specified during the installation process in Module 04; typically this is the *Farm Service Account* or the installation account that you are using. Because your administrator toolkit includes both Project Professional 2010 and Project Web App, you must be able to connect to Project Server using Project Professional 2010. Before you can use Project Professional 2010 in your Project Server environment, you must create a login account for the Project client application on your local machine.

> If you did not specify your own login account during the installation process, you should log in to your workstation using the account you specified as the Project Server Administrator, or first create an account for yourself on the Project Server instance. I cover creating resources and users in Module 09.

You have two options available to you for creating a Project Server login account. You can do this by launching the *Microsoft Project Server 2010 Accounts* tool under the *Office Tools* folder in the *Office* folder from your start menu, or you can launch Project Professional 2010 and complete the following steps:

1. From Project Professional 2010, click the *File* tab and select the *Info* tab on the left hand navigation menu, and then click the *Manage Accounts* button in the *Project Server Accounts* section of the *Information* page shown in Figure 5 - 41.

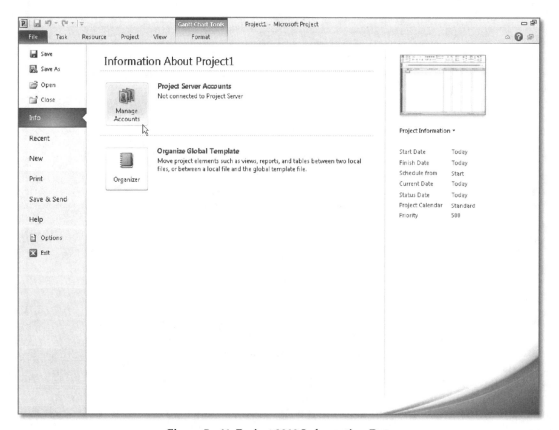

Figure 5 - 41: Project 2010 Information Page

Notice that the *Information* page carries two types of content: 1) Navigation tools for accessing Project Server accounts and the organizer, and 2) Summary informaton about the current project. If you close the default Project 1 file, the system displays only the navigation buttons and the title becomes simply "Information."

2. After you click the *Manage Accounts* button, the system displays the *Project Server Accounts* dialog shown in Figure 5 - 42.

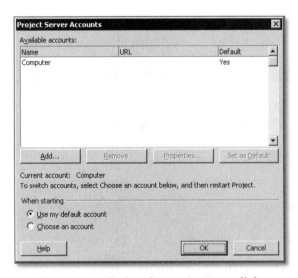

Figure 5 - 42: Project Server Accounts dialog

3. Project Server 2007 users will notice that Microsoft updated this dialog for Project 2010. Click the *Add* button and the system displays the *Account Properties* dialog shown in Figure 5 - 43.

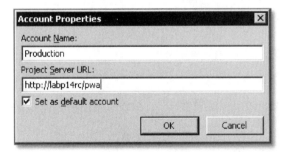

Figure 5 - 43: Account Properties dialog

4. Enter a friendly name for your new account in the *Account Name* field and enter a valid URL in the *Project Server URL* field. You must enter the URL with the **http:// or https://** prefix. Select the *Set as default account* option. Figure 5 - 43 shows the completed *Account Properties* dialog for the new account that connects to my organization's Production Project Server instance.

5. Click the *OK* button. If you enter a URL using the http:// protocol rather than the secure https:// protocol,

6. The system displays the warning dialog shown in Figure 5 - 44. Ignore the warning unless your server requires a secure URL. Click the *Yes* button to continue if you see this warning.

Figure 5 - 44: Security warning dialog

7. The system redisplays the *Project Server Accounts* dialog with your new account, as shown in Figure 5 - 45.

Figure 5 - 45: Project Server Accounts dialog
with new account

8. In the *Project Server Accounts* dialog, select the *Choose an account* option. This is particularly important if you connect to multiple Project Server instances and if you want to completely control the connection state.

 MsProjectExperts recommends that you always select the *Choose an account* option. This provides better control for users who connect to multiple instances and allows for better control of off-line feature use.

9. Create an additional Project Server login account for each instance of your Project Server 2010 system, such as for test or training Project Server instances, and then click the *OK* button.

After you create your Project Server login account profiles in Project Professional 2010, exit and then re-launch the software. This is a necessary step because creating your login accounts does not connect you to a Project Server instance. The system displays the *Login* dialog shown in Figure 5 - 46. Because you selected the *Choose an account* option in the *Project Server Accounts* dialog, the system allows you to select the Project Server instance for connection. Had you not chosen this option, the system automatically connects to the instance you set as default.

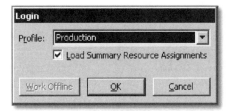

Figure 5 - 46: Login dialog

The *Login* dialog pre-selects the account you set as the default account in the *Project Server Accounts* dialog. If you wish to connect using a different login account, click the *Profile* pick list and select a different account as shown in Figure 5 - 47. Note that the first time you connect to a Project Server instance, the *Work Offline* option is not available.

Figure 5 - 47: Select a different Profile

 You can select the *Computer* profile to use Project Professional 2010 without connecting to a Project Server instance. This causes the software to function in "desktop only" mode and disables all enterprise features.

Click the *OK* button to connect to your desired Project Server instance. If the system cannot connect to the selected Project Server instance, it displays the *Could not connect to Server* dialog shown in Figure 5 - 48.

Figure 5 - 48: Could not connect to Server warning

If you see the dialog shown in Figure 5 - 48, click the *Cancel* button to return to the *Login* dialog and then click the *Cancel* button in the *Login* dialog. At this point, you must troubleshoot the cause of the login problem, which is likely one of the four possible reasons previously shown in the *Could not connect to Server* warning.

Performing Basic Functional Tests

Now that you have verified basic Project Server connectivity in Project Professional 2010, it is time to confirm that you can exercise basic system input, such as creating, saving, and publishing a project. To verify that you can create and save a project, launch Project Professional 2010 and select the login account that you created in the previous section of this module. Use the Project 1 file that Project opens automatically, or click the *File* tab and then click the *New* tab from the sidepane, as shown in Figure 5 - 49.

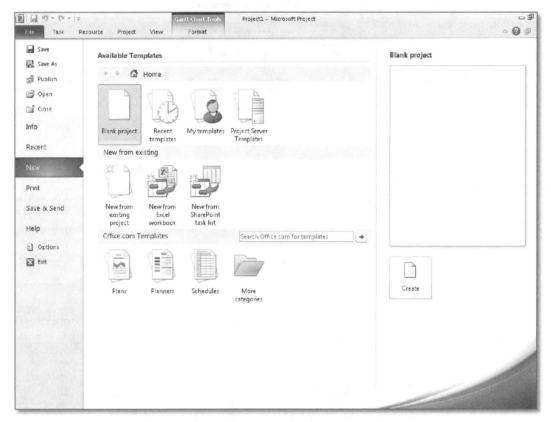

Figure 5 - 49: Project Professional with New Project options displayed

In the *Available Templates* section, click the *Blank project* link. The system opens the blank project as shown in Figure 5 - 50.

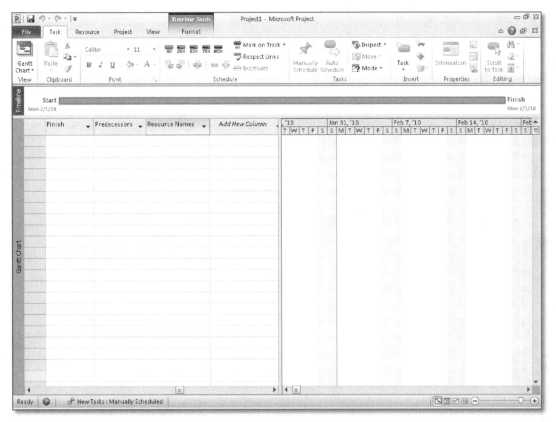

Figure 5 - 50: New Project

Add a few tasks to your new project. Click the *File* Tab and then click *Save* from the menu. The system displays the *Save to Project Server* dialog shown in Figure 5 - 51.

Note that unless you have selected otherwise, the system defaults all new tasks to *Manually Scheduled*, which is a new feature in Project Server 2010. To learn about *Manually Scheduled* tasks and the other new features in Microsoft Project Professional 2010, refer to the *Ultimate Study Guide to Microsoft Project 2010: Foundations,* ISBN: 978-1-934240-13-7.

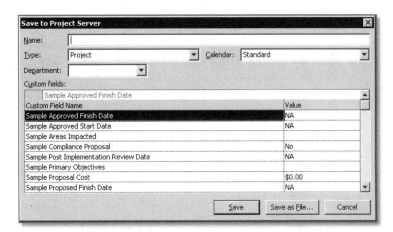

Figure 5 - 51: Save to Project Server

159

Enter a name for your test project in the *Name* field and then click the *Save* button. Watch the message in the lower tray of the application frame where the system reports the save status as shown in Figure 5 - 52. Wait until you see the message, *Save completed successfully*.

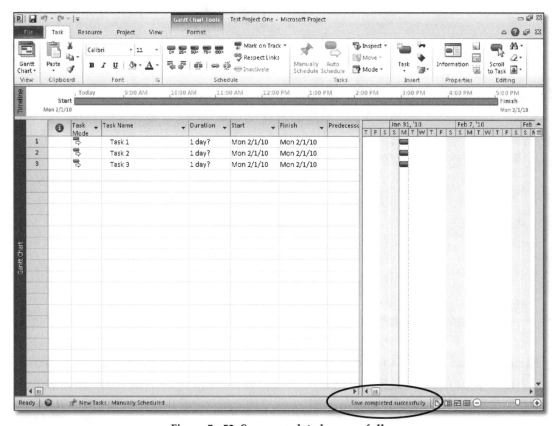

Figure 5 - 52: Save completed successfully

Next, build a team using enterprise resources in the Enterprise Resource Pool. Click the *Resource* tab and click the *Add Resources* button and select the option to *Build Team from Enterprise* on the menu as shown in Figure 5 - 53.

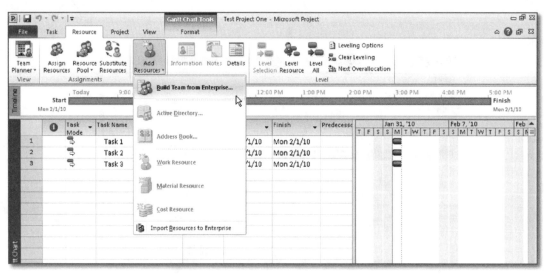

Figure 5 - 53: Add resources to project

The system opens the *Build Team* dialog shown in Figure 5 - 54.

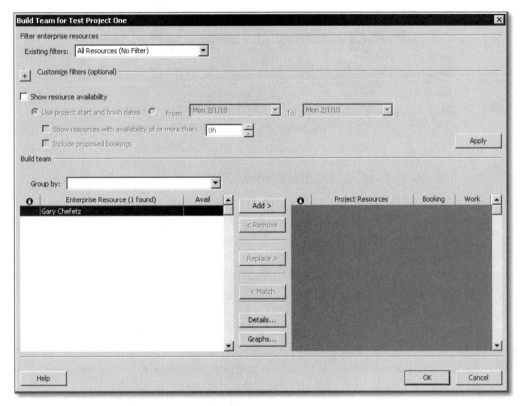

Figure 5 - 54: Build Team dialog

The dialog should contain only one resource, which is your current login. Select the account representing your current logon on the left, and click the *Add* button in the center of the dialog to add this resource to the team. Click the *OK* button to complete the action. In your new project schedule, add the current resource to the test tasks you entered in your project using the *Resource Names* field as shown in Figure 5 - 55. Note that assigning resources using this method is not a best practice for your users, but it is adequate for testing purposes.

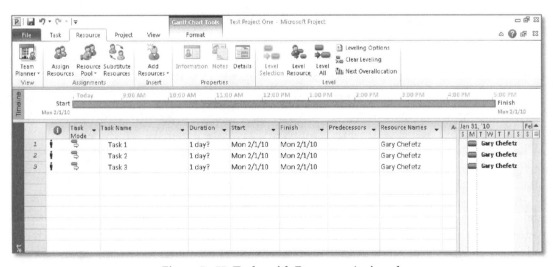

Figure 5 - 55: Tasks with Resources Assigned

Next, click the *Project* tab and then click the *Project Information* button to display the *Project Information* dialog shown in Figure 5 - 56.

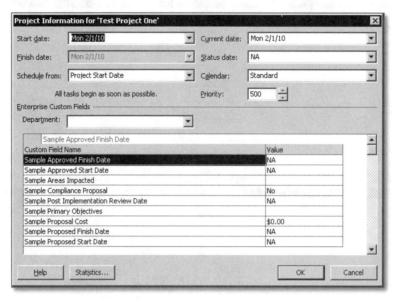

Figure 5 - 56: Project Information dialog

In the *Start date* field, set the project start date to today, if it is not the default, using the date picker and then click the *OK* button. Note that you want to use a current start date so that your new task assignments appear in the current period in PWA.

Next, click the *File* tab and select the *Publish* menu item to publish the project. The system displays the *Publish Project* dialog shown in Figure 5 - 57.

 Note that Project Professional 2010 initiates a save job if you haven't saved changes to your project plan immediately prior to publishing. You see this in the status tray at the bottom of the Project Professional window in the same place where the system reports the publish job status.

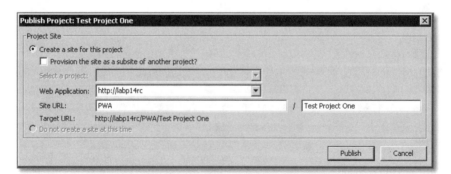

Figure 5 - 57: Publish Project dialog

Accept the defaults in the dialog and click the *Publish* button to continue. The system announces the publish status and percentage in the Status bar at the bottom of the application window. When the system indicates that the publish job completed successfully, click the File tab and then click the *Close* menu item. The system displays the dialog shown in Figure 5 - 58.

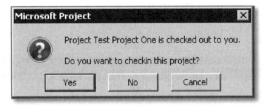

Figure 5 - 58: Check-in dialog

Click the *Yes* button to check in the project schedule. Launch your Internet Explorer application, if necessary, and navigate to your Project Server home page or refresh this page if you already have it displayed. The page should now look something like the page shown in Figure 5 - 59. Notice that you now have one or more new tasks assigned to you as highlighted in the figure.

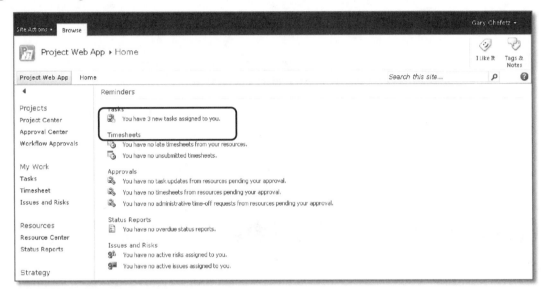

Figure 5 - 59: Project Web App home page after publishing a test project

Click the *Tasks* link in the *My Work* section to go to the *Tasks* page shown in Figure 5 - 60. You should see the new assignment(s) in the *Tasks* page.

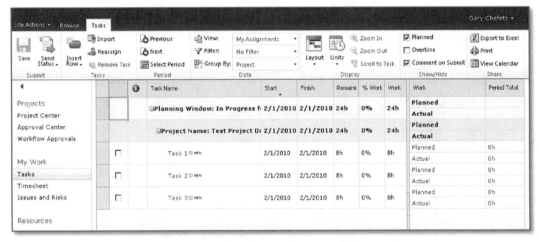

Figure 5 - 60: Tasks page showing new task assignments

Click the *Project Center* link from the Quick Launch menu. The system opens the *Project Center* page shown in Figure 5 - 61. You should see your test project in this view.

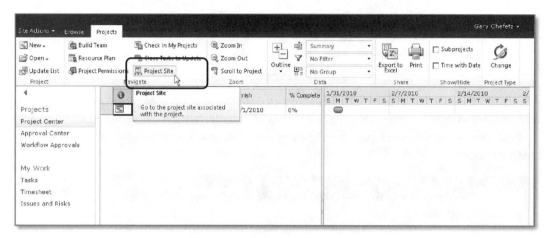

Figure 5 - 61: Project Center Page

On the *Project Center* page, make sure that your test project is selected in the grid, or select the project by clicking on the row header. You can also select any cell in the row that does not contain a hyperlink. (If you click a cell with a hyperlink, you will navigate away from the page.) In the *Navigate* section of the ribbon, click the *Project Site* button to navigate to your new Project site. The system spawns a new window and displays your new site in the window as shown in Figure 5 - 62.

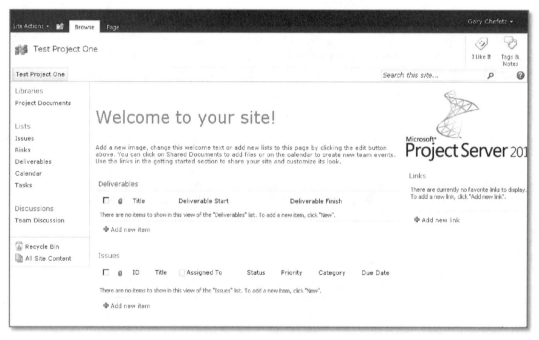

Figure 5 - 62: New Project Site

Once you verify that the Project site displays properly, close the *Project Site* window and return to the Project Web App home page. You have now verified basic Project Server functionality by proving that you can create, save, and publish a project, and that the data is flowing through the system correctly and that the system is creating Project Sites correctly.

Verifying Cube Building Capability

Now that you have verified basic functionality for Project Server 2010, you should also verify your ability to build OLAP cubes by configuring your analysis services connection and initiating the first build. To set up the OLAP cube building parameters in the system, navigate to your Project Web App home page and click the *Server Settings* link in the Quick Launch menu. The system displays the *Server Settings* page shown in Figure 5 - 63.

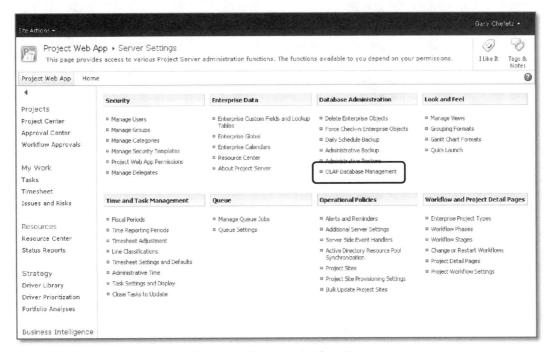

Figure 5 - 63: Server Settings Page

In the *Database Administration* section of the *Server Settings* page, click the *OLAP Database Management* link. The system displays the *OLAP Database Management* page shown in Figure 5 - 64.

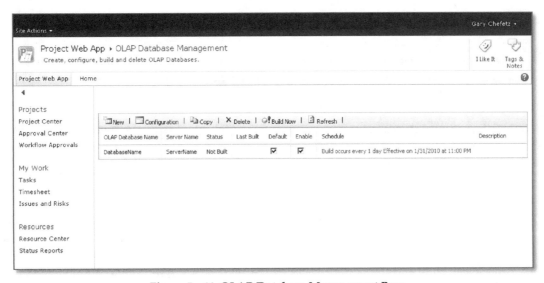

Figure 5 - 64: OLAP Database Management Page

Notice that Project Server 2010 now supports multiple cubes, which means that you can create cubes for specific audiences, such as departments. You can manage all of your cubes from this page. By default, the system creates a single cube configuration entry with generic names. You must configure this entry to actually build a cube. To configure the build settings for a cube for the first time, click the *DatabaseName* link below the *OLAP Database Name* header column. The system displays the *OLAP Database Build Settings* page shown in Figure 5 - 65.

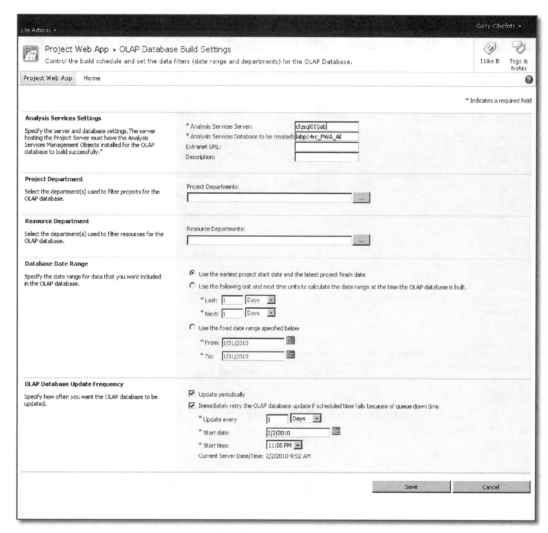

Figure 5 - 65: OLAP Database Build Settings

Enter your Analysis Services machine name in the *Analysis Services Server* field. In the *Analysis Services Database to be created* field, enter a name for the cube database you want to create (example: <PWAInstanceName>). Note that there are two new sections on this page, *Project Department* and *Resource Department*. These allow filtering by department, a new feature in Project Server 2010 that I cover in depth in Module 07. For now ignore these selections, as you must configure your system to use department filtering correctly. Accept the default selection of *Use the earliest project start date and the latest project finish date* option in the *Database Date Range* section. For now you can either accept the default selections in the *OLAP Database Update Frequency* section or deselect the *Update Periodically* check box, as there is no sense in wasting server resources until you have actual data in the system. Click the *Save* button to save your cube build settings. The system re-displays the *OLAP Database Management* page reflecting your changes, as shown in Figure 5 - 66.

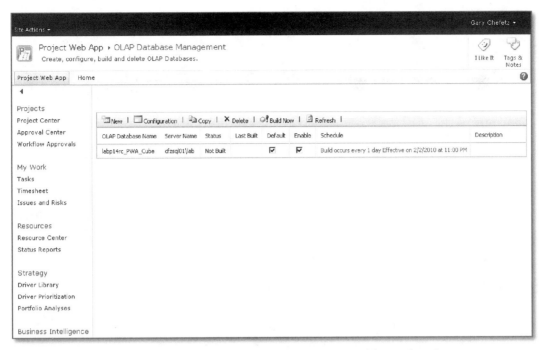

Figure 5 - 66: OLAP Database Management page with saved settings

On the *OLAP Database Management* page, select the Cube configuration that you just created and click the *Build Now* button. Notice that the *Status* column changes to *Processing*. If you would like to follow the build progress, click the *Processing* link to open the *Build Status* window shown in Figure 5 - 67.

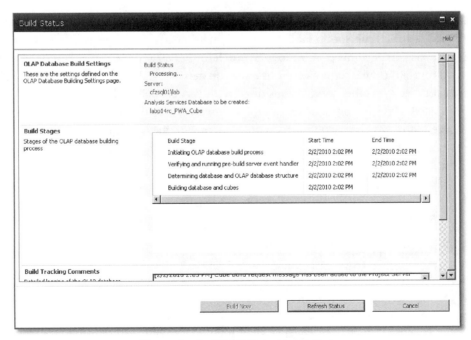

Figure 5 - 67: OLAP Cube Build Status

When the cube build completes successfully, your *Build Status* page should look something like Figure 5 - 68.

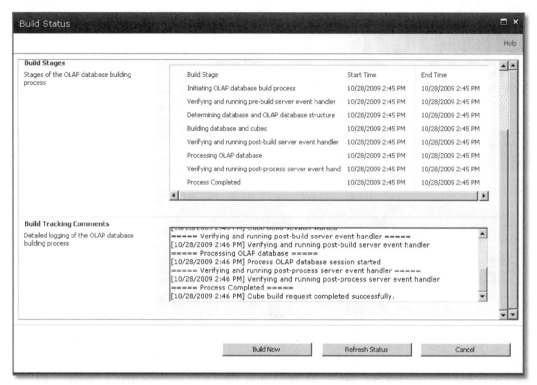

Figure 5 - 68: Build Status window displaying successful cube build completion

When your initial cube build succeeds, your system is ready to deliver analysis on the portfolio of projects you will soon add to the server. The initial cube build takes practically no time at all because you have only one resource and one project in your database. Expect this process to take **much longer** as you build up your database of projects and resources. You should revisit the cube settings options after you determine the best time to run the cube building routine, when it does not conflict with other service windows on the server such as daily backups. For now, you have accomplished what you need to verify your configuration; however, you will return to the cube configuration later in the configuration process, after you have configured your system with the custom taxonomic information that makes the information in the cubes interesting and applicable to your users.

Verifying Reporting Capability in the BI Center

The final verification step that I suggest you take before proceeding with your Project Server configuration is to verify that your Business Intelligence Center is functioning correctly and you are able to make connections to the sample reports. From Project Web App, select the *Business Intelligence* link from the *My Work* section of the Quick Launch menu. The system displays the *Business Intelligence Center* home page shown in Figure 5 - 69.

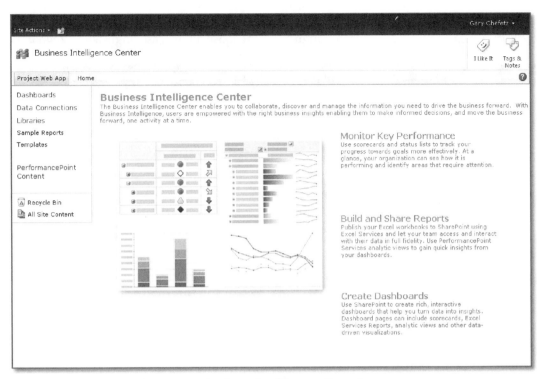

Figure 5 - 69: Business Intelligence Center home page

From the menu on the left, click on the *Sample Reports* link. The system displays the *Sample Reports* page shown in Figure 5 - 70.

Figure 5 - 70: Sample Reports home page

Click the link named *English (United States)* or the appropriate sample reports link for your installation language. The system displays the sample reports page for the language you choose, in my case English as shown in Figure 5 - 71.

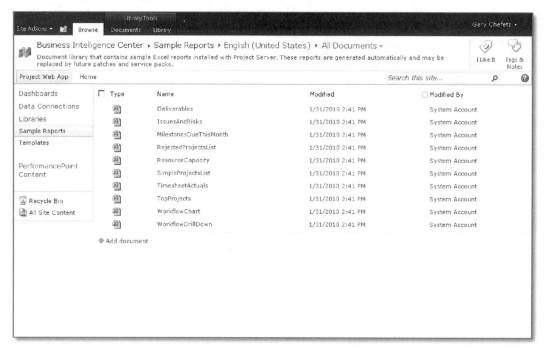

Figure 5 - 71: Sample Reports for English

Select the *SimpleProjectList* link to load the *Simple Projects List* report shown in Figure 5 - 72. When the system prompts to refresh external data connections, click the *Yes* button to proceed with displaying the report.

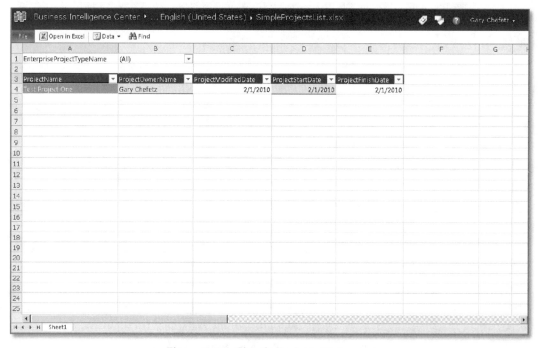

Figure 5 - 72: Simple Projects List report

You should see the test project that you created earlier in this module showing in the report. You can also test the *Resource Capacity* report which will contain only one resource at this time. All of the other reports will show no results, as no data exists in the system meeting the selection criteria for the other reports. The main point of this exercise is to verify that you configured Excel Services and the Secure Store Service correctly for normal operations.

Congratulations, you now have a fully functioning SharePoint Server 2010 and Project Server 2010 installation. Next, you take on the more difficult and time-consuming task of configuring your Project Server for your organization's specific requirements. The modules that follow walk you through this process.

Creating Additional Project Server Instances

Creating additional Project Server instances on your farm is quite simple once you have learned how to perform the post installation configuration steps that are the primary subject of this module. Before you create your new Project Server instance, you must consider whether your new instance targets the same audience as your first site, or whether it will serve a different user community. **Review this entire topical section before creating an additional instance, to properly prepare yourself and your security environment based on its target audience**.

To begin the process of creating an additional Project Server instance, open your SharePoint Central Administration site and click on the *Manage service applications* link in the *Application Management* section. The system displays the *Manage Service Applications* page. Select the *Project Server Service Application* link and the system displays the *Manage Project Web App Sites* page shown in Figure 5 - 73.

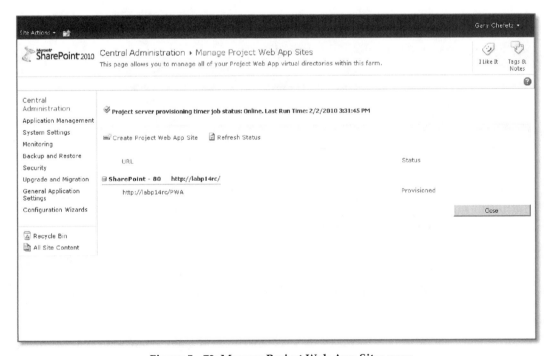

Figure 5 - 73: Manage Project Web App Sites page

Click the *Create Project Web App Site* link, just as you did previously on this page to create your first PWA site in Module 04. The system displays the *Create Project Web App Site* page shown in Figure 5 - 74.

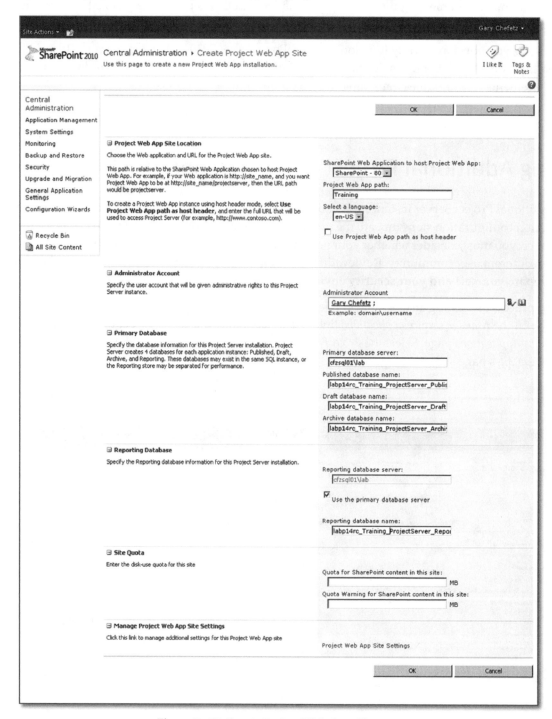

Figure 5 - 74: Create Project Web App Site page

Notice that I gave the site a new name in the *Project Web App Path* field. Likewise, you must choose a unique value for this field and then change the database names from the default names to a unique and identifiable name for your system. In this case, I chose to prefix the database names with the server and instance name because my SQL Server instance hosts databases from multiple Project Server farms. These identifiable labels display nicely in SQL Server Management Studio. Click the *OK* button to create your new site. The system returns to the *Manage Project Web App Sites* page shown in Figure 5 - 75. Notice that a line item now shows for your new site and the *Status* field changes as the site provisioning walks through the following steps:

- Waiting for resources

- Creating Project Web App Site

- Provisioning Databases

- Configuring the new Project Web App Site

- Provisioned

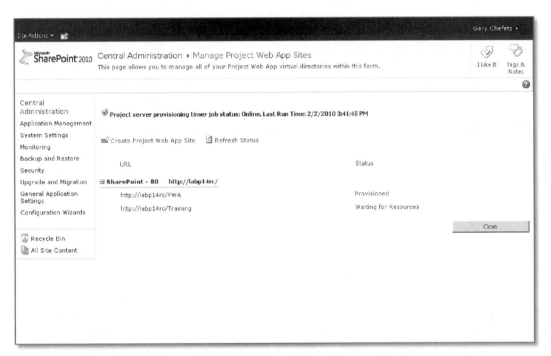

Figure 5 - 75: Manage Project Web App Sites while provisioning a new site

Configuring Your New Project Server Instance

Once the system completes the new site provisioning, you must repeat the post-configuration steps you completed for your first PWA site, for your new site. To view the specific steps for each of the following, refer back to the detailed instructions earlier in this module.

- Add login to Project Server Reporting Database for Domain Global Groups: If you create new domain global groups for a Project Server instance, you must add a login for these groups in SQL Server, repeating the steps you took for your first instance.

- Add login to Project Server Reporting Database for Secure Store Account: If your new site is intended for a separate audience, you will want to create a new instance of Excel Services service application and create a new Secure Store Target Application for the new instance. If your new Target Application will use unique credentials, then you must also create a SQL Login for this account following the same steps you used to do this for the first instance.

- Add a Trusted Data Connection Library to Excel Services: You must now add the URL for your new site's Trusted Data Connection library on the *Excel Services Trusted Data Connection Libraries* page. The easiest way to accomplish this is to open the existing record, copy the URL and paste it into the *Add Trusted Data Connection Library* page. Change the portion of the URL that represents the instance name to your new site before saving the record.

- Add Trusted File locations to Excel Services: As you did with your first site, you must add the trusted libraries to your Excel Services Trusted File Locations. The easiest way to accomplish this is to harvest the URLs from your first entry and duplicate the entries, changing the portion of the URL that points to the specific instance.

- Create a SQL Login for the OLAP Services account for the new instance reporting database: Just as for your first instance, the account running OLAP services requires access to the reporting database for the new instance in order to generate the OLAP cube.

- Implement SQL Server performance settings: Use the same rules you applied to your first instance to your new instance.

> **Warning:** Creating a new instance of Project Server provisions all built-in trusted data connections, templates, and sample reports with the same Secure Store Service ID value "ProjectServerApplication," resulting in all new Project Server instances pointing to the first Secure Store Service Application you created above. In order to segregate Report Readers and Report Authors of various instances, each instance requires its own set of domain global groups and each requires its own Excel Services Aplication instance and Secure Store Target Application; otherwise users automatically gain access to the reporting databases of other instances.

- Optionally create new domain global groups for report authors and report viewers: I call this an optional step because you must first determine whether you are accommodating a separate security audience in your new site. If your new site serves a distinctly different audience than your first site, you must create new domain global groups to segregate the reporting user authorities for your instances.

- Optionally create a new Secure Store Target Application for the instance: When your new instance serves a separate audience than your first site, you should create a new Secure Store Target Application for your new site following the steps in the *Create Secure Store Target Application* section earlier in this module. You can use any Application ID you want, but you must alter the connection strings for your Data Connections Library and the documents in the Sample Reports and Templates libraries to point to this Application ID using the following procedure.

Creating a New Excel Services Application Instance

If you need to segregate reporting security between your Project Server 2010 instances, the first step in the process is to create a new Excel Services Application. From your SharePoint Central Administration homepage, select *Manage service applications* from the *Application Management* section. The system displays the *Manage Service Applications* page shown previously in Figure 5 - 9. Click on the *New* button from the *Create* section of the ribbon, and select the *Excel Services Application* item. The system opens the *Create New Excel Services Application* dialog shown in Figure 5 - 76.

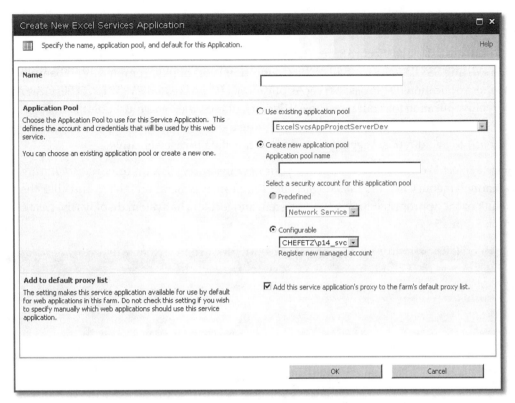

Figure 5 - 76: Create New Excel Services Application dialog

Type a name for your new instance in the *Name* field. Determine whether to create a new application pool or use an existing one, and set the credentials for the new application pool if you choose the *Create new application pool* option. Leave the *Add this service application's proxy to the farm's default proxy list* selected, and click the *OK* button to create your new instance. The system displays a processing dialog while it creates your new instance. This may take a minute or two.

At this point you must complete the configuration steps I covered previously at the beginning of this module. Work through the topical headings in this module in the following order:

- Prepare to Configure Excel Services

- Configure Excel Services

- Harvest URLs

- Configure Excel Services Global Settings (Note that this is where you specify new SSSID for your new instance)

- Configure Trusted Data Connection Libraries

- Configure Trusted File Locations

- Create a new Secure Store Target Application (Using your new SSID)

- Set Secure Store Credentials

Pointing Data Connections to the New Secure Store Target Application

When you elect to create a separate Secure Store Target Application with a distinct Secure Store Service ID value, you must update the existing SSS ID values for all of the Connection Workbooks, Templates and Sample Reports, which always point to the Application ID "ProjectServerApplication." If you created a new Excel Services Application and Secure Store Target Application for your new Project Server instance, then you must point your Project Server reporting artifacts at your new Target Application. Before executing the following steps, copy your new Target Application ID to your clipboard to avoid typos, keeping in mind that this data is case-sensitive.

1. From the Project Web App home page for your new instance, click on the *Business Intelligence* link on the Quick Launch menu. Click the *Data Connections* link from the menu on the left and click the *English (United States)* link or the appropriate link for your system and locale. The system displays the *Data Connections* page shown in Figure 5 - 77.

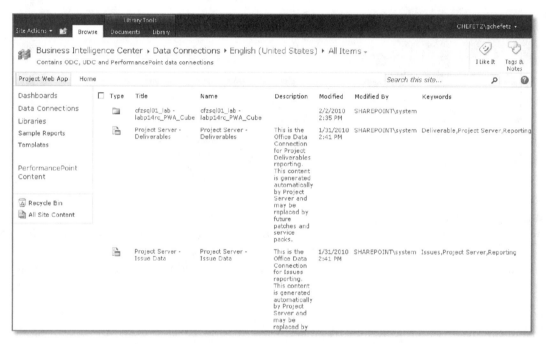

Figure 5 - 77: BI Center Data Connections page (partial)

2. On the *Data Connections* page, click the first data connection document link to open the file in Microsoft Excel. The system launches Excel. Enter your logon credentials if the system prompts. Click the *Enable* button if you see the warning shown in Figure 5 - 78.

Figure 5 - 78: Excel Security Warning

3. After you click the *Enable* button, the system displays the selected workbook in Excel as shown in Figure 5 - 79. The system warns you that the document is open read-only, but you can ignore this because you will save your updated file locally before uploading it to the Data Connections library.

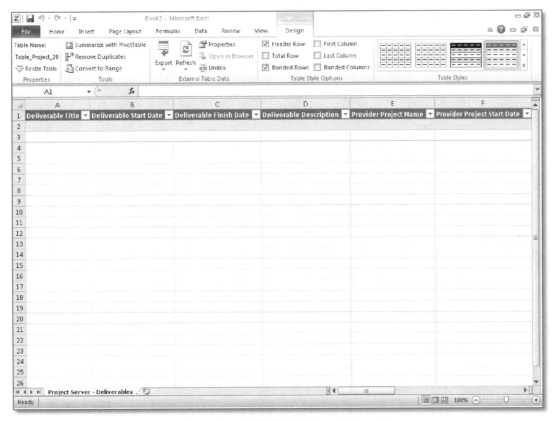

Figure 5 - 79: ODC File Open in Excel

4. From the *Design* tab, select the *Properties* button from the *External Table Data* section or select the *Data* tab and select the *Properties* button from the *Connections* section of the ribbon. The system displays the *Workbook Connections* dialog shown in Figure 5 - 80.

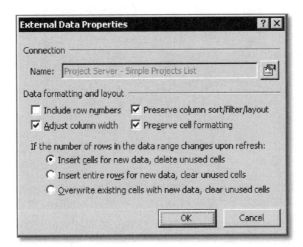

Figure 5 - 80: External Data Properties dialog

5. Click the button on the right side of the *Connection* section of the dialog. The system displays the *Connection Properties* page. Select the *Definition* tab to display the connection details as shown in Figure 5 - 81.

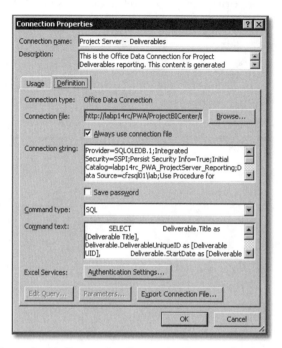

Figure 5 - 81: Connection Properties Page Definition Tab

6. Click the *Authentication Settings* button in the *Excel Services* section of the page. The system displays the *Excel Services Authentication Settings* dialog shown in Figure 5 - 82.

**Figure 5 - 82: Excel Services
Authentication Settings dialog**

7. In the *SSS ID* field, change the *Application ID* to the one that you assigned to your new Secure Store Target Application for your new instance. Click the *OK* button to return to the *Connection Properties* page shown previously in Figure 5 - 81. On the *Connection Properties* page, click the *Export Connection File* button. The system opens the Excel *File Save* dialog shown in Figure 5 - 83.

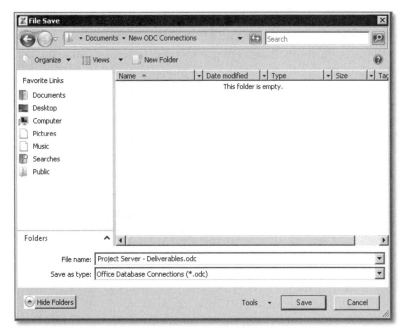

Figure 5 - 83: Excel File Save dialog

8. Click the *Save* button to save the new .odc file to a directory on your local machine. Click the *OK* button to close the *Connection Properties* dialog and then click the *Close* button on the *Workbook Connections* dialog. Close the workbook, and the system prompts you to save as shown in Figure 5 - 84.

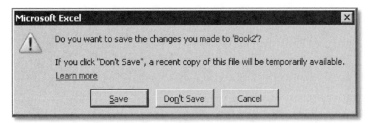

Figure 5 - 84: Excel save prompt

9. Click the *Don't Save* button. Complete the preceding steps for each of the connection documents in the Data Connections Library until you have created new .odc files containing the new Secure Store Target Application pointer for each connection in the library. After you complete the new file set, use the *Upload Document* button on the *Document* tab of the ribbon in the Connections Library to upload your new versions of the connection files.

 Warning: Do not forget that you must update the .odc files for your connections to any OLAP databases that you create in the system. The system does not create connection files for OLAP cubes until you build an OLAP database. Because Project Server 2010 supports multiple OLAP database, you must update 14 connection files for each OLAP database that you create.

You can not only use this technique to segregate authentication authorities between instances, you can also use this technique to segregate authentication authorities within a Project Web App instance. This is a very powerful construct that provides you with enormous flexibility in targeting your reports and available data connections to specific audiences using Excel Services and the Secure Store Service in SharePoint Server 2010.

Module 06

Understanding the Project Web App Interface

Learning Objectives

After completing this module, you will be able to:

- Understand and use the Project Web App user interface
- Log in to Project Web App from the workstation of another user
- Become familiar with Project Server ribbon navigation
- Use the new grid objects in Project Web App pages
- Access the Project Web App administration features

Inside Module 06

Tools for Configuration 183

Using the Project Web App User Interface 183

Logging into Project Web App from another Workstation 186

Using the Quick Launch Menu 186

Using the Ribbon Menus 188

Manipulating the Data Grid.. 197

Printing the Data Grid 200

Exporting the Data Grid to Excel... 201

Using the Project Web App Administration Interface...202

Tools for Configuration

In Project Server 2010, you must perform the initial configuration of your system from two locations:

- Project Web App
- Project Professional 2010

You use Project Web App to define custom fields and to set various system configuration options. You use Project Professional 2010 to create custom enterprise views, tables, filters, and groups for the Enterprise Global file. You use a combination of both tools to define a custom field containing a formula, to create custom enterprise calendars, and to add resources to the Enterprise Resource Pool.

Before you begin configuring Project Server 2010, you must become familiar with both the Project Web App user interface in general and the *Server Settings* interface in particular. You must also create a Project Server login account in Project Professional 2010, which I covered in the previous module.

Using the Project Web App User Interface

When you log in to Project Web App with a valid user account, the system presents the Home page. Figure 6 - 1 shows the Home page for a user with Project Server administrator permissions. The Project Web App *Home* page consists of two parts: a Quick Launch menu on the left and a main content area in the middle.

If you are already familiar with SharePoint websites, you will instantly recognize the Project Web App user interface as a standard SharePoint site layout. In Project Server 2010, the entire Project Web App interface is fully embedded into SharePoint. All of the Project Web App pages function just like any other SharePoint site. In fact, you can quickly and easily customize your Project Web App site by dragging and dropping web parts from the SharePoint web part gallery just as you would for any other SharePoint application.

The Quick Launch menu contains links to all areas of Project Web App that you can reach based on your security permissions. The main content area contains *Reminders* about your action items including Tasks, Timesheets, Approvals, Status Reports, and Issues and Risks. Across the top of the page, Project Server 2010 offers you a number of additional options and selections:

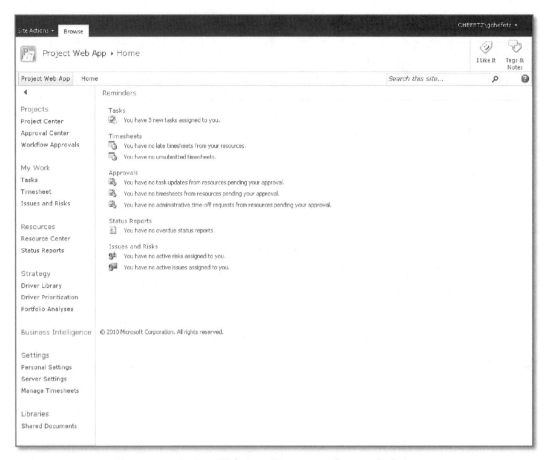

Figure 6 - 1: Project Web App Home page for an administrator

Starting at the upper left of the screen and working across, you first see the *Site Actions* menu, a SharePoint artifact that provides standard SharePoint options a shown in Figure 6-2. These include:

1. The *Edit Page* selection allows you to put the page into edit mode to introduce additional web parts or change the page layout. When you edit the page from this menu selection, all users are affected by the changes.

2. The *New Document Library* selection allows you to create a new document library to attach to the PWA site.

3. The *New Site* option allows you to create a new sub-site of the PWA site. The former two selections are the most popular content types.

4. You can access the full range of available content types that you can create by selecting the *More Options* menu item, which includes new sites and document libraries.

5. The *View All Site Content* selection allows you to see the entire site's content in one page.

6. The *Edit in SharePoint Designer* selection allows you to edit the site using SharePoint Designer. Note that you cannot edit the PWA site using SharePoint Designer; however you can edit subordinate sites and Project sites using SharePoint Designer.

7. The *Site Permissions* selection allows you to manage site permissions through SharePoint, but security synchronization with SharePoint is handled through Project Server, and it is not a good practice to change settings here other than for rare exceptions.

8. Finally, the *Site Settings* selection takes you to the full administration page for the SharePoint site underlying your Project Server instance. You learn more about SharePoint administration in Module 17.

Figure 6 - 2: Site Actions Menu

- Project Web App inherits the *Browse* tab from SharePoint, and it is visible throughout the site. In PWA, this contains title information only, and serves no functional purpose in the PWA user interface other than to provide you with a quick way to access the Project Web App homepage from any page in the system.

- In the far upper-right corner, shown in Figure 6 - 3, notice that your name appears with a pull down menu shown in Figure 6 - 4. This menu contains selections that allow you to change your personal settings, personalize the page, sign out or sign in as a different user.

**Figure 6 - 3: Personal Menu
and Social Media options**

Figure 6 - 4: Personal Menu

- Immediately below the social media functions is a Search tool you can use to search for specific information in the Project Web App site. To use this tool, enter your search terms in the *Search* field and then click the Magnifying Glass icon.

- The two buttons below the logon menu, *I Like It* and *Tags & Notes,* are part of SharePoint's new social media features. The *I Like It* button tags pages for yourself, while *Tags & Notes* allows you to add both private and public tags and notes.

- To the right of the search tool, click the *Help* icon   to see context-sensitive help displayed in a floating window.

Logging into Project Web App from another Workstation

Project Server 2010 allows you to log in to Project Web App from another user's workstation while the user is logged on to your corporate network with his/her own network user ID. To log in to Project Web App from another user's workstation, click the *Sign in as Different User* from the *Personal Menu* pick list at the bottom of the menu, shown previously in Figure 6 - 4.

The system displays the standard Windows network logon dialog shown in Figure 6 - 5: Connect dialog. In the *Connect to* dialog, enter your Domain and user ID in the *User name* field, enter your network password in the *Password* field, and then click the *OK* button.

Figure 6 - 5: Connect dialog

The system automatically logs you in to Project Web App using your network user credentials, and displays your name in the upper right hand corner of the screen.

Using the Quick Launch Menu

The Project Web App user interface offers a Quick Launch menu on the left side of every primary page. This menu lists your viewable selections based on your role in the project management environment. In Figure 6 - 6, shown below, the Quick Launch menu contains menu options for a user with Project Server administrator permissions. The options available on the Quick Launch menu include:

The **Project Web App** tab returns you to the home page. In all cases, clicking on the header link in each section navigates you to the first item below the header.

The **Projects** section contains three links. Click the *Project Center* link to navigate to the Project Center page where you can view your project portfolio. Click the *Approval Center* link to view and navigate to the Task Updates page, where you approve task updates (task progress) from your team members. Click the *Workflow Approvals* link to navigate to the *Project Server Workflow Tasks* page where you approve or reject steps in the workflow for new proposed projects.

The **My Work** section contains three subordinate links depending on your security permissions. Click the *Tasks* link to view tasks assigned to you. Click the *Timesheet* link to view your timesheet for the current reporting period. Click the *Issues and Risks* link to view issues and risks assigned to you in all of your projects.

The **Resources** section contains two links. Click the *Resource Center* link to navigate to the Resource Center page where you can view and work with resource information. Click the *Status Reports* link to navigate to the Status Reports page where you can create or respond to a Status Report request.

The **Strategy** section contains three links. Click the *Driver Library* link to navigate to the Driver Library page and view a list of your organization's business drivers for projects. Click the *Driver Prioritization* link to navigate to the Driver Prioritization page and see your organization's priorities for business drivers. Click the *Portfolio Analyses* link to navigate to the Portfolio Analyses page and access the executive decision making tool provided separately as Portfolio Server in the previous Project Server version.

Click the **Business Intelligence** link to access the Business Intelligence center in Project Server, where you can view reports and perform project data analysis.

The **Settings** section contains three links. Click the *Personal Settings* link to navigate to the *Personal Settings* page where you can set up e-mail subscriptions for Alerts and Reminders, manage queued jobs, setup Alerts and Reminders for your resources, manage your delegates or act as a delegate. Click the *Server Settings* link to navigate to the Server Settings page and configure nearly all options available in your Project Server 2010 system. Click the *Manage Timesheets* link to view a list of all of your past, current, and future Timesheets.

Figure 6 - 6:
Quick Launch Menu

The **Libraries** section contains only one link. Click the *Shared Documents* link to navigate to the Shared Documents page where you can share public documents with everyone using the Project Server system. Click the **Libraries** section heading to navigate to the All Site Content page where you can see all available public content. In all cases except for the **Libraries** link, clicking the header selection takes you to the first subordinate link.

A new addition to the Quick Launch menu for Project Server 2010 is the ability to collapse the menu to open up the screen real estate. This feature is particularly handy when you view pages that expose the data grid object. You can use the small left-pointing triangle image shown in Figure 6 - 7 to completely collapse the Quick Launch menu. When you collapse the menu, the system reverses the direction of the triangle image to indicate that you can reopen the menu by clicking on the image.

**Figure 6 - 7: Collapse
the Quick Launch menu**

Using the Ribbon Menus

Every Project Web App page that contains a data grid includes a *Ribbon* with one or more *Ribbon* tabs at the top of the page. When you click a *Ribbon* tab, Project Server 2010 displays one or more buttons on the *Ribbon*, depending on your Project Server permissions. For example, Figure 6 - 8 shows the *Project Center* page for a user with administrator permissions. Notice the *Projects* ribbon at the top of the page showing under the *Projects* tab.

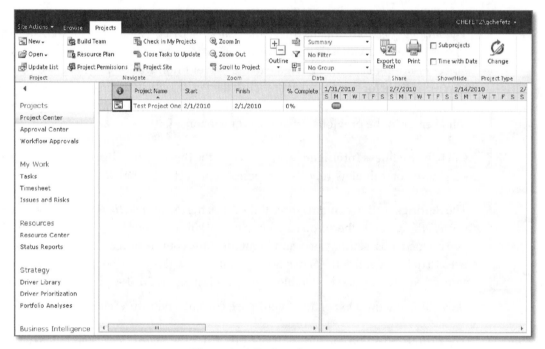

Figure 6 - 8: Project Center page

Notice that the Project Center has one context-sensitive tab, the *Projects* tab. Some pages contain only the *Browse* tab when their functionality is handled within the page itself. In one particular case, the *Browse* tab actually contains an additional navigation element, but I will cover that momentarily. The *Projects* ribbon contains menu selections in seven sections: *Project, Navigate, Zoom, Data, Share, Show/Hide* and *Project Type.* If you have used prior versions of Project Server, you can see right away that Project Web App has a much richer set of available functionality than ever before, because Project Web App now supports project editing in the browser, a new feature in Project Server 2010. The *Project* section gives you the ability to create new proposals and projects, open projects for editing in the browser or Project Client, as well as the ability to synchronize data between projects and SharePoint lists, another new feature for 2010. The *Navigate* section provides familiar functions carried forward from previous versions including *Build Team, Resource Plan, Check in My Projects, Close Tasks to Update* and a button to navigate to the *Project Site* for a selected project, formerly known as the *Project Workspace* in Project Server 2007.

Some pages contain more than one context-sensitive tab, such as the *Project Details* page, which contains three such tabs, *Project* as well as *Task* and *Options,* which are grouped together under *Schedule Tools,* as shown in Figure 6 - 9. You navigate to the *Project Detail* page by clicking on the name of a project from the *Project Center* page. The *Project Detail* page contains both a *Project* and a *Task* tab because you must access both project-level and task-level functions to fully leverage the features on this page. Notice the convenient *Status* bar notification just below the ribbon.

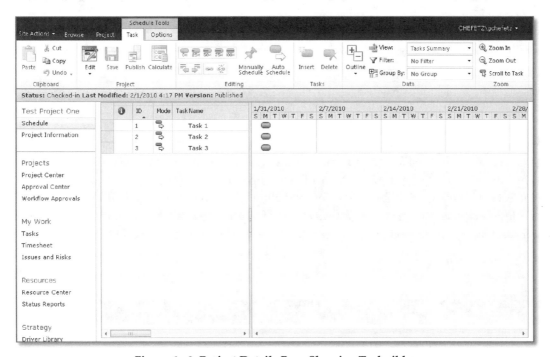

Figure 6 - 9: Project Details Page Showing Task ribbon

 Note that the *Projects* tab in the *Project Center* differs significantly from the *Project* tab you see in the *Project Details* page. The operations available in the *Project Center* apply to all projects available in the *Project Center* while the *Project* tab available in a *Project Details* page contains operations that you use to act on a selected project.

In the new *Task* ribbon shown in Figure 6 - 9 notice the *Clipboard* section on the far left and the *Editing* and *Tasks* Sections in the center. These three sections contain the new web-based project editing tools available in Project Server 2010 using familiar iconography similar to what you find in the Project client. This exciting new capability supports a much stronger project management collaboration story for Project Server 2010, allowing numerous users to participate in project schedule development, or even manage simple projects from end-to-end, including project tracking, without using the Project 2010 client. I say "simple" projects as these tools are a small subset of the editing capabilities you find in the Project client and are limited in their functionality. Most notably, while you can assign resources or even multiple resources to a task, you cannot control the percent-units value for assignments with 100% as your only choice. Similarly, you can create task dependencies; however you are limited to creating Finish-to-Start dependencies and cannot enter lag values as you can in the Project client and you cannot manage constraints. Despite these limitations, this new capability represents a giant advance in Project Web App usability and is likely to please many Project Server users. Notice that the *Data* and *Zoom* sections provide you with tools to manipulate the data display and Gantt chart displays respectively. Finally, the *Project* section makes the most common Project-level functions conveniently available without the need to switch to the *Project* tab.

Click the *Options* tab and the system displays the *Options* ribbon shown in Figure 6 - 10.

Figure 6 - 10: Project Details Page Options Ribbon

From the *Share* section, you can choose to print the project or export to Excel. The *Link To* section contains buttons that allow you to create links from tasks to Documents, Issues and Risks contained in the Project's *Project Site*. You can even create any one of these objects and link them all in one operation. The *Show/Hide* option allows you to select to display the project summary task in the current view and allows you to change the date/time format. Finally, this ribbon also provides quick access to the *Close Tasks to Updates* feature also available from the Project Center. Click the *Project* tab to reveal the *Project* ribbon for the *Project Details* page shown in Figure 6 - 11.

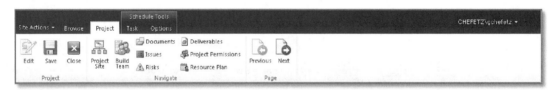

Figure 6 - 11: Project Details Page Project Ribbon

The *Project* ribbon on the Project Details page provides redundant *Edit* and *Save* buttons and provides the only way to close and check-in a project after editing on the web via the *Close* button in the *Project* section. The *Navigate* section provides navigation to the Project Site homepage using the *Project Site* button or to any of the four primary Project Site features using the *Documents, Issues, Risks* and *Deliverables* buttons to reach their respective destinations. You also find *Build Team* and *Resource Plan* buttons to activate these two features and a new *Project Permissions* button that allows you to set project-level permissions specific to your selected project. Finally, the *Previous* and *Next* buttons allow you to switch between schedule pages and the *Project Fields* page where you can edit the *Project Name, Project Start Date* and *Project Owner* fields as well as any enterprise custom fields applicable to the specific project. Note in the figure that the *Edit* button is grayed out because the project is open for editing.

Working your way down through the Quick Launch menu, the next stop is the *Approval Center*. To navigate to the *Approval Center* click the *Approval Center* link. The system displays the *Approval Center* homepage where you process task status updates, Administrative Time requests, Timesheet Lines and Timesheet updates from your resources as shown in Figure 6 - 12.

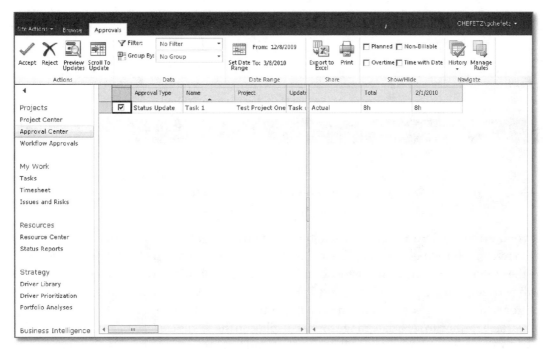

Figure 6 - 12: Approval Center

Notice that the *Approvals* ribbon contains tools in the *Actions* section to accept, reject, and preview the impact that updates have on your schedule. In the *Data* section, you can filter or group the data on the page. Use the *Date Range* section to set a date range for the data display. Like many pages in PWA, the *Approvals* ribbon contains a *Share* section for exporting the data to Excel or to print the data grid. The *Show/Hide* section contains checkboxes to selectively control data display options such as showing planned work values, non-billable work entries, overtime work entries, and to display the time with the date. Finally, you can use the *Navigate* section to call the *Manage Rules* page or navigate to either the *Status Updates* history or the *Timesheet* updates history pages. Clicking the *Preview Updates* button navigates you to the *Preview Updates* window containing the *Preview* ribbon shown in Figure 6 - 13.

Figure 6 - 13: Preview Ribbon

The *Preview Updates* page contains a Gantt chart displaying a tracking view of the project that you select to preview, and therefore the ribbon contains buttons in the *Navigate* section to allow you to zoom in or out as well as scroll to the selected task on the Gantt chart. The *Data* section contains controls to switch views, set a filter or group by value, and to select the Outline level displayed. You can select to show or hide Summary Tasks and select whether to show the time as well as the date in date fields from the *Show/Hide* section. Finally, the ribbon contains the standard *Share* section for exporting to Excel or printing the data grid to a printer.

When you select the *History* button from the *Approvals* page shown previously in Figure 6 - 12, you have a choice of either *Status Updates* or *Timesheets*. These display their respective update histories. When you select Status Updates or Timesheets, the system displays the following two ribbons shown in Figure 6 - 14 and Figure 6 - 15.

Figure 6 - 14: Status Updates History Ribbon

Figure 6 - 15: Timesheets History Ribbon

Both ribbons contain the standard *Share* section and both contain a *Navigate* section. In both cases, clicking the *Approval Center* button returns you to the *Approvals Center* shown previously in Figure 6 - 12. When you click the *History* button you have the option to navigate to the history details page that is not currently displayed. You use these to toggle back and forth between *Status Updates History* and *Timesheets History*. On the *Status Updates* ribbon, you can use the *Delete Item* button to delete a history entry, or the *Publish* button to publish the selected items from the *Actions* section. Use the *Set Date Range* button to set a date range for the display on the *Status Updates* page. The *Timesheets History* ribbon allows you to use the *Recall* button to recall a timesheet, and it allows you to use the *Filters* button in the *Data* section to set filter criteria for the data displayed on the page.

Finally, the last selection on the *Approvals Center* ribbon in the *Navigate* section is the *Manage Rules* button that navigates you to the *Rules* page where you can create rules for automatically approving updates. The *Rules* menu ribbon is shown in Figure 6 - 16.

Figure 6 - 16: Rules Ribbon

Like most ribbon menus in the system, the *Rules* ribbon contains the standard *Share* section. In the *Rule* section, the ribbon contains buttons for creating, editing and deleting rules including *New, Edit, Copy* and *Delete* selections. The *Run* section contains the *Run Selected* button to run rules that you select in the page and a *Run All* button to immediately run all of your rules.

Workflow Approvals is the last selection in the *Projects* section of the Quick Launch menu. When you click the *Workflow Approvals* selection the system displays the *Workflow Approvals* page with the ribbon menu shown in Figure 6 - 17.

Figure 6 - 17: Workflow Approvals Browse Ribbon

This page defaults to the *Browse* tab, an oddball arrangement among the other ribbons in Project Server. Notice also that this tab contains a special navigation element at the end of the page location string at the top of the ribbon, which is also unique to this page. This navigational element immediately allows you to refine the dataset shown in the page. Because this page uses a standard SharePoint list to contain its data, it inherits the standard SharePoint *List Tools* ribbons for manipulating SharePoint lists. It also inherits the *Navigate Up* feature that allows you to navigate back to the PWA homepage using a breadcrumb trail. You find this feature on most native SharePoint pages and occasionally in PWA as in this example. You will encounter these menu ribbons when you use any standard SharePoint list. The *Items* ribbon is shown in Figure 6 - 18 and the *List* ribbon appears in Figure 6 - 19.

Figure 6 - 18: List Tools Items Ribbon

Figure 6 - 19: List Tools List Ribbon

> Note that not all standard SharePoint menu items are applicable to Project Server pages where they might appear. Further, your permissions in the system may prevent you from selecting various actions from the menu.

The next stop on the Project Web App interface tour is the *Work* section of the Quick Launch menu. The *Tasks* selection takes you to the *Tasks* page, which contains a single ribbon menu that provides functionality for manipulating data and the display in the page. Team members use the *Tasks* page to submit progress updates to the project managers whose projects they are assigned to. The *Tasks* page ribbon is shown in Figure 6 - 20.

Figure 6 - 20: Tasks Page Tasks Ribbon

In the *Submit* section of the ribbon you can save your updates for later submission using the *Save* button, or send a status update for all tasks or selected tasks using the *Send Status* pick list. The *Tasks* section contains an *Insert Row* pick list that allows you to add a new task, assign yourself to an existing task, or add a team task to your Tasks reporting screen. Use the *Import* button to import data from your timesheet, or the *Reassign* button to assign a selected task to another resource and the *Remove Task* button to remove a task from your Tasks page. The buttons in the *Period* section allow you to navigate to other reporting periods using the *Previous* and *Next* buttons or the *Select Period* button. The *Data* section provides selectors to choose a view, filter, and group-by values for the view. The *Display* section contains a *Layout* selector that allows you to choose between three layouts: Gantt chart, Time-phased and Sheet layout. The *Units* selector allows you to choose a format for displaying Duration, Work and Dates in the page and the *Zoom* buttons and *Scroll to Task* button provide familiar navigation options when the Gantt chart layout is active. The *Show/Hide* section contains checkboxes that allow you to selectively show Planned and Overtime rows as well as to determine whether you are prompted for comments when submitting updates. The *Share* section contains the typical *Export to Excel* and *Print* selections as well as a special *View Calendar* button that activates a calendar view of your Tasks page.

The *Timesheet* ribbon, shown in Figure 6 - 21, contains functionality you need to manipulate the display and data in the *Timesheet* page.

Figure 6 - 21: Timesheet Ribbon

From the *Submit* section, you can use the *Save* button to save your entries for a later date or use the *Send Status* button to send status on specific tasks. The *Send Timesheet* button locks and submits your entire timesheet. The *Tasks* section contains an *Insert Row* button, *Import* button, and *Remove Task* button that provide the same abilities that I discussed in the *Tasks* ribbon. In the *Period* section, the *Previous* and *Next* buttons allow you to navigate forward and backward through time periods and the *Select Period* button opens a dialog that allows you to quickly navigate to a specific time period. The *Data* section includes selectors to change the view or group-by values while the *Show/Hide* section contains checkboxes to show or hide data rows for Planned work, Overtime work, Non-Billable work. The *Totals* checkbox lets you determine whether or not to show totals by day in daily timesheet columns, and the *Units* selector allows you to define how the system displays duration, work and dates on this page. Finally, the *Share* section provides the standard options for exporting to Excel or printing.

The last selection in the *Work* section is *Issues and Risks*, which navigates you to the *Issues and Risks* page that does not contain a specialized ribbon.

The next place you find a specialized ribbon menu is in the *Resource Center* that you reach by clicking on the *Resources* heading or *Resource Center* link from the Quick Launch menu. The *Resources* ribbon is shown in Figure 6 - 22.

Figure 6 - 22: Resources Ribbon

From the *Editing* section of the *Resources* ribbon, you select the *New Resource* button to create a new resource, select the *Edit Resource* button to edit both an individual resource and multiple resources by batch. The *Bulk Edit* button takes you to a screen that allows you to bulk-edit resources by providing values for resources that apply to multiple entries. The *Open* button opens the selected resources for editing in the Project client. Familiar selections adorn the *Data* section with options to choose an outline level for the display, and selectors to choose a view, filter and group-by values. The *Show/Hide* section contains checkboxes to show the list of selected resources alongside the selection grid and add the time to the date format. The *Share* section provides the usual *Share* options while the *Navigate* section provides links to two resource views via the *Resource Assignments* and *Resource Availability* buttons. Click the *Resource Assignments* button to reach the *Resource Assignments* page containing the ribbon shown in Figure 6 - 23.

Figure 6 - 23: Resource Assignments Ribbon

The *Resource Assignments* ribbon contains display and navigation options as this page is not actionable. Note that the *Display* section provides buttons to change the view to *Gantt Chart* or *Timephased Data*. The *Set Date Range* button allows you to select a date range for the display while the buttons in the *Zoom* section control zooming on the Gantt chart as well as a *Scroll to Task* button to quickly scroll the Gantt chart to the selected task. The *Data* section contains buttons to set the Outline level display, select a view or set filter and group-by options. The *Show/Hide* section contains checkboxes to show time with date, summary tasks, overtime work and work. Use the options in the *Share* section as you would with any other ribbon and the *Navigate* section to go back to the Resource Center page, or click the *Resource Availability* button to navigate to the *Resource Availability* page with the ribbon shown in Figure 6 - 24.

Figure 6 - 24: Resource Availability Ribbon

The *Availability* ribbon contains a view selector to choose a view in the *View* section. The usual *Share* options are available from the ribbon and the *Navigate* section allows you to return to the *Resource Center* page or the *Resource Assignments* page.

The final stop on the ribbon tour is a quick look at the ribbon menus for the *Strategy* section. The selections you find under *Strategy* are the pages that contain the Portfolio analysis capability previously found in Microsoft Portfolio Server, which is now fully integrated into Project Server. Select *Driver Library* from the *Strategy* section to see the *Driver Ribbon* shown in Figure 6 - 25.

Figure 6 - 25: Business Driver Ribbon

The ribbon functionality for Business Drivers is very simple; you can either create a new Business Driver, or delete an existing one. You have the exact capabilities with the first ribbon you encounter in Business Driver Prioritization process as shown in Figure 6 - 26.

Figure 6 - 26: New Driver Prioritization Ribbon

The second ribbon menu that you encounter during the Business Driver Prioritization process is shown in Figure 6 - 27. This ribbon contains icons for the logical steps involved in the process: *Define Properties*, *Prioritize Drivers* and *Re-*

view Priorities. These align with the steps that the system walks you through while performing a prioritization exercise. Note that all three of these ribbons contain the *Share* section with the usual options and that the Prioritization ribbon contains a *Close* button to complete the prioritization.

Figure 6 - 27: Driver Prioritization Ribbon

The last selection in the Quick Launch menu that contains Project-Server-specific ribbon menus is *Portfolio Analyses*. This is the top-down decision making tool formerly contained in Portfolio Server 2007. The first step in the analysis process is to create a new analysis or work with an existing one. The ribbon menu shown in Figure 6 - 28 contains *New* and *Delete* buttons for creating new or deleting existing portfolios in the *Analysis* section. The *Project Dependencies* button allows you to define dependencies and inclusive or exclusive relationships between projects in your analysis.

Figure 6 - 28: Portfolio Analysis Ribbon

Once you have created the initial analysis and defined your project dependencies, the system walks you through the analysis process. The next step is to define the properties for the analysis such as what projects to consider, and to set other properties and constraints for the analysis. The ribbon menu that supports this process is shown in Figure 6 - 29. Note that the next two steps that follow use almost identical ribbon menus, as shown in Figure 6 - 30 for prioritizing your selected projects and in Figure 6 - 31 for reviewing your priorities before you use the system tools to perform the actual analysis.

Figure 6 - 29: Define Properties

Figure 6 - 30: Prioritize Projects

Figure 6 - 31: Review Priorities

Note that the *Share* section appears on pages with data grids. Pages, such as the *Define Properties* page, do not contain data grids and, therefore, do not display ribbon menus that include the *Share* section.

After you have defined your analysis selections, the next step you take is to perform the analysis using the tools provided by the system. The first analysis is cost-driven. The ribbon menu for cost analysis, shown in Figure 6 - 32, introduces two new sections to the ribbon including *Portfolio Selection* and *Projects*. The *Portfolio Selection* section is common to both cost analysis and resource analysis as shown in the *Analyze Resources* ribbon in Figure 6 - 33 with the only difference being that the *Analyze Resource* ribbon also contains a *Reports* selector. Both ribbons also include a *Projects* section that offers additional tools that pertain to the specific type of analysis.

Figure 6 - 32: Analyze Cost

Figure 6 - 33: Analyze Resources

In the previous two figures, notice that both contain an additional tab selection, the *Options* tab showing the *Options* ribbon in Figure 6 - 34. This ribbon provides additional option settings for both cost and resource analysis scenarios.

Figure 6 - 34: Options Tab

You have now explored the major components for the Project Server PWA user interface, focusing on the various ribbon menus that you encounter in the system. If you have used one of the prior versions of Project Server, by this time you are no doubt impressed by both the breadth of the new functionality available in Project Server 2010 and by the way the new ribbons surface this functionality in a more intuitive arrangement than prior versions.

Manipulating the Data Grid

As I previously mentioned, a number of Project Web App pages contain a data grid that displays task, resource, and assignment data. Some data grids, such as the Project Center page, have a vertical split bar separating the grid into two sections, while other pages contain a single grid only. For example, notice that the Project Center page, shown previously in Figure 6 - 8, consists of two sections: the project list on the left side of the split bar, and the Gantt Chart on the right side. To work with the data in the grid most effectively, it is important to know how to take the following actions:

- **Move the Split Bar**: You move the split bar in the grid by floating your mouse pointer anywhere over the split bar itself. When the mouse pointer changes from a single arrow to a double-headed arrow, click and hold the mouse button to "grab" the split bar, and then drag it to the new position on the screen. Figure 6 - 35 shows the mouse pointer hovering over the *split bar*.

**Figure 6 - 35: Mouse Pointer
over Split Bar**

- **Change Column Widths**: To change the width of any column in the grid, position the mouse pointer anywhere on the right edge of the column in the header row. The mouse pointer changes from a single arrow to a double-headed arrow. Click and hold to "grab" the right edge of the column, and drag the edge of the column to the proper width. Figure 6 - 36 shows that I am increasing the column width of the *Project Name* column.

Figure 6 - 36: Widen the Project Name Column

 To widen any column to "best fit" the data in the column, you can use the Microsoft Office Excel trick by double-clicking the gridline on the right edge of the column.

- **Move Columns**: To move any column in the grid, click and hold the column header of the column you want to move, then drag the column and drop it into its new position in the grid. The column snaps to the grid at the locations where you can place the column. Notice in Figure 6 - 37 that I am dragging the % Complete column to a new position. Notice how the column floats over the other columns in a transparent format as I move it across the other columns.

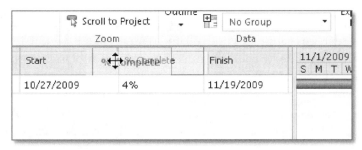

Figure 6 - 37: Dragging the %Complete Column

- **Hide and Unhide Columns**: To hide any column, float your mouse pointer over the column header of the column you want to hide, and then click the pick list button that appears at the right edge of the column. Project Server 2010 displays the pick list menu shown in Figure 6 - 38. On the pick list menu, click the *Hide Column* item.

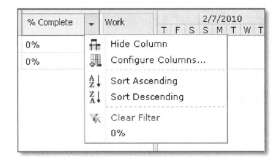

Figure 6 - 38: Hide Column

- To unhide a column, float your mouse pointer over any column header, click the pick list button, and click the *Configure Columns* item on the pick list menu shown previously in Figure 6 - 38. The system displays the *Configure Columns* dialog shown in Figure 6 - 39. In the *Configure Columns* dialog, select the option checkbox for the column(s) you want to unhide and then click the *OK* button.

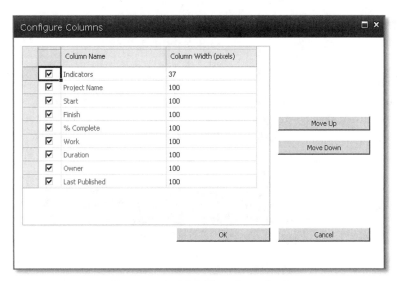

**Figure 6 - 39: Unhide column in the
Configure Columns Dialog**

- Notice in the dialog shown in Figure 6 - 39 that Project Server 2010 also allows you to set column widths and the column display order. To change the width of any column, enter the width in pixels in the *Column Width* field. To change the display order of columns, select any column and use the *Move Up* and *Move Down* buttons. Click the *OK* button when finished.

- **Sort Columns:** To sort the data in the grid, float your mouse pointer over the column header of the column that you want to sort, click the pick list button, and then click the *Sort Ascending* or *Sort Descending* item on the pick list menu.

Project Server 2010 automatically saves any changes you make to the layout of a grid (such as column order, column width, etc.) in your user profile. The layout of the grid reappears the next time you return to the page. These changes affect the current user only. A Project Server administrator must use the *Manage Views* selection from the *Server Settings* menu to make these changes universal for all users.

Printing the Data Grid

Project Server 2010 allows you to print a report from a data grid or export the data grid information to Microsoft Office Excel. To print a data grid, click the *Print* option in the *Share* section on the Ribbon. The system opens the Print Grid window in its own Internet Explorer window. Figure 6 - 40 shows the Print Grid window for the *Project Center* page.

Figure 6 - 40: Print Grid Window

Notice that the *Print Grid* window is a duplicate of the grid in the parent window. In this window, you can rearrange and resize the columns using the same techniques you used to move columns in the parent window, however you cannot hide columns. Instead, you must hide the columns that you do not wish to print before you open the *Print Grid* window. If you do hide columns for printing, don't forget to restore them in your view.

Project Server 2010 prints both the data grid and the Gantt chart components. The ability to print the Gantt chart is new for 2010. In prior versions you could apply additional formatting to the grid prior to printing, however that feature is not available in Project Server 2010.

Warning: If you attempt to print a data grid, and the data grid exceeds 100 lines of information, Project Server 2010 does not allow you to print the data grid. Instead, the system forces you to export the data grid to Microsoft Office Excel. From Excel, you can then print the data grid.

Exporting the Data Grid to Excel

In addition to printing the data grid, you can also export the data grid to a Microsoft Office Excel workbook by clicking on the *Export to Excel* button from the *Share* section of the ribbon on a page containing a data grid. When you select this option, the system displays the *File Download* dialog shown in Figure 6 - 41.

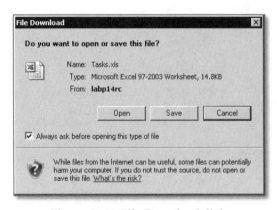

Figure 6 - 41: File Download dialog

Click the *Open* button to open the file in Microsoft Excel. The system opens Excel and exports the grid as shown in Figure 6 - 42.

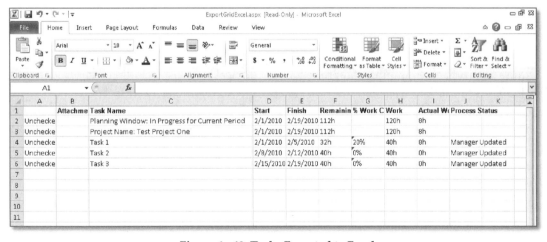

Figure 6 - 42: Tasks Exported to Excel

Using the Project Web App Administration Interface

To access the administration features of the system, log in to Project Web App using an account with administrator permissions and then click the *Server Settings* link in the Quick Launch menu. The system displays the *Server Settings* page shown in Figure 6 - 43.

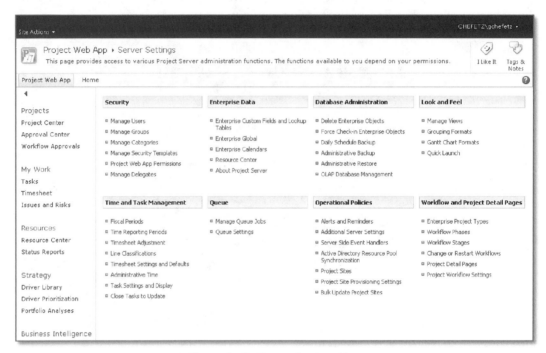

Figure 6 - 43: Server Settings Page

The *Server Settings* page organizes administrator functions into logical sections, including *Security, Enterprise Data, Database Administration, Look and Feel, Time and Task Management, Queue, Operational Policies* and *Workflow and Project Detail Pages*. Each section contains links for the functions you perform as the Project Server administrator. For example, use the functions in the Security section to manage Users, Groups, Categories, Security Templates, Project Web App Permissions, and to manage delegates. Tables 6 - 1 through 6 - 8 contain brief descriptions of the functions available in each section of the *Server Settings* page.

Security Functions	
Function	**Description**
Manage Users	Add, modify, and deactivate users. Set Groups, Categories, Permissions, and Custom Field values.
Manage Groups	Add, modify, and delete user Groups. Set Active Directory Group mappings for user Groups with synchronization frequencies. Manage user and Category associations to Groups and global permissions.
Manage Categories	Add, modify, and delete Categories. Associate users, Groups, projects, resources, and Views with each Category.
Manage Security Templates	Add, modify, and delete the security templates used to set Category Permissions and Global Permissions in Groups.
Project Web App Permissions	Enable or disable the high-level permissions that are available in Project Server 2010 for Category and Global permissions.
Manage Delegates	Add or delete delegates in the system.

Table 6 - 1: Security Functions

Enterprise Data Functions	
Function	**Description**
Enterprise Custom Fields and Lookup Tables	Create, modify, and delete custom enterprise fields and Lookup Tables. Modify built-in custom enterprise fields and Lookup Tables.
Enterprise Global	Navigate to Project Professional 2010 to modify the Enterprise Global file.
Enterprise Calendars	Create, modify, and delete custom enterprise Calendars. Modify the built-in enterprise Standard calendar.
Resource Center	Navigate to the Resource Center page to create new resources, to modify existing resource information individually or using a bulk modification, or to view resource availability and resource assignments.
About Project Server	Display the current number of active Project Server users and Project Professional users.

Table 6 - 2: Enterprise Data Functions

Database Administration Functions	
Function	**Description**
Delete Enterprise Objects	Delete projects, resources and user accounts, Status Report responses, Timesheets, and User delegations from the Project Server database.
Force Check-in Enterprise Objects	Check in projects, resources, custom fields, Calendars, Lookup Tables, or Resource Plans left in a checked-out state.
Daily Schedule Backup	Schedule daily backup of objects to support item-level restoration of projects, the Enterprise Resource Pool, Calendars, fields, the Enterprise Global file, View definitions, system settings, and Category/Group settings.
Administrative Backup	Manually back up projects, the Enterprise Resource Pool, Calendars, fields, the Enterprise Global file, View definitions, system settings, and Category/Group settings.
Administrative Restore	Manually restore individual items backed up automatically or manually.
OLAP Database Management	Create, modify, and delete OLAP databases. Set the parameters, dimensions, and measures used for automated OLAP cube generation for each database. Initiate the process of building the OLAP cubes and view their status.

Table 6 - 3: Database Administration functions

Look and Feel Functions	
Function	**Description**
Manage Views	Create, modify, copy, or delete any type of View displayed in Project Web App.
Grouping Formats	Customize the grouping formats used in Project Web App views.
Gantt Chart Formats	Customize the formats for Gantt charts used in Project Web App views.
Quick Launch	Add, edit, delete, or reorder the links in the Quick Launch menu in Project Web App.

Table 6 - 4: Look and Feel functions

Time and Task Management Functions	
Function	**Description**
Fiscal Periods	Define, modify, and delete financial periods and set Fiscal Year options.
Time Reporting Periods	Define Time Periods used for Timesheets in Project Web App.
Timesheet Adjustment	Alter submitted timesheets.
Line Classifications	Create duplicate timesheet lines for business or accounting purposes.
Timesheet Settings and Defaults	Specify all options related to Timesheet display and usage in Project Web App. Tie the My Timesheet page to the My Tasks page for a single point of time entry in Project Web App.
Administrative Time	Add and delete categories used for tracking administrative time.
Task Settings and Display	Specify the default and/or locked-down reporting methods for reporting and tracking task progress in Project Web App.
Close Tasks to Update	Lock down completed or cancelled tasks to prevent entry of progress against them.

Table 6 - 5: Time and Task
Management functions

Queue Functions	
Function	**Description**
Manage Queue Jobs	View the current status of Queue jobs and take administrative action on them.
Queue Settings	Specify custom settings for Queue job processing or restore default settings.

Table 6 - 6: Queue functions

Operational Policies Functions	
Function	**Description**
Alerts and Reminders	Set up a connection to an SMTP mail server, specify e-mail message information, and set the time for e-mail Reminder service to run.
Additional Server Settings	Specify connectivity options for users with Project Professional 2007. Specify whether to allow master project publishing and allow project managers to use local base calendars, set the default currency, specify Resource Capacity and Resource Plan Work Day settings, and determine the behavior of the built-in custom State field. Synchronize Project Web App tasks with each user's Exchange Server account.
Server Side Event Handlers	Add, modify, or delete custom Event Handlers.
Active Directory Resource Pool Synchronization	Set options for synchronizing the Enterprise Resource Pool with Active Directory.
Project Sites	Create, edit, and delete SharePoint sites and synchronize user access to a site. Link to Site Administration page for a specific SharePoint site.
Project Site Provisioning Settings	Manipulate automation settings for WSS site creation when users publish a project to Project Server.
Bulk Update Project Sites	Update the URL path for one or more project sites after restoring or migrating content, Update content types after migration, and synchronize project site permissions.

Table 6 - 7: Operational Policies functions

Workflow and Project Detail Pages Functions	
Function	**Description**
Enterprise Project Types	Create, modify, and delete project types used with an associated Workflow process to approve Proposal projects.
Workflow Phases	Create, modify, and delete the Phases used in the Workflow process.
Workflow Stages	Create, modify, and delete the Stages used in each Phase of the Workflow process.
Change or Restart Workflows	Change or restart the Workflow process for individual Proposal projects or enterprise projects.
Project Detail Pages	Change the Properties or modify the layout of the Project Detail pages used in the Workflow process in Project Web App. **Warning:** You must have Microsoft Office SharePoint Designer to edit the Project Detail pages.
Project Workflow Settings	Enter the Workflow Proxy User Account information for your Project Server 2010 system.

**Table 6 - 8: Workflow and
Project Detail Pages functions**

Your overview tour of the Project Web App user interface is complete. Although you haven't seen every ribbon menu in the system, you have covered most of them, including those for the most significant pages. Some of the pages that you use to administer Project Server also contain ribbon menus, however they are very simple and you learn about them as you encounter them in upcoming modules.

In the next module, you learn how to begin building your Project Management Information system by laying the foundation with custom taxonomies that reflect your specific business requirements and provide the system metadata necessary to provide valuable output from the system.

Module 07

Creating System Metadata and Calendars

Learning Objectives

After completing this module, you will be able to:

- Understand project types

- Understand department filtering

- Understand the importance of custom enterprise fields

- Edit built-in lookup tables

- Create a custom lookup table

- Create custom enterprise fields using lookup tables, formulas, and graphical indicators

- Edit custom enterprise fields and lookup tables

- Delete custom enterprise fields and lookup tables

- Set the working schedule on the enterprise standard calendar

- Create custom enterprise base calendars

- Import a base calendar from a non-enterprise project

Inside Module 07

Understanding Significant Changes to Project Server 2010 Metadata Architecture 211

Introducing Departments 211

Introducing Project Types 213

Introducing Business Drivers...214

Working with Enterprise Custom Fields and Lookup Tables...214

Understanding Enterprise Field Types...215

Understanding Built-In Fields and Lookup Tables..215

Modifying Built-In Lookup Tables 218

Modifying the Cost Type Lookup Table 222

Modifying the Health Lookup Table 223

209

Modifying the RBS Lookup Table 224

Creating the Team Names Lookup Table... 226

Creating and Modifying Custom Lookup Tables...**228**

Creating a New Lookup Table 229

Modifying a Custom Lookup Table 233

Creating Custom Fields **233**

Creating Free Entry Custom Fields..**234**

Making Fields Required 236

Creating a Custom Field with a Lookup Table **237**

Modifying Built-In Project and Resource Department Fields... 240

Creating a Custom Field with a Formula...**243**

Understanding Field Types with Formulas... 243

Creating a Formula Using Project Web App 246

Creating a Formula Using Project Professional 2010 250

Importing a Local Field as a Custom Enterprise Field **257**

Displaying Graphical Indicators in Custom Fields...**259**

Creating Graphical Indicators Using Project Web App.. 259

Creating Graphical Indicators Using Project Professional 2010 263

Understanding the Connection between Formulas and Graphical Indicators.............................. 266

Deleting a Custom Field or Lookup Table...**267**

Planning for Matching Generic Resources **268**

Creating Enterprise Calendars **270**

Setting Company Holidays 271

Setting the Daily Working Schedule 274

Creating a New Base Calendar 278

Importing a Base Calendar from a Project 280

Understanding Significant Changes to Project Server 2010 Metadata Architecture

Just as at its heart Microsoft Project 2010 is a scheduling tool, Microsoft Project Server 2010 is a Project management information system, one that is transitioning from a singular focus on project management to an all encompassing work management system capable of delivering project, work, and resource management capabilities. More than ever, Project Server requires a carefully planned metadata architecture, which is especially true for leveraging Project Server 2010's demand management, lifecycle management and portfolio management capabilities.

As with an ERP system, you must mold the raw functionality provided in Project Server 2010 to shape and channel information to your organization's specific requirements. Although the built-in generic information streams provide useful tracking and statistical data, the information becomes meaningful only when you seed the database with custom attributes. These attributes exist in Project Server 2010 as custom fields, which come in two flavors: enterprise and local. For the most part, you manage enterprise field definitions centrally using the Project Web App interface rather than through Project Professional 2010. Only administrators or users specifically granted administrator permissions can modify these fields. Project Managers can modify local custom fields for their projects on a project-by-project basis, as well as in project templates and in their local Global.mpt file. If you are familiar with field customization in Project Server 2007, you will find that the process for customizing enterprise fields is identical in most ways; however, you have many more built-in enterprise custom fields to consider and significantly more data that requires attribution.

For instance, the purpose of implementing demand management is to capture structured information that supports the structured decision making process that the portfolio management capabilities provide. This most often requires additional data collection. Likewise, you must create additional metadata to support the portfolio selection process itself. If you intend to take advantage of these exciting new features in Project Server 2010, expect to spend more time planning your information architecture for Project Server 2010 than you spent on prior versions, much more.

Introducing Departments

Microsoft Project 2010 introduces two powerful new constructs to the Project Server metadata arena, *Departments* and *Project Types*. Beginning with *Departments*, this construct is meant to overcome a limitation that made it difficult to deploy Project Server with a single instance serving multiple departments with diverse metadata requirements. In previous versions of Project Server, every custom field was visible to every user. This could become particularly annoying when project managers have to enter this information in the *Project Information* dialog where they might have to find their ten departmental fields among a selection of fifty or more. In Project Server 2010, *Departments* overcome that limitation by providing a **master content filtering** system.

Warning: The functionality provided by *Departments* does not leverage the security system in Project Server and therefore does not provide a secure environment behind this construct. For most organizations, *Departments* provides a very satisfactory solution to what becomes information overload for users, but it is not a satisfactory solution if your organization must provide a security framework behind the visibility issue in order to comply with some regulatory or voluntary industry standards.

You can see the physical manifestation of *Departments* in Project Server right away by selecting *Enterprise Custom Fields and Lookup Tables* from the *Enterprise Data* section of the *Server Settings* page. The system displays the *Enterprise Custom Fields and Lookup Tables* page shown in Figure 7 - 1.

Figure 7 - 1: Enterprise Custom Fields and Lookup Tables page

Notice in the figure that under the *Enterprise Custom Fields* section you find two fields referencing "departments," *Project Departments* and *Resource Departments*. These two built-in custom enterprise fields both use the *Department* lookup table you see in the *Lookup Tables for Custom Fields* section at the bottom of the page. The *Department* lookup table is blank when you install Project Server. Notice also the *Department* column in the *Enterprise Custom Fields* section. If you plan on using this feature, you should consider it first before you create other objects in Project Server 2010 because it applies to important system artifacts including:

- Projects

- Resources

- Enterprise Custom Fields

- Project Types

- Business Drivers

- OLAP Cubes

As you might have surmised by now, your design for the *Department* lookup table determines the granularity of your filtering capability using *Departments* in Project Server 2010. When you use department attribution, both the *Enterprise Resource/User* and the *Enterprise Object* (Project, Custom Field...) must have matching attribution or the object is not visible in the system. I cover editing the *Department* lookup table later in this module.

Warning: Data filtering applies to users who are administrators as well as ordinary users. Those administrators who need visibility to all data in the system should have all departments associated with their user accounts.

Introducing Project Types

Project Types, a second important innovation in the Project Server 2010 metadata architecture, gives you the ability to establish, as the feature name suggests, project types. The important thing to know about *Project Types* is that you use them to connect workflows with *Enterprise Project Templates* and *Project Site Templates*. This is a very big advance in Project Server's capabilities. Previous versions of Project Server were limited to using only one template for all *Project Workspaces* (Project Server 2007). The system now supports multiple *Project Site* (Project Server 2010) templates connected through *Project Types*, which also gives you the ability to specify a unique base project template for each project type.

As you can already see, you need to consider *Project Types* when designing your *Department* structure. The more significant impact on the metadata requirements comes from potential *Enterprise Custom Fields* that you may need when you start connecting *Project Types* and workflows. Notice in Figure 7 - 1, shown previously, that the *Field* column contains thirteen fields beginning with the word *Sample*. All of these fields are used to capture data for sample workflow that ships with Project Server 2010. Imagine that you have three departments wanting to manage three different project types each. While there will be overlapping and common field requirements, you can easily imagine that each of the resulting nine project types would have some information requirements that would be completely unique to that need. If each *Project Type* required only three unique fields, you nonetheless have 27 additional fields plus the growth incurred in adding the common fields. When you consider the likely growth in your enterprise custom field base, you quickly appreciate the power of department attribution in Project Server 2010. I show you how to create *Project Types* in the next module, Module 08, *Configuring Lifecycle Management*.

It's interesting to note that the only other two new fields in the list for Project Server 2010 are *Project Department* and *Resource Department*. More noticeable is that the *State* field is gone in 2010.

Introducing Business Drivers

Business Drivers are used by management stakeholders to measure projects by the way they impact business strategy. Defining *Business Drivers* is an exercise you must conduct through structured meetings with the executive stakeholders who will use Project Server 2010 for portfolio decision making support in determining which projects to select for execution among those requested by the business. Because defining and maintaining *Business Drivers* is a business responsibility, it appears on the *Quick Launch* menu in the *Strategy* section. *Business Drivers* are very easy to enter and maintain, but can be quite a challenge to determine and then prioritize. As an Implementer, you may be called upon to orchestrate the *Business Driver* definition sessions, and as an Administrator, you may be called upon to physically maintain the *Business Driver* library, or more likely show your business colleagues how to do so.

Working with Enterprise Custom Fields and Lookup Tables

Enterprise Custom Fields provide the necessary building blocks for making Project Server data interesting to your every-day users, as well as management stakeholders. Without metadata attribution, management would have difficulty accessing relevant project information across a portfolio of projects. Project Web App gives you the opportunity to capture and display this information in custom Views and through a plethora of reporting capabilities leveraging OLAP cubes and Reporting Database data through Excel Services. Metadata brings project information to life, such as budget and schedule variance. In the *Project Center* view shown in Figure 7 - 2, I added the project *Cost Status* and project *Schedule Status* custom enterprise project fields to enrich the view. Each of these fields displays a green, yellow, or red stoplight indicator to show the severity of budget or schedule variance. Using this view, project stakeholders and executives can easily determine the variance for each project across the portfolio of projects.

Figure 7 - 2: Project Center View

 When initially building your custom field set in Project Server 2010, you work with the Custom Fields section of the Requirements and Configuration Specification document deliverable.

Understanding Enterprise Field Types

Project Server 2010 offers six types of custom enterprise fields at the Task, Resource, and Project levels. Previous versions of Microsoft Project Server before 2007 offered you a limited number of custom fields; however, Project Server 2010 offers you an **unlimited number** of each of the following field types:

- Enterprise **Cost**

- Enterprise **Date**

- Enterprise **Duration**

- Enterprise **Flag**

- Enterprise **Number**

- Enterprise **Text**

For those of you upgrading from Project Server 2003, Project Server 2010 treats text fields the same way Project Server 2007 does, and does not offer outline codes, but offers the same functionality using enterprise fields containing a hierarchical lookup table structure.

Understanding Built-In Fields and Lookup Tables

Project Server 2010 contains twenty built-in fields and six built-in Lookup Tables. To view the built-in fields and Lookup Tables, complete the following steps:

1. Log in to Project Web App with administrator permissions.

2. Click the *Server Settings* link in the Quick Launch menu.

3. Click the *Enterprise Custom Field Definition* link in the *Enterprise Data* section of the *Server Settings* page.

The system displays the *Enterprise Custom Fields and Lookup Tables* page shown in Figure 7 - 3. The *Enterprise Custom Fields and Lookup Tables* page consists of two sections. Use the options in the *Enterprise Custom Fields* section to create new enterprise fields, or to copy, edit, or delete an existing field. Use the options in the *Lookup Tables for Custom Fields* section to create a new lookup table, or to copy, edit, or delete an existing lookup table. Project Server 2010 users will find this page largely unchanged since 2007, however you should note the important addition of the *Behavior* column in this page which replaces the *Required* column in 2007 and indicates one of three possible values: "Not required," "Required," or "Workflow-controlled." When custom fields indicate that they are *Workflow-controlled*, users cannot edit these outside the context of a workflow in the system. Consequently, these appear as read-only in all views except for *Project Detail Pages* when custom fields are presented as part of *workflow stages*. You learn more about workflows in Module 8, *Configuring Lifecycle Management*.

Figure 7 - 3: Custom Fields and Lookup Tables page

Project Server 2010 contains twenty built-in custom fields and seven built-in lookup tables. Thirteen of these fields and two of these lookup tables are specifically used in the *Sample Project Lifecycle Workflow* that ships with Project Server 2010. These specific built-in custom fields and lookup tables are as follows:

- The **Sample Approved Finish Date field** is a project date field used in the sample workflow process.

- The **Sample Approved Start Date field** is a project date field used in the sample workflow process.

- The **Sample Areas Impacted field** is a project text field containing the **Areas Impacted lookup table**, and is used in the sample workflow process. The *Areas Impacted* lookup table contains a single-level code mask, with five values in the actual lookup table. You can use these values "as is," or you may customize them according to your organization's project workflow approval requirements.

- The **Sample Assumptions field** is a project text field used in the sample workflow process.

- The **Sample Business Need field** is a project text field used in the sample workflow to capture information about the business need.

- The **Sample Compliance Proposal field** is a project flag field used in the sample workflow process.

- The **Sample Goals field** is a project text field used in the sample workflow process.

- The **Sample Post Implementation Review Date field** is a project date field used in the sample workflow process.

- The **Sample Post Implementation Review Notes field** is a project text field used in the sample workflow process.

- The **Sample Primary Objectives field** is a project text field containing the **Primary Objective lookup table**, and is used in the sample workflow process. The *Primary Objective* lookup table contains a single-level code mask, with seven values in the actual lookup table. You can use these values "as is" or you may customize them according to your organization's project workflow approval requirements.

- The **Sample Proposal Cost field** is a project cost field used in the sample workflow process.

- The **Sample Proposed Finish Date field** is a project date field used in the sample workflow process.

- The **Sample Proposed Start Date field** is a project date field used in the sample workflow process.

Warning: Before you make any changes to the sample custom enterprise fields, read Module 8, Configuring Lifecycle Mangement, in its entirety. Modifying these before you understand how the sample workflow uses them may jeopardize your ability to use the sample workflow.

These fields are included with the sample workflow to demonstrate the capability of the system and to provide users with a starting point for customizing the workflow's detail pages to meet their specific needs. The type of data represented in these fields is very typical of the data most organizations want to collect when they embark on a demand capture endeavor. You can use this as a conversation starter, or you can use these as a solution starter to craft your demand management process. You can also opt to completely replace or modify the sample workflow, which may require programming with Visual Studio. You may also choose to start fresh with custom fields and delete the sample workflow and the sample custom fields. Many users new to demand management will find these sample fields invaluable in helping them get started with demand management in Project Server 2010. Other built-in enterprise custom fields include:

- The **Cost Type field** is a resource text field containing the **Cost Type lookup table**. The *Cost Type* lookup table contains a single-level code mask, but contains no values in the actual lookup table. You must customize the *Cost Type* lookup table to mold its functionality to your organization's requirements. You can use this field, or any other resource filed, to match resources in the enterprise resource pool to roles in Portfolio Analyses in Project Server 2010.

- The **Health field** is a task text field containing the **Health lookup table**. The *Health* lookup table contains a single-level code mask with six values in the actual lookup table. You can use these values "as is" or you may customize them according to your organization's task tracking requirements.

- The **Project Departments field** is a project text field containing the **Departments lookup table**. The *Departments* lookup table contains a single-level code mask, but contains no values in the actual lookup table. You must customize the *Departments* lookup table according to your organization's requirements for filtering the view of enterprise objects by department.

- The **RBS field** is a resource text field containing the **RBS lookup table**. The *RBS* lookup table contains a single-level code mask, but contains no values in the actual lookup table. If you want to use the RBS to define and manage relationship-based Project Server 2010 security, you must customize the *RBS* lookup table to reflect the reporting structure in your organization.

Keep in mind that the RBS **rarely** reflects the exact structure of an organization. Rather, it is a "pseudo organizational chart" that can be anything from representative to nearly literal.

- The **Resource Departments field** is a resource text field containing the **Departments lookup table**. The *Departments* lookup table contains a single-level code mask, but contains no values in the actual lookup table. You must customize the *Departments* lookup table according to your organization's requirements for filtering enterprise objects by department.

- The **Team Name** field is a resource text field that does not contain a lookup table. I recommend that you create a lookup table for this field if you want to use the *Team Name* field to assign a group of resources (a team) to tasks. Obviously, you must customize the lookup table to match the teams available in your organization.

Warning: Project Server 2010 **does not** include an empty Lookup Table associated with the *Team Name* field. Because the *Edit Custom Field* page defaults to the last lookup table in the list, it is very easy to accidentally assign the *Sample Primary Objective* lookup table to this field if you absentmindedly open and save the *Team Name* field. MSProjectExperts recommends that you immediately create a *Team Names* lookup table and then assign it in the *Team Name* field to avoid this problem. This is a serious vulnerability because the system does not allow you to change the lookup table assigned to a custom field once you apply it, requiring you to delete the custom field instead. Because you cannot delete the built-in custom fields, the misapplication of an incorrect lookup table must be repaired directly in the database.

Modifying Built-In Lookup Tables

As I noted earlier in this module, Project Server 2010 includes six built-in lookup tables: *Cost Type, Department, Health, RBS, Sample Areas Impacted* and *Sample Primary Objective* If you need to use *Cost Type, Department* or *RBS* built-in lookup tables, you must enter the lookup table values. If you are going to deploy Portfolio Analyses capabilities in Project Server 2010 you must create lookup table values for the *Cost* Type field. If you plan on using the sample workflow, you will likely want to modify or replace values in the two sample lookup tables.

If you intend to use this feature, I recommend that you begin the process of working with custom fields and lookup tables by determining and modifying the values in the *Department* lookup table, as many of the enterprise custom fields you create will require this attribution. Although you can always go back and edit your enterprise custom fields to add the *Department* value later, you save a lot of time by enabling yourself to complete your definitions during field creation. Next, I recommend you immediately create a new *Team Names* lookup table if your organization wants to use the *Team Resource* feature in Project Server 2010. After completing these two important first steps, you can begin creating the other custom lookup tables your organization requires.

To modify any of the built-in lookup tables, complete the following steps:

1. Navigate to the *Enterprise Custom Fields and Lookup Tables* page in Project Web App.

2. In the *Lookup Tables for Custom Fields* section in the bottom half of the page, click the name of the lookup table you want to edit. The system displays the *Edit Lookup Table* page for the selected lookup table. For example, Figure 7 - 4 shows the *Edit Lookup Table* page for the *Department* lookup table.

3. Edit the *Code Mask* as needed.

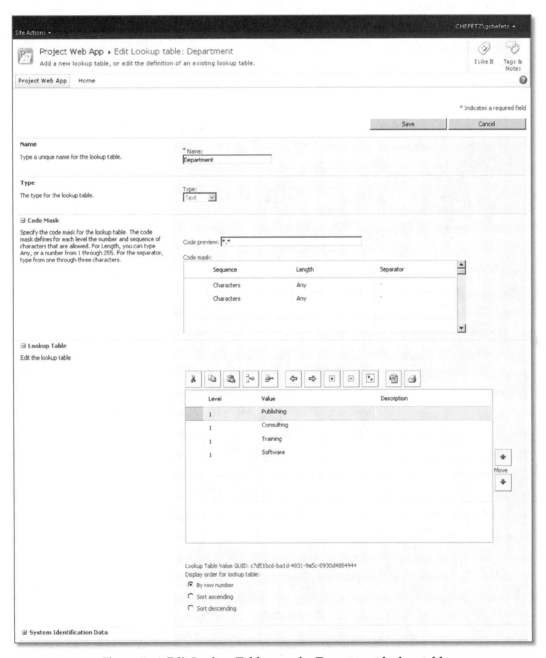

Figure 7 - 4: Edit Lookup Table page for Department lookup table

You enter the values in the *Lookup Table* section according to the structure you build in the *Code Mask*. If you need only a "flat file" list of values, you can use the single-level *Code Mask* included by default in each built-in lookup table. If you want a hierarchical lookup table, however, you must add additional lines to the *Code Mask* as I did in the figure.

Project Server 2010 defaults the *Department* field to a single-level *Code Mask* that uses characters of any length with the period character as the separator in the *Code Mask*. You may edit this first level and add additional levels as needed. To create a new level in the *Code Mask*, click the first blank line in the *Sequence* column, click the pick list button, and select the type of data for the outline code segment. You may select *Numbers, Uppercase Letters, Lowercase Letters,* or *Characters*. When you select any of these, the values for each code segment must adhere to the type of data specified. Selecting the *Characters* item gives you the most flexibility, as you may use any character in defining your values. Use one of the other selections to reflect non-flexible formalized values in your enterprise.

Click in the *Length* column on the selected line and enter the length for the code segment. The default choice allows any length, but you can delete this choice and enter a number representing the maximum number of characters allowed, up to a maximum of 255 characters.

Click in the *Separator* column on the selected line and enter the character used as the separator between code segments. You can use up to three characters as the separator, including characters like the period (the default option), a dash, a plus sign, or a forward slash. You can also use other non-numeric and non-alphabetic characters, such as those found above the number keys on your keyboard.

4.   Edit the existing values in the *Lookup Table* section or add new values as needed.

5.   Add optional information in the *Description* field for each of the lookup table values.

When you select any existing value in the *Lookup Table* section, the system activates the toolbar at the top of the *Lookup Table* section, as shown in Figure 7 - 5. The first three buttons on the toolbar are the standard *Cut, Copy,* and *Paste* buttons found in Microsoft Office products. Use the *Insert Row* and *Delete Row* buttons to add a new row between two existing rows or to delete an existing row. Use the *Outdent* and *Indent* buttons to control the level of indenture for any row of information in the lookup table and to build a hierarchical structure. Use the *Expand, Collapse,* and *Expand All* buttons to expand or collapse a hierarchical lookup table. Use the *Export to Excel* and *Print* buttons to export the data to Excel or to print the data on paper.

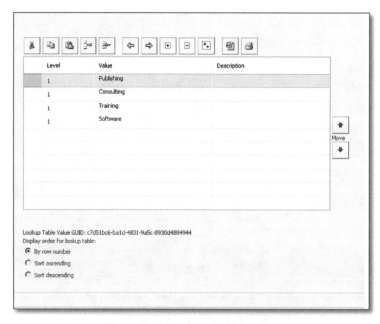

Figure 7 - 5: Lookup Table toolbar

To export the lookup table data to Microsoft Office Excel, click the *Export to Excel* button. The system displays the *File Download* dialog shown in Figure 7 - 6.

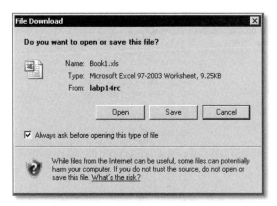

**Figure 7 - 6: File Download dialog
for export to Excel**

Click the *Open* button to continue the export process or click the *Save* button to save the lookup table data as a Microsoft Office Excel 97-2003 Worksheet file to a location that you choose. If you click the *Open* button, the system displays the Microsoft Office Excel warning dialog shown in Figure 7 - 7.

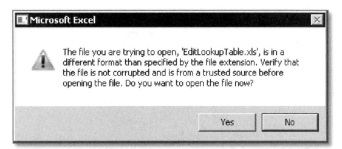

Figure 7 - 7: Microsoft Office Excel warning dialog

Click the *Yes* button in the dialog to continue the process of exporting the lookup table data to Excel. When finished, the system displays the exported lookup table data in an Excel workbook. For example, Figure 7 - 8 shows the exported data in Excel for my new *Departments* lookup table.

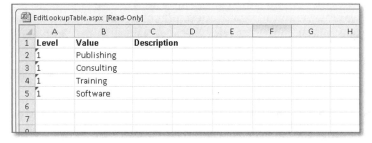

Figure 7 - 8: Lookup Table exported to an Excel workbook

To print the lookup table, click the *Print* button in the *Lookup Table* section of the *Edit Lookup Table* page. The system displays the lookup table data as a web page in Internet Explorer as shown in Figure 7 - 9. To print the lookup table data, you must use Internet Explorer's print functionality.

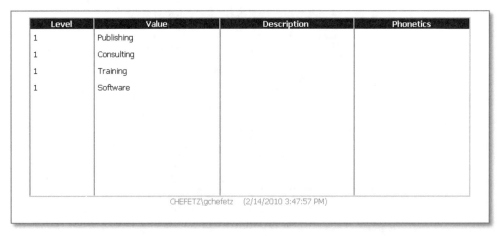

Figure 7 - 9: Print Preview page displays Lookup Table data

To complete the process of editing the *Lookup Table*, continue with the following final steps:

6. Change the sorting order of the values in the *Lookup Table* as needed. Project Server 2010 allows you to sort the data in the lookup table in three ways: by row number, ascending order, and descending order. The system offers you these three sort options at the bottom of the lookup table list. If you select the *By row number* option, the system retains the order in which you entered the values in the lookup table. Use this option when you need to display the lookup table in a specific order that is neither ascending nor descending. When you select the *Sort ascending* option, the system sorts the lookup table list in ascending order (A-Z and 0-9). When you select the *Sort descending* option, the system sorts the lookup table list in descending order (Z-A and 9-0).

7. Click the *Save* button to save your changes to the selected built-in lookup table.

Modifying the Cost Type Lookup Table

The *Cost Type* field is potentially a very special field in Project Server 2010, as it is eligible to provide the *Roles* values for *Portfolio Analyses.* You can use this field or any other resource field. If you decide to use this field for Portfolio Analyses, you must take care in defining the values in the *lookup table* to match your portfolio analysis requirements. If you choose to use this field for this special purpose, you cannot make this a multi-value field and you cannot apply a multi-level code mask. If you do not intend to use the Portfolio Analyses capabilities, or you choose to use a different field for those capabilities, then you can use this field for integrating data with a third-party financial application, such as Microsoft Dynamics or SAP. You can also use the *Cost Type* field to do financial analysis on your organization's resources by cost types. For example, a typical organization might have only three types of resources from a financial perspective: billable resources, non-billable resources, and outside contractors. Billable resources generate revenue, while the other two types of resources generate expenditures only. Of course, you can use any *Resource* custom field to accomplish this.

When you open the *Cost Type* lookup table for editing, you find a single-level code mask with no values in the lookup table. If you want to use the *Cost Type* field for Portfolio Analyses, you must add a list of resource types in your organization, and you should not change the code mask; you must also assign a *Cost Type* value to every resource you want to include in your portfolio head count. If you want to use the same values you use for *Generic* resources, you can also consider using this field in lieu of creating other fields for matching resources. You can edit the *Cost Type* field (not the lookup table) by selecting the *Use this field for matching generic resources* checkbox in the *Edit Custom Field* page. Note that many organizations require multi-value skill matching fields for this purpose, particularly for large resource pools. Consider these requirements carefully, as Project Server allows you to model resourcing portfolio analyses at a different level than you use for actual resource matching in projects, providing significant flexibility. If your organization wants to use the *Cost Type* field with a financial application, you must add values to the *Cost Type* lookup table to match the specifications of your financial application. If you do not need to use the *Cost Type* field, then you do not need to edit the *Cost Type* lookup table.

Modifying the Health Lookup Table

Organizations use the *Health* field to monitor the current condition of task progress in terms of the project management process. For example, the *Health* field communicates whether a task is on schedule, late, early, etc. The default *Health* lookup table contains a single-level code mask with six values in the lookup table. These values are:

- Not Specified
- On Schedule
- Late
- Early
- Blocked
- Completed

You may modify these values to match your organization's criteria for monitoring the current condition of tasks in each project. In our organization, we categorize the current condition of project tasks using only five values, which are:

- Not Specified
- In Progress
- On Hold
- Cancelled
- Completed

On Hold means that someone interrupted work on the task temporarily and the task will resume at a later date. We use this when a project team or team member is pulled off one project to assist with another project with higher urgency or priority. To meet our organization's reporting needs about the current condition of each project, I removed all of the default *Health* lookup table values and replaced them with our own, as shown in Figure 7 - 10.

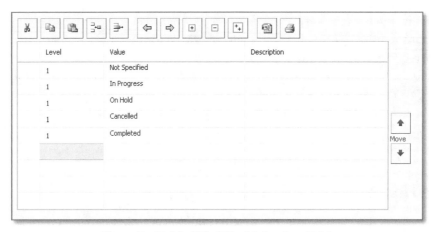

Figure 7 - 10: Modified Health Lookup Table

Warning: The *Health* field uses a default value from the *Health* lookup table. When you modify the entries in the *Health* lookup table, you should immediately edit the *Health* field to set this value. On the *Custom Fields and Lookup Tables* page, click the name of the *Health* field to open the field for editing. Select a value from the *Default Value* pick list in the *Custom Attributes* section of the *Edit Custom Field* page and then click the *Save* button. You **must** perform this step because the system does not allow the *Default Value* field to contain a null value.

Modifying the RBS Lookup Table

You use the *RBS* field to control Project Server security by defining a pseudo-org chart for your organization. Refer to Module 12, Configuring Project Server Security for other RBS design decisions you must tackle while creating your Requirements and Configuration Specification deliverable. You should populate your *RBS* lookup table before importing your resource pool so that you are able to attribute resources correctly after loading them.

Like assigning each resource a place in an org chart, the *RBS* field shows Project Server 2010 "who reports to whom." You can control a manager's ability to see project and resource data through subordination in the *RBS* field. These resource reporting constructs drive very powerful Project Server 2010 relationship-based security features.

When you open the *RBS* lookup table for editing, you find a single-level code mask with no values in the lookup table. Because the *RBS* lookup table is a blank slate by default, it is your responsibility to design and configure it specifically for your organization. Keep in mind that lookup table values can be hierarchical, which is exactly what you need for this purpose.

Based on your requirements, you should create an *RBS* lookup table that reflects your organization's management reporting structure. For example, an organization that uses Project Server 2010 only in the IS department may have a very simple reporting structure within IS. Based on that reporting structure, I created a 3-level *Code Mask* and populated the *RBS* lookup table shown in Figure 7 - 11.

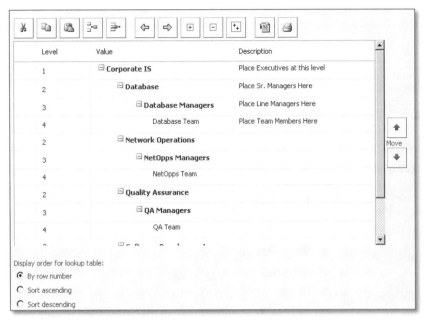

Figure 7 - 11: Sample RBS Lookup Table structure

Notice that in the *Description* column in the *RBS* lookup table shown in Figure 7 - 11, I added information to indicate how to configure Project Server security when you select an RBS value for each resource in the enterprise resource pool. Based on the information in the *Description* column, you can configure the Project Server security environment as follows:

- Place company executives and Project Server administrators at the Corporate IS level and they can view resource information for all resources in the system because all of the resources fall below them in the RBS structure.

- Place senior managers at the Database, Network Operations, Quality Assurance, or Software Development levels. Senior managers can see only those resources below them in their branch of the RBS structure. For example, the senior manager of the Database branch sees only those resources at the Manager and Team Member levels of the Database branch.

- Place project managers and resource managers at the Manager level of the appropriate branch of the RBS structure. For example, place the Project Managers for the Software Development team at the Manager level of the Software Development branch. The Software Development project managers see only those resources at the Team Member level of the Software Development branch.

- Place team members at the Team Member level of the branch to which they belong.

Depending on how you set up security Categories, you can configure Project Server 2010 so that people can see other people at the same level of the RBS lookup table. This means that senior managers at the Database level can see all resources below them in their branch, plus all other senior managers at the Database level. I discuss Project Server 2010 security in Module 12.

I show you how to set up the Enterprise Resource Pool and use the RBS field in Module 9.

Warning: Be very careful about the placement of project managers in your organization's RBS. Any project manager who manages cross-functional project teams must be placed at a high level in the RBS to access resources across the organization. Using the previous example, if a project manager must manage projects that include members of all four departmental teams, the project manager must be placed at the Corporate IS level of the RBS to gain access to the resources for all four teams.

Your RBS complexity follows your deployment scope. If you are deploying a single implementation across many departments, and each department distributes resource maintenance to its managers, your RBS structure may have many top-level branches with many descending levels. On the other hand, if your installation is for a single department, and only one person is responsible for handling resource data, then you may not need to use the RBS field at all, or you may need to use it for reporting only. Assessing the value of the RBS to your organization is an important system design decision. You should fully understand the Project Server security model to make these decisions.

Creating the Team Names Lookup Table

You can use the *Team Name* field to allow project managers to assign a team of resources to tasks in a project. Before you can use this field, you must create a *Team Names* (or similarly named) lookup table and populate the lookup table with names of the various teams in your organization.

The sample organization I'm modeling the lookup table for has four standard teams used to assign work that anyone on the team can perform, plus the organization uses "ad hoc" teams created according to the skills required for each project. Included are a standard Database team, standard Network Operations team, a QA team, and a Software Development team. Each team includes the appropriate project manager and team members with the necessary skills. I therefore must create the *Team Names* lookup table with the names of the four standard teams for the organization. To create a new *Lookup Table* follow these steps:

1. From the *Server Settings* page select *Enterprise Custom Fields and Lookup Tables* from the *Enterprise Data* section of the page. Scroll to the bottom of the page to reveal the *Lookup Tables for Custom Fields* section shown in Figure 7 - 12.

Lookup Tables for Custom Fields

New Lookup Table | Copy Lookup Table | ✕ Delete Lookup Table |

Lookup Table ▲	Type	Last Updated
Cost Type	Text	1/31/2010
Department	Text	2/14/2010
Health	Text	2/15/2010
RBS	Text	2/15/2010
Sample Areas Impacted	Text	1/31/2010
Sample Primary Objective	Text	1/31/2010

Figure 7 - 12: Lookup Tables for Custom Fields section

2. Click the *New Lookup Table* button on the toolbar above the grid. The system displays the *New Lookup Table* page shown in Figure 7 - 13.

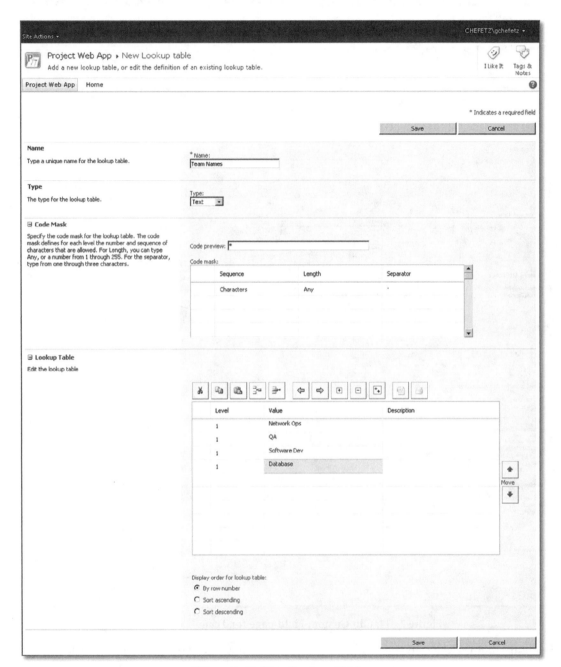

Figure 7 - 13: New Lookup Table page

3. Notice in the figure that I entered the *Team Names* for my organization in the *Lookup Table* section. Click the *Save* button to save your changes.

After creating and saving the *Team Names* lookup table, I must edit the *Team Name* field and apply the new *Team Names* lookup table. To edit an existing field, navigate to the *Enterprise Custom Fields and Lookup Tables* page and click in the *Team Name* field. The system opens the *Edit Custom Field: Team Name* page shown in Figure 7 - 14.

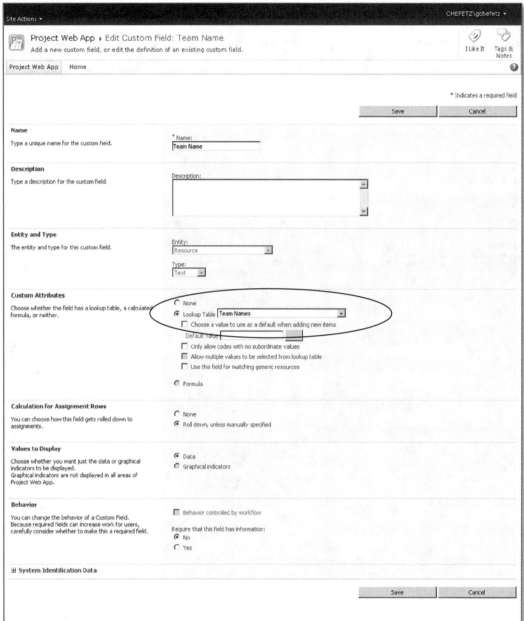

Figure 7 - 14: Edit Custom Field page for Team Name field

Notice in the figure that I selected the new *Team Names* lookup table I created in the last step, and assigned it to the *Team Name* enterprise custom field as highlighted in the image. Click the *Save* button to save your changes.

Creating and Modifying Custom Lookup Tables

Before defining any new custom enterprise fields, you must determine whether your fields require a lookup table. Therefore, I recommend you create your lookup tables first and then apply the lookup tables when you create new custom enterprise fields that require them, as I did for the *Team* field in the previous example.

Creating a New Lookup Table

In my organization, we need several lookup tables in custom fields to meet our reporting needs for tracking tasks, resources, and projects. For example, we need a *Risks* lookup table containing a list of project risk levels (High, Medium, and Low). We need a *Locations* lookup table containing the locations of our company's regional offices in the US and Europe.

To create a new Lookup Table, complete the following steps from the *Custom Fields and Lookup Tables* page:

1. Click the *New Lookup Table* button. The system displays the *New Lookup Table* page shown in Figure 7 - 15. The *New Lookup Table* page contains sections in which to enter the *Name* of the lookup table, select the *Type* of lookup table, set up the *Code Mask*, and enter the actual lookup table values.

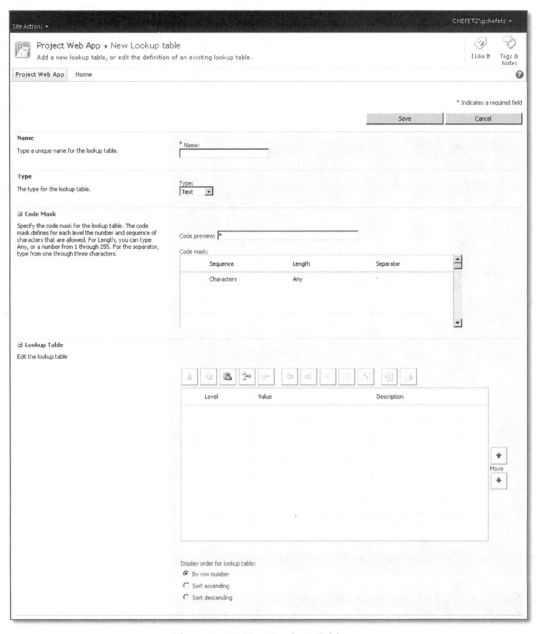

Figure 7 - 15: New Lookup Table page

2.   Enter a name for the lookup table in the *Name* field.

3.   Click the *Type* pick list and select the type of lookup table you want to create. Project Server 2010 allows you to create five types of Lookup Tables: *Cost, Date, Duration, Number,* and *Text*. If you select the *Text* option, the system presents the *New Lookup Table* page shown previously in Figure 7 - 15 and requires you to supply a code mask for the lookup table. If you select any of the other four types, the system allows you to define a single-level lookup table and displays the *New Lookup Table* page shown in Figure 7 - 16 for the *Cost* type.

Figure 7 - 16: New Lookup Table page for the Cost type

4.   If you selected the *Text* type, create the code mask required for the type of lookup table you want to create.

To create a code mask you must supply values for each level in the *Sequence, Length,* and *Separator* columns. Project Server 2010 defaults to a single-level code mask that uses characters of any length with the period character as the separator in the code mask. You may edit this first level and add additional levels as you need.

To create a new level in the code mask, click the first blank line in the *Sequence* column, click the pick list button, and select the type of data for the outline code segment. You may select *Numbers, Uppercase Letters, Lowercase Letters,* or *Characters*. When you select any of these, the values for each code segment must adhere to the type of data specified. Selecting the *Characters* item gives you the most flexibility, as you may use any character in defining your values. Use one of the other selections to reflect non-flexible formalized values in your enterprise.

Click in the *Length* column on the selected line and enter the length for the code segment. The default choice allows any length, but you can delete this choice and enter a number representing the maximum number of characters allowed, up to a maximum of 255 characters.

Click in the *Separator* column on the selected line and enter the character used as the separator between code segments. You can use up to three characters as the separator, including characters like the period (the default option), a dash, a plus sign, or a forward slash. You can also use other non-numeric and non-alphabetic characters, such as those found above the number keys on a keyboard.

In the *Lookup Table* section of the page, you can use any of the buttons at the top of the section to modify the data you enter. For example, use the *Indent* and *Outdent* buttons to structure the lookup table entries to match your code mask.

Tip: You can use the *Paste* button to paste values into the lookup table from another application, such as Microsoft Office Word or Excel.

5. Enter data in the *Lookup Table* section of the page and confirm that the lookup table data conforms to the code mask that you specified. Figure 7 - 17 shows the completed definition of the *Locations* lookup table. Notice that I specified a two-level code mask that accepts any type of characters on the first level and any type of characters on the second level. Notice also that my lookup table values conform to the code mask.

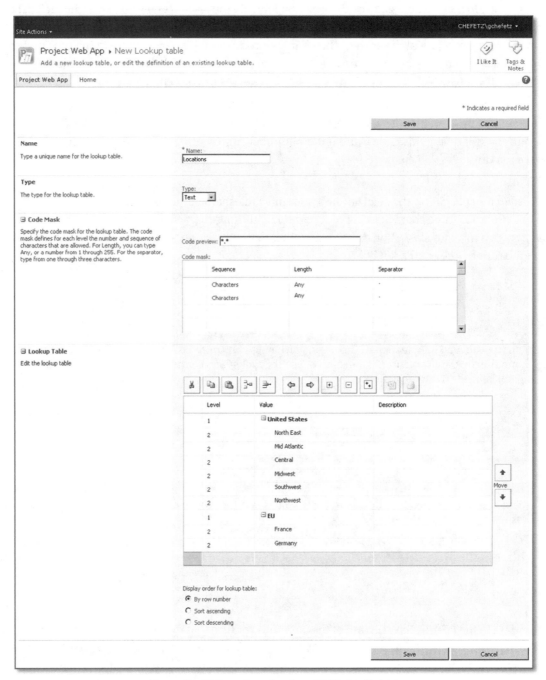

Figure 7 - 17: Locations Lookup Table Definition

6. Select a sort order at the bottom of the *Lookup Table* section as needed.

7. Click the *Save* button to save your new lookup table.

If you attempt to save the lookup table with an illegal character as a separator in the code mask, the system displays the error message shown in Figure 7 - 18. The system displayed the warning dialog when I attempted to use a comma character as a separator character in the code mask.

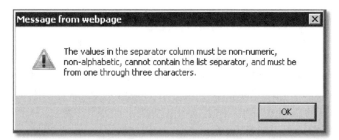

Figure 7 - 18: Warning dialog about illegal Separator character

If you do not enter the lookup table values according to your specified code mask, the system presents an error message in red text at the top of the page as shown in Figure 7 - 19. The system does not allow you to save the lookup table until you correct the errors.

Figure 7 - 19: Lookup Table values do not conform to the Code Mask

Modifying a Custom Lookup Table

To modify an existing custom lookup table, click the name of the existing lookup table in the *Enterprise Custom Fields and Lookup Tables* page. Project Server 2010 displays the *Edit Lookup Table* page for the selected lookup table. You learned how to edit a lookup table in the example for editing the *Department* field so I do not show you this page again.

Creating Custom Fields

After you edit the built-in lookup tables and create custom lookup tables for the fields you want to create with value lists, you are ready to create custom enterprise fields. Organizations typically need custom fields to track unique information about projects, resources, and tasks in projects. You can create all types of custom enterprise project, resource, and task fields, including the following:

- Free entry fields that allow the user to manually enter any value.
- Fields that require the user to select a value from a lookup table of allowable values.
- Fields that contain a formula that automatically calculates a value using data in other fields.
- Fields that display graphical indicators instead of data.

I discuss how to create all of these types of fields in the succeeding sections of this module. Project Server 2010 allows you to create custom enterprise fields in two locations:

- You can create custom enterprise project, resource, and task fields using Project Web App.
- You can use Project Professional 2010 to create only task and resource fields, which you can then import into Project Server.

Using the Project Web App interface, I show you how to create free entry fields and fields that contain a lookup table. Using the Project Professional 2010 interface, I show you how to create fields that contain a formula and/or display graphical indicators instead of data.

233

Creating Free Entry Custom Fields

Use a free entry custom field to allow users to manually enter any value in the field, as defined by the field type. This means that the system allows a user to enter any alphanumeric data in a text field, but permits the user to only enter numeric cost data in a cost field. Our organization needs a custom enterprise task text field into which users can type an optional billing department number for each task. To create this task text field, complete the following steps from the *Enterprise Custom Fields and Lookup Tables* page:

1. Click the *New Field* button. Project Server 2010 displays the *New Custom Field* page shown in Figure 7 - 20.

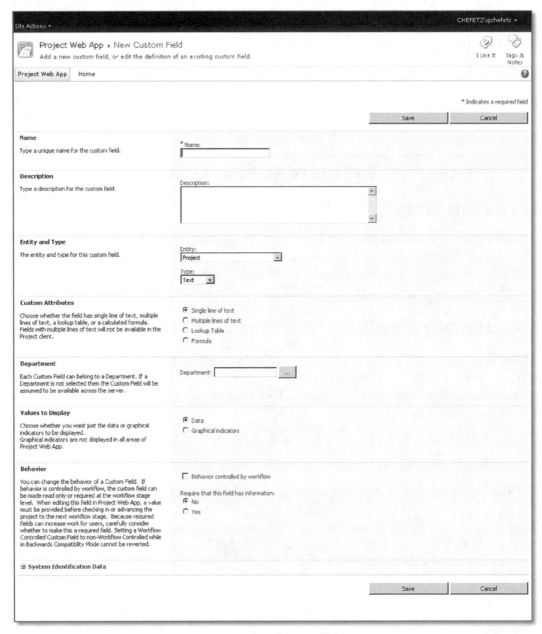

Figure 7 - 20: New Custom Field page

2. Enter a name for the new custom field, such as Billing Department, in the *Name* field and enter an optional description in the *Description* field.

3. Click the *Entity* pick list and select the *Task* entity from the pick list. When you select the *Task* entity (or the *Resource* entity), Project Server 2010 refreshes the *New Custom Field* page to include two additional sections, as shown in Figure 7 - 21. The *Calculation for Summary Rows* section contains options used with a formula. If you do not include a formula in the field, the system allows only the *None* option in this section. The *Calculation for Assignment Rows* section offers options that determine whether the system displays editable information for task assignments in the *Tasks* page.

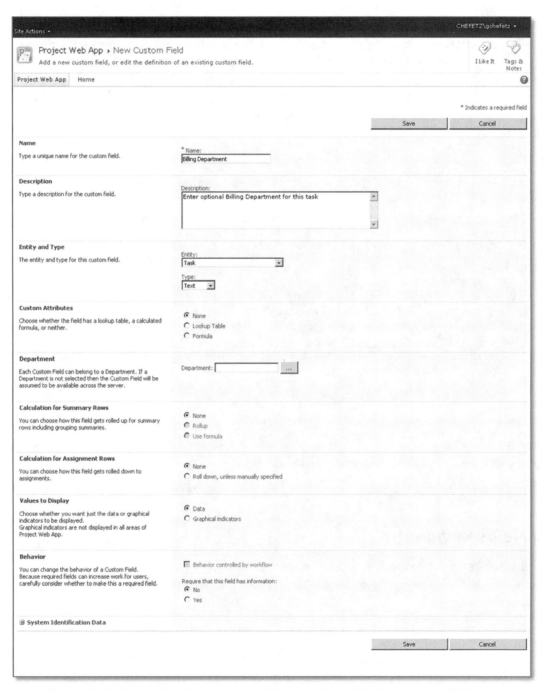

Figure 7 - 21: Calculation for Assignment Rows option on the New Custom Field page

4. Click the *Type* pick list and select the *Text* type from the pick list.

For custom enterprise project, resource, and task fields, Project Server 2010 allows you to create Cost, Date, Duration, Flag, Number, and Text fields.

5. In the *Custom Attributes* section, select the *None* option.

When you create a new custom enterprise project text field, the system offers two special options in the *Custom Attributes* section. Select the *Single Line of Text* option to limit users to entering only a single line of text in the field. Select the *Multiple Lines of Text* option to allow users to enter two or more lines of text in the field.

6. If you want to control user visibility to this field using the *Department* filter, click the *Department* button and select the *Department(s)* that can see this field.

If you do not select a value in the *Department* list, all users in your Project Server 2010 system can see the field.

7. In the *Calculation for Assignment Rows* section, select one of the available options.

Warning: If you intend to include a custom enterprise Task field in the *Tasks* page and need to allow users to enter a value in the field, you must select the *Roll Down, Unless Manually Specified* option in the *Calculation for Assignment Rows* section. For a free entry field, this allows users to manually type a value in the field. For a field containing a lookup table, this allows users to select a value from the list of values in the lookup table. This also makes the data available in assignment views such as the *Resource Usage* and *Task Usage* views

8. In the *Values to Display* section, select the *Data* option.

9. In the *Behavior* section, select the *Yes* option to require the user to enter a value in the field. Select the *No* option if you want to make data entry optional in the field.

10. When you finish, click the *Save* button to save the new custom field.

Making Fields Required

When you select the *Yes* option in the *Behavior* section for a custom enterprise field, this makes the field required and forces users to provide a value before Project Server 2010 writes a record to the database. Required fields impact users in the following manner:

*   For a required enterprise project field, project managers must enter or select a value in the field before they can save a new project to the Project Server database.

*   When you define a required enterprise task field, project managers must enter or select a value for **every task** in the project before they can save the project.

*   For a required enterprise resource field, your Resource Pool administrators must enter or select a value for **every resource** before they can save the resource in the enterprise resource pool.

Warning: If you plan to use Active Directory synchronization to help maintain your resource pool, using required resource fields can prevent the synchronization job from completing successfully, as these values cannot be mapped from AD using the built-in functionality provided in the system.

If users fail to enter a value in any required field, the system warns them in a dialog and then documents the error in the required field. For example, Figure 7 - 22 shows the warning dialog the system displays when I fail to enter a value in a required project field before saving a new enterprise project. Before the system allows me to save my project, I must select a value for this project.

Figure 7 - 22: Required field dialog

Using Required Fields

You must give careful thought to your organization's use of required fields. For example, it must be reasonable to expect that users have a value for a required field when they encounter them. You must also anticipate exceptions to validated values when opting to use them. In the case of required resource fields for instance, you must consider whether you have applicable values for *Generic, Material*, and *Cost* resources, if your configuration includes them. For example, a required *Regional Office* field does not make sense for a Generic resource unless you are creating a geographically specific generic resource. In this case, providing an "NA" value in the lookup table may suffice.

Creating a Custom Field with a Lookup Table

You use lookup tables to control the values users enter into a custom field. You can also use a lookup table to allow your users to select a valid value from a list rather than forcing them to manually type values into the field. For example, our organization needs a custom enterprise project field containing the *Locations* lookup table. Using the lookup table in this field, users must select the office location for which they are performing the project. In addition, our organization uses a custom enterprise resource field that also contains the *Locations* lookup table. Using the lookup table in this field, the Project Server administrator can specify an office location value for each resource in the enterprise resource pool.

To create a custom project field using the *Locations* lookup table, complete the following steps from the *Custom Fields and Lookup Tables* page:

1. Click the *New Field* button. Project Server 2010 displays the *New Custom Field* page shown previously in Figure 7 - 20.

2. Enter a name for your new custom field, such as Office Location, in the *Name* field.

3. Click the *Entity* pick list and select the *Project* entity from the pick list.

4. Click the *Type* pick list and select the *Text* type.

5. In the *Custom Attributes* section, select the *Lookup Table* option and then select the *Locations* lookup table from the *Lookup Table* pick list. The system expands the *Custom Attributes* section to include lookup table information as shown in Figure 7 - 23.

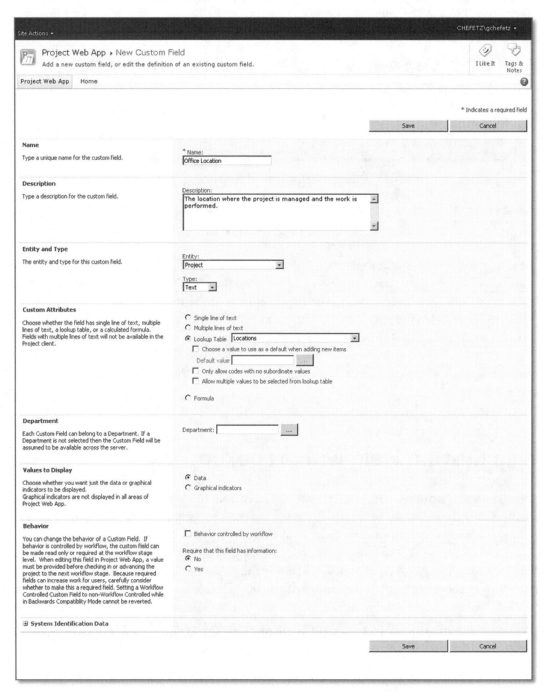

Figure 7 - 23: Custom Attributes Section with Lookup Table options

The *Custom Attributes* section offers three additional settings for the lookup table you select. Use these options as follows:

• Select the *Choose a value to use as a default when adding new items* option to specify the default value for the field. When you select this option you must click the *Select Value* (...) button to the right of the *Default Value* field and then pick a value from the Lookup Table, as shown in Figure 7 - 24.

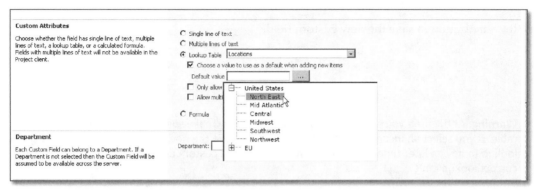

Figure 7 - 24: Select a Default Value for the Office Location field

 If you enter desicriptions for your field values, the system displays the *Description* field information for each value in the Lookup Table.

• Select the *Only allow codes with no subordinate values* option to require users to select a value at the lowest level of the lookup table. If you select this option for the *Locations* field, the system allows users to select the values below the United States and EU selections; however it does not allow them to select the United States or EU values themselves because they have subordinate values.

• Select the *Allow multiple values to be selected from lookup table* option to make the field a Multi-Value (MV) field. When you create an MV field, users can select one or more values in the field. If you do not select this option, the system allows users to select only a single value in the field.

 Warning: If you intend to use a custom field with a *Lookup Table* for data analysis, do not select the *Allow multiple values to be selected from lookup table* option. Selecting this option makes the field inelligible to be used as a dimension in an OLAP cube.

 If you create a custom enterprise Resource field with a Lookup Table, the *Custom Attributes* section contains one additional option: the *Use This Field for Matching Generic Resources* option. Select this option if you want Project Server 2010 to use this field to match human resources with generic resources, such as with skill matching. Users can use the system's resource matching capabilities in either the *Build Team* dialog or the *Resource Substitution* Wizard.

6.   In the *Values to Display* section, select the *Data* option.

7.   In the *Behavior* section, select the *Yes* option to require users to enter a value in the field or select the *No* option to make data entry optional for the field. You can also select the *Behavior controlled by workflow* option to control the new custom enterprise project field in a workflow process.

8.   Click the *Save* button to save the new custom field.

Warning: At the time you select the *Lookup Table* option, make sure that you select the **correct** lookup table. If you select an incorrect lookup table and then save the new custom field, you cannot change the lookup table at a later time. Instead, you must delete the custom field and create a new one using the correct lookup table.

When you create a custom enterprise project field, you have the option to select the *Behavior controlled by workflow* checkbox in the *Behavior* section for fields that use a *Lookup Table*. When you select this option, Project Server 2010 adds the field to the list of fields controlled by workflow. After creating a custom enterprise field controlled by workflow, you must also add the field to one of the *Project Detail Pages* managed by a workflow or it will not be accessbile from anywhere else in the system except for administration pages.

Modifying Built-In Project and Resource Department Fields

In Project Server 2010, you may need to modify some of the built-in enterprise fields that contain a lookup table. Specifically, if your organization intends to use the Department filtering feature to limit the display of projects, resources, enterprise custom fields, project types, business drivers and OLAP cubes, you may need to edit the *Project Departments* field and the *Resource Departments* field. Each of these fields contains the *Departments* lookup table. By default, these two fields allow users to select multiple values from the pick list and this default behavior cannot be changed. In addition, you may need to specify a default value for each field, or you may want to make it a required field. In the case of the *Resource Departments* field, you may also want to use the field for resource matching.

To modify either one of these fields, click the name of the field in the *Enterprise Custom Fields* section of the *Enterprise Custom Fields and Lookup Tables* page. The system opens the field for editing in the *Edit Custom Field* page shown in Figure 7 - 25. Notice that the page does not contain a *Departments* section or selector, as all other enterprise custom fields do.

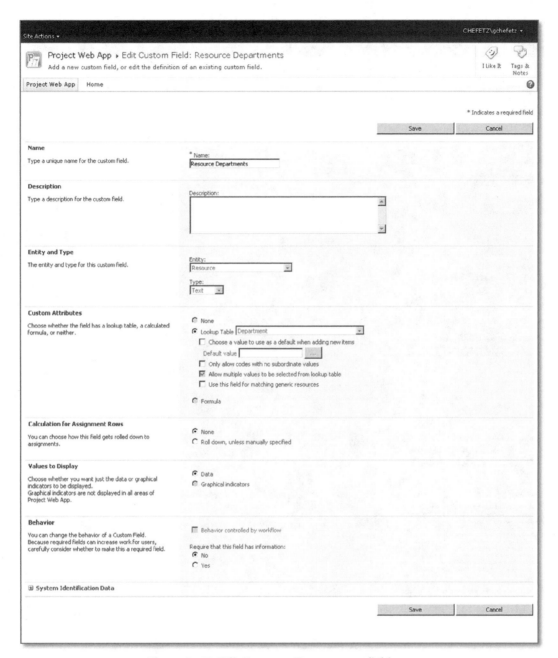

Figure 7 - 25: Edit Resource Departments field page

In the *Custom Attributes* section, notice that *Allow multiple values to be selected from lookup table* is selected and grayed out. You can set a default value for the field and you can select the *Use this field for matching generic resources* option as well as the *Only allow codes with no subordinate values* option, but you cannot change any other field *Custom Attributes*, and you cannot delete this field. You may optionally set the field to be required and you can set the option in the *Calculation for Assignment Rows* section to *Roll down, unless manually specified*. You can also add a description to the field.

The *Project Departments* field uses a similarly limited *Edit Custom Field* page shown in Figure 7 - 26.

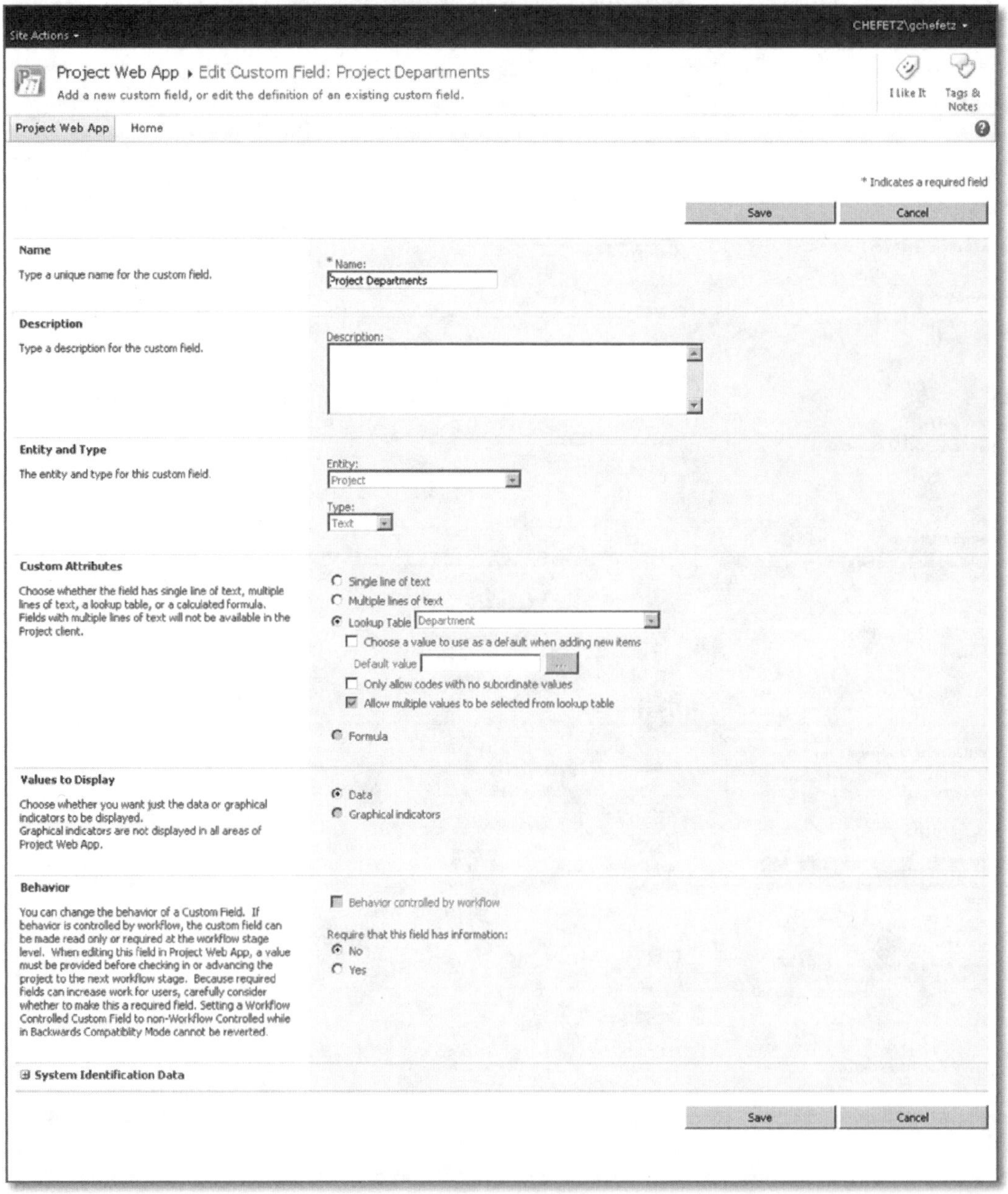

Figure 7 - 26: Edit Project Departments field page

Notice that the *Custom Attributes* section appears to allow you to select either the *Single line of text* or the *Multiple lines of text* options; however, the field will not save with either of these options if selected, and the system displays *An unknown error has occurred* error message at the top of the page. While the resource-specific option to use the field for matching generic resources does not apply here, you can set the same additional options for this field as you can for the *Resource Departments* field. It is worth noting that the option to control both the *Project Departments* and *Resource Departments* fields via workflow is also grayed out for these fields.

Creating a Custom Field with a Formula

Using a custom field with a formula provides a very flexible way to influence the output of views in both Project Professional 2010 and Project Web App. By using a formula in a custom field, you can perform compound financial calculations such as net present value or build business-specific key performance indicators (KPI's). You can also provide data conditioned to a specific business interpretation to accommodate non-project standard displays of duration and effort facts.

As you create each custom enterprise field containing a formula, keep in mind that the formula can reference most standard or custom enterprise fields, but they cannot reference local custom fields. This is because local custom fields are not reliable data sources.

To define a custom field containing a formula, the system provides two methods:

- Use Project Web App.

- Use Project Professional 2010.

The Project Web App interface is limited by the fact that the system neither allows you to import a formula from another custom field or to test a formula in a project, nor does it allow you to access the *Help* articles to assist you with writing your formula. On the other hand, you can use Project Professional 2010 to define the field and create the formula, and then import the new custom field into Project Server 2010. The advantage of this approach is that you can you can import a formula from another custom field, you can test your formula on a real project before you import it, and you can access the *Help* library of documentation about all fields and functions available for use in your formulas. For the purpose of thoroughness, I document how to create a formula using both interfaces.

MsProjectExperts recommends that you always use Project Professional 2010 to define custom fields containing a formula. The user interface for creating a formula is much better than the one provided in Project Web App.

Before you create a field and formula using Project Professional 2010, MsProjectExperts recommends that you open any production project saved as an MPP file in Read-Only mode. This allows you to create and test your formulas in custom enterprise task fields. When finished, you can import the new field into Project Server 2010 and close the project without saving the changes.

Understanding Field Types with Formulas

Remember that Project Server 2010 offers you the following field types for formulas: *Cost, Date, Duration, Flag, Number*, and *Text*. Although you can create a formula in any of these field types, the mystery for most users is determining which field type to use for your formula. Consider the following examples on how to use formulas with each field type:

- Use a **Cost** field when you need to calculate any type of custom cost using your organization default currency type. For example, our organization defines two custom enterprise task cost fields, *Internal Cost* and *Client Billable Cost*, to track project costs. I can define a third custom enterprise task cost field called *Profit* and create the following formula to calculate the profit:

```
[Client Billable Cost] - [Internal Cost]
```

- Use a **Date** field when you need to calculate any type of project date. For example, our organization defines a "drop dead" date for the completion of each task as the date 5 days later than the original *Baseline Finish* date. I can define a custom enterprise task date field called *Drop Dead Date* and use the following formula to calculate the drop dead date:

```
ProjDateAdd([Baseline Finish], "5d", "Standard")
```

In the preceding formula, I used the ProjDateAdd function to add 5 working days to the *Baseline Finish* date, as defined by the schedule shown in the enterprise *Standard* calendar.

- Use a **Duration** field when you need to calculate the duration between two dates. For example, our organization needs to calculate the time span (duration) between the *Baseline1 Finish* date and the *Baseline Finish* date for every task after a change control procedure. I can define a custom enterprise task duration field called *Baseline Slippage* and use the following formula to calculate the duration:

    ProjDateDiff([Baseline1 Finish], [Baseline Finish], "Standard")

In the preceding formula, I used the ProjDateDiff function to determine the number of working days between the *Baseline1 Finish* date and the *Baseline Finish* date, as defined by the schedule shown in the enterprise *Standard* calendar.

- Use a **Flag** field to calculate a value where the answer must be in a Yes/No or True/False format. For example, our organization needs to flag new tasks that the project manager failed to baseline after a change control procedure. I can define a custom enterprise task *Flag* field called *Is Baselined* and use the following formula to determine whether each task has a *Baseline Finish* date value:

```
IIf([Baseline Finish]<>ProjDateValue("NA"), True, False)
```

- Use a **Number** field to calculate any type of unformatted numeric value. For example, our organization needs to calculate the percentage of duration variance for every task. I can define a custom enterprise task *Number* field called *Percent Duration Variance* and use the following formula to calculate that value:

```
IIf([Milestone], 0, IIf([Baseline Finish]<>ProjDateValue("NA"), [Duration Va-
riance]/[Baseline Duration], 0))
```

The preceding formula uses the IIf function to determine whether a task is a milestone. If so, the formula returns a 0 value. If the task is not a milestone, then the formula uses a second IIf function and the ProjDateValue function to determine whether the task has a *Baseline Finish* value, indicating that the task has been baselined. If so, the formula calculates the percentage of duration variance. If not, the formula returns a 0 value.

- Use a Text field to generate textual information resulting from a calculation, or to apply numeric formatting to a formula that generates a number. For example, our organization needs to calculate the percentage of duration variance for every task, but wants to display the number as an actual percentage value, such as 20%. I can define a custom enterprise task *Text* field called *Percent Duration Variance* and use the following formula to calculate that value and format the result as a percentage:

```
IIf([Milestone],"NA",IIf([Baseline Finish]<>ProjDateValue("NA"), ([Duration Va-
riance]/[Baseline Duration]) * 100 & "%", "0%"))
```

The preceding formula uses the IIf function to determine whether a task is a milestone. If so, the formula returns an "NA" text value. If the task is not a milestone, the formula uses another IIf function and the ProjDateValue function to determine whether the task has a *Baseline Finish* value, indicating that the task has a baseline. If so, the formula calculates the percentage of duration variance, multiplies the resulting value by 100, and appends the text string with the percent sign (%) to show a percentage value. If not, the formula returns a "0%" text value.

Using the type of formulas shown in last two examples you can also calculate the percentage of work variance or cost variance by substituting [Work Variance]/[Baseline Work] or [Cost Variance]/[Baseline Cost] in either of the preceding formulas.

Even though Project Professional 2010 does not allow you to create and import custom enterprise project fields, you can use this application to help you create Project fields that include a formula. Because a custom enterprise project field is essentially a special type of custom enterprise task field, do the following:

In Project Professional 2010, define a custom enterprise task field that mimics the custom enterprise project field you need.

1. Create the formula in the task field.
2. Test the formula by examining the resulting value shown in the Project Summary Task (Row 0).
3. If the formula calculates correctly, then copy and paste the formula into a Notepad file.
4. Close the temporary read-only project file in Project Professional 2010.
5. Begin the process of creating the custom enterprise project field in Project Web App.
6. Copy and paste the formula from the Notepad file.

MSProjectExperts recommends this process as a best practice because it allows you to test the functionality of the field (and its formula) before you actually define the field in Project Web App.

Creating a Formula Using Project Web App

As I stated earlier, you can create a custom enterprise field with a formula in either Project Web App or in Project Professional 2010. While creating the formula in Project Web App, you cannot test the formula before you save it to confirm that the formula functions as desired. This makes it much more difficult to create a formula for a custom enterprise task field, making Project Professional 2010 a much better option for creating the formula. On the other hand, Project Server 2010 does not allow you to use Project Professional 2010 to create a custom enterprise project field with a formula, which makes the Project Web App interface a better option.

As a part of our organization's project tracking methodologies, I must calculate percentage of cost variance for each project. To accomplish this, I need to define a custom enterprise Project field containing a formula to perform the calculation. Because the field requires a formula, I can use either a custom enterprise task *Number* or *Text* field. For the purpose of this example, I plan to use a *Number* field, and I want the formula to "trap" for tasks that do not have a baseline value set and for milestone tasks.

Before I show you how to create this custom field I need a formula to calculate the percentage of cost variance. The formula is simply:

Cost Variance/Baseline Cost

How did I determine this formula? If the project cost is $125,000 when the baseline cost is only $100,000, then the cost variance is $25,000 (Cost – Baseline Cost). Applying the percentage of cost over budget formula, the task is 25% over budget (25,000/100,000 = .25 = 25%).

To create a custom enterprise field with a formula in Project Web App, complete the following steps:

1. Click the *New Field* button on the *Enterprise Custom Fields and Lookup Tables* page.

Project Server 2010 displays the *New Custom Field* page shown previously in Figure 7 - 20.

2. Enter a name for your new custom field, such as Percent Cost Variance, in the *Name* field.

3. Click the *Entity* pick list and select the *Project* entity from the pick list.

4. Click the *Type* pick list and select the *Number* type.

5. In the Custom Attributes section, select the *Formula* option.

The system refreshes the *New Custom Field* page to show the formula workspace (blank canvas) and the formula tools in the *Custom Attributes* section, as shown in Figure 7 - 27. The formula tools include the *Pick field* button, the *Pick Function* button, and the *Pick Operator* button.

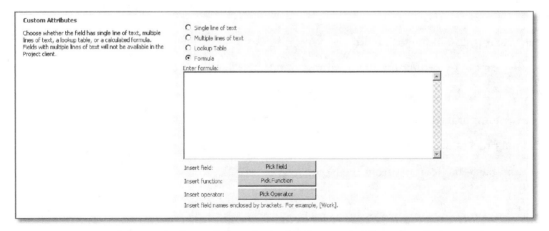

Figure 7 - 27: Formula buttons in the Custom Attributes section

6. Use the formula tools buttons to build your formula using custom enterprise fields, functions, and operators.

When you click the *Pick field* button, the system displays a list of all default and custom fields available. The system groups the default and custom fields into six categories, including *Cost, Date, Duration, Flag, Number,* and *Text*. Figure 7 - 28 shows the list of field types available by clicking the *Pick field* button.

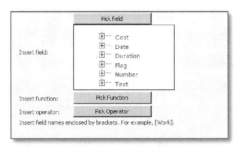

**Figure 7 - 28: Field types available
using the Pick field button**

When you click the *Expand* (+) button, the system displays the list of all fields available in that group. Figure 7 - 29 shows the list of *Cost* fields.

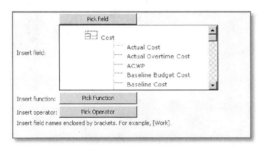

Figure 7 - 29: Cost Fields

From the list of fields in the expanded section, click the first field you want to use in the formula. The system adds the field to the formula workspace and collapses the *Pick field* list, as shown in Figure 7 - 30.

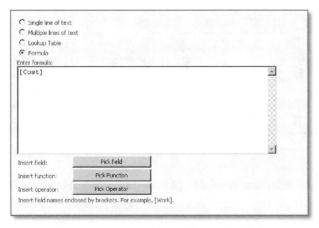

**Figure 7 - 30: Formula workspace includes
first selected field**

247

If you need to use mathematical operators, such as multiplication or division operators, you can click the *Pick Operator* button. The system displays the list of available mathematical and Boolean operators, as shown in Figure 7 - 31. Select the operator you want to use in your formula and the system adds the operator to the formula workspace.

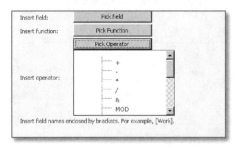

**Figure 7 - 31: Mathematical operators
on the Pick Operator list**

Project Server 2010 includes a number of mathematical and logical functions to help you create your formula. When you click the *Pick Function* button, the system displays the list of all functions available. The system groups these functions into six categories, including *Conversion, Date/Time, General, Math, Microsoft Project*, and *Text*. Figure 7 - 32 shows the list of functions available by clicking the *Pick Function* button.

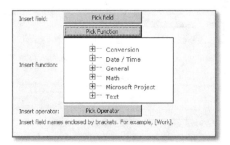

**Figure 7 - 32: Functions available using
the Pick Function button**

When you click the *Expand* (+) button, the system displays the list of all functions available in that group. Figure 7 - 33 shows the list of functions in the General section.

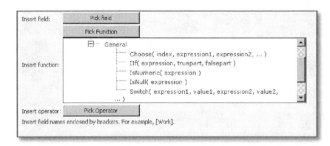

Figure 7 - 33: Functions in the General section

Several categories contain functions that are very helpful in building useful formulas in Project Professional 2010 and Project Web App. In the **Date/Time** category, consider using the following functions:

- Use the **Day** or **Month** function to isolate the day or month value in any date. For example, Day (10/21/2008) returns the 21 value.

- Use the **Now** function to return the current date, as specified on the system clock in your workstation.

In the **General** category, consider using the following functions:

- Use the **IIf** function to test for a condition, and then to return a certain value if the condition is true, or a different value if the condition is false. You can also nest IIf functions.

- Use the **Switch** function to test for a series of conditions, and to return a value for the first condition that generates a *True* value. In some cases, using the Switch function is much simpler than using a series of nested IIf functions.

In the **Microsoft Project** category, consider using the following functions:

- Use the **ProjDateAdd** function to add a specific number of days to a date using the working schedule on the calendar you specify.

- Use the **ProjDateDiff** function to determine the number of working days between two dates using the working schedule on the calendar you specify.

- Use the **ProjDateValue** function to test for the presence (or lack) of baseline information for a task. Project Professional 2010 indicates the lack of a baseline on a task by an NA value in either the *Baseline Start* or *Baseline Finish* fields. You normally use this function as part of a formula using an IIf statement. For example, the following formula tests for a Baseline:

```
IIf([Baseline Finish] = ProjDateValue("NA"), truepart, falsepart)
```

From the list of functions in the expanded section, select a function that you want to use in the formula. The system adds the function to the formula workspace and collapses the *Pick Function* list. After I built a formula using functions, fields, and mathematical operators, Figure 7 - 34 shows the following completed formula in the formula workspace:

```
IIf([Baseline Finish] = ProjDateValue("NA"), -16000, [Cost Variance] / [Baseline
Cost])
```

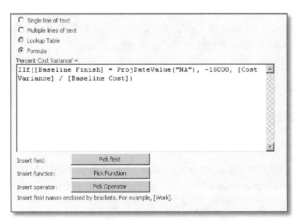

Figure 7 - 34: Percent Project Cost Variance formula

I used the following logic to create this formula:

- I used IIf([Baseline Finish] = ProjDateValue("NA") to test for the presence of a Baseline Finish date for each task.

- If there is no *Baseline Finish* date for the task, the formula returns a value of -16,000. I selected this value because the odds of it occurring as a result of the [Cost Variance] / [Baseline Cost] calculation are slim to none. In order for the [Cost Variance] / [Baseline Cost] calculation to return a value of -16,000, the task would need to be 1,600,000% under budget! Because I cannot use text in a *Number* field, I had to use a number that would indicate that a task has no *Baseline Finish* date.

- If the task has a *Baseline Finish* date, the formula applies the [Cost Variance] / [Baseline Cost] calculation to determine the percentage of cost variance.

Finish the process of creating the new field with a formula by completing the following steps:

7. In the *Values to Display* section, select the *Data* option.

8. Click the *Save* button.

Creating a Formula Using Project Professional 2010

If you need a custom enterprise task or resource field containing a formula, you can use Project Professional 2010 to create the field and formula initially in a project that you open read-only. This process creates a local field in the project, and you can then test the formula in the project to confirm its validity. When you confirm the formula works as intended, you can import the local field into Project Server 2010 as a new enterprise field containing a formula, and close the read-only project without saving it.

In addition to tracking the percentage of cost variance in each project, I must also calculate the percentage of cost variance for **each task** in every project. To meet this reporting need, I can create a custom task field using a formula very similar to the one I used in the *Percent Project Cost Variance* field that I created in the previous section.

To define this custom field and use a formula to calculate percent of task cost variance, launch Project Professional 2010 and log in to Project Server, and then complete the following steps:

1. Open a project in read-only mode so that you cannot save changes to this project.

2. Click on the *Custom Fields* button on the *Project* ribbon.

The system displays the *Custom Fields* dialog shown in Figure 7 - 35. Notice that the dialog shows the built-in custom Health field, along with the Billing Department field I created earlier in this module.

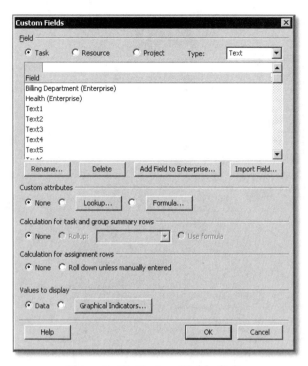

Figure 7 - 35: Custom Fields dialog

3. Select the *Task* option and then select the *Number* value from the *Type* pick list.

4. Select the first available Number field and then click the *Rename* button. The system displays the *Rename Field* dialog shown in Figure 7 - 36.

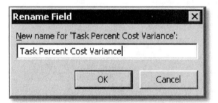

Figure 7 - 36: Rename Field dialog

5. Enter a new name for the custom field, such as Task Percent Cost Variance, and then click the *OK* button. Figure 7 - 37 shows the *Custom Fields* dialog after renaming the Number1 field. Notice that the system lists the new name for the field (Task Percent Cost Variance) plus the field's original name (Number1).

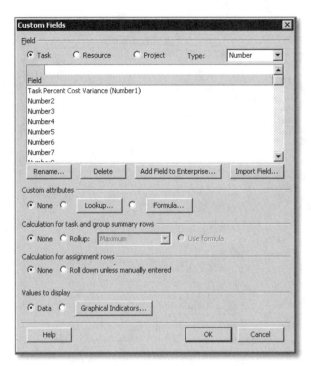

**Figure 7 - 37: Custom Fields dialog
with the renamed Number1 field**

6. Click the *Formula* button and Project Professional 2010 displays the *Formula* dialog for the new Task Percent Cost Variance field shown in Figure 7 - 38.

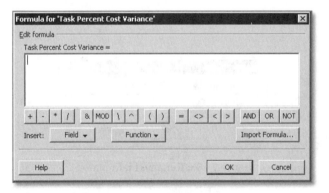

Figure 7 - 38: Formula dialog

7. The *Formula* dialog contains a number of tools to assist you with creating the formula. If another field contains a formula you wish to reuse in the current field, you can import the formula into the *Formula* dialog. If the field containing the formula is a local field in a project, you must close the *Formula* dialog and then close the *Customize Fields* dialog, open the project to make the formula available for import, and then return to the *Formula* dialog to customize the field. Otherwise, to import a formula click the *Import Formula* button in the lower right corner of the *Formula* dialog. Project Professional 2010 displays the *Import Formula* dialog shown in Figure 7 - 39.

Figure 7 - 39: Import Formula dialog

8. Click the *Project* pick list and select one of the project files that you currently have open. Select the *Field type* option for the type of field containing the formula. Click the *Field* pick list and select the field containing the formula you want to import. Click the *OK* button when finished. In the case of the Percent Task Cost Variance field, no other field contains the necessary formula, so I must create the formula manually using some of the other tools available in the *Formula* dialog.

9. Click the *Field* button to access a list of all default and custom fields available in Project Professional 2010. The system groups the default and custom fields into nine categories, including *Cost, Date, Duration, Flag, ID/Code, Number, Project, Text,* and *Work.* Figure 7 - 40 shows the list of field types available by clicking the *Field* button.

The *Project* category contains three sub-categories: *Date, Number,* and *Text.* In the *Date* sub-category, you can find useful Date fields such as Creation Date or Last Update. In the *Number* sub-category, you can find useful Number fields such as Minutes Per Day or Minutes Per Week. In the *Text* sub-category, you can find useful Text fields such as Author or Title.

**Figure 7 - 40: Field
types available**

10. Click the *Function* button to access a list of all available Functions. The system groups the functions into six categories, including *Conversion, Date/Time, General, Math, Microsoft Project,* and *Text.* Figure 7 - 41 shows the list of functions available by clicking the *Function* button.

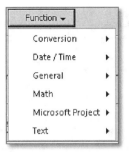

**Figure 7 - 41: Function
types available**

In addition to the fields and functions available in the *Formula* dialog, you can click any of the operand buttons to add mathematical or logical operators to your formula.

11. Using any of the available tools in the *Formula* dialog, create the formula for your custom field. Figure 7 - 42 shows the completed Percent Task Cost Variance formula in the *Formula* dialog as follows:

```
IIf([Baseline Finish] = ProjDateValue("NA"), -16000, IIf([Milestone], 0, [Cost Va-
riance] / [Baseline Cost]))
```

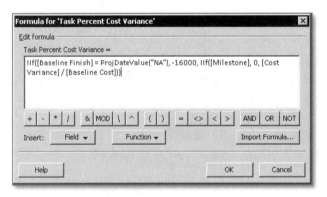

Figure 7 - 42: Completed Task Percent Cost Variance formula

The logic behind the structure of this formula is as follows:

- I used IIf([Baseline Finish] = ProjDateValue("NA") to test for the presence of a baseline finish date for each task.

- If there is no baseline finish date for the task, the formula returns a value of -16,000. I explained in the previous section why I selected this number.

- If the task has a baseline finish date, I use IIf([Milestone] to test whether the task is a milestone. The Milestone field is a default calculated flag field in Project Server 2010, and contains either a True or False value for every task.

- If the task is a milestone, the formula returns a 0 value.

- If the task is not a milestone, the formula applies the [Cost Variance] / [Baseline Cost] calculation to determine the percentage of cost variance.

12. Click the *OK* button to close the *Formula* dialog.

Project Professional 2010 displays the warning dialog shown in Figure 7 - 43. This warning indicates that the system will delete all values in the Percent Task Cost Variance field and will calculate all values using the formula. In this dialog, always click the *OK* button to return to the *Custom Fields* dialog.

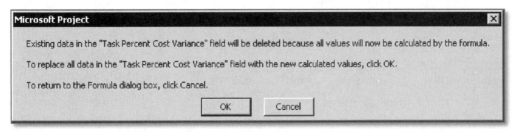

Figure 7 - 43: Warning dialog about using a formula in a custom field

13. In the *Calculation for Task and Group Summary Rows* section of the *Custom Fields* dialog, select your calculation option for summary tasks.

When you define a custom enterprise field using a formula, you must choose how the system calculates the formula in summary tasks and when you apply grouping to the project. You have three options in the *Calculation for Task and Group Summary Rows* section: *None*, *Rollup*, and *Use formula*.

If you do not want to apply the formula to group and summary rows, select the *None* option. To apply the literal formula to group and summary rows, select the default *Use formula* option. To apply the formula in a different manner, select the *Rollup* option and then select a rollup value from the pick list shown in Figure 7 - 44. Rollup options apply to all custom fields except text fields. I present a thorough explanation of rollup options in the next subsection.

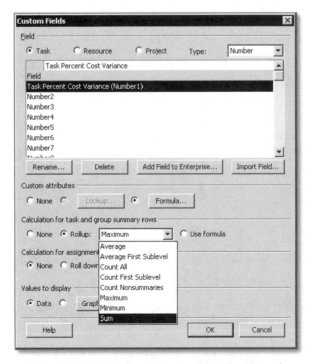

**Figure 7 - 44: Rollup options in the Calculation for
Task and Group Summary Rows section**

Understanding Rollup Methods for Enterprise Custom Fields

As I stated in the previous section, when you define a custom enterprise field using a formula, you must choose the calculation behavior for the field in summary tasks and groupings. When you select the *Rollup* option in the *Calculation for Task and Group Summary Rows* section of the *Custom Fields* dialog, the system displays the *Rollup* pick list shown previously in Figure 7 - 44. Your choices on the *Rollup* pick list vary by field type. The system offers no rollup choices for text fields. Table 7 - 1 lists the available field types and their rollup applicability.

Rollup Type	Cost	Date	Duration	Flag	Number
Average	X		X		X
Average First Sublevel	X		X		X
Count All					X
Count First Sub-level					X
Count Non-summaries					X
Maximum	X	X	X		X
Minimum	X	X	X		X
Sum	X		X		X
And				X	
Or				X	

Table 7 - 1: Custom Field Rollup Types

Now that you know which *Rollup* methods apply to each field type, use the following rollup method descriptions to assist you with choosing the appropriate method for your new field. Keep in mind that there is no particular right or wrong answer. The choice you make must simply follow the function that you intend for the field. Choose from the following *Rollup* methods in Project Server 2010:

- **Average**: Causes the rollup to be an average of all non-summary values beneath the summary row.

- **Average First Sublevel**: Causes the rollup to be an average of both the non-summary and summary values on just the first level of subtasks or grouped tasks.

- **Count All**: Causes the rollup to be a count of all summary and non-summary items beneath the summary row.

- **Count First Sublevel**: Causes the rollup to be a count of both the summary and non-summary tasks on only the first level beneath the summary row.

- **Maximum**: The rolled up value is the maximum value of values beneath the summary row.

- **Minimum**: The rolled up value is the minimum value of all values beneath the summary row.

- **Sum**: The rolled up value is the sum of all non-summary values beneath the summary row.

- **AND**: The rolled up value is the logical AND of all the flag values appearing beneath the summary row. For example, if all flags in the subtasks are set to *Yes*, then the rollup in the summary task is *Yes*; if any flags in the subtasks are set to *No*, then the rollup in the summary task is *No*. If any flag is set to *No*, then the rollup in the summary task is *No*.

- **OR**: The rolled up value is the logical OR of all flag values appearing beneath the summary row. If any flags in the subtasks are set to *Yes*, then the rollup is *Yes*.

Notice in Figure 7 - 45 that I selected the *Use formula* option in the *Calculation for Task and Group Summary Rows* section of the *Custom Fields* dialog. By selecting this option, I force Project Server 2010 to use the formula for all tasks, including summary tasks and the Project Summary Task (Row 0).

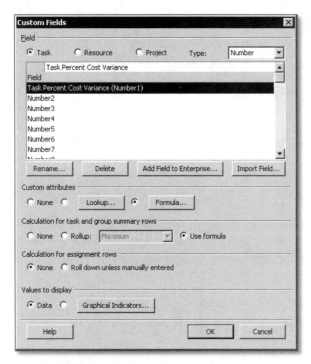

Figure 7 - 45: Completed formula in the Custom Fields dialog

Importing a Local Field as a Custom Enterprise Field

When you finish defining the custom field with a formula using Project Professional 2010, along with the rollup options for summary tasks and grouped tasks in your custom field, the field exists only in the project in which you created it. Now you must import the local task field into Project Server 2010 as a new custom enterprise task field. To import the custom field, verify that you are logged in to Project Server with administrator credentials and then click the *Add Field to Enterprise* button at the top of the *Custom Fields* dialog shown previously in Figure 7 - 45. Project Professional 2010 displays the *Add Field to Enterprise* dialog shown in Figure 7 - 46.

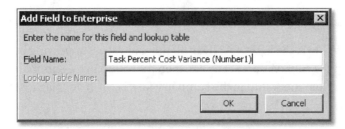

Figure 7 - 46: Add Field to Enterprise dialog

The *Add Field to Enterprise* dialog displays the *Field Name* and *Lookup Table Name* if applicable. Leave the information "as is" in the dialog and then click the *OK* button to add the new custom field to the system. After the system adds the new field to Project Server 2010, it displays the confirmation dialog shown Figure 7 - 47.

Figure 7 - 47: Confirmation dialog after adding new field to enterprise

 Notice in the confirmation that you must exit and restart Project Professional 2010 before you can use the new custom enterprise field. This procedure is necessary to refresh your cached Enterprise Global file so that you gain access to the new custom enterprise field.

After completing the process of adding the new custom field to the enterprise system, click the *OK* button in the confirmation dialog and again in the *Custom Fields* dialog and then exit Project Professional 2010. You can now see the new custom field in the *Custom Fields and Lookup Tables* page in Project Web App shown in Figure 7 - 48.

**Figure 7 - 48: Custom Fields and Lookup Tables page
shows new Task Percent Cost Variance field**

 Warning: Notice that the Task Percent Cost Variance field includes the (Number1) text string in the field name. After you import a custom field from Project Professional 2010, the system imports the entire field name as listed in the *Add Field to Enterprise* dialog. After importing fields into the enterprise from Project Professional 2010, you must edit the name of each field individually to remove unwanted information (such as "Number1") from the field name.

Using the Custom Fields dialog in Project Professional 2010, you can also import a lookup table by selecting the *Outline Code* field type. In the *Outline Code*, you must create the *Code Mask* and *Lookup Table*, and then import the *Outline Code* field as a new *Enterprise Lookup Table*.

Warning: If you add a new calculated field to an existing Project Server 2010 environment, your project managers must open each of their enterprise projects, press the **F9** function key to recalculate the project, and then save and publish their projects.

Displaying Graphical Indicators in Custom Fields

Graphical indicators lend a powerful, popular, and eye-pleasing impact to views in both Project Professional 2010 and Project Web App. Many users find graphical indicators easier to understand than the raw numerical data. For example, almost anyone can figure out that a red stoplight indicator is not a good thing; while a green "smiley face" indicator is a sign of something very good indeed!

As with custom enterprise fields that contain a formula, there are two ways to create a custom enterprise field that uses graphical indicators:

- Use Project Web App.

- Use Project Professional 2010.

The advantages of using Project Professional 2010 are that you can import graphical indicators from another custom enterprise field, you can test your graphical indicators on a real project, and you can access the system's *Help* documentation. The Project Web App interface does not provide any of these three features. For the purpose of thoroughness, I document how to create graphical indicators using both interfaces.

Creating Graphical Indicators Using Project Web App

For ease of variance analysis, our company's project reporting methodology requires the use of stoplight indicators to show the percentage of project cost variance. Users need to see this information in a *Project Detail* view reached from the *Project Center* and in a custom view in Project Professional 2010. Therefore, I want to display a green, yellow, or red stoplight indicator for each value in the new *Percent Task Cost Variance* field that I created previously in this module. Our company's criteria for displaying stoplights in this field are as follows:

- If the task has no *Baseline Finish* date (indicating that the project is not baselined), display a clock face icon.

- If the *Task Percent Cost Variance* is less than 20%, then display green smiley face icon.

- If the *Task Percent Cost Variance* value is greater than or equal to 20% but less than 50%, then display yellow serious face icon.

- If the *Task Percent Cost Variance* value is greater than or equal to 50%, then display red unhappy face icon.

In addition, users need to be able to see the underlying value in the field for any task by floating the mouse pointer over the graphical indicator. To add graphical indicators to the *Task Percent Cost Variance* field, complete the following steps:

1. Click the name of the *Task Percent Cost Variance* field on the *Enterprise Custom Fields and Lookup Tables* page to open the field for editing.

2. In the *Values to Display* section of the page, select the *Graphical indicators* option. The system displays a graphical indicators data grid as shown in Figure 7 - 49.

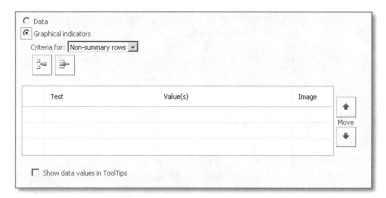

**Figure 7 - 49: Graphical Indicators data grid
on the Edit Custom Fields page**

3. Enter your graphical indicator criteria in the Graphical indicators data grid.

 Warning: If you use the Project Web App interface to create graphical indicators for a *Task* field, you must individually specify the criteria used for non-summary tasks (subtasks), summary tasks (such as phases and deliverables), and the *Project Summary Task* (Row 0). Using the items on *Criteria for* pick list, the system allows you to set completely different criteria for each of the three types of tasks, or to specify that all summary rows (including the Project Summary Task) inherit their criteria from the non-summary rows.

To set up the criteria for the graphical indicators, you must specify multiple tests using the pick lists in the data grid. The order in which you enter your criteria is very important because the system processes the criteria list from the top to the bottom of the grid. When the system encounters the first "true" condition for a test, it stops processing the criteria and displays the graphical indicator for that test. This means that in some cases, you may need to enter the criteria in reverse order from your reporting requirements.

When you click the first blank cell in the *Test* column and then click the pick list, the system offers the following tests:

*   Equals

*   Does not equal

*   Is greater than

*   Is greater than or equal to

- Is less than

- Is less than or equal to

- Is within

- Is not within

- Contains

- Does not contain

- Contains exactly

- Is any value

The *Is Any Value* test yields a positive result in all cases. This makes it useful as a "catchall" test to include at the bottom of the criteria list, as it will display an indicator to represent a value not otherwise defined.

The tests you select in the *Test* column apply to the values you select or enter in the *Value(s)* column. In the *Value(s)* column, you can select a standard or enterprise field, or you can enter a literal value. In the *Image* column, select a graphical indicator for each test. Table 7 - 2 shows the types of multi-colored graphical images available and the number of each type of image.

Image Type	Number
Blank indicator	1
Stoplights	13
Flags	8
Solid color squares	5
Plus signs	5
Minus signs	6
Solid color diamonds	3
Blue arrows	5
Semaphores	7
Light bulbs	2
Miscellaneous	5
"Smiley face" icons	6

Table 7 - 2: Graphical Indicators

As you create your Graphical Indicator criteria, you need more than three default rows in the data grid. You can click the *Insert Row* button to add as many rows as you need.

To meet our organization's reporting requirements, the correct order of my graphical indicator criteria is as follows in Table 7 - 3:

Test	Value(s)	Image
Equals	-16000	Clock face
Is greater than or equal to	.50	Red unhappy face
Is greater than or equal to	.20	Yellow neutral face
Is less than	.20	Green smiley face

Table 7 - 3: Correct order for Graphical Indicator criteria

Because Project Server 2010 processes the graphical indicator criteria in the order listed, the system processes the above criteria as follows:

- The system first determines if the value for the task equals -16,000. If true, it displays the Clock face graphical indicator and stops processing the list.

- If the previous test returns false, the system determines if the percent cost variance for the task is greater than or equal to 50%. If true, it displays the red unhappy face graphical indicator and stops processing the list.

- If the previous test returns false, the system determines if the percent cost variance for the task is greater than or equal to 20%. If true, it displays the yellow neutral graphical indicator and stops processing the list.

- If the previous test returns false, the system determines if the percent cost variance for the project is less than 20%. Again, if true, it displays the green smiley face graphical indicator and stops processing the list.

- If all test conditions return false, the system displays no symbol at all.

Because of how I created the formula and structured the graphical indicator criteria, the system will find a true condition for one of the four criteria for every project and will always display a resulting graphical indicator. Figure 7 - 50 shows the four criteria for the graphical indicators in the *Percent Project Cost Variance* field.

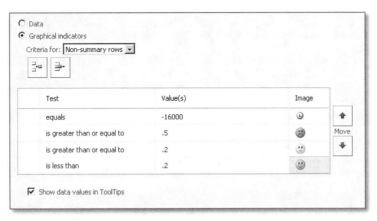

**Figure 7 - 50: Completed graphical indicator criteria
for the Task Percent Cost Variance field**

4. If you want users to see the underlying data values by floating their mouse pointer over the graphical indicator, select the *Show data values in ToolTips* option.

5. Click the *Save* button to save the graphical indicator criteria as a part of the *Percent Task Cost Variance* field.

Creating Graphical Indicators Using Project Professional 2010

For ease of variance analysis, our company's project reporting methodology requires the use of stoplight indicators to show the percentage of task cost variance. Users need to see this information in a *Project Detail* view in Project Web App. Therefore, I want to display a green, yellow, or red stoplight indicator for each value in the new *Percent Cost Variance* field. This example is identical to the field I created using Project Web App. Here I show you how to set graphical indicators using the Microsoft Project 2010. I do not show you how to enter the formula in this example, as I covered that previously. Our company's criteria for displaying stoplights in this field are as follows:

*   If the project has no *Baseline Finish* date (indicating that it is not baselined), display a clock face icon.

*   If the Percent Cost Variance value is less than 10%, then display green smiley face icon.

*   If the Percent Cost Variance value is greater than or equal to 10% but less than 20%, then display yellow serious face icon.

*   If the Percent Cost Variance value is greater than or equal to 20%, then display the red unhappy face icon.

In addition, users need to be able to see the underlying value in the field for any task by floating the mouse pointer over the graphical indicator. To add graphical indicators to the *Percent Cost Variance* field, complete the following steps:

1. Click the *Custom Fields* button on the *Project* ribbon to open the *Custom Fields* dialog. In the *Custom Fields dialog* in Project Professional 2010, select the Percent Cost Variance custom field and then click the *Graphical Indicators* button. Project Professional 2010 displays the *Graphical Indicators* dialog for the Percent Cost Variance field, shown in Figure 7 - 51.

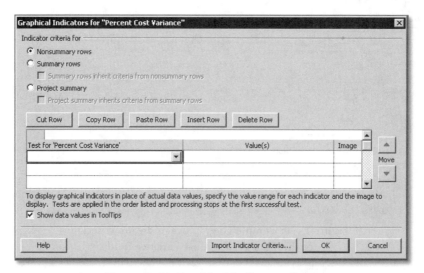

Figure 7 - 51: Graphical Indicators dialog

In the *Indicator criteria for* section of the *Graphical Indicators* dialog, you **must** specify your graphical indicator criteria for three types of tasks:

- Non-summary tasks (subtasks)

- Summary tasks (such as Phases and Deliverables)

- Project Summary Task (Row 0)

Using the *Indicator criteria for* options at the top of the dialog, the system allows you to set completely different criteria for each of the three types of tasks, or to specify that all summary rows (including the Project Summary Task) inherit their criteria from the non-summary rows.

2. Select the *Project Summary* option and enter graphical indicator criteria for the Project Summary task in the *Test*, *Value(s)*, and *Image* columns of the data grid.

3. Select the *Summary rows* option and then select the *Summary rows inherit criteria from nonsummary rows* option.

The system displays the warning dialog shown in Figure 7 - 52.

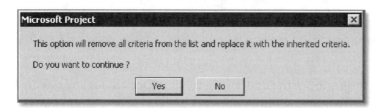

Figure 7 - 52: Warning dialog for inherited criteria
from non-summary rows

4. Click the *Yes* button in the warning dialog. The system automatically imports the criteria specified for non-summary tasks into the data grid for summary tasks and "grays out" the criteria so you cannot change them.

If you want to set up different graphical indicator criteria for summary tasks, do not select the *Project summary inherits criteria from summary rows* option, and then enter a new set of criteria in the *Test*, *Value(s)*, and *Image* columns of the data grid.

5. Select the *Project summary* option and then select the *Project summary inherits criteria from summary rows* option.

6. Click the *Yes* button in the warning dialog.

The system automatically imports the criteria specified for summary tasks into the data grid for the Project Summary Tasks and "grays out" the criteria so you cannot change them.

If you want to set up different graphical indicator criteria for the Project Summary Task, do not select the *Project summary inherits criteria from summary rows* option, and then enter a new set of criteria in the *Test*, *Value(s)*, and *Image* columns of the data grid.

To meet our organization's reporting requirements, the correct order of my graphical indicator criteria for non-summary tasks is as follows in Table 7 - 4:

Test	Value(s)	Image
Equals	-16000	Clock face
Is greater than or equal to	.20	Red unhappy face
Is greater than or equal to	.10	Yellow neutral face
Is less than	.10	Green smiley face

Table 7 - 4: Correct order for Graphical Indicator criteria

Because Project Server 2010 processes the graphical indicator criteria in the order listed, the system processes the above criteria as follows:

- The system first determines if the value for the task equals -16,000. If true, it displays the clock face graphical indicator and stops processing the list.

- If the previous test returns false, the system determines if the percent cost variance for a task is greater than or equal to 20%. If true, it displays the red unhappy face graphical indicator and stops processing the list.

- If the previous test returns false, the system determines if the percent cost variance for a task is greater than or equal to 10%. If true, it displays the yellow neutral graphical indicator and stops processing the list.

- If the previous test returns false, the system determines if the percent cost variance for a task is less than 10%. Again, if true, it displays the green smiley face graphical indicator and stops processing the list.

- If all test conditions return false, the system displays no symbol at all.

Because of how I created the formula and structured the graphical indicator criteria, the system will find a true condition for one of the three criteria for every task and will always display a graphical indicator. Figure 7 - 53 shows the first three criteria for the graphical indicators in the *Percent Cost Variance* field.

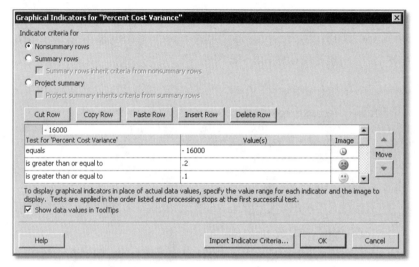

Figure 7 - 53 : Completed graphical indicator criteria for the Percent Cost Variance field

7. If you want your users to see the underlying data values by floating their mouse pointer over the graphical indicator, select the *Show data values in ToolTips* option.

8. Click the *OK* button to close the *Graphical Indicators* dialog and return to the *Custom Fields* dialog.

Understanding the Connection between Formulas and Graphical Indicators

If you know in advance that you need to create graphical indicators in a custom field with a formula, give careful thought to the interaction between the formula and the graphical indicator criteria. Your reporting requirements ultimately determine what type of fields to use, how to write the formula, and how to list the graphical indicator criteria. Make sure you structure your formula to return consistent values that the system can test with graphical indicator criteria.

Keep in mind that Project Web App allows users to export data in a data grid to Microsoft Office Excel. The Project Center page contains a data grid, for example, and is often the location for using custom enterprise project fields that contain a formula and display graphical indicators. When exporting to Excel from a data grid that displays graphical indicators, the system **does not** export the graphical indicators. Instead, it exports only the underlying value in each cell. Because of this, you may opt to use a text field rather than a number field when creating a formula with graphical indicators in the field.

For example, following are the three most common variance formulas you might want to use with graphical indicators in either task fields or project fields. To use any of these formulas, you must select a *Text* field type, rather than a

Number field type. When exporting to Excel from a Project Web App data grid, keep in mind that the system exports the text values, giving useful information to the user in Excel.

Percent Cost Variance

```
Switch(([BaselineFinish]=ProjDateValue("NA")),"NoBaseline",[Milestone],
"Green",[CostVariance]<([BaselineCost]*0.05),"Green", [Cost Variance]<([Baseline
Cost]*0.1), "Yellow", [Cost Variance]>=([Baseline Cost]*0.1), "Red")
```

The Percent Cost Variance formula shown above uses the Switch function to determine what text value to display in the field. It tests for the following conditions:

- Baseline Finish date = NA
- Milestone
- Percent cost variance < 5%
- Percent cost variance < 10%
- Percent cost variance >= 10%

The first condition that generates a "True" response forces the system to display the text specified for that test.

Percent Work Variance

```
Switch(([Baseline Finish]=ProjDateValue("NA")), "No Baseline", [Milestone], "Green",
[Work Variance]<([Baseline Work]*0.05), "Green", [Work Variance]<([Baseline
Work]*0.1), "Yellow", [Work Variance]>=([Baseline Work]*0.1), "Red")
```

Percent Duration Variance

```
Switch(([Baseline Finish]=ProjDateValue("NA")), "No Baseline", [Milestone], "Green",
[Duration Variance]<([Baseline Duration]*0.05), "Green", [Duration Va-
riance]<([Baseline Duration]*0.1), "Yellow",[Duration Variance]>=([Baseline Dura-
tion]*0.1), "Red")
```

If you use any of the above formulas in your own custom fields, you must specify your own organization's criteria for calculating how much variance results in a green, yellow, or red value in the formula. After creating these formulas in a field, you can create matching graphical indicator criteria.

Deleting a Custom Field or Lookup Table

To delete a custom enterprise field or lookup table, first navigate to the *Custom Fields and Lookup Tables* page in Project Web App. If you want to delete a custom field, select it in the data grid and then click the *Delete Field* button. When prompted, click the *Yes* button in the warning dialog to delete the field. If you want to delete a custom lookup table, select it in the data grid and then click the *Delete Lookup Table* button. When the system prompts, click the *Yes* button in the warning dialog to delete the Lookup Table.

Planning for Matching Generic Resources

Consider the following scenario in my organization to understand the need for matching human resources with generic resources:

- Project managers in our organization routinely plan projects that do not start until three months or more in the future.

- During the initial planning for a new project, project managers add generic resources to their project team and then assign the generic resources to the tasks.

- The generic resources are skill-based or placeholder resources that indicate the IT skills needed to perform each task.

- As the project start date approaches, project managers need to match generic resources with human resources who possess the same IT skills and have the availability to work on the project.

The preceding scenario is very common across the EPM community. Most organizations find generic resources a useful planning tool and need to do some form of matching between generic resources and human resources as they move project into execution. The most common need, as presented above, is to match skills between generic and human resources. Other common needs involve matching resources by availability, by position in the RBS structure, by region or location, and by language proficiency.

Scale is everything when you plan for matching generic resources with human resources. Project Server 2010 provides tools that instantly sift through hundreds or thousands of resources to locate one that has the preferred attributes for the job. If your organization does not have a large number of resources, then you may take a very light-handed approach to this capability or choose to ignore it completely.

Project Server 2010 provides project managers and planners two tools for skill matching generic-to-human or human-to-human resources: the *Build Team from Enterprise* tool and the *Resource Substitution Wizard*. Using either tool, the system matches skills and other resource attributes by comparing enterprise resource fields that contain lookup tables and other criteria that the individual user can apply through the interface. Skill matching uses "contains" logic as it compares a generic resource with possible matching human resources, and does not require an exact match between the resources.

Your challenge as the Project Server business analyst or administrator is to provide thoughtful attribution values to enhance Project Server's team-building tools. If you are working with a large enterprise resource pool, it is possible to build a significant matrix of attributes for team building. Distributed organizations may want location codes, while large organizations may want seniority codes and secondary skill identifiers. Remember that once you create a new attribute, you obligate yourself to provide a value for it for each resource in your enterprise resource pool.

My organization's primary need is to match generic resources with human resources using IT skills. Using a skills assessment provided by our human resources staff, we categorized four types of IT skills with specific IT skills as follows:

- **Database** – DB2, Oracle, SQL Server

- **Network Operations Center** – Network Engineer, Network Hardware Engineer, Server Engineer

- **Quality Assurance** – QA Analyst, Tester

- **Software Development** – Dot Net Developer, RPG Developer, Java Developer

Based on the above information, I can use a single enterprise field containing a lookup table to represent the available skills across the IT department. Because Project Server 2010 allows the use of multiple values in the lookup table, I can select multiple skills for each resource. To enable skill matching in my organization, I first created the IT Skills lookup table shown partially in Figure 7 - 54

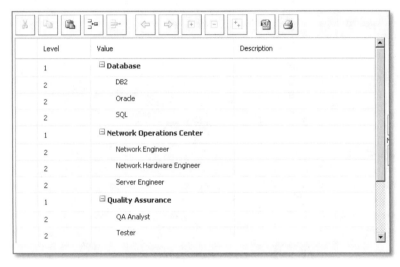

**Figure 7 - 54: IT Skills lookup table with Database,
Network, and QA skills visible**

After creating the Skills lookup table, I created a custom enterprise resource field called Primary IT Skill using the Skills lookup table shown in Figure 7 - 54. I set up the options in the IT Skills field shown in Figure 7 - 55 to match the following requirements:

- The enterprise resource pool administrator must select a specific IT skill for each resource and cannot select one of the six categories only.

- The field must not allow the user to select multiple values for each resource. I mandate this requirement because I intend to use this field as a dimension in the OLAP cubes, which do not display data for Multi-Value (MV) fields.

- The field must be used for matching generic resources with human resources.

- The field must not be a required field, so the system does not require the enterprise resource pool administrator to select an IT Skill value for every resource in the pool. I mandate this requirement because the enterprise resource pool will contain other types of resources, including material resource and cost resources that do not have an IT Skill value.

269

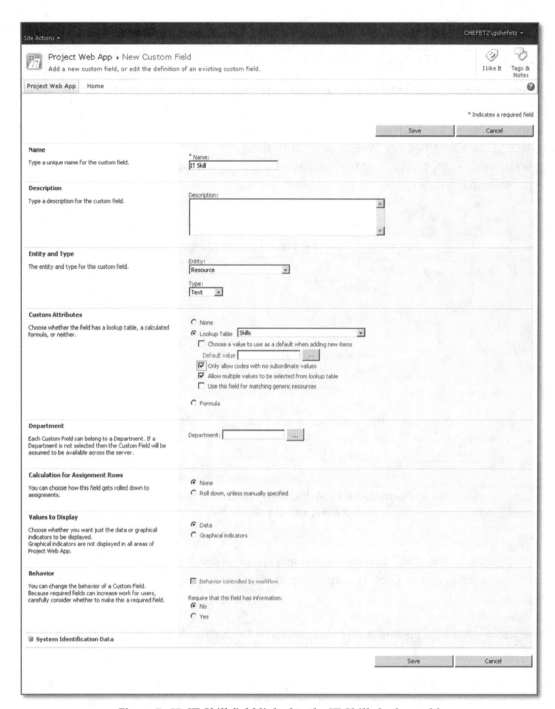

Figure 7 - 55: IT Skill field linked to the IT Skills lookup table

Creating Enterprise Calendars

Before you add resources and projects to your Project Server 2010 database, you must configure your organization's enterprise *Standard* calendar and create new base calendars as indicated in your Requirements and Configuration Specification document. The enterprise *Standard* calendar serves as the default project calendar for all new projects created in the system, and provides the base calendar for all resources as well. You create additional base calendars for the unique scheduling needs of your organization, such as for a resource who works four 10-hour work days each week, or for tasks that must occur on weekends only. At a minimum, you must add your company's holidays to the enterprise *Standard* calendar so that your project managers have realistic project schedules.

To work with enterprise calendars, navigate to the *Server Settings* page in Project Web App and then click the *Enterprise Calendars* link in the *Enterprise Data* section of the page. The system displays the *Enterprise Calendars* page shown in Figure 7 - 56.

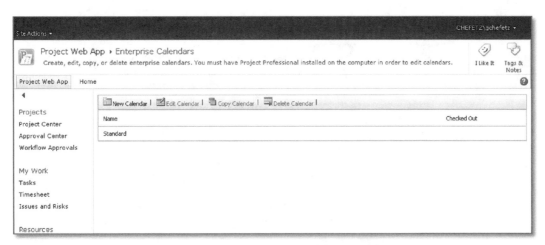

Figure 7 - 56: Enterprise Calendars page

Setting Company Holidays

To edit the *Standard* calendar, select the *Standard* calendar in the list of calendars and then click the *Edit Calendar* button. The system launches Project Professional 2010 and opens the *Standard* calendar for editing in the Change Working Time dialog shown in Figure 7 - 57.

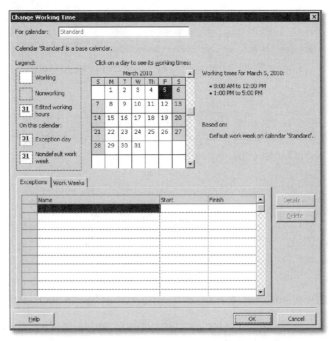

**Figure 7 - 57: Change Working Time dialog
for the Standard calendar**

To add a non-working company holiday on the *Standard* calendar, complete the following steps:

1. In the calendar data grid, select the date of the next company holiday.

 To set consecutive nonworking days, drag your mouse pointer to select a block of days. To select noncontiguous dates, select the first date, press and hold the **Control** key, and then select additional dates.

2. On the *Exceptions* tab in the bottom half of the page, enter a name for the holiday, and then press the Right-Arrow key. Notice in Figure 7 - 58 that I set May 31, 2010 as the Memorial Day company holiday.

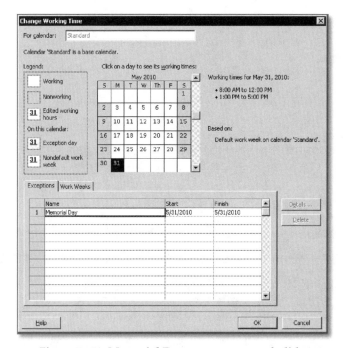

Figure 7 - 58: Memorial Day set as company holiday

3. Click the *Details* button.

The software displays the *Details for* dialog for the selected holiday, as shown in Figure 7 - 56. You use the *Details for* dialog to create a recurring company holiday for a specified number of years into the future. For example, you might set each company holiday to recur for the next 5 years.

 The right side of the *Recurrence Pattern* section allows you to specify a hard date every year, such as January 1, or a floating date, such as the fourth Thursday of every November (Thanksgiving Day).

4. In the *Recurrence Pattern* section, select the *Yearly* option and then select your pattern of recurrence.

5. In the *Range of Recurrence* section, select the *End after* option and then select the number of years to repeat the holiday. Figure 7 - 59 shows the *Recurrence pattern* values set to *Yearly* on *The Last Monday of May* and the *Range of recurrence* values set to *End after 5 occurrences*.

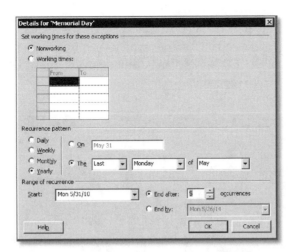

Figure 7 - 59: Details dialog for Memorial Day

6. Click the *OK* button. The system displays the *Change Working Time* dialog with the Memorial Day holiday set as shown in Figure 7 - 60.

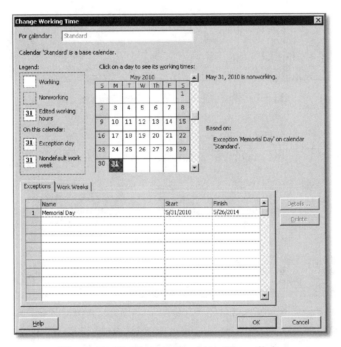

Figure 7 - 60: Change Working Time dialog
with Memorial Day holiday

Warning: When you set a hard date as nonworking time, such as January 1, and then set the holiday to recur multiple times, some of the nonworking dates may fall on a weekend. Project Server 2010 **does not** automatically reset a Saturday holiday to the previous Friday, or reset a Sunday holiday to the following Monday. Instead, you must set these weekend occurrences as additional holidays on the Exceptions tab.

7. After you set a recurring company holiday on a hard date, such as January 1, scroll through the calendar grid looking for weekend occurrences and then set additional exceptions according to your organization's policies. For example, notice in Figure 7 - 61 that I set an additional New Year's Day holiday for January 3, 2011 because January 1, 2011 falls on a weekend.

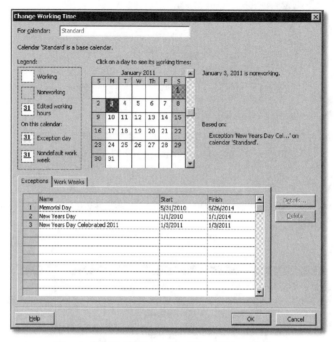

**Figure 7 - 61: Change Working Time dialog
with New Years Day Holiday Exceptions**

8. Set additional nonworking time occurrences for the holiday when it falls on a Saturday or Sunday.

9. Repeat steps #1-7 for each company holiday.

10. Click the *OK* button to close the *Change Working Time* dialog and save the changes to the *Standard* calendar.

Setting the Daily Working Schedule

After setting your company holidays, you may also need to establish the daily working schedule for your company. By default, the *Standard* calendar in Project Server 2010 assumes a daily working schedule of 8:00 AM – 5:00 PM with one hour off for lunch, Monday through Friday, with Saturday and Sunday as nonworking times. Some organizations want to change the working schedule on the *Standard* calendar to match their exact working schedule, such as 7:00 AM – 3:30 PM with a half-hour for lunch. Other organizations want to change the working schedule to match a typical worker's productive working day (6 hours of productive work/day) by using a 9:00 AM – 4:00 PM schedule with one hour for lunch.

In the previous example, I am not recommending the use of a "productive working time" construct, such as setting the *Standard* calendar schedule to 6 hours per work day. Instead, I merely use it for illustration purposes. You must carefully make such decisions during your design phase.

To change the working schedule on the Standard calendar from the *Enterprise Calendars* page in Project Web App, complete the following steps:

1. Select the *Standard* calendar in the list of calendars and then click the *Edit Calendar* button.

The system launches Project Professional 2010 and opens the *Standard* calendar for editing in the *Change Working Time* dialog shown previously in Figure 7 - 61.

2. In the *Change Working Time* dialog, click the *Work Weeks* tab and then click the *Details* button. The software displays the *Details* dialog for the Default working schedule shown in Figure 7 - 62.

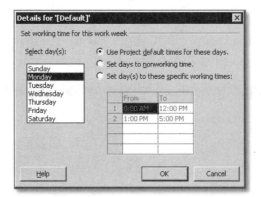

**Figure 7 - 62: Details dialog for the
Default working schedule**

3. In the *Select day(s)* section, select and drag Monday through Friday in the list of days.

4. Select the *Set day(s) to these specific working times* option at the top of the dialog. The software displays the default 8:00 AM – 5:00 PM working time in the Working times grid, shown in Figure 7 - 63.

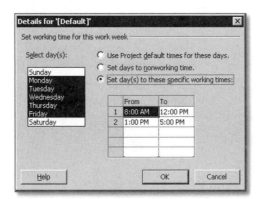

**Figure 7 - 63: Default working schedule
in the Details dialog**

5. Change the *From* and *To* times to reflect your organization's working schedule. For example, Figure 7 - 64 shows a standard working schedule of 9:00 AM to 4:00 PM with an hour for lunch as if I wanted to reflect the productive working time of 6 hours per day for resources in our organization.

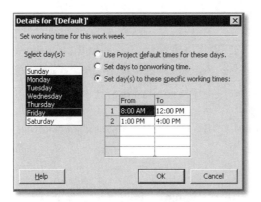

**Figure 7 - 64: New default working schedule
in the Details dialog**

6. Click the *OK* button to close the Details dialog and return to the *Change Working Time* dialog. When you click any date in the calendar grid at the top of the *Change Working Time* dialog, you can see the new working schedule for the *Standard* calendar shown in Figure 7 - 65.

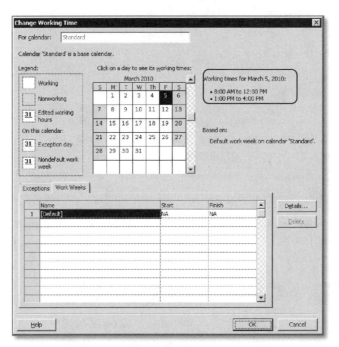

**Figure 7 - 65: Change Working Time dialog
with new working schedule**

7. Click the *OK* button to close the *Change Working Time* dialog and save the new working schedule on the Standard calendar.

Warning: Synchronizing Working Time with Project Options

If you change the working schedule on the *Standard* calendar to any schedule different from the default 8:00 AM – 5:00 PM working schedule, and the *Standard* calendar is the default Project calendar for individual projects, your project managers must synchronize the calendar options in **every existing enterprise project** to match the schedule in the *Standard* calendar. To synchronize the calendar options, your project managers must complete the following steps:

1. Open an enterprise project.

2. Click File ➤ Options and then select the *Schedule* tab. Figure 7 - 66 shows the *Project Options* dialog with the *Schedule* page selected.

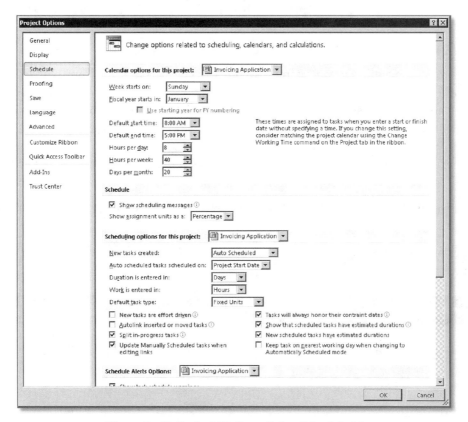

Figure 7 - 66: Project Options dialog Schedule tab

3. Set the *Default start time* and *Default end time* values to match the project calendar start time and end time.

4. Set the *Hours per day* and *Hours per week* values to match the working hours per day and per week on the project calendar.

5. Click the *OK* button and then save the project.

For example, I set the working schedule on the *Standard* calendar from 9:00 AM to 4:00 PM, representing only a 7-hour working day and a 35-hour working week. In every enterprise project, each project manager must perform the following steps on the *Options* dialog *Calendars* page:

*   Set the *Default start time* to 9:00 AM.

*   Set the *Default end time* to 4:00 PM.

*   Set the *Hours per day* value to 7 hours.

*   Set the *Hours per week* value to 35 hours.

The *Hours per day* setting on the *Schedule* tab determines how Project Professional 2010 calculates the duration of **every task** in the project. The formula used to calculate duration is called the duration equation and written as follows:

$$\text{Duration} = \text{Work} \div (\text{Hours Per Day} \times \text{Units})$$

$$D = W \div (HPD \times U)$$

The HPD value in the duration equation is actually the *Hours per day* value on the *Schedule* tab of the *Options* dialog. Therefore, if the length of a working day in the *Standard* calendar is "out of sync" with the *Hours per day* setting on the *Schedule* page, you will see confusing duration values calculated in your Project Professional 2010 plans.

Creating a New Base Calendar

A *Base* calendar is a master calendar that represents a unique working schedule for your company. You should create custom base calendars to show a project schedule different than the one shown on the *Standard* calendar. Before you create a new *Base* calendar, you must determine whether to create it by copying an existing *Base* calendar or by creating the *Base* calendar from scratch. If you copy an existing *Base* calendar, such as the *Standard* calendar, the new *Base* calendar inherits the working schedule and holidays from the original *Base* calendar. If you create a new *Base* calendar from scratch, Project Server 2010 creates a new blank calendar with a work schedule from 8:00 AM – 5:00 PM with an hour for lunch, and with Saturdays and Sundays set as nonworking time.

To create a copy of an existing calendar, complete the following steps from the *Enterprise Calendars* page in Project Web App:

1. Select an existing calendar and then click the *Copy Calendar* button. The system displays the *Copy Calendar* dialog shown in Figure 7 - 67.

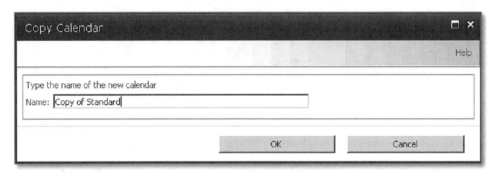

Figure 7 - 67: Copy Calendar dialog

2. Enter a name for the calendar in the *Name* field and then click the *OK* button. Project Server 2010 adds the new *Base* calendar to the list of calendars on the *Enterprise Calendars* page, as shown in Figure 7 - 68. Notice that I created a new *Base* calendar named 4 X 10 to reflect the working schedule of resources who work four 10-hour days.

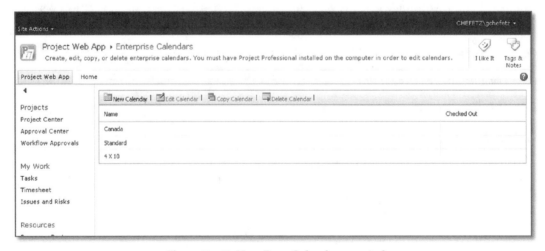

Figure 7 - 68: New Base Calendars created

3. Select the new *Base* calendar and click the *Edit Calendar* button. Project Server 2010 displays the *Change Working Time* dialog shown previously.

4. Click the *Work Weeks* tab and then click the *Details* button. Project Server 2010 displays the *Details* dialog shown previously.

5. In the *Details* dialog, select the daily working schedule for each day of the week. Figure 7 - 69 and Figure 7 - 70, together, show the *Details* dialog after I set the working schedule with 10 hours of work Monday through Thursday, with no work on Friday.

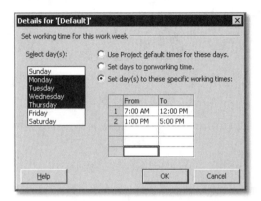

**Figure 7 - 69: Details dialog shows
Monday - Thursday schedule**

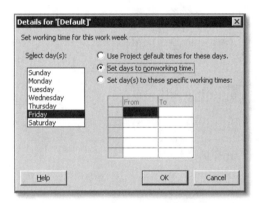

**Figure 7 - 70: Details dialog
shows Friday schedule**

6. Click the *OK* button to close the *Details* dialog and return to the *Change Working Time* dialog.

7. Click the *OK* button to close the *Change Working Time* dialog and save the new *Base* calendar.

When you create a new blank *Base* calendar by clicking the *New Calendar* button on the *Enterprise Calendars* page, you must perform the same steps presented earlier in this section to set up your new blank *Base* calendar.

Importing a Base Calendar from a Project

Project Server 2010 allows you to import *Base* calendars created in local (non-enterprise) projects. For example, prior to our organization's implementation of Project Server 2010, a project manager created a special Weekend Work base calendar in a project to schedule tasks that must occur only on a Saturday or Sunday. To import this Base calendar as an enterprise Base calendar, I must complete the following steps:

1. Launch Project Professional 2010 and log in to Project Server with administrator permissions.

2. Open the local (non-enterprise) project.

3. Click the *Change Working Time* button on the project ribbon.

4. In the *Change Working Time* dialog, click the *For calendar* pick list and select the local *Base* calendar. Notice in Figure 7 - 71 that I selected the Weekend Work local Base calendar.

 You can create additional Base calendars in the *Change Working Time* dialog using the *Create New Calendar* button and the *Add Calendar to Enterprise* button.

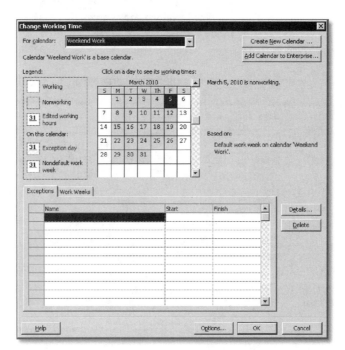

**Figure 7 - 71: Change Working Time dialog
shows local Base calendar**

5. Click the *Add Calendar to Enterprise* button.

The system displays the *Add to Enterprise* dialog. In the *Add to Enterprise* dialog, enter a new name that conforms to your organizational standard for naming base calendars and then click the *OK* button.

6. Click the *OK* button to close the *Change Working Time* dialog.

Figure 7 - 72 shows the new Weekend Only Work calendar added to the calendars list on the *Enterprise Calendars* page in Project Web App.

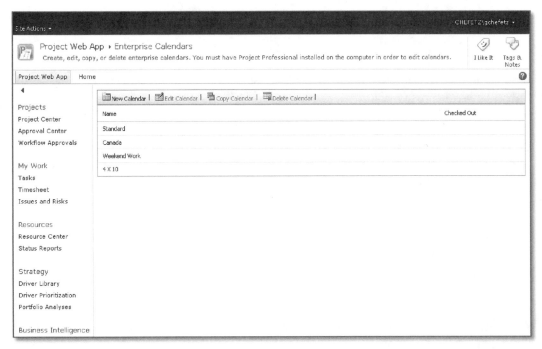

Figure 7 - 72: Enterprise Calendars page includes Weekend Work calendar

Module 08

Configuring Lifecycle Management

Learning Objectives

After completing this module, you will be able to:

- Understand Lifecycle Management

- Understand Demand Management

- Understand Decision Management

- Understand the configuration process for Lifecycle Management

- Create and manage new Enterprise Project Types

- Create Project Detail Pages (PDPs)

- Create new Phases and Stages

- Understand the Sample workflow

- Create and Manage Dynamic workflows

Inside Module 08

Understanding Lifecycle Management..**285**

    Understanding Demand Management...285

    Understanding Decision Management...285

    Understanding Project Types and Lifecycle Management...286

    Understanding Phases and Stages...287

    Understanding Project Detail Pages..288

    Understanding the Lifecycle Management Configuration Process...288

Creating Lifecycle Management Elements..**289**

    Creating and Editing Project Detail Pages..296

    Sample Project Detail Pages in Action...300

    Creating Business Drivers..304

    Configuring Workflow Phases...306

Configuring Workflow Stages 307

Creating Enterprise Project Templates **312**

Creating an Enterprise Project Template Manually 312

Creating and Modifying Enterprise Project Types... 314

Editing an Enterprise Project Type... 319

Working with the Sample Workflow..**319**

Adapting the Sample Workflow for Your Needs.. 327

Configuring Project Workflow Settings..**328**

Working with the Dynamic Workflow Solution Starter **329**

Deploying the Dynamic Workflow Solution Starter... 330

Creating and Configuring a Dynamic Workflow Instance 331

Considerations for Working with the Dynamic Workflow Tool.. 334

Understanding Lifecycle Management

One of the most exciting new capabilities Project Server 2010 provides is a sophisticated demand, decision making and lifecycle management system. This system allows your organization to capture project requests and work through a manual or automated procedure to collect information about proposed projects and ultimately use Project Server 2010's new Portfolio decision making tools to intelligently select the organization's portfolio of projects and then manage each project through an appropriate governance lifecycle.

Project Server 2010 provides a complete cradle-to-grave lifecycle management capability by combining a built-in proposal creation process with the decision-making tools that were formerly included with Microsoft Office Portfolio Server 2007, and the ability to govern the end-to-end process using a workflow that moves projects through a series of user-defined *Stages*. You can define lifecycles (workflows) to control all types of governance or process lifecycles.

The sample workflow that ships with Project Server 2010 uses the predefined enterprise custom fields I mentioned in the previous module with the names that start with the word *sample*. The system also contains pre-defined *Phases*, *Stages*, and *Project Detail Pages (PDPs)* used to construct an example of an end-to-end lifecycle. Microsoft provides this sample to help you understand how lifecycle management works, so I use this as my example for this module as well.

The highest form of automated governance you can achieve using Project Server 2010 is to apply workflows to your project types specifically customized for each type of project you allow into the system. With a workflow, you can automate business logic, interact with external data systems, and create multiple branching decision trees–all of this limited only by your development capabilities. Even when you use only simple linear workflows, you can establish powerful governance control of your organization's project lifecycle(s). To get up and running quickly with workflows in Project Server 2010, you can customize the sample workflow to some extent, you can explore 3rd-party solutions that provide graphical interfaces for building sophisticated workflows, or you can use Microsoft's Dynamic Workflow starter solution, which I cover later in this module.

Understanding Demand Management

Project Server 2010 provides you with the tools for very basic demand management without using workflows by providing the ability to display multiple *Project Detail Pages* in the project drilldown window in Project Web App. Those of you who have worked with earlier versions of Project Server will be astounded with the changes Microsoft made to this window, which now has the ability to display multiple project information pages as well as provide an interface to edit the project itself. The most basic form of demand management you can perform uses this window to display *Project Detail Pages* that expose required fields for a specific *Project Type*. When a user creates an instance of that *Project Type*, the system compels the user to fill in the required fields before completing the initial save. When you add workflows, you can build extremely complex demand and lifecycle management scenarios.

Understanding Decision Management

Project Server provides decision support tools integrated from previous versions of Portfolio Server. Unlike previous versions, you can use the Project Server Interface (PSI) to interact with the decision-making tools rather than being limited by the read-only API provided previously. To force projects through a selection process that includes a portfolio analysis step, you must govern your projects using a workflow. You can, of course, use the portfolio analysis capabilities without a workflow, without limiting your analysis ability, which is largely driven by the metadata you capture and create for use in your analyses. You may even choose to implement Project Server strictly for portfolio analysis and not for project management.

Understanding Project Types and Lifecycle Management

In Module 7, I introduced you to *Project Types*, which are a key element to the demand and lifecycle management story and an important consideration in determining your metadata requirements. In this module, you learn how to use these to build a demand and lifecycle management governance process for your organization. To refresh your memory, a *Project Type* consists of a *Project Template*, a set of *Project Detail* pages, an optional *Workflow* and a *Project Site* template. You can associate a *Project Type* with one or more departments in Project Server. Figure 8 - 1 shows an illustration of the collection of objects contained in the definition of a *Project Type*.

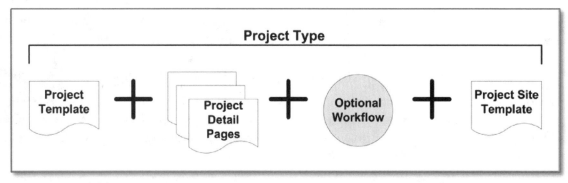

Figure 8 - 1: Project Type Representation

When an *Enterprise Project Type* does not have an associated workflow, an Administrator must specifiy the PDPs that display for the EPT. When an *Enterprise Project Type* does have a workflow, the display of PDPs is controlled by the workflow.

- A **Project Template** is a pre-built schedule model that ideally contains a well-structured schedule with generic resources assigned to tasks as well as duration and effort information that the author estimated in the template. To the degree that the template can eliminate manual schedule building, the more valuable it is to the managers who use them. When you do not specify a specific project template for a *Project Type*, the system uses a blank project template.

- **Project Detail Pages** are web-part based web pages that you create to display and collect project related information. You display *Project Detail Pages* in Project Server Web App in the Project drilldown window. You can control the display of PDPs using a workflow, or simply allow users to select through the pages manually without governing the order of their access using a workflow. *Project Detail Pages* can contain Project Server 2010 enterprise custom fields and other web parts that display information, or interact with data such as an Excel Services workbook. You can also create InfoPath forms and integrate them with PDPs programmatically. You must specify a *New Project Detail Page* for a Project Type.

- **Workflows** are code-based solutions that you can use to control the entire lifecycle flow of projects in Project Server 2010, from proposal through project closure. Workflows can contain very sophisticated business logic such as processing a project request through an automated criteria-based selection or rejection process. Complex workflows can contain multi-branching process logic and can interact with external data sources. Microsoft Project Server 2010 contains one sample workflow that is used with the *Sample Proposal* that ships with the system. The sample workflow interacts with the portfolio analysis and selection tool in Project Server 2010, forcing project approval through that process. The system requires a workflow to accomplish this. You can adapt the sample workflow to some extent through manipulating its contents; however, you must use Visual Studio to make programmatic changes to the source code, which is available in the Project Server 2010 SDK. Microsoft also provides a downloadable solution starter that builds dynamic workflows. This tool allows nonprogrammers to create simple, non-branching linear workflows complete with approval check points. I cover the sample workflow and solution starter in more depth later in this module. If you do not associate a workflow with a Project Type, the user manually selects from the *Project Detail Pages* defined by the administrator for the specific Project Type.

- **Project Site Templates** are what Project Server uses to create project sites for new projects (formerly named *Project Workspaces* in previous editions). You can build new project site templates to meet the specific requirements of your project types, rather than living with the one-size-fits-all model used in previous Project Server versions. It is important to build new project site templates based on the out-of-box standard project site template, as this contains custom web parts and modifications that support the documents, risks, issues and deliverables-management capabilities for project collaboration. Your customized templates can include features such as additional data presentation, pre-loaded content, and content integrated from external data sources. Your vision for these is bound only by the limits of SharePoint. See Module 17 to learn how to create a custom *Project Site* template. If you do not specify a *Project Site* template for a *Project Type*, the system uses the default *Project Site* template.

Understanding Phases and Stages

When you apply a workflow to a *Project Type*, you generally do so to establish governance of a complete project lifecycle. There is no limit to the lifecycles you can model using Project Server 2010, whether it be a manufacturing process or a methodological process such as a typical software development lifecycle (SDLC). To help you build and manage your lifecycles, Microsoft Project Server 2010 provides standard lifecycle elements *Phases* and *Stages*. *Phases* are a collection containing at least one *Stage* that contains at least one *Project Detail Page*. While *Phases* primarily serve as containers or groupings, *Stages* contain a number of properties and constituents that help you build your governance flow.

To view the built-in sample *Phases* and *Stages* Microsoft ships to support the sample work flow, from the *Server Settings* page, select the *Workflow Stages* link from the *Workflows and Project Details* section. The system displays the *Workflow Stages* page shown in Figure 8 - 2.

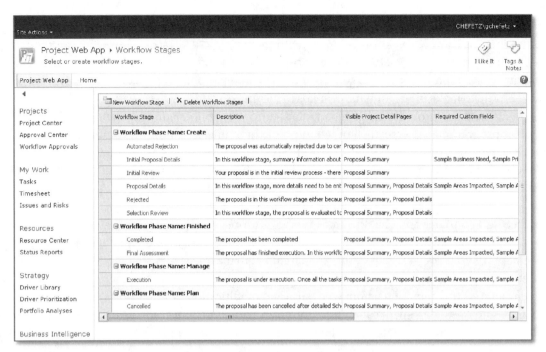

Figure 8 - 2: Workflow Stages page

Notice in the figure that the sample *Stages* are grouped by their respective *Phase*. Notice also that the *Create* workflow phase contains six stages: Automated Rejection, Initial Proposal Details, Initial Review, Proposed Details, Rejected and Selection Review. Each of these *Stages* represents a step in the sample workflow and contains at least one PDP. You can define *Project Detail Pages* in a variety of ways to include required fields as well as to apply automated progress control in and out of stages using workflow.

Understanding Project Detail Pages

The base element of the Phase/Stage construct is the *Project Detail Page* or PDP. A PDP is a special kind of web part page that you can display in the project drilldown window. Project Server 2010 provides a number of special web parts specifically for use within PDPs; however, you can also use standard SharePoint web parts like the *Content Editor* web part or the *Page Viewer* web part on PDP pages. You use *Project Detail Pages* both to display and collect information relevant to the stage and project to which you associate it. While *Stages* can contain more than one PDP, they must contain at least one PDP. You can associate PDPs with more than one stage. In fact it is common to always display a page that shows the current state of the workflow in every stage, it is also common to display the schedule page within numerous stages.

Understanding the Lifecycle Management Configuration Process

Now that you have a high-level understanding of the elements you use in Project Server 2010 to build a lifecycle management process and how they relate to each other, you should understand the logical order in which you need to create and configure these elements. In order to proceed with your configuration process, you need to create the building blocks first. I recommend that you configure Lifecycle Management elements in the following order:

1. Create the custom enterprise project fields you need to govern your lifecycle process.

2. Create the *Project Detail Pages* required to support your *Stages*.

3. Create your *Phases* and then *Stages*.

4. Create or import enterprise project templates.

5. Create *Project Site* templates.

6. Create workflows.

7. Create *Enterprise Project Types*.

MSProjectExperts recommends that you fully map out your project types and workflow processes before you begin creating elements to support them, otherwise you are likely to find yourself having to account for changes across many objects when you make even a simple change to one.

Creating Lifecycle Management Elements

Because Module 07 is devoted to custom field creation, I do not cover that subject again in this module. Instead I assume that you are comfortable with that process, and have already created the enterprise custom fields you need to create your own custom workflow or to enhance the sample workflow. Before I show you how to create PDPs, you should understand how *Project Detail Pages* display in Project Web App and how they can be controlled by workflow. I use the sample workflow and its associated *Phases, Stages* and *Project Detail Pages* for demonstration purposes throughout this section.

From the Project Web App Quick Launch menu, select the *Project Center* link from the *Project* section. The system displays the *Project Center* shown in Figure 8 - 3.

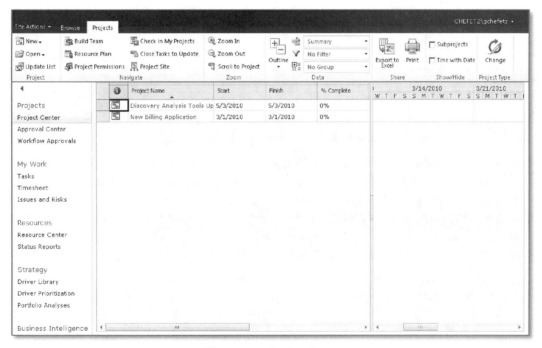

Figure 8 - 3: Project Center

To invoke the sample workflow you must create a new project of the sample project type by using the *New* menu in the upper left on the *Projects* ribbon and selecting the *Sample Proposal* item from the pick list shown in Figure 8 - 4.

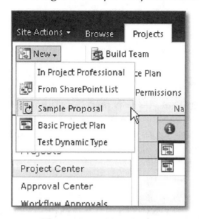

Figure 8 - 4: New menu

When you click on the selection, the system starts a new instance of the *Sample Proposal* workflow and displays the first *Project Detail Page* shown in Figure 8 - 5.

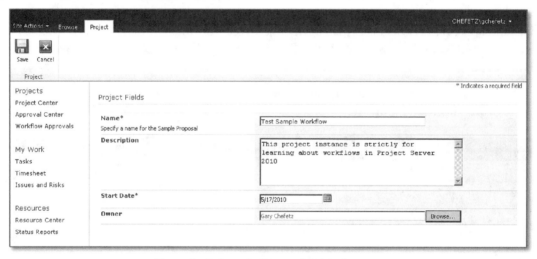

Figure 8 - 5: Sample Proposal Initiation page

Notice that this page contains only three fields accepting user entry, *Name, Description* and *Start Date.* Notice, also, the asterisks at the end of the *Name* field and *Start Date* field, which indicate that these are marked as required. You cannot save your entries on this page until you provide information in these fields. After you complete your entries, click the *Save* button in the *Project* section of the *Project* ribbon. Note that after clicking the button, the system displays a series of messages in upper right hand corner of the screen to indicate that it is working on your request. The fist message you see is *Processing* followed by *Creating Sample Proposal* as shown in Figure 8 - 6.

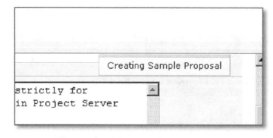

Figure 8 - 6: Processing messages

When the processing completes, the system displays the *Workflow Status* page shown in Figure 8 - 7. This is the second *Project Detail Page* that the system displays in this particular workflow process. You determine what pages display in each phase and stage of the project workflow.

Figure 8 - 7: Workflow Status page

Keep in mind that you are still looking at and working in the project drilldown window in Project Web App, which now displays multiple pages for a single project. Notice that above the top left section of the Quick Launch you now see an additional navigation section for the project that you are in the process of creating, in my case "Test Sample Workflow," and that the project displays as selected in the menu. Every stage in a workflow must have a *Workflow Status* page. You can use the one provided in the system or make your own. The *Workflow Status* page always displays by default when you first enter a stage. Below the project name selection is another link, *Proposal Summary*. This link corresponds with the one shown in the table in the middle of the page in the *Available Pages in this Workflow Stage* section. All *Project Detail Pages* that are available for the current stage are accessible from either the left hand navigation or the *Workflow Status* page when it is included in the stage. When you click the link in one of the sections, the system displays the selected *Project Detail Page*. In this case, the *Proposal Summary* is shown selected in Figure 8 - 8.

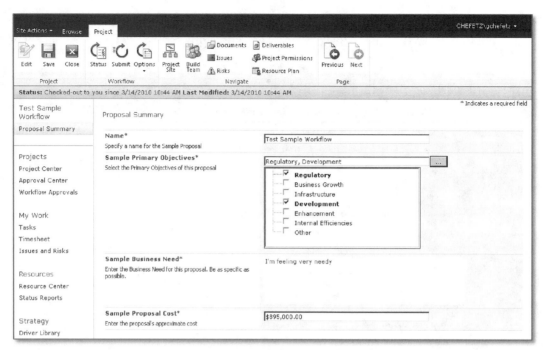

Figure 8 - 8: Proposal Summary page

Enter your own clever choices and remarks in these fields, including a value in the *Sample Proposal Cost* field that is below one million dollars. It is very important that you **do not enter a value over a million dollars** if you wish to completely work through the sample workflow, as crossing this cost threshold will cause your project to be automatically rejected. I selected the *Regulatory* item from the *Sample Primary Objective* area. Notice the options available in the *Project* and *Workflow* sections of the *Project* ribbon. At this point you can save your information and submit it later, or you can save and then click the *Submit* button. To proceed to the next workflow stage, click the *Submit* button. The system displays the *Message from webpage* dialog shown in Figure 8 - 9.

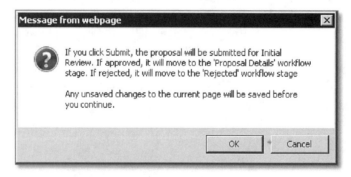

Figure 8 - 9: Message from webpage

Click the *OK* button to continue. The system accepts your input and moves the workflow to an approval checkpoint where an authorized approver must approve the initial request before it moves to the next stage in the workflow. To both view and approve the request, select the *Workflow Approvals* link from the *Projects* section of the Quick Launch menu. The system displays the *Project Server Workflow Tasks My Tasks* page, which contains the *Workflow Approvals* page, shown in Figure 8 - 10.

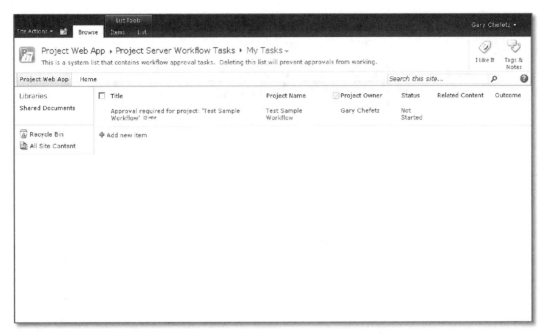

Figure 8 - 10: Workflow Approvals page

Notice the *Approval required for project: 'Test Sample Workflow'* item that appears on the list. Note also that this is a standard SharePoint task list. Hover over the item to reveal the checkbox next to the item and select the checkbox. The page display changes to reveal the *Workflow Approvals* ribbon shown in Figure 8 - 11.

Figure 8 - 11: Workflow Approvals page with item selected

After you select the item, the *List Tools* ribbon appears. Select the *Edit Item* button from the *Manage* section of the ribbon. The system opens the item for editing in the dialog shown in Figure 8 - 12.

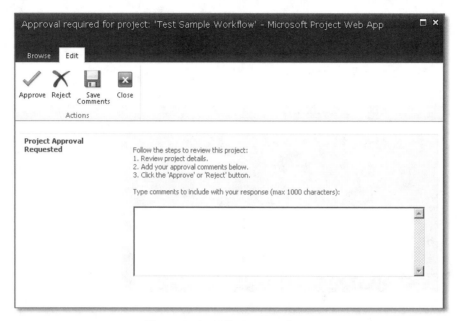

Figure 8 - 12: Edit Approval Item

The *Sample Workflow* requires that one person with approval rights approve the request. The system also supports *Majority* and *Consensus* approval types. Notice that you can approve, reject, or simply add and save comments before closing the item. In this case, you want to select the *Approve* button from the *Actions* section of the ribbon to approve the request and move it forward in the workflow. The system redisplays the *Workflow Approvals* page, which now shows that the request has been approved to move to the next workflow stage after the *Initial Request* stage as shown in Figure 8 - 13.

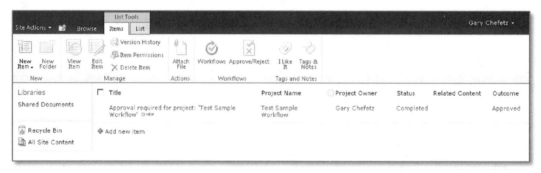

Figure 8 - 13: Workflow request approved

Once approved, the project proposal advances to the *Proposal Details* stage, which displays five *Project Detail Pages* in addition to the *Workflow Status* page as shown in Figure 8 - 14. Notice the series of pages listed in the left-hand navigation as well as the grid in the *Available Pages in this Workflow Stage* section of the page. Notice the status of each page in the grid display. Before you can advance to the next workflow stage, you must complete the pages marked as incomplete. After completing the required information for all of the PDPs shown in the *Proposal Details* stage, the workflow moves the project into the *Select* phase, where the workflow waits for selection using the portfolio analysis tools where your new project must be committed to the portfolio before you can move on to the *Planning* phase.

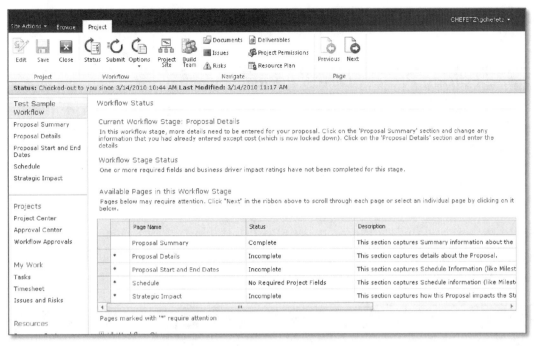

Figure 8 - 14: Project Details Workflow Stage

Behind the scenes, the workflow has already processed some custom business logic included in the automated rejection stage. The stages of the workflow that you advanced through are as shown in Figure 8 - 15.

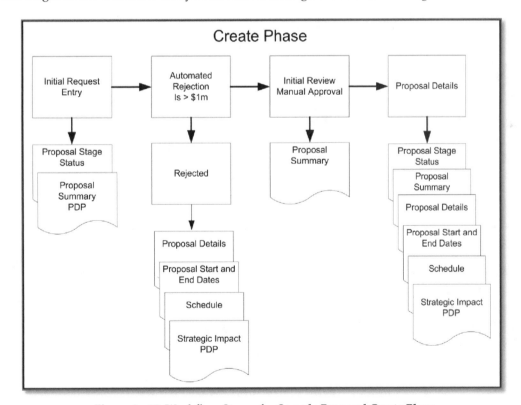

Figure 8 - 15: Workflow Stages for Sample Proposal Create Phase

Behind the scenes, the system created a project file, in this case the default blank project file because the sample does not specify an enterprise project template. It also created a *Project Site* using the custom enterprise template specified for the workflow; in this case it used the default *Project Site* template because the sample does not specify a custom *Project Site* template.

Creating and Editing Project Detail Pages

Now that you have a sampling of how you move through stages in a project using Project Detail Pages, it is time to explore creating and maintaining these pages in Project Server 2010. Before you can organize your process into phases and stages, you must first create the *Project Detail Pages* used in each stage of the workflow. During each stage, users enter, modify, review, or process data on the *Project Detail Page(s)* used in that Stage. To create a new *Project Detail Page* or edit an existing one, complete the following steps:

1. Click the *Server Settings* link in the Quick Launch menu.

2. Click the *Project Detail Pages* link in the *Workflow and Project Detail Pages* section of the *Server Settings* page.

The system displays the *Project Detail Pages* library shown in Figure 8 - 16. Notice that the *Project Detail Pages* library contains nine default *Project Detail Pages* used in Project Server 2010.

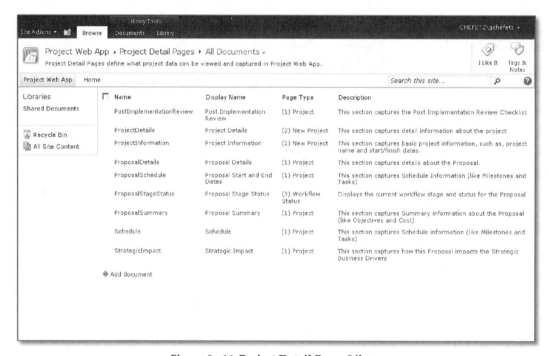

Figure 8 - 16: Project Detail Pages Library

3. Click the *Documents* tab in *Library Tools* super section on the ribbon menu. The system displays the *Documents* ribbon menu on the page as shown in Figure 8 - 17. Notice that I selected the *PostImplementationReview* page in the document list in order to light-up the button on the *Documents* Ribbon. Notice also that there is an additional *Library* menu tab. This is a standard menu for working with elements of a document library in SharePoint. I cover working with standard SharePoint menus in Module 17.

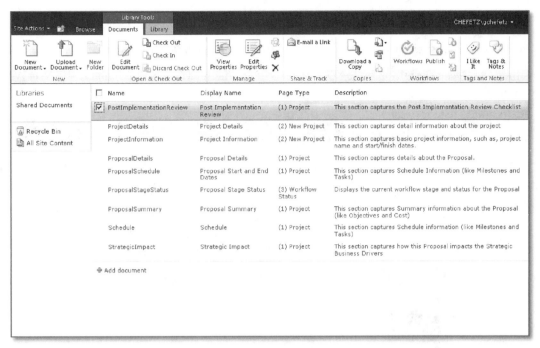

Figure 8 - 17: Documents Ribbon options

4. Click the *Edit Properties* button from the *Manage* section of the *Documents* ribbon. The system displays the *Project Details Pages properties* dialog shown in Figure 8 - 18.

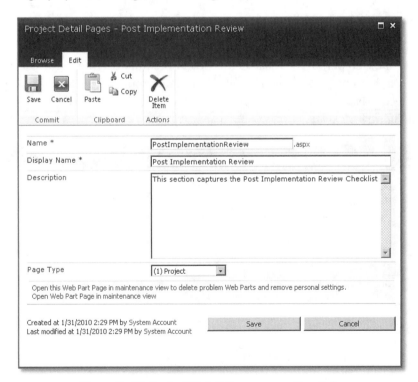

Figure 8 - 18: Project Detail Pages properties dialog

5. Notice the pick list in the *Page Type* section. The available *Page Types* include:

    - **Project**: Use for PDPs that display during the execution of a project including closing a project.

- **New Project:** Use for PDPs that display during the create project or proposal stages.

- **Workflow Status**: Use for PDPs that display the *Workflow Status* web part.

6. Click the *New Document* button on the *Documents* ribbon menu. The system displays the *New Web Part Page* shown in Figure 8 - 19.

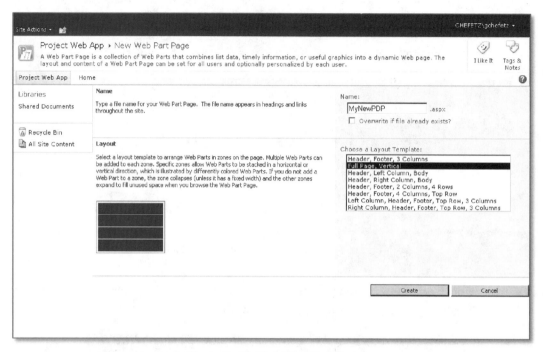

Figure 8 - 19: New Web Part Page

7. Enter a name for the web part in the *Name* field, choose a template in the *Choose a Layout Template* list, and then click the *Create* button. You can use any layout that suits your specific needs, however selecting the *Full Page, Vertical* selection is a practical choice for most PDP pages. The system displays the new blank web part page shown in Figure 8 - 20.

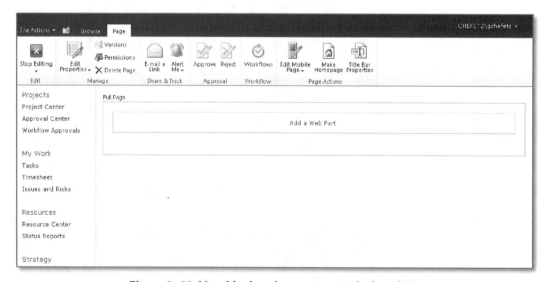

Figure 8 - 20: New blank web part page ready for editing

8. Click the *Add a Web Part* link in the center of the page. The system redisplays the page to show the SharePoint web part gallery shown in Figure 8 - 21.

Figure 8 - 21: SharePoint Web Part Gallery

9. In the list of web part categories on the left side of the display, select the *Project Web App* folder to see the web parts that are specifically designed for use with Project Web App. Several of these are designed specifically for use with *Project Detail Pages* as follows:

-   **Project Details** web part allows you to drill down into a project's schedule. You use this web part when you view or edit a schedule in Project Web App.

-   **Project Fields** web part displays project custom fields, project summary fields, and project intrinsic fields such as project name and description. Users can edit these fields when they are enabled in a *Project Detail Page*.

-   **Project Fields (Backwards Compatible)** web part emulates the Project Server 2007 *Edit Project Properties* page. Use this web part for *Project Detail Pages* when your system is running in backwards compatibility mode (BCM).

-   **Project Strategic Impact** web part allows users to set the business driver priorities for a specific project. Use this web part to collect strategic impact data for use with portfolio analysis.

-   **Workflow Status** web part displays important data about the workflow status of a project that is subject to workflow management. You typically make this web part available on a page at almost every stage of a web flow.

10. In the list of web parts that ship with Project Server 2010, select a web part and then click the *Add* button. You are not limited to using the web parts provided specifically for *Project Detail Pages*. You can use generic SharePoint Server 2010 web parts as well as custom web parts you can obtain from third parties. To illustrate

this, in the example shown in Figure 8 - 22, I selected the *Excel Web Access* web part from the *Business Data* folder and pointed it at the *Resource Capacity* sample report before clicking the *Stop Editing* button from the *Page* ribbon.

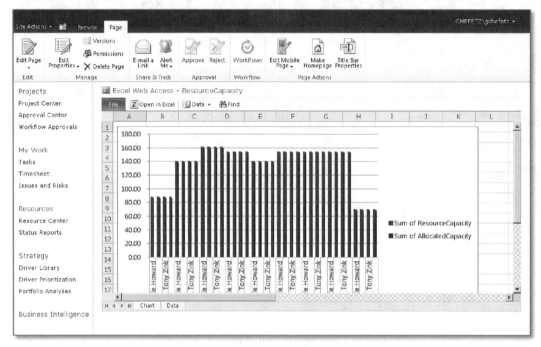

Figure 8 - 22: Completed New Project Details Page

You can use this technique to connect *Project Detail Pages* to other content in the PWA site collection or other trusted data sources. For instance, you might design your *Project Site* template for a specific project type to include a pre-populated cost benefit analysis Excel workbook. You can then create a *Project Detail Page* that exposes this in a stage during the lifecycle workflow. Consider how powerful this construct becomes. When you build new *Project Detail Pages*, there is no real limit on what you can achieve by using the correct web parts and a workflow to govern the stage transitions.

Sample Project Detail Pages in Action

The sample workflow that you started earlier in this module is now in the *Proposal Details* stage, a point at which numerous PDPs are exposed, many of which require attention from the user. You must provide required information before the system will allow you to submit your proposal to the next stage of the workflow unless your proposal was already rejected by either the automated or manual initial selection process. When you select your started proposal from the *Project Center*, your started proposal should open to the *Proposal Status Page* shown previously in Figure 8 - 14. Notice that there are three pages marked as incomplete and one that has no required fields. Select the *Proposal Details* link from either the left hand navigation or the grid in the middle of the page. The system displays the *Sample Proposal Details* page shown in Figure 8 - 23.

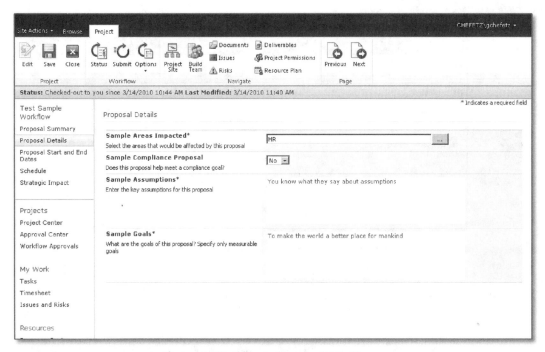

Figure 8 - 23: Sample Proposal Details page

The *Sample Proposal Details* page uses the *Project Fields* web part set to display only the fields that you see in the previous figure. If you put the page into edit mode and put the web part into edit mode, you can see how simple this configuration is, as shown in Figure 8 - 24. Notice that only the fields selected in the *Displayed Project Fields* window show in the *Project Detail Page*.

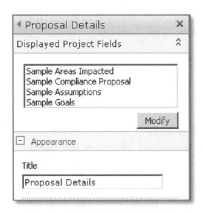

Figure 8 - 24: Project Details
web part panel

To make changes to the web part when you use it in your own *Project Detail Pages,* click the *Modify* button to open the *Choose Project Fields* dialog shown in Figure 8 - 25.

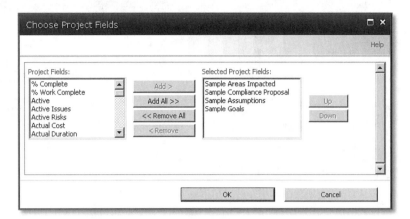

Figure 8 - 25: Choose Project Fields dialog

To continue your tour of the sample workflow, add entries to the page and use the *Save* button on the *Project* ribbon to save your entries on each page. The next page that requires attention is the *Proposal Start and End Dates* page shown in Figure 8 - 26.

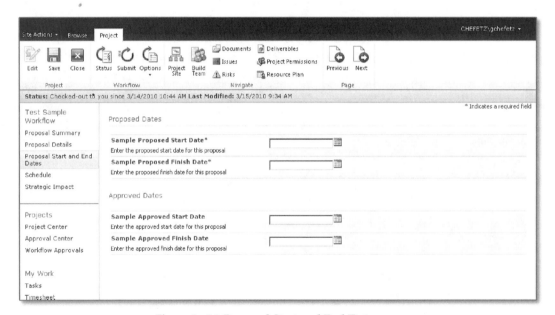

Figure 8 - 26: Proposal Start and End Dates page

This page also uses the *Project Fields* web part to display four custom enterprise project fields. Provide information in the required fields marked with an asterisk and click the *Save* button to save your entries. Click on the *Schedule* page link and the system displays the *Schedule* page shown in Figure 8 - 27.

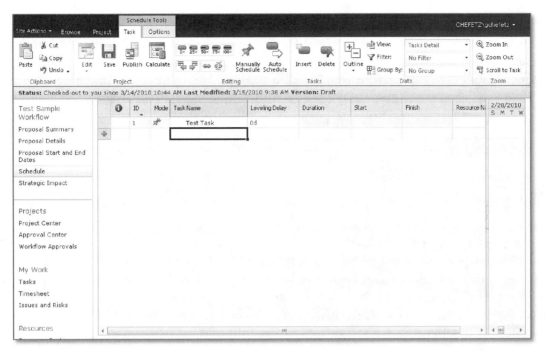

Figure 8 - 27: Schedule Page

The *Schedule* page is an out of the box *Project Detail Page* that uses the *Project Details* web part to expose the project schedule for editing. Notice in Figure 8 - 27 that I entered a "Test Task" name to create a single task in the new schedule. You must expose this page during any workflow stage that allows users to edit the project, including early planning stages and while the project is managed through its active lifecycle. At this point in the workflow, there is no requirement for the project to have a developed schedule and there are no required entries for this page. If the sample workflow had an enterprise project template attached, the template schedule would display now. When you click on the *Strategic Impact* link on the left hand menu, the system opens the *Strategic Impact* page shown in Figure 8 - 28.

Figure 8 - 28: Strategic Impact page

The *Strategic Impact* page is a PDP that contains the *Project Strategic Impact* web part. The purpose of this web part is to allow the users to rank the project based on its impact on the organization's Strategic Business Drivers that you must define for your organization. The *Project Strategic Impact* web part displays the appropriate business drivers based on the department that the *Project Type* and Business Drivers are assigned to. This is an important web part to include in your workflow if you intend to analyze your portfolio using strategic alignment analysis. The sample workflow includes this page because it is designed to use the portfolio analysis capability to select the projects to execute. Because the system does not include any predefined business drivers, you must create some before you can submit your new proposal into the selection process.

Creating Business Drivers

In order to advance your sample workflow and to use the portfolio analysis engine to align your portfolio selection to your business strategy, you must create some business drivers. Notice in Figure 8 - 28 shown previously that I defined two business drivers that are very typical business strategies: *Launch New Products* and *Open New Markets*. Other common business drivers include: Increase Employee Satisfaction, Increase Customer Satisfaction, Improve Product Quality, Improve Service Quality, etc. Defining business drivers is not an administrative function, and you must have input from C-level management to make this effective at the enterprise level. You can also deploy and use portfolio analysis at the departmental level, and this requires input from all of VP and Director-level management to create an effective set of business drivers.

It is not surprising, then, that the path to defining business drivers is not through the *Server Settings* page. Rather, you access these by selecting the *Driver Library* link from the *Strategy* section of the Quick Launch menu. The system displays the *Driver Library* page shown in Figure 8 - 29.

Figure 8 - 29: Driver Library page

The *Driver Library* page allows you to create, edit and delete business drivers. To create a new business driver, click the *New* button in the *Driver* section of the *Driver* ribbon. The system displays the *New Business Driver* page shown in Figure 8 - 30. Enter a name and description in the appropriate fields. Next you must select the departments that this business driver applies to. You can create a business driver that applies to the entire company or to only specific departments. In order to use departmental filtering, you should have your departments defined before creating content in Project Server 2010 that requires this filtering. When you do not assign a department, the business driver applies to all users. Notice in the *Status* section that you can deactivate a driver by selecting the *Inactive* button. You want to make a driver inactive when you no longer need it for future analysis, but need to preserve it for historical data purposes such as reviewing historic data analyses. Finally, you should enter *Project Impact Statements* to help your users understand how to use the business driver. While these can be abstract as the example in the figure, they can also contain metrics. For instance, *Project Impact Statements* for a Grow Revenue business driver might define a low impact as having less than $500K growth impact, while moderate might be defined as between $500K and $1M, and so on. Click the *Save and Close* button on the *Driver* ribbon to save and close your new business driver.

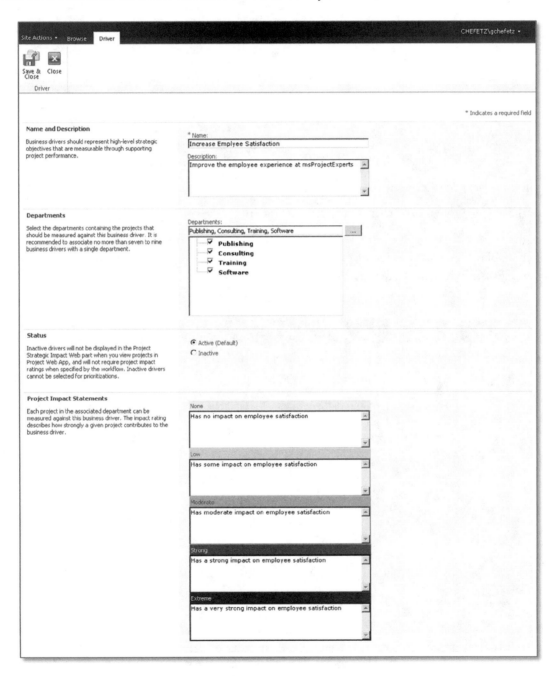

Figure 8 - 30: New Business Driver page

After configuring a few sample business drivers, return to your instance of the sample workflow and complete your required entries on each PDP, using the *Save* button to save your entries on each page. When you complete your entries, click the *Submit* button to submit your new project for *Proposal Selection*, the next stage in the workflow.

Configuring Workflow Phases

Phases are an organizational unit for a collection of workflow stages. In Project Server 2010, you associate stages with phases, each of which represents a step in the workflow process. The default phases in the system support the Sample Proposal workflow. In the order in which you work through the workflow, these include:

- Create

- Select

- Plan

- Manage

- Finished

To view the system's default phases, or to create a new phase, complete the following steps:

1. Log into Project Web Access with administrator permissions.

2. Click the *Server Settings* link in the Quick Launch menu.

3. Click the *Workflow Phases* link in the *Workflow and Project Detail Pages* section of the *Server Settings* page. The system displays the *Workflow Phases* page shown in Figure 8 - 31. Notice that the page displays five sample *Workflow Phases*, which are Create, Finished, Manage, Plan, and Select. Note that the system displays the default phases in alphabetical order rather than logical sequential order.

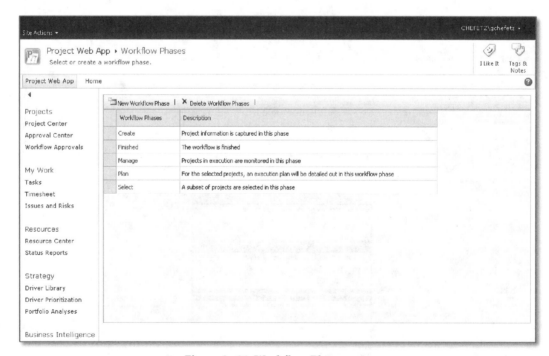

Figure 8 - 31: Workflow Phases page

If your organization needs to define a new phase for a workflow, click the *New Workflow Phase* button on the toolbar. The system displays the *Add Workflow Phase* page shown in Figure 8 - 32.

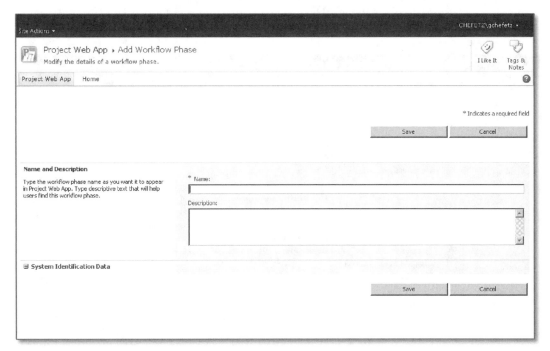

Figure 8 - 32: Add Workflow Phase page

To create the new *Phase*, enter the name of the *Phase* in the *Name* field and enter an optional description in the *Description* field. Click the *Save* button when finished. As you can see, a *Phase* is nothing more than a grouping item containing a name, optional description and a system identification number in the form of a system-assigned GUID. Workflows reference stages by their GUIDs and not their names. Therefore, deleting one of the pre-defined phases or stages will break the sample workflow. Simply recreating the stage or phase by the same name will not restore this functionality. If you save your new phase, the system displays the new Phase on the *Workflow Phases* page, shown previously in Figure 8 - 31.

To edit an existing *Phase*, click the name of the *Phase*. The system displays the selected *Phase* in editing mode. With the exception of the title, the page looks identical to the *Add Workflow* page shown previously in Figure 8 - 32. You can change the *Name* field and *Description* field for a phase without breaking the sample workflow.

Configuring Workflow Stages

Workflow stages allow you to configure the way users interact with workflow transitions and *Project Detail Pages*. Each stage represents a step in the workflow process. Each stage uses one or more *Project Detail Pages* to display or capture the information during that stage. Stages contain characteristics and properties that affect the way the *Project Detail Pages* behave and how the workflow interacts with users. To better understand how these interrelate, follow these steps:

1. From the *Server Settings* page, select the *Workflow Stages* link from the *Workflow and Project Detail Pages* section of the page. The system displays the *Workflow Stages* page shown in Figure 8 - 33.

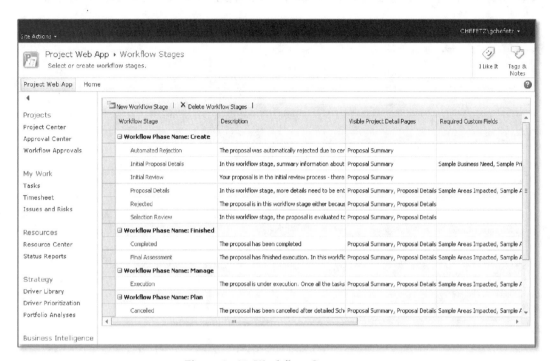

Figure 8 - 33: Workflow Stages page

2. From the grid, click on the *Initial Proposal Details* stage to open the stage for editing as shown in Figure 8 - 34 and Figure 8 - 35. I break these into two images to accommodate the length.

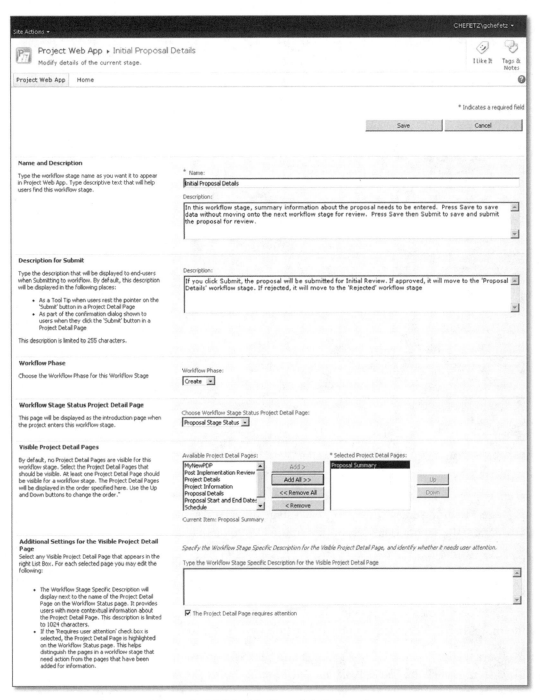

Figure 8 - 34: Modify Stage details top of page

Module 08

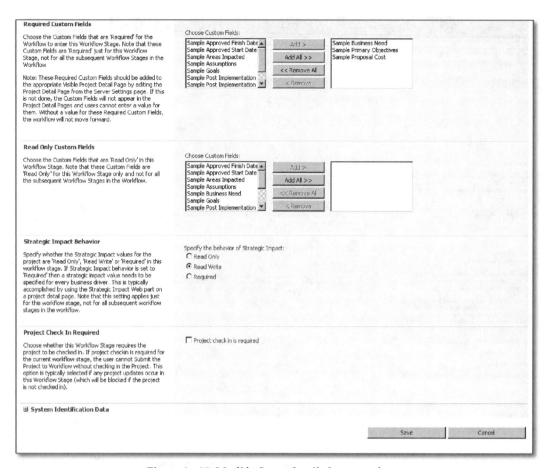

Figure 8 - 35: Modify Stage details bottom of page

The workflow stage page is the same for creating new stages and editing existing ones. Whether you are creating a new workflow stage, or editing an existing stage, each stage must be assigned to a *Phase*. Enter the name of the Stage in the *Name* field, and enter an optional description in the *Description* field.

The *Description for Submit* section contains a second *Description* field into which you enter the description that Project Server 2010 displays when a user clicks the *Submit* button to move beyond the current stage. The system displays your description as a Tooltip when the user floats the mouse pointer over the *Submit* button, and displays the text you enter here in the confirmation dialog shown previously in Figure 8 - 9 after the user clicks the *Submit* button. The system limits you to no more than 255 characters in the description you enter in this section *Description* field.

In the *Workflow Phase* section, click the *Phase* pick list and select the phase for the stage. In the *Workflow Stage Status Project Detail Page* section, click the *Choose Workflow Stage Status Project Detail Page* pick list and choose a *Project Detail Page* that is the *Workflow Status* Type and contains the *Workflow Status* web part from the list. The system always makes this page visible during this stage of the workflow process. The example uses the *Proposal Stage Status* project detail page that ships with the product.

In the *Visible Project Detail Pages* section, you select the *Project Detail Pages* you want visible to users during this stage of the workflow process. By default, the system selects no *Project Detail Pages* other than the *Workflow Stage Status Detail Page* you selected, so you must select at least one *Project Detail Page* you need to support your data gathering and communication for this stage, because a stage cannot have only a *Workflow Status* page and no others. You can select each *Project Detail Page* individually or use multi-selection techniques in the *Available Project Detail Pages* list and then click the *Add* button to add your selected pages to the list on the right. After adding the first page or all of your pages, you should enter a description for the page in the *Type the Workflow Stage Specific Description for the Visible Project Detail*

310

Page text field. Note that the value changes for this field as you select each page in the right hand side of the *Choose Project Detail Pages* section. The system displays the *Stage Specific Description* with the name of the *Project Detail Page* in the *Workflow Status* page. The system limits you to no more than 1,024 characters in the description. If you need to mandate the user to take action in the *Project Detail Page*, select the option checkbox named *The Project Detail Page requires attention*. After completing this process for the first *Project Detail Page* in the *Visible Project Detail Pages* section, repeat the process for each additional *Project Detail Page* you added to this Stage. The system allows you to enter a *Stage Specific Description* and to select the option checkbox for each *Project Detail Page* individually.

The *Required Custom Fields* section allows you determine the behavior of the fields in the *Project Details Pages* and the stage. To make fields required for this stage, select one or more custom fields in the *Choose Custom Fields* list and then click the *Add* button to add them to the list on the right. If you want to include all of the available custom fields, click the *Add All* button.

Warning: *The Project Detail Page(s)* used in this stage must include the custom fields you select in the *Required Custom Fields* section. If you fail to include these custom fields in *the Project Detail Page(s)*, users cannot enter required values, and Project Server 2010 does not allow the workflow process to continue beyond this stage.

In the *Read Only Custom Fields* section, choose the fields that the system displays as read-only during this workflow stage. Select one or more custom fields in the *Choose Custom Fields* list and then click the *Add* button to add them to the list on the right. If you want to include all of the available custom fields, click the *Add All* button. When you mark a field as read-only for a stage, the field will not be editable when displayed in the *Project Details* web part on any *Project Detail Page* included in this stage. *Required* and *read-only* attributes for fields are an important control in managing the information flow within your workflow.

In the *Strategic Impact Behavior* section, the system allows you to specify the behavior of *Strategic Impact* values for the project proposal. Select the *Read Only* option or *Read Write* option as you require. If you select the *Required* option, users must select a *Strategic Impact* value for **every** Business Driver in order to determine strategic alignment using portfolio analysis.

If you select the *Required* option in the *Strategic Impact Behavior* section, make sure that you included the *Strategic Impact* web part on at least one of the Project Detail Page(s) used in this Stage.

In the *Project Check In Required* section, you must choose whether the stage requires the user to check in the project. If you select the *Project check in is required* option, the user cannot submit the project Proposal to the workflow without first checking in the project. You typically select this option if any updates occur to the project Proposal in this Stage. If you select the *Project check in is required* option and the user does not check in the project proposal, Project Server 2010 prevents the user from submitting the project to the next stage in the workflow. One reason for setting this flag is to allow the workflow to modify the project. If your workflow edits the project after the user hits submit, the project must first be checked in. Otherwise, the workflow cannot check out the project, edit it, then check it back in. Setting this option is also a good way to ensure that the project is available for editing by the next person who needs to work the project through the next workflow stage. If you do not require the check in, you may find that you have a lot of people complaining that they can't edit the project to shepherd it though the next stage. Click the *Save* button when you complete your entries to save your new stage or modified stage.

Creating Enterprise Project Templates

Before you create your enterprise *Project Types*, you may want to create or import the enterprise project templates for use with your enterprise *Project Types*. To take full advantage of the power of *Project Types*, you should create a corresponding enterprise project template for each enterprise *Project Type*. As the Project Server administrator, you can create an enterprise project template in one of two ways:

- Create the enterprise project template manually.

- Import an existing project as an enterprise project template.

Before you attempt to create or import enterprise project templates, msProjectExperts recommends that you enlist the aid of key project managers and executives to determine which types of projects must be governed through workflow. Once you determine your requirements, ask your project managers to help in the creation of appropriate enterprise project templates.

Creating an Enterprise Project Template Manually

To create an enterprise project template from scratch, launch Project Professional 2010 and log in to Project Server. Create a project template according to your organization's project standards. At a minimum, your enterprise project templates should contain the following elements:

- Project tasks with duration estimates.

- Summary tasks to organize the tasks into phase and deliverable sections.

- Milestone tasks to represent significant points in the project.

- Task dependencies linking tasks to one another.

- Task notes, where applicable.

- Generic Resources assigned to tasks.

Including generic resources with effort estimates, if applicable, reduces the workload on your project schedulers when creating a new project from the template. At the very least, add generic resources to the project team and assign them to tasks to indicate the skill types required for each task. Your enterprise project template **should never** include constraints or deadline dates on tasks, as your project managers need to add these according to the requirements for each individual production project.

When you finish creating the template, click File ➤ Save. The system displays the *Save to Project Server* dialog shown in Figure 8 - 36.

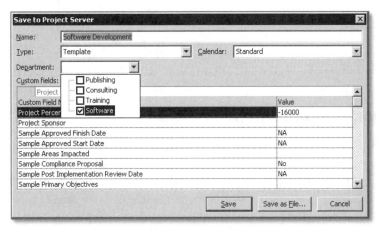

Figure 8 - 36: Save to Project Server dialog

In the *Save to Project Server* dialog, enter a name for the enterprise project template in the *Name* field. Click the *Type* pick list and select the *Template* item from the list. Select a *Calendar* value if the template uses a project calendar other than the *Standard* calendar. Optionally, enter default custom field information in the *Custom fields* section and assign the template to the same department as its intended *Project Type*. In the example above, I am saving a new template for *Software Development* that will be visible to members of the *Software* department only. Ultimately, I will assign this to a new *Project Type* I am creating called *Software Development* as well.

When you save a project as an enterprise template, the system does not force you to enter values in required fields. If you choose to enter values in any custom enterprise fields, these become the default values for new projects created from the template. Project managers can then change these values when creating a new project. To guarantee that project managers supply a value for all required enterprise fields, do not enter any value in the required fields when you save the enterprise template. This forces your project managers to enter values in those fields before they can save an enterprise project in the Project Server database.

Click the *Save* button. The system displays the *Save As Template* dialog shown in Figure 8 - 37.

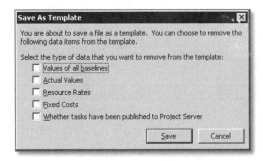

Figure 8 - 37: Save As Template dialog

In the *Save As Template* dialog, select as many options as are appropriate. If you are saving a template based on a completed production project, you may wish to select every option in the *Save As Template* dialog. If your template contains planned Fixed Costs in the task Costs table, do not select the *Fixed Costs* option. Because I am creating a new template, I do not need to select any of these options. Click the *Save* button to save your new enterprise project template.

313

You can also import an enterprise project template or existing project schedule as a template using the *Import Wizard*. Using the wizard gives you the ability to map local custom fields and resources to enterprise fields and resources. The wizard also forces some integrity checking on the schedule; however, I do not cover importing projects and templates in this module. You learn about this technique and other tactics for building your project environment in Module 13.

Creating and Modifying Enterprise Project Types

Typically, organizations manage multiple types of projects, such as IT projects, engineering projects, HR projects, new product development projects, etc. In fact, each of these departments may have several types of projects that they manage. To meet the lifecycle management needs of an organization, Project Server 2010 allows you to create multiple enterprise project types to address each specific requirement. Each enterprise project type can include an enterprise project template, a workflow, a collection of project detail pages and an enterprise project site template. Project Server 2010 ships with two enterprise project types:

- Sample Proposal
- Basic Project Plan

The *Sample Proposal* template includes a workflow process, while the *Basic Project Plan* template does not include a workflow or custom elements. Beyond these two enterprise project types, you can create one or more additional project types to meet your organization's lifecycle management needs. To create a new *Enterprise Project Type*, complete the following steps:

1. Log into Project Web Access with administrator permissions.
2. Click the *Server Settings* link in the Quick Launch menu.
3. Click the *Enterprise Project Types* link in the *Workflow and Project Detail Pages* section of the *Server Settings* page.

The system displays the *Enterprise Project Types* page shown in Figure 8 - 38. Notice that the page displays the two default enterprise project types available in Project Server 2010, plus one additional type that I created.

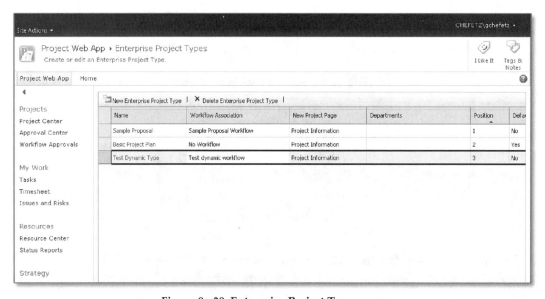

Figure 8 - 38: Enterprise Project Types page

4. To create a new *Project Type*, click the *New Enterprise Project Type* button. The system displays the *Add Enterprise Project Type* page shown in Figure 8 - 39. The *Add Enterprise Project Type* page contains ten sections in which you must edit or select configuration information for the new project type.

Enter a name for the Enterprise Project Type in the *Name* field and enter an optional description in the *Description* field. Click the *Site Workflow Association* pick list and select a workflow to associate with the enterprise project type. The pick list includes only two default Workflows:

- Sample Proposal Workflow

- No Workflow

If you need additional workflows, you must create the workflows in Visual Studio or by using another tool that is capable of building SharePoint workflows. You must then deploy you new workflow(s) to the server hosting Project Server 2010. To associate a workflow with the enterprise project type, select a workflow from the *Site Workflow Association* pick list.

If you select the default *Sample Proposal Workflow* or other workflow in the *Site Workflow Association* pick list, the system allows you to choose only a single option in the *New Project Page/Project Detail Pages section* pick list. In a freshly installed Project Server instance, the *Project Information* item is your only choice. If you created additional pages that are *New Project Types*, the selector populates with these pages as well. When attaching to a workflow, this option represents the first project detail page that users see when they create a new project proposal in the *Project Center* page using your new enterprise project type.

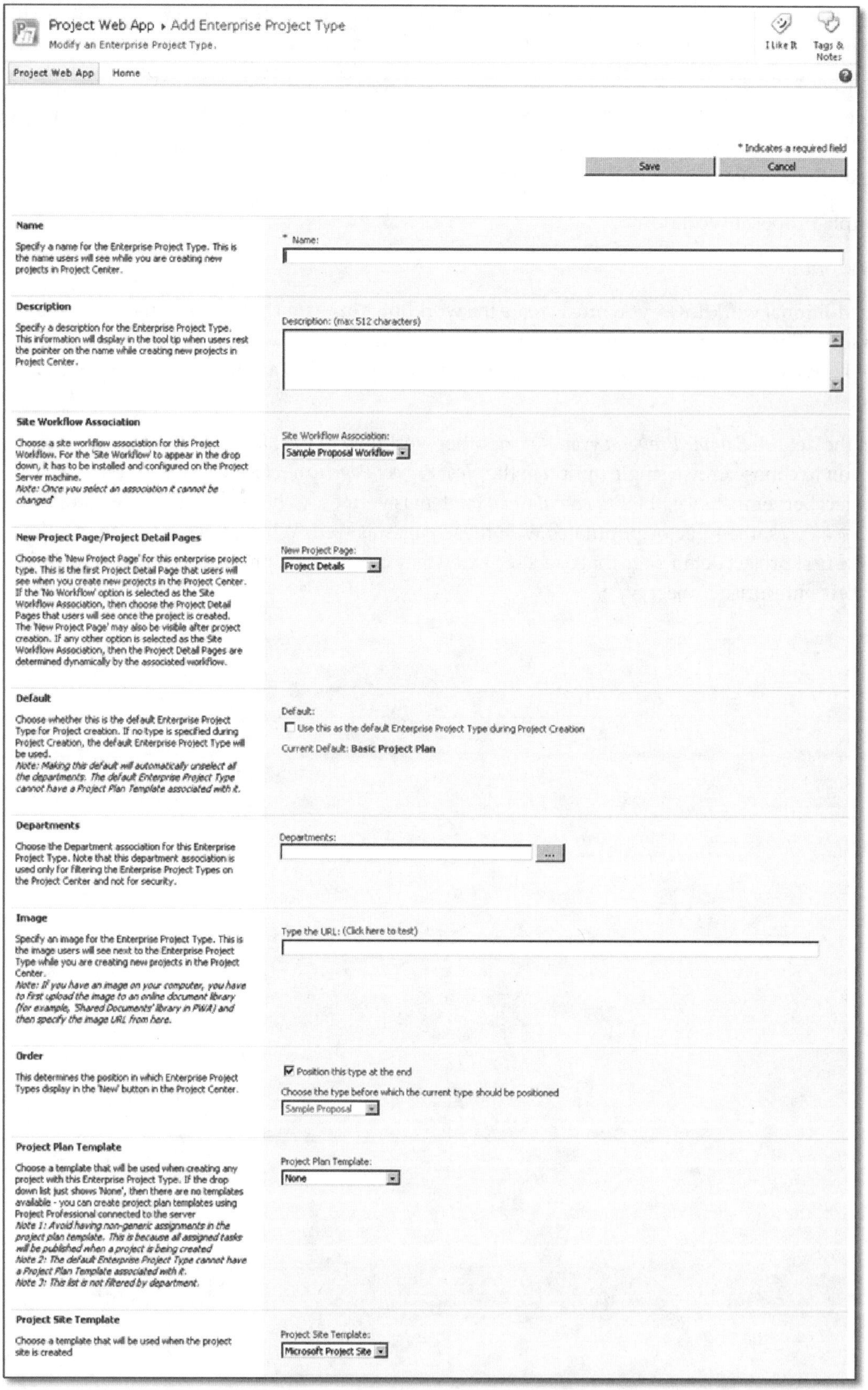

Figure 8 - 39: New Enterprise Project Type page

If, on the other hand, you select the *No Workflow* item in the *Site Workflow Association* pick list, the system refreshes the *New Project Page/Project Detail Pages* section as shown in Figure 8 - 40. In the *Available Project Detail Pages* list, select one or more project detail pages and then click the *Add* button. Alternatively, click the *Add All* button to add all available project detail pages.

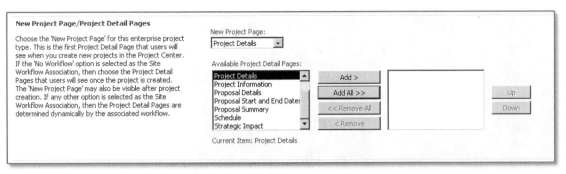

Figure 8 - 40: New Project Page/Project Detail Pages section

When you do not select a workflow association, the pages you select from the *Available Project Detail Pages* list are visible for new projects in the Project Center when a user selects a specific project to edit or view. You do not specify these pages for project types associated with workflows at this point, because you associate pages with stages in the workflow instead. In the case of workflow-connected project types, the *New Project Page* selection is the page that users encounter first when creating a new project from your project type.

Warning: If you are creating a non-workflow associated Enterprise Project Type, you must select at least one item on the *Available Project Detail Pages* list and add it to the list on the right. If you fail to do so, Project Server 2010 does not allow you to save the *new Enterprise Project Type* and reminds you to select at least one item on the *Available Project Detail Pages* list.

The default *Enterprise Project Type* for creating a new project proposal is the *Basic Project Plan* type. Project Server 2010 allows you to set your new enterprise project type as the new default by selecting the *Use this as the default Enterprise Project Type during Project Creation* option. When you select this option, however, the system locks both the *Departments* field and the *Project Plan Template* field, because the default project type must be available to all users and must have a blank project plan as the template.

If you need to limit the users who can see the new *Enterprise Project Type*, click the *Select Value* button for the *Departments* field and select one or more department values. If you do not select a value in the *Departments* field, the new *Enterprise Project Type* becomes available for all users.

In the *Image* section of the page, you have the option to associate the new enterprise project type with an image file. The system displays the image you select when a user creates a new project proposal using the new enterprise project type. Before you associate an image with the *Enterprise Project Type*, you must upload the image file to a document library in Project Server 2010. The document library for public documents is one choice; however, you may want to save files like this in a separate library that you create specifically for this purpose. I like to create a separate document library for this purpose without displaying it on the Quick Launch menu so that users do not accidentally modify or delete these objects. After uploading the image file to the document library, click the image file, and then copy the URL for the image file to the clipboard. On the *New Enterprise Project Type* page, paste the URL into the *Type the URL* field in the *Image* section. After making your entry, click the *Click here to test* hyperlink to confirm the URL for the image file. Figure 8 - 41 shows my new *Test New Project Type* on the *New* menu with my added image. Above it, note that I did not specify an image for the *Test Dynamic Type*.

**Figure 8 - 41: New
Project Type with image**

 The images you choose to associate with enterprise project types must be scaled for the intended purpose, which is to display as an icon next to the selection on a pick list menu. Therefore you should choose a graphic that works well as an icon in a very small format. Scale your images to 18px. X 18px. for this purpose.

In the *Order* section of the page, the system allows you to position the new *Enterprise Project Type* on the *New pick list* when a user clicks on the *New* button in the Project Center. The system selects the *Position this type at the end* checkbox by default. To position the new enterprise project type anywhere else in the list, deselect this checkbox. The system enables the *Choose the type before which the current type should be positioned* pick list. Click the pick list and select the location for the new *Enterprise Project Type*.

In the *Project Plan Template* section, you can optionally associate your new *Enterprise Project Type* to a specific enterprise project template. When you associate a *Project Plan* template to a project type, the system converts the project proposal into an enterprise project using the enterprise project template you select when it is approved. Click the *Project Plan Template* pick list and select an enterprise project template from the list. If you leave the default *None* value selected in this field, the system creates a new blank project when users select the project type.

In the *Project Site Template* section, your final option is to select the project site template to use when creating the *Project Site* for projects created using your new *Enterprise Project Type*. By default, the system selects the *Microsoft Project Site* item in the *Project Site Template* field. If you want to use additional project site templates, you must create them. I teach you how to do this in Module 17.

Click the *Save* button to complete your entries. The system saves the new *Enterprise Project Type* and displays it on the *Enterprise Project Types* page. Notice in Figure 8 - 42 that I created two new enterprise project types called *Test New Project Type* and *Test Dynamic Type*. I associated the *Test New Project Type* with no workflow, and with no specific department selected. This means that all users in all departments can create a new project proposal for a *Test New Project Type* project, and that the project is not governed by a workflow process. Notice also that I did associate the *Test Dynamic Type* with a workflow called *Test Dynamic Workflow*. This means that new projects based on this project type are governed by workflow. I discuss dynamic workflows later in this module.

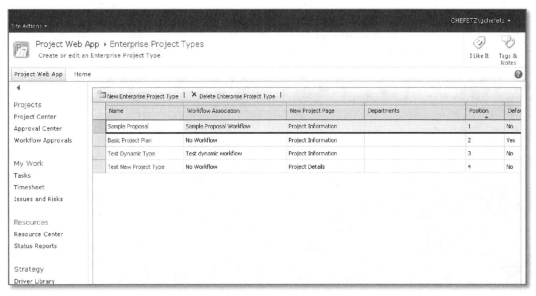

Figure 8 - 42: Enterprise Project Types page shows new Test New Project Type entry

Editing an Enterprise Project Type

To edit an existing Enterprise Project Type, complete the following steps:

1. Click the *Server Settings* link in the Quick Launch menu.

2. Click the *Enterprise Project Types* link in the *Workflow and Project Detail Pages* section of the *Server Settings* page.

3. On *the Enterprise Project Type page,* click the name of the enterprise project type you want to edit.

The system displays the selected enterprise project type in editing mode. With the exception of the title, the page looks identical to the *Add Enterprise Project Type* page shown previously in Figure 8 - 39. Change any of the editable values on the page and then click the *Save* button.

Working with the Sample Workflow

Now that you have a broad understanding of how Project Server 2010 uses workflow in lifecycle management, I take you through the rest of the steps in the sample workflow proposal that you started earlier in this module so that you can determine whether you need or want to adapt it for your own purposes. Understand that if you cannot adapt it to your needs, and you want to have a workflow that interacts with the portfolio decision making engine in Project Server, you must develop it using Visual Studio or a third-party tool. At this point your first sample workflow should be completely through the *Proposal Details* stage and *Create* phase as shown previously in Figure 8 - 15. If you haven't completed all the project detail pages in the *Proposal Details* stage and submitted your new proposal, do so at this time.

The next phase in the process is the *Select* phase. The *Select* phase has only two stages: *Selected* or *Not Selected.* In order for the proposal to move forward, it must be selected and committed through a Portfolio Analysis commit action. The point of the next thirteen steps is to show you how the sample workflow works and is not intended to teach you about using the *Portfolio Analyses* feature in 2010. Complete the following steps to move your proposal to the next phase in the workflow:

1. You first need to create a driver prioritization using the business drivers you defined in the *Creating Business Drivers* section earlier in this module. Click the *Driver Prioritization* selection in the *Strategy* section of the Quick Launch menu. The system displays the *Driver Prioritization* page shown in Figure 8 - 43.

Figure 8 - 43: Driver Prioritization page

2. Click the *New* button on the *Prioritizations* ribbon. The system displays the *New Driver Prioritization* page shown in Figure 8 - 44.

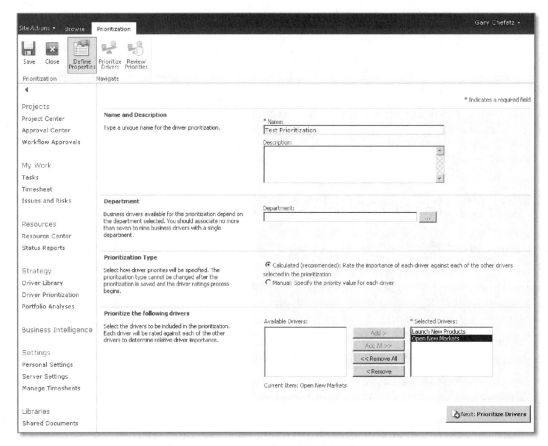

Figure 8 - 44: New Driver Prioritization page

3. Enter a name for your new prioritization, leave the *Department* selections blank, and add all of your drivers to the *Select Drivers* list in the *Prioritize the following drivers* section; then click the *Next: Prioritize Drivers* button to advance to the next page. The system displays the *Prioritize Drivers* page shown in Figure 8 - 45.

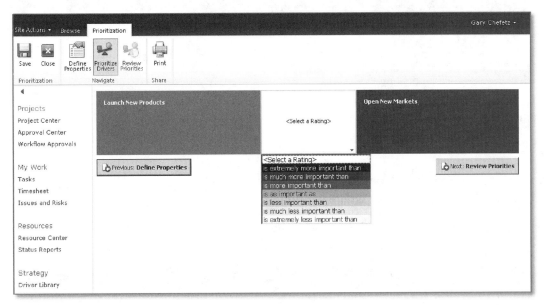

Figure 8 - 45: Prioritize Drivers Page

4. Use the *Select a Rating* pick list to prioritize your drivers. Depending on how many drivers you defined, you may need to work through more than one pair-wise comparison. Click the *Next: Review Priorities* button when you complete your entries. The system displays the *Review Priorities* page shown in Figure 8 - 46.

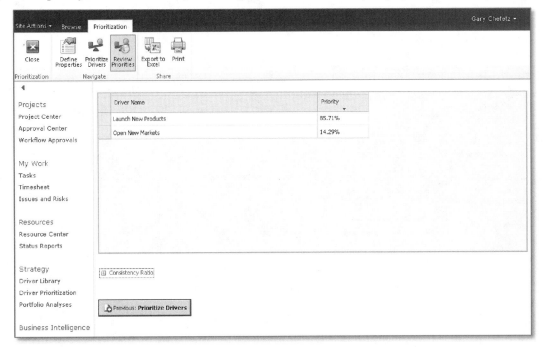

Figure 8 - 46: Review Priorities page

5. Click the *Close* button on the *Prioritization* ribbon.

6. From the Quick Launch menu, select *Portfolio Analyses* from the *Strategy* section. The system opens the *Portfolio Analyses* page shown in Figure 8 - 47.

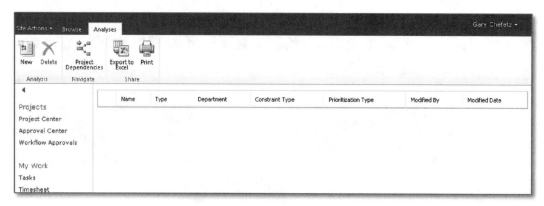

Figure 8 - 47: Portfolio Analyses page

7. Click the *New* button in the *Analysis* section of the *Analyses* ribbon. The system displays the *New Portfolio Analysis* page shown in Figure 8 - 48.

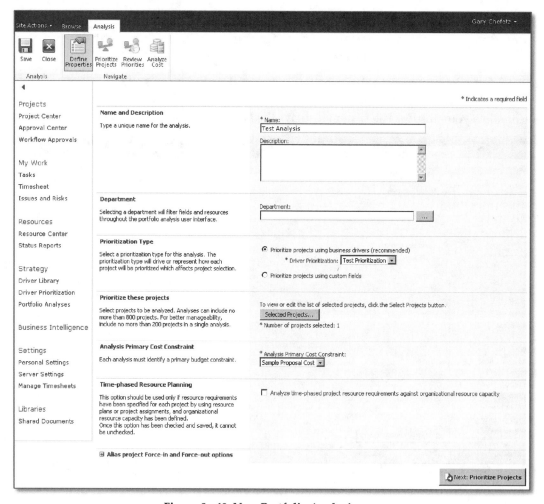

Figure 8 - 48: New Portfolio Analysis page

8. Give your new analysis a name, leave the *Department* field blank, and in the *Prioritization Type* section select the *Prioritize projects using business drivers* option. Click the *Selected Projects* button and the system displays the *Select Projects* dialog shown in Figure 8 - 49.

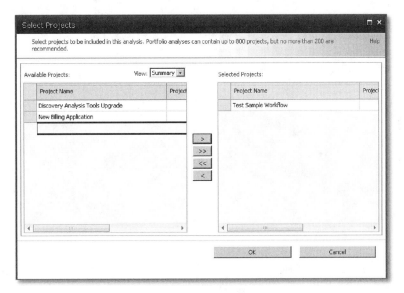

Figure 8 - 49: Select Projects dialog

9. As I did in the example in the figure, select your new proposal and use the arrow button to move it to the *Selected Projects* section on the right. Click the *Ok* button when you are done, and the system returns you to the *New Analysis* page shown previously in Figure 8 - 48. Leave the default selection in the *Analysis Primary Cost Constraint* section, and do not select the option for *Time-phased Resource Planning*. Note that this is for demonstration purposes only and that not selecting this option will ultimately stall this new project in the workflow, as without this analysis, the workflow cannot proceed. Click the *Next: Prioritize Projects* button to continue. The system displays the *Driver Strategic Impact* page shown in Figure 8 - 50.

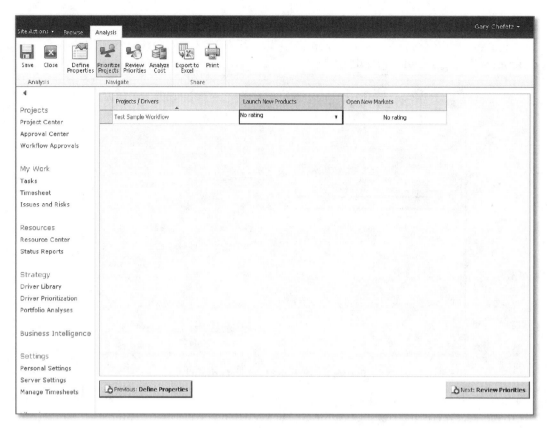

Figure 8 - 50: Driver Strategic Impact page

10. Select at least one rating for your project and click the *Next: Review Priorities* button to continue. The system displays the *Project Prioritization Summary* page shown in Figure 8 - 51.

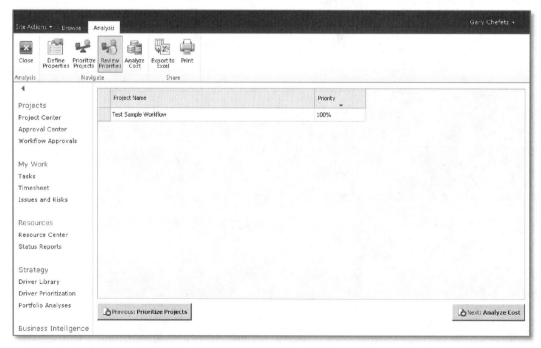

Figure 8 - 51: Project Prioritization Summary page

11. Click the *Next: Analyze Cost* button to continue. The system advances to the *Cost Constraint Analysis* page shown in Figure 8 - 52.

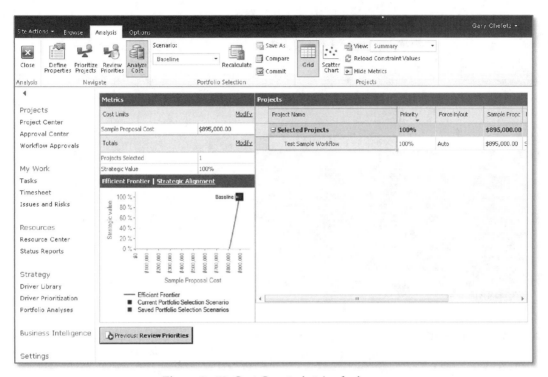

Figure 8 - 52: Cost Constraint Analysis page

12. In the *Portfolio Selection* section of the *Analysis* ribbon, click the *Commit* button. The system displays the *Message from webpage* warning shown in Figure 8 - 53.

Figure 8 - 53: Message from webpage dialog

13. Click the *OK* button to continue.

Because the sample workflow is coded to hook into portfolio analysis, you cannot move to the next stage of the workflow until your project is committed through this process. Return to the *Project Center* and select your new proposal project in the grid. You should now see that the project has advanced to the *Resource Planning* stage, as shown for my new project proposal in Figure 8 - 54.

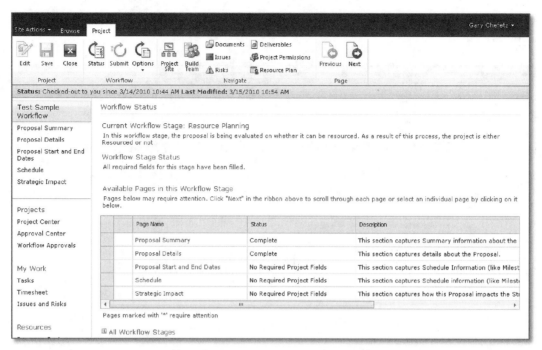

Figure 8 - 54: Workflow Status after Project Selection

The resource planning phase requires a portfolio manager to perform a resource analysis on the project using the portfolio analysis tools as well, and the manager must commit the project through this process to move it into the scheduling stage. The rest of the workflow progresses following the diagram shown in Figure 8 - 55.

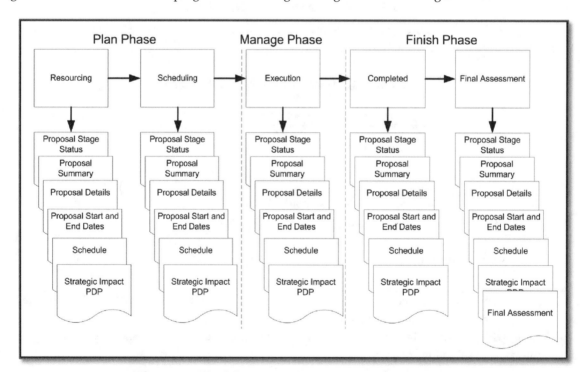

Figure 8 - 55: Workflow Stages for Sample Proposal continued

As you can see in the diagram, the project detail pages that the workflow uses remain constant until the final stage, which introduces a *Final Assessment* page which captures some lessons learned information. Before the plan can move from the *Scheduling* stage to the *Execution* stage, the system requires a manual approval after the project manager submits the project from the *Scheduling* stage. The project manager cannot submit the project from the *Execution* stage to the *Completed* stage until all of the tasks in the project are marked 100% complete. Any attempt that the project manager makes to submit the project to this stage while there are incomplete tasks in the plan is immediately rejected by the workflow logic. Once the project manager marks all tasks complete, the project is eligible for submission to the *Finish* phase.

Adapting the Sample Workflow for Your Needs

Perhaps the most important thing to know about adapting the sample workflow for your own needs is what you cannot and must not change. If you make any of the following changes, you break your workflow and you cannot recover from this without a deep dive into the published database. In order to recover from this, you must redeploy the sample workflow using Visual Studio and a copy of the workflow from the Project SDK.

- **Do not delete** any of the sample workflow *Stages*. Like all objects in the system, workflows reference these by globally unique identifiers (GUIDs).

- **Do not delete** any of the sample required fields. Once again, these are referenced by GUID, so you cannot recreate these.

You can change lots of characteristics of the sample workflow, to adapt it to your methodology and organizational vernacular. Have fun changing the following as long as you do not delete and recreate them:

- Project Phases if you are careful to provide new Phases first, as each stage must maintain a connection to a phase. You need to disassociate all stages from a Phase before you can delete it.

- Project Type Name and description information.

- Names of Phases and descriptive information.

- Names of Stages and descriptive information.

- Project Detail Page Names and configurations.

- Sample Custom Field Names.

By changing the above items, you can significantly personalize the presentation of the workflow objects to your constituency. You can also add additional custom fields and standard project fields to the existing project detail pages, and you can add additional web parts to the project detail pages as well.

 Warning: The sample workflow uses the *Sample Proposal Cost* field for its automated rejection. If you need to manage projects that cost over one million dollars, you should add a new enterprise custom cost field and add it to the appropriate project detail pages. Train your users not to enter costs in the *Sample Proposal Cost* field, and consider renaming it to something like "Enter Zero Field." You can use any custom enterprise cost field to perform cost analysis; in fact, you can use more than one for running various analysis scenarios.

Certain items are hard-coded in the workflow and you cannot change these without using Microsoft Visual Studio. These include the following:

- Email Subjects.

- Email Bodies.

- Some messages shown in SharePoint that are embedded in the workflow.

- Workflow task outcomes (approved, rejected, etc.).

- Automated Rejection set to $1 million dollars.

> The sample workflow solution is available in the Project SDK downloadable from MSDN. If you want to make changes to any of the above items, you can download the solution files and modify them to meet your needs, or use the sample workflow as a basis for creating a completely new version.

Modify the Areas Impacted and Primary Objective Lookup Tables

Microsoft provided these two lookup tables to serve as an example of the type of Project Custom fields that are typical in a project lifecycle workflow solution. You should modify these to reflect your company's organizational structure and objectives respectively.

Configuring Project Workflow Settings

All workflows that you initiate in Project Server 2010 run under an account. One last step you should take in the process of configuring the lifecycle management process is to set the *Workflow Proxy User Account*. Click the *Project Workflow Settings* link in the *Workflow and Project Detail Pages* section of the *Server Settings* page. The system displays the *Project Workflow Settings* page shown in Figure 8 - 56. Notice that this page includes only a single option, which is the *Workflow Proxy User account* field. In this field, enter the Windows user ID of the account used by Project Server Interface (PSI) to make calls during the workflow process.

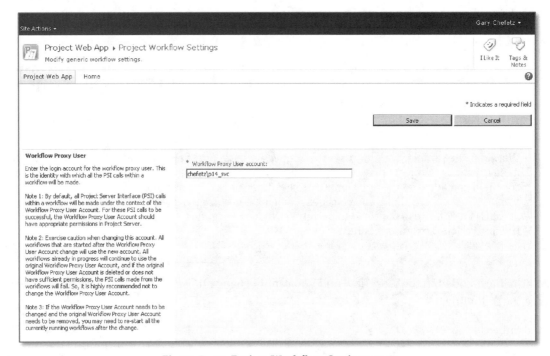

Figure 8 - 56: Project Workflow Settings page

Notice that this page contains numerous warnings about the Windows user account you select. In short, these warnings are:

- Make sure the Workflow Proxy User Account has the proper permissions in Project Server 2010. The minimum rights needed for the account to execute PSI-calls (regarding Project Server security) are:

  Global permissions:

  - Log On

  - Manage Users And Groups

  - Manage Workflow

  Category permissions:

  - Open Project

  - Save Project

  - View Enterprise Resource Data

  - Edit Project Properties

  - View Enterprise Resource Data

> **Warning:** The account you use as the workflow proxy must have a logon in Project Server2010 with the minimum permissions listed above. You can use your applicaiton service account for this purpose, but you must first add it as a Project Server 2010 user. The system does not allow you to enter an account that is not a Project Server user. Because some of the permissions this account needs are administrator privileges, you can simply add it to the *Administrators* group in Project Server.

- Do not change the *Workflow Proxy User* account after people begin using Project Server 2010, due to possible adverse consequences to workflows already running in the system.

- If you must change the *Workflow Proxy User* account after people begin using Project Server 2010, and you need to delete the original *Workflow Proxy User* account, plan on restarting all workflows that are currently running in the system.

Working with the Dynamic Workflow Solution Starter

You can use simple linear workflow solutions to build elegant stage-gate workflows in your system using the **DynamicWorkflow** solution starter available from the MSDN code gallery. This is a free solution starter provided by Microsoft that you can use to quickly and easily create new workflows for Project Server without any knowledge of programming. If you want to take the solution to a higher level, Microsoft provides the source code in the download. With developer skills, you can customize the solution to meet your requirements. I cannot provide you with a link to the download as it was not available to the public at the time of this writing. Inasmuch as Microsoft download links tend to change, if I did list a URL, it would likely be different by the time you read this.

Deploying the Dynamic Workflow Solution Starter

After downloading and unzipping the solution starter package, you find the following elements in the *Dynamic-Workflow* folder:

1. **DMDynamicWorkflow folder** containing the files for the Visual Studio 10 source code.

2. **InfoPath folder** containing the InfoPath form and the code-behind project for (VSTO) for the *Workflow Association Details* page.

3. Deployment files located in the DynamicWorkflow folder itself including a ReadMe.docx file containing basic installation and customization notes.

In the DynamicWorkflow folder, you find two important files: *Deploy.ps1* and the *Deploy_DynamicWorkflow.bat*. The .bat file calls the .ps1 file, which is a PowerShell script that deploys the solution. Before you can deploy the solution, you must first unblock these two files:

- Right click on the file and choose *Properties* from the shortcut menu.

- In the *Properties dialog* click the *Unblock* button at the bottom.

Next, you must edit the batch file to point to your instance name. The contents of the batch file appear below:

```
@echo off
Set DeploymentPackageFolder="."

Set SiteUrl="http://localhost/pwa"
Set SolutionFolder="./"
Set SolutionName="DMDynamicWorkflow.wsp"
Set FeatureName="DMDynamicWorkflow_DynamicWorkflow"

cd %DeploymentPackageFolder%
powershell "& set-executionpolicy remotesigned"
PowerShell -file .\Deploy.ps1 %SiteUrl% %SolutionFolder% %SolutionName% %Feature-
Name%

Pause
```

In the line containing **Set SiteUrl=http://localhost/pwa**, you must change the value of the instance name unless you named your instance by default "pwa." Once you change this value to your instance name, you are ready to deploy the solution. Simply double click on the .bat file and the PowerShell script takes care of everything for you. The script runs very quickly. If your system does not respond to the "localhost" in the URL, you can provide your server name instead.

Warning: If you receive an error during the deployment "There has been an error processing the form..." your system may not support the "localhost" protocol. Try chaning "localhost" to your server name instead. You can also enable the localhost protocol by configuring Alternate Access Mappings for your server by adding internal URLs.

If you have more than one instance of Project Web App, you must change the .bat file and run it for each instance individually. Deploying to one instance does not make the solution available to all instances on the server.

Creating and Configuring a Dynamic Workflow Instance

Once you deploy the solution, you must configure it in your system. From any page in your Project Web App instance, select the *Site Settings* link in upper left hand corner and select *Site Settings* from the menu. The system displays the *Site Settings* page shown in Figure 8 - 57.

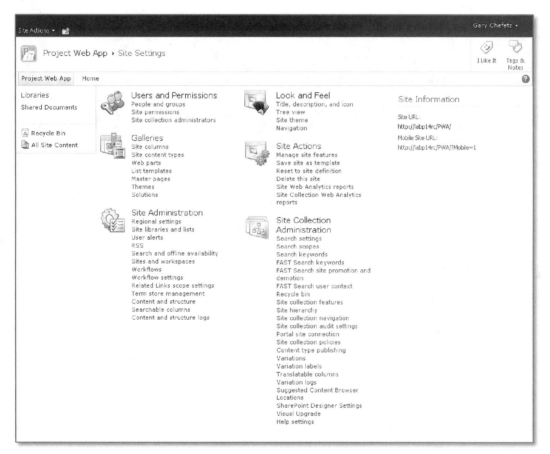

Figure 8 - 57: Site Settings page

From the *Site Administration* section click on the *Workflow settings* link. The system displays the *Workflow Settings* page shown in Figure 8 - 58.

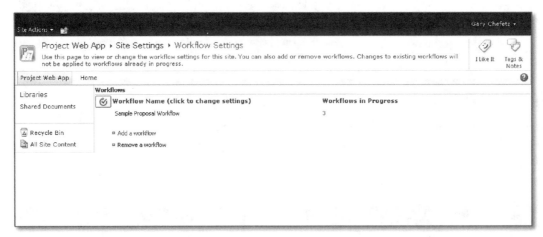

Figure 8 - 58: Workflow Settings page

Click on the *Add a workflow* link and the systems opens the *Add a Workflow* page shown in Figure 8 - 59.

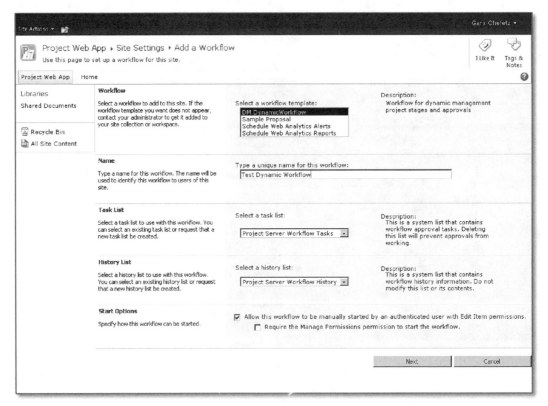

Figure 8 - 59: Add a Workflow page

You should now see the *DM DynamicWorkflow* template in the *Select a workflow template* selector in the *Workflow* section at the top of the page. Make sure to select this and complete the following steps:

- Enter a name for your new instance of the workflow in *Name* section of the page.

- Select the *Project Server Workflow Tasks* item in the *Select a task list* selector in the *Task List* section.

- Select the *Project Server Workflow History* in from the *Select a history list* selector in the *History List* section of the page.

- Leave the *Allow this workflow to be manually started by an authenticated user with Edit Item permissions* check box selected.

- Click the *Next* button to continue. The system displays the *Change a Workflow* page shown in Figure 8 - 60.

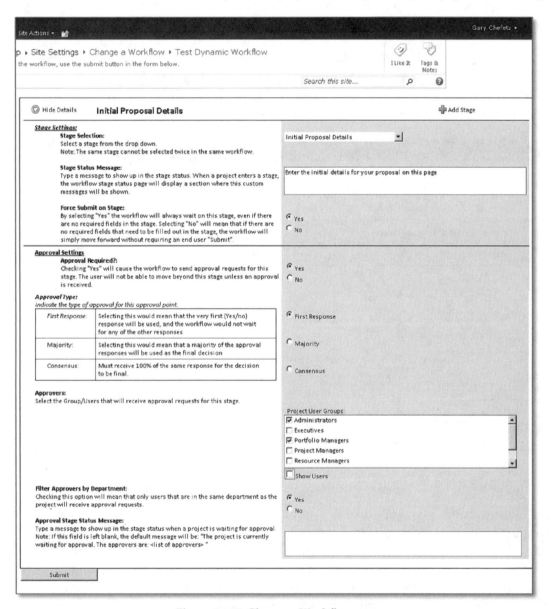

Figure 8 - 60: Change a Workflow page

In the *Stage Settings* section at the top of the page, you must select a stage for the first step of the workflow, so you must create your stages and project detail pages before you create the workflow. For demonstration purposes, I use the sample workflow *Initial Proposal Details* stage. Enter a S*tage Status Message* to display in the *Workflow Status* page. When you select the *Yes* option in the *Force Submit on Stage* section, the workflow waits until the user clicks the *Submit* button before allowing the workflow to progress. Because this is the first stage in the workflow, I selected *Yes*. You should select *No* only when there are no required fields in the stage.

In the *Approval Settings* section you have the option to require approval or to not require approval. When you select *No*, everything on the page below the *Approval Settings* selector does not display. In Figure 8 - 60, I selected *Yes*, which causes the system to display the detailed information below. Notice that you have three options in the *Approval Type* section, *First Response*, *Majority* and *Consensus*. The instructional notes on the page describe these adequately, and they are fairly intuitive by name. I selected the *First Response* option, as my business rules do not require a committee or half a committee to respond to the request. Next, you must select your approvers group(s) by selecting the check box next to the Project Server security groups in the *Project User Groups* section. All members of the groups you select are then able to act on approvals for this stage of the workflow. Note that you can use the *Show Users* check box to see all users in Project Web App. Now you must decide whether to apply department filtering to the approval requests. When you select this option, only eligible approvers with the same *Department* tag as the project can see and act upon the approval request. Finally, you can set a message to display for the stage status display when the stage is waiting for approval in the *Approval Stage Status Message* section. Click the *Add Stage* button in the upper right to continue to create another stage in your workflow. The system redisplays the page as shown in Figure 8 - 61.

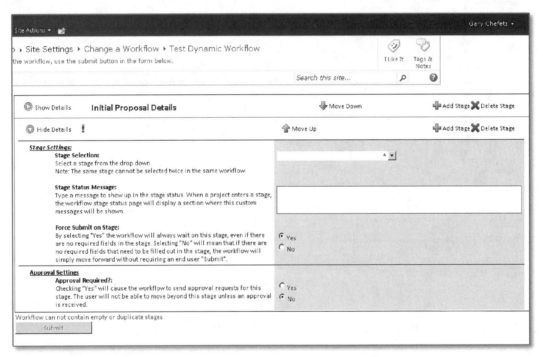

Figure 8 - 61: Change a workflow page redisplayed

Notice that the system builds a stack of workflow stages as you progress. Your new stage is now ready for definition and is open and visible, while the stage you just created is now collapsed and displays above the stage you are currently creating. Notice also that you now have the ability to delete a stage, as well as reorganize stages by moving them up and down using the *Arrow* buttons in the center of the top display area. Create as many stages as you need to support your workflow design by repeating the above process until you configure a complete workflow. The process of assembling a workflow using this dandy tool is very easy.

Considerations for Working with the Dynamic Workflow Tool

There are always trade-offs when you design for simplicity, so the Dynamic Workflow tool has its limitations. You can create only simple linear workflows using the tool, so you cannot add multi-branching logic, and you have no way of hooking into the portfolio analysis functions when you construct your workflow. Nonetheless, you can accomplish a lot with this tool. Here are some tips to help you create your dynamic workflows:

- Map your process first. If necessary, use Visio or PowerPoint to map your workflow and the phases and stages it requires, including the project detail pages and custom fields that you want to use in your PDPs.

- Create your enterprise custom fields first. If you want the fields to be available only in your workflow, don't forget to select the *Behavior controlled by workflow* option in the *Behavior* section of the *Custom Fields* page when you create your fields. You learned about this previously in Module 07.

- Create your *Project Detail Pages* next. You must define these before you create your stages.

- After creating your custom fields and project detail pages, create your workflow *Phases*. Remember that these are simply organizational buckets, but you need these when you create your stages, as you assign stages to phases.

- Create your *Stages* as the last step before assembling the workflow using the Dynamic Workflow tool.

- Do not reuse the Sample workflow pages except for those I note are good to use, as some of these contain code behind them that invoke approvals. When you use them in a stage that requires approval, they can create a double approval condition that can prevent the workflow from progressing.

- Remember to create a project detail page that exposes the *Proposals Stage Status* web part to display the workflow status. You can reuse the existing *ProposalScheduleStatus* PDP in the system or create your own.

- Remember to include a PDP that contains the *Project Details* web part in stages where users need access to the schedule for viewing and editing in the *Project Center*. You can reuse the existing *Schedule* PDP or create your own.

- If you want to include a decision-making step using portfolio analysis tools, be sure to include a PDP that exposes the *Strategic Impact* web part, as portfolio analysis requires this data. You can use the existing *StrategicImpact* PDP or create your own.

- Remember to set an approval point on the stage for portfolio analysis. Although you cannot use the *Commit* feature in portfolio analysis, you can use a manual approval to control this process.

I could easily devote an entire book to this subject, so to learn more about using workflows with SharePoint and Project Server, be sure to explore the resources on TechNet and MSDN. If you are a developer interested in diving deeper into this topic for Project Server 2010, Stephen Sanderlin provides good coverage in the *Developers Guide to Project Server 2007 and 2010*, ISBN 978-1-934240-08-3.

Module 09

Building and Managing the Enterprise Resource Pool

Learning Objectives

After completing this module, you will be able to:

- Understand the importance and purpose of the Enterprise Resource Pool

- Understand the difference between enterprise and local resources

- Understand resource types

- Create Work, Material, Generic, Cost, and Team resources

- Open the Enterprise Resource Pool and check out resources

- Edit existing enterprise resources

- Mass edit enterprise resources from the Resource Center

- Prepare resource data for import into the Enterprise Resource Pool

- Import resource data

- Deactivate enterprise resources

Inside Module 09

Enterprise Resource Pool Overview 339
   Understanding Enterprise vs. Local Resources 339
Understanding Enterprise Resource Types...340
Working with the Resource Center Data Grid 341
   Creating an Ad Hoc Filter 342
   Using AutoFilter 344
   Sorting the Data in the Grid 344
   Configuring Columns 345
   Applying Views 346
Creating Resources Using Project Professional 2010 346

Entering General Information...350

Changing Working Time...352

Using the Custom Fields Page..361

Creating Non-Work Resources..362

Editing Enterprise Resources Using Project Professional 2010 ....**367**

Checking Out Enterprise Resources for Editing...368

Using Project Web App to Create an Enterprise Resource.....................................**369**

Setting Type Options..371

Setting Identification Information Options..371

Setting User Authentication Options...372

Setting Assignment Attributes Options...372

Setting Exchange Server Details Options..373

Setting Departments Options...373

Setting Resource Custom Fields Options..374

Setting Security Options...374

Setting Group Fields Options..375

Setting Team Details Options..376

Mass Editing Enterprise Resources..**376**

Bulk Editing Enterprise Resources...377

Individually Editing Enterprise Resources by Batch..379

Adding Resources Using Active Directory Synchronization **382**

Preparing to Import Enterprise Resources **384**

Importing Resources from Active Directory..386

Importing Resources from Your Address Book 390

Verifying a Windows Account for a Resource...392

Preparing Custom Field Data..394

Importing Enterprise Resources...**398**

Deactivating an Enterprise Resource **400**

Enterprise Resource Pool Overview

The *Enterprise Resource Pool* in Microsoft Project Server 2010 should contain all of the enterprise resources needed to perform project work in your organization. Defined in simple terms, resources are the people, equipment, and materials required to execute a project. Defined in accounting terms, resources are the elements of project direct costs. As such, resource pool attribution drives the ability to track activity-based project costs as well as material consumption. Project cost drives meaningful performance measures in the system, generating cost data that can enhance business decisions.

Building a well-structured *Enterprise Resource Pool* enables you to use the important resource management features of Project Server 2010. Meaningful output from the system depends on enterprise custom fields. Before you build your *Enterprise Resource Pool*, you want to make certain that you create adequate attribution for your resource pool using the techniques you learned in Module 07. Before you build the Enterprise Resource Pool, you need to know where to obtain your organization's resource data, and whether to create the resources manually, import them automatically through Active Directory synchronization, or import them from existing projects.

Whether you pull this data from Active Directory, Exchange, Outlook, Excel, or from any other source, chances are that you will be doing significant manual updating. This is mostly because the custom fields you apply are very likely to be new constructs for your organization. Those that are not new to the organization may come from a variety of sources, such as your organization's HR and accounting departments.

Understanding Enterprise vs. Local Resources

Project Server 2010 allows your organization to use both local and enterprise resources within the system:

- **Enterprise resources** exist in the enterprise resource pool and are available for use across the portfolio of projects. Only those users with specific permissions in the system can create enterprise resources.

- **Local resources** are non-enterprise resources that exist only in a local project plan and are not part of the enterprise resource pool. Anyone who manages an enterprise project using Project Professional 2010 can create local resources.

You can maintain tighter control over the system when you manage all your resources through the enterprise resource pool. Because you cannot prevent project managers from entering local resources in their project plans, at least not without using custom software code, this becomes a training and policy issue. Therefore, you should establish a workflow for how your organization handles the creation of resources.

Understanding Enterprise Resource Types

Project Server 2010 defines resources in a variety of ways, and organizes them in the resource hierarchy shown in Figure 9 - 1.

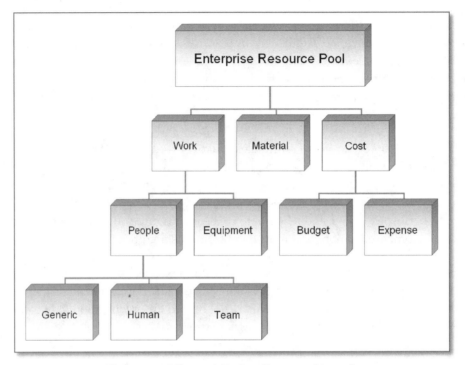

Figure 9 - 1: Microsoft Project Resource hierarchy

Project Server 2010 allows you to define three basic resource types: work, material, and cost. You use work resources to model people and equipment, while you use material resources to represent the supplies consumed during the project lifecycle. In Project Server 2010, you can use cost resources to track budget costs and budget expenses unrelated to the work resources assigned to tasks. Work resources affect both the schedule and the cost of the project, while material and cost resources affect only the project cost.

Project Server 2010 organizes work resources into three groups: generic, non-generic (or human resources), and team resources. A human resource is a specific individual you can identify by name. A generic resource is a skill-based placeholder resource, such as a "C++ software developer," that represents one or more human resources. Generic resources allow you to specify the skills required for a task assignment before you know which specific human resources are available to work on the task. Your project managers can use skill-set matching and availability matching, as well as resource substitution to replace generic resources with available human resources who possess the same skills. Generic resources are particularly useful in project templates, which can save many hours of schedule development.

A team resource is a special type of generic resource that represents a team of people. You should create team resources in either of the following situations:

- Your organization uses dedicated project teams, and the team members do not change from project to project. For instance, these are perfect for scrum projects, providing a mechanism for team members to pick up work during a sprint.

- Your organization needs to track work that might not be resource-specific, such as maintenance tasks flowing from a trouble ticket system.

Team resources support the construct of "pickup" work, whereby any one of a number of people can do the work and can self-assign their tasks. Before you can create and use team resources, you must create a custom lookup table, populate it with a list of team names in your organization, and then attach the lookup table to the *Team Name* built-in custom field.

> Project Server 2010 has no way to distinguish between work resources that are people and those that are equipment. Because of this, the system counts every work resource as a Project Server user when calculating its internal license count requirement. You may also want to add an enterprise custom resource field and lookup table to provide metadata attribution to distinguish between people and equipment resources in order to separate them in views and reports.

Project Server 2010 allows you to create all types of enterprise resources using either Project Professional 2010 or Project Web App. For the sake of simplicity, I demonstrate how to create all types of enterprise resources using Project Professional 2010 first, and then I demonstrate how to use the Project Web App interface to create a new enterprise resource.

Working with the Resource Center Data Grid

Unlike previous versions of the Project Server system, which contained functions for opening the enterprise resource pool directly in Project Professional, you must use the *Resource Center* page, shown in Figure 9 - 2, to launch all of your resource pool maintenance activities. This is the case whether you want to use Project Professional or Project Web App to add or modify resources. For this reason, you should know how to use the data grid most effectively.

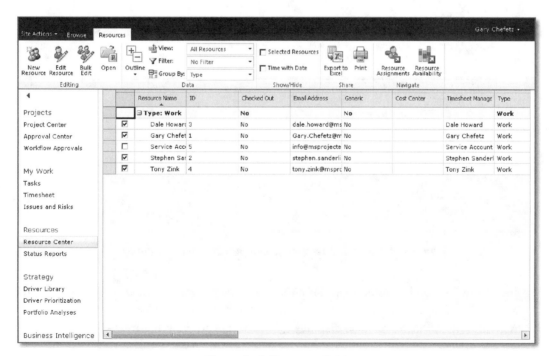

Figure 9 - 2: Resource Center

Creating an Ad Hoc Filter

To create an ad hoc filter, complete the following steps:

1. Click the *Filter* pick list in the *Data* section of the *Resources* ribbon, and select the *Custom Filter* item. The system opens the *Custom Filter* dialog shown in Figure 9 - 3.

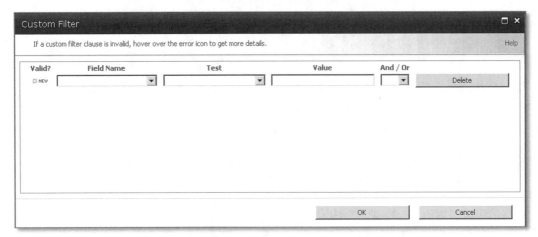

Figure 9 - 3: Custom Filter dialog

2. From the *Field Name* pick list, select a field to enter your first criteria, select a *Test* value from the *Test* pick list, and enter a value in the *Value* field. Use the *And/Or* pick list to continue building your filter criteria, or click the *OK* button to apply your filter. In Figure 9 - 4, I set filter criteria to show only *Generic* resources. Notice that you can use the *Delete* button to delete a row in your filter if necessary.

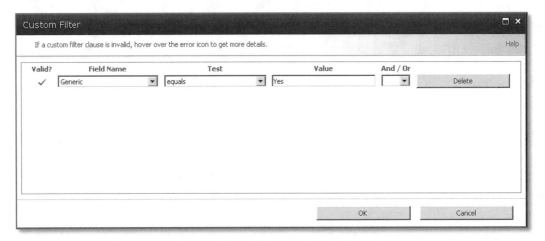

Figure 9 - 4: Custom Filter dialog testing for Generic resources

3. Before you apply your ad hoc filter, make sure that the *Valid* column displays a check mark indicating that you created a valid filter. If your filter is invalid, then the system displays an X in this column. If you try to apply an invalid filter, the system also displays the warning shown in Figure 9 - 5.

Figure 9 - 5: Invalid Filter Warning

4. Click the *OK* button to apply your valid ad hoc filter. Figure 9 - 6 shows the Resource Center page after applying the ad hoc filter to show only Generic resources.

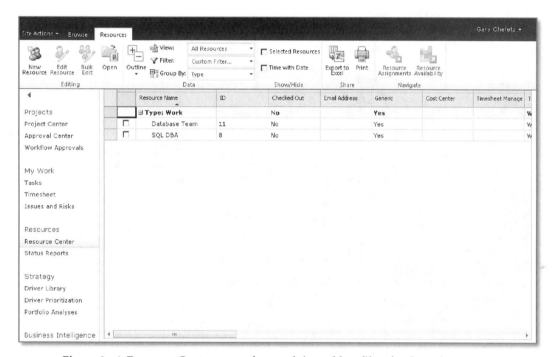

Figure 9 - 6: Resource Center page after applying ad hoc filter for Generic resources

 Project Server 2010 does not allow you to save ad hoc filters. Therefore, you must recreate the filter every time you want to use it.

5. To clear the ad hoc filter click the *Filter* pick list and select the *No Filter* item from the list.

Using AutoFilter

To apply and use an AutoFilter in the data grid, float your mouse pointer over the column header of any data column in the grid. The system displays the auto filter button in the column header as shown in Figure 9 - 7.

**Figure 9 - 7: Mouse pointer
floating over column header**

Click the column header to display the menu. The system displays the multipurpose menu shown in Figure 9 - 8.

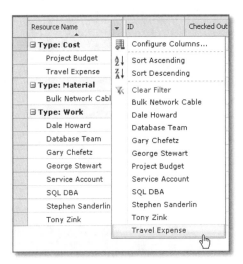

Figure 9 - 8: Multipurpose menu

To apply an *AutoFilter* select a value in the bottom section of the menu below the *Clear Filter* selection. To remove the *AutoFilter*, select the *Clear Filter* item in the menu.

Sorting the Data in the Grid

You can sort the data in the grid using the same multipurpose menu shown previously in Figure 9 - 8. Select the *Sort Ascending* or *Sort Descending* item from the pick list to apply sorting to the grid based on the column you selected. Figure 9 - 9 Shows the *Resource Center* page after I applied *Sort Ascending* on the *Resource Name* field. Notice that the system sorts the data within the existing groupings.

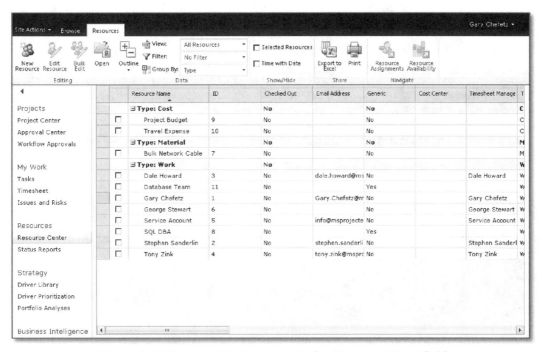

Figure 9 - 9: Resource Center page sorted on Resource Name field

Configuring Columns

You can also rearrange and resize the columns in the view using the same multipurpose menus shown previously in Figure 9 - 8. Select the *Configure Columns* item to open the *Configure Columns* dialog shown in Figure 9 - 10. Use the *Move Up* and *Move Down* buttons to reorder the columns, and use the *Column Width (pixels)* field to specify the field widths in pixels. You can also rearrange columns using the dragging technique I showed you in Module 6.

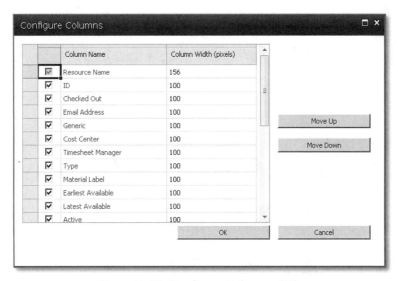

Figure 9 - 10: Configure Columns dialog

When you make changes to a view using this method, you are changing your personal version of the view, and these changes do no affect how others see the view. Project Server remembers your preferences and always redisplays the view based on your new arrangement. If you need to change the view for all users in the system, you must modify the master copy of the view. You learn how to create and manage system views in Module 14.

Applying Views

To apply one of the default *Resource Center* views, click the *View* pick list from the *Data* section of the *Resource* ribbon as shown in Figure 9 - 11.

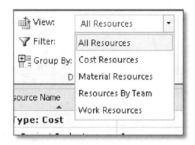

**Figure 9 - 11: Choose a View
from the View pick list**

The View pick list offers five default Resource Center views, including:

- All Resources

- Cost Resources

- Material Resources

- Resources By Team

- Work Resources

Creating Resources Using Project Professional 2010

Before you can manually enter your organization's enterprise resources, you must open the *Enterprise Resource Pool*. To open the *Enterprise Resource Pool* in Project Professional 2010, complete the following steps from Project Web App:

1. In your web browser, select *Resources* or *Resource Center* from the Quick Launch menu. The system opens the *Resource Center* page shown in Figure 9 - 12.

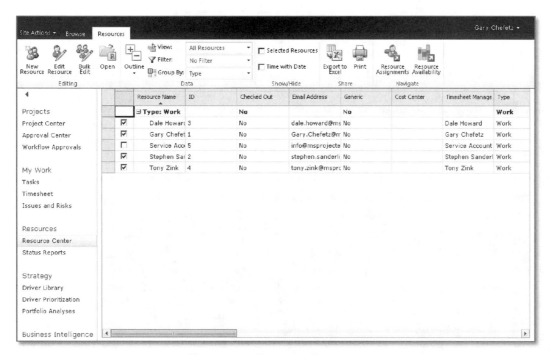

Figure 9 - 12: Resource Center page

2. On the page you can select any resources for editing, or you can select none. I want to call your attention to the hidden selector menu that appears over the checkbox column in the grid only when you float your mouse pointer over the column header. Make note of this, as this is a characteristic of the grid object and applies to many pages in the system. Otherwise this feature is not easily discoverable.

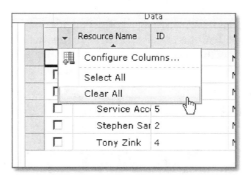

Figure 9 - 13: Hidden Column Header Selector

3. Once you make or clear your selections, (in this case clear any selected resources), click on the *Open* button in the Editing section on the *Resources* ribbon. The system opens the *Enterprise Resource Pool* for editing as shown in Figure 9 - 14. Notice that the Project displays "Checked-out Enterprise Resources – Microsoft Project" at the top of the screen.

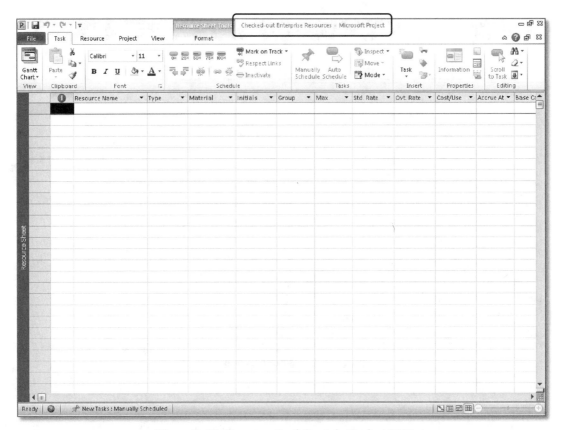

Figure 9 - 14: Resource Pool Open in Project 2010

4. Project 2010 opens to the *Resource Sheet* view. This is the view that you use to enter resource information. As I stated before, you should create all of your resource custom fields prior to entering resources, otherwise you will find yourself going back and forth attributing your resources.

> The *Resource Sheet* view contains only standard project fields out of the box. In order to enter your custom field information, you must manually add the columns you need in the current view, which will not persist from session to session. MSProjectExperts recommends that you create a new enterprise resource sheet view containing the necessary fields so that you can reuse it. You learn about building views in Module 14.

The first step in defining enterprise work resources is to enter basic resource information. Enter this information in the following fields of the *Resource Sheet* view for each enterprise work resource:

*   In the **Resource Name** field, enter the full name of each work resource.

*   In the **Type** field, leave the value set as the default work value.

*   In the **Initials** field, enter the initials of each resource. By default, Project Professional 2010 enters only the first initial of the first word in the *Resource Name* column.

*   In the **Group** field, enter the skill, team, department, or some other manner to group the resources.

*   In the **Max. Units** field, enter a percentage representing the maximum amount of an average working day the resource is available for project work on this project. Enter 100% or your discounted availability only for re-

sources that are available for full-time project work, and enter a value less than 100% for resources who are available to work less than full-time.

- In the ***Std. Rate*** field, enter the rate at which you cost the resource's work. The default measure is hourly cost, such as $50.00/hr, but you may also enter a cost using any other time units, such as $2,000/wk.

- In the ***Ovt. Rate*** field, enter the rate at which you cost overtime work. In Project Server 2010, overtime work is any work the user or project manager enters explicitly in the *Overtime Work* field.

- In the ***Cost/Use*** field, enter the "flat rate" that accrues each time a project manager uses the resource in the project. The *Cost/Use* field is similar to the "trip charge" billed by a plumber to get the plumber to show up at your home. The system applies the *Cost/Use* rate in addition to any applicable hourly rate you set.

> **Warning:** msProjectExperts recommends that you **never** enter a resource's actual salary in any of the resource *Cost* fields. Doing so may result in privacy issues with your company's HR department and could even cause dissension and morale problems with project staff. In fact, some European Union countries have laws prohibiting this practice. Instead, use "blended" or average rates for resources within a team, a department, or even across your entire organization.

- In the ***Accrue At*** field, select a value that determines how Project Server 2010 realizes the costs when you assign the selected resource to a task. You can realize the cost at the beginning of the task by selecting the *Start* value, or realize the cost at the end of the task by selecting the *End* value. The default value, *Prorated,* realizes the cost evenly across the duration of the task.

- In the ***Base Calendar*** column, select the *Base Calendar* that Project Server 2010 uses to set up the resource's personal calendar. If you entered your company holidays on the *Standard* calendar, and then you specify this calendar as the resource's *Base Calendar,* the resource's personal calendar automatically inherits all company holidays.

- The ***Code*** field is a free text field in which you may enter any type of additional information about the resource, such as the cost center code or work phone number for the resource.

> Similar to Microsoft Excel, you can speed up the entry of resources by using the *Fill Handle* to fill data from one cell to consecutive cells above or below it. Do this by selecting a cell, and then click and hold the *Fill Handle* in the lower right corner of the selected cell, dragging up or down to fill as many cells as you like.

> **Warning:** When entering your resource names, avoid using non-alphanumeric characters other than the underscore or a semicolon to separate first and last names. Special characters can cause problems with project names and resource names in Project Server 2010. If your company's naming convention uses the "last name, first name" form, use a semicolon instead of a comma in the resource name. Because the comma character is the list separator for standard English SQL Server deployments, you cannot use a comma in resource names.

Figure 9 - 15 shows the Resource Sheet view after I added basic resource information about a new work resource named George Stewart. Notice that I entered specific information about him in the *Initials, Group, Std. Rate,* and *Ovt. Rate* columns.

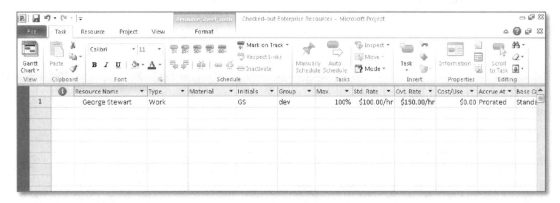

Figure 9 - 15: Work resource entered in Resource Sheet view

The second step in defining enterprise work resources is to enter custom resource information for each resource using the *Resource Information* dialog. To access this dialog, double-click the resource and the system opens the *Resource Information* dialog shown in Figure 9 - 16. Notice that the *Resource Information* dialog includes four tabbed pages of information for the selected resource, including the *General, Costs, Notes,* and *Custom Fields* pages. I discuss each of these pages separately.

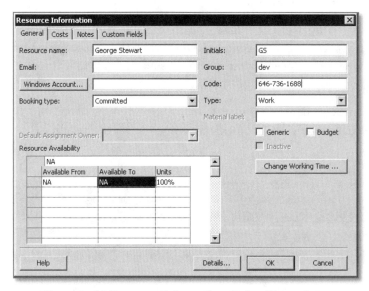

Figure 9 - 16: Resource Information dialog General page

Entering General Information

The General page includes some of the basic information you already entered in the *Resource Sheet* view, such as *Resource Name, Type, Initials, Group,* and *Code*. Notice in Figure 9 - 16 that I used the *Code* field for the resource's office phone number. The *General* page also allows you to enter additional information, such as the resource's e-mail address, windows account, resource availability information and booking type. You can also select the *Generic* checkbox to make the resource a *Generic* resource, a *Budget* resource, or an *Inactive* resource. Note that you cannot make a resource inactive until you save the resource for the first time. Therefore the *Inactive* option is grayed out in the figure.

Use the *Resource Availability* section to enter changes in the availability for the selected resource, such as when a part-time employee becomes a full-time employee on a specific date. The system accepts up to 100 entries in the *Resource Availability* section.

Figure 9 - 17 shows the changes in availability for George Stewart, who goes from full-time to part-time to attend graduate school during the 2010-2011 school year. Notice in the figure how his availability changes from 100% *Units* to 50% *Units* and then returns to 100% *Units* again. The software automatically updates these availability changes in the *Max. Units* field for the resource.

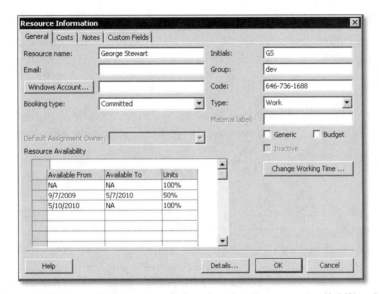

Figure 9 - 17: Resource Information dialog showing Resource Availability changes

 MSProjectExperts recommends that you always document changes in *Resource Availability* with a Note.

Project Server 2010 allows you to indicate a default *Booking Type* for each resource. The choices for the *Booking Type* field are *Proposed* or *Committed*. When a project manager assigns a resource to a task, and the resource has a "Proposed" booking type, the system interprets each of the resource's assignments as a "tentative commitment." When a project manager assigns a resource with a "Committed" booking type, the system interprets the assignments as "firm commitments." Project managers can change the *Booking Type* value for each project team member on a project-by-project basis. You should set the *Booking Type* value to committed for all resources in the Enterprise Resource Pool; otherwise, Project Managers must remember to do this in order for the assignments to affect resource availability.

Booking Type Consequences

When a project manager books a team member as a proposed resource on a project, the system handles all task assignments for the proposed resource as proposed assignments. The consequences within Project Server 2010 are as follows:

1. Published task assignments do not display for proposed resources on their *Tasks* and *Timesheet* pages.

2. The projects in which a resource is booked as proposed do not display in the *View Resource Availability* page, and the resource's work hours do not display for proposed task assignments.

3. Proposed bookings do not affect resource availability. Consequently, these do not appear in the *View Resource Availability* page.

4. Booking type is a dimension of the OLAP Cube and is available for use in building views.

A correct e-mail address and Windows account are essential for human work resources that collaborate through Project Server. If you are using a Work resource to represent equipment or other asset usage, do not specify Windows authentication, because you will not likely have active directory accounts for equipment--not to mention that getting equipment to log on to Project Web App would be quite an engineering feat!

When creating a work resource, you may manually enter the Windows Account information or pull it from an available address book. If you have Outlook or any other MAPI–compliant mail client installed on your workstation connected to a company mail server, clicking the *Windows Account* button provides you with options to connect to your address book in Outlook or Lotus Notes. Note that a mail client must have a Windows mail profile in order for Project Professional 2010 to find it on the workstation. Lotus Notes, for example, does not create a Windows mail profile during installation, so you must do this manually.

Changing Working Time

There are several situations that require you to change the working schedule for a resource, such as:

- The resource works a schedule different from the schedule on the enterprise *Standard* calendar.

- You need to add nonworking time for the resource, such as vacation or planned sick leave.

- You need to make minor modifications to the resource's working schedule, such as adding Saturday work for a specific period of time.

I discuss how to configure each of these scheduling requirements separately.

Setting an Alternate Working Schedule

If you need to create an alternate working schedule for a resource, and the schedule differs from the enterprise standard calendar, there are two ways to accomplish this. To use the first method, you must first create a custom enterprise base calendar in the system. Refer back to Module 07, if necessary, for the steps to create a custom base calendar.

After you create the custom base calendar, simply select that new calendar in the *Base Calendar* column for the selected resource.

> If you have multiple resources that need the same alternate working schedule, create a new base calendar with the alternate schedule, and set this calendar as the base calendar for each of the resources that work the alternate schedule.

If you do not want to create a custom base calendar with the new schedule, you can specify the non-standard working schedule for the resource by completing the following steps:

1. Click the *Change Working Time* button on the *General* page of the *Resource Information* dialog.

The system displays the *Change Working Time* dialog for the selected resource, such as for George Stewart shown in Figure 9 - 18.

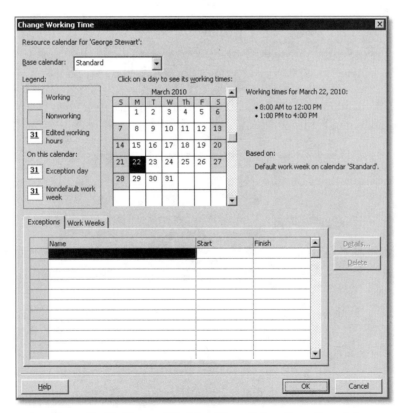

Figure 9 - 18: Change Working Time dialog, Exceptions tab

2.   Click the *Work Weeks* tab. Figure 9 - 19 shows the *Work Weeks* tab in the *Change Working Time* dialog for George Stewart.

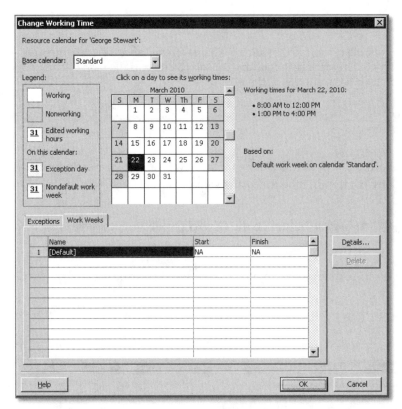

Figure 9 - 19: Change Working Time dialog, Work Weeks tab

3.   Select the *[Default]* item in the Work Weeks data grid and then click the *Details* button. The software displays the *Details* dialog shown in Figure 9 - 20.

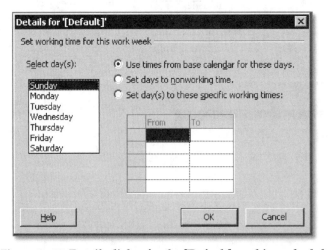

Figure 9 - 20: Details dialog for the [Default] working schedule

4.   In the *Select day(s)* list, select the days for which you want to change the schedule.

5. Select one of the three working times options in the upper right corner of the dialog, such as the *Set day(s) to these specific working times* option.

6. Enter the alternate working schedule in the *From* and *To* fields in the data grid.

Figure 9 - 21 shows the *Details* dialog for a working schedule where the resource works 10 hours per day from Monday through Friday. Because George Stewart is a Senior Project Manager, this is not an atypical working schedule.

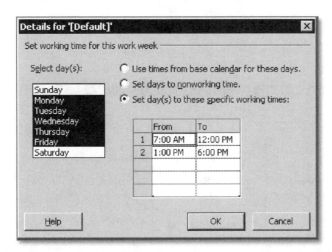

Figure 9 - 21: Details dialog shows alternate working schedule

7. Click the *OK* button to close the Details dialog.

Figure 9 - 22 shows the *Change Working Time* dialog with the new alternate working schedule for George Stewart.

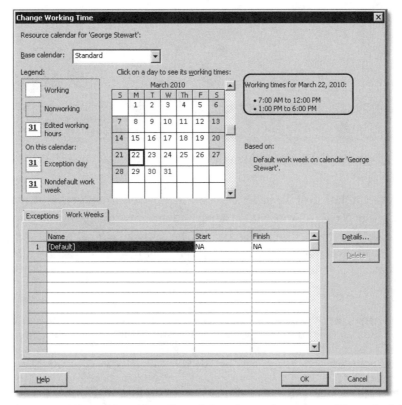

Figure 9 - 22: Change Working Time dialog shows alternate working schedule

Entering Nonworking Time

Project Server 2010 allows you to enter nonworking time, such as vacations and sick leave, for each individual resource in the enterprise resource pool. To enter nonworking time for a selected resource, complete the following steps:

1. Click the *Change Working Time* button on the *General* page of the *Resource Information* dialog.

2. Click the *Exceptions* tab. Figure 9 - 23 shows the *Exceptions* tab of the *Change Working Time* dialog for George Stewart.

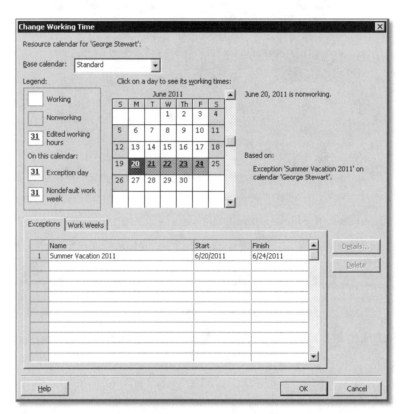

Figure 9 - 23: Change Working Time dialog with vacation exception

3. In the calendar object at the top of the page, select the days to set as nonworking time as I did in Figure 9 - 23. In the first blank line of *Name* column, enter a name for the nonworking time instance, such as "Summer Vacation." Press the right-Arrow key on the keyboard. The software automatically sets the selected time period as nonworking time, such as the summer vacation time scheduled in August 2011 for George Stewart shown in Figure 9 - 23.

If your organization uses the planned Sick time and Vacation categories of Administrative time, Project Server 2010 automatically adds a nonworking time instance for approved Sick time and Vacation submissions for each resource. For example, if George Stewart submitted one week of Vacation time to his timesheet manager, and the manager approved the submission, the week of vacation would appear as a nonworking time instance on George Stewart's calendar in the enterprise resource pool, similar to that shown in Figure 9-23.

Setting Working Schedule Changes

To set a change to the regular working schedule for the resource, such as when a resource might be asked to extend their work week, or needs to reduce it for a specified period of time, complete the following steps:

1. Click the *Change Working Time* button on the *General* page of the *Resource Information* dialog.

2. Click the *Work Weeks* tab.

3. In the first blank line of the *Name* column, enter a name for the schedule change and then press the right-arrow key.

4. Enter the starting date of the schedule change in the *Start* field and enter the ending date in the *Finish* field. For example, Figure 9 - 24 shows an extended working schedule change for George Stewart during the month of October 2010 only, when he works Saturdays from 7:00 to 12:00.

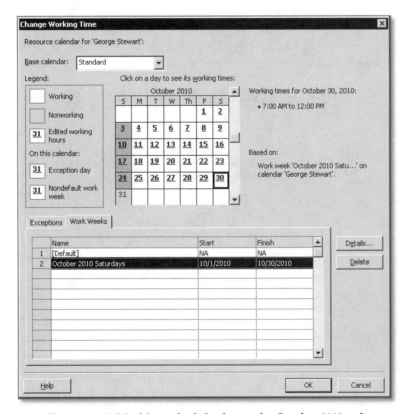

Figure 9 - 24: Working schedule change for October 2010 only

5. Click the *Details* button. The software displays the *Details* dialog as shown in Figure 9 - 25.

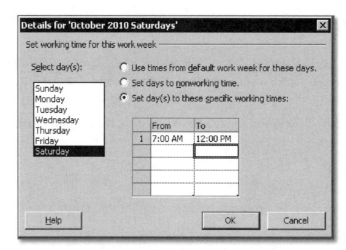

Figure 9 - 25: Details dialog for the October 2010 schedule change

6. In the *Select day(s)* list, select the days for which you want to change the schedule, and then click the *Set day(s) to these specific working times* option.

7. Enter the alternate working schedule in the *From* and *To* fields in the data grid, and press the *Enter* key on the keyboard after you enter the time value for the final *To* field. Figure 9 - 25 now shows that George Stewart must work 5 hours each Saturday during October 2010 only, in addition to the 10 hours that he works each day Monday through Friday.

8. Click the *OK* button to close the *Details* dialog. Figure 9 - 26 shows the *Change Working Time* dialog with the October 2010 schedule change for George Stewart.

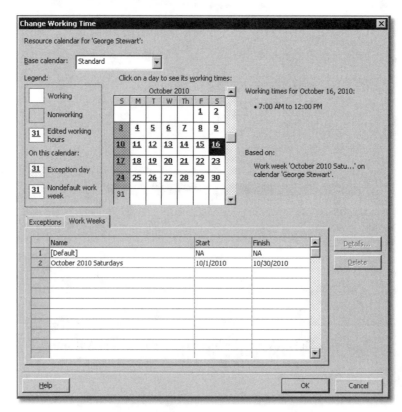

**Figure 9 - 26: Change Working Time dialog
with October 2010 schedule change**

Entering Cost Information

In the *Resource Information* dialog, click the *Costs* tab to view the cost rates for the selected resource, as shown in Figure 9 - 27. The *Costs* page displays the Standard Rate, Overtime Rate, and Per Use Costs for the selected resource. In addition, this page also contains five Cost Rate tables labeled A through E. Cost Rate Table A contains the default rates you entered in the *Resource Sheet* view for Standard, Overtime, and Per Use Cost rates. You can use Cost Rate Tables B through E for alternate cost rates. You can set any of the rates on Cost Rate Tables A through E so that the rate changes on a given day.

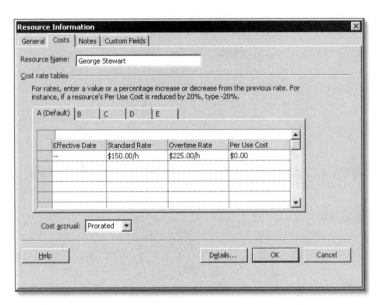

Figure 9 - 27: Resource Information dialog Costs page

As a part of your organization's project-costing model, you may need to change cost rates on a specific date for a selected resource. For example, on January 1, 2011, the Standard and Overtime Rates increase for George Stewart due to a change in seniority. To define a new cost rate that begins on a specific date, enter the date in the *Effective Date* field on the first blank line of the data grid and then enter the new rates on the same line, as shown in the example in Figure 9 - 28.

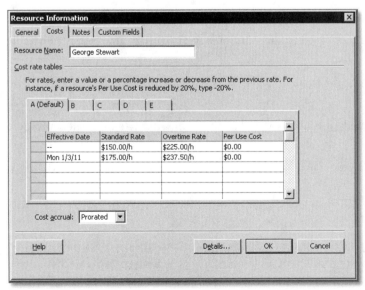

Figure 9 - 28: Resource Information dialog Cost rate increase on 1/3/11

When you enter a cost rate change for a resource, Project Server 2010 automatically costs all project work after the effective date at the new cost rate for that resource. For example, for George Stewart's tasks the system costs all work prior to 1/3/11 at $150/hour and costs all work after 1/3/11 at $225/hour.

You might also have an enterprise resource that plays multiple roles in a project, where cost depends on the role. For example, we cost George Stewart's work on project management tasks at $150/hour but cost his work at $300/hour on tasks where he must serve as an expert witness in legal hearings. To specify an alternate cost rate for a selected resource, select one of the alternate Cost Rate Table tabs (B through E) and enter the alternate rate(s) on the first line of the data grid on that tab as shown for George Stewart in Figure 9 - 29.

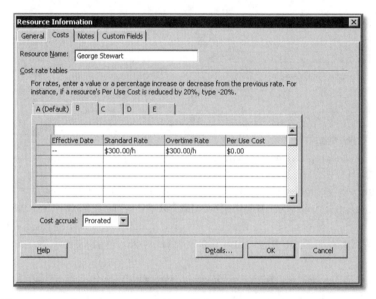

Figure 9 - 29: Resource Information dialog Alternate cost rate on Table B

msProjectExperts recommends that you document your use of alternate *Cost Rate Tables* with a Note. The Note should explain how and when to use the alternate rates shown on *Cost Rate Tables B through E*.

Entering Resource Notes

Click the *Notes* tab in the *Resource Information* dialog to record additional information about the selected resource, such as changes in availability and notes about how to use the rates in the alternate Cost Rate Tables. Figure 9 - 30 shows the *Notes* page with documentation on the Cost rates for Cost Rate Table B.

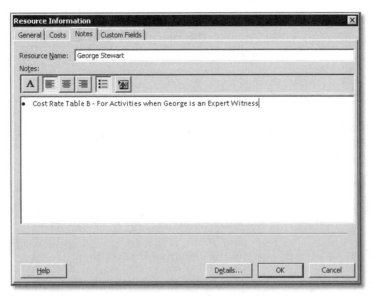

Figure 9 - 30: Resource Information dialog Notes page

MSProjectExperts recommends that you use resource notes to document important resource information such as changes in availability and your use of alternate cost rates. This makes it easier for others to understand how Project Server 2010 calculates both the schedule and the cost of tasks to which you assign the resource.

Using the Custom Fields Page

Click the *Custom Fields* tab in the *Resource Information* dialog to see all of the custom enterprise resource fields available for resources in your organization. Figure 9 - 31 shows the *Custom Fields* page for George Stewart. Notice that the dialog contains the custom field IT Skill, and three built-in fields (RBS, Team Name, and Cost Type).

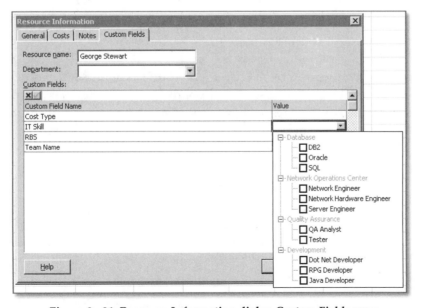

Figure 9 - 31: Resource Information dialog Custom Fields page

When you finish selecting values for custom enterprise fields for the selected resource, click the *OK* button to close the *Resource Information* dialog and return to the *Resource Sheet* view in the Checked-out Enterprise Resources file.

Creating Non-Work Resources

Project Server 2010 allows you to create several different types of non-work resources, including material resources, generic resources, cost resources, and team resources. I discuss how to create each of these resources individually.

Creating Material Resources

To create a material resource, open the enterprise resource pool and complete the following steps in the *Resource Sheet* view:

1. Enter the name of the material resource in the *Resource Name* column.

2. Click the *Type* pick list button and select the *Material* value from the pick list.

3. Enter a value in the *Material Label* column to indicate how you measure the consumption of the material resource.

The *Material Label* field allows you to define your own consumption units corresponding with the costs that you set. For instance, concrete for a construction project might be labeled "cubic yard," while an electronic component might be labeled "each," or "assembly." The point is to make the label correspond to the cost. In Figure 9 - 32, notice that I entered a material resource called Bulk Network Cable whose consumption we measure in feet with a cost of $0.25/foot.

	ⓘ	Resource Name	Type	Material Label	Initials	Group	Max.	Std. Rate	Ovt. Rate	Cost/Use	Accrue At
1	🖉	George Stewart	Work		GS	dev	100%	$150.00/hr	$225.00/hr	$0.00	Prorated
2		Bulk Network Cable	Material	Feet	B			$0.25		$0.00	Prorated

Figure 9 - 32: Bulk Network Cable Material resource

Creating Generic Resources

Generic resources support key resource features in Project Server 2010, including skill matching in the *Build Team* dialog and the *Resource Substitution Wizard*. They also create resource demand for projects in early phase development, and this demand aggregated with the named resources you specify is what portfolio analytics use to measure resource demand against availability. Generic resources serve as placeholders for actual resources before you identify your actual resources.

In previous versions of Microsoft Project Server, the system counted both generic and regular work resources when calculating capacity. In Microsoft Project Server 2010, generic resources affect only demand and are not counted in determining resource capacity. Users of previous versions may have to to adjust certain views and analysis techniques to account for this change when upgrading to Microsoft Project Server 2010.

You can use generic resources to model project costs before you assign human resources. When you assign generic resources to tasks in project plans, Project Server 2010 calculates costs based on the rates set in the enterprise resource pool. To create a generic resource, complete the following steps:

1. Enter the name of the generic resource in the *Resource Name* column.

2. Enter all other basic information in the columns of the *Resource Sheet* view as you would for a non-generic resource.

3. Double-click the resource.

4. On the *General page* in the *Resource Information* dialog, select the *Generic* option.

5. Specify cost information on the *Costs* page.

6. Specify custom field values on the *Custom Fields* page.

7. Click the *OK* button.

Step #6 is extremely important if you intend to use generic resources for skill matching and portfolio analytics. You must specify values for the custom enterprise resource fields that you created to match generic resources with human resources.

Figure 9 - 33 shows the *Resource Information* dialog for a Generic resource called SQL DBA.

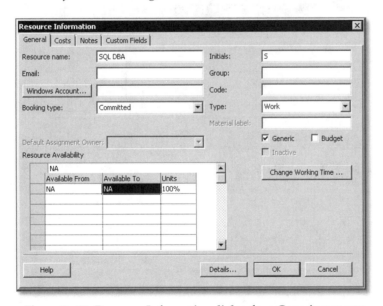

Figure 9 - 33: Resource Information dialog for a Generic resource

Creating Cost Resources

Microsoft introduced Cost resources in Project Server 2007. You generally use cost resources in three situations:

- Your organization needs to connect cost data in your project to a third-party financial system.

- Your organization specifies a budget for each project, and your project managers enter actual project costs manually in their Project Professional 2010 plans.

- Your organization needs to track additional project expenditures, such as travel expenses, across all enterprise projects.

The system provides you with two types of cost resources: *Budget Cost* resources and *Expense Cost* resources. To create a *Budget Cost* resource, complete the following steps:

1. Enter the name of the *Budget Cost* resource in the *Resource Name* field.

2. Click the *Type* pick list and select the *Cost* item from the list. Notice in Figure 9 - 34 that I am creating a *Budget Cost* resource named Project Budget.

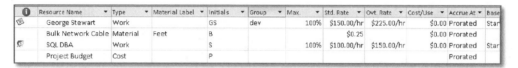

	Resource Name	▼	Type	▼	Material Label	▼	Initials	▼	Group	▼	Max.	▼	Std. Rate	▼	Ovt. Rate	▼	Cost/Use	▼	Accrue At	▼	Base
	George Stewart		Work				GS		dev		100%		$150.00/hr		$225.00/hr		$0.00		Prorated		Star
	Bulk Network Cable		Material		Feet		B						$0.25				$0.00		Prorated		
	SQL DBA		Work				S				100%		$100.00/hr		$150.00/hr		$0.00		Prorated		Star
	Project Budget		Cost				P												Prorated		

Figure 9 - 34: Enter Budget Cost resource information in the Resource Sheet view

3. Enter additional information for the *Budget Cost* resource in the *Initials, Group, Accrue At*, and *Code* fields, as needed.

4. Double-click the name of the *Budget Cost* resource.

5. On the *General* page of the *Resource Information* dialog, select the *Budget* option as shown in Figure 9 - 35.

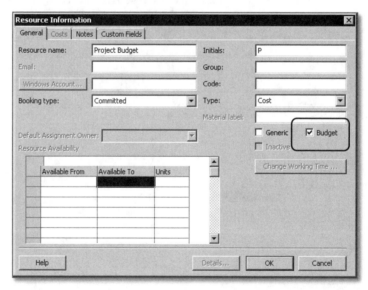

Figure 9 - 35: Budget Cost resource in the Resource Information dialog

6. Click the *OK* button.

To create an *Expense Cost* resource, complete the following steps:

1. Enter the name of the *Expense Cost* resource in the *Resource Name* field in the *Resource Sheet* view.

2. Click the *Type* pick list and select the *Cost* item from the list.

3. Enter additional appropriate information for the *Expense Cost* resource in the *Initials, Group, Accrue At*, and *Code* fields. Figure 9 - 36 shows my new cost resources named Project Budget and Travel Expense.

ⓘ	Resource Name	Type	Material Label	Initials	Group	Max.	Std. Rate	Ovt. Rate	Cost/Use	Accrue At	Base
	George Stewart	Work		GS	dev	100%	$150.00/hr	$225.00/hr	$0.00	Prorated	Star
	Bulk Network Cable	Material	Feet	B			$0.25		$0.00	Prorated	
	SQL DBA	Work		S		100%	$100.00/hr	$150.00/hr	$0.00	Prorated	Star
	Project Budget	Cost		P						Prorated	
	Travel Expense	Cost		T						Prorated	

Figure 9 - 36: Completed Budget Cost and Expense Cost resource

Recommendations for Using Cost Resources

Cost resources have a number of behavioral characteristics you should be familiar with in Project Server 2010, including:

- Cost resources can determine the start and finish dates for tasks. This occurs when a user manually contours cost or actual cost information in the timephased grid in the *Task Usage* and *Resource Usage* views.

- Users have full control over cost and actual cost contours in the *Task Usage* and *Resource Usage* views. This means a user can manually contour the planned cost for a cost resource, and then manually contour a different pattern for the actual cost for the cost resource.

- When a user manually contours actual cost information that is less than the original planned cost for the cost resource, the system does not automatically reschedule unspent money. Instead, the system allows the user to reschedule the unspent money.

- If a user manually contours cost information at a monthly level in the timephased grid, the system correctly applies the cost from the start date of the task to the finish date of the task.

Cost resources have some limitations. Therefore, ask your project managers to follow Microsoft's recommendations for using cost resources effectively in their enterprise projects:

- Do not assign a cost resource on the same task as a work resource if the resource reports actual progress from Project Web App.

- Although you can manually contour planned cost information at a monthly level for cost resources in the *Task Usage* or *Resource Usage* views, **do not** enter actual cost information at the monthly level. Instead, enter the actual cost information at a finer granularity level, such as on a daily or weekly basis.

- Do not assign a task calendar using 24-hour elapsed days (eDays) to a task assigned to a cost resource.

- Do not disable the *Actual costs are always calculated by Microsoft Project* option in your project from the *Calculations for this Project* section of the *Schedule* tab of the *Project Options* page in the backstage.

- Avoid using the *Undo* feature if you edit the *Remaining Duration* field for a task assigned to a cost resource.

Creating Team Resources

Another resource type in Project Server 2010 is a special type of generic resource called a *Team* resource. You should create team resources only if your organization uses dedicated project teams and the team members do not change from project to project, or if your organization needs to model pick-up work that any team member can perform. Before you can create and use team resources, you must create a custom *Lookup Table*, populate it with a list of team names in your organization, and then attach the *Lookup Table* to the *Team Name* built-in custom field. Your project managers can then assign a team resource to tasks in a project. After the manager publishes the project with a team resource assignment, all members of the team can self-assign team tasks from their *Tasks* page in Project Web App.

To create a team resource, complete the following steps:

1. Enter the name of the team resource in the *Resource Name* column.

2. Enter all other basic information in the columns of the *Resource Sheet* view.

3. Double-click the resource and select the *Generic* option in the *Resource Information* dialog.

4. Specify cost information on the *Costs* page.

5. Specify custom field values on the *Custom Fields* page and then click the *OK* button.

> **Warning:** When you specify custom field values for the team resource, make sure that you select a value from the *Team Name* field. Project Server 2010 uses the *Team Name* field to match team members with the team resource.

6. In the *Resource Sheet* view right-click on the *Type* column header and select *Insert Column* from the shortcut menu.

7. Click the *Field Name* pick list, select the *Team Assignment Pool* field name from the list, and then click the *OK* button.

8. In the *Team Assignment Pool* column, select the *Yes* value for the team resource. Figure 9 - 37 shows the new Database Team resource as I select the *Yes* value in the *Team Assignment Pool* column.

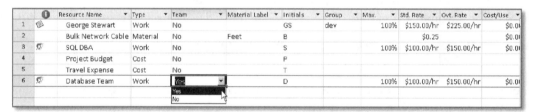

	ⓘ	Resource Name	Type	Team	Material Label	Initials	Group	Max.	Std. Rate	Ovt. Rate	Cost/Use
1		George Stewart	Work	No		GS	dev	100%	$150.00/hr	$225.00/hr	$0.0
2		Bulk Network Cable	Material	No	Feet	B			$0.25		$0.0
3		SQL DBA	Work	No		S		100%	$100.00/hr	$150.00/hr	$0.0
4		Project Budget	Cost	No		P					
5		Travel Expense	Cost	No		T					
6		Database Team	Work	Yes		D		100%	$100.00/hr	$150.00/hr	$0.0
				Yes							
				No							

Figure 9 - 37: Team resource added to Enterprise Resource Pool

After you create a team resource, you must indicate the members of the team by selecting the correct *Team Name* value for each human resource that serves on the team. For example, Figure 9 - 37 shows that I created a team resource named Database Team that represents a dedicated team that works on database tasks. The team consists of four DBA's; therefore, I must set the correct *Team Name* value for each of the four resources to make them members of Database Team.

**Using Generic, Material, Cost, and Team
Resources with Required Enterprise Fields**

When you define generic, material, cost, or team resources, you must provide a value for all **Required** custom enterprise resource fields. Therefore, it is very important that you provide appropriate custom field values for use specifically with these types of resources at the time you are defining your custom fields. If you do not provide appropriate required field values, the system displays an error warning when you attempt to save the generic, material, cost, or team resources in the enterprise resource pool.

Editing Enterprise Resources Using Project Professional 2010

To edit existing enterprise resources in Project Professional 2010, you must first check them out from the enterprise resource pool. When you check out an enterprise resource, the system locks the resource to prevent anyone else from editing it at the same time.

> Checking out a resource does not prevent project managers or resource managers from using the resource as a member of a project team or from assigning the resource to a task in a project plan.

To check out one or more existing resources, navigate to the *Resource Center* in Project Web App shown in Figure 9 - 38.

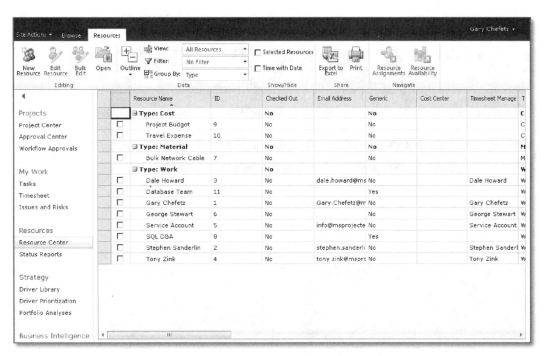

Figure 9 - 38: Resource Center page in Project Web App 2010

By default, the *Resource Center* page displays all resources in the enterprise resource pool grouped by resource type. For example, notice in Figure 9 - 38 that my enterprise resource pool includes work, material, and cost resources.

> Notice in Figure 9-38 that Project Server 2010 groups standard generic resources with other work resources. Because you may want to separate generic resources from human resources, you can create a custom *Resource Center* view for this purpose. I discuss how to create custom views in Module 14.

Checking Out Enterprise Resources for Editing

To check out resources for editing, select the option checkbox to the left of each resource that you want to check out. Notice in Figure 9 - 39 that I selected Stephen Sanderlin and Tony Zink.

 To select all resources in the Enterprise Resource Pool quickly, float your mouse pointer over the selection column header and use the pick list and click the *Select All Resources* item as I showed you earlier in this module.

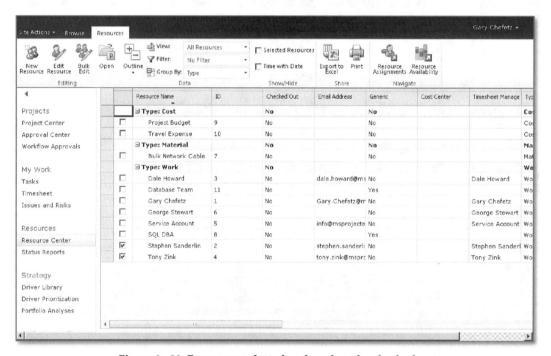

Figure 9 - 39: Resources selected and ready to be checked out

To check out the selected resources, click the *Open* button from the *Editing* section of the *Resources* menu. The system opens the Checked-out Enterprises Resources in Project Professional 2010 as shown in Figure 9 - 40.

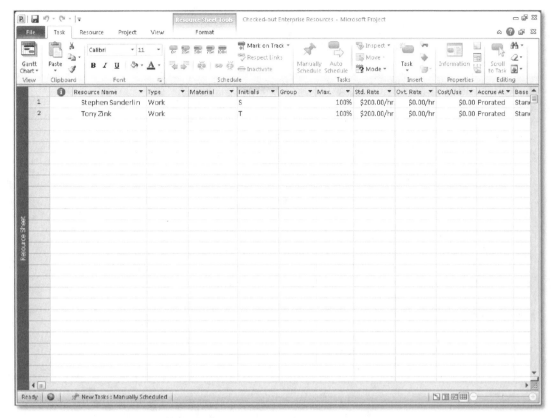

Figure 9 - 40: Checked-out enterprise resources in the Resource Sheet view

To edit the information for any resource, simply edit the basic information presented in the *Resource Sheet* view, or double click the resource and edit the custom resource information in the *Resource Information* dialog. If you also want to add new enterprise resources, follow the steps detailed in the previous topical sections to create *Work, Material, Generic, Cost,* or *Team* resources. When you are finished working with the enterprise resource pool, save and close the file.

Using Project Web App to Create an Enterprise Resource

Now that you know how to create each type of enterprise resource using the Project Professional 2010 interface, you should also understand how to create an enterprise resource using the Project Web App interface. Log into Project Web App with administrator permissions, and then navigate to the *Resource Center* page. To create a new enterprise resource, click the *New Resource* button from the *Editing* section of the *Resources* ribbon. The system displays the *New Resource* page. Because the page is so long, I cropped the image slightly, and the additional *Save* and *Cancel* buttons at the bottom of the page do not show in Figure 9 - 41.

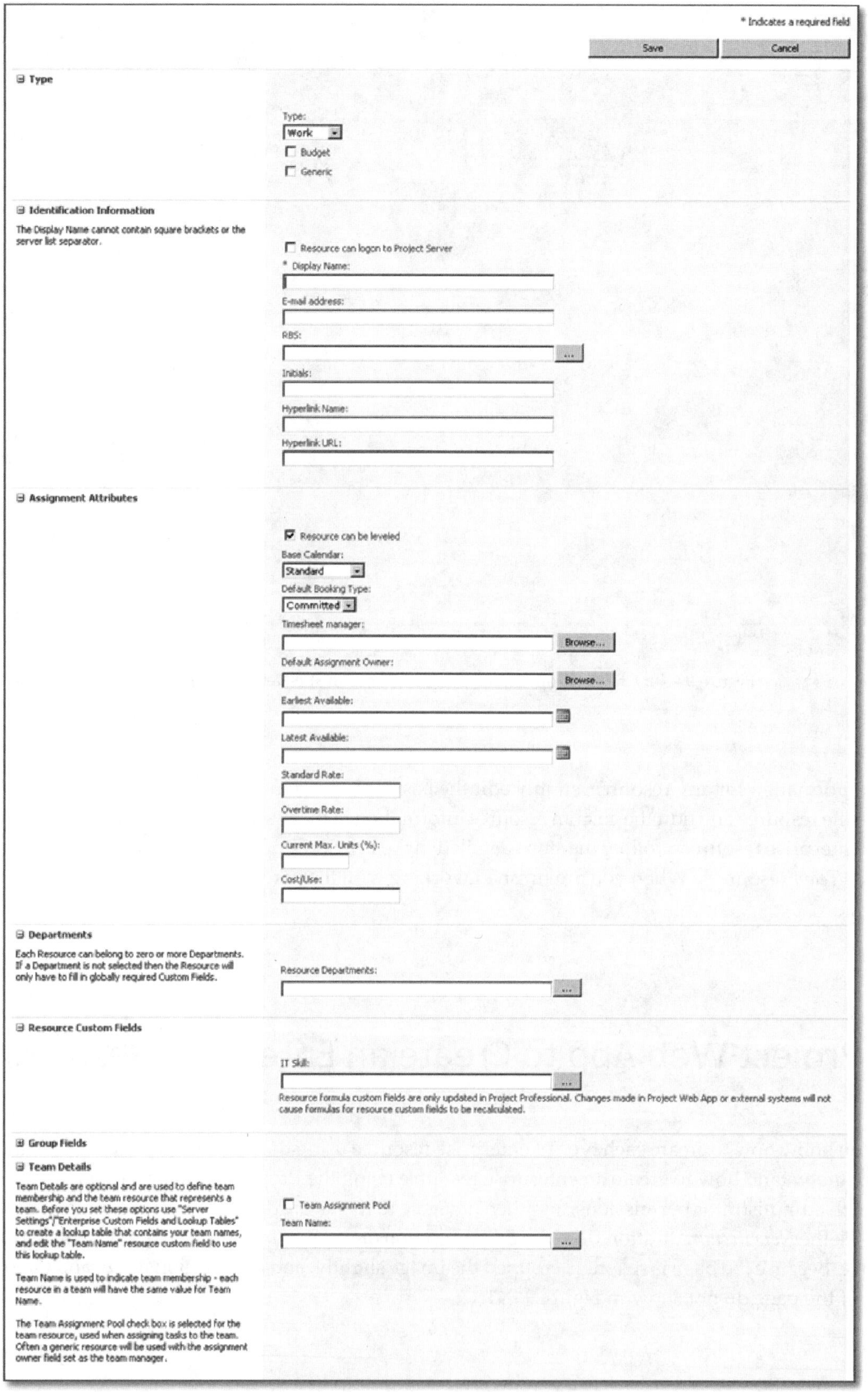

* Indicates a required field

| Save | Cancel |

Type

Type:
Work

☐ Budget
☐ Generic

Identification Information

The Display Name cannot contain square brackets or the server list separator.

☐ Resource can logon to Project Server

* Display Name:

E-mail address:

RBS:

Initials:

Hyperlink Name:

Hyperlink URL:

Assignment Attributes

☑ Resource can be leveled

Base Calendar:
Standard

Default Booking Type:
Committed

Timesheet manager:
[Browse...]

Default Assignment Owner:
[Browse...]

Earliest Available:

Latest Available:

Standard Rate:

Overtime Rate:

Current Max. Units (%):

Cost/Use:

Departments

Each Resource can belong to zero or more Departments. If a Department is not selected then the Resource will only have to fill in globally required Custom Fields.

Resource Departments:

Resource Custom Fields

IT Skill:

Resource formula custom fields are only updated in Project Professional. Changes made in Project Web App or external systems will not cause formulas for resource custom fields to be recalculated.

Group Fields

Team Details

Team Details are optional and are used to define team membership and the team resource that represents a team. Before you set these options use "Server Settings"/"Enterprise Custom Fields and Lookup Tables" to create a lookup table that contains your team names, and edit the "Team Name" resource custom field to use this lookup table.

Team Name is used to indicate team membership - each resource in a team will have the same value for Team Name.

The Team Assignment Pool check box is selected for the team resource, used when assigning tasks to the team. Often a generic resource will be used with the assignment owner field set as the team manager.

☐ Team Assignment Pool

Team Name:

Figure 9 - 41: New Resource Page

Setting Type Options

In the *Type* section of the *New Resource* page, begin creating a new enterprise resource by clicking the *Type* pick list and selecting one of the three primary resource types. Use the following as your guide to create the proper type of resource:

- If you need to create a human or equipment resource, select the *Work* item from the *Type* pick list.

- If you need to create a material resource, select the *Material* item from the *Type* pick list.

- If you need to create an expense cost resource, select the *Cost* item from the *Type* pick list.

- If you need to create a budget cost resource, select the *Cost* item from the *Type* pick list, and then select the *Budget* checkbox.

- If you need to create a generic resource, select the *Work* item from the *Type* pick list, and then select the *Generic* checkbox.

When you select either the *Material* or *Cost* item on the *Type* pick list, the system refreshes the *New Resource* page to show only the relevant fields used for the selected resource type. When you choose to create a material resource, for example, the system removes irrelevant options such as the *Resource Can Logon to Project Server* checkbox in the Identification section and most of the options in the *Assignment Attributes* section, and removes irrelevant sections such as the *User Authentication* section.

Setting Identification Information Options

In the *Identification Information* section, first determine whether the resource needs to use Project Web App. By default, the system selects the *Resource can logon to Project Server* checkbox, which means that the resource will use Project Web App to report task progress. If you have a resource that does not have a Windows network user ID, such as an external consultant or contractor, then you should deselect the *Resource can logon to Project Server* checkbox to show that the resource will not use Project Web App to report task progress.

Enter the name of the resource in the *Display Name* field (a required field), and enter the resource's e-mail address in the *E-mail address* field (a non-required field). You must enter an e-mail address for any resource that needs to receive *alert* and *reminder* e-mail messages from Project Server 2010. To enter a value in the *RBS* field, click the *Select Value* button to the right of the field. Expand the RBS lookup table to locate the value you need, and then select an RBS value for the resource, as shown in Figure 9 - 42.

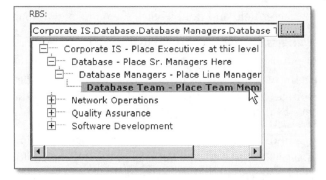

Figure 9 - 42: Select a value in the RBS field

When you select a value in the *RBS* field, the system enters a value in the field and collapses the lookup table. To complete the information in the *Identification Information* section of the page, optionally enter the resource's two or three letter initials in the *Initials* field, and enter hyperlink information in the *Hyperlink Name* and *Hyperlink URL* fields.

Setting User Authentication Options

In the *User Authentication* section, leave the default *Windows Authentication* option selected, and then enter the resource's Windows network user ID in the *User logon account* field. If you intend to use Active Directory Synchronization with Project Server 2010, the system automatically synchronizes the resource with Active Directory by default. If you do not want to synchronize the resource with Active Directory, then select the *Prevent Active Directory synchronization for this user* checkbox.

Setting Assignment Attributes Options

The *Assignment Attributes* section contains a number of important options that control how Project Server 2010 uses the resource. Select the *Resource can be leveled* option to allow project managers to level overallocations for the resource. To exempt the resource from leveling, deselect the *Resource can be leveled* option. When you deselect this option, the system sets a *No* value in the *Can Level* field for the resource in Project Professional 2010. Click the *Base Calendar* pick list and select the enterprise calendar that specifies the working schedule for the resource. Click the *Default Booking Type* pick list and select either a *Committed* value or a *Proposed* value from the list. If you select the *Proposed* value, project managers can change the *Booking Type* value for the resource in the *Build Team* dialog in Project Professional 2010 when they add the resource to their project team.

The *Default Booking Type* option controls the behavior of Project Server 2010 when a project manager publishes a project with the resource assigned to tasks in the project. If the resource is a *Committed* resource, the system displays all of the resource's assignment information in Project Web App. If the resource is a *Proposed* resource, the system does not display the resource's assignments in Project Web App. This means that the *Proposed* resource cannot see his/her task assignments on either the *Timesheet* page or the *Tasks* page in Project Web App.

The next two options are extremely important in Project Server 2010. When you enter the name of the resource in the *Display Name* field, the system pre-populates the resource's name in the *Timesheet Manager* and *Default Assignment Owner* fields. The system uses the *Timesheet Manager* field to determine who approves the resource's timesheets. If the resource does not require timesheet approval, leave the resource's name in the field. Otherwise, click the *Browse* button to the right of the *Timesheet Manager* field and double-click the name of a manager in the *Pick Resource* dialog.

Project Server 2010 uses the *Default Assignment Owner* field to determine whose *Tasks* page the system displays the assignments of when a manager publishes a project. If the resource is responsible for reporting progress on his/her own task assignments, then leave the resource's name in the *Default Assignment Owner* field. On the other hand, if you need to designate a different resource to enter progress on behalf of the resource, then click the *Browse* button to the right of the *Default Assignment Owner* field and double-click the name of the resource in the *Pick Resource* dialog.

If the resource is available during only a specific time period, you can specify this time period by entering the dates in the *Earliest Available* and *Latest Available* fields. Click the *Calendar* button for each field and select a date. If the resource is continually available for project work, you do not need to select a date in either of these fields.

To specify additional time periods for availability, you must open the Enterprise Resource Pool and edit the resource availability information in Project Professional 2010.

If your organization uses resource cost rates to cost projects, then enter these rates for the resource in the *Standard Hourly Rate* and *Overtime Hourly Rate* fields. In Project Professional 2010, the system displays this information in the *Standard Rate* and *Overtime Rate* fields on Cost Rate Table A for the selected resource.

To specify additional Standard and Overtime Rate information on Cost Rate Tables B-E, you must open the Enterprise Resource Pool and edit the cost rate information in Project Professional 2010.

Finally enter a percentage value in the *Max. Units* field, reflecting the resource's availability for project work. If the resource is available full-time for project work, then enter 100% in the field. If the resource is only available to work part time on projects, then enter a value that is less than 100%. Typically, you might enter part-time values such as 25%, 50%, or 75%, for example.

Setting Exchange Server Details Options

The options you select in this section determine whether Project Server 2010 synchronizes Project Web App tasks with Microsoft Exchange. The system displays Project Web App tasks on the Tasks list in Microsoft Office Outlook, and the resource can status these from Outlook using the percent complete tracking method. To set up task synchronization with Microsoft Exchange for the resource, select the *Synchronize Tasks* option and then enter the resource's e-mail account display name in the *User Principal Name* field. If you do not want to use synchronization with Microsoft Exchange, do not select the *Synchronize Tasks* option for the resource.

Do not select the *Sychronize Tasks* option unless and until you configure both Project Server and Exchange Server for synchronization. Use this option on this page when creating new resources on a system already configured for Exchange synchronization. Note that additonal configuration is required for each user in Exchange Server.

Setting Departments Options

The *Departments* section of the *New Resource* page contains only a single option: the *Resource Departments* field. Project Server 2010 uses the *Resource Departments* field to filter a resource's access to built-in and custom enterprise fields and other Project Server objects. If you need the resource to access all enterprise fields and objects, leave the *Resource Departments* field blank. To limit the resource's access to objects tagged for their department only, click the

Select Value button to the right of the field and select one or more values, such as shown in Figure 9 - 43.

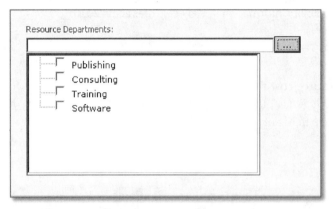

Figure 9 - 43: Select a Resource Departments value

 You can select multiple values in the *Resource Departments* field if you made the field a multi-value (MV) field.

Setting Resource Custom Fields Options

The *Resource Custom Fields* section contains any custom enterprise resource fields you created previously, including both free entry fields and fields containing a lookup table. Enter or select a value for each of your custom enterprise resource fields, as shown for my *IT Skill* field in Figure 9 - 44.

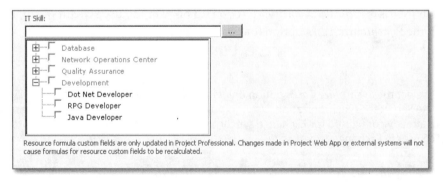

Figure 9 - 44: Select a value in the IT Skill field

Setting Security Options

You control each resource's security access to projects, other resources, and views by adding the resource to one or more security groups in the *Security Groups* section of the *New Resource* page. By default, Project Server 2010 adds each new resource to the *Team Members* group. To add the resource to additional groups, select one or more groups in the *Available Groups* list and click the *Add* button. To remove a resource from a security group, select the group in the

Groups that contain this user list and then click the *Remove* button. You can also use the *Add All* button or the *Remove All* button to handle a mass addition or removal of all groups.

Notice the options available in the *Security Categories* and *Global Permissions* sections of the *New Resource* page. I strongly recommend against adding a resource to a *Category* or setting individual *Global Permissions* for the resource. Either of these actions constitutes setting an "override" to the permissions inherited from the security groups to which the resource belongs. The more overrides you have, the more complicated you make your security environment. Instead, control all security in Project Server 2010 only by adding resources to security groups!

Setting Group Fields Options

Immediately below the *Resource Custom Fields* section of the *New Resource* page, the system includes a collapsed *Group Fields* section. Expand this section to enter information in the fields in this section, shown in Figure 9 - 45.

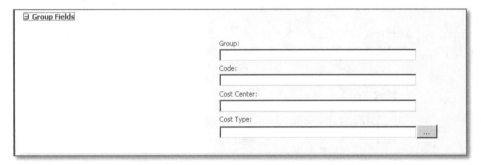

Figure 9 - 45: Expanded Group Fields section

Enter the resource's team, department, or role in the *Group* field. Enter any type of required code information for the resource in the *Code* field. Enter the resource's cost center in the *Cost Center* field. All three of these fields are free entry fields that allow you to enter any combination of text and/or numbers in the field. If your organization tracks resource information by cost type, click the *Select Value* button for the *Cost Type* field and select a value as shown in Figure 9 - 46.

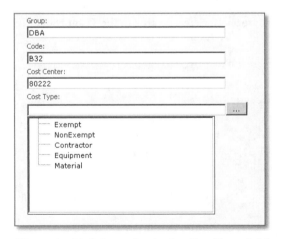

Figure 9 - 46: Select value in the Cost Type field

Notice in Figure 9 - 46 that I entered *DBA* in the *Group* field, indicating that the resource is part of the DBA team. Notice also that I entered *832* in the *Code* field, as our organization uses this field to show the location of the resource on our corporate campus. Notice also that I entered *80222* in the *Cost Center* field, indicating the cost center number for this resource.

Setting Team Details Options

You use the *Team Details* section to create a *Team* resource or to add a resource to a team represented by a *Team* resource. Before you can create a *Team* resource, you must create a *Team Names* lookup table and attach it to the *Team Name* built-in enterprise field. To create a *Team* resource, complete the following steps:

1. Confirm that you selected the *Generic* option in the *Type* section of the page.

2. Select the *Team Assignment Pool* option.

3. Click the *Select Value* button for the *Team Name* field and select a value.

To add a resource to a team represented by a Team resource, complete the following steps:

1. **Do not** select the *Team Assignment Pool* option.

2. Click the *Select Value* button for the *Team Name* field and select the same value selected for the team resource, as shown in Figure 9 - 47.

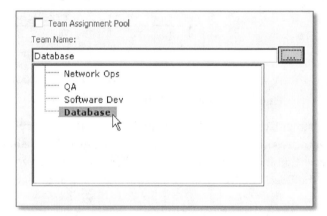

Figure 9 - 47: Select a value in the Team Name field

Notice in Figure 9 - 47 that I am adding the resource to a team represented by a *Team* resource for the Database team. When you finish creating the new resource on the *New Resource* page, click the *Save* button to save the resource in the enterprise resource pool in Project Server 2010.

Mass Editing Enterprise Resources

Project Server 2010 offers you two methods to edit the information for multiple resources using the *Resource Center* page:

- Bulk edit the enterprise resources as a group.

- Individually edit the enterprise resources as a batch.

To begin the process of editing a group of enterprise resources in bulk or individually as a batch, in the *Resource Center*, select the option checkbox to the left of the name of each resource you want to edit. You can quickly select all or clear all using the techniques I showed you earlier in this module.

Bulk Editing Enterprise Resources

Remember that when you Bulk Edit resources, you apply the same change to every selected resource. After you select two or more resources, click the *Bulk Edit* button from the *Editing* section of the *Resources* ribbon. Project Server 2010 displays the *Bulk Edit* page for the selected resources shown in Figure 9 - 48.

The *Bulk Edit* page contains six sections: *Assignment Attributes, Built-In Custom Fields, Exchange Server Details, Departments, Resource Custom Fields,* and *Resources Selected.* As I mentioned in the previous section, the two fields in the *Assignment Attributes* section are extremely important to the timesheet and task progress reporting functionality in Project Server 2010. When you create a new enterprise resource, the system automatically enters the resource's name in the *Timesheet Manager* and *Default Assignment Owner* fields. On the *Bulk Edit* page, you can change the values in either of these fields in bulk for all of the selected resources.

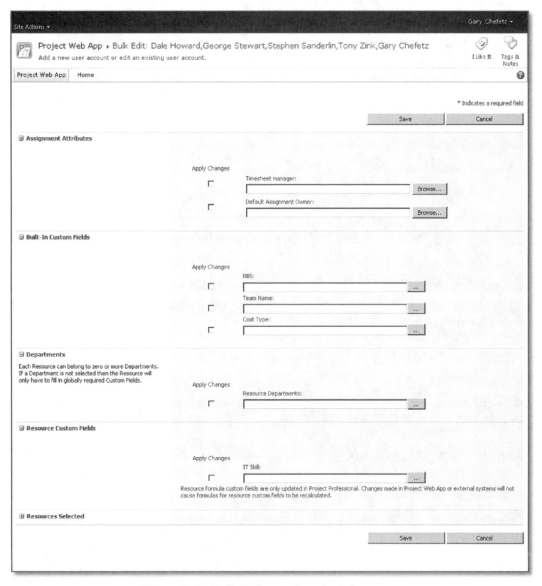

Figure 9 - 48: Bulk Edit page for selected resources

To change the value for either the *Timesheet Manager* or *Default Assignment Owner* field, click the *Browse* button to the right of the field. The system displays the *Pick Resource* window. Figure 9 - 49 shows the *Pick Resource* window for the *Timesheet Manager* field.

Figure 9 - 49: Pick Resource window

The *Pick Resource* window for the *Timesheet Manager* field shows of the all resources that have the *Approve Timesheets* permission and can serve as a timesheet manager for other resources. In this window, double-click the name of the person responsible for approving the resource's timesheets to select that person.

 If the *Pick Resource* window displays a long list of resources, you can quickly locate a speicific resource by entering a partial name in the text field at the top of the page and clicking the *Search* button.

 Warning: After you select a manager in the *Timesheet Manager* field, you must manually select the *Apply Changes* checkbox to the left of the field. This system does not automatically select this checkbox for you.

In some organizations, team members do not enter and submit task progress to the project manager. Instead, a designated person such as a team leader is responsible for entering and submitting task progress on behalf of each team member. If this describes your organization, enter the name of the designated team leader in the *Default Assignment Owner* field for the group of resources. This action places the group's task assignments on the *Tasks* page of the team leader.

Warning: After you select a resource in the *Default Assignment Owner* field, you must manually select the *Apply Changes* checkbox to the left of the field. This system does not select this checkbox for you automatically.

Warning: If you want all team members to see their own task assignments on the *Tasks* page, then leave the *Default Assignment Owner* field blank on the Bulk Edit page.

The *Built-In Custom Fields* section contains three built-in custom enterprise resource fields that ship with Project Server 2010, including the *RBS*, *Team Name*, and *Cost Type* fields. To select a value in any of these three fields, click the *Select Value* button to the right of the field and choose your value. The system automatically selects the *Apply Changes* checkbox for you.

The *Departments* section contains only a single field. In the *Departments* section, click the *Select Value* button to the right of the *Resource Departments* field and select one or more *Departments* as needed for all of the selected resources. The system automatically selects the *Apply Changes* checkbox for you.

The *Resource Custom Fields* section contains any custom enterprise resource fields that you created. Notice in Figure 9 - 48, shown previously, that the *Resource Custom Fields* section contains the custom enterprise field I created earlier, *IT Skill*. Click the *Select Value* button to the right of any field that you want to specify a value for all selected resources, and then select a value. Once again, the system automatically selects the *Apply Changes* checkbox for you.

The final section is the *Resources Selected* section. The system collapses this section by default, as this section does not contain any editable fields. After you enter or select values on the *Bulk Edit* page, click the *Save* button. Project Server 2010 applies the field changes to each of the resources in the group you selected.

Individually Editing Enterprise Resources by Batch

Sometimes you need to edit a group of resources, but need to specify values for each resource individually. To batch edit resources individually, select the option checkbox to the left of each resource name in the *Resource Center* page, and then click the *Edit Resource* button from the *Editing* section of the *Resources* ribbon. Project Server 2010 displays the *Edit Resource* page for the first selected resource. Because the page is so long, I must break into two parts, as shown in

Figure 9 - 50 and Figure 9 - 51. Notice that the *Edit Resource* page now contains three buttons at the top and bottom of the page. You use these three buttons to edit and navigate through each of the selected resources individually.

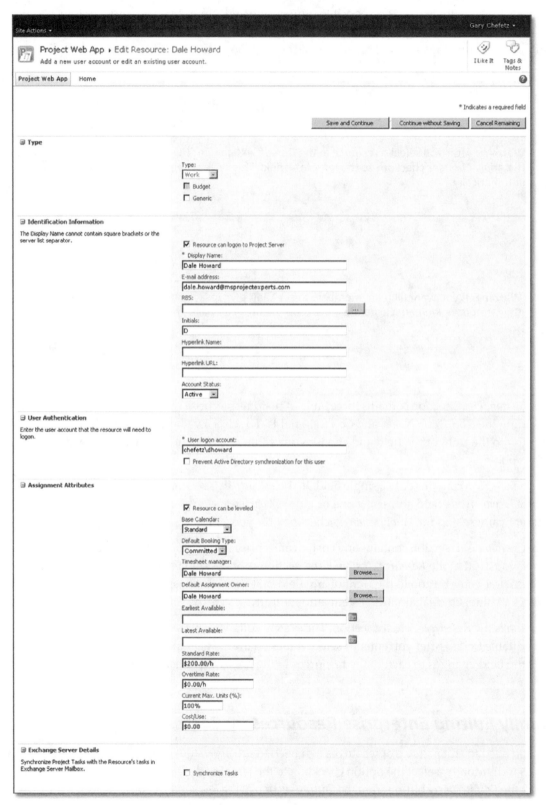

Figure 9 - 50: Top of Edit Resource page for first selected resource

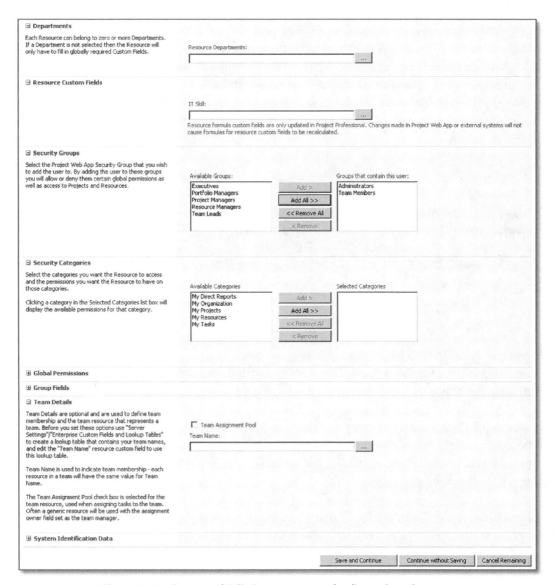

Figure 9 - 51: Bottom of Edit Resource page for first selected resource

On the *Edit Resource* page for the first selected resource, you cannot change the value in the *Type* pick list, and you cannot deselect the *Resource can logon to Project Server* option. Beyond these two restrictions, you can change the values in other fields on the page. When you finish editing the first resource, click the *Save and Continue* button.

The system displays the *Edit Resource* page for the next selected resource. Continue editing each selected resource and click the *Save and Continue* button on each page. On the *Edit Resource* page for the last selected resource, edit the resource and then click the *Save* button. If you do not want to make any edits for the selected resource on any page, click the *Continue without Saving* button. To stop batch editing at any time, click the *Cancel Remaining* button.

Adding Resources Using Active Directory Synchronization

In addition to manual resource entry, you can configure Project Server 2010 to add new resources to the enterprise resource pool automatically using Active Directory synchronization. When your organization's Active Directory administrator adds a new resource to a designated Active Directory group, the system automatically adds the new resource to the enterprise resource pool during the next synchronization. Conversely, if your Active Directory administrator removes a resource from the designated Active Directory group, the system automatically deactivates the resource during the next synchronization. This makes a fairly quick and easy method for adding resources and making them inactive in the system.

Warning: Active Directory synchronization requires that the servers running both Active Directory and Project Server 2010 are working across trusted domains.

How does this synchronization process work? During each synchronization cycle, one or more of following activities occur:

- If a user exists in the designated Active Directory group that does not exist in the enterprise resource pool, the system adds the new user to the enterprise resource pool.

- If a user exists in both Active Directory and the enterprise resource pool, the system compares the user's metadata with the user's Active Directory GUID (Globally Unique Identifier). If there is a match between the user's metadata and Active Directory GUID, the system writes Active Directory data to the enterprise resource pool entry for that user.

- If a user with an Active Directory GUID exists in the enterprise resource pool but does not exist in Active Directory, the system deactivates the user account in the Project Server database.

If you wish to use Active Directory synchronization with the enterprise resource pool, complete the following steps to configure Project Server 2010 to perform the synchronization process:

1. Log in to Project Web App with administrator permissions.

2. Click the *Server Settings* link in the Quick Launch menu.

3. Click the *Active Directory Resource Pool Synchronization* link in the *Operational Policies* section of the *Server Settings* page.

Project Server 2010 displays the *Active Directory Enterprise Resource Pool Synchronization* page shown in Figure 9 - 52.

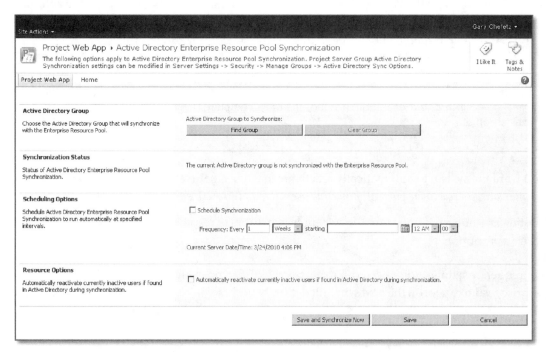

Figure 9 - 52: Active Directory Enterprise Resource Pool Synchronization page

4. Click the *Find Group* button. The system displays the *Find Group in Active Directory* dialog shown in Figure 9 - 53.

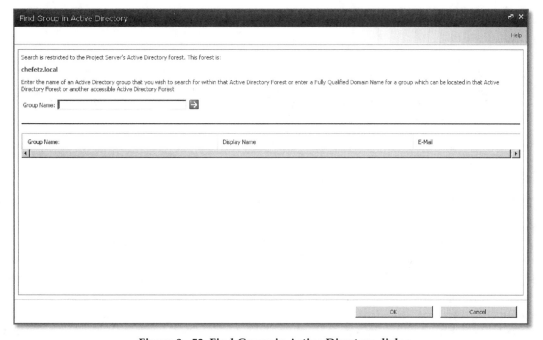

Figure 9 - 53: Find Group in Active Directory dialog

5. In the *Find Group in Active Directory* dialog, enter the AD group you want to use to synchronize the resources in the enterprise resource pool, and then click the *OK* button.

6. Select the *Schedule Synchronization* option from the *Scheduling Options* section of the *Active Directory Enterprise Resource Pool* page, and then set the frequency for synchronizing AD resources with the enterprise resource pool. Project Server 2010 allows you to schedule the synchronization on a daily, weekly, or monthly frequency. You can set a start date and the time of day for the synchronization to run.

> If you want to synchronize AD resources manually with the enterprise resource pool, do not select the *Schedule Synchronization* option. Instead, you must complete these steps **every time** you wish to synchronize resources.

7. If you want the system to automatically reactivate inactive resources if the resources exist in AD, then select the *Automatically reactivate currently inactive users if found in Active Directory during synchronization* option.

8. Click the *Save* button. If you want the system to synchronize resources immediately, click the *Save and Synchronize Now* button.

Based on the frequency settings you selected, Project Server 2010 synchronizes resources between Active Directory and the enterprise resource pool on the next scheduled date. Note that you must attribute your resources with custom field information manually after they are added by Active Directory synchronization.

> **Warning:** Becuase Active Directory synchronization is not capable of synchronizing custom field data, you must not define custom enterprise resource fields as required if you intend on using this feature. Required fields cause resource synchronization to fail.

> **Warning:** In addition to using AD synchronization to add resources to the enterprise resource pool, you can also use AD synchronization to add the new enterprise resources to the correct Security Groups in Project Web App. See Module 12, (Configuring Project Server Security), where I discuss how to use AD synchronization to add resources to Security Groups.

Preparing to Import Enterprise Resources

As I stated earlier in this module, you can create enterprise resources using three methods: you can create them manually, import them automatically using Active Directory synchronization, or import them manually from external sources such as existing project plans. Prior to implementing Project Server 2010, many organizations use earlier versions of the Microsoft Project desktop application to track standalone projects. Some organizations use a shared resource pool along with their Microsoft Project plans. In either situation, you may find a list of your organization's resources in individual projects or in the shared resource pool file. Using these projects, Project Server 2010 provides a conduit for importing resource data directly into the enterprise resource pool.

Keep in mind that importing enterprise resources from various file types, such as Excel, can be an inefficient and potentially dangerous method, because you have a much higher risk of corrupting your database than with manually entering the resources. Instead, a much better approach is to stage your resource data in a simple project file until you verify that the data is ready to import into the enterprise resource pool.

Using a project file provides two benefits. First, you have an opportunity to catch bad data characters in the file without affecting your production database. Data characters that might be acceptable to an ODBC database or in an Excel file, for instance, might cause Project Server 2010 to choke or crash during the import process. Second, using a project file is the easiest way to establish importable custom field data. This approach works when you acquire the resource data from a foreign system, such as an SAP Human Resources database, and is a good option for organizations that have their resource information in an existing shared resource pool file, or for organizations that have resources distributed across existing stand-alone project files.

Organizations that already use a shared resource pool in a well-established project management system need only make a copy of the shared pool file for import purposes. Now is a good time to clean up the existing data for typos, name changes, and the like. Add the new enterprise attributes and their values to the shared resource pool file by mirroring the attributes using local custom fields. These become available for you to map to enterprise fields in the *Import Wizard* during the final import process.

If your organization has resources defined across project plans, but not in shared resource pools, you should first consider whether there is enough consistency in the plans to make the effort of obtaining the data worthwhile. The most important consistency to look for is the resource naming convention. If resource naming is not consistent across plans, or cost rates vary, the value of using them for input diminishes. You also want to verify that they contain enough information to make them worthwhile. Accurate Windows accounts and e-mail addresses are highly valuable here.

If your plans pass this test, the approach to take is to create a new resource pool from existing projects by completing the following steps:

1. Launch Project Professional 2010, select your account in the Project Server accounts dialog, and click the *Offline* button. Working in offline mode helps you to avoid the possibility that you might accidentally publish the plan or that you might prematurely import resources into the enterprise resource pool.

2. Click the *File* menu and open a project plan containing resources that you want to harvest.

3. Apply the *Resource Sheet* view.

 To use this method, you must expose all of the data you want to copy from the source file in the view by adding the appropriate columns to the view. You also must make sure that you configure the destination file *Resource Sheet* view with the same columns in the same order as the source file.

4. Click the *Select All* button in the upper left corner of the *Resource Sheet*, and then click the *Copy* button to copy all resources to the clipboard.

5. Click the *New* button to open a new blank project, or open a file you previously set up for this purpose, and then apply the *Resource Sheet* view.

6. Select the first cell in the *Indicators* column for the first blank resource line.

7. Click the *Paste* button to paste all resources from the existing project into the new project.

8. Clean up the data by repairing minor inconsistencies and omissions, and then add the new attributes and values.

9. Save the new project for importing into the enterprise resource pool.

If you are not starting out with an existing collection of Microsoft Project plans, and project management is new to your company, you can find any type of data source to begin with, such as a resource listing in Excel or Access, or you can simply choose to enter your resources manually. Consider your resource naming convention in light of Microsoft Project's default alphabetical sorting, which makes no distinction between a first name and a last name in the *Resource Name* field.

Importing Resources from Active Directory

Project Professional 2010 communicates with your company's Active Directory whether you have logged in to Project Server or not. If you use this feature when connected to Project Server 2010, then the application makes several assumptions about the resources that you add. For example, when you have the enterprise resource pool open, the system assumes that the resources you add are new enterprise resources and automatically adds them to the pool. If you have only one project open, the system automatically marks the new resources as local resources. When you are using this feature early in the process to build an interim resource pool, remember to work with Project Professional offline from Project Server.

To add resources from Active Directory, apply the *Resource Sheet* view in either a blank project or a project containing resources. Click the *Add Resources* button from the *Insert* section of the *Resource* ribbon. The system displays the *Add Resources* pick list shown in Figure 9 - 54.

Figure 9 - 54: Add Resources pick list

From the pick list, select the *Active Directory* item. The system displays the *Select Users or Groups* dialog shown in Figure 9 - 55.

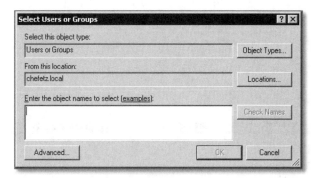

Figure 9 - 55: Select Users or Groups dialog

Click the *Object Types* button in the upper right corner of the dialog to display the *Object Types* dialog. Select the type of objects you want displayed in the *Object Types* dialog, and then click the *OK* button. For this example, I will select only Users in the *Object Types* dialog, as shown in Figure 9 - 56.

Figure 9 - 56: Object Types dialog

Click the *Locations* button in the *Select Users* dialog. The system displays the *Locations* dialog shown in Figure 9 - 57. In this dialog, select from the various Active Directory trees and then click the *OK* button.

Figure 9 - 57: Locations dialog

In the Select Users dialog shown previously in Figure 9 - 55, you can also click the *Advanced* button in the lower left corner of the dialog. The system displays the *Select Users* dialog with the *Common Queries* tab expanded, as shown in Figure 9 - 58.

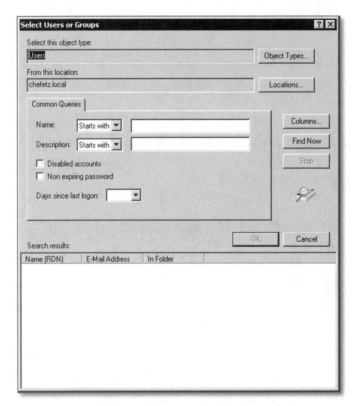

Figure 9 - 58: Select Users dialog, Build a query to find resources

Use the options in the *Common Queries* section to build a query to locate your resources and then click the *Find Now* button. Figure 9 - 59 shows resources located through my search.

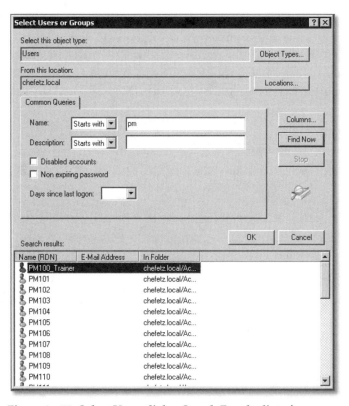

Figure 9 - 59: Select Users dialog Search Results list of resources

In the Search Results pane, select the resources you want to import, and then click the *OK* button. From the list, I selected resources PM101 through PM110. Figure 9 - 60 shows the *Select Users* dialog with the resources selected.

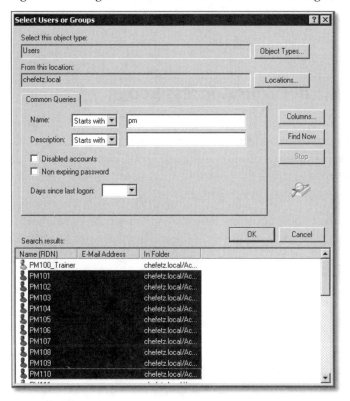

Figure 9 - 60: Select Users dialog with resources selected

Click the *OK* button to close the query window, and then click the *OK* button on the *Select Users or* Groups dialog to add the users to the *Resource Sheet* view of the active project. Figure 9 - 61 shows the users added to the project from Active Directory. Notice that the system adds the resources as local resources, as indicated by the icon to the left of each resource's name. You must save this file to your local drive or a file share, and then use the *Import Enterprise Resources* wizard to save the resources to the enterprise resource pool.

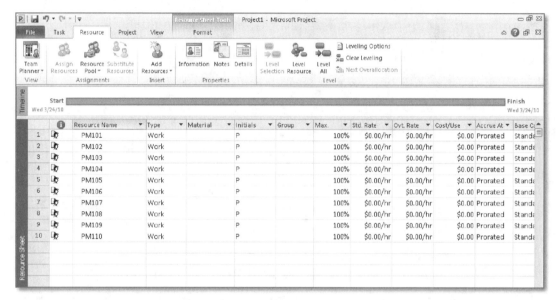

Figure 9 - 61: New resources added from Active Directory

Importing Resources from Your Address Book

Project Professional 2010 can communicate with your company's address book whether you log in to Project Server 2010 or not. If you use this feature when connected to Project Server, the application makes several assumptions about the resources that you add. If you have the enterprise resource pool open, the system assumes that these are new enterprise resources and adds them directly to the pool. If you have only a project open, the system automatically adds the new resources as local resources in the active project.

To add resources from the address book, apply the *Resource Sheet* view in either a blank project or a project containing resources. Click the *Add Resources* button from the *Insert* section of the *Resource* ribbon. The system displays the *Select Resources* dialog shown in Figure 9 - 62.

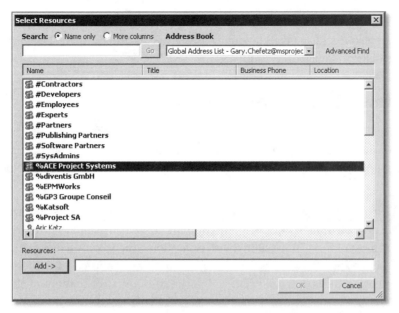

Figure 9 - 62: Select Resources dialog

At the top of the dialog, click the *Address Book* pick list to select from the various address books available to you on your network. After you choose an address book, select the resources you want to add to the project from the selected address book, and then click the *Add* button. The system displays the selected resources in the text field to the right of the *Add* button, as shown in Figure 9 - 63.

Figure 9 - 63: Select Resources dialog with selected resource

When you complete your selections, click the *OK* button. The system imports the selected resources from your address book into the *Resource Sheet* view of the active project, as shown in Figure 9 - 64.

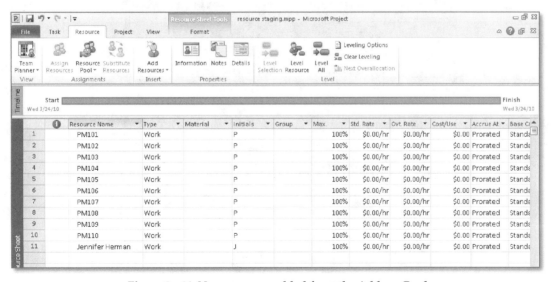

Figure 9 - 64: New resource added from the Address Book

Notice in Figure 9 - 64 that the system adds the new resources using the *Display Name* as the name for the resource. If you use this method to add resources to a project, you may need to clean up the name of each resource before importing the resources into the enterprise resource pool.

Verifying a Windows Account for a Resource

The importance of an accurate Windows account should cause you to look at how you might merge information from more than one source. For instance, if you hope to obtain all the information you need from the company address book, and you then discover the information is not current, you have a dilemma. Is it worth obtaining the data from this source?

You can browse Active Directory to search for users one by one to find and fill in missing information if you import from a less than complete and accurate source. If your company uses consistent naming conventions through the years, you can likely guess most of these, but dealing with exceptions can become a difficult task when the naming is unpredictable. Therefore, make sure that your potential data source has a valid Windows logon contained in it before you decide to use it as an import basis. If it does not, weigh the consequences of manual cleanup.

 Warning: When you use external data sources, be very wary of data containing non-alphanumeric characters and leading or trailing spaces. Leading spaces are the more troublesome issue. Also be wary of hidden charcters, such as soft return characters in Excel and Word files.

Project Professional 2010 provides the means to verify Windows logons by connecting to your company address book. Following this path to the address book is different than the one described in the previous topic. Adding the *Windows Account* and *e-mail address* fields to the *Resource Sheet* view makes editing the data more convenient. To connect to the company address book, double-click the resource in the *Resource Sheet* view. The system opens the *Resource Information* dialog. In this dialog, complete the following steps:

1. Click the *Windows Account* button shown in Figure 9 - 65 to link to your company's address book through your e-mail client.

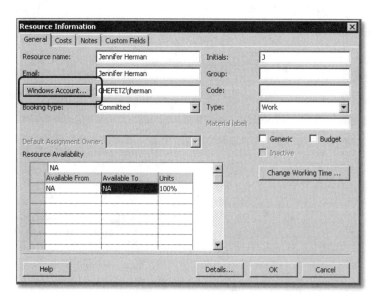

Figure 9 - 65: Windows Account button in the Resource Information dialog

2. If your system displays the *Choose Profile* selection dialog, select a profile name and click the *OK* button.

> Not all mail clients create mail profiles on a workstation during installation. For Lotus Notes, for instance, you must manually configure a Windows mail profile in order for Project Professional 2010 to see it on the client machine. Any MAPI-compliant mail client will work.

3. Depending on your mail client security settings, the system may prompt you for a logon. The default security settings in Microsoft Outlook cause the system to display a dialog prompting for access to your Outlook client. Click the *Allow* button to allow access to e-mail addresses in Outlook.

4. Project Professional 2010 attempts to match the name with an entry in the company address book. The results display in the dialog shown in Figure 9 - 66. If the name entered in the *Resource Sheet* matches a name found in the address book, you can simply click the *Yes* button to enter the Windows Account for the resource.

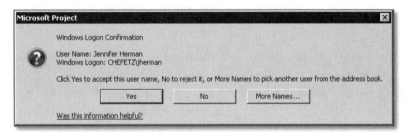

Figure 9 - 66: Windows Logon Confirmation

5. If the name does not generate a match, the system displays *(No Suggestions)* as shown in Figure 9 - 67 where there is no match for the name Allen Pettit.

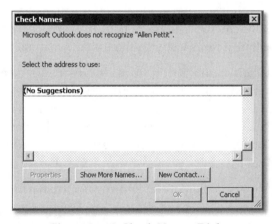

Figure 9 - 67: Check Names Dialog

6. If the system does not find a matching name, click the *Show More Names* button to display the Address Book dialog shown in Figure 9 - 68. Notice that the Address Book lists Allen Pettit by his nickname, Al Pettit. Select the resource and then click the *OK* button.

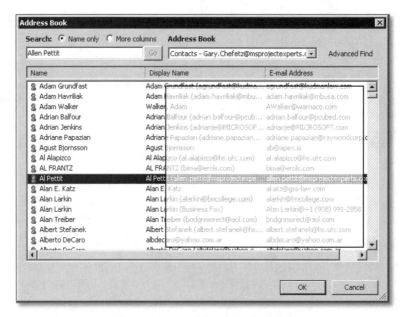

Figure 9 - 68: Address Book dialog

The system displays the *Resource Information* dialog with the Windows user account information in the *Windows Account* field. Click the *OK* button to return to the *Resource Sheet* view. For the most part, you use your connection to the company address book to populate Windows Accounts and e-mail addresses. The Windows Account name in the format domainname\username or the Active Directory name is key information. This information must be correct or your enterprise resource import fails. A bad e-mail address does not create an import problem, but it prevents Project Server 2010 from sending e-mail notifications for the impacted resources and causes error messages on the server. It is not worth importing bad data, so make sure that you get it right the first time.

Preparing Custom Field Data

After you gather the Windows User account and e-mail address information, you need to stage the custom field data before importing your resources into the enterprise resource pool. As I previously mentioned, this is likely to be new to your organization, so plan for the time it takes to assign these values manually.

When importing resources to the enterprise resource pool from a Microsoft Project .mpp file, Project Professional 2010 allows you to map local custom fields and outline codes to enterprise custom fields for each resource in the project. The structures of any local outline codes must exactly match the lookup table in the corresponding enterprise field. You can map any available local outline code to any available enterprise field containing a lookup table, however, so the name you give the local code and the enterprise code you select is inconsequential beyond identifying the code for your own recognition.

Getting the values for enterprise fields with lookup tables into your source file has the added benefit of being useful when you are assigning non-related values as well. For instance, the *Skill* field may be useful in manually setting resource cost rates, as you can use this code in your current view to sort the resources by like values. Generally, resource cost rates are usually consistent within these classifications.

To help build the local fields and outline codes in your temporary resource pool, you can import the corresponding enterprise fields you created earlier in Project Server 2010. To create local outline codes, complete the following steps:

1. Launch Project Professional 2010 and log in to Project Server with administrator permissions.

2. Open your temporary resource pool file.

3. Click the *Custom Fields* button from the *Properties* section of the *Project* ribbon.

4. Select the *Resource* option and then click the *Type* pick list and select the *Outline Code* item from the list.

5. Select any custom resource outline code field and rename it to a name similar to the enterprise field with which it corresponds. For example, in Figure 9 - 69, I renamed the resource *Outline Code1* field as the *Local RBS* field.

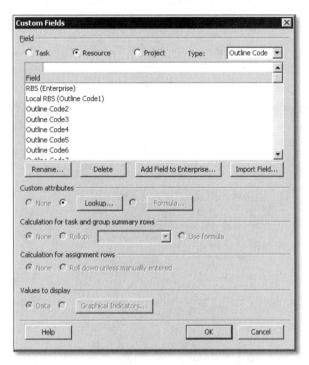

**Figure 9 - 69: Custom Fields dialog
for the temporary resource pool**

6. Click the *Import Field* button to display the *Import Custom Field* dialog shown in Figure 9 - 70.

Figure 9 - 70: Import Custom Field dialog

7. In the Import Custom Field dialog, select the *Global (+ non-cached Enterprise)* file as the *Project*, select the *Resource* option, and then select the enterprise custom field that you wish to import. Notice in Figure 9 - 71 that I am importing the *RBS* field along with its corresponding RBS lookup table.

Figure 9 - 71: Import Custom Field dialog for RBS

8. Click the *OK* button to import the *RBS* field data into the *Local RBS* outline code. During the import process, the system imports both the code mask and lookup table into the local outline code, as shown in Figure 9 - 72.

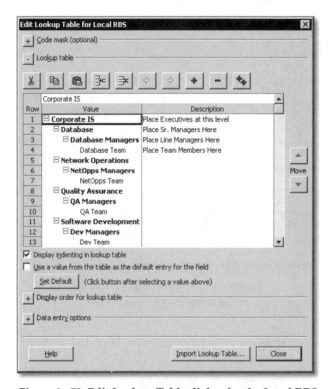

Figure 9 - 72: Edit Lookup Table dialog for the Local RBS

Following this process guarantees that the outline code structures between the temporary resource pool and the enterprise global match exactly. This minimizes problems during the process of importing enterprise resources into the enterprise resource pool from the temporary resource pool.

Once you set up the necessary local outline codes and import the enterprise field values into them, you must specify the local outline code values for each resource. Insert each local outline code field into the *Resource Sheet* view to facilitate entry. For example, to insert the *Local RBS* field into the *Resource Sheet*, complete the following steps:

1. Right-click the any column header or click on the *Add Column Header* on the far right.

2. If you chose to right click, from the shortcut menu select *Insert Column*.

3. From the field list, select the *Local RBS* field.

4. Once the field is added to the resource sheet, right click on the column header and select the *Field* Definition item from the shortcut menu to open the *Field Settings* dialog shown in Figure 9 - 73.

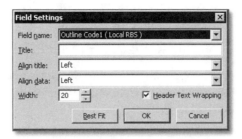

Figure 9 - 73: Field Settings dialog

5. Set the *Align Title* value to *Left* and the *Align Data* value to *Left*.

6. Set the *Width* value to *50*.

7. Click the *OK* button.

8. Repeat steps #2-6 for every local field and outline code you created in your temporary resource pool file.

After you insert each of your local fields and outline codes into the *Resource Sheet* view, you can begin entering values in those fields for each resource. For example, Figure 9 - 74 shows that I am setting a value in the *Local RBS* field for Jennifer Herman to indicate that she is a team member on the Software Development team. Notice also that I inserted two additional local outline codes for data entry: *Local Departments* and *Local Skills*. These local outline codes coincide with the enterprise *Resource Departments* and *Skills* fields.

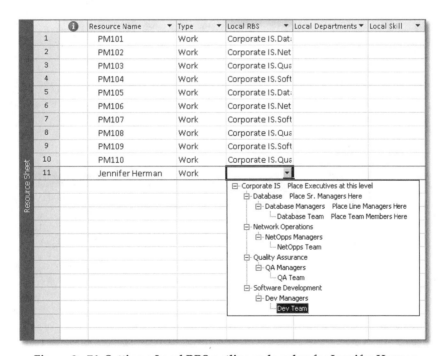

Figure 9 - 74: Setting a Local RBS outline code value for Jennifer Herman

After you enter all of your resources in the temporary resource pool, and set resource values for both standard and custom fields, you are ready to import your resources as enterprise resources into the enterprise resource pool. Save and close the temporary resource pool before you attempt to import the resources.

Importing Enterprise Resources

Because your temporary resource pool now contains values for mapping all required field values, the import process itself completes very quickly. To import resources using the *Import Resources Wizard*, complete the following steps:

1. Launch Project Professional 2010 and log in to Project Server using an administrator account.

2. With your local resource staging file open, click the *Add Resources* button from the *Insert* section of the *Resource* ribbon and the select the *Import Resources to Enterprise* item on the pick list. The system opens the *Import Resources Wizard* side pane shown in Figure 9 - 75.

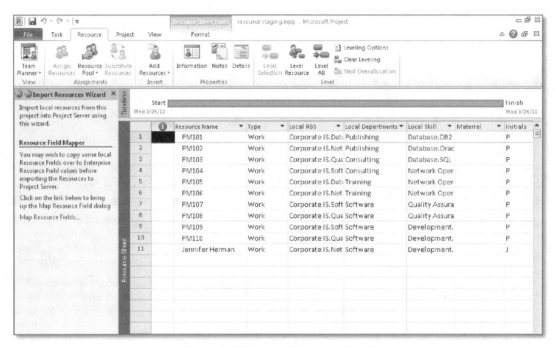

Figure 9 - 75: Import Resource Step 1

3. Click the *Map Resource Fields* link in the middle of the side pane. The system displays the *Map Custom Fields* dialog shown in Figure 9 - 76.

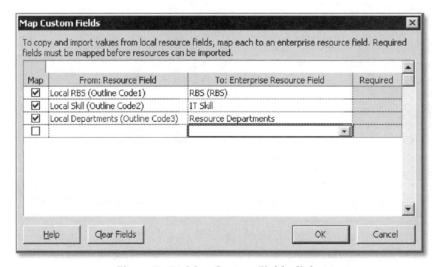

Figure 9 - 76: Map Custom Fields dialog

4. In the *From* column, select each of your local custom fields or outline codes and in the *To* column, select each of the corresponding enterprise custom fields. Figure 9 - 76 shows the *Map Custom Fields* dialog set up to map three local outline codes with three enterprise custom fields. Notice that I mapped the *Local RBS* outline code to the *RBS* enterprise field, the *Local Departments* outline code to the *Resource Departments* enterprise field, and the *Local Skills* outline code to the *IT Skill* enterprise field.

5. Click the *OK* button to close the *Map Custom Fields* dialog and return to the *Import Resources Wizard* side pane.

6. Click the *Continue to Step 2* link at the bottom of the side pane.

Project Server 2010 validates each of the resources in the temporary resource pool file, confirming valid Windows user accounts, and verifying that the local fields and outline codes precisely match their corresponding enterprise fields. The system also looks for duplicate resources. When finished, the system displays the *Confirm Resources* page of the *Import Resources Wizard* side pane shown in Figure 9 - 77.

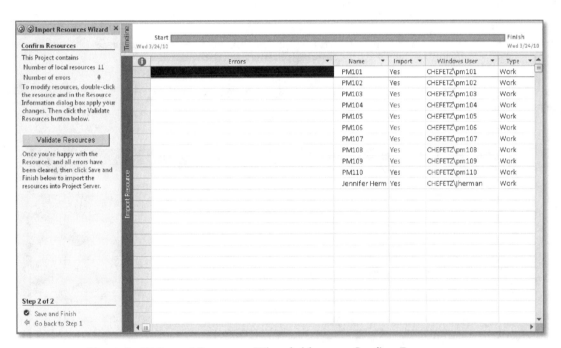

Figure 9 - 77: Import Resources Wizard side pane, Confirm Resources page

If Project Server 2010 detects any errors with the resources in the temporary resource pool file, it lists the number of errors found at the top of the *Import Resources Wizard* side pane, and documents the type of error to the left of each problematic resource in the *Errors* column. Before you can import the resources, you must correct these errors. To fix the problem, double-click the name of a resource and change any erroneous information in the *Resource Information* dialog. After you fix each problematic resource, click the *Validate Resources* button to confirm that no errors remain.

7. Click the *Save and Finish* link at the bottom of the *Import Resources Wizard* side pane.

8. When the system completes the import process, close the temporary resource pool file.

Deactivating an Enterprise Resource

When a resource leaves the company, or is no longer available for project work, it may become necessary to deactivate the resource within Project Server 2010. Before you deactivate any resource, you should confirm with your project managers that the resource has no remaining work value greater than 0 hours in any project in the portfolio.

> **Warning:** If you fail to complete this important first step, your project managers will receive a warning message **every time** they open a project in which the deactivated resource has Remaining Work greater than 0 hours.

To deactivate a resource, you can use either the Project Web App interface or Project Professional 2010. To deactivate a resource using Project Web App, complete the following steps:

1. Log into Project Web App with administrator permissions and click the *Server Settings* link in the Quick Launch menu.

2. Click the *Manage Users* link in the *Security* section of the *Server Settings* page. The system displays the *Manage Users* page shown in Figure 9 - 78.

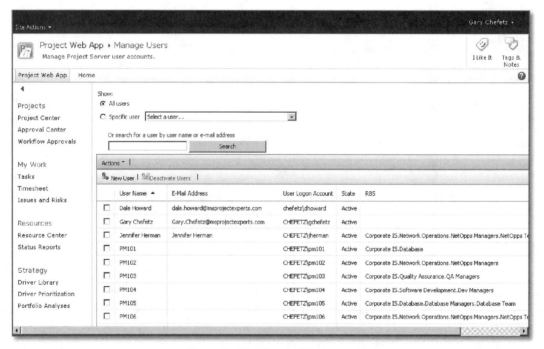

Figure 9 - 78: Manage Users page

3. On the *Manage Users* page, select the option checkbox to the left of each resource that you want to set to inactive.

4. Click the *Deactivate Users* button on the toolbar above the data grid. The system displays the warning message shown in Figure 9 - 79.

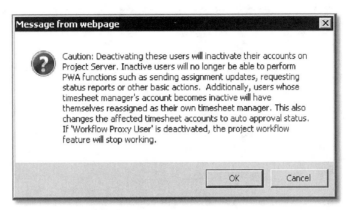

Figure 9 - 79: Warning dialog about deactivating enterprise resources

5. Click the *OK* button to inactivate the selected resources.

To set the resource to inactive using Project Professional 2010, you must first open the resource for editing from the enterprise resource pool. You can start in Project Professional or Project Web App, but both starting points take you to Project Web App first. To begin this process in Project Professional, click the *Resource Pool* button from the *Assignments* section of the *Resource* ribbon and select the *Enterprise Resource Pool* item on the pick list. The system opens Project Web App in a new browser window as shown in Figure 9 - 80.

Figure 9 - 80: Open Enterprise Resource pool

1. Select the resources you want to set to inactive and click the *Open* button in the *Editing* section of the *Resources* menu. The system opens your selected resources for editing in the *Resource Sheet* view in Project Professional.

2. Double-click the name of the first resource.

3. In the *Resource Information* dialog, select the *Inactive* option as shown in Figure 9 - 81.

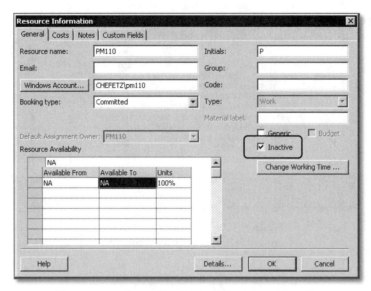

Figure 9 - 81: Set an Enterprise Resource to Inactive

4. Click the *OK* button. The system denotes the inactive resource with an *Inactive* indicator to the left of the resource's name, as shown in Figure 9 - 82.

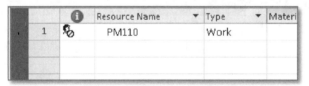

Figure 9 - 82: Inactive resource

5. Complete steps #2 through #4 for each resource you want to inactivate.

6. Save and close the Enterprise Resource Pool.

You now have the "know how" to build your organization's enterprise resource pool using the various techniques covered in this module. Do not rush through this process, as the Enterprise Resource Pool is your system's most important asset.

Module 10

Initial Project Server Configuration

Learning Objectives

After completing this module, you will be able to:

- Understand the functional approach for configuring Project Server 2010 options
- Set options for Enterprise Features
- Configure Project Server's notification engine
- Configure Exchange Server synchronization
- Set options for OLAP cube building and resource availability information
- Configure custom Event Handlers
- Configure Quick Launch menus

Inside Module 10

Configuring Project Server 2010 405

Setting High-Level Enterprise Functionality 405

Changing the Project 2007 Compatibility Mode 407

Specifying Project Professional Versions 407

Specifying Enterprise Settings Options 408

Specifying Currency Settings Options 409

Specifying Resource Capacity Settings 410

Specifying the Resource Plan Work Day Option 410

Specifying the Exchange Server Details Option 411

Specifying Task Mode Settings 411

Configuring Exchange Server Synchronization 412

Determine the Account running the Queue Service for Project Server 412

Configure Exchange Server 412

Create a Project Web App Account for each Exchange Client Access Server 413

403

Configure Exchange Users 414

Configure a Project Web App User for Exchange Server Synchronization 415

Special Considerations for Test Environments... 416

Understanding How Exchange Synchronization Works 417

Configuring Alerts and Reminders..**418**

Setting Options for the OLAP Cube **420**

Configuring the OLAP Database... 423

Deleting an Existing OLAP Database 427

Configuring Event Handlers..**428**

Configuring the Quick Launch Menu **431**

Configuring Project Server 2010

After you create system metadata and calendars, including project types and workflows, and populate the enterprise resource pool, you are ready to configure Project Server 2010. The order in which you configure the system makes a difference to some degree; therefore, I suggest that you approach things in this order:

1. Set application options.

2. Configure timesheet and tracking options.

3. Configure security using Groups and Categories.

4. Build the project environment.

5. Build custom Views.

6. Build custom Reports.

This module shows you how to set application options. Successive modules teach you how to work through the other five steps listed above. Here, I teach you how to configure the following Project Server 2010 application options:

- High-level enterprise functionality

- Notifications and reminders

- Exchange Server synchronization

- OLAP and Resource Availability settings

- Event Handlers

- Quick Launch menus

Setting High-Level Enterprise Functionality

Your logical first step is to make sure that, at a high level, you configure Project Server 2010 to match your organization's requirements. To configure these high-level options, log in to Project Web App with administrator permissions. Click the *Server Settings* link in the Quick Launch menu and then click the *Additional Server Settings* link in the *Operational Policies* section of the *Server Settings* page. The system displays the *Additional Server Settings* page shown in Figure 10 - 1.

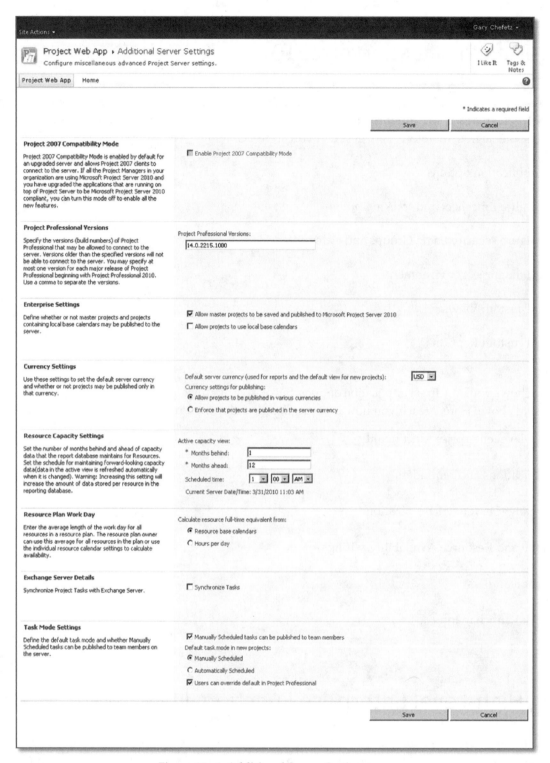

Figure 10 - 1: Additional Server Settings page

The *Additional Server Settings* page contains eight sets of options that affect Project Server 2010 usage from a very high level. These sections are:

- Project 2007 Compatibility Mode

- Project Professional Versions

- Enterprise Settings

- Currency Settings

- Resource Capacity Settings

- Resource Plan Workday

- Exchange Server Details

- Task Mode Settings

Changing the Project 2007 Compatibility Mode

If you upgrade to Project Server 2010 from Project Server 2007, the system automatically selects the *Enable Project Server Compatibility Mode* option. You cannot select this mode directly, as it applies only when you upgrade from Project Server 2007. (You can also migrate from Project Server 2003; however the path to 2010 is always through the 2007 version.) When selected, this option allows users of Project Professional 2007 to connect to the Project Server, and provides a transition time for upgrading your users' desktops to Project Professional 2010. Once all your organization's project managers are using Project Professional 2010, you can deselect this option. If you deselect this option, the system displays the *Warning* dialog shown in Figure 10 - 2. In the *Warning* dialog, click the *OK* button to disable the *Enable Project Server Compatibility Mode* option.

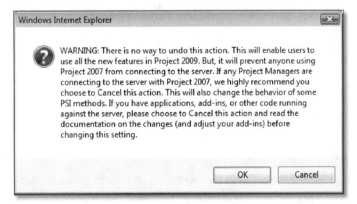

Figure 10 - 2: Warning dialog about disabling Compatibility Mode

Warning: When running in *Compatibility Mode,* Project Server disables all new functionality in Project Professional 2010 when users connect to the server, and disables all new functionality in Project Server 2010 that Project Professional 2007 is unaware of. Use this mode only for transitioning your user desktops when it is impossible to address your desktop upgrade in a quick and easy manner, such as may be the case when your organization does not employ a push system for updating desktops remotely, or the number of Project users exceeds the threshold that your orgaznization can upgrade quickly.

Specifying Project Professional Versions

In previous versions of Project Server, the system provided no way to control which versions of Project Professional could connect to the server. This was particularly troublesome after service pack upgrades to the server where project managers had a different Service Pack (SP) level on Project Professional than the Service Pack level on the Project

Server system. One of the problems in this situation was project corruption. This new feature allows you to control connectivity by specifying major build of Project Professional as the lowest build number that a user must have to connect to Project Server 2010. In the *Project Professional Versions* field, you can specify one or more versions of Project Professional that can connect to your Project Server system. Enter no more than one version for each major release of Project Professional beginning with Project Professional 2007. For example two major versions you might specify in the *Project Professional Versions* field if you are using BCM are:

- 12.0.6425.1000 (Project Professional 2007 with Service Pack 2)

- 14.0.4763.1000 (Project Professional 2010 RTM)

Once you specify acceptable versions, Project Server 2010 does not allow users with older versions to connect to the system using Project Professional.

Specifying Enterprise Settings Options

The first selection in the *Enterprise Settings* section is the *Allow master projects to be saved and published to Microsoft Project Server 2010* option. The system enables the option by default. Before you disable the use of master projects, you should know whether master projects are a necessary part of your organization's project management methodologies.

In Project Professional 2010 terms, a "master project" is a single project containing two or more inserted projects (also known as subprojects). Project managers generally create master projects to analyze a program of projects they manage, or to create cross-project dependencies when tasks in one project are dependent on tasks in one or more other projects. The default setting allows project managers to save and publish master projects to the Project Server database. If your organization prohibits the use of master projects in the Project Server database, deselect this option. Otherwise, leave this option enabled.

> Using Project Professional 2010, users create a master project by completing the following steps:
> 1. Launch Project Professional 2010 and log in to Project Server.
> 2. Open a new blank project file.
> 3. Apply the *Project* ribbon and click the *Subproject* button from the *Insert* section.
> 4. In the *Insert Project* dialog, navigate to an existing project and select it, then click the *Insert* button.
> 5. The system inserts the project as a sub-project of the master project.
> 6. Repeat step #3 for each project that you want to use as a subproject of the Master.
> 7. Click the *File* tab and select *Save* from the menu to save the master project.
> 8. When prompted, click the *Yes to All* button to save each of the subprojects.

The other option in the *Enterprise Settings* section is the *Allow projects to use local base calendars* option, which controls the use of *Base* calendars in your Project Server 2010 environment. The system disables the option by default. This means that your project managers cannot create their own *Base* calendars, restricting them to only the enterprise *Base* calendars in the system. Enable this feature if your company has calendar requirements that vary by project and that you cannot easily standardize using only enterprise *Base* calendars. If you enable this feature, your project managers can create and use their own *Base* calendars in each enterprise project, along with the enterprise *Base* calendars you create in the system. In most cases, you should leave this unselected, as using local *Base* calendars can lead to odd duration calculations and user confusion.

Specifying Currency Settings Options

The options in the *Currency Settings* section determine how Project Server 2010 handles the currencies used for project costing. To select the default currency for your organization, click the *Default server currency* pick list on the right side of the section and then select a currency from the list. The default setting for this field in the US version of Project Server 2010 is *USD* (US dollars).

If your company is a multinational organization that uses multiple currencies for costing projects, use the default *Allow projects to be published in various currencies* option. Selecting this option allows your project managers to select their own currencies on a project-by-project basis.

> To change the currency for any project, your project managers must complete the following steps:
> 1. Launch Project Professional 2010 and log in to Project Server.
> 2. Open an enterprise project.
> 3. Click the *File* tab and select the *Options* item from the menu.
> 4. In the *Project Options* dialog, select the *Display* tab.
> 4. In the *Currency options for this project* section, change the *Currency* option.
> 5. Click the *OK* button and then save the project.

If your organization costs all project work using a single currency, then select the *Enforce that projects are published in the server currency* option. Selecting this option prevents your project managers from changing the currency in all enterprise projects, and forces them to use the currency you specify. When you select this option, Project Server 2010 displays the warning dialog shown in Figure 10 - 3.

Figure 10 - 3: Warning dialog for
enforce currency setting change

Click the *OK* button in the warning dialog and the system redisplays the *Currency Settings* section as shown in Figure 10 - 4.

Figure 10 - 4: Currency Settings section shows projects with conflicting currency

409

Notice the area at the bottom of the *Currency Settings* section in Figure 10 - 4. This area lists projects with a currency setting that is in conflict with the server currency. In my situation, there are no conflicting projects because I am in the process of setting up Project Server 2010 prior to loading any projects. However, if you change the option in the *Currency Settings* section **after** you have production projects in the system, and you then see projects listed in this section, your project managers must open each project, change the currency settings and republish the conflicting projects to resolve the currency conflict.

Warning: When you support multiple currencies in your system, you should consider the metadata requirements for building system artifacts that display project costs. Specifically you should think about rolling up cost data in views as well as filtering criteria you may need to support your presentation of this data in views, reports and OLAP analysis.

Specifying Resource Capacity Settings

The options in the *Resource Capacity Settings* section control the past and future time span that Project Server 2010 uses to calculate resource capacity (availability for project work). The system determines resource capacity based on each resource's calendar, including the number of hours each day shown on the resource's *Base* calendar, the *Max. Units* value specified for the resource, and the nonworking time, such as vacations, that you enter on the resource's calendar.

For example, if a resource's *Base* calendar shows 8 hours of work per day and you set the resource's *Max. Units* value at 50%, the system shows the resource's capacity as 4 hours per day (50% x 8 hours/day). If you specify a week of nonworking time for the resource from July 5-8, 2011, then the system shows that resource's capacity as 0 hours during the week of nonworking time.

The system maintains resource availability by running a daily processing job. The default *Months behind* option setting is *1 month*, while the default *Months ahead* option setting is *12 months*. Change these options to see further into the past/future, but be aware that if you increase either of the default settings, it increases the amount of data stored for each resource in the reporting database and increases the processing time for the daily job. The *Scheduled time* option determines the time at which the system processes the latest resource capacity information each day. The default *Scheduled time* option is *1:00 AM*. You can adjust this timing to avoid conflicts with other processing jobs, such as your daily back-up process.

Users can see resource capacity information in Project Server 2010 by completing the following steps:

1. Log in to Project Web Access and navigate to the Resource Center page.
2. Select the option checkbox for one or more resources.
3. Click the *Resource Availability* button on the *Resources* ribbon.
4. The *Resource Availability* page shows resource capacity as a black line in the chart.

Specifying the Resource Plan Work Day Option

The *Resource Plan Work Day* section contains a single option, the *Calculate resource full-time equivalent from* option with two possible selections. You use this option to govern how Project Server 2010 determines working days in *Resource*

Plans associated with projects. Project managers can use a *Resource Plan* to communicate the high-level resource needs for a project. Select the default *Resource base calendars* option to have the system calculate resource FTE based on each resource's *Base* calendar. Select the *Hours per day* option to calculate FTE availability based on the hours per day you specify. When you select the *Hours per day* option, the system redisplays the *Resource Plan Work Day* section as shown in Figure 10 - 5.

**Figure 10 - 5: Resource Plan Work Day section
with Hours per day option selected**

In the *Hours per day* text field, specify the number of hours in a standard working day for your organization. Remember that the option you select in this section affects every *Resource Plan*.

Specifying the Exchange Server Details Option

Project Server 2007 allowed team members to display their tasks in Microsoft Office Outlook, either as appointments on the Outlook Calendar or as To-Do List items on the Outlook Tasks page. To use this functionality, however, the system required each user to download and install an Outlook Add-in. As you might surmise, this requirement was simply too "labor intensive" for many organizations, and the Outlook Add-in was fraught with stability issues.

In Project Server 2010, Microsoft streamlined the task synchronization process down to a single option specified by the Project Server administrator. The *Exchange Server Details* section contains the *Synchronize Tasks* option, which the system deselects by default. To set up automatic task synchronization between Project Web App and each user's Outlook task list, select the *Synchronize Tasks* option. Keep in mind that you must also configure Exchange Server 2007 or Exchange Server 2010 for task synchronization, and you must set the synchronize option for each user individually by editing the resources shown in the *Resource Center* page. I cover configuring Exchange Server synchronization in the next main topical section in this module.

Specifying Task Mode Settings

Manually scheduled tasks are a new feature in Microsoft Project 2010. The options in the *Task Mode Settings* section allow you to control or restrict their use in Project Server 2010. The first option, *Manually Scheduled tasks can be published to team members* is selected by default, and indicates to the system that project managers may publish these to team members. Because *Manually Scheduled* tasks can accept % complete progress status only, you may want to disable this option by deselecting it if time tracking for all tasks in your goal. The next option, *Default task mode in new projects*, allows you to set the default mode for new tasks when Project Professional 2010 is connected to your Project Server instance. You can select the *Manually Scheduled* (default) or *Automatically Scheduled* option. Your selection here overrides the user preference set in Project Professional 2010. Finally, the system allows you to restrict the task type to either *Manually Scheduled* or *Automatically Scheduled* by deselecting the default *Users can override default in Project Professional* check box. If you set the default task mode to *Automatically Scheduled* and deselect the *Users can override default in Project Professional* check box, you force all projects published to Project Server to use *Automatically Scheduled* tasks only. When you finish setting the options in each of the eight sections on the *Additional Server Settings* page, click the *Save* button to save the changes.

Configuring Exchange Server Synchronization

The first step in configuring both Project Server 2010 and Exchange Server 2007 or Exchange Server 2010 for task synchronization is to select the *Exchange Server Details* option on the *Additional Server Settings* page that I covered in the last section. The next step is to create a PWA user account for each *Exchange Client Access* server in your Exchange farm. Using the directions I provided in Module 9 for creating new users from the *Manage Users* page in Project Web App, create a new user for each *Exchange Client Access* server in your Exchange farm using Windows authentication. Deselect the option *User can be assigned as a resource*, and add each user to the *Administrators* group. In the examples below, I use the same service account that I used to install and run Project Server.

Determine the Account running the Queue Service for Project Server

In order for Exchange synchronization to work, you must grant the account running your *Project Server Queue Service* impersonation rights in Exchange server, as the *Queue Service* makes the actual calls. In all likelihood, this is the service account you specified at installation. If you know that you used only one service account for your setup, you can safely assume that your specified service account is running the *Project Server Queue Service*. If you do not remember the account that you used for this purpose, you can discover it using *Task Manager* on your front-end server. To verify this, execute the following steps:

1. Right click on the *Taskbar* on your front-end server and select the *Start Task Manager* item.

2. In the *Windows Task Manager* select the *Processes* tab.

3. Scroll to locate the *Microsoft.Office.Project.Server.Queuing.exe* item and note the name in the *User Name* column.

Configure Exchange Server

Log on to your Exchange Server with an administrator account. Click the *Start* button and select *All Programs* and expand the *Microsoft Exchange Server 2007* item on the programs list. Select the *Exchange Management Shell* item shown in Figure 10 - 6.

**Figure 10 - 6: Launch Exchange Management Shell
from All Programs list**

The system launches the *Exchange Management Shell* command window shown in Figure 10 - 7.

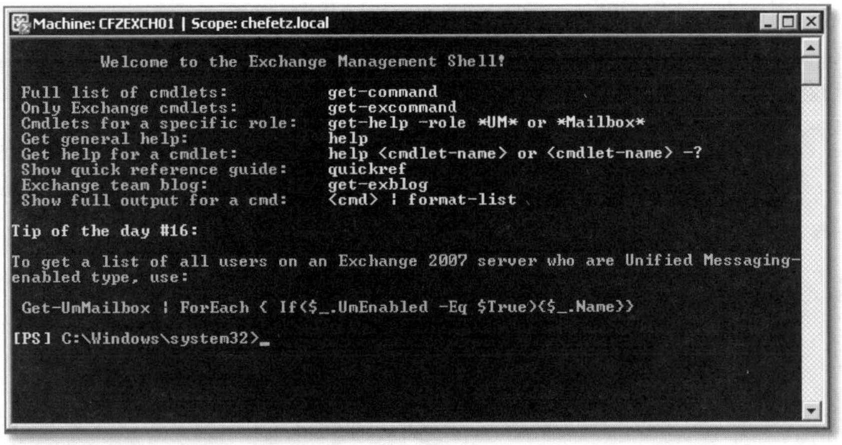

Figure 10 - 7: Exchange Management Shell command window

In the *Exchange Management Shell* command window, type the command shown in the following command example replacing the string <queuingserviceaccount> with the name of the account running the Project Server queuing service.

```
add-adpermission -identity (get-exchangeserver).distinguishedname -user (get-
user -identity <queuingserviceaccount>| select-object).identity -extendedrights
ms-exch-epi-impersonation
```

If you type the command accurately and then press the *Enter* key, the system reports a successful impersonation permission grant as shown in Figure 10 - 8.

```
Identity            User             Deny   Inherited Rights
--------            ----             ----   --------- ------
CFZEXCH01           CHEFETZ\p14_svc  False  False     ms-Exch-EPI-Impers...
```

Figure 10 - 8: Exchange Management Shell displays impersonation rights success

You must repeat this process for each *Exchange Client Access* server in your Exchange farm.

Create a Project Web App Account for each Exchange Client Access Server

Each Exchange Client Access server in your Exchange farm must have a user account in Project Web App, which allows the Exchange to call the *Project Server Exchange Web* service. To create a user account for an Exchange server, complete the following steps:

1. From the *Server Settings* page in Project Web App, select *Manage Users* from the *Security* section. From the *Manage Users* page, click *New User* from the menu above the grid. The system displays the *New User* page shown in Figure 10 - 9.

2. On the *New User* page, clear the *User can be assigned as a resource* check box and type the name of the Exchange Client Access server in the *Display Name* field.

3. In the *User Authentication* section, enter the Windows account for the Exchange Client Access server computer account in the *User logon account* field.

4.   In the *Security Groups* section, add the user to the Administrators group.

5.   Click the *Save* button to save your new account.

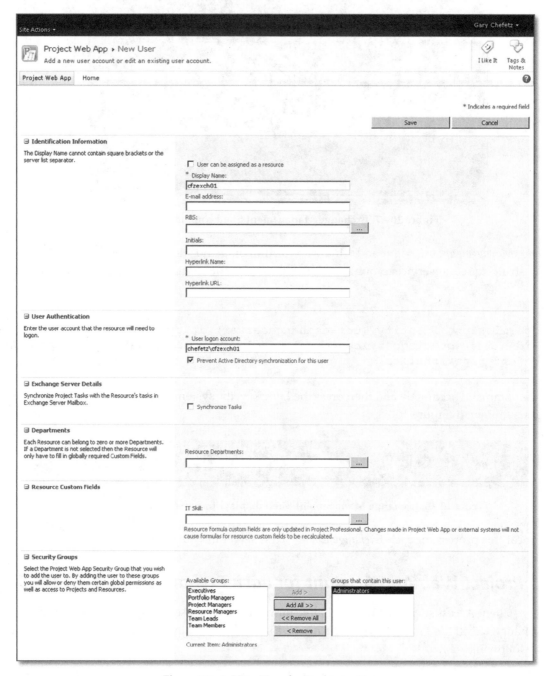

Figure 10 - 9: New User for Exchange Server

Configure Exchange Users

For each Exchange user that you want to configure for Project Server task synchronization, you must also execute the following *Exchange Management Shell* command, where you replace the string <projuser> with the Project Server User's Windows **display name** and the string <queuingserviceaccount> with the account you granted impersonation rights in the previous command procedure. This gives the *Project Server Queuing Service* account, to which you granted general impersonation rights in the previous procedure, specific rights to impersonate the user you specify in the command line.

```
add-adpermission -identity"<projuser>"-user<queuingserviceaccount>-
extendedrights ms-exch-epi-may-impersonate
```

If you type the command accurately and then press the *Enter* key, the system reports a successful impersonation grant as shown in Figure 10 - 10.

Figure 10 - 10: Impersonation Success for specific user

If you have a single server Exchange farm, you can close the *Exchange Management Shell* command window and proceed to the next step.

Configure a Project Web App User for Exchange Server Synchronization

From the *Server Settings* page in Project Web App, select *Manage Users* from the *Security* section. The system displays the *Manage Users* page shown in Figure 10 - 11.

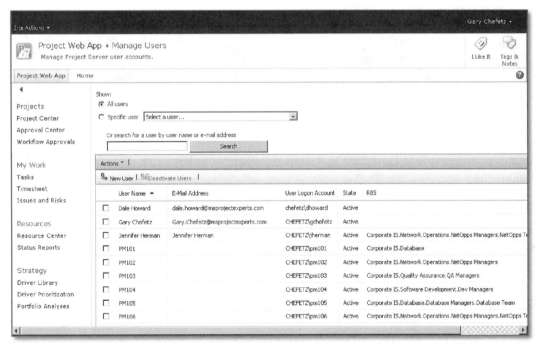

Figure 10 - 11: Manage Users page

Select a user by clicking on the *User Name.* The system opens the *Edit User* page. In the *Exchange Server Details* section, select the *Synchronize Tasks* checkbox as shown in Figure 10 - 12.

Figure 10 - 12: Edit User Exchange Server Details section

After selecting the checkbox, click the *Save* button to save your changes.

> To make this setting change for multiple resources, you can use the *Batch Edit* feature that I showed you in the previous module, by selecting multiple resources from the *Resource Center* page.

Special Considerations for Test Environments

The Active Directory *directory service* runs a process each hour that ensures that members of protected groups are not subject to security descriptors manipulation. If a security descriptor for a user account that is a member of a protected group, such as *Domain Admins,* does not match the security descriptor on the AdminSDHolder object, the system overwrites the user's security descriptor with a new security descriptor taken from the AdminSDHolder object. The *Send As* right is delegated by modifying the security descriptor of a user object. Therefore, if the user is a member of a protected group, the system overwrites this permission.

> **Warning:** Applying exceptions of this type directly to the *AdminSDHolder* object violates security best practices. Best practice dictates that users who are members of protected groups, such as Domain Admins, use separate logons for their activities as users. You should take this measure only if you are using single logons in test or development domains and not in your production domain.

To work around this issue you must grant the May-Impersonate permission to the adminSDHolder object. To do this, execute the following steps:

1. On your Exchange server open the *Exchange Management Shell.*

2. Run the following PowerShell command before you run the command for individual users who are members of protected groups. Note that this is the same command you run for individual users; however, you run this on the *adminsdholder* object rather than an individual user.

```
add-adpermission -identity "adminsdholder" -user <account> -extendedrights ms-
exch-epi-may-impersonate
```

Protected Groups in Active Directory include:

- Account Operators

- Administrator

- Administrators

- Backup Operators

- Domain Admins

- Domain Controllers

- Enterprise Admins

- Print Operators

- Read-only Domain Controllers

- Replicator

- Schema Admins

- Server Operators

Understanding How Exchange Synchronization Works

Once you configure Exchange synchronization, each time a project manager publishes task assignments, the system kicks off a synchronization job for tasks in that project, synchronizing Project Server assignments with the Outlook tasks list for each user in the schedule that has the *Synchronize Tasks* option selected in their Project Server user record. The synchronization process supports synchronization to the Outlook task list only, and you are limited to tracking tasks by percent complete only. Exchange synchronization does not support collecting time against tasks. Figure 10 - 13 shows a project assignment displayed as an Outlook task.

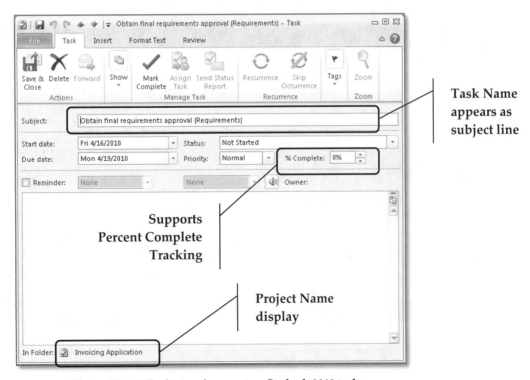

Figure 10 - 13: Project assignment as Outlook 2010 task

Exchange synchronization runs a full synchronization job nightly. In addition a range of events trigger point synchronizations, including adding, deleting and modifying tasks in Outlook; modifying tasks in the *Tasks* page; and accepting and rejecting task updates in the *Approval Center*. Project actions such as deleting a published project, deleting a resource, activating or deactivating resources, and enabling and disabling the site-level exchange setting also trigger a synchronization event. Exchange synchronization supports users who work with the Outlook desktop client as well as Outlook Web App.

To force a full synchronization with Exchange, deselect the option to *Synchronize Tasks* in the *Exchange Server Settings* section of the *Additional Server Settings* page and click the *Save* button. Return to the page and reselect the option and click the *Save* button. Do not do this while users are active on the system.

Configuring Alerts and Reminders

Before you can use the built-in notification engine in Project Server 2010 to send e-mail messages to system users, you must configure the settings for *Alerts and Reminders*. An *Alert* is an e-mail message that the system sends immediately after a triggering event, such as when a project manager publishes a new project. The system notifies all project team members about their new assignments with an *Alert* e-mail message. A *Reminder* is an e-mail message that the system sends once a day to remind team members of events, such as upcoming tasks or overdue status reports.

To access these settings, click the *Alerts and Reminders* link in the *Operational Policies* section of the *Server Settings* page. The system displays the *Alerts and Reminders* page shown in Figure 10 - 14.

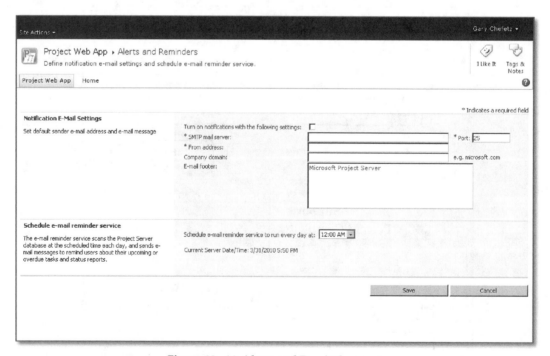

Figure 10 - 14: Alerts and Reminders page

To enable and configure the notifications engine, complete the following steps:

1. Select the *Turn on notifications with the following settings* check box.

2. Enter a server name in the *SMTP mail server* field.

3. Change the number in the *Port* field if your e-mail server is set to use a number other than the standard Port 25.

4. Enter an e-mail address in the *From address* field to indicate that Project Server is the e-mail sender.

5. Enter your organization's domain in the *Company domain* field.

6. Change the text in the *E-mail footer* field if you want more or less information in the footer of each e-mail message.

7. Click the *Schedule e-mail reminder service to run every day at* pick list, and then select from the list the time of day that you want the reminder service to run.

Remember to consider other server maintenance processes such as backups and your OLAP cube generation settings when you select the processing time for generating reminders. The daily Reminder process does not generally require a long window of operation, unlike the OLAP cube generation, resource capacity, and backup processes.

Warning: After configuring the system settings for *Alerts* and *Reminders*, you may also need to configure your SMTP server to relay messages from Project Server 2010.

8. When you complete your selections click the *Save* button and the system displays the confirmation dialog shown in Figure 10 - 15.

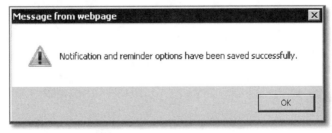

**Figure 10 - 15: Confirmation dialog
for Alerts and Reminders options**

Setting Options for the OLAP Cube

You must set the criteria for publishing OLAP cube data in your system, including the date range for the data and its update frequency. Project Server 2010 uses data from the OLAP cube for data analysis using Excel workbooks and leverages Excel Services to present these in Project Web App. To configure the OLAP cube settings, click the *OLAP Database Management* link in the *Database Administration* section in the *Server Settings* page. The system displays the *OLAP Database Management* page shown in Figure 10 - 16.

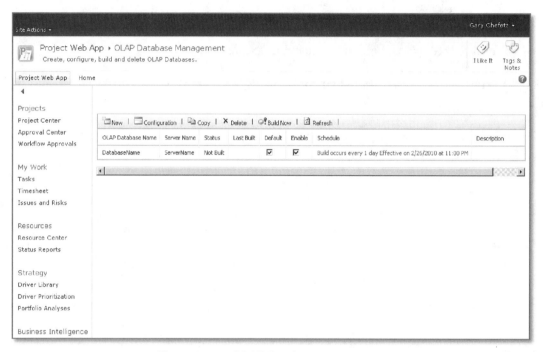

Figure 10 - 16: OLAP Database Management

By default, the *OLAP Database Management* page contains one default, but incomplete, cube record. To begin the process of setting OLAP cube information in your organization's Project Server 2010 system, you must configure the default OLAP database build settings and then configure the OLAP database according to your organization's reporting requirements. Project Server 2010 allows you to build multiple OLAP databases, each of which might meet an individual set of reporting requirements or serve different audiences such as for various departments. Remember that you can attribute OLAP databases using Project Server's *Departments* filtering.

To configure the default OLAP cube, click the *DatabaseName* entry in the *OLAP Database Name* field. The system displays the *OLAP Database Build Settings* page shown in Figure 10 - 17. Notice that the *OLAP Database Build Settings* page consists of five sections of options:

- Analysis Services Settings
- Project Department
- Resource Department
- Database Date Range
- OLAP Database Update Frequency

420

Project Server 2010 requires you to enter information in the *Analysis Services Settings, Database Date Range,* and *OLAP Database Update Frequency* sections. You may optionally enter information in the *Project Department* and *Resource Department* sections if you want to restrict the list of projects and/or resources in the OLAP database.

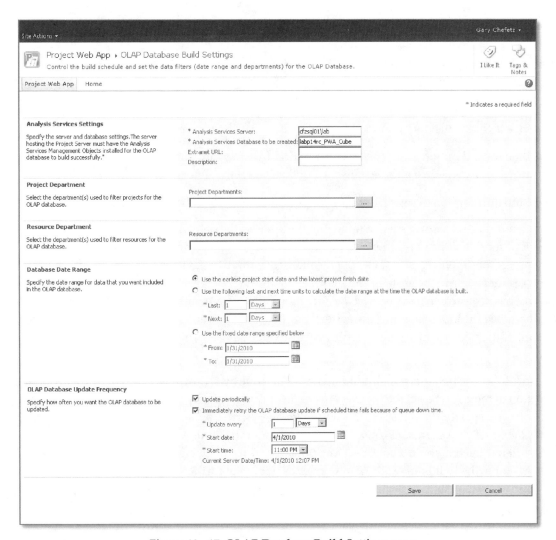

Figure 10 - 17: OLAP Database Build Settings page

To configure the OLAP database, begin by entering information in the *Analysis Services Settings* section of the *OLAP Database Build Settings* page. Enter the name of the server running Analysis Services in the *Analysis Services Server* field, replacing the default value "ServerName." Enter a name for your cube in the *Analysis Services Database to be created* field, replacing the default "DatabaseName" entry. Enter an optional extranet address for the server running Analysis Services in the *Extranet URL* field. Enter an optional description in the *Description* field.

If you need to restrict the list of projects included in the OLAP database, click the *Project Departments* pick list and select one or more *Departments*. If you need to restrict the list of resources included in the OLAP database, click the *Resource Departments* pick list and select one or more *Departments*.

You can select multiple values in the *Project Departments* pick list or the *Resource Departments* pick list **only** if you modified these two built-in enterprise fields to allow users to select multiple values.

In the *Database Date Range* section, you must decide on a date range for your OLAP cube data. You may choose to set the date range in one of three ways:

- Select the first option to set the date range from the *earliest project start date to the latest project finish date*. The system sets this as the default option in the *Database Date Range* section.

- Select the second option to set specific time period forward and backward from the current date, enter the amount of time in the *Last* and *Next* fields, and then select the time units on the *Units* pick list for each field .

- Select the third option to set a fixed date range and then enter the dates in the *From* and *To* fields.

When making your date selections, keep in mind that the broader the date range you select, the more data the system must process and store. This has a profound effect on data storage requirements and processing times. Further, these activities are processor–intensive, so your server resource consumption is a factor of your server's power, the amount of project and resource data in the system, and the extent of the date range you require the system to generate. On the other hand, when you more narrowly restrict the date range, the system must build a more complex query to retrieve the data for the cube build. Occasionally, the system-built query is less efficient than it should be, in which case you lose some or all of the performance gain of retrieving a smaller dataset. This is an unpredictable condition, so your mileage may vary.

Your final step is to set the frequency for updating the OLAP cube by setting the options in the *OLAP Database Update Frequency* section of the page. Select the *Update periodically* option to specify automatic updating using the frequency and time options you specify. **Do not** select this option if you wish to update the OLAP cube manually. Select the *Immediately retry the OLAP database update if scheduled time fails because of queue down time* option to force the system to re-try the build when it fails. If you do not select this option, and if the Queue is down when the system attempts to build the OLAP cube, the build fails and the system does not make further attempts.

Set the frequency and schedule for building the OLAP cube in the *Update every*, *Start date*, and *Start time* fields. Where system activity is brisk and project status is changing frequently, a daily build might be your best selection. If you have a slower-paced project environment and updates are occurring on a weekly basis, then you might want to choose a weekly build. Assuming that you have no project data in your Project Server 2010 database, click the *Save* button after completing your selections. The system displays the new OLAP database in the data grid on the *OLAP Database Analysis Administration* page. For example, in Figure 10 - 18, I created a new default OLAP database to show all resources and projects. Notice that I used my server name and instance name in my naming convention to make this easily identifiable in the list and in the Analysis Services console. Notice also that I built the cube by clicking on the *Build Now* button on the toolbar above the grid. You should verify your entries by building your new cube. This should proceed very quickly because you have very little data in the system

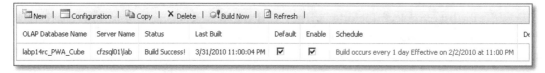

Figure 10 - 18: New Default OLAP database

Until you have projects in your Project Server 2010 database, msProjectExperts recommends that you do not select the *Update Periodically* option. This puts the cube building process into manual mode. After you have projects in the database, you can reselect the *Update Periodically* option to build the OLAP cube automatically.

Remember that the system pushes data to the OLAP database based on the settings you choose. The build process is slow and consumes system resources when it runs. Most administrators set this operation to run at a time of day when the system is idle, as performance degradation can be substantial on your SQL Server unless you have a dedicated server for Analysis Services.

If you previously created an OLAP database, you can create a new OLAP database by selecting it and clicking the *Copy* button. The system displays the OLAP Database Build Settings page for the new OLAP database, shown previously in Figure 10-16. Specify your settings for the new OLAP database and click the *Save* button when finished.

If you create multiple OLAP databases, you must specify one of them as the default OLAP database by selecting its *Default* option. The system allows you to have only one default OLAP database. You can also enable or disable data processing on an OLAP database by selecting or deselecting its *Enable* option.

Configuring the OLAP Database

In Project Server 2010, each OLAP database contains fourteen OLAP cubes. For example, when you build the OLAP database the system creates Project, Resource, Task, and Assignment cubes, including a Timephased and Non-timephased version of each cube, where appropriate. After you create a new OLAP database, you must also configure the OLAP cubes in that database to include the custom enterprise fields you want to include as dimensions and measures. To customize the OLAP database, select the new OLAP database and then click the *Configuration* button on the toolbar. Project Server 2010 displays the *Database Configuration* page for the selected database, such as the one shown in Figure 10 - 19. Notice that the *Database Configuration* page includes five sections: *Cube Dimensions*, *Cube Measures*, *Built-In Measures*, *Inactive Tasks*, and *Calculated Measures*.

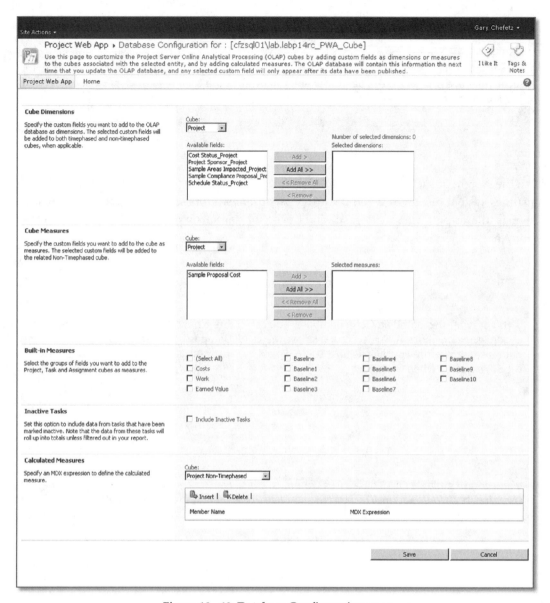

Figure 10 - 19: Database Configuration page

In the *Cube Dimensions* section, you select the custom enterprise project, resource, task, and assignment fields that you want to include as dimensions in each OLAP cube. By default, the system displays the built-in and custom enterprise project fields first. Notice in Figure 10 - 19 that the *Available fields* list in the *Cube Dimensions* section includes all the custom enterprise project fields containing lookup tables. The system lists only those custom enterprise fields that are a single-value field containing a lookup table. These are eligible to become dimensions in the cube.

Warning: If you create a custom enterprise project field, the system does not include the field in the available fields list if the field meets one of the following criteria:

- The field is a free-entry field.
- The field contains a single line or multiple lines of text.
- The field contains a formula.
- The field is a multi-value (MV) field containing a lookup table.

The only available custom enterprise project fields are those that are single-value fields that contain a lookup table.

From the list of Project fields shown in the *Available fields* list, select the fields you want to include in the OLAP cube and then click the *Add* button. Click the *Cube* pick list and select the *Resource* type from the pick list, as shown in Figure 10 - 20. Notice that I previously selected all of the available custom enterprise Project fields.

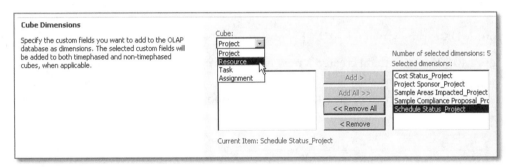

Figure 10 - 20: Cube pick list

From the *Available fields* list, select the custom enterprise resource fields you want to add as dimensions in the OLAP cube and then click the *Add* button. Repeat this process to select custom enterprise task fields and assignment fields.

An assignment contains both task information and resource information created when a project manager assigns a resource to a task. When you select the *Assignment* item from the *Cube* pick list, the system displays a list containing both custom enterprise Task and Resource fields.

In the *Cube Measures* section, you must select the custom enterprise project, resource, task, and assignment fields you want included as measures in the OLAP cube build. The system displays only those built-in and custom enterprise fields that contain a numeric value, including cost, duration, and number fields. These fields **cannot** contain a formula or a lookup table. Notice in Figure 10 - 19, shown previously, that the *Cube Measures* section lists one built-in Project field: the *Sample Proposal Cost* field.

In the *Built-in Measures* section, select the data you want included as total fields (facts) in your OLAP cubes in the OLAP database. The more measures you select, the longer it takes to build your OLAP database, generating a larger OLAP database in the process. By default, Project Server 2010 selects none of these options. At a minimum, I recommend you select the *Work* and *Baseline* options. If your organization tracks project costs, I recommend that you select the *Cost* option. If your organization uses Earned Value Analysis to measure project variance, I recommend that you select the *Earned Value* option. If your organization uses any of the additional sets of baseline fields (Baseline 1 to Baseline 10), you should select the additional baseline fields as well.

Project Server 2010 allows project managers to mark a task as inactive in their enterprise project, a new feature in this version. An inactive task might represent a cancelled task or a task that is delayed and is "on hold" until a future time period. In the *Inactive Tasks* section, you have the option to include these tasks in your OLAP database. If you select the *Include Inactive Tasks* option, the system includes work, cost, and baseline data for the inactive tasks in the OLAP database. When you include inactive tasks, users can still filter out the inactive task data, as *Inactive* becomes a dimension in the cube.

In the *Calculated Measures* section, you can create custom calculated measures using the <u>M</u>ulti<u>d</u>imensional <u>E</u>xpressions (MDX) query language. MDX is the query language you use to work with and retrieve multidimensional data in Microsoft SQL Server Analysis Services for SQL Server 2005 and 2008. To create a calculated measure, complete the following steps:

1. Click the *Cube* pick list and select the OLAP cube to add the calculated measure.

2. Click the *Insert* button.

3. Enter a descriptive name for the calculated measure in the *Member Name* field.

4. Enter your MDX expression in the *MDX Expression* field.

For example, Figure 10 - 21 shows that I created a new calculated measure called *Remaining Capacity* for the virtual cube *Portfolio Analyzer*. Notice the simple MDX expression: [capacity] – [work] subtracting the planned work value in the cube from the capacity represented in the cube. This is a common request and a calculated measure I always add to client systems.

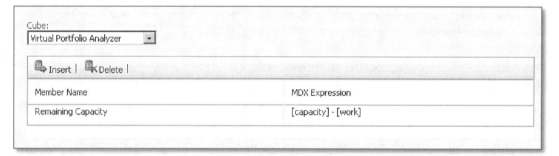

Figure 10 - 21: Calculated Measure added to the cube

Warning: If you enter an invalid expression in the *MDX Expression* field, Project Server 2010 **does not** perform validation on your expression and does not warn you of the error when you save your Cube Configuration information. In fact, you do not see the error until you attempt to use the custom calculated measure in a Data Analysis view. Further, a faulty MDX entry may cause your cube build to fail. Therefore, before entering an MDX expression, you should first test the expression as a local cacluated field first using an Excel workbook connected to the cube.

When you complete your entries for defining database configuration information, click the *Save* button. The system redisplays the *OLAP Database Management* page. If you haven't already done so, test your cube configuration by clicking on the *Build Now* button on the toolbar above the grid. When you build your cube for the first time, the system adds connection (.odc) files in a new folder in your *Data Connections* library. You use the .odc files to connect a workbook to your cubes. When you add and build additional OLAP databases, the system adds a corresponding folder to your *Data Connections* library for each new cube.

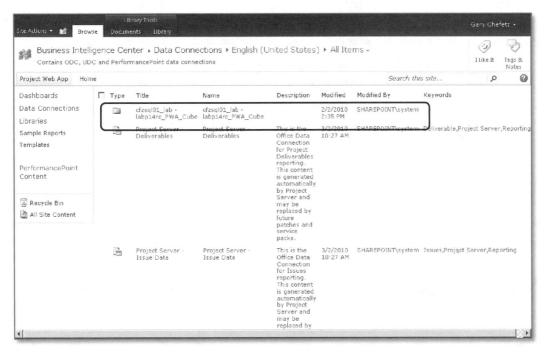

Figure 10 - 22: Data Connections library shows new folder for OLAP database

If you drill down into the folder, you find a new connection file for each of the 14 cubes in the OLAP database. You learn how to use these in Module 16, Creating and Managing Reports.

Deleting an Existing OLAP Database

To delete an existing OLAP database, select the OLAP database on the *OLAP Database Management* page and then click the *Delete* button. The system displays the confirmation dialog shown in Figure 10 - 23. Click the OK button to confirm the deletion process.

Figure 10 - 23: Confirmation dialog
to delete an OLAP database

Configuring Event Handlers

The *Microsoft Project Server Events Service* manages events in the system, controlling all major system operations through pre-defined events and custom *Event Handlers*. The Microsoft *Project Server Queue Service* handles the flow of data between the four system databases, using two different queues to process the data transfer.

The Microsoft *Project Server Events Service* allows you to extend Project Server 2010 by adding new business logic. When changes occur in business object data, the system fires numerous events. When you associate an *Event Handler* with an *Event*, the system executes the *Event Handler* every time that particular event occurs. Using a custom *Event Handler*, you can add custom validation routines, data processing, or notification services, and you can initiate and sustain additional workflows as well.

Before you add a custom *Event Handler* to an event, someone in your organization (such as a software developer) must create the actual *Event Handler*. *Event Handlers* for Project Server 2010 are class library assemblies built on the .NET Framework 3.5 with Service Pack 1.

To add a custom *Event Handler* to an event, click the *Server-Side Event Handlers* link in the *Operational Policies* section of the *Server Settings* page. The system displays the *Server Side Event Handlers* page shown in Figure 10 - 24.

Figure 10 - 24: Server Side Event Handlers page

On the *Events* page, Project Server 2010 provides 18 categories of events, including:

- Admin
- Calendar
- CubeAdmin
- Custom Fields

- Lookup Table

- Notifications

- Optimizer

- Project

- Reporting

- Resource

- Resource Plan

- Rules

- Security

- Statusing

- Status Reports

- Timesheet

- UserDelegation

- Workflow

- WSSInterop

There are actually two types of events among the events listed in the 18 categories: pre-events and post-events. Business objects raise pre-events before saving data to the Project Server database, and you can use a custom event handler to add business logic processing before the event occurs or cancel any operation that raises a pre-event. The system raises post-events after saving data in the Project Server database. You cannot cancel a post-event operation, but you can add a custom event handler that triggers an action in response to a post-event, such as sending an e-mail message to a pre-defined list of users or processing additional business logic.

 To determine whether an event is a pre-event or a post-event, look at its name in the *Event Name* field. The system displays post-events with a verb in **past tense**, such as **changed, created, or deleted.** The system displays pre-events using the present progressive tense, such as changing, creating, or deleting.

In the list of events in the *Events* section, click the name of the event that you want to associate with your new *Event Handler*. Notice in Figure 10 - 25 that I want to associate a custom *Event Handler* with the *Calendar Changed* post-event to trigger an action every time someone changes a calendar in Project Server.

Figure 10 - 25: Events page with Changed event selected in Calendar section

After selecting an event from the list, click the *New Event Handler* button. The system displays the *New Event Handler* page shown in Figure 10 - 26.

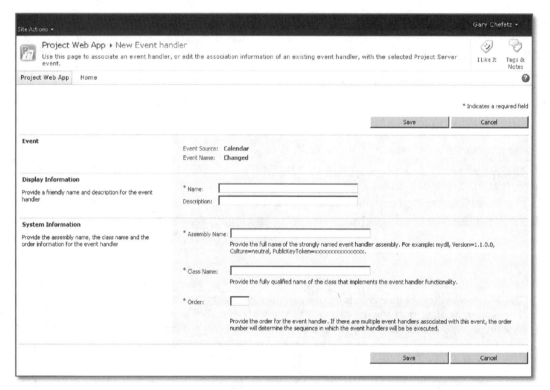

Figure 10 - 26: New Event Handler page for the Calendar Created event

On the *Event Handler* page, enter the relevant information to attach the custom *Event Handler* to the selected event. Enter a friendly name for the *Event Handler* in the *Name* field, along with an optional description in the *Description* field. In the *Assembly Name* field, enter the full name for the *Event Handler* assembly. Enter the fully qualified name for the class that implements the functionality of the *Event Handler* in the *Class Name* field. Provide the order for processing the *Event Handler* in the *Order* field. If you have multiple *Event Handlers* associated with an event, the *Order* field determines the order in which Project Server 2010 processes the *Event Handlers*. When you complete your entries, click the *Save* button.

To learn more about creating and deploying custom *Event Handlers*, see the *Developers Guide to Microsoft Project Server 2007 and 2010* by Stephen Sanderlin, ISBN 978-1-934240-08-3.

Configuring the Quick Launch Menu

Changing the order and layout of your Quick Launch menu is not likely to be at the top of your list of implementation tasks, yet customizing the menu is a useful way to tailor Project Server 2010 to the your user-specific requirements. To change the Quick Launch menu in Project Web App, click the *Quick Launch* link in the *Look and Feel* section of the *Server Settings* page. The system displays the *Quick Launch* page shown in Figure 10 - 27.

Figure 10 - 27: Quick Launch page

The *Quick Launch* page includes two sections for configuring the Quick Launch menu: the *Configure Quick Launch Behavior* section and the *Set Menu Item Details* section. The *Configure Quick Launch Behavior* section controls how the system presents the Quick Launch menu for each user. You have several options to control this behavior, including:

- Set the *Expand menu items for* option to the *Current section only* setting to collapse all main menu sections and expand only the main menu section currently selected. When you select this option, the system displays the full Quick Launch menu when a user logs in to Project Web App, but then collapses the main menu sections when the user selects a menu item. Figure 10 - 28 shows the Quick Launch menu with all main menu sections expanded, while Figure 10 - 29 shows the Quick Launch menu with only the *Project Center* main menu section expanded.

Figure 10 - 29: Quick Launch menu collapsed from Project Center

Figure 10 - 28: Quick Launch menu completely expanded

- Set the *Expand menu items for* option to the default *All sections* setting to force the system to always display the Quick Launch menu with all main menu sections expanded. This guarantees that users see all menus at all times in Project Web App.

- Select or deselect the *Show menu items from Windows SharePoint Services* option to show or hide menu items driven by Windows SharePoint Services features. If you deselect this option, the system hides the *Documents* menu item.

The *Set Menu Item Details* section allows you to edit the default menu items, create new menu items, and set the display order of all menu items. To edit a default menu, click the hyperlink for the name of the menu. For example, click the *Issues and Risks* menu hyperlink in the data grid. The system displays the *Add or Edit Link* page for the *Issues and Risks* menu shown in Figure 10 - 30.

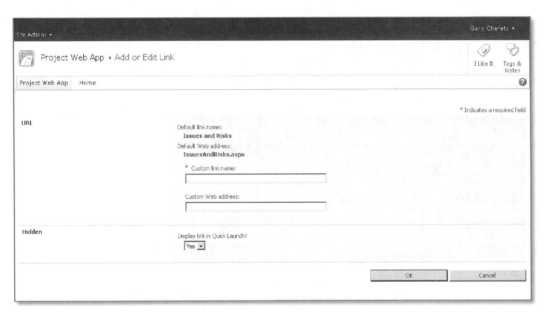

Figure 10 - 30: Add or Edit Link page

If you want to change the name of the menu, enter a new name in the *Custom link name* field. To redirect the menu to a URL containing custom content, enter the URL in the *Custom Web address* field. To hide the menu so that it does not appear in the Quick Launch menu, click the *Display link in Quick Launch* pick list and select the *No* value. Click the *OK* button to save your changes to the default menu.

To create a new menu item, you must either add the menu to an existing main menu section or create a new main menu section. For example, our organization needs a new main menu section called PM Help, with two sub-menus that point to the web sites for Project Server Experts and for the Project Management Institute. To create the new *PM Help* main menu section, complete the following steps:

1. Click the *New Link* button on the toolbar at the top of the grid. Project Server 2010 displays the *Add or Edit Link* page shown in Figure 10 - 31.

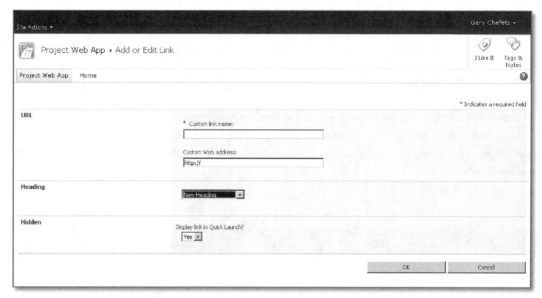

Figure 10 - 31: Add or Edit Link page for a new menu section

2. Enter a name for the main menu section in the *Custom link name* field.

3. Enter a URL for the main menu section in the *Custom Web address* field.

4. Click the *Heading* pick list and select the *New Heading* item.

5. Click the *Display link in Quick Launch* pick list and select the *Yes* item.

6. Click the *OK* button.

> You **must** specify a URL for every main menu section. The URL is the default location to which Project Web Access navigates if a user clicks the main menu link. For example, if you click the *Projects* main menu, the system navigates to the *Project Center* page. If you do not want the main menu section to point anywhere outside of Project Web App, simply enter the URL for the Project Web App Home page.

Project Server 2010 adds the new *PM Help* main menu section in the Quick Launch menu as shown in Figure 10 - 32. To create a new submenu in the new main menu section, complete the following steps:

1. Click the *New Link* button on the toolbar at the top of the grid.

Project Server 2010 displays the *Add or Edit Link* page shown previously in Figure 10 - 31.

2. Enter a name for the menu in the *Custom link name* field.

3. Enter a URL for the menu in the *Custom Web address* field.

4. Click the *Heading* pick list and select the *PM Help* item.

5. Click the *Display link in Quick Launch* pick list and select the *Yes* item.

6. Click the *OK* button.

Project Server 2010 adds the new submenu items in the PM Help section of the Quick Launch menu shown in Figure 10 - 33.

Figure 10 - 32: PM Help section added to Quick Launch menu

Figure 10 - 33: PM Help sub-menus added to Quick Launch menu

To move a submenu or a main menu section, select the item you want to move and then click the *Move Up* or *Move Down* button. To delete a submenu or a main menu, select the item and then click the *Delete Link* button. If you select a main menu section and delete it, the system deletes all submenus in that section as well. Click the *Save* button to save the latest menu changes.

When you add a new heading item to the Quick Launch menu and then add submenu items, the system automatcially adds space between the last submenu item and the following heading item. The system does not add space between two heading items automatically. Instead, you must create a new blank heading item to add space between two heading items. Notice that Microsoft added a blank heading item between *Business Intelligence* and *Settings* to create the space between them.

Warning: To create a main menu containing submenus that point to websites outside of Project Web App, you must use a main menu URL that points to a Project Web Access page. Otherwise, the system does not display the submenus. To create the two submenus for the Help menu shown in Figure 10-32, I pointed the *PM Help* main menu URL to the Project Web App Home page. This is a bug in the release version.

Module 11

Configuring Time and Task Tracking

Learning Objectives

After completing this module, you will be able to:

- Understand the difference between task tracking and time tracking
- Define financial periods
- Define Timesheet periods
- Configure Timesheet options
- Configure the use of Administrative time
- Specify the default method for tracking task progress

Inside Module 11

Understanding Tracking 439
Defining Financial Periods 439
Defining Time Reporting Periods 442
Configuring Timesheet Options 446
    Creating Line Classifications...446
    Setting Timesheet Options 447
Configuring Administrative Time...450
Disabling the My Timesheet Functionality 452
Setting the Task Tracking Method 454
    Specifying the Tracking Method 456
    Locking Down the Tracking Method 460
    Setting the Reporting Display 461
    Protecting User Updates...461
    Defining the Near Future Planning Window 462
Setting Up the Timesheet Page 463

Customizing the My Tasks Page...**466**

Using Percent of Work Complete...466

Using Actual Work Done and Work Remaining...470

Using Hours of Work Done per Period 471

Tips for Using Tracking Methods **472**

Using Percent of Work Complete...472

Using Actual Work Done and Work Remaining...473

Summary **473**

Understanding Tracking

The configuration you choose for tracking in Project Server 2010 has a tremendous impact on everyone in your organization. Therefore, it is vitally important that you know the tracking requirements of your organization before you configure tracking settings for your system. Plan to meet with your project managers, executives, and accounting department to determine the task and time tracking needs of each, and then configure the system based on these requirements.

Project Server 2010 supports the two classic approaches to task assignment tracking: effort-based tracking fundamentally supported by time collection, and duration-based tracking fundamentally supported by collecting status based on percentage of completion. Within this dichotomy, Project Server provides you the ability to create variations of these tracking methods and to create blended methods to support very specific requirements and collect all types of standard and custom tracking data.

In a normal repetitive cycle, the organization must require project team members to enter task-tracking information for enterprise projects. Organizations may need to collect time information in a daily timesheet to track the amount of time spent on activities such as non-project work, billable and non-billable time, or time spent on administrative work. Project Server 2010 also interfaces with third party ERP systems to support articulation of timesheet information to a billing, payroll, or accounting system.

 Warning: Your organization's greatest challenge is **culture** when introducing the use of timesheets for the first time. If your organization has not previously used timesheets of any type, you will likely face a great deal of "pushback" from team members, and possibly even from project managers as well. Your leaders **must address this issue and plan accordingly**, or face the possibility of failure in implementing Project Server 2010 in your organization.

To configure Project Server 2010 for tracking, you must specify your organization's settings in each of the following areas, which I discuss individually:

- Financial periods
- Time periods for timesheets
- Timesheet options
- Default method of tracking task progress

Defining Financial Periods

If your organization intends to use Project Server 2010 with a third-party financial system, or if you need to create OLAP views that include financial periods, you must define financial periods that match your organization's method for reporting financial information. This means you must create fiscal years with fiscal months. To configure financial periods, click the *Financial Periods* link in the *Time and Task Management* section of the *Server Settings* page. Project Server 2010 displays the *Fiscal Periods* page shown in Figure 11 - 1.

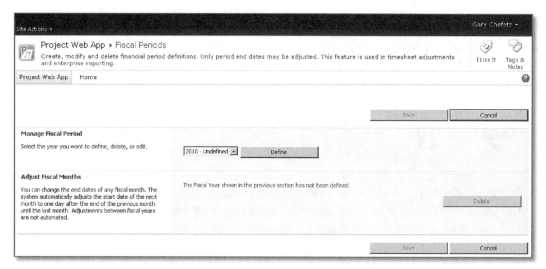

Figure 11 - 1: Fiscal Periods page

You use the *Fiscal Periods* page to create the fiscal years and fiscal months used for reporting financial information. If, for instance, your organization's fiscal year begins on July 1 for the next fiscal year, then July 1, 2010 begins FY2011. So if your Project Server 2010 implementation began January 1, 2010, you need to create two fiscal years for reporting purposes, FY2010 (the current fiscal year) and FY2011 (the next fiscal year).

To create a new fiscal year, click the *Manage Fiscal Period* pick list, select the fiscal year you want to create, and then click the *Define* button. The system displays the *Define Fiscal Year Parameters* page shown in Figure 11 - 2.

On the *Define Fiscal Year Parameters* page, begin by entering the starting date of the selected fiscal year in *The fiscal year begins on* field. You can type the date, or you can click the *Calendar* button to select the date from a calendar date picker. Because our organization's FY2010 began January 1, 2010, I enter that date in the field.

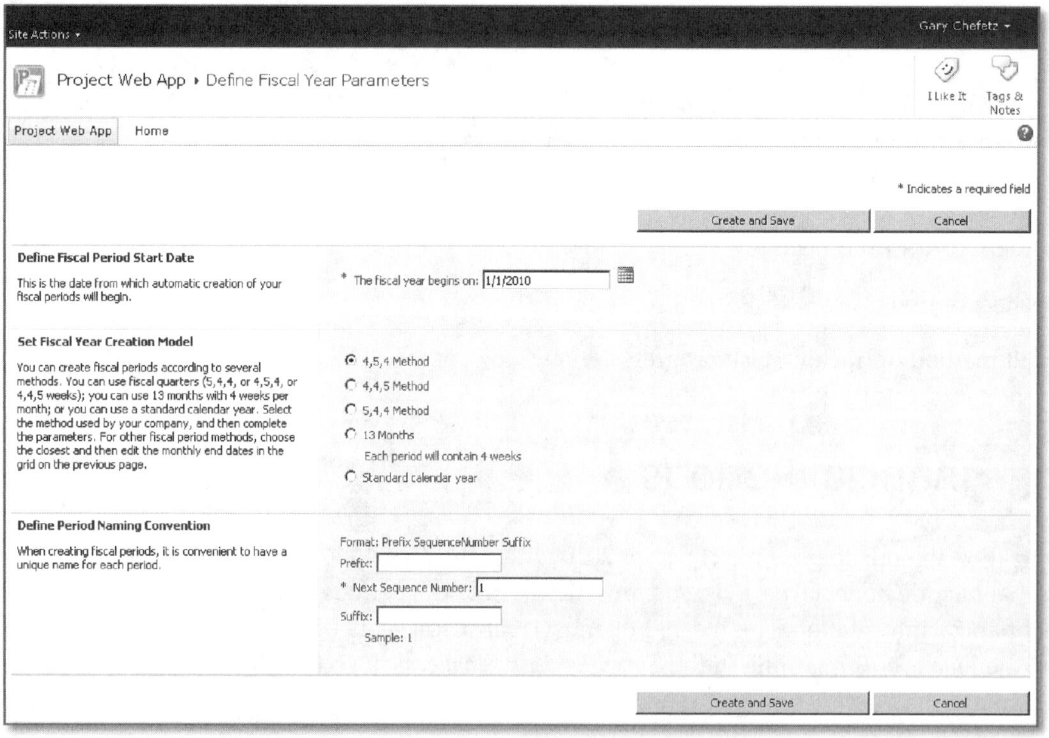

Figure 11 - 2: Define Fiscal Year Parameters page

In the *Set Fiscal Year Creation Model* section of the page, select the fiscal periods that best match your organization's approach to managing fiscal periods. Project Server 2010 allows you to create fiscal quarters using one of three accounting methods (4-5-4, or 4-4-5, or 5-4-4), using 13 months where each month represents 4 weeks, or using the standard calendar with 12 monthly periods. Our organization uses fiscal months that follow the calendar, so I selected the *Standard calendar year* option.

If you select the *4-5-4* option, the system sets up fiscal quarters consisting of a 4-week month, a 5-week month, and a 4-week month. The *4-4-5* or *5-4-4* options work in a similar manner. The months created by the system may or may not coincide with actual calendar months.

In the *Define Period Naming Convention* section, enter your organization's naming convention in the *Prefix, Next Sequence Number*, and *Suffix* fields. For example, our organization uses the following naming convention to represent January 2010: FY10-1. To set up this naming convention, I enter "FY10-" (minus the quotes) in the *Prefix* field, enter 1 in the *Next Sequence Number* field, and enter nothing in the *Suffix* field.

Notice that I follow the FY10 text string with a dash character to separate the fiscal year from the fiscal month. Of the three fields, the only one required is the *Next Sequence Number* field.

Project Server 2010 allows you to enter up to 15 characters in either the *Prefix* or *Suffix* fields, and to enter a number up to six digits in the *Next Sequence Number* field.

The system displays a sample of your naming convention directly below the *Suffix* field. Use this sample to confirm that the system names your fiscal periods the way you want before you actually create the fiscal periods.

When you complete your entries, click the *Create and Save* button. The system creates fiscal periods according to your specifications, and displays them on the *Fiscal Periods* page shown in Figure 11 - 3.

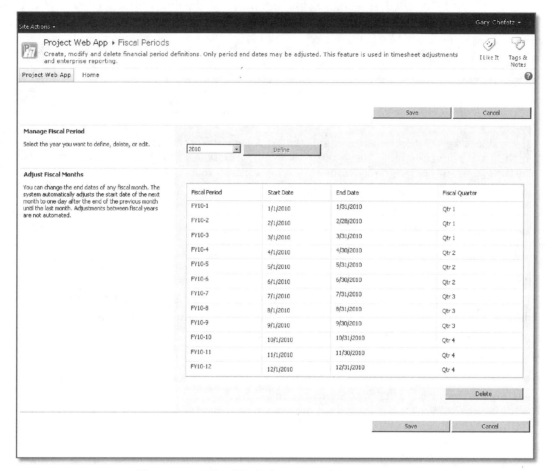

Figure 11 - 3: Fiscal Periods page with FY2010 periods

If the system does not create the fiscal periods as you expected, click the *Delete* button immediately. The system removes all of the fiscal periods you just created, and you must recreate the fiscal periods. When you are satisfied with the results, click the *Save* button.

Warning: When you create fiscal periods for a new fiscal year, Project Server 2010 **does not** assume that the first fiscal period begins immediately after the last fiscal period of the last fiscal year. You must always select the starting date for the current year of fiscal periods.

Defining Time Reporting Periods

If your organization plans to use the Project Server 2010 timesheet system or the *Tasks* page to record time in addition to task progress, you must define *Time Reporting Periods* that match your organization's method for collecting time. To define *Time Reporting Periods*, click the *Time Reporting Periods* link in the *Time and Task Management* section of the *Server Settings* page. The system displays the *Time Reporting Periods* page shown in Figure 11 - 4.

In the *Timesheet Reporting Periods* page, the system allows you to define time periods individually, or to create them in bulk. If your organization uses weekly or bi-weekly time reporting periods, it is much easier to create the time reporting periods in bulk.

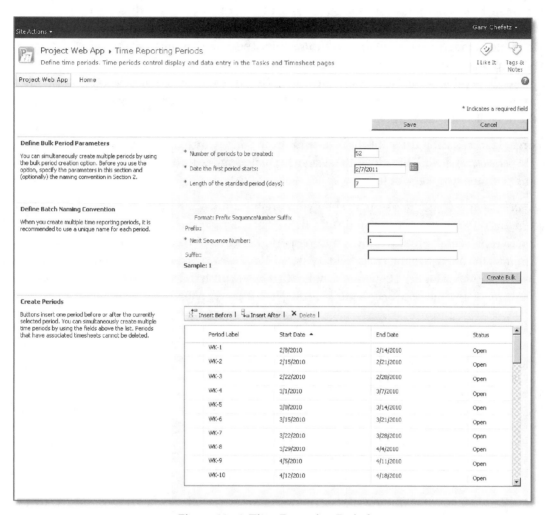

Figure 11 - 4: Time Reporting Periods

If you want to create time reporting periods manually, simply click the *Insert Before* button at the top of the *Create Periods* grid to create the first time period. The system creates a one-week unnamed time reporting period for the current date, as shown in Figure 11 - 5.

Figure 11 - 5: New unnamed time reporting period

443

After creating the new unnamed time reporting period, you must manually enter a name for it in the *Period Label* field, enter a start date for the period in the *Start Date* field, and enter an end date in the *End Date* field. After you finish editing the first time period, click the *Insert After* button to create and edit each new successive time period. Notice that if you insert a new time reporting period before a list of existing time reporting periods, the system automatically sets up a new time reporting period contiguous with the first time reporting period that follows it.

If you want to create time reporting periods in bulk, begin by entering data in the three required fields in the *Define Bulk Period Parameters* section at the top of the *Time Reporting Periods* page. Enter the number of periods for Project Server 2010 to create in the *Number of periods to be created* field. The default number in this field is *52*. Type the date of the first timesheet period in the *Date the first period starts* field, or click the *Calendar* button to select the date from a calendar date picker. The value in this field always defaults to today, so remember to select the date of the first day of the first reporting period. Enter the length of each reporting period in the *Length of the standard period (days)* field. The system sets the default value as 7 days in this field.

Because our organization's standard reporting week runs from Sunday through Saturday, I entered January 3, 2010 in the *Date the first period starts* field. This allows the system to create Sunday through Saturday time reporting periods in bulk, beginning with the first week of January 2010.

In the *Define Batch Naming Convention* section, enter your organization's naming convention for each time reporting period in the *Prefix*, *Next Sequence Number*, and *Suffix* fields. For example, our organization uses the **FY10-WK-1** naming convention to represent the first weekly reporting period in 2010. To set up this naming convention, I entered "FY10-WK-" (minus the quotes) in the *Prefix* field, I entered 1 in the *Next Sequence Number* field, and entered nothing in the *Suffix* field as shown in Figure 11 - 6. Again, notice that I use a dash character to separate the year from the week number. Of the three fields, the only one required is the *Next Sequence Number* field.

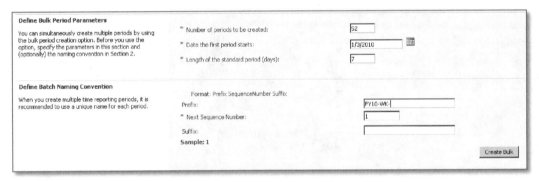

Figure 11 - 6: Define Bulk Parameters and Naming Convention

When you complete your entries, click the *Create Bulk* button. The system creates the number of specified time reporting periods, as shown in Figure 11 - 7.

 Project Server 2010 allows you to enter up to 15 characters in either the *Prefix* or *Suffix* fields, and to enter a number up to six digits in the *Next Sequence Number* field.

The system displays a sample of your naming convention directly below the *Suffix* field. Inspect this sample to confirm that the system names your timesheet periods correctly before you actually create the time periods.

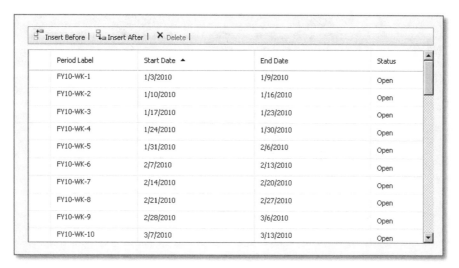

Figure 11 - 7: Time Reporting Period settings page after creating 52 periods

After creating time reporting periods in bulk, you may need to delete one or more periods. To delete a single period, click the gray row header of a single time reporting period and then click the *Delete* button. To delete multiple timesheet periods, press and hold the *Control* key and select the row headers of each period you want to delete in bulk, and then click the *Delete* button. If you do not go live with your implementation until later in the year for which you created bulk time reporting periods, you may want to delete or close the periods prior to the go-live date, as these open time periods will show up as unsubmitted timesheets in the reminders web part on the homepage for each user.

 Warning: After your organization "goes live" with Project Server 2010 and users begin submitting timesheets for approval, you **cannot** delete any time period for which any user submitted a timesheet. This includes future time periods in which a user submitted planned nonworking time, such as planned vacation or planned sick leave.

After you create time reporting periods in bulk, the system sets the value in the *Status* field to *Open* for each period. If you want to allow your organization's resources to enter future time for planned vacation and planned sick leave, you need to leave every timesheet period open for data entry. As a part of your regular operational duties, you must eventually set the *Status* field value to *Closed* for past timesheet periods to prevent resources from entering time against past closed time periods. When you finish setting up your time reporting periods, click the *Save* button to close the *Time Reporting Periods* page.

Configuring Timesheet Options

Two sets of options allow you to configure timesheets for your organization in Project Server 2010. You can create *Line Classifications*, if necessary, for business purposes or accounting needs such as tracking work done on-site and off-site. You may also change the default options for displaying timesheet periods in Project Web App.

Creating Line Classifications

To create additional timesheet line classifications, click the *Line Classifications* link in the *Time and Task Management* section of the *Server Settings* page. The system displays the *Line Classifications* page shown in Figure 11 - 8.

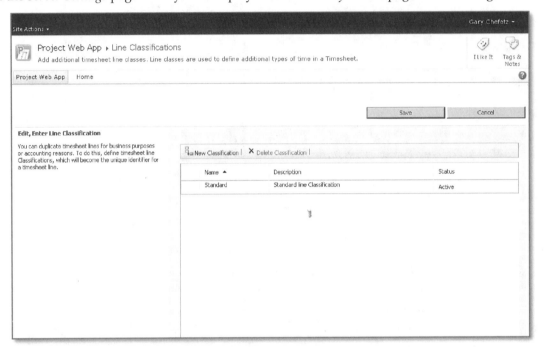

Figure 11 - 8: Line Classifications page

In the data grid, the system displays the *Standard* line classification for timesheet tasks. If your organization requires additional line classifications, click the *New Classification* button at the top of the data grid. Project Server 2010 adds the new, unnamed line classification as shown in Figure 11 - 9.

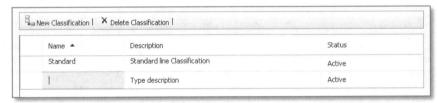

Figure 11 - 9: New unnamed line classification

Edit the information for the new line classification line by entering data in the *Name* and *Description* fields. If you do not want to use the new classification immediately, set its *Status* value to *Inactive*; otherwise, leave the *Status* value set to *Active*. Create as many additional line classification as you need and then click the *Save* button when finished.

 Warning: To preserve historical data, Project Server 2010 does not allow you to delete the new classification after you save it, If you create a new line and no longer need it, set the *Status* value to *Inactive*. The *Delete Classification* button works only until you save your new entry.

Setting Timesheet Options

To set the options for displaying Project Server 2010 timesheets, click the *Timesheet Settings and Defaults* link in the *Time and Task Management* section of the *Server Settings* page. The system displays the *Timesheet Settings and Defaults* page shown in Figure 11 - 10. Notice that the first section of the page determines how the system displays the timesheet in Project Web App.

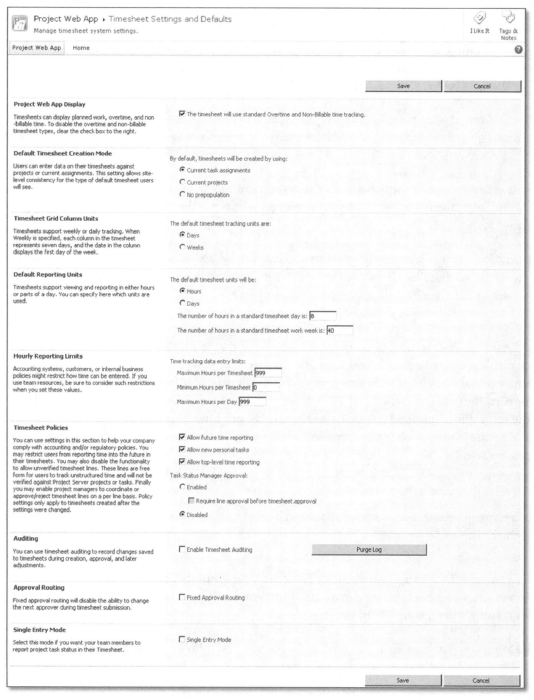

Figure 11 - 10: Settings and Defaults page

In the *Project Web App* display section, leave the default *The timesheet will use standard Overtime and Non-Billable tracking* option to track Billable, Non-Billable, and Overtime work. When selected, this option allows users to add the *Overtime, Non-Billable,* and *Overtime nonbillable* fields to their timesheets as needed. Deselect this option to track only actual work and scheduled work.

In the *Default Timesheet Creation Mode* section, Project Server 2010 offers three options for timesheet creation. The system uses the option you select when a user creates a new timesheet using the *Create with Default Setting* option. The three options in the *Default Timesheet Creation Mode* section are:

- Select the default *Current task assignments* option to force the system to create timesheets that include both administrative tasks and current task assignments. By default, a current task is any task with planned work during the time period for which the user creates a timesheet.

- Select the *Current projects* option to force the system to create timesheets that include both administrative tasks and only a single top-level line item for each project containing a current task. This option is for organizations that do not track time at the task level, and do not use time to drive task progress.

- Select the *No prepopulation* option to force the system to create blank timesheets that include only administrative tasks. Selecting this option forces the users to insert the tasks they want to see after they create a new timesheet.

In the *Timesheet Grid Column Units* section, select the default *Days* option to specify daily tracking with seven days/week on each user's timesheet. Selecting this option forces the system to set up timesheets with a 7-day data grid using the dates you selected for each timesheet period. Select the *Weeks* option to specify weekly tracking, where each column in the timesheet represents a seven day time period.

In the *Default Reporting Units* section, select the default *Hours* option to display planned work in hours, or select the *Days* option to display planned work in days. Regardless of which option you choose, Project Server 2010 allows team members to enter actual work in either hours or days. If a team member enters actual work in days, such as 1d, then the system converts the value to hours using the number you specify in *The number of hours in a standard timesheet day is* field. The default value in this field is *8*, so if a user enters .5d in a timesheet cell, the system converts the value to 4 hours. If you select the *Weeks* option in the *Timesheet Grid Column Units* section, and a user then enters an actual work value in weeks, such as 1w, the system converts the value to hours using the number you specify in *The number of hours in a standard timesheet week is* field. The default value in this field is 40, so if a user enters .75w in a timesheet cell, the system converts the value to 30 hours.

In the *Hourly Reporting Limits* section, set your upper and lower limits for time entry based on your organization's policies for time entry. These options are:

- In the *Maximum Hours per Timesheet* field, enter the largest number of hours each user can enter in a single timesheet. On a timesheet spanning one week, the theoretical upper limit is 168 hours (7 days x 24 hours/day). To set no upper limit, enter 999 in the field.

- In the *Minimum Hours per Timesheet* field, enter the smallest number of hours each user can enter in a single timesheet. The default value in this field is 0 hours, meaning that users are not required to enter more than 0 hours in any timesheet.

If your organization mandates that each user enter a minimum number of hours during each timesheet period, such as 40 hours, enter that number in the *Minimum Hours per Timesheet* field. The system enforces this minimum value when the user attempts to submit the timesheet.

- In the *Maximum Hours per Day* field, enter the largest number of hours each user can enter in a single timesheet day. On a one day time period, the theoretical upper limit is 24 hours since there are only 24 hours in a day. If you wish to set no upper limit, enter 999 in the field.

 Setting either the *Maximum Hours per Timesheet* value or *Maximum Hours per Day* value to *999* makes no sense unless your entries represent more than one actual resource. Therefore, determine your organization's policy for tracking time and enter those numbers accordingly.

In the *Timesheet Policies* section, Project Server 2010 offers options that you can set according to your organization's policies for using the Timesheet functionality. These options are:

- Select the *Allow future time reporting* option to allow resources to enter time for tasks in the future, such as for vacation or planned sick leave. Deselect this option to allow resources to report time only in their current timesheet and in past open timesheets.

- Select the *Allow new personal tasks* option to permit users to create timesheet entries for personal tasks. A personal task is any task not included in any project in Project Server 2010. Deselect this option to prevent users from adding personal tasks to their timesheets.

- Select the *Allow top-level time reporting* to allow users to enter time at the project level.

- Enable the *Task Status Manager Approval* option to include members of the Project Managers group in timesheet line item approvals.

- If you select the previous option, the system activates the *Require line approval before timesheet approval* option. Select this option to force project managers to approve timesheet lines from the projects they manage, or leave it deselected to make the timesheet line approval process optional.

- In the *Auditing* section, select the *Enable Timesheet Auditing* option to allow timesheet auditing. The default state of this option is deselected. If you select the *Enable Timesheet Auditing* option, the system creates an auditing log of timesheet usage which is not accessible through any standard view or report in Project Web App. You must write your own queries or application to retrieve and use this data. You can click the *Purge Log* button at any time to clear the auditing log file of all entries.

In the *Approval Routing* section, select the *Fixed Approval Routing* option to prevent users from manually selecting the next timesheet approver when they submit their timesheets for approval. Deselect this option to allow users to select the next timesheet approver when they submit their timesheets for approval, such as when your organization uses multiple timesheet approvers and users are allowed to select the approver.

The *Single Entry Mode* section contains one very important option that controls the behavior of the *Timesheet* page and the *Tasks* page. If you select the *Single Entry Mode* option, Project Server 2010 works as follows:

- A user enters time on Task A on the *Timesheet* page.

- The system automatically updates the task progress on Task A on the *Tasks* page.

- When the user submits the timesheet for approval to the timesheet manager, the system automatically sends the task update for approval to the *Status Manager* for the task.

If you select the *Single Entry Mode* option, the system locks the options in the *Tracking Method* section of the *Task Settings and Display* page that I cover in the upcoming section, *Setting the Tracking Method*. These locked options force synchronization between the time entered on the *Timesheet* page and the task progress shown on the *Tasks* page. Keep in mind that when you select the *Single Entry Mode* option, the system automatically selects the *Hours of Work Done Per Period* option. You can still set the *Reporting Display* options to determine whether users enter their time in daily increments or in weekly buckets.

Configuring Administrative Time

You can configure Project Server 2010 to track administrative time. Administrative time consists of activities such as non-project time, unplanned work, support work, meetings, training, and non-working time such as vacation and sick leave. To configure the system to track administrative time on each user's timesheet, click the *Administrative Time* link in the *Time and Task Management* section of the *Server Settings* page. The system displays the *Edit or Create Administrative Time* page shown in Figure 11 - 11.

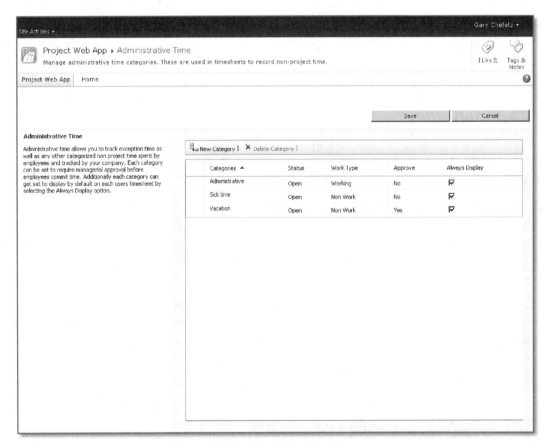

Figure 11 - 11: Administrative Time page

The *Administrative Time* data grid includes three default categories: Administrative, Sick time, and Vacation. You can edit each of these categories and add new categories. For each category of administrative time, you can set the following values:

- Enter a descriptive name for the category in the *Categories* field.

- In the *Status* field, set the status for the category as either *Open* or *Closed*. If you close a category, you prevent resources from entering time against it, even though it still appears on each user's timesheet.

- In the *Work Type* field, set the type to *Working* or *Non Work*.

- In the *Approve* field, select either the *Yes* or *No* value to indicate whether category submissions require managerial approval.

- Select the *Always Display* option to display the administrative time category on each user's timesheet. Deselect this option for a new category that you do not want users to see, and then select this option when you want users to see the category on their timesheets.

msProjectExperts strongly recommends that you determine your organization's default categories of administrative time, and then configure these categories before users actually begin using timesheets. If you deselect the *Always Display* option for a category after users create timesheets, the category continues to appear on existing timesheets, and does not appear on new timesheets.

Warning: If your organization intends to use the planned *Sick time* and *Vacation* categories of administrative time, understand that Project Server 2010 reschedules project tasks around a resource's nonworking time automatically. When a resource submits planned *Sick time* or *Vacation*, and the timesheet manager approves the submission, the system automatically adds the planned *Sick time* or *Vacation* as a new nonworking time exception on the resource's calendar in the enterprise resource pool. Unfortunately, Project Server 2010 **does not** indicate whether the nonworking time is *Sick time* or *Vacation* on the resource's calendar, simply labeling the exception as "Timesheet." At least at this point you can guess that it must be planned time for one of your non-working administrative time categories.

msProjectExperts recommends that you maintain a relatively **short list** of administrative time categories. The more categories you add, the longer the list of tasks on each user's timesheet, and the more cumbersome the time entry process becomes.

Figure 11 - 12 shows the administrative time categories that our organization needs to use. Notice that I added a new category called *Training*. Because training is nonworking time in our organization, it requires approval. After you create your organization's administrative time categories, click the *Save* button.

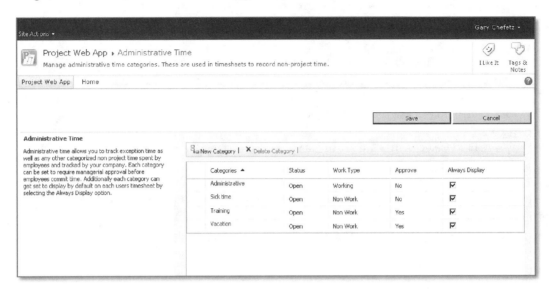

Figure 11 - 12: New categories on the Administrative Time page

Warning: To preserve historical data, Project Server 2010 does not allow you to delete the new administrative time category after you create it and then click the *Save* button. If you create a new category and do not need it, set the *Status* value to *Closed* and then deselect the *Always Display* option. You can use the *Delete Category* button in the toolbar to delete a new category before you click the *Save* button on the page.

Disabling the Timesheet Functionality

The Timesheet functionality is available by default in Project Server 2010. If your organization does not want to use this functionality, and wants to disable it completely so that users cannot access the *Timesheet* page, then complete the following steps:

1. Navigate to the *Server Settings* page in Project Web App and click the *Project Web App Permissions* link in the *Security* section of the page.

2. Deselect the following permissions in the *Resource* section of the page:

   • Adjust Timesheet

   • Approve Timesheets

3. Deselect the following permissions in the *Time and Task Management* section of the page:

   • Accept Timesheets

- View Project Timesheet Line Approvals

- View Resource Timesheet

4. Deselect the following permission in the Views section of the page:

- View Timesheets

5. Click the *Save* button.

Completing this first set of steps disables the timesheet functionality at the top level in the system. Next, you must hide the *Timesheet* link in the Quick Launch menu by completing the following steps:

1. Navigate to the *Server Settings* page and click the *Quick Launch* link in the *Look and Feel* section.

2. On the *Quick Launch* page, click the *Timesheet* link to open it for editing.

3. Click the *Display link in Quick Launch* pick list and select the *No* item on the list.

4. Click the *OK* button.

5. Click the *OK* button and then click the *Save* button.

Finally, you must remove the Timesheet reminders from the *Home* page by modifying the *Reminders* web part using the following steps:

1. Navigate to the *Home* page in Project Web App.

2. Click the *Reminders Web Part Menu* pick list in the upper right corner of the *Reminders* web part and then click the *Edit Web Part* item, as shown in Figure 11 - 13.

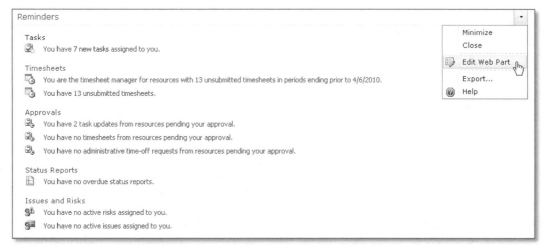

Figure 11 - 13: Edit Page of the Reminders Web Part

The system opens the Project Web App Home page for editing; notice that when you have the *Home* page open in editing mode, the system shows all of the available drop areas into which you can drop a web part. These drop areas include the *Header, Footer, Left, Middle,* and *Right* drop areas.

1. In the *Reminders* side pane on the right side of the page, scroll to the bottom and then expand the Project Web App section as shown in Figure 11 - 14.

Figure 11 - 14: Reminders Web Part
Project Web App section

2. Deselect each of the following options in the Project Web App section:

    *   Show timesheets from resources pending approval

    *   Show administrative time off requests to approve

    *   Show my unsubmitted timesheets

    *   Show late timesheets from resources

    *   Show project timesheet lines pending approval

3. Click the *OK* button.

 The only timesheet functionality you **cannot** disable is the *Import* button on the *Tasks* page. Because there is no way to hide or disable this button through the user interface without custom coding, you must make this a training issue with your staff and tell them not to click the button.

Setting the Task Tracking Method

The tracking method your organization chooses has a significant impact on project team members and their interaction with the *Tasks* page in Project Web App. Not only do some of these options control what data a resource reports, but they also determine the appearance of the *Tasks* page. You must understand both the interface impact and your organization's tracking requirements to determine tracking method settings.

 Warning: If you selected the *Single Entry Mode* option on the *Timesheet Settings and Defaults* page, keep in mind that Project Server 2010 locks the *Tracking Settings* options at the top of the *Task Settings and Display* page.

As part of the Project Server 2010 implementation, your organization must make two important decisions about tracking method settings:

- Determine which method of progress tracking to set as the default.

- Determine whether to "lock down" the default method of tracking, or to allow individual project managers to select their own tracking method for each project.

Project Server 2010 offers four methods for tracking task progress. The difference between each tracking method is the progress information entered by resources:

- **Percent of Work Complete** allows resources to enter an estimated *% Work Complete* value for each task assignment.

- **Actual Work Done and Work Remaining** allows resources to enter the cumulative amount of *Actual Work* and *Remaining Work* for each task assignment.

- **Hours of Work Done per Period** allows resources to enter the hours of *Actual Work* completed on a daily or weekly basis for each task assignment.

- **Free Form** allows resources to enter task progress using any of the three previous methods for each task assignment.

In addition, each of the four methods for tracking task progress also allows resources to adjust the *Remaining Work* estimate for each task assignment.

 Percent of Work Complete is the system default method of tracking progress unless your organization selects another method.

 Warning: The *Percent of Work Complete* and the *Actual Work Done and Work Remaining* methods of tracking progress impose tracking limitations on your project managers. Neither of these methods is date sensitive, which means that Project Server 2010 does not automatically reschedule uncompleted work for tasks that started late. Because of this limitation, I recommend that you customize the setup of the *Tasks* page to include the *Actual Start* and *Actual Finish* fields to make each method of tracking date sensitive. I document the recommended setup of the *Tasks* page in the next section of this module.

To configure the default method of tracking progress for your organization, click the *Task Settings and Display* link in the *Time and Task Management* section of the *Server Settings* page. Project Server 2010 displays the *Task Settings and Display* page shown in Figure 11 - 15. The *Task Settings and Display* page contains four sections of tracking options. I discuss the options in each section separately.

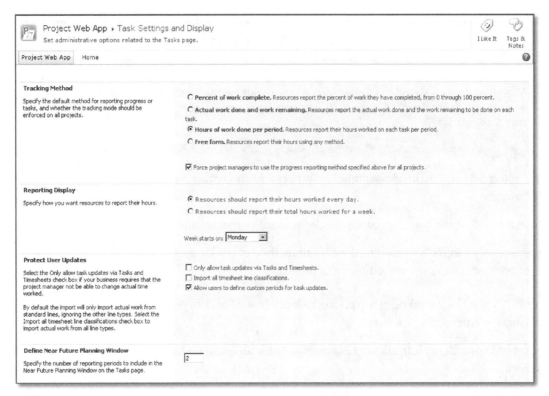

Figure 11 - 15: Task Settings and Display page

Specifying the Tracking Method

In the *Tracking Method* section, specify one of the four tracking methods for your organization. If you select the **Percent of Work Complete** method of tracking, the system displays the *Tasks* page shown in Figure 11 - 16.

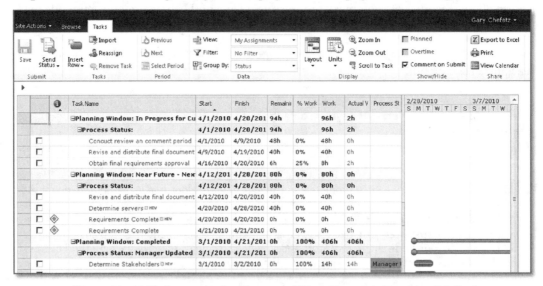

Figure 11 - 16: Tasks page using Percent of Work Complete Tracking Method

On the *Tasks* page, resources enter their cumulative *Percent Work Complete* value in the *% Work Complete* column. When you use the *Percent of Work Complete* tracking method, the system locks the *Actual Work* column and locks the cells in the timephased grid if the user selects to display the timephased grid by selecting this option from the *Layout* button pick list. Users can click on a *Task Name* to display the *Assignment Details* page for the selected task, shown in Figure 11 - 17.

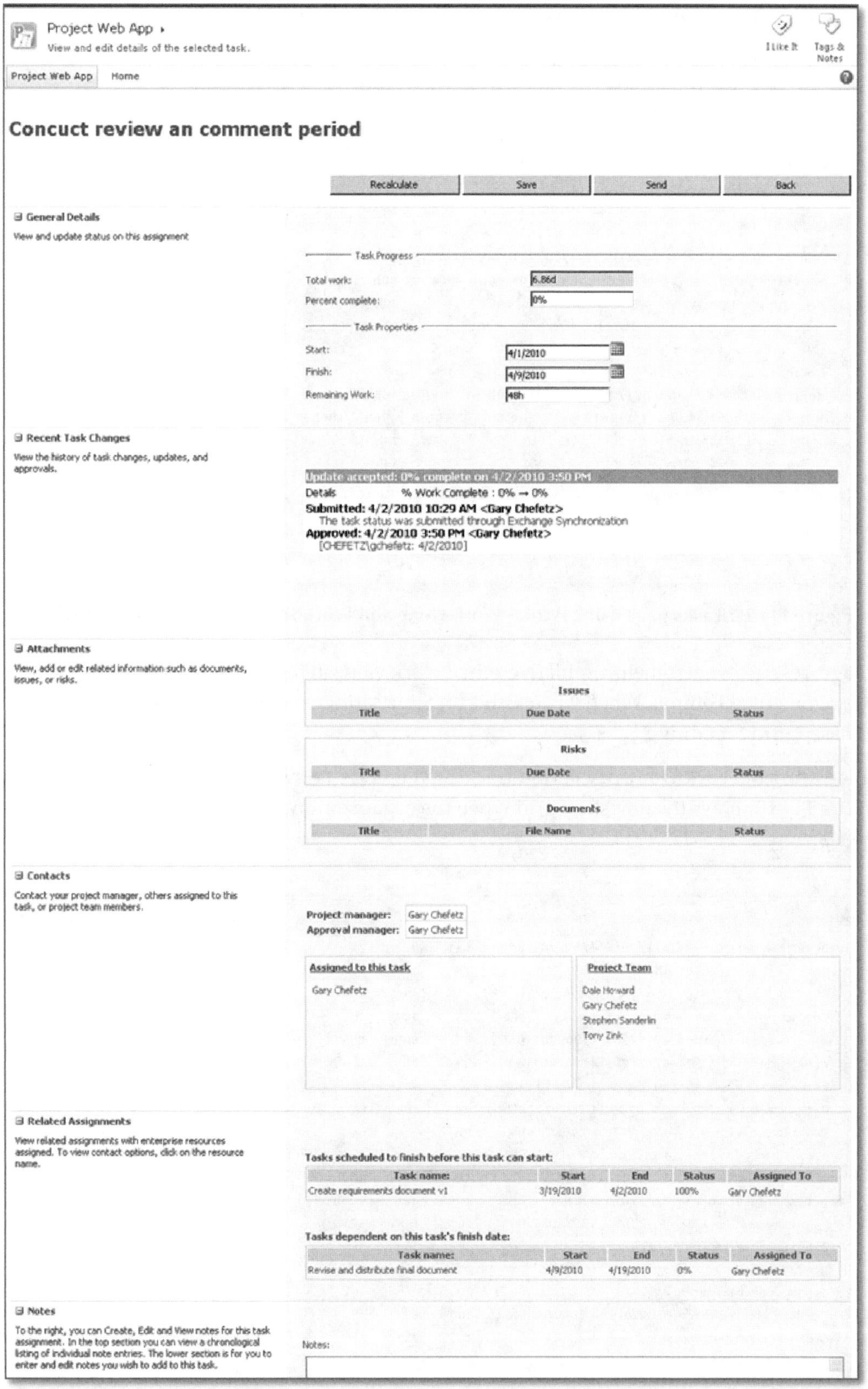

Figure 11 - 17: Task Details page for a selected task

If you select the **Actual Work Done and Work Remaining** method of tracking, the system displays the *Tasks* page shown in Figure 11 - 18.

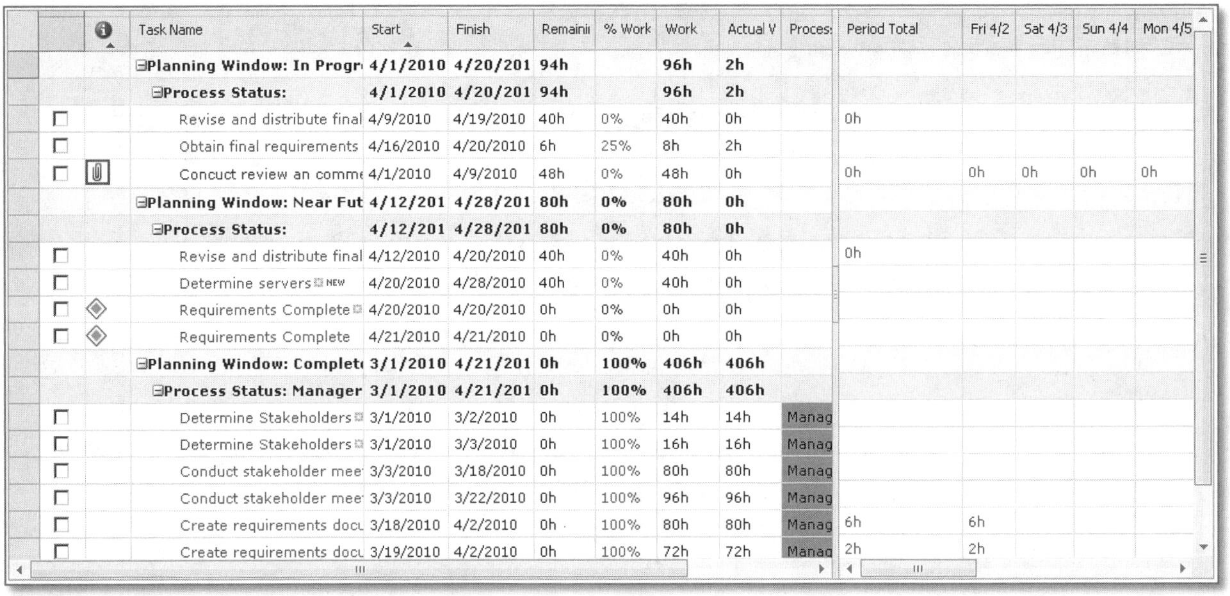

Task Name	Start	Finish	Remainii	% Work	Work	Actual V	Proces:	Period Total	Fri 4/2	Sat 4/3	Sun 4/4	Mon 4/5
⊟Planning Window: In Progr	**4/1/2010**	**4/20/201**	**94h**		**96h**	**2h**						
⊟Process Status:	**4/1/2010**	**4/20/201**	**94h**		**96h**	**2h**						
Revise and distribute final	4/9/2010	4/19/2010	40h	0%	40h	0h		0h				
Obtain final requirements	4/16/2010	4/20/2010	6h	25%	8h	2h						
Concuct review an comm	4/1/2010	4/9/2010	48h	0%	48h	0h		0h	0h	0h	0h	0h
⊟Planning Window: Near Fut	**4/12/201**	**4/28/201**	**80h**	**0%**	**80h**	**0h**						
⊟Process Status:	**4/12/201**	**4/28/201**	**80h**	**0%**	**80h**	**0h**						
Revise and distribute final	4/12/2010	4/20/2010	40h	0%	40h	0h		0h				
Determine servers NEW	4/20/2010	4/28/2010	40h	0%	40h	0h						
Requirements Complete	4/20/2010	4/20/2010	0h	0%	0h	0h						
Requirements Complete	4/21/2010	4/21/2010	0h	0%	0h	0h						
⊟Planning Window: Complet	**3/1/2010**	**4/21/201**	**0h**	**100%**	**406h**	**406h**						
⊟Process Status: Manager	**3/1/2010**	**4/21/201**	**0h**	**100%**	**406h**	**406h**						
Determine Stakeholders	3/1/2010	3/2/2010	0h	100%	14h	14h	Manag					
Determine Stakeholders	3/1/2010	3/3/2010	0h	100%	16h	16h	Manag					
Conduct stakeholder mee	3/3/2010	3/18/2010	0h	100%	80h	80h	Manag					
Conduct stakeholder mee	3/3/2010	3/22/2010	0h	100%	96h	96h	Manag					
Create requirements docu	3/18/2010	4/2/2010	0h	100%	80h	80h	Manag	6h	6h			
Create requirements docu	3/19/2010	4/2/2010	0h	100%	72h	72h	Manag	2h	2h			

Figure 11 - 18: Tasks page using Actual Work Done and Work Remaining method of tracking

On the *Tasks* page, resources enter their cumulative actual work value in the *Actual Work* column and remaining work value in the *Remaining Work* column. When you use this tracking setting, the system locks the *%Work Complete* column and the timephased grid for editing.

If you select the **Hours of Work Done per Period** tracking method, the system displays the *Tasks* page with a timesheet grid. Figure 11 - 19 shows the timesheet grid when the organization's method of tracking progress requires resources to enter progress on a daily basis.

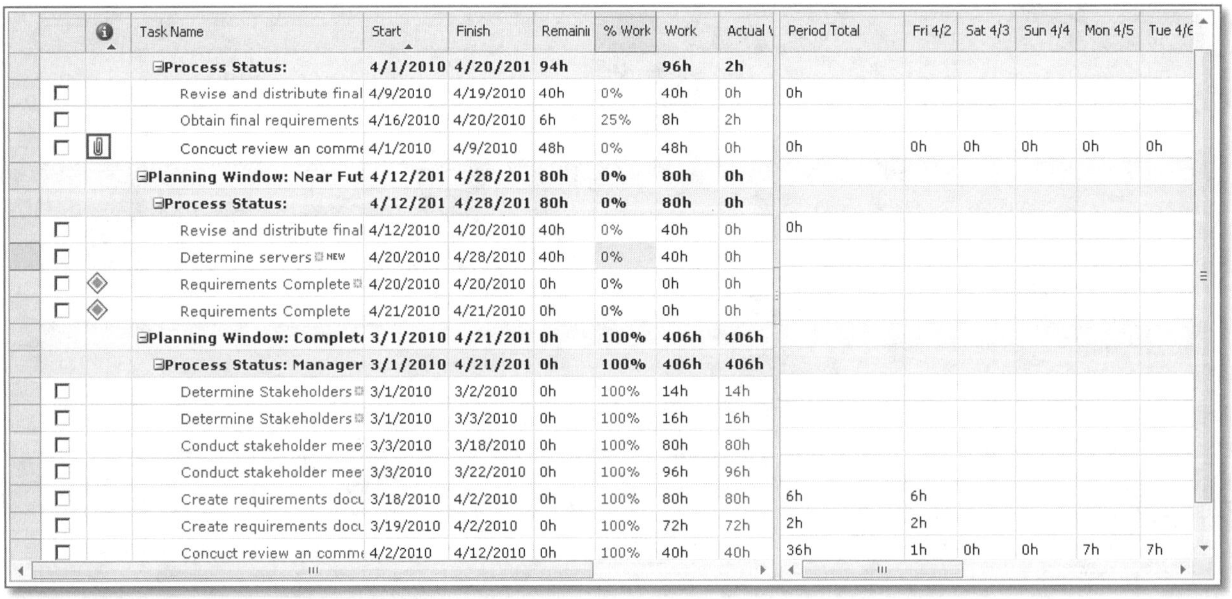

Task Name	Start	Finish	Remainii	% Work	Work	Actual \	Period Total	Fri 4/2	Sat 4/3	Sun 4/4	Mon 4/5	Tue 4/6
⊟Process Status:	**4/1/2010**	**4/20/201**	**94h**		**96h**	**2h**						
Revise and distribute final	4/9/2010	4/19/2010	40h	0%	40h	0h	0h					
Obtain final requirements	4/16/2010	4/20/2010	6h	25%	8h	2h						
Concuct review an comm	4/1/2010	4/9/2010	48h	0%	48h	0h	0h	0h	0h	0h	0h	0h
⊟Planning Window: Near Fut	**4/12/201**	**4/28/201**	**80h**	**0%**	**80h**	**0h**						
⊟Process Status:	**4/12/201**	**4/28/201**	**80h**	**0%**	**80h**	**0h**						
Revise and distribute final	4/12/2010	4/20/2010	40h	0%	40h	0h	0h					
Determine servers NEW	4/20/2010	4/28/2010	40h	0%	40h	0h						
Requirements Complete	4/20/2010	4/20/2010	0h	0%	0h	0h						
Requirements Complete	4/21/2010	4/21/2010	0h	0%	0h	0h						
⊟Planning Window: Complet	**3/1/2010**	**4/21/201**	**0h**	**100%**	**406h**	**406h**						
⊟Process Status: Manager	**3/1/2010**	**4/21/201**	**0h**	**100%**	**406h**	**406h**						
Determine Stakeholders	3/1/2010	3/2/2010	0h	100%	14h	14h						
Determine Stakeholders	3/1/2010	3/3/2010	0h	100%	16h	16h						
Conduct stakeholder mee	3/3/2010	3/18/2010	0h	100%	80h	80h						
Conduct stakeholder mee	3/3/2010	3/22/2010	0h	100%	96h	96h						
Create requirements docu	3/18/2010	4/2/2010	0h	100%	80h	80h	6h	6h				
Create requirements docu	3/19/2010	4/2/2010	0h	100%	72h	72h	2h	2h				
Concuct review an comm	4/2/2010	4/12/2010	0h	100%	40h	40h	36h	1h	0h	0h	7h	7h

Figure 11 - 19: Tasks page using Hours of Work Done per Period with daily time entry

When you select this tracking method, the system locks the *%Work Complete* column and the *Actual Work* column from editing on the left-hand data grid, while unlocking the timephased grid.

Figure 11 - 20 shows the timesheet grid when resources enter progress on a weekly basis. Notice that the system locks the same columns as it does when the reporting periods are daily.

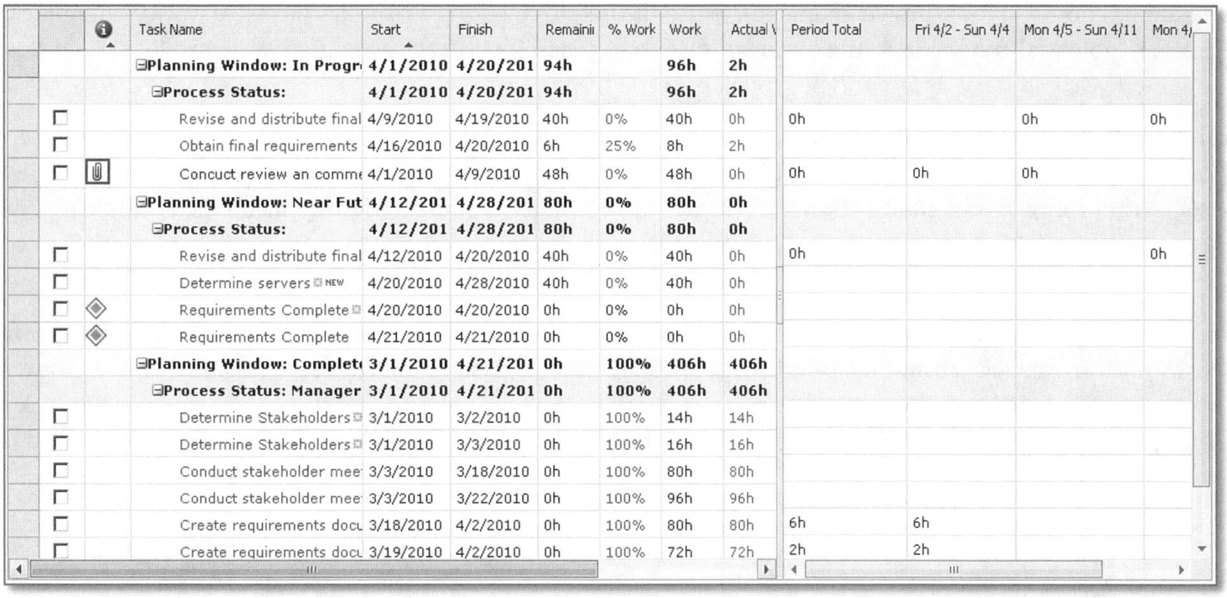

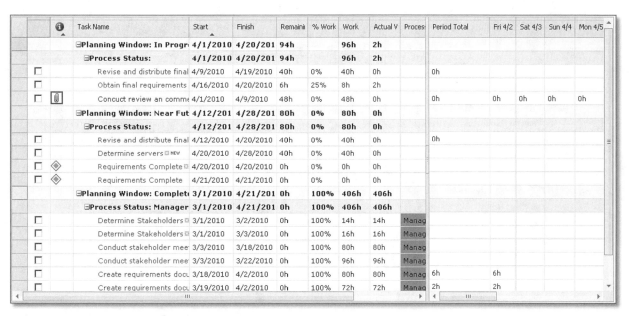

Figure 11 - 20: Tasks page using Hours of Work Done per Period with weekly time entry

If you select the **Free Form** method of tracking, the system displays the *Tasks* page shown in Figure 11 - 21.

Figure 11 - 21: Tasks page using Free Form entry

When you use the Free Form tracking method the system unlocks all progress columns for editing. Users must choose which columns to edit.

Locking Down the Tracking Method

As I mentioned previously, your organization must decide whether to "lock down" the default method of tracking, or to allow individual project managers to select their own method of tracking for each project. To lock down the tracking method, select the *Force project managers to use the progress reporting method specified above for all projects* option. Most organizations choose to force project managers to use the default tracking method. The consequence of not locking this down is potential confusion in the minds of resources when their *Tasks* page displays tasks that use different tracking methods and have different fields available for editing.

If you do not lock down the default tracking method for the organization, a resource must know how to report progress using the different methods available. In certain implementations where project teams are static entities, or where specific groups represented within the system follow different uniform tracking methods, multiple reporting methods may be a viable option. As a general rule, however, I recommend you strive for simplicity rather than complexity in setting up Project Server 2010 for tracking task progress.

When you do not lock down the default tracking method, a project manager can change the method of tracking for a project by clicking the *File* tab and the selecting the *Info* tab in the *Backstage* in Project Professional 2010 as shown in Figure 11 - 22. The project manager can then select any one of the four methods of tracking progress in the pick list. After selecting the new method of tracking progress in the project, the project manager must save the project and then publish it to make the change apparent in Project Web App.

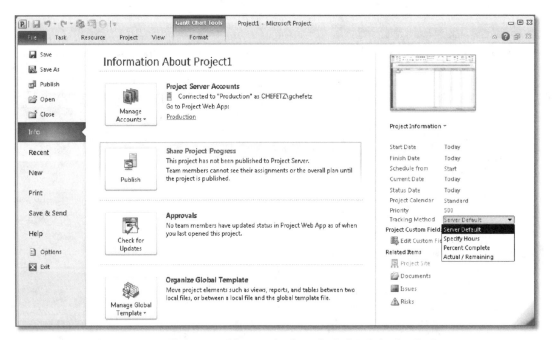

Figure 11 - 22: Change tracking method on the Info tab in the Backstage

 Notice in the figure above that the default method of tracking progress is *Server Default.* Therefore, it only makes sense to select one of the three other options: *Specify Hours, Percent Complete*, or *Actual/Remaining*.

Setting the Reporting Display

The *Reporting Display* section of the *Task Settings and Display* page allows you to determine how Project Server 2010 displays the data grid when you select the *Hours of Work Done per Period* method of tracking. In this section, you must specify whether to show a daily grid or a weekly grid, and then specify the first day of each reporting period.

If you select the default *Resources should report their hours worked every day* option, the system displays a daily timesheet grid spanning seven days on the *Tasks* page, as shown previously in Figure 11 - 21. If you select the *Resources should report their total hours worked for a week* option, the system displays a weekly timesheet data grid spanning four weeks on the *Tasks* page, as shown previously in Figure 11 - 20.

In the *Reporting Display* section of the *Task Settings and Display* page, you must also select an option from the *Week starts on* pick list. If you select the default *Monday* value, the system sets up workweeks from Monday through the following Sunday. If you select the *Sunday* option, the system sets up workweeks from Sunday through the following Saturday.

Protecting User Updates

In the *Protect User Updates* section, you specify how Project Server 2010 handles task updates from the *Tasks* page. If you select the *Only allow task updates via Tasks and Timesheets* option, you prevent your project managers from manually entering actual progress in their enterprise projects in Project Professional 2010. If your project managers need to enter actual progress manually in their enterprise projects, you must not select this option. Selecting this option enables the "Managed Time Periods" feature used previously in Project Server 2003 and 2007.

By default when users import their time entered in the *Timesheet* page to the *Tasks* page, the import will only import actual work from standard lines, ignoring the other line types. Select the *Import all timesheet line classifications* check box to import actual work from all line types when your organization tracks both time and task progress using both the *Timesheet* page and the *Tasks* page in Project Web App.

The *Allow users to define custom periods for task updates* option allows users to define custom time reporting periods when you enable this option. For example, Figure 11 - 23 shows the *Select Period* dialog that a user reaches by clicking the *Select Period* button from the *Period* section of the *Tasks* ribbon.

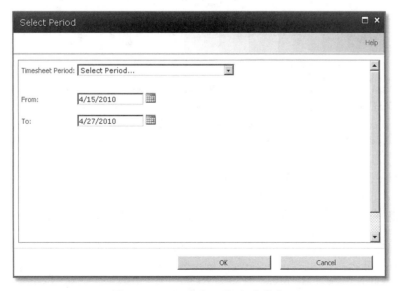

Figure 11 - 23: Select Period dialog

Notice in Figure 11 - 23 that the *From* and *To* fields display and are available for editing. When you select this option, each user can define their own reporting periods as they use the system. When you do not select this option, the *From* and *To* fields and their date pickers do not display in the *Select Period* dialog. Users are limited to using the *Timesheet Period* selector. If you combine this option with the *Free Form* reporting option, your Project Server tracking system is really "unleashed." This is the first version of Project Server to accommodate an unstructured time reporting paradigm.

Defining the Near Future Planning Window

In the *Define Near Future Planning Window* section, enter the number of reporting periods that constitute the *Near Future Planning Window*. The default value in this section is 2 reporting periods, representing a two-week "look ahead" into the future. The system uses the value in this section to group the tasks on the *Tasks* page, as shown in Figure 11 - 24.

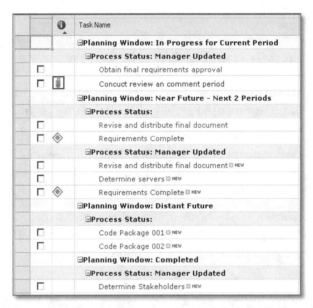

Figure 11 - 24: Planning Windows displayed on the Tasks page

Notice in Figure 11 - 24 that the system organizes all tasks on the *Tasks* page into four groups: *In Progress for Current Period*, *Near Future*, *Distant Future* and *Completed*. The *In Progress* group includes any unstarted task with a start date in a previous reporting period or in the current reporting period, plus any task that is currently in-progress. The *Near Future* group includes tasks with a start date in the next "N" reporting periods where "N" is the value you set. The *Distant Future* group includes all tasks with a start date that falls after the *Near Future* grouping. Of course, the *Completed* group shows tasks that are marked 100% complete.

After you set your organization's task tracking settings, click the *Save* button. As you can clearly see, the tracking settings you select have a major impact on how team members interact with the system when entering actual progress. Before your project managers publish any projects, you should carefully consider how your organization measures project progress and then select the appropriate tracking settings values.

Warning: Carefully choose your method of tracking progress. If you choose the wrong method and then later need to change it in an environment where you force all project managers to use the Project Server default, all project managers must open each of their projects and publish to force the new method to each team member's *Tasks* page in Project Web App. In an environment with a large number of projects, changing the default method of tracking progress may prove very frustrating to your project managers!

Setting Up the Timesheet Page

By default, the *Timesheet* page in Project Server 2010 includes two views, *My Timesheet* and *My Work*. The *My Work* view contains the following default fields: (Note: The *My Timesheet* view contains only the first five fields on the list.)

- Task Name

- Project Name

- Comment

- Billing Category

- Process Status

- Start

- Finish

- Remaining Work

- % Work Complete

- Work

- Actual Work

- Duration

If you are tracking time in weekly buckets rather than daily time tracking and you use *Single Entry Mode,* when a resource updates a task through the timesheet, the system cannot determine the actual start date and actual end date for a task. This isn't a problem for daily time reporting because the system recognizes that the first date a user reports time against a task is the actual start date, and the last date of time reporting that causes the task to become 100% complete is the actual finish date. In the case of weekly reporting buckets, you need to capture this information from your users if you want the project schedule to reflect these dates accurately. You can modify both timesheet views or create your own views for this purpose. To modify one of the existing timesheet views, select the *Manage Views* item from the *Look and Feel* section of the *Server Settings* page. The system displays the *Manage Views* page shown in Figure 11 - 25. Notice in the figure that I highlighted two sections, one containing the views that appear in the *Timesheet* page and the other containing the views for the *Tasks* page, which I cover next. I also cover creating and managing views in more depth in Module 14.

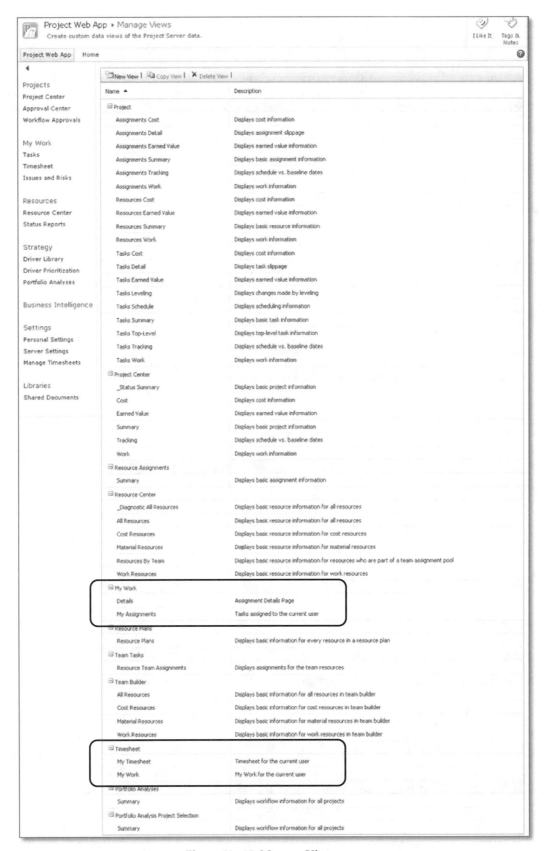

Figure 11 - 25: Manage Views page

From the *Timesheet* section, click on the *My Work* view to open it for modification. The system displays the *Edit View* page for the *My Work* view shown in Figure 11 - 26.

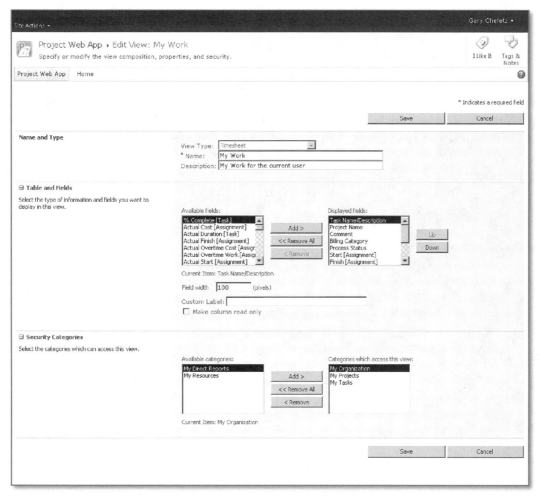

Figure 11 - 26: Edit View page for My Work

To add the *Actual Start* and *Actual Finish* dates to the view, in the *Table and Fields* section, locate and select the fields in the *Available fields* list on the left and click the *Add* button to add them to the *Displayed Fields* list on the right. Use the *Up* and *Down* buttons to move the fields to the position where you want them to appear. Notice the controls below the field selectors in the *Table and Fields* section. You can further tailor the display of fields by selecting a *Displayed field* on the right and changing three attributes:

1. **Field Width** in pixels: Allows you to set the field width in the display.

2. **Custom Label**: Allows you to change the label for the field in the column header display.

3. **Make column read only**: Allows you to lock the field for editing in the view.

By default, a user can edit any field in the view except for the *Project Name* and *Task Name/Description* fields and the fields that the system locks based on the tracking method options you select. You can prevent users from editing other fields using the *Make column read only* checkbox. Use this feature, for instance, if you do not want to allow your users to change planned start or finish dates. Do not change any values in the *Security Categories* section until you understand the impacts of this action, which I teach you in the next module, *Configuring Project Server Security*.

Customizing the Tasks Page

As I stated earlier, Project Server 2010 offers your organization four methods for tracking task progress. Because the default layout of the *My Assignments* view for the *Tasks* page is static, MSProjectExperts recommends that you create a custom layout of this view based on your tracking method. The key action is to modify the *Tasks* page layout to capture the most relevant information about task progress for each project manager. This is particularly important if you are not using timesheets in Project Server, or if you use the manual import from timesheets to populate progress in the *Tasks* page, and you require additional input from your users regarding the status of tasks. The *My Assignments* view contains the following default fields:

- Task Name

- Start

- Finish

- Remaining Work

- % Work Complete

- Actual Work

- Process Status

Using Percent of Work Complete

To capture the most relevant information about task progress using the *Percent Work Complete* method of tracking, MSProjectExperts recommends that you modify the *My Assignments* view layout by completing the following steps:

1. Log in to Project Web App with administrator permissions.

2. Click the *Server Settings* link in the Quick Launch menu.

3. Click the *Manage Views* link in the *Look and Feel* section of the *Server Settings* page.

4. Click the *My Assignments* link in the *My Work* section of the *Manage Views* page to open the *My Assignments* view for editing, as shown in Figure 11 - 27.

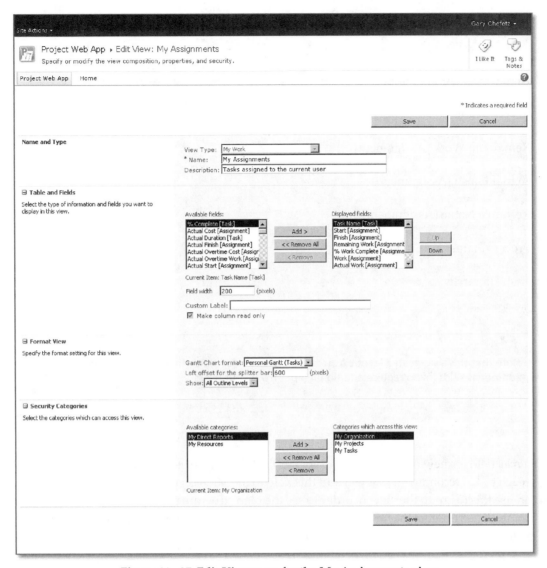

Figure 11 - 27: Edit View page for the My Assignments view

5. Select the *Start [Assignment]* field and *Finish [Assignment]* field in the *Displayed fields* list on the right and click the *< Remove* button.

6. Select the following fields in the *Available fields* list and then click the *Add >* button to add them to the *Displayed fields* list:

    *   Actual Finish [Assignment]

    *   Actual Start [Assignment]

    *   Actual Work [Assignment]

    *   Work [Assignment]

    *   Task Hierarchy

467

7. Use the *Up* and *Down* buttons to move the fields in the *Displayed fields* list into the following order:

    - Task Name [Task]

    - Actual Start [Assignment]

    - % Work Complete [Assignment]

    - Remaining Work [Assignment]

    - Actual Finish [Assignment]

    - Resource Name [Assignment]

    - Process Status

    - Task Hierarchy

Note that this a suggested layout. You can choose to keep fields that I suggest removing, or you can add additional fields if you require additional input from your users.

The *Task Hierarchy* field is a new field in Project Server 2010, added to give users the ability to show the summary task hierarchy for each task. I recommend that you add this field to the *My Assignments* view for the convenience of your users, who can use this to group the view in order to see the plan structure around their assignments. Figure 11 - 28 shows the recommended order of the fields in the *My Assignments* view. The fields you select for this view appear on the *Tasks* page for each resource in Project Web App.

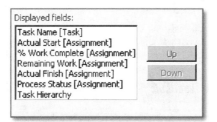

**Figure 11 - 28: Displayed fields list
for the My Assignments view
using Percent of Work Complete**

8. Click the Save button to complete the changes. Figure 11 - 29 shows a user's *Tasks* page with the custom layout applied.

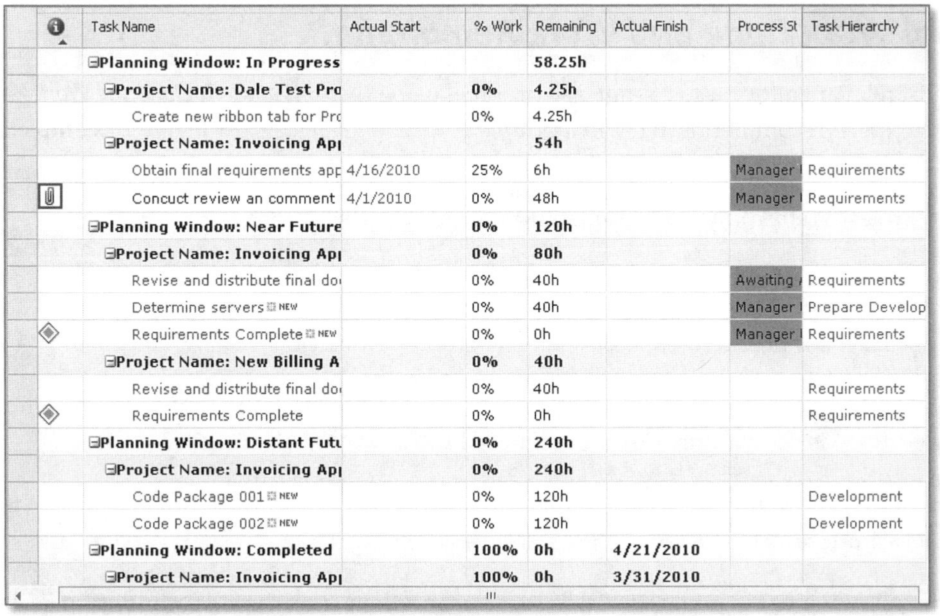

Task Name	Actual Start	% Work	Remaining	Actual Finish	Process St	Task Hierarchy
Planning Window: In Progress			**58.25h**			
Project Name: Dale Test Pro		**0%**	**4.25h**			
Create new ribbon tab for Prc		0%	4.25h			
Project Name: Invoicing Ap			**54h**			
Obtain final requirements apr	4/16/2010	25%	6h		Manager	Requirements
Concuct review an comment	4/1/2010	0%	48h		Manager	Requirements
Planning Window: Near Future		**0%**	**120h**			
Project Name: Invoicing Ap		**0%**	**80h**			
Revise and distribute final do		0%	40h		Awaiting	Requirements
Determine servers NEW		0%	40h		Manager	Prepare Develop
Requirements Complete NEW		0%	0h		Manager	Requirements
Project Name: New Billing A		**0%**	**40h**			
Revise and distribute final do		0%	40h			Requirements
Requirements Complete		0%	0h			Requirements
Planning Window: Distant Futu		**0%**	**240h**			
Project Name: Invoicing Ap		**0%**	**240h**			
Code Package 001 NEW		0%	120h			Development
Code Package 002 NEW		0%	120h			Development
Planning Window: Completed		**100%**	**0h**	**4/21/2010**		
Project Name: Invoicing Ap		**100%**	**0h**	**3/31/2010**		

Figure 11 - 29: Tasks page with custom Percent of Work Complete layout

Users with Project Server 2007 experience may note the absence of grouping options for both the *Tasks* and *Timesheet* views. In order to use the *Task Hierarchy* field to change the display of the *Tasks* page, each user must apply the grouping manually. The interface no longer allows you to control this aspect of the views. Figure 11 - 30 shows the same view as Figure 11 - 29 with custom grouping applied by the user in the view. I expanded the *Task Name* view to better show the task hierarchy display.

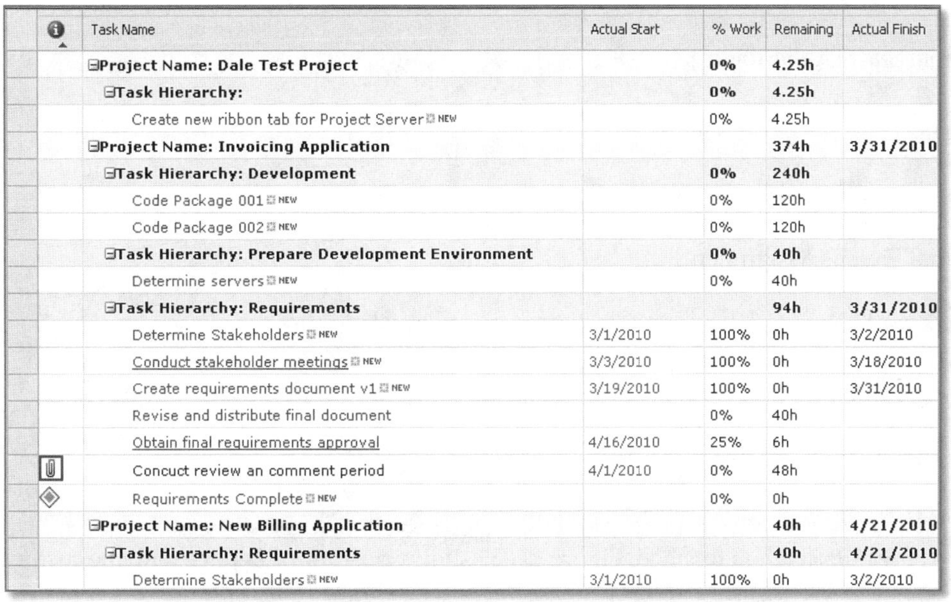

Task Name	Actual Start	% Work	Remaining	Actual Finish
Project Name: Dale Test Project		**0%**	**4.25h**	
Task Hierarchy:		**0%**	**4.25h**	
Create new ribbon tab for Project Server NEW		0%	4.25h	
Project Name: Invoicing Application			**374h**	**3/31/2010**
Task Hierarchy: Development		**0%**	**240h**	
Code Package 001 NEW		0%	120h	
Code Package 002 NEW		0%	120h	
Task Hierarchy: Prepare Development Environment		**0%**	**40h**	
Determine servers NEW		0%	40h	
Task Hierarchy: Requirements			**94h**	**3/31/2010**
Determine Stakeholders NEW	3/1/2010	100%	0h	3/2/2010
Conduct stakeholder meetings NEW	3/3/2010	100%	0h	3/18/2010
Create requirements document v1 NEW	3/19/2010	100%	0h	3/31/2010
Revise and distribute final document		0%	40h	
Obtain final requirements approval	4/16/2010	25%	6h	
Concuct review an comment period	4/1/2010	0%	48h	
Requirements Complete NEW		0%	0h	
Project Name: New Billing Application			**40h**	**4/21/2010**
Task Hierarchy: Requirements			**40h**	**4/21/2010**
Determine Stakeholders NEW	3/1/2010	100%	0h	3/2/2010

Figure 11 - 30: Tasks page with custom grouping applied

Using Actual Work Done and Work Remaining

To capture the most relevant information about task progress using the *Actual Work Done and Work Remaining* tracking method, MSProjectExperts recommends that you modify the *My Assignments* view layout by completing the following steps:

1. Log in to Project Web App with administrator permissions.

2. Click the *Server Settings* link in the Quick Launch menu.

3. Click the *Manage Views* link in the *Look and Feel* section of the *Server Settings* page.

4. Click the *My Assignments* link in the *My Work* section of the *Manage Views* page to open the *My Assignments* view for editing, as shown previously in Figure 11 - 27.

5. Select the *Start [Assignment]* field and *Finish [Assignment]* field in the *Displayed fields* list on the right and click the *< Remove* button.

6. Select the following fields in the *Available fields* list and then click the *Add >* button to add them to the *Displayed fields* list:

   - Actual Finish [Assignment]

   - Actual Start [Assignment]

   - Task Hierarchy

7. Use the *Up* and *Down* buttons to move the fields in the *Displayed fields* list into the following order:

   - Task Name [Task]

   - Actual Start [Assignment]

   - % Work Complete [Assignment]

   - Remaining Work [Assignment]

   - Actual Finish [Assignment]

   - Resource Name [Assignment]

   - Process Status

   - Task Hierarchy

8. Click the *Save* button when finished. Figure 11 - 31 shows a user's *Tasks* page with the custom layout applied.

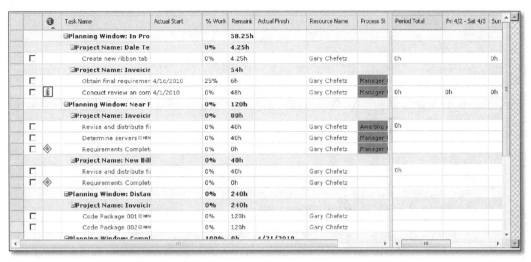

		!	Task Name	Actual Start	% Work	Remaini	Actual Finish	Resource Name	Process St	Period Total	Fri 4/2 - Sat 4/3	Sun
			⊟Planning Window: In Pro			58.25h						
			⊟Project Name: Dale Te		0%	4.25h						
☐			Create new ribbon tab		0%	4.25h		Gary Chefetz		0h		0h
			⊟Project Name: Invoicir			54h						
☐			Obtain final requiremer	4/16/2010	25%	6h		Gary Chefetz	Manager			
☐	📎		Conduct review an com	4/1/2010	0%	48h		Gary Chefetz	Manager	0h	0h	0h
			⊟Planning Window: Near F		0%	120h						
			⊟Project Name: Invoicir		0%	80h						
☐			Revise and distribute fir		0%	40h		Gary Chefetz	Awaiting	0h		
☐			Determine servers ⊠ NEW		0%	40h		Gary Chefetz	Manager			
☐	◈		Requirements Complete		0%	0h		Gary Chefetz	Manager			
			⊟Project Name: New Bill		0%	40h						
☐			Revise and distribute fir		0%	40h		Gary Chefetz		0h		
☐	◈		Requirements Complete		0%	0h		Gary Chefetz				
			⊟Planning Window: Distan		0%	240h						
			⊟Project Name: Invoicir		0%	240h						
☐			Code Package 001 ⊠ NEW		0%	120h		Gary Chefetz				
☐			Code Package 002 ⊠ NEW		0%	120h		Gary Chefetz				
			⊟Planning Window: Compl		100%	0h	4/21/2010					

Figure 11 - 31: Tasks page with custom Actual Work Done and Work Remaining layout

Using Hours of Work Done per Period

To capture the most relevant information about task progress using the *Hours of Work Done per Period* method of tracking, MSProjectExperts recommends that you modify the *Tasks* page layout by completing the following steps:

1. Log in to Project Web App with administrator permissions.

2. Click the *Server Settings* link in the Quick Launch menu.

3. Click the *Manage Views* link in the *Look and Feel* section of the *Server Settings* page.

4. Click the *My Assignments* link in the *My Work* section of the *Manage Views* page to open the *My Assignments* view for editing, as shown previously in Figure 11 - 27.

5. Select the following fields in the *Displayed fields* list on the right and click the < *Remove* button:

   - Start [Assignment]

   - Finish [Assignment]

   - Resource Name [Assignment]

 Warning: If your organization intends to use assignment owners that are not the actual resource, such as team leaders or administrative assistants, to submit task progress on behalf of team members, then **do not** remove the *Resource Name [Assignment]* field. Each assignment owner must see the name of the resource assigned to each task in the *Tasks* page in order to submit task progress on behalf of the assigned resource.

6. Use the *Up* and *Down* buttons to move the fields in the *Displayed fields* list into the following order:

   - Task Name [Task]

   - % Work Complete [Assignment]

   - Remaining Work [Assignment]

- Actual Work

- Process Status

- Task Hierarchy

7. Click the *Save* button when finished. Figure 11 - 32 shows the recommended layout of fields in the *Tasks* page.

8. Click the *Save* button to complete your changes.

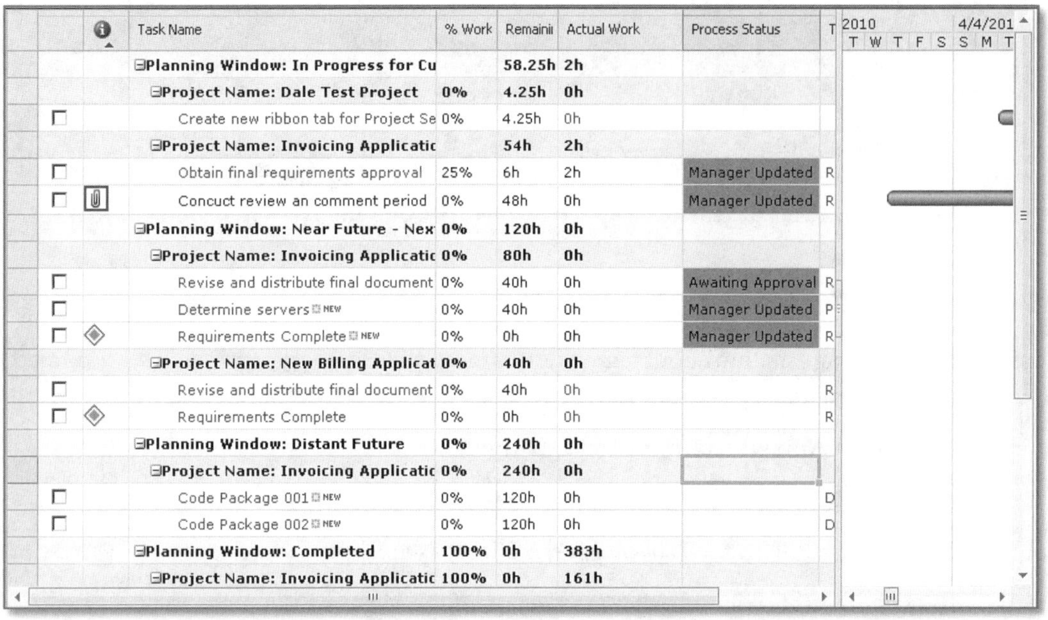

		Task Name	% Work	Remaini	Actual Work	Process Status	T	2010 T W T F S S M T	4/4/201
		⊟Planning Window: In Progress for Cu		58.25h	2h				
		⊟Project Name: Dale Test Project	0%	4.25h	0h				
☐		Create new ribbon tab for Project Se	0%	4.25h	0h			●	
		⊟Project Name: Invoicing Applicatic		54h	2h				
☐		Obtain final requirements approval	25%	6h	2h	Manager Updated	R		
☐	🗎	Conduct review an comment period	0%	48h	0h	Manager Updated	R	━	
		⊟Planning Window: Near Future - Nex	0%	120h	0h				
		⊟Project Name: Invoicing Applicatic	0%	80h	0h				
☐		Revise and distribute final document	0%	40h	0h	Awaiting Approval	R		
☐		Determine servers ▣ NEW	0%	40h	0h	Manager Updated	P		
☐	◈	Requirements Complete ▣ NEW	0%	0h	0h	Manager Updated	R		
		⊟Project Name: New Billing Applicat	0%	40h	0h				
☐		Revise and distribute final document	0%	40h	0h		R		
☐	◈	Requirements Complete	0%	0h	0h		R		
		⊟Planning Window: Distant Future	0%	240h	0h				
		⊟Project Name: Invoicing Applicatic	0%	240h	0h				
☐		Code Package 001 ▣ NEW	0%	120h	0h		D		
☐		Code Package 002 ▣ NEW	0%	120h	0h		D		
		⊟Planning Window: Completed	100%	0h	383h				
		⊟Project Name: Invoicing Applicatic	100%	0h	161h				

Figure 11 - 32: My Assignments view using Hours of Work Done per Period

Tips for Using Tracking Methods

If your organization uses either the *Percent of Work Complete* method or the *Actual Work Done and Work Remaining* method of tracking, you should be aware of the default behavior of both Project Server 2010 and Project Professional 2010 when using these two methods. In the following sections I present some tips for effectively using these two tracking methods after setting up the custom layout of the *Tasks* page detailed in the previous topical section.

Using Percent of Work Complete

The Percent of Work Complete method of tracking progress does not automatically capture an *Actual Start* date or an *Actual Finish* date when resources enter progress on tasks. Instead, when the resource enters a percentage value in the *Progress* field, the system assumes the task **started as scheduled**. When the resource enters 100% in the *% Work Complete* field, the system assumes the task **finished as scheduled**.

For example, Rhonda Epperson was to perform 40 hours of work beginning on Monday, but completed only 50% of her work because she actually started work on Wednesday. When she enters 50% in the *% Work Complete* field for the task, the software **assumes she started on Monday** even though she actually started on Wednesday. The result is that, even though the task will probably finish at least two days late, the system does not show the potential late finish.

MSProjectExperts recommends as a best practice that your organization require each resource to use the following methodology for entering progress on the *Tasks* page using this tracking method:

1. In the *Actual Start* field, enter the actual date when the resource began work on the task.

2. In the *% Work Complete* field, enter the cumulative percentage of how much work the resource completed to date.

3. Adjust the estimate in the *Remaining Work* field, if necessary.

4. If the resource adjusts the *Remaining Work* estimate, the resource should add a note to document the reason for the change.

5. In the *Actual Finish* field, enter the actual date when the task is complete, which causes the system to set the *% Work Complete* field to 100% for the task.

Using this methodology, resources should never enter 100% in the *% Work Complete* field because when the user enters an *Actual Finish* date, the system marks the task 100% complete automatically. The only time a user can safely enter 100% in the *% Work Complete* field is when the task starts and finishes as scheduled.

Using Actual Work Done and Work Remaining

The *Actual Work Done and Work Remaining* tracking method does not automatically capture an *Actual Start* date or an *Actual Finish* date when resources enter progress on tasks. Instead, when the resource enters actual hours, the system assumes the task **started as scheduled**. When the resource enters as many actual hours as originally planned in the *Actual Work* field or in the timephased grid, causing the *Remaining Hours* value to hit zero, the system assumes the task **finished as scheduled**.

For example, Rhonda Epperson was to perform 40 hours of work beginning on Monday. Rhonda completed only 20 hours of work because she actually started work on Wednesday. When she enters 20 hours in the *Actual Work* field for the task, the software **assumes she started on Monday** even though she actually started on Wednesday. The result is that the system does not show the potential late finish even though the task will probably finish at least two days late.

MSProjectExperts recommends as a best practice that your organization require each resource to use the following methodology for entering progress on the *Tasks* page using this tracking method:

1. In the *Actual Start* field, enter the actual date when the resource began work on the task.

2. In the *Actual Work* field, or in the timephased grid, enter the cumulative number of hours of actual work completed to date.

3. Adjust the estimate in the *Remaining Work* field, if necessary.

4. If the resource adjusts the *Remaining Work* estimate, the resource should add a note to document the reason for the change.

5. In the *Actual Finish* field, enter the actual date when the resource finishes work on the task.

Summary

As you can see, there are numerous options available to you when selecting tracking methods and configuring the system for task updates and time entry. I have tried to give you some pointers toward best practices, but each implementation and each organization has its own unique requirements. If you completely identify these before you begin your configuration, your configuration will take less time.

Module 12

Configuring Project Server Security

Learning Objectives

After completing this module, you will be able to:

- Understand each aspect of Project Server 2010 security
- Set Organizational permissions
- Manage individual User accounts
- Deactivate a User account
- Understand the relationship between Groups and Categories
- Understand the Allow, Deny, and Not Allow permission states
- Manage security with Groups
- Create a custom Group
- Manage security with Categories
- Create a custom Category
- Use Categories in conjunction with the RBS field
- Set permissions with security templates
- Create a new security template
- Manage Active Directory synchronization for Groups

Inside Module 12

Project Server Security Overview 477

Setting Organizational Permissions...477

Understanding Users vs. Resources 491

    Users and Resources Can Be the Same Person 491

Managing User Accounts 492

    Creating a New User Account 493

    Editing User Information...498

Deactivating a User Account...499

Controlling Security with Groups and Categories...**499**

   Associating Multiple Groups and Categories..505

   Understanding Built-in Groups...506

   Understanding Built-in Categories..506

Understanding Permissions...**509**

   Understanding Global Permissions and Category Permissions..509

   Understanding Denied, Allowed and Not Allowed...509

   Understanding Permissions Cumulative Behavior..510

Managing Permissions through Groups...**511**

   Creating a New Group..516

   Deleting a Group..517

Managing Permissions through Categories...**518**

   Creating a New Category..527

   Deleting a Category..530

Using and Managing Security Templates..**530**

   Creating a New Security Template..531

   Deleting a Security Template...534

Managing AD Synchronization for Groups..**534**

Resolving Common Security Requirements..**538**

Project Server Security Overview

One of your most important configuration efforts is mapping your organizational security requirements to the security constructs within Project Server 2010. You must give yourself time to understand the underlying concepts so that you can apply them in a way that not only meets your organizational requirements but also enables easier maintenance. The system provides a flexible set of security management tools, which at first glance may seem obscure and complex. Therefore, I provide you with a step-by-step, clear and thorough explanation of security management within Project Server 2010.

In Project Server 2010 security, the system uses each of the following features to control security:

- **Organizational permissions** represent the complete collection of permissions at the highest level in the system and make features available or unavailable to all users in the system.

- **Global permissions** represent a collection of functional permissions for a group of users.

- **Category permissions** are a collection of permissions that grant access to security objects that you set for specific groups within specific categories.

- A **Group** is a collection of users with identical global permissions for each member.

- A **User** is an individual who has a logon account in Project Server 2010.

- A **Resource** is a person, equipment or material that can be used or consumed on a task assignment.

- A **Category** is a collection of security objects and permissions that you can assign to a user or group.

- **Security objects** include projects, resources, and views with access controlled by categories.

- **Security rules** are access permissions that you may assign based on Project Server relationships.

Project Server 2010 also uses the *Project Departments* field and the *Resource Departments* field to control visibility to enterprise projects, the enterprise resources and other system objects associated with each *Department*. Because I discussed *Department Filtering* previously, and because this is not a security feature, I do not discuss this topic in Module.

Setting Organizational Permissions

Your first step in configuring Project Server 2010 security is to set organizational permissions. Organizational permissions exist at the highest level in the system and make features available or unavailable to everyone using the system. If you enable an organizational permission, the permission is available to users in the system, based on the permissions in the groups to which each user belongs. If you disable an organizational permission, that function is unavailable to every user in the system regardless of the permissions in the groups to which each user belongs.

To set organizational permissions, click the *Project Web App Permissions* link in the *Security* section of the *Server Settings* page. Project Server 2010 displays the *Project Web App Permissions* page shown in Figure 12 - 1 and Figure 12 - 2. Because of the page length, I break the page into two separate figures.

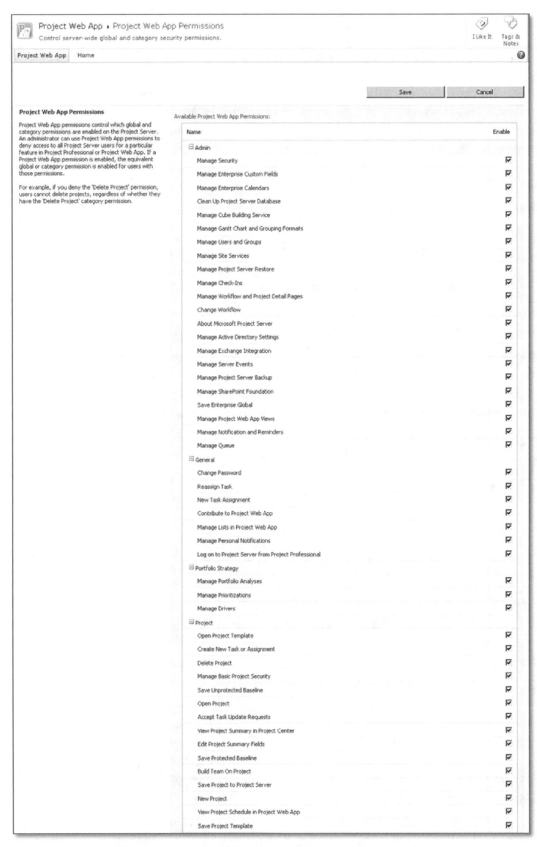

Figure 12 - 1: Project Web App Permissions page, top of page

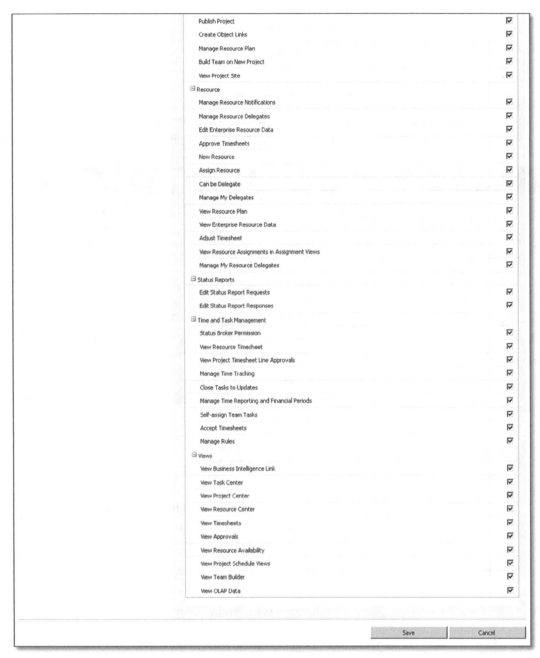

Figure 12 - 2: Project Web App Permissions page, bottom of page

The *Project Web App Permissions* page contains all available permissions in Project Server 2010 affecting both Project Professional 2010 and Project Web App. The system groups these organizational permissions into eight topical sections:

- Admin
- General
- Portfolio Strategy
- Project
- Resource

- Status Reports

- Time and Task Management

- Views

In each of these eight topical sections, the system enables all organizational permissions by default in Project Server 2010. To disable any permission, simply deselect the *Enable* option for that permission. Table 12 - 1through Table 12 - 8 document each of the permissions found in all sections of the *Project Web App Permissions* page in alphabetical order.

Admin	
Permission	**Description**
About Microsoft Project Server	Displays the *About Project Server* link on the *Server Settings* page in PWA. Allows a user to access the *About Project Server* page in PWA.
Change Workflow (New for 2010)	Allows a user to change or restart the workflow stage for a project type governed by workflow. Users must also have *Manage Workflow and Project Detail Pages* global permission enabled to use this permission.
Clean up Project Server Database	Displays the *Delete Enterprise Objects* link on *the Server Settings* page in PWA. Allows a user to access the *Delete Enterprise Objects* page in PWA to delete projects, resources, status report responses, timesheets, and user delegations.
Manage Active Directory Settings	Displays the *Active Directory Resource Pool Synchronization* link on the *Server Settings* page in PWA, activates the *Active Directory Synch Options* button on the *Manage Groups* page, and displays *Active Directory Group to Synchronize* subsection at the top of the *Add or Edit Group* page in PWA. Allows a user to manage all Active Directory (AD) settings to synchronize AD with the enterprise resource pool and with security groups in PWA.
Manage Check-Ins	Displays the *Force Check-In Enterprise Objects* link on the *Server Settings* page in PWA. Allows a user to access the *Force Check-in Enterprise Objects* page in PWA to check in projects, resources, custom fields, calendars, lookup tables, and resource plans.

Admin	
Permission	**Description**
Manage Cube Building Service	Displays the *OLAP Database* section on the *Server Settings* page in PWA. Allows a user to specify the settings for OLAP cube creation and to build the OLAP cube.
Manage Enterprise Calendars	Displays the *Enterprise Calendars* link on the *Server Settings* page in PWA. Allows a user to access the *Enterprise Calendars* page in PWA to create, modify, and delete enterprise calendars.
Manage Enterprise Custom Fields	Displays the *Enterprise Custom Fields and Lookup Tables* link on the *Server Settings* page in PWA. Allows a user to access the *Custom Fields and Lookup Tables* page in PWA to create, modify, and delete custom enterprise fields and lookup tables.
Manage Exchange Integration (New for 2010)	Allows the user to select or deselect the *Exchange Server Details* item on the *Additional Server Settings* page.
Manage Gantt Chart and Grouping Formats	Displays the *Grouping Formats* link and the *Gantt Chart Formats* link on the *Server Settings* page in PWA. Allows a user to access the *Grouping Formats* page and the *Gantt Chart Formats* page in PWA.
Manage Notification and Reminders	Displays the *Alerts and Reminders* link on the *Server Settings* page in PWA. Allows a user to access the *Alerts and Reminders* page in PWA to set up the e-mail settings used for sending alerts and reminders.
Manage Project Server Backup	Displays the *Daily Schedule Backup* link and the *Administrative Backup* link on the *Server Settings* page in PWA. Allows a user to access the *Daily Backup Schedule* page and *Administrative Backup* page in PWA to backup Project Server objects, such as projects, the enterprise resource pool, custom enterprise fields, etc.
Manage Project Server Restore	Displays the *Administrative Restore* link on the *Server Settings* page in PWA. Allows a user to access the *Administrative Restore* page in PWA to restore Project Server objects, such as

Admin	
Permission	**Description**
	projects, the enterprise resource pool, custom enterprise fields, etc.
Manage Project Web App Views	Displays the *Manage Views* link on the *Server Settings* page in PWA.
	Allows a user to access the *Manage Views* page to create, modify, and delete views in PWA.
Manage Queue	Displays the *Queue* section on the *Server Settings* page in PWA.
	Allows a user to specify queue settings and to manage queue jobs.
Manage Security	Displays the *Manage Categories* link and the *Manage Security Templates* link on the *Server Settings* page in PWA.
	Allows a user to access the *Manage Categories* page to create, modify, and delete security Categories in PWA.
	Allows a user to access the *Manage Templates* page to create, modify, and delete security Templates.
Manage Server Events	Displays the *Server Side Event Handlers* link on the *Server Settings* page in PWA.
	Allows a user to access the *Server Side Event Handlers* page to create, modify, and delete event handlers.
Manage SharePoint Foundation (Replaces 2007: Manage Windows SharePoint Services)	Displays the *Project Sites* link, *Bulk Update Project Sites* link, and the *Project Site Provisioning Settings* link on the *Server Settings* page in PWA.
	Allows a user to access the *Project Site Provisioning Settings* page in PWA to specify how the system provisions project workspaces.
	Allows a user to access the *Project Sites* page in PWA to manage each project workspace individually.
	Allows a user to create or delete a project site, or to specify the permissions and all settings on the current SharePoint Site.
Manage Site Services (New for 2010)	Allows users to change server settings that could adversely affect performance in a multi-tenancy environment such as a hosted system.

Admin	
Permission	**Description**
	Allows users to manage OLAP Database Management, Queue Settings, Server Side Event Handlers, Active Directory Resource Pool Synchronization, and Bulk Update Project Sites. Without this permission a user cannot change such things as a site URL, or elevate user permissions beyond PWA.
Manage Users and Groups	Displays the *Manage Users* link and the *Manage Groups* link on the *Server Settings* page in PWA. Allows a user to access the *Manage Users* page to create, modify, and deactivate user accounts in PWA. Allows a user to access the *Manage Groups* page to create, modify, and delete security groups.
Manage Workflow and Project Detail Pages (New for 2010)	Displays the *Workflow and Project Detail Pages* section and links on the *Server Settings* page. Allows a user to access all functions in *Workflow and Project Detail Pages* section.
Save Enterprise Global	Allows a user to open, modify, and save the *Enterprise Global* file using Project Professional 2010.

Table 12 - 1: Project Web App permissions, Admin section

General	
Permission	**Description**
Change Password	Displays the *Change Password* link on the *Personal Settings* page in PWA only for users who log in to Project Server 2010 using claims-based authentication. Allows a user to change his/her password.
Contribute to Project Web App	Allows a user to edit list items in a Windows SharePoint site for a project in Project Web App.
Log On to Project Server from Project Professional	Allows a user to log in to Project Server 2010 using Project Professional 2010.
Manage Lists in Project Web App	Allows a user to create, modify, and delete lists in any Windows SharePoint site for a project in Project Web App.
Manage Personal Notifications	Displays the *Manage My Alerts and Reminders* link on

	the *Personal Settings* page in PWA.
	Allows a user to subscribe to e-mail alerts and reminders from Project Server 2010.
New Task Assignment	Enables the *Create a New Task* and *Join a Task* menu items on the *Insert Task* menu on the *Tasks* page in PWA.
	Allows a user to access the *New Task* page to create a new task assignment or to self assign to an existing task.
Reassign Task	Enables the *Reassign* button on the *Tasks* page in PWA.
	Allows a user to access the *Task Reassignment* page to delegate a task assignment to another resource.

Table 12 - 2: Project Web App permissions, General section

Portfolio Strategy (New for 2010)	
Permission	**Description**
Manage Drivers	Allows a user to access the *Driver Library* page in PWA to create, modify, and delete business drivers.
Manage Portfolio Analyses	Allows a user to access the *Portfolio Analyses* page in PWA to create, modify, and delete portfolio analyses and use all available analysis tools.
Manage Prioritizations	Allows a user to access the *Driver Prioritization* page in PWA to create, modify, and delete driver prioritizations.

Table 12 - 3: Project Web App permissions, Portfolio Strategy section

Project	
Permission	**Description**
Accept Task Update Requests	**Category Permission:** Allows a user to accept task updates on the *Approvals* page in PWA for only those projects specified in the categories to which the user is associated.
Build Team on New Project	Allows the user to access the *Build Team* dialog in an *unsaved* project in Project Professional 2010.
Build Team on Project	**Category Permission:** Allows the user to access the *Build Team* dialog in Project Professional 2010 for *exist-*

Project	
Permission	**Description**
	ing projects specified in the categories to which the user is associated.
Create New Task or Assignment	**Category Permission:** Allows the user to create new tasks or assignments in only those projects specified in the categories to which the user is associated.
Create Object Links	**Category Permission:** Allows a user to create, modify, or delete links between project site items (Risks, Issues, Documents, or Deliverables) and tasks in the projects specified in the categories to which the user has access.
Delete Project	**Category Permission:** Allows users to delete projects in the *Open* dialog in Project Professional. The user can delete only those projects specified in the categories to which the user is associated.
Edit Project Summary Fields	**Category Permission:** Allows a user to display the *Project Information* page for a project from the *Project Center* page in PWA and then to edit fields on the *Project Fields* page by clicking the *Edit* button. The user can edit the project fields' data for only those projects specified in the categories to which the user is associated.
Manage Basic Project Security (New for 2010)	**Category Permission:** Enables the *Project Permissions* button on the *Project Center* page. Allows a user to create specific project security permissions for only those projects specified in the categories to which the user has access.
Manage Resource Plan	**Category Permission:** Enables the *Resource Plan* button on the *Project Center* page. Allows a user to create and edit a resource plan for the projects specified in the categories to which the user has access.
New Project	Allows a user to create and save a new project in the Project Server database using Project Professional 2010. **Note:** Users with this permission appear on the list of managers shown in the *Owner* field on the *Project Details* page in PWA.
Open Project	**Category Permission:** Allows a user to open an enterprise project using either Project Professional 2010 or PWA for only those projects specified in the categories

Project	
Permission	**Description**
	to which the user is associated.
Open Project Template	Allows a user to create a new enterprise project from an enterprise template.
Publish Project	**Category Permission:** Allows a user to publish a project in Project Professional 2010. This permission allows a user to publish only those projects specified in the categories to which the user is associated.
Save Project Template	Allows the user to save a project template in the Project Server database using Project Professional 2010.
Save Project to Project Server	**Category Permission:** Allows a user to save an enterprise project in the Project Server database using Project Professional 2010 for only those projects specified in the categories to which the user is associated.
Save Protected Baseline	**Category Permission:** Allows a user to save or clear a protected baseline in Project Professional 2010 for only those projects specified in the categories to which the user is associated. "Protected Baseline" refers to only the *Baseline* and *Baseline 1-5* sets of fields.
Save Unprotected Baseline	Allows a user to save or clear an unprotected baseline in an enterprise project using Project Professional 2010 in only the *Baseline 6-10* sets of fields.
View Project Schedule in Project Web App (Replaces 2007: View Project Details in Project Center)	**Category Permission:** Allows a user to see project detail pages reached from the *Project Center* page in PWA for only those projects specified in the categories to which the user is associated.
View Project Site (Replaces 2007: View Project Workspace)	**Category Permission:** Allows the user to see the Project Site for only those projects specified in the categories to which the user has access.
View Project Summary in Project Center	**Category Permission:** Allows a user to see *Project Center* views in PWA for only those projects specified in the categories to which the user is associated.

Table 12 - 4: Project Web App permissions, Project section

Resource	
Permission	**Description**
Adjust Timesheet	**Category Permission:** Allows a user to adjust the entries on a submitted timesheet on the *Review Timesheet Detail* page in PWA for only those resources specified in the categories to which the user is associated.
Approve Timesheets	**Category Permission:** Allows a user to approve a submitted timesheet for only those resources specified in the categories to which the user is associated.
Assign Resource	**Category Permission:** Allows a user to add resources to a project using the *Build Team* dialog in Project Professional 2010. In the *Build Team* dialog, this permission displays only the resources specified in the categories to which the user is associated.
Can be Delegate (New for 2010)	Allows a user to serve as a delegate for another user. Adds the user to the list of names in the *Delegate Name* field on the *Add Delegation* page in PWA.
Edit Enterprise Resource Data	**Category Permission:** Allows the user to edit enterprise resource data using the *Resource Center* page in PWA or by opening the enterprise resource pool in Project Professional 2010. This permission allows the user to edit only those resources specified in the categories to which the user is associated.
Manage My Delegates (New for 2010)	Displays the *Manage Delegations* link on the *Personal Settings* page. Allows a user to create a delegation for him/herself, but relies on someone else to pick up and act on the delegation.
Manage My Resource Delegates (Replaces 2007: Create Surrogate Timesheet)	Allows a user to act as a resource delegate on behalf of another user who created the delegation. Displays the *User Name* field on the *Add Delegation* page.
Manage Resource Delegates	**Category Permission:** Allows a user to manage resource delegates for only those users specified in the categories to which the user is associated. Displays this list of users in the *User Name* field on the *Add Delegation* page.
Manage Resource Notifications	Displays the *Manage My Resource's Alerts and Reminders*

Resource	
Permission	**Description**
	link in the *Personal Settings* page in PWA.
New Resource	Allows a user to add a new resource to the enterprise resource pool using either Project Professional 2010 or the *Resource Center* page in PWA.
View Enterprise Resource Data	**Category Permission:** Allows a user to see enterprise resources in the *Build Team* dialog using Project Professional 2010 and in the *Resource Center* page of PWA. This permission allows the user to see data for only those resources specified in the categories to which the user is associated.
View Resource Assignments in Assignment Views	**Category Permission:** Allows the user to see resource assignments in the *Resource Assignments* page of PWA for only those resources specified in the categories to which the user is associated.
View Resource Plan	Enables the *Resource Plan* button where ever it appears in PWA. Allows a user to see a *Resource Plan* for a selected project.

Table 12 - 5: Project Web App permissions, Resource section

Status Reports	
Permission	**Description**
Edit Status Report Requests	Allows a user to see the *Requests* section on the *Status Reports* page in PWA to create, view, and delete status report requests.
Edit Status Report Responses	Allows a user to see the *Responses* section on the *Status Reports* page in PWA to respond to a status report request.

Table 12 - 6: Project Web App permissions, Status Reports section

Time and Task Management	
Permission	**Description**
Accept Timesheets	Allows a user to view a timesheet, but not approve the timesheet. Once accepted, the user can forward the timesheet to another user who has the *Approve Timesheets* permission and can approve the timesheet.
Close Tasks to Updates	Displays the *Close Tasks to Update* link on the *Server Settings* page in PWA.
	Allows a user to access the *Close Tasks to Update* page in PWA to close a task to prevent resources from entering additional progress against the task.
Manage Rules	Enables the *Manage Rules* button on the *Approvals* page.
	Allows a user to access the *Rules* page to create rules to process task updates automatically.
Manage Time Reporting and Financial Periods (Replaces 2007: Manage Timesheet and Financial Periods)	Displays the *Financial Periods* link and the *Time Reporting Periods* link on the *Server Settings* page in PWA.
	Allows a user to access the *Fiscal Periods* page to create fiscal periods, and to access the *Time Reporting Periods* page to create time reporting periods.
Manage Time Tracking	Displays the *Line Classifications* link, the *Timesheet Settings and Defaults* link, the *Administrative Time* link, and the *Task Settings and Display* link on the *Server Settings page* in PWA.
	Allows a user to configure every option to control time and task tracking.
Self-assign Team Tasks	Enables the *From Team Tasks* item on the *Insert Task* pick list on the *Tasks* page.
	When a user is a member of a *Team* resource, this permission allows the user to access the *Team Tasks* page to accept a team assignment as his/her individual assignment.
Status Broker Permission	Allows an account to impersonate users during Exchange synchronization. Used with Exchange synchronization only.
View Project Timesheet Line Approvals	Allows a user who is a project manager to view and approve new lines added to the *Timesheet* page for

Time and Task Management	
Permission	**Description**
	projects managed by the user.
View Resource Timesheet	Allows a user to view the timesheets for those resources specified in the categories to which the user is associated.

Table 12 - 7: Project Web App permissions, Time and Task Management section

Views	
Permission	**Description**
View Approvals	Displays the *Approvals* section in the Quick Launch menu. Allows a user to access the *Approvals Center* in PWA to approve task updates and administrative time submissions.
View Business Intelligence Link (New for 2010)	Displays the *Business Intelligence Center* link in the Quick Launch menu.
View OLAP Data	Allows a user to connect to views that use OLAP data in the *BI Center*.
View Project Center	Allows a user to access the *Project Center* page in PWA to view *Project Center* views.
View Project Schedule Views (Replaces 2007: View Project View)	Allows a user to access the schedule page and other *Project Detail Pages* for a project by clicking the name of the project in the *Project Center* page. The user must also have the *View Project Center* permission enabled to use this permission.
View Resource Availability	Allows a user to access the *Resource Availability* page for resources selected in the *Resource Center* page of PWA.
View Resource Center	Allows a user to access the *Resource Center* page in PWA.
View Task Center	Allows a user to access the *Tasks* page in PWA.
View Team Builder	Enables the *Build Team* button on the *Project Center* page in PWA. Allows a user to access the *Build Team* page for the selected project in the *Project Center* page.

Views	
Permission	**Description**
View Timesheets	Allows a user to access the *Timesheets* page or the *My Timesheet* page for the current time period in PWA.

Table 12 - 8: Project Web App permissions, Views section

MSProjectExperts recommends that you disable the *Delete Project* permission to prevent anyone from accidentally deleting an enterprise project in the *Open* dialog of Project Professional 2010. Disabling this permission does not prevent you, as the Project Server administrator, from deleting enterprise projects using the *Delete Enterprise Objects* page in PWA.

Understanding Users vs. Resources

A **User** is a person who can log in to Project Server and use its features and functions. Depending upon the person's role within the organization, a user may need to log in to Project Web App and mark a task complete or submit a status report. Another user may need to create, save, and publish a new project schedule with Project Professional so that it will be visible to others through the web interface. Yet another user may want to log in to PWA and view the status of a project or a program.

A **Resource** is a person, material or other non-human tool that a Project requires for execution. A resource can be a piece of equipment such as a bulldozer which is used to excavate a job site, or it may be a human being such as a carpenter who builds the walls of a house, or a resource may be consumable materials such as pallets of shingles for the roof of a new building.

Users and Resources Can Be the Same Person

By way of example, George Stewart needs to log in to Project Web App to update tasks on his *Tasks* page. To accommodate this requirement George needs to be both a resource and user in the Project Server system. His user account is tied to his resource record in the system. If George's team lead is responsible for updating George's tasks, then George may not require access to Project Server. If the latter is the case, you can set George up as a resource and not a Project Server user.

You may also have people in your organization who are users, but not resources. For example, a senior manager may require access to PWA to view the status of projects, programs and portfolios in the system, but be too senior to be assigned project-level tasks in the system. You need to make this senior manager a user in the system, but not a resource.

The Project Server security model allows you to control which users can access the system, the system functions they can use, the data that they can access, and the actions that they can take upon the data. You can organize similar types of users into groups for easier security management. You then grant a specific set of system permissions to each group of users. For example, you can organize all project participant users into a *Team Members* group, and then you grant permissions to the entire group to view their project work and update the status of their assigned tasks. You can also organize all senior-level manager users into an *Executives* group, and then grant permissions to the entire group to view the status of all projects in the system.

Managing User Accounts

Many of your account creation duties occurred when you created the resources in your enterprise resource pool using Project Professional 2010. When you saved your enterprise resource pool, Project Server 2010 automatically created a user account in Project Web App for each resource with a Windows user account. Beyond these accounts, you may also need to create user accounts for users who are not in the enterprise resource pool but need to access the system through Project Web App, such as executives or customers.

To manage individual user accounts, click the *Manage Users* link in the *Security* section of the *Server Settings* page. Project Server 2010 displays the *Manage Users* page, shown in Figure 12 - 3.

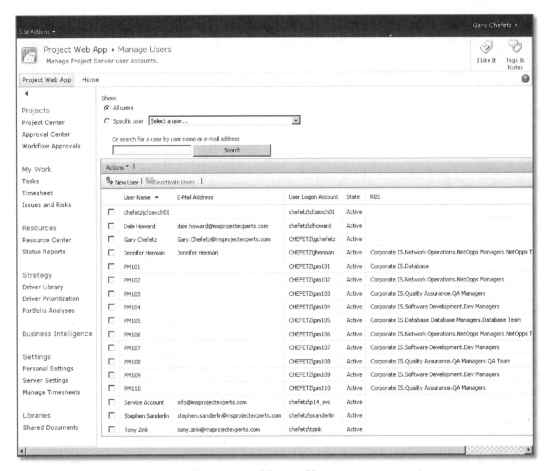

Figure 12 - 3: Manage Users page

The *Manage Users* page does not display more than 400 users. If your number of users exceeds the limit of 400 users, then the system displays a blank page with no users. In this situation, you can locate a user account by selecting a user from the *Specific User* pick list or by entering a full or partial user name in the *Search* field.

On the *Manage Users* page, you can add, modify, or deactivate user accounts, but you may not delete user accounts. Deactivating a user does not remove the resource from the enterprise resource pool. Instead, it deactivates the user account and resource, preventing project managers from using the deactivated resource for project assignments.

On the *Manage Users* page, select the default *All users* option at the top of the page to view all users currently in your Project Server 2010 system, up to the limit of 400 users. To show one specific user, select the *Specific user* option and then click the *Specific user* pick list and select a user, as shown in Figure 12 - 4.

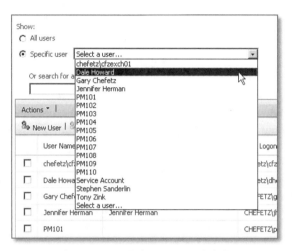

Figure 12 - 4: Select a user pick list

To search for a user, enter at least a partial name or e-mail address in the *Search* field and then click the *Search* button. The system reveals the results of the search on the *Manage Users* page, as shown in Figure 12 - 5.

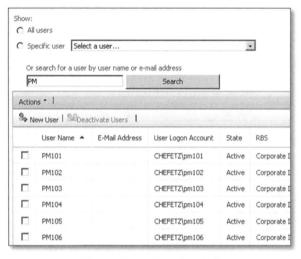

Figure 12 - 5: Search results

Creating a New User Account

To create a new user account to Project Server 2010, click the *New User* button at the top of the data grid. The system displays the *New User* page shown in Figure 12 - 6 and Figure 12 - 7. Because of the length of this page, I must break the page into two separate figures.

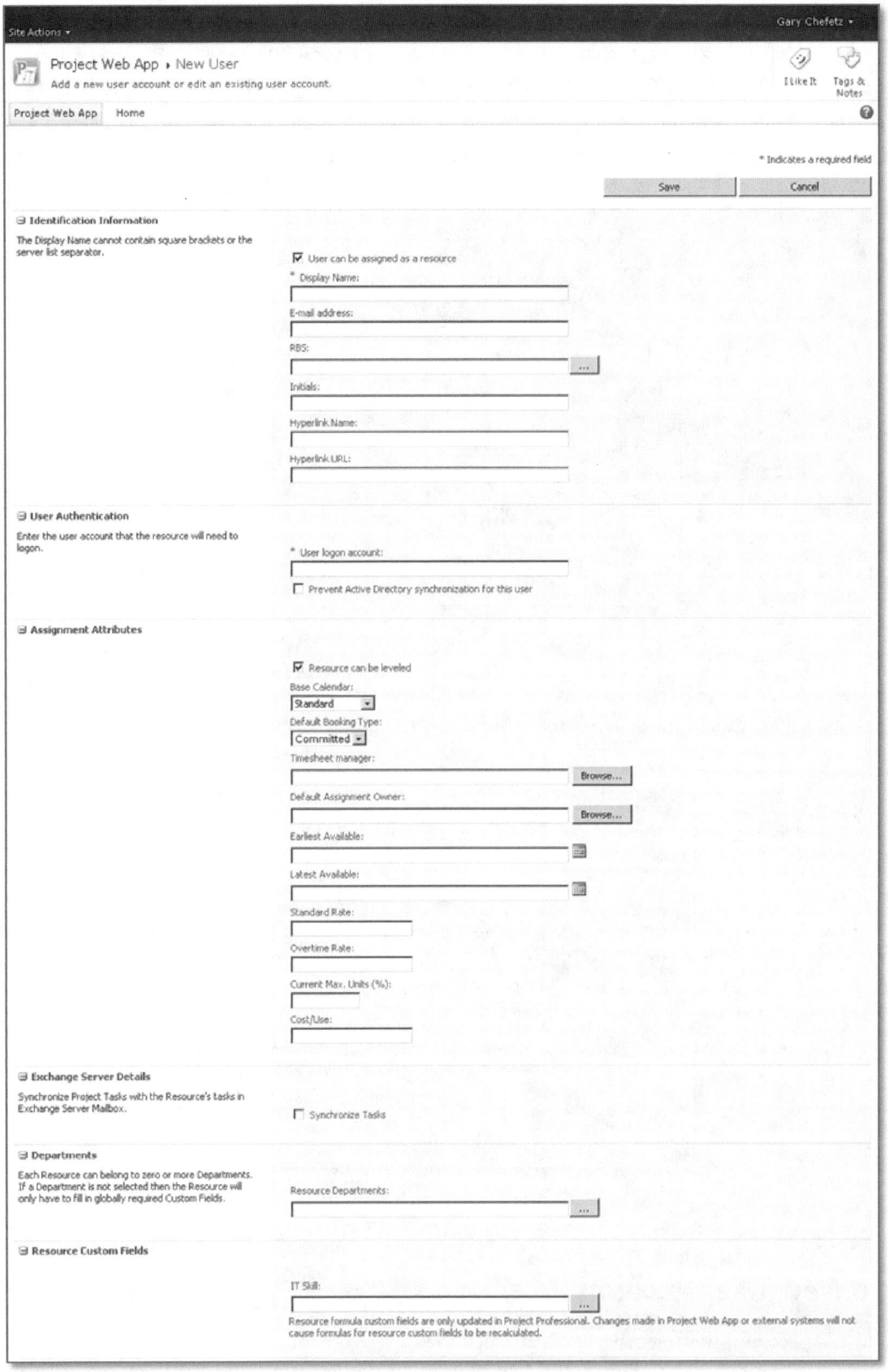

Figure 12 - 6: New User page, top of page

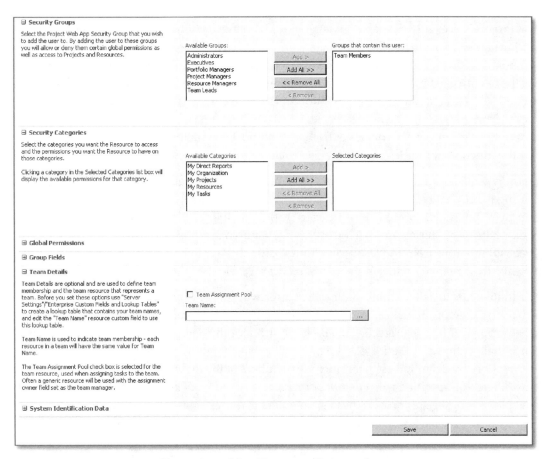

Figure 12 - 7: New User page, bottom of page

When creating a user account, you have the option to create a corresponding resource in the enterprise resource pool by selecting the default *User can be assigned as a resource* option at the top of the page. If you select this option, Project Server 2010 displays the *Assignment Attributes* section and the *Team Details* section of the *Add User* page. When you save the new user account, the system automatically creates a same-named resource in the enterprise resource pool. If you want to create a user account that is not a resource in the enterprise resource pool, such as for an executive or a customer, then deselect the *User can be assigned as a resource* option immediately.

MSProjectExperts recommends that you **deselect** the *User can be assigned as a resource* option so that you do not create enterprise resources from the *Add User* page. This is particularly important when you add the service account as a user in Project Server. Instead of creating resources from this page, create all enterprise resources by opening the enterprise resource pool in Project Professional 2010.

In the *Identification Information* section, enter a name for the user account in the *Display Name* field. Enter any other information in this section as required. If your organization uses the *RBS* field to manage security, be sure to select a value for the *RBS* field.

In the *User Authentication* section, in the *User login account* field, enter the necessary login account information. If you use a *Windows Account* in the form domain\username, you may optionally select the *Prevent Active Directory synchronization for this user* option. When selected, this option forces the AD synchronization process to ignore the user account.

Remember that Project Server 2010 displays the *Assignment Attributes* section only if you select the *User can be assigned as a resource* option at the top of the page. Enter resource information in this section to determine how the system handles task assignments for the resource. Select the default *Resource can be leveled* option if you want project managers to be able to level the resource in Project Professional 2010 should the resource become overallocated. Click the *Base Calendar* pick list and select an alternate base calendar other than the enterprise standard calendar, if required. Otherwise, leave the enterprise standard calendar selected. Click the *Default Booking Type* pick list and select either the default *Committed* option or *Proposed* option. Refer back to Module 9, Managing Enterprise Resources, to refresh your memory about the function of the *Default Booking Type* field.

In the *Assignment Attributes* section, the next two fields are very important to the timesheet reporting and task progress reporting functionality in Project Server 2010. The value you specify in the *Timesheet Manager* field determines who approves timesheets submitted by the user. By default, the system sets the value in the *Timesheet Manager* field to the name of the user. This means that the user is his/her own timesheet approver, which causes the system to accept timesheet submissions from the resource automatically. If you do not intend to use the timesheet approval functionality, leave the resource's name in the *Timesheet Manager* field.

If your organization wants to use the built-in timesheet approval process, then you must select a new timesheet approver for each user. Generally, the timesheet approver is the user's functional manager or resource manager. To specify the timesheet approver for the user, click the *Browse* button for the *Timesheet Manager* field. The system displays the *Pick Resource* dialog shown in Figure 12 - 8. The *Pick Resource* window shows all users that have the Approve Timesheets permission. By default, these users include members of the *Resource Managers* group and *Administrators* group, plus any others you specified with custom permissions. In the *Pick Resource* window, when you double-click the name of the user's timesheet approver, the system enters this user's name in the *Timesheet Manager* field.

Figure 12 - 8: Pick Resource window

If the *Pick Resource* window displays a long list of resources, you can quickly locate the desired resource by entering a partial name in the text field at the top of the page and clicking the *Search* button.

The system uses the value in the *Default Assignment Owner* field to determine on whose *Tasks* page to display task assignments when a project manager publishes a project. By default, the system enters the name of the resource in the *Default Assignment Owner* field. If the resource is responsible for reporting progress on his/her own task assignments, leave the resource's name in the *Default Assignment Owner* field. This means that when a manager publishes a project, tasks assigned to the resource appear on the resource's *Tasks* page in Project Web App.

Warning: Make sure that the system enters a name in the *Default Assignment Owner* field. If you leave this field blank, when a project manager assigns the resource to tasks in a project and publishes the project, Project Server 2010 adds the task assignments to the *Tasks* page **of the project manager and not the assigned resource**. Although this feature allows for much flexibility in the system, it can create untold confusion for everyone involved when the field is blank!

In some organizations, the resource does not submit task progress. Instead, a designated individual, such as a team leader or an administrative assistant, must enter the time on behalf of each team member. To set up your system for a scenario such as this, click the *Browse* button to the right of the *Default Assignment Owner* field and in the *Pick Resource* window, select the name of the individual who enters progress on behalf of the user.

The next two fields in the *Assignment Attributes* section are the *Earliest Available* and *Latest Available* fields. By default, the system leaves these two fields blank. Enter values in one or both of these fields only if a resource's availability for project work is limited to a particular time window. This might be the case for a temporary or contract resource. Otherwise, leave these two fields blank.

The last four fields in the *Assignment Attributes* section are the *Standard Rate, Overtime Rate, Current Max. Units (%)*, and *Cost/Use* fields. In these first two rate fields, enter the standard and overtime rates at which you cost the resource's work. These set the values for cost rate table "A" for the resource. In the *Current Max. Units (%)* field, enter a percentage representing the maximum amount of an average working day the resource is available for project work. Enter 100% or your discounted availability only for resources that are available for full-time project work, and enter a value less than 100% for resources who are available to work less than full-time. In the *Cost/Use* field, enter an amount if the resource incurs a cost per-use, such the "trip charge" you pay a plumber to show up, before any charges related to work. Refer to Module 9, Managing Enterprise Resources, to refresh your memory about these last four fields in the *Assignment Attributes* section.

The single options in *Exchange Server Details* section allow you to set up Project Server 2010 to synchronize the user's Project Web App tasks with the user's Microsoft Outlook task list. If you want to use this synchronization functionality, select the *Synchronize Tasks* option. Refer back to Module 10, Initial Project Server Configuration, for more information on configuring resources for Exchange Server synchronization. If you do not intend to use this functionality, do not select the *Synchronize Tasks* option.

The *Departments* section is a new feature in Project Server 2010 that filters user's visibility to enterprise projects and enterprise fields. If you set up the *Departments* lookup table with your organization's departments, you can specify the *Departments* to which the user belongs in the *Resource Departments* field. Click the *Select Value* button for the *Resource Departments* field and then select one or more values in the pick list. After selecting at least one value, click the *Select*

Value button again to enter the values in the field. If your organization does not use the departments functionality in Project Server 2010, then leave the *Resource Departments* field blank for each user.

The *Resource Custom Fields* section displays any custom enterprise resource fields you created during the process of setting up your organization's custom enterprise fields. Enter or select values in any of the fields shown in this section. If you set any of your organization's custom enterprise resource fields as multi-value fields, you can select multiple values for the resource.

The *Security Groups* section allows you to add this user to one or more of the available security groups in the system. Select one or more groups from the *Available Groups* list and click the *Add* button to add the selected group(s) to the *Groups that contain this user* list. By default, the system adds each new user to the *Team Members* group only. You may remove the user from this group by selecting the *Team Members* group in the *Groups that contain this user* list and then clicking the *Remove* button.

Warning: You should not use the *Security Categories* and *Global Permissions* sections to attribute resources individually. Just because you can do so does not mean it is a wise thing to do. When you set individual permissions for a user in either of these sections, you may override the permissions specified by the user's group permissions, and the inherited *Category* relationships from the user's *Groups*. Therefore, I strongly recommend that you **do not** attempt to manipulate individual permissions, as this creates a very complex security environment that is difficult for you to manage.

By default, Project Server 2010 collapses the *Group Fields* section. However, this section does contain some important fields in which you should enter information. Therefore, remember to expand this section when you are creating a new user. In the *Group Fields* section, enter or select relevant information in the *Group, Code, Cost Center*, and *Cost Type* fields.

Warning: You can use the *Team Details* section as an alternate method to create a *Team* resource or to add members to a team. On the other hand, I strongly recommend that you create *Team* resources in the enterprise resource pool, as this method is quicker and easier. I presented this information previously in Module 9.

The *System Identification Data* section contains internal information about the user in the Project Server 2010 database. At the time you save the user, the system generates the information in all of the fields in this section except for the *External ID* field. You may enter information in the *External ID* field, if necessary.

When you complete your entries for the new user account, click the *Save* button and Project Server 2010 creates the user account. If you selected the *User can be assigned as a resource* option, the system creates both a user account and a same-named resource in the enterprise resource pool. If you deselected the *User can be assigned as a resource* option, the system creates only a user account.

Editing User Information

To edit the information for any user account, click the name of the resource in the data grid shown on the *Manage Users* page. The system displays the *Edit User* page for the selected resource. The *Edit User* page is identical to the *New User* page shown previously in Figure 12 - 6 and Figure 12 - 7. Change any information, as you require, and then click the *Save* button.

Deactivating a User Account

When a resource leaves the company, or is no longer available for project work, it may become necessary to deactivate the resource within Project Server 2010. Before you deactivate any resource, you should confirm with the resource's project managers that the resource has no remaining work value greater than 0 hours in any project in the system.

> **Warning:** If you fail to complete this important first step, your project managers will receive a warning message any time they open an enterprise project in which the deactivated resource has remaining work greater than 0 hours.

You can deactivate an enterprise resource from two locations: from the Project Professional 2010 client and from Project Web App. In Module 09, I presented the steps necessary to deactivate an enterprise resource using Project Professional 2010; therefore, I will not present those steps again. To deactivate a resource using Project Web App, complete the following steps:

1. Click the *Manage Users* link in the *Security* section of the *Server Settings* page.

2. On the *Manager Users* page, select the checkbox to the left of the name of each resource you wish to set to inactive.

3. Click the *Deactivate Users* button.

The system displays the warning dialog shown in Figure 12 - 9. Click the *OK* button to deactivate the selected resources.

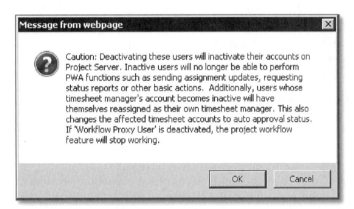

Figure 12 - 9: Warning dialog when deactivating enterprise resources

Controlling Security with Groups and Categories

You control security for all users in Project Server 2010 using *Categories* and *Groups*. A *Category* is a collection of data such as projects, resources, and views. A *Group* is a collection of users who have similar needs for information and functionality. Simply stated, you may think of *Categories* and *Groups* as follows:

*   *Categories* control what you can **access** in Project Server 2010.

*   *Groups* control what you can **do** in Project Server 2010.

- The overlap between *Categories* and *Groups* controls **what you can do with what you can access** in Project Server 2010.

A *Group* in Project Server 2010 simply represents a collection of users, or a collection of people who will be logging in and accessing the features of Project Server, as represented in Figure 12 - 10.

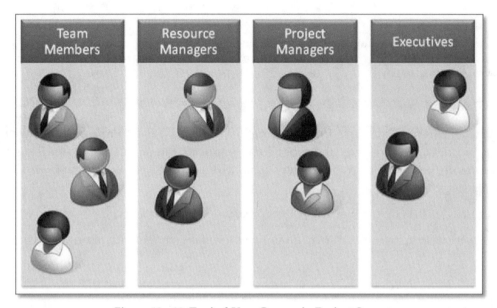

Figure 12 - 10: Typical User Groups in Project Server

Project Server 2010 ships with seven built-in *Groups*. Along with the groups represented in Figure 12 - 10, Administrators, Team Leads, and Portfolio Managers round out the built-in selections. Although using *Groups* is not a requirement for setting up security for your Project Server system, it simplifies the system administration significantly. MSProjectExperts highly recommends that you use *Groups* rather than adding a new user to the system and manually granting them the individual permissions to access various system functions. To follow best practices, proceed as follows when determining and creating your security *Groups*:

1. Identify and analyze the various roles of people who will be using the tool (Team Members, Project Managers, Executives, etc.).

2. Create a Project Server *Group* that represents each role or use a built-in *Group*.

3. Identify the system functions that each role will need in order to carry out their work.

4. Grant the appropriate system permissions to each *Group* as a whole.

5. Add a new user to the system and enter a few key pieces of descriptive data, such as their Name, Email Address, Windows User Account, etc.

6. Add the new user to the appropriate *Group(s)*, based on the role(s) that they will fill.

This might sound like a lot of work, but if done correctly, the up-front work required for creating the various *Groups* in the system needs to be done only once. From that point forward, whenever you add a new user to the system, you simply need to create the user and associate the user to the appropriate group or groups.

A Project Server user can be a member of multiple *Groups* if they wear different hats within the organization. For instance, on one project a person may be participating as a Team Member, and on another project that same person may be the Project Manager. Therefore, you can drop their user account into both the Team Members group and the Project Managers group to grant them the necessary permissions in the system.

When you configure a new instance of Project Server 2010, you typically need to control which data certain people can access. More specifically, you control people's access to certain projects and resources. For example, you may want Project Managers to have access only to their own projects, but you may want Executives to have the ability to access all of the projects in the system. You may also want Resource Managers to have access to their own resources, but you may want Executives to have the ability to access all of the resources in the system.

As you can see, you need a mechanism to distinguish between different collections of projects and resources, and then selectively grant access to those collections or *Categories* of data. Just as a default Project Server 2010 instance contains a number of predefined *Groups*, it also contains built-in *Categories*:

- My Direct Reports
- My Organization
- My Personal Projects
- My Projects
- My Resources
- My Tasks

Each of these *Categories* represents a collection of data that people need to access, view, and act upon. Think of the *My Organization* category as a collection of all projects in the system, whereas the *My Projects* category might consist of a smaller subset of projects owned by an individual as shown in Figure 12 - 11.

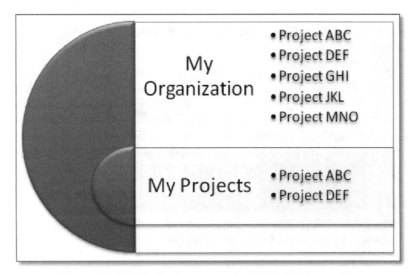

Figure 12 - 11: My Projects is a subset of My Organization

Likewise, you can think of the *My Resources* category as a collection of all of the resources in the system that report up to you, whereas the *My Direct Reports* category represents a subset of those resources that report directly to you as illustrated in Figure 12 - 12.

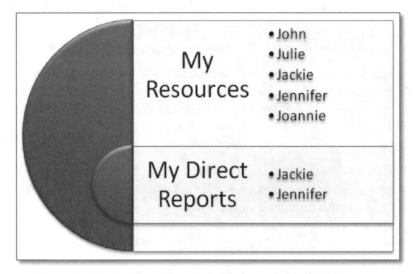

Figure 12 - 12: My Direct Reports is likely a subset of My Resources

Assuming that you captured your business requirements and analyzed those requirements and defined your *Groups* (collections of people using Project Server) and *Categories* (collections of projects and resources), you now need to associate your *Groups* with your *Categories* in order to grant people (users) access to projects and resources (data).

For example, the *My Projects* category represents a collection of projects in the system that someone owns. If you want to grant a group of Project Managers access to the projects that they own, then you associate the *My Projects* category with the *Project Managers* group. The *Project Managers* group defines which people will act as Project Managers in the system. The *My Projects* category defines which projects they will be able to access, view, and act upon.

Similar to the previous example, the *My Resources* category represents a collection of resources in the system that someone owns. If you want to grant a group of Resource Managers access to the resources that they own, you associate the *My Resources* category with the *Resource Managers* group. The *Resource Managers* group defines which people act as Resource Managers in the system. The *My Resources* category defines which resources they can access, view, and act upon.

Categories and *Groups* work interactively to control what a user can access and do in Project Server 2010. Within the system's security environment, *Groups* can be "associated" or "linked" with *Categories*. You can manage these links from *Manage Groups* or *Manage Categories,* but it is easier to manage these via *Manage Categories*. When a user is a member of a *Group*, and the *Group* links to a *Category*, the interaction between the *Group* and the *Category* determines precisely what the user can access and do within Project Server 2010.

As I stated previously, *Categories* control what you can access in Project Server 2010. Specifically, *Categories* control precisely which projects, resources, and views users can access in Project Server 2010. Figure 12 - 13 illustrates how a *Category* functions by controlling access to projects, resources, and views of those projects and resources.

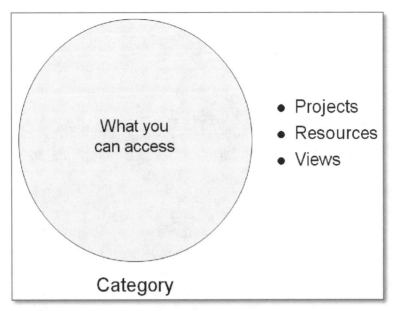

Figure 12 - 13: Categories control what users can access

Groups control what you can do in Project Server 2010. Specifically, *Groups* specify the non-project-specific and non-resource-specific system features and functions that a user can access within the system. Figure 12 - 14 illustrates how a *Group* functions, including six typical permissions that members of a group might need within the system. The *Manage Queue* permission typically belongs to the *Administrators* group, while the *Self-Assign Team Tasks* permission typically belongs to the *Team Members* group. The *New Project* permission typically belongs to the *Portfolio Managers* and *Project Managers* groups. The *View Resource Plan* permission typically belongs to the *Resource Managers* and *Project Managers* groups, while the *Manage Drivers* permission typically belongs to the *Executives* group.

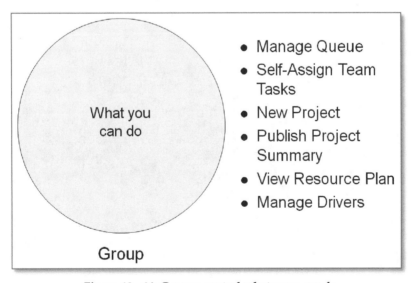

Figure 12 - 14: Groups control what users can do

The overlap between *Categories* and *Groups* controls what you can do with what you can access in Project Server 2010. Because *Categories* are associated with *Groups*, and *Groups* are associated with *Categories*, Figure 12 - 15 shows how *Categories* and *Groups* interact with one another.

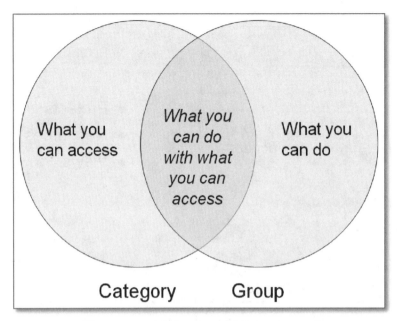

**Figure 12 - 15: Categories and Groups control
what you can do with what you can access**

Figure 12 - 16 shows a specific example of how a *Category* and a *Group* interact. The *My Projects* category determines which projects belong to me. In general terms, a project is "my project" if I have a direct relationship with it, such as I own/manage the project, I am a status manager for a task in the project, or I am a team member in the project. The *Project Managers* group allows me to open projects. The interaction between the *Category* and *Group* determines that I can open any project belonging to me.

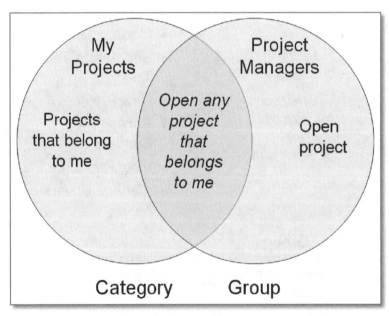

**Figure 12 - 16: Interaction between the My Projects category
and the Project Managers group**

Associating Multiple Groups and Categories

In an ideal scenario, each *Group* of users needs access to only one *Category* of data in the system. However, this often is inadequate to model the business requirements for your organization. For example, a *Group* of users, such as resource managers, may need to access multiple collections of data. The resource managers may not only be managing a group of resources as defined by the *My Resources* category, but they may also be managing a group of departmental projects as defined by a new category I created, *My Departmental Projects*. By adding projects to this category, I securely grant the group of resource managers access to all of their department's projects. Keep in mind that even though I can do something similar using *Departments* filtering in Project Server 2010, this method uses the Project Server security model.

An example of two different groups of people requiring association with the same category can be seen in the fact that executives and administrators both usually need and receive access to everything in the system. By default, both the built-in *Administrators* group and the *Executives* group are associated with the *My Organization* category, which grants access to all content by default if you don't modify it. In situations like these, you take advantage of the commonality of the categorical need and connect both groups to the same category. Notice in Figure 12 - 17 that the *Executives* group gets only read access to projects and resources through this category, while the *Administrators* group gets write access. Under this arrangement administrators can do anything they want, while executives can merely view the results.

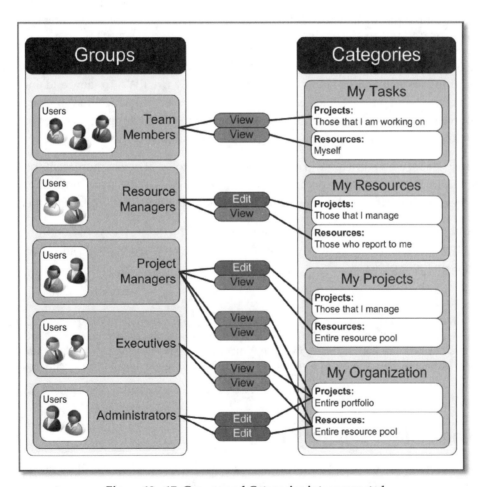

Figure 12 - 17: Groups and Categories interconnected

Understanding Built-in Groups

Project Server 2010 installs with seven built-in security *Groups*. These represent the most common generalized roles in a project management environment. As such, they are very useful starting points for configuring your own Project Server security matrix. Although the definitions of these roles often differ from company to company, they are often quite similar to Microsoft's default vision and what I describe below.

- **Administrators:** People who are responsible for managing the configuration and daily maintenance activities of the Project Server application. Users in this group typically have the ability to edit all projects and resources stored in the system, and use PWA and Project Pro on a daily basis to manage the system.

- **Executives:** People who need high-level visibility into the status of work being performed in the organization. Users in this group typically have the ability to view all projects and resources stored in the system and use PWA on a periodic basis.

- **Portfolio Managers:** People who are responsible for managing one or more programs or portfolios, a collection of related projects and proposed projects within the organization. Users in this group typically have the ability view all of the work within their portfolio using PWA, and they may also have the ability to edit schedules using Project 2010.

- **Project Managers:** People who are responsible for managing one or more projects within the organization. Users in this group typically have the ability to edit their own project schedules using Project 2010, and they sometimes have the ability to view other projects and resources using PWA.

- **Resource Managers:** People who are responsible for managing a group of resources, usually human resources, within an organization. Users in this group typically use PWA to view and analyze the resources who report to them and their assigned work, as well as the projects in which they are participating. Occasionally resource managers will also manage departmental projects or support, maintenance, and operations work schedules, in which case they may have permissions similar to those granted to project managers.

- **Team Leads:** People who participate in projects and act as leaders of one or more teams of resources. Users in this group typically have the same permissions as team members, with a few elevated permissions, such as allowing them to view all of their team's work or to delegate tasks to individuals on their teams.

- **Team Members:** People who participate in projects and perform the 'real work' on those projects. Users in this group typically can use PWA to view the status of their own projects and to submit updates for their task assignments on those projects.

You do not need to shoehorn your people into Project Server's default security *Groups*, but rather you should configure Project Server 2010 to support the roles of the people in your organization. The preset permissions in the default security groups in Project Server may need to be tweaked to meet your needs. Review the Global Permissions for each security *Group* and adjust them accordingly.

Understanding Built-in Categories

The default security *Categories* included in a new instance of Project Server 2010 represent collections of data that users can access, view, and act upon. Some users need the ability to access all of the projects in the system, some need the ability to access all of the resources in the system, and others need access to select subsets of projects and resources.

Figure 12 - 18 shows the *Add or Edit Category* page referenced in the following list of built-in *Categories* and their descriptions.

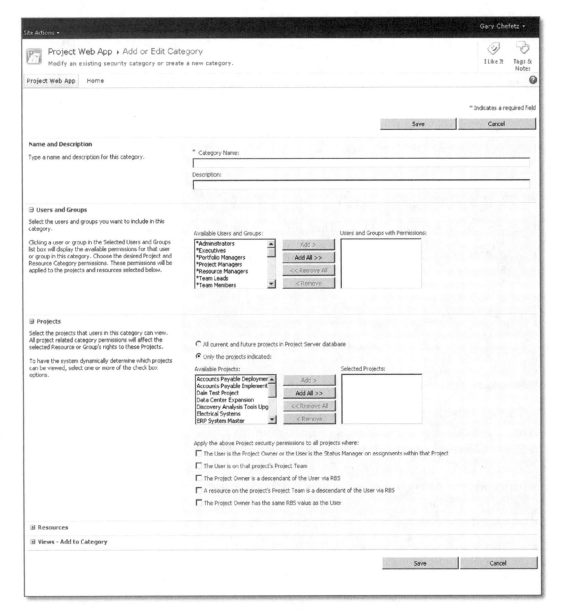

Figure 12 - 18: Add or Edit Category page

- **My Direct Reports:** By default, this category is associated with the *Resource Managers* group and grants access to a select collection of resource data. More specifically, it gives any users associated with the category the ability to access data for the resources who report directly to them as defined by their RBS value. This category does not grant access to any project data. The *Projects* section of the *Add or Edit Category* page for this category contains no specific individual projects and none of the conditional statements are used to indicate user access to projects. In the *Resources* section no specific individual resources are selected for this category, but the conditional statement, *They are direct descendants of the User via RBS* is selected. In short, users associated with this category are granted access to the resources who report directly to them.

- **My Organization:** This category, associated with the *Administrators, Executives, Portfolio Managers, Project Managers,* and *Resource Managers* groups, grants access to a large collection of project and resource data. More specifically, it gives any users associated with this category the ability to access all projects and all resources in the system. In the *Projects* section of the *Add or Edit Category* page for *My Organization, All current and future projects in the Project Server database* is selected. In the *Resources* section, *All current and future resources in the Project Server database* is selected. Users associated with this category are granted access to all projects and all resources in the system.

- **My Projects:** By default, this category associates with the *Project Managers, Resource Managers*, and *Team Leads* security groups and grants access to a select collection of project and resource data. More specifically, it gives any users associated with this category the ability to access their own projects and their own resource records in the system. In the *Projects* section of the *Add or Edit Category* page, no specific individual projects are selected for this category, but three conditional statements are selected:

  - *The User is the Project Owner* or *The User is the Status Manager on assignments within that Project*

  - *The User is on that project's Project Team*

  - *A resource on the project's Project Team is a descendant of the User via RBS*

  In the Resources section no specific individual resources are selected for this category, but two of the conditional statements are selected:

  - *The User is the resource*

  - *They are members of a Project Team on a project owned by the User*

  Users associated with this category are granted access to projects that they own, projects on which they participate as an assignment owner, and projects belonging to people who work for them, as well as their own resource data and the resource data of anyone working on their projects.

- **My Resources:** This category, typically associated with the default Resource Managers security group, grants access to a select collection of resource data. More specifically, it gives any users associated with this category the ability to access data for the resources who report to them. By default it does not grant access to any project data. In the *Projects* section of the *Add or Edit Category* page, no specific individual projects are selected for this category, and none of the conditional statements are used to indicate projects. In the *Resources* section of the *Add or Edit Category* page, no specific individual resources are selected for this category, but one conditional statement is selected:

  - *They are descendants of the user via RBS*

  Users associated with this category are granted access to the resources who report up to them.

- **My Tasks:** This category associates with the *Team Members* group and grants access to a select collection of project and resource data. More specifically, it gives any users associated with the category the ability to access data for their own projects and data about themselves. In the *Projects* section of the *Add or Edit Category* page, no specific individual projects are selected for this category, but one conditional statement is selected:

  - *The User is on that project's Project Team*

  In the *Resources* section of the *Add or Edit Category* page, no specific individual resources are selected for the category, but one conditional statement is selected.

  - *The User is the resource*

  Users associated with this category are granted access to the projects in which they participate as team members, as well as to their own resource data.

Understanding Permissions

At this point, you should have a high-level understanding of how groups and categories interact to define what a user can do and to determine what data the user can see only and what data the user can act upon. In the next two topical sections I take a deep dive into setting permissions in groups and categories. You learn the nitty-gritty mechanics of how to build a security matrix in Project Server, but before you take that plunge, there are a few high-level concepts you should understand about permissions in Project Server 2010.

Understanding Global Permissions and Category Permissions

I began this module by showing you the complete system-wide permissions list for Project Server 2010 followed by tables containing the permissions and descriptive information. In the tables you may have noticed that I note when a permission is a *Category* permission. Permissions come in two basic flavors in Project Server 2010, *Global* permissions and *Category* permissions. The system allows you to set *Global* permissions (permissions you set it in Groups) for both groups and individual users. You set *Category* permissions at the intersection between groups and categories. You can think of *Global* permissions as the high-level "what-you-can-dos" in the system, while *Category* permissions are granular to the object collection of a specific category. In other words, you can have the *Global* permission allowing you to open projects in the system, but you may not have it for every category that belongs to the collection of groups of which you are a member. This makes for a rich- but-confusing security concept, but I assure you that you will understand how this works after reading the deep dive.

At the risk of sounding repetitive, do not set permissions on individual users; instead work with groups exclusively when you set *Global* permissions. Just because you can do so doesn't mean you should. Allow those words to echo in your head at all times while working with Project Server security.

Understanding Denied, Allowed and Not Allowed

When you encounter permissions in the administration interface, except for the presentation in the *Project Web App Permissions* page, every permission has two checkboxes associated with it: *Allow* and *Deny*. To understand how to use these two checkboxes correctly, you must understand that permissions in Project Server 2010 have three possible value states. Those of you familiar with database logic might compare this to 3-value field logic. With one or the other of the checkboxes selected, you create the explicit states of "Allowed" or "Denied," and by deselecting both checkboxes you create the implicit state of "Not Allowed."

- Allowed

- Not Allowed

- Denied

To set a permission, use the following approach:

- To set a permission to Allowed, select the *Allow* checkbox for that permission.

- To set a permission to Denied, select the *Deny* checkbox for that permission.

- To set a permission to Not Allowed, deselect both the *Allow* and *Deny* checkboxes (do not select either option).

For example, Figure 12 - 19 shows the *Project* and *Resources* sections of the *Global Permissions* grid for the *Project Managers* group. Notice that all permissions in the *Project* section are explicitly set to *Allowed*. Notice also that the only permissions in the *Resource* section explicitly set to *Allowed* are *Manage Resource Notifications* and *View Resource Plan*. The other four resource permissions are, therefore, implicitly set to *Not Allowed*.

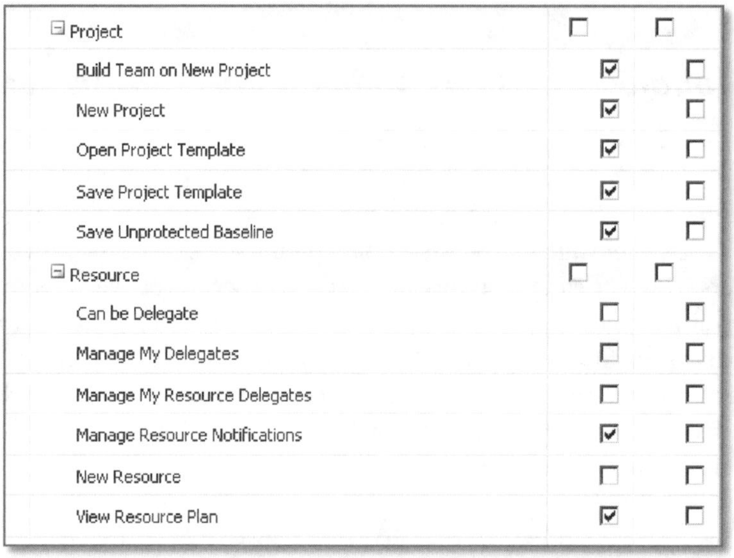

**Figure 12 - 19: Global Project and Resource Permissions
for the Project Managers group**

The difference between the *Denied* and *Not Allowed* permission states is a great source of confusion to less experienced Project Server administrators. If a user is a member of only one security group, then there is no practical difference between the two permission states. In this case, when a permission is set to either *Denied* or *Not Allowed*, the user cannot do what the permission describes. Understanding the difference between these two states becomes extremely important when you assign users to more than one group, which is a common requirement. I address this topic in more detail in the next section.

Understanding Permissions Cumulative Behavior

When a user is a member of multiple security groups and those groups grant access to multiple categories, then the difference between the *Denied* and *Not Allowed* permission states lies in how the system calculates a **cumulative permission** for the user. To calculate the cumulative permission state for any user, Project Server 2010 uses an order of precedence based on the strength of each permission state. The order of precedence from strongest to weakest is as follows:

1. Denied (*Deny* checkbox selected)

2. Allowed (*Allow* checkbox selected)

3. Not Allowed (neither checkbox selected)

Notice in the order of precedence that the *Denied* state overrides the *Allowed* state, and that the two explicit states, *Denied* and *Allowed*, both override the implicit *Not Allowed* state.

Based on this information, how do you determine how Project Server 2010 calculates a cumulative permission when a user is a member of multiple security groups? Suppose a user is a member of two groups called Team Members and Project Managers. In each group, the Project Server administrator sets a different permission state for the *View Project Center* permission. Table 12 - 9 documents how the system calculates the cumulative permission state for the *View Project Center* permission across the two Groups.

View Project Center permission			
Team Members Permission	Not Allowed	Allowed	Not Allowed
Project Managers Permission	Allowed	Denied	Denied
Cumulative	**Allowed**	**Denied**	**Denied**

Table 12 - 9: Cumulative Permissions

In the first scenario, *Not Allowed* in one group and *Allowed* in the other, the cumulative permission is *Allowed* because *Allowed* overrides *Not Allowed*. Because the cumulative permission is *Allowed*, the user can view the *Project Center* page. In the second scenario, *Allowed* in one group and *Denied* in the other, the cumulative permission is *Denied* because *Denied* overrides *Allowed*. This means the user cannot view the *Project Center* page. The third scenario yields the same result as the second, because *Denied* is essentially the trump card. This again means the user cannot view the *Project Center* page.

The fact that permissions are cumulative across groups and categories gives you a lot of flexibility in using a "layered" approach to granting permissions. Every bit of time you spend designing and simplifying your security approach yields manifold maintenance benefits in managing your system.

Because the *Denied* permission state overrides both the *Allowed* and *Not Allowed* states, MSProjectExperts recommends that you rarely set any permission to *Denied*. Most of the time, setting a *Not Allowed* permission addresses your security needs.

Managing Permissions through Groups

All of the organizational permissions I documented at the beginning of this module are available for you to set to *Allow, Not Allow,* or *Deny* at the group level. An individual user inherits permissions from the groups to which he/she is assigned. Once again, the rules of precedence apply when a user belongs to more than one group.

Remember that if you set a permission to *Deny* in one group, you deny that permission for a user across all of the groups to which he/she belongs, regardless of permission settings in all other groups.

To view or edit an existing group in Project Server 2010, click the *Manage Groups* link on the *Server Settings* page. The system displays the *Manage Groups* page shown in Figure 12 - 20.

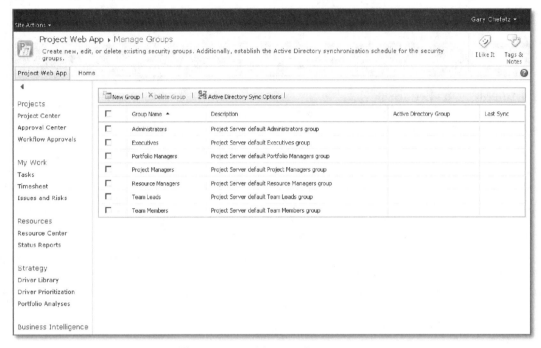

Figure 12 - 20: Manage Groups page

You can see on the *Manage Groups* page that Project Server 2010 contains the seven built-in groups I mentioned when I introduced you to *Groups* and *Categories* previously. In the data grid on the *Groups* page, click the name of the group you want to view or edit. The system displays the *Add or Edit Group* page for the selected group. Figure 12 - 21 shows the *Add or Edit Group* page for the *Project Managers* group.

The system divides the *Add or Edit Group* page into four sections. The *Group Information* section contains general information about the group, including the *Group Name* field, the *Description* field, and the *Find Group* and *Clear Group* buttons used to synchronize the group with an Active Directory group.

The *Users* section lists the users that belong to the group. Notice in Figure 12 - 21 that there are no users in this group. As part of your setup of Project Server 2010, you must add users to the *Selected Users* list **in every group** by selecting one or more users in the *Available Users* list and then clicking the *Add* button.

Note: You can also add users to groups by editing user accounts from the *Manage Users* page.

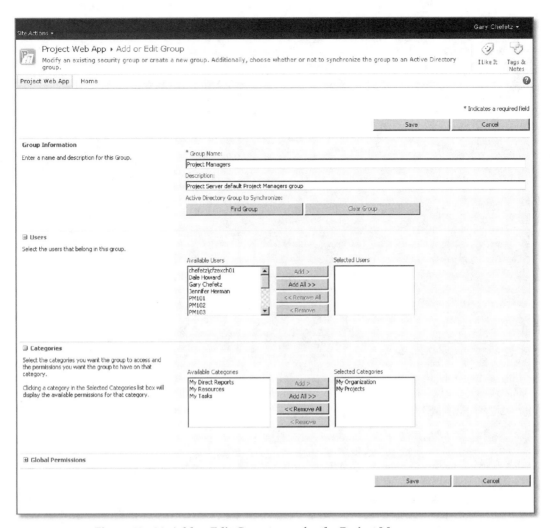

Figure 12 - 21: Add or Edit Group page for the Project Managers group

The *Categories* section lists the security categories to which members of this group have access, along with the specific permissions for each category in the group. It is extremely important for you to understand that when you select a category in the *Selected Categories* list, Project Server 2010 displays the *Permissions* grid for the selected category. Figure 12 - 22 shows the *Category Permissions* grid for the *My Organization* category. This shows you the difference between *Global* permissions and *Category* permissions and how they display in different places. In order to set *Global* permissions for the *Project Managers* group, you must expand the *Global Permissions* section.

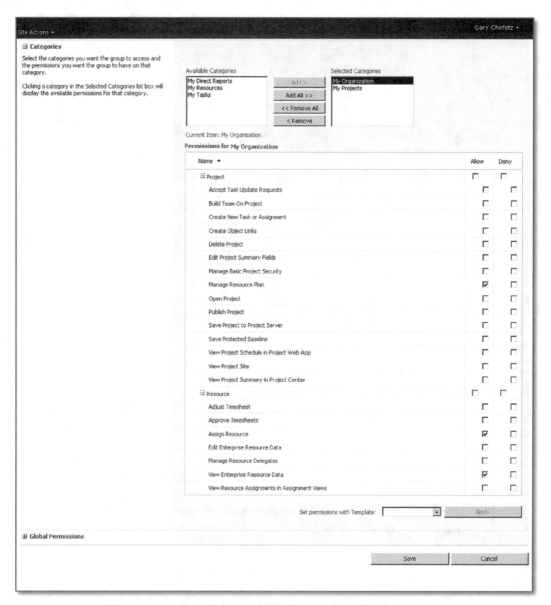

Figure 12 - 22: Permissions grid for the My Organization category

For each category, you can set the *Project* and *Resource* permissions for the objects specified by the category. You can set each of these permissions to *Allow, Deny,* or *Not Allowed*. For example, notice in Figure 12 - 22 that the default permissions are set to *Allow* for the *Manage Resource Plan* permission in the *Project* section, along with the *Assign Resource* and *View Enterprise Resource Data* permissions in the *Resource* section, while all other permissions are set *to Not Allowed*. Because the *My Organization* category grants blanket access to all projects and all resources, this means that members of the *Project Managers* group can manage a resource plan for all projects and can see and assign all resources in the *Build Team* dialog.

MSProjectExperts recommends that you set *Category* permissions when you are editing or creating a category rather than while you are editing or creating a group. Although the system allows you to do this from either location, it is easier and more intuitive to skip the *Categories* section of this page and enter this information when configuring the security from the *Add or Edit category* page, where you can also see the relevant collection of objects or the context for which you are granting permissions.

The *Global Permissions* section shows the global permissions for members of the selected group. By default, Project Server 2010 collapses the permissions grid in the *Global Permissions* section. To expand the *Global Permissions* section, click the name of the section, or click the expand indicator (+) to the left of the section name. Figure 12 - 23 and Figure 12 - 24 show the *Global Permissions* grid for the *Project Managers* group. Because of the length of this section, I break the page in two images. Notice in Figure 12 - 23 that I also collapsed the *Admin* section to shorten an otherwise lengthy section that does not apply to the *Project Managers* group.

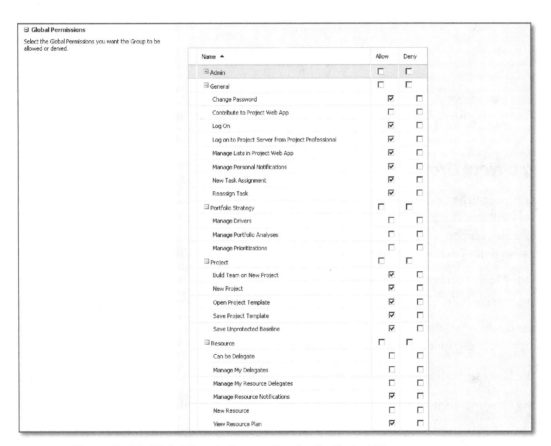

Figure 12 - 23: Global Permissions section for the Project Managers group, top

As you examine the *Add or Edit Group* page for the *Project Managers* group, you can see that every group has its own collection of *Category* permissions and *Global* permissions. Always remember that the combination of category and group membership determines what a user can do with what the user can access in Project Server 2010.

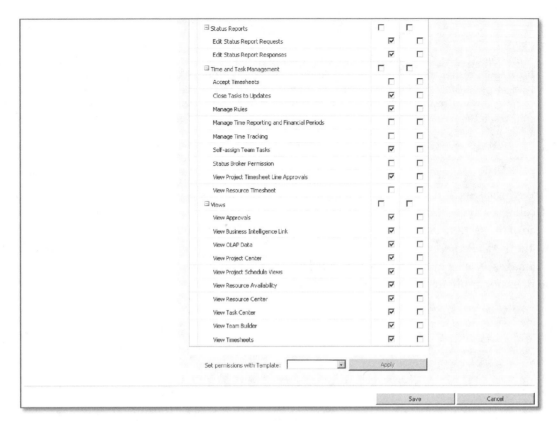

Figure 12 - 24: Global Permissions section for the Project Managers group, bottom

Creating a New Group

Depending on your organization's unique security requirements, you may need to create new security groups in Project Server 2010 to accommodate your needs. There are two ways you can use groups when you build your security matrix; the most obvious purpose a group can serve is to "grant access" to data, but you can also use groups to "deny access" to data. To create a new group, complete the following steps:

1. On the *Manage Groups* page shown previously in Figure 12 - 20, click the *New Group* button. The system displays the *Add or Edit Group* page as shown previously in Figure 12 - 21.

2. In the *Group Information* section of the *Add or Edit Group* page, enter a name in the *Group Name* field and enter an optional description in the *Description* field.

3. In the *Users* section, select the users you want to add to the new group, and then click the *Add* button.

4. In the *Categories* section, select the categories you want to add to the new group, and then click the *Add* button.

5. In the *Categories* section, select each category individually and then set the permissions for the selected category in the permissions grid. You must do this for each category, either through this page or the *Add or Edit Category* page.

6. In the *Global Permissions* section, select your settings for members of the new group.

7. Click the *Save* button when finished.

To set permissions rapidly in either the Permissions grid or the *Global Permissions* grid, select a *Security Template* from the *Set Permissions with Template* pick list at the bottom of the grid, and then click the *Apply* button. There are eight standard *Security Templates* available, one representing the default permissions in each default group in Project Server 2010. This assumes that the built-in security templates are configured correctly to meet your organization's business requirements, and they should be carefully reviewed before using them. I discuss *Security Templates* in the next section of this module.

KISS My Security

The old rule "Keep It Simple, Stupid" applies to setting security in Project Server 2010. Your goal in using groups and categories to control security is to simplify your security schema maintenance as much as possible. This allows you to leverage the relationship-based security rules in categories to automate user access to project data, resource data, views, and system features.

Deleting a Group

If you create a custom group and later need to delete it, complete the following steps:

1. On the *Manage Groups* page, select the checkbox to the left of the group or groups you want to delete.

2. Click the *Delete Group* button on the toolbar. Project Server 2010 displays the warning dialog shown in Figure 12 - 25.

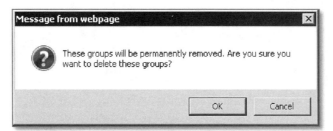

Figure 12 - 25: Warning dialog when deleting a Group

3. Click the *OK* button to delete the selected Group.

 Warning: If you delete a group accidentally, the system provides no way to undo the deletion unless you backed up the category and group settings using either the *Schedule Backup* or *Administrative Backup* tools. If you did back up these settings, you can restore all backed up categories and groups using the *Administrative Restore* tool in the *Database Administration* section of the *Server Settings* page. If you did not back up the category and group settings, then you must manually recreate the group using the information presented in this module.

517

For a summary of all default *Global* permissions for all Project Server 2010 built-in group, refer to the book download package. The download details follow the book's introduction.

MSProjectExperts recommends that if you you do not need any of the default groups that ship with Project Server 2010, that you set the description for those groups to "Not Used." If you do not wish to use a group, simply remove any users included in the *Users* section of the group. You can create a replica of each standard group using *Security Templates* if you do not alter the templates. This is a strategy you can apply both before and after the first time you make changes to the built-in security groups. .

Managing Permissions through Categories

To access *Categories* in Project Web App, click the *Manage Categories* link in the *Security* section of the *Server Settings* page. Project Server 2010 displays the *Manage Categories* page shown in Figure 12 - 26.

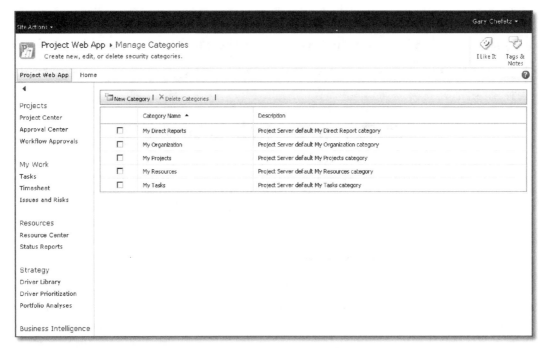

Figure 12 - 26: Manage Categories page

Project Server 2010 installs with the five default categories I discussed earlier in this module under the topic, Understanding Built-in Categories. These consist of *My Direct Reports, My Organization, My Projects, My Resources,* and *My Tasks.* To view or edit the security settings for any category, click the link in the *Category Name* field in the data grid. Project Server 2010 displays the *Add or Edit Category* page for the selected category. The *Add or Edit Category* page contains five sections:

- The **Name and Description** section contains setup information about the *Category*.

- The **Users and Groups** determines which users or groups have access to the category as well as the permissions that each user or group is given for the category.

- The **Projects** section determines which projects are accessible within the system by users and groups that have access to the category.

- The **Resources** section determines which resources are accessible within the system by users and groups that have access to the category.

- The **Views – Add to Category** section determines which views are accessible within the system for users and groups that have access to the category.

Following are the recommended steps for configuring a security category:

1. Identify a collection of project and resource data that a group of Project Server users needs to view or act upon.

2. Select the group(s) of people that need access to the category of data in the *Users and Groups* section of the page.

3. Define which project-related actions those people need to take on the category of data by granting the appropriate permissions in the *Users and Groups* section of the page.

4. Define which projects those people will be able to take the project-related actions upon in the *Projects* section of the page.

5. Define which resource-related actions those people need to take on the category of data by granting the appropriate permissions in the *Users and Groups* section of the page.

6. Define which resources those people will be able to take the resource-related actions upon in the *Resources* section of the page.

7. Define which views those people will be able to use in the *Views* section of the page.

Figure 12 - 27 shows the *Add or Edit Category* page for the *My Projects* category. Notice that the system collapses the *Resources* section and the *Views – Add to Category* section by default.

The *Name and Description* section contains the *Category Name* field and the *Description* field. The *Users and Groups* section contains the names of both groups and individual users who belong to this category. Notice in Figure 12 - 27 that the *Project Managers, Resource Managers*, and *Team Leads* groups belong to this category. More importantly, notice that I do not assign users directly to the category, and I strongly advise you to follow this best practice as well.

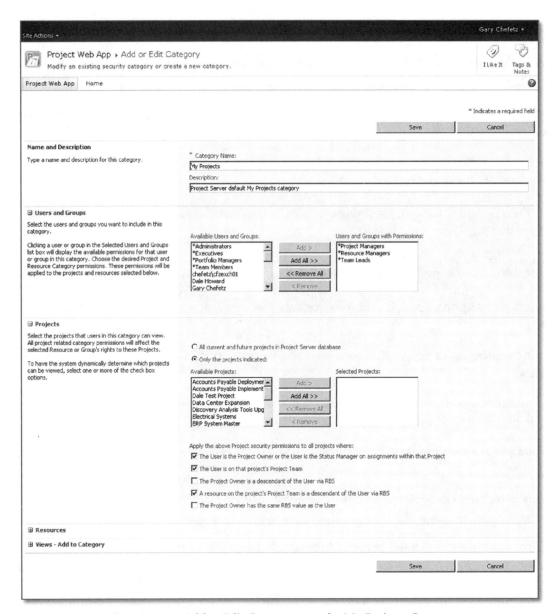

Figure 12 - 27: Add or Edit Category page for My Projects Category

In the *Users and Groups* section, Project Server 2010 prefixes an asterisk character (*) at the beginning of each group name. This asterisk character pushes the group names to the top of the list, making it easier for you to locate the groups you want to include in the category.

If you select the name of one of the groups (or users) listed in the *Users and Groups with Permissions* list, the system expands the *Users and Groups* section to include a permissions grid, as shown in Figure 12 - 28. Notice that the label for the permissions grid shows that the permissions specified in the grid are for the *Project Managers* group only.

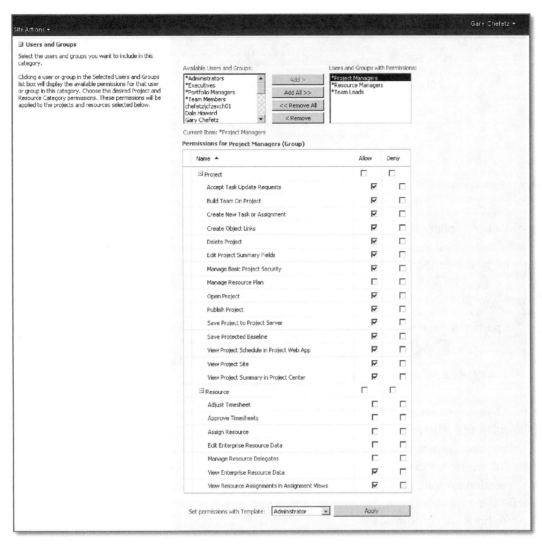

Figure 12 - 28: Category Permissions grid in the Users and Groups with Permissions section

The permissions grid for the *Users and Groups with Permissions* section represents the "overlap" or "interaction" between the category and the groups that have access to the category. Just as you saw when you were learning to edit groups, you can display the *Category Permissions* section simply by selecting the group in the *Users and Groups with Permissions* list. In the case of editing groups, of course, you selected the category. What you see in this *Category Permissions* grid directly determines "what you can do with what you can access." Notice also in Figure 12 - 28 that the *Project Managers* group has 14 of the 15 possible permissions in the *Projects* section of the permissions grid, and has 2 of the 7 possible permissions in the *Resources* section.

Figure 12 - 29 shows only the *Projects* section of the *Add or Edit Category* page for the *My Projects* category. This section defines which projects that the selected users and groups are able to see or act upon through this category (as specified through the previously defined project-related category permissions).

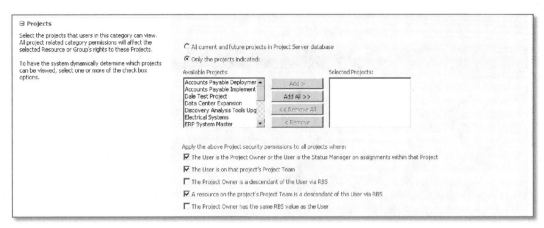

Figure 12 - 29: Projects section for the My Projects Category

You have two available options for associating projects to this category. If you select the *All current and future projects in Project Server database* option, the system does exactly what the option name implies: it gives universal access to every current and future project in the Project Server database.

Important Note: If you select the *All current and future projects in Project Server database* option, the rest of the section becomes irrelevant and it appears grayed-out.

If you select the *Only the projects indicated* option, the system offers a number of additional choices. You may select only specific projects from the list on the left and click the *Add* button to copy them to the list on the right. This is certain to be a labor intensive arrangement unless you use this approach for creating exceptions rather than rules. The additional choices allow you to select one or more of the five checkboxes in the *Apply the above Project security permissions to all projects where* section to create relationship-based associations with projects in the system. This is a much more powerful way of defining the concept of *"My Projects"* and does not require manual maintenance to maintain the security matrix. Your options are as follows:

- **The User is the Project Owner or the User is the Status Manager on assignments within that Project** – Select this option to allow each user to see those projects for which he/she is the owner of the project or is the status manager of task assignments in the project.

- **The User is on that project's Project Team** – Select this option to allow each user to see those projects in which he/she is a member of the project team.

- **The Project Owner is a descendant of the User via RBS** – Select this option to allow each user to see those projects owned by users who fall below them in their branch of the *RBS*. For example, if George Stewart is below Mickey Cobb on her branch of the *RBS* field and George is the owner of the project, selecting this option allows Mickey to see George's projects.

- **A resource on the project's Project Team is a descendant of the User via RBS** – Select this option to allow each user to see those projects in which users below them in their branch of the *RBS* field have task assignments in a project. For example, if George Stewart is below Mickey Cobb on her branch of the *RBS* field, and George is a member of the project team in a project not owned by Mickey, selecting this option allows Mickey to see that project.

- **The Project Owner has the same RBS value as the User** – Select this option to allow each user to see projects owned by a resource at the same position in the *RBS* field. For example, Mickey Cobb and George Stewart are project managers. Both Mickey and George use resources from the same pool of resources, and both of them have exactly the same *RBS* field value. Selecting this option allows Mickey to see George's projects and allows George to see Mickey's projects.

Notice in Figure 12 - 29 shown previously that the default settings for the *My Projects* category allow users to access the projects that they own or manage, access the projects in which they are a team member, and access the projects in which resources below them in the RBS are team members. By default, the *My Projects* category does not allow users to access projects managed by resources below them in the RBS, or access projects owned by resources at the same RBS level.

To expand the *Resources* section, click the section name or click the expand indicator (+) to the left of the section name. Figure 12 - 30 shows the expanded *Resources* section for the *My Projects* category. This section defines which resources that the selected users and groups can see or act upon through this category (as specified through the previously defined resource-related category permissions).

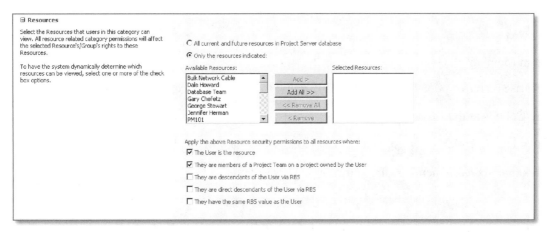

Figure 12 - 30: Resources section for the My Projects Category

The *Resources* section first lists the resources that are accessible to users who have access to the selected category. The *Available Resources* list includes all resources in the enterprise resource pool, plus any user accounts you created for users who do not serve on project teams such as executives. As with the *Projects* section, two options are available for the resource list. If you select the *All current and future resources in Project Server database* option, the system does exactly what the name implies: it gives universal access to every current and future resource in the Project Server database. If you select the *All current and future resources in Project Server database* option, the rest of the section becomes irrelevant and appears grayed-out.

If you select the *Only the resources indicated* option, the system offers a number of additional choices. One choice is to select only specific resources from the list on the left and then to click the *Add* button to copy them to the list on the right. The other choices are to select one or more of the five checkboxes in the *Apply the above Resource security permissions to all resources where* section. These options are as follows:

- **The User is the resource** – Select this option to allow each user to see his/her own resource and assignment data.

- **They are members of a Project Team on a project owned by the User** – Select this option to allow each user to see the resources in each project for which he or she is the Owner.

- **They are descendants of the User via RBS** – Select this option to allow each user to see every resource below him/her on his/her branch of the *RBS* field.

- **They are direct descendants of the User via RBS** – Select this option to allow each user to see only those resources one level below him/her on his/her branch of the *RBS* field.

- **They have the same RBS value as the User** – Select this option to allow each user to see other users at the same position on their branch of the *RBS* field. For example, Mickey Cobb is a project manager and George Stewart is a resource manager, and both of them have exactly the same RBS value. This means that Mickey can see George and George can see Mickey.

The first two options are simple to understand, while the last three require some additional explanation. To understand the differences between the last three options, consider the organizational chart structure shown in Figure 12 - 31 and the explanations on how the *RBS* structure and *Category* permissions work together to control "who sees whom within the system." I set up an *RBS* field against this org chart by defining a top level for Executives, a second level for Project Managers and Resource Managers, and a third level for Team Members, as follows:

Executive

    PM and RM

        Team Member

In the enterprise resource pool, I attributed an RBS value for each resource shown in Figure 12 - 31 as follows:

- Ray Cobb is at the *Executive* level.

- Terry Uland, Helen Howard, and Mickey Cobb are at the *PM and RM* level.

- The other six team members are at the *Team Member* level.

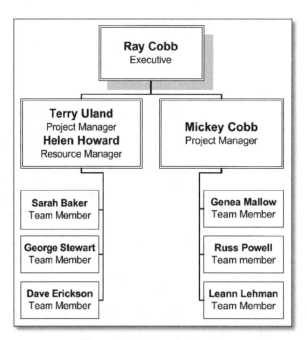

Figure 12 - 31: RBS structure

If you select only the *They are descendants of the User via RBS* option, the system grants each user access to view resource and assignment information as follows:

- Ray Cobb can see every resource below him.

- Terry Uland and Helen Howard can see Sarah Baker, George Stewart, and Dave Erickson.

- Mickey Cobb can see Genea Mallow, Russ Powell, and Leann Lehman.

- The six team members cannot see resource and assignment information for anyone.

If you select only the *They are direct descendants of the User via RBS* option, the system grants each user access to view resource and assignment information as follows:

- Ray Cobb can see only Terry Uland, Helen Howard, and Mickey Cobb.

- Terry Uland and Helen Howard can see Sarah Baker, George Stewart, and Dave Erickson.

- Mickey Cobb can see Genea Mallow, Russ Powell, and Leann Lehman.

- The six team members cannot see resource and assignment information for anyone.

If you select only the *They have the same RBS value as the User* option, the system grants each user access to view resource and assignment information as follows:

- Ray Cobb and Mickey Cobb cannot see anyone.

- Terry Uland can see Helen Howard, and Helen Howard can see Terry Uland.

- Sarah Baker, George Stewart, and Dave Erickson can see one another. Genea Mallow, Russ Powell, and Leann Lehman can see one another.

Notice that the *They have the same RBS value as the User* option does not allow Terry Uland and Helen Howard to see Mickey Cobb, even though they are at the same level of the RBS. This permission does not allow users to see others at the same level on different branches of the RBS. It allows users to see one another only if they are at the same RBS level **on the same branch**.

If you want to make any type of view accessible to users who have access to this category, you must select the views you want them to see. A view is a special type of web-based report. I cover creating and managing views in detail in Module 14, Creating and Managing Views. Figure 12 - 32 shows the *Views – Add to Category* section for the *My Projects* category.

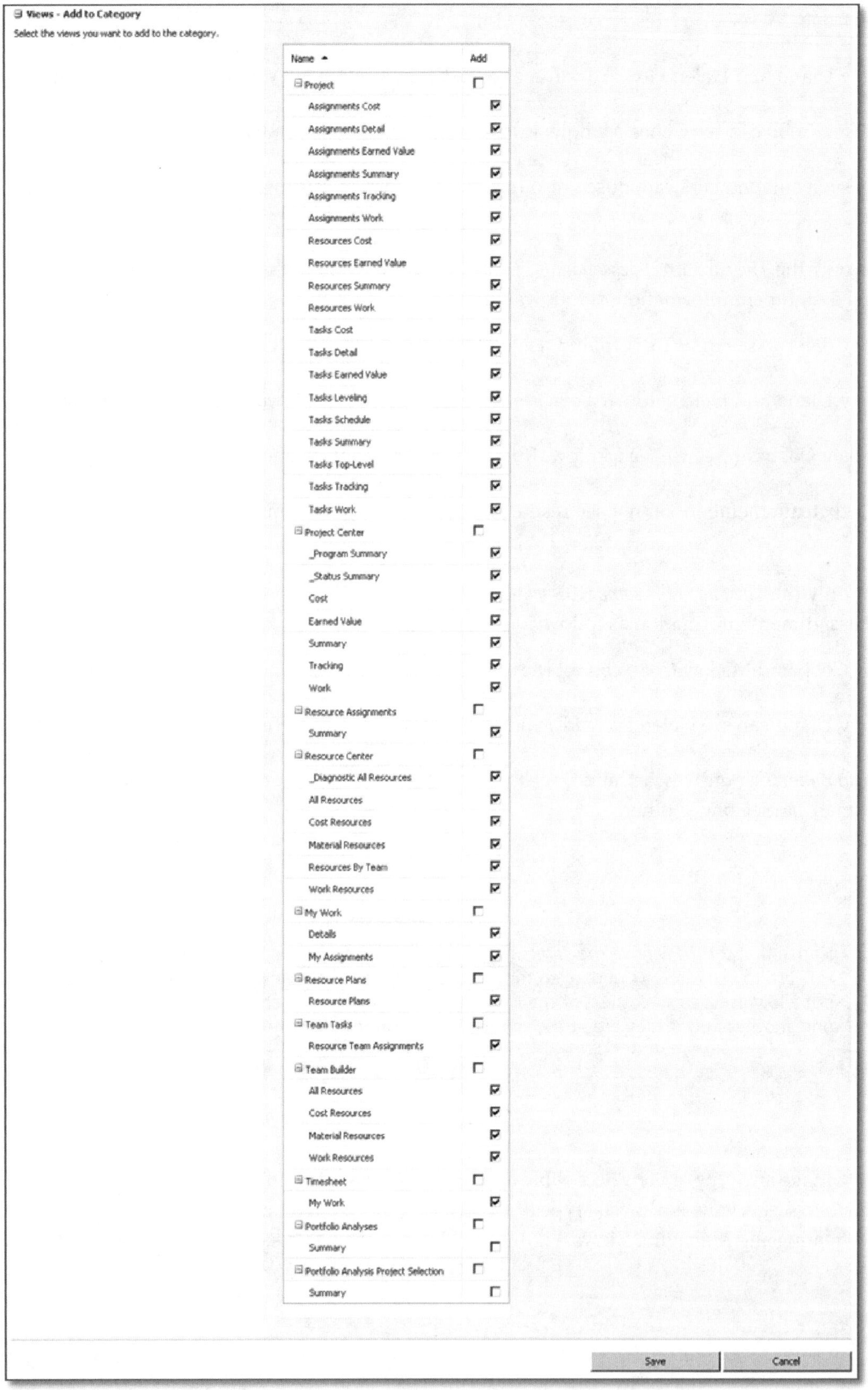

Figure 12 - 32: Views – Add to Category section for the My Projects Category

Notice in Figure 12 - 32 that the *My Projects* category grants access to almost every type of view within the system except for Portfolio Analyses and Portfolio Analysis Selection views. The types of available views include:

- **Project** views, accessed by clicking the name of a project in the *Project Center* page.

- **Project Center** views, visible on the *Project Center* page.

- **Resource Assignments** views, accessed from the *Resource Center* page by selecting one or more resources and then clicking the *Resource Assignments* button.

- **Resource Center** views, visible on the *Resource Center* page.

- **My Work** views, visible on the *Tasks* page or by clicking the name of a task on the *Tasks* page.

- **Resource Plans** views, accessed from the *Project Center* page by selecting a project and clicking the *Resource Plan* button.

- **Team Tasks** views, accessed from the *Tasks* page by clicking the *Insert Task* pick list button and then clicking the *From Team Tasks* item on the pick list.

- **Team Builder** views, accessed from the *Project Center* page by selecting a project and clicking the *Build Team* button.

- **Timesheet** views, visible on the *Timesheet* page.

To a large degree, your ability to manage category configuration determines your success with simplicity. Although you can assign individual users and groups to categories, as a rule you should assign only groups to categories. When you begin adding individual users to categories, you have crossed the line from a security environment that is simple to maintain and into a high-maintenance environment instead.

MSProjectExperts recommends that you add only groups to categories. Rarely, if ever, should you add an individual user to a category, and only under the most unusual of circumstances. This assumes that the built-in security templates are configured correctly to meet your organization's business requirements. You should arefully review these before using them.

Creating a New Category

Based on your organization's unique security requirements, you may need to create one or more new categories. To create a new category, complete the following steps:

1. On the *Manage Categories* page shown previously in Figure 12 - 26, click the *New Category* button. The system displays the *Add or Edit Category* page shown previously in Figure 12 - 27 through Figure 12 - 30.

2. In the *Name and Description* section of the *Add or Edit Category* page, enter a name in *Category Name* field and enter an optional description in the *Description* field.

3. In the *Users and Groups* section, select the groups you want to add to the new category, and then click the *Add* button.

4. In the *Users and Groups* section, select each group individually, and then set the permissions for the selected group in the permissions grid. You must do this for each group that you added in the previous step.

You can set permissions very quickly by selecting a *Security Template* from the *Set Permissions with Template* pick list at the bottom of the permissions grid, and then clicking the *Apply* button. There are seven standard *Security Templates* available, one for each default group in Project Server 2010.

5. In the *Projects* section, select your security settings for access to projects in this category.

6. In the *Resources* section, select your security settings for access to resources in this category.

7. In the *Views – Add to Category* section, select the views you want users to see who have access to this category.

8. Click the *Save* button when finished.

Figure 12 - 33 shows the *Add or Edit Categories* page for a new custom *My Generic Resources* category. To shorten the length of the page, I collapsed the *Projects and Views – Add to Category* sections. I selected no options in the *Projects* section, because this category gives access to only resources, as indicated by the resources I selected manually in the *Resources* section. I also selected the relevant resource-related views in the *Views – Add to Category* section, such as all available views in the *Resource Center* section of the data grid.

I created the *My Generic Resources* category shown in Figure 12 - 33 because of the following security requirements:

•   Our organization intends to use RBS to control Project Server 2010 security to limit access to projects and resources. This means that we allow project managers to see only those resources directly below them in the same branch of the RBS.

•   We attribute generic resources with an RBS value on the same branch as the resources whose skills they represent. For example, I attributed the VB dot Net Developer generic resource with the same RBS value as our team of software developers.

•   Our project managers need access to all generic resources across all branches of the RBS.

The third point in our security situation drives the need for the custom *My Generic Resources* category. The first two points prevent project managers from seeing all generic resources in our enterprise resource pool. However, by adding the *Project Managers* group to the *My Generic Resources* category, project managers have access to their own resources, and they have access to all generic resources as well.

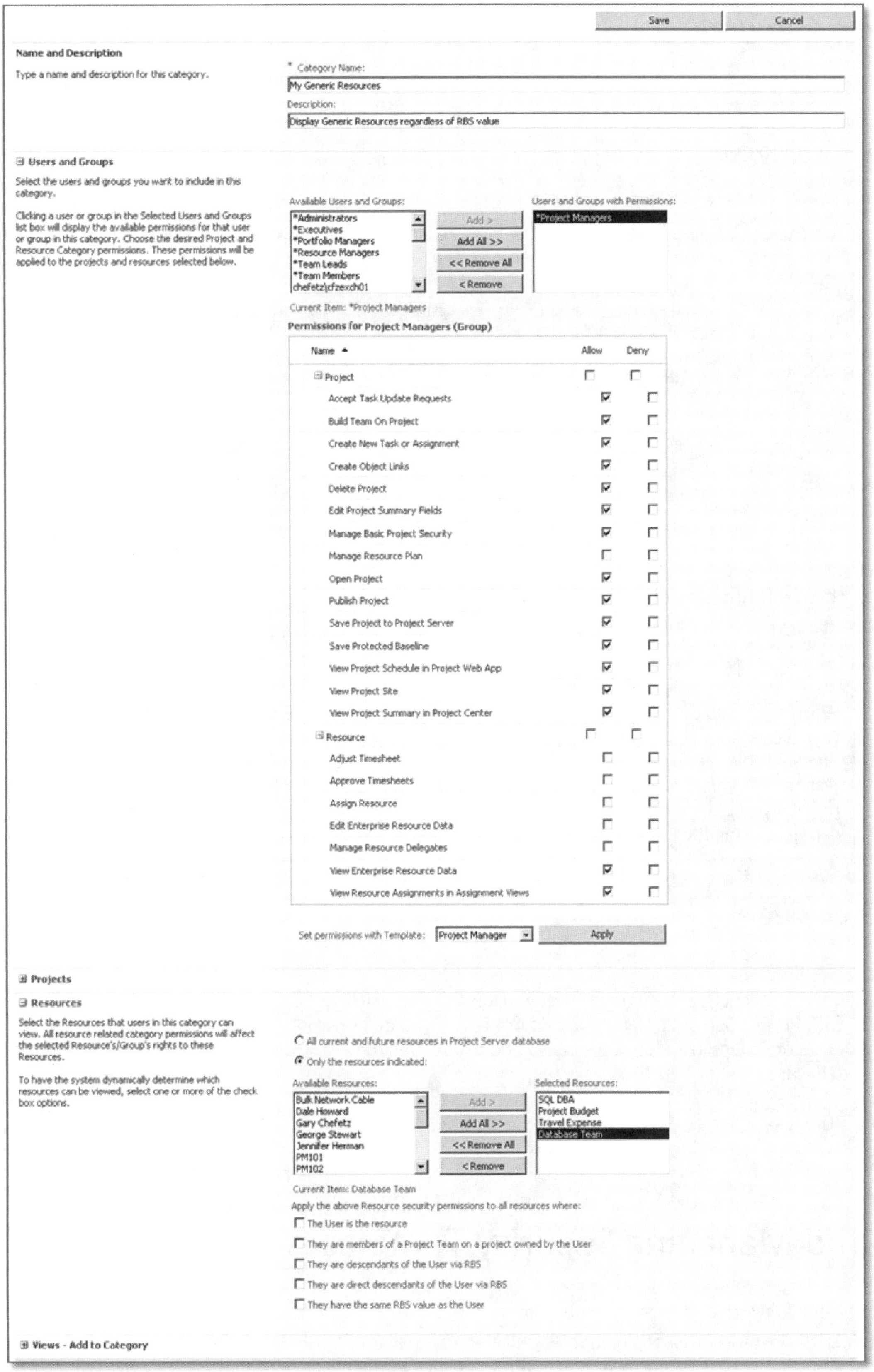

			Save		Cancel	

Name and Description

Type a name and description for this category.

* Category Name:

My Generic Resources

Description:

Display Generic Resources regardless of RBS value

⊟ Users and Groups

Select the users and groups you want to include in this category.

Clicking a user or group in the Selected Users and Groups list box will display the available permissions for that user or group in this category. Choose the desired Project and Resource Category permissions. These permissions will be applied to the projects and resources selected below.

Available Users and Groups:

```
*Administrators
*Executives
*Portfolio Managers
*Resource Managers
*Team Leads
*Team Members
chefetz\cfzexch01
```

| Add > |
| Add All >> |
| << Remove All |
| < Remove |

Users and Groups with Permissions:

*Project Managers

Current Item: *Project Managers

Permissions for Project Managers (Group)

Name ▲	Allow	Deny
⊟ Project	☐	☐
Accept Task Update Requests	☑	☐
Build Team On Project	☑	☐
Create New Task or Assignment	☑	☐
Create Object Links	☑	☐
Delete Project	☑	☐
Edit Project Summary Fields	☑	☐
Manage Basic Project Security	☑	☐
Manage Resource Plan	☐	☐
Open Project	☑	☐
Publish Project	☑	☐
Save Project to Project Server	☑	☐
Save Protected Baseline	☑	☐
View Project Schedule in Project Web App	☑	☐
View Project Site	☑	☐
View Project Summary in Project Center	☑	☐
⊟ Resource	☐	☐
Adjust Timesheet	☐	☐
Approve Timesheets	☐	☐
Assign Resource	☐	☐
Edit Enterprise Resource Data	☐	☐
Manage Resource Delegates	☐	☐
View Enterprise Resource Data	☑	☐
View Resource Assignments in Assignment Views	☑	☐

Set permissions with Template: | Project Manager ▼ | | Apply |

⊞ Projects

⊟ Resources

Select the Resources that users in this category can view. All resource related category permissions will affect the selected Resource's/Group's rights to these Resources.

To have the system dynamically determine which resources can be viewed, select one or more of the check box options.

○ All current and future resources in Project Server database
● Only the resources indicated:

Available Resources:

```
Bulk Network Cable
Dale Howard
Gary Chefetz
George Stewart
Jennifer Herman
PM101
PM102
```

| Add > |
| Add All >> |
| << Remove All |
| < Remove |

Selected Resources:

```
SQL DBA
Project Budget
Travel Expense
Database Team
```

Current Item: Database Team

Apply the above Resource security permissions to all resources where:

☐ The User is the resource

☐ They are members of a Project Team on a project owned by the User

☐ They are descendants of the User via RBS

☐ They are direct descendants of the User via RBS

☐ They have the same RBS value as the User

⊞ Views - Add to Category

Figure 12 - 33: My Generic Resources custom Category

Deleting a Category

If you create a custom category and later need to delete it, complete the following steps:

1. On the *Manage Categories* page shown previously in Figure 12 - 26, select the checkbox to the left of the category you want to delete.

2. Click the *Delete Category* button. Project Server 2010 displays the warning dialog shown in Figure 12 - 34.

Figure 12 - 34: Warning dialog before deleting a Category

3. Click the *OK* button to delete the selected Category.

Warning: If you delete a category accidentally, the system provides no way to undo the deletion unless you backed up the category and group settings using either the *Schedule Backup* or *Administrative Backup* tools. If you did back up these settings, you can restore all backed up *Categories* and *Groups* using the *Administrative Restore* tool in the *Database Administration* section of the *Server Settings* page. If you did not back up the category and group settings, then you must manually recreate the category using the information presented in this module.

MsProjectExperts recommends that you change the description of any of the default categories that ship with Project Server 2010 that you do not use. If you do not want to use a category, simply remove any users or groups included in the *Users and Groups* section of the category and change the description to "Not Used."

Using and Managing Security Templates

To make life easier for you, and to support better standardization of permissions settings across your organization, Project Server 2010 provides *Security Templates* that you can use to quickly set permissions in groups and categories. Notice the *Set permissions with Template* pick list at the bottom of the *Global Permissions* data grid in Figure 12 - 35. The appearance of this selector is identical in the *Category* permissions grid, so I do not show that separately.

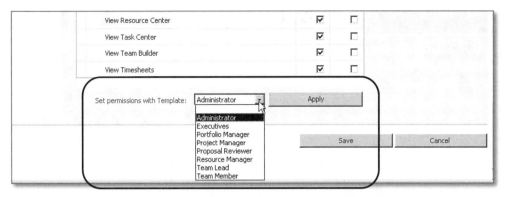

Figure 12 - 35: Set Permissions with Template pick list in Global Permissions grid

Security Templates allow you to manage permissions based on pre-configured records. Project Server 2010 provides a default *Security Template* for each of the seven default groups and one for a deprecated group, *Proposal Reviewers*. To add or modify a *Security Template,* click the *Manage Security Templates* link in the *Security* section of the *Server Settings* page. The system displays the *Manage Templates* page shown in Figure 12 - 36. Notice in the figure that someone at Microsoft forgot to remove the *Proposal Reviewer* template, which is no longer used in Project Server 2010.

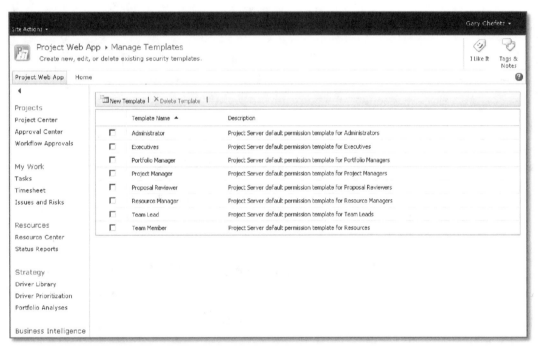

Figure 12 - 36: Manage Templates page

Creating a New Security Template

To create a new Security Template, click the *New Template* button on the *Manage Templates* page. The system displays the *Add or Edit Template* dialog shown in Figure 12 - 37. To reduce the size of this lengthy page, notice that I collapsed the *Project* section in the *Category Permissions* grid and the *Admin, General,* and *Views* sections in the *Global Permissions* grid. Note that I collapsed the permission areas in both the *Category Permissions* and *Global Permissions* sections.

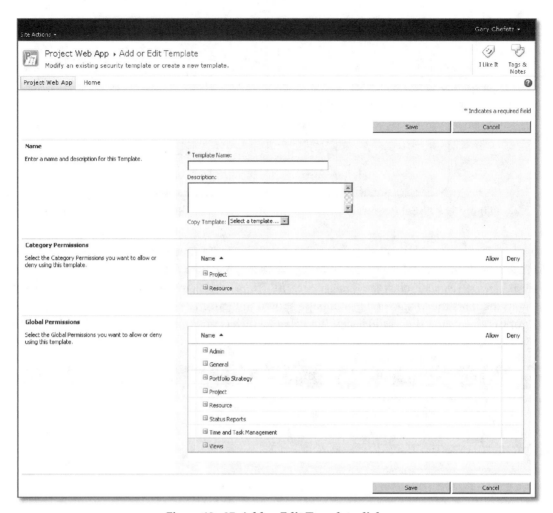

Figure 12 - 37: Add or Edit Template dialog

In the *Add or Edit Template* dialog, enter values in the *Template Name* and *Description* fields. If you want to copy an existing *Security Template,* click the *Copy Template* pick list and select an existing template from the list. Project Server 2010 displays the confirmation dialog shown in Figure 12 - 38.

Figure 12 - 38: Confirmation dialog
when copying a security template

Click the *OK* button to copy the selected template permissions to the new *Security Template.* The benefits you gain from using the *Copy Template* feature include:

- It allows you to quickly configure a new *Security Template* based on the settings of an existing template.

- It allows you to preserve the prior configurations of an existing *Security Template* for backup purposes.

Set the *Category Permissions* and the *Global Permissions* and then click the *Save* button to save the new *Security Template*. Figure 12 - 39 shows the *Manage Templates* page after I created a new security template called Business Administrators. Notice in the *Description* column that I use this new template to set up group and category permissions for groups of business administrators, for whom I redact the more technical administration permissions in the system.

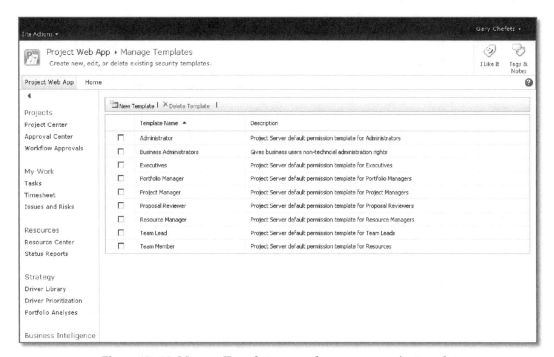

Figure 12 - 39: Manage Templates page shows new security template

Many self-taught users of Project Server 2010 attempt to configure user permissions by adding categories and setting global permissions for every user account individually. This process is a **huge mistake,** and leads to a security environment that is too complex to manage easily. If you configured security this way in your own system, you must undo these settings for every user account. Begin this process by creating a *No Permissions* security template, a security template with no permissions. You can then use the *No Permissions* security template to "undo" the global permissions set individually for each user account. You must also remove any categories you added to each user account.

Before you modify the permissions in a default *Security Template*, MSProjectExperts recommends that you always make a backup copy of the template before you change it. This strategy allows you to redeploy a copy of the original *Security Template* should your modifications fail to deliver the results you seek.

To modify a security template, click the name of the template in the data grid on the *Manage Templates* page. The system displays the *Add or Edit Template* page for the selected template, such as the page shown previously in Figure 12 - 37. Edit the permissions to meet your requirements and then click the *Save* button when finished.

Deleting a Security Template

If you create a new Security Template and later need to delete it, complete the following steps:

1. On the *Manage Templates* page, select the checkbox to the left of the security template you want to delete.

2. Click the *Delete Template* button. Project Server 2010 displays the warning dialog shown in Figure 12 - 40.

Figure 12 - 40: Warning dialog before deleting a Security Template

3. Click the *OK* button to delete the selected security template.

Warning: If you delete a security template accidentally, the system provides no way to undo the deletion. Therefore, you must manually recreate the security template.

MSProjectExperts recommends that you do not delete the default security templates that ship with Project Server 2010.

Managing AD Synchronization for Groups

In addition to providing Active Directory synchronization with the enterprise resource pool, Project Server 2010 also offers synchronization between Active Directory groups and Project Server security groups. Because the synchronization process involves the mapping of security groups in Active Directory to security groups in Project Server 2010, it may be easier for your organization to create custom Active Directory groups that match the default and custom Project Server 2010 security groups.

Before you can use the Active Directory synchronization feature with Project Server groups, you must match each Project Server security group with an Active Directory group. Begin by clicking the *Manage Groups* link in the *Security* section of the *Server Settings* page. On the *Manage Groups* page, click the name of the first group that you want to match to an Active Directory group. Figure 12 - 41 shows the top two sections of the *Add or Edit Group* page for the administrators group.

MSProjectExperts recommends that you avoid using special characters, such as dashes and ampersands, in naming your Active Directory groups. The SQL engine may misinterpret these characters, resulting in AD synchronization failure.

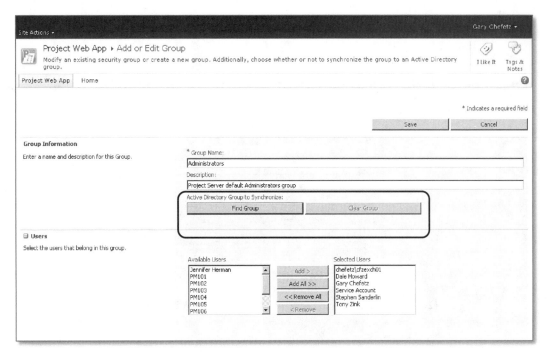

Figure 12 - 41: Modify Group page, find an Active Directory Group

In the *Group Information* section of the page, click the *Find Group* button. The system displays *Find Group in Active Directory* dialog shown in Figure 12 - 42.

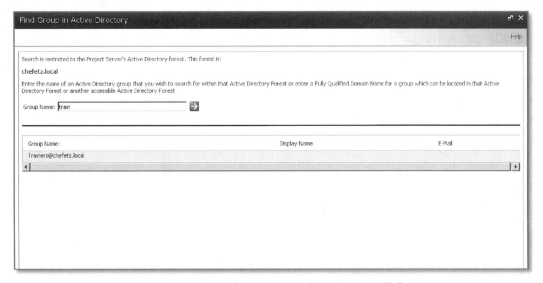

Figure 12 - 42: Find Group in Active Directory dialog

In the *Find Group in Active Directory* dialog, search for and select an Active Directory group, and then click the *OK* button. The system redisplays the *Add or Edit Group* page and lists the selected Active Directory group in the *Active Group to Synchronize* field, as shown in Figure 12 - 43.

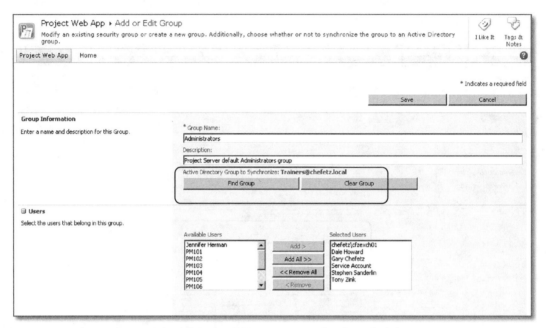

Figure 12 - 43: Selected Active Directory group for the Administrators group

Click the *Save* button to save the Active Directory synchronization information for the selected group. Repeat this process for **every** Project Server 2010 security group you want to synchronize with AD. After you specify an Active Directory group for each Project Server 2010 security group, you must also configure the schedule for Active Directory synchronization. On the *Manage Groups* page, click the *Active Directory Synch Options* button at the top of the data grid. The system displays the *Synchronize Project Server Groups with Active Directory* window, shown in Figure 12 - 44.

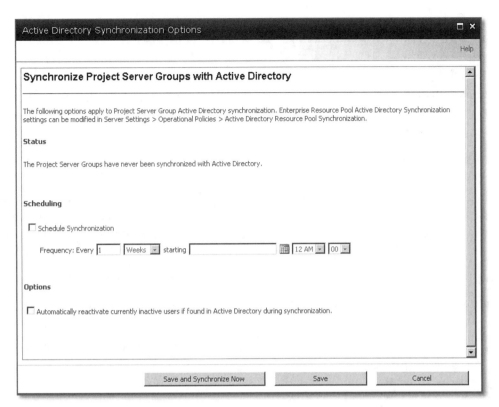

Figure 12 - 44: Active Directory Synchronization Options for groups

Select the *Schedule Synchronization* option and then set the frequency for synchronizing Active Directory groups with the Project Server 2010 security group. The system allows you to schedule the synchronization on a daily, weekly, or monthly frequency.

 If you want to synchronize AD groups with Project Server 2010 Security groups manually, do not select the *Schedule Synchronization* option. Instead, you must complete these steps every time you wish to synchronize resources manually.

If you want the system to reactivate inactive user accounts automatically if they still exist in AD, select the *Automatically reactivate currently inactive users if found in Active Directory during synchronization* option. Click the *Save* button when you finish your selections. Based on the frequency settings you selected, the system synchronizes Active Directory groups and the Project Server 2010 security groups at the next scheduled date.

 If you want the system to synchronize resources immediately, click the *Save and Synchronize Now* button.

 MSProjectExperts recommends as a best practice that you do not synchronize AD groups with Project Server groups at the same time as you synchronize the Enterprise Resource Pool with AD. Instead, offset the time of the two AD synchronizations by at least an hour.

537

Resolving Common Security Requirements

I provide the following real-world scenarios as examples of how you can tweak the security model to accommodate typical security requirements in Project Server 2010. All of the examples are questions that users frequently ask in the Microsoft forums and community newsgroups.

Q: How do I set up Project Server 2010 so that project managers can see only the resources they manage, as defined by the *RBS* field?

A: Before you can use the *RBS* field to control "who sees whom" in Project Server 2010, you must build your company's "pseudo org chart" in the *RBS* field, and then you must set an *RBS* field value for every resource in the Enterprise Resource Pool. After you complete these steps, continue with the following steps to configure the Project Managers group:

1. Click the *Manage Groups* link in the *Security* section of the *Server Settings* page.

2. Click the name of the *Project Managers* group to display the *Add or Edit Group* page for the *Project Managers* group.

3. In the *Categories* section, select the *My Organization* category and set the following permissions to *Not Allowed* (neither *Allow* nor *Deny* is selected):

   - Manage Resource Plan

   - Assign Resource

   - Manage Resource Delegations

   - View Enterprise Resource Data

4. In the *Categories* section, select the *My Projects* category and then set the following permissions to *Allow*:

   - Manage Resource Plan

   - Assign Resource

   - Manage Resource Delegations

   - View Enterprise Resource Data

5. Click the *Save* button.

The preceding set of steps configures the *Project Managers* group to display only the resources specified in the *My Projects* category. Complete these additional steps to configure the *My Projects* category:

1. Click the *Manage Categories* link in the *Security* section of the *Server Settings* page.

2. Click the name of the *My Projects* category to display the *Add or Edit Category* page for the *My Projects* category.

3. In the *Resources* section of the page, select the following options:

   - The User is the resource

   - They are members of a Project Team on a project owned by the User

   - They are descendants of the User via RBS

- They have the same RBS value as the User

4.   Click the *Save* button.

The last set of steps configures the *My Projects* category to show only the resources below each manager in the RBS, and to show any other manager at exactly the same level on the same branch of the RBS.

Q: The default settings in Project Server 2010 allow users in the Project Managers group Read/Write access only to their own projects. Our project managers also need read-only access to the projects belonging to other project managers. How do I configure Project Server to make this happen?

A: To allow Read-Only access to other managers' projects, complete the following steps:

1.   Click the *Manage Groups* link in the *Security* section of the *Server Settings* page.

2.   Click the name of the *Project Managers* group to display the *Add or Edit Group* page for the *Project Managers* group.

3.   In the *Categories* section, select the *My Organization* category and then set the *Open Project permission* to *Allow*.

4.   Click the *Save* button.

The first set of steps allows read-only access to projects managed by other project managers because it allows a project manager to open a project but not save the project. Next, complete the following steps to configure the *My Projects* category so that it allows access only to projects owned or managed by the project manager:

1.   Click the *Manage Categories* link in the *Security* section of the *Server Settings* page.

2.   Click the name of the *My Projects* category to display the *Add or Edit Category* page for the *My Projects* category.

3.   In the *Projects* section, deselect the following permissions:

- The User is on that project's Project Team

- A resource on the project's Project Team is a descendant of the User via RBS

4.   Click the *Save* button.

The last set of steps configures the *My Projects* category to show only those projects directly owned or managed by each project manager. This allows your project managers read/write access to their own projects and read-only access to projects belonging to other project managers.

Q: Although our organization allows only the Project Server administrators to modify the enterprise resource pool, we have one project manager who needs to be able to change the working time calendars for team members, entering information like vacation and sick leave. How do we configure Project Sever 2010 to make this happen?

A: To give an individual project manager the authority to make read/write changes to the enterprise resource pool, complete the following steps:

1.   Click the *Manage Users* link in the *Security* section of the *Server Settings* page.

2.   Click the name of the project manager to display the *Edit User* page for the selected project manager.

3.   Expand the *Security Categories* section, and then add the *My Resources* category to the *Selected Categories* list.

4.   In the Permissions grid for the *My Resources* category, set the following permissions to *Allow*:

- Edit Enterprise Resource Data

- View Enterprise Resource Data

5. Click the *Save* button.

Q: How do I set up a "chain" of timesheet approvers, so that a manager must first approve a resource's timesheet, and submit the timesheet to a senior manager for final approval?

A: Before I show you how to set up the "chain" of timesheet approvers, consider the following roles in an organization:

Senior Manager A

  Resource Manager A

    Team Member A

In the preceding list, Team Member A must submit a timesheet to Resource Manager A for approval. Once approved, Resource Manager A must submit the Timesheet to Senior Manager A for final approval. To set up this process, you must create a new custom group called *Timesheet Reviewers* using the following steps:

1. Click the *Server Settings* link in the Quick Launch menu and then click the *Manage Groups* link.

2. Click the *New Group* button.

3. Enter the name *Timesheet Reviewers* as the name the new group.

4. Add Resource Manager A to the new group.

5. In the *Categories* section, add the *My Resources* category to the list on the right.

6. In the *Permissions for My Resources* grid, select the *Resource Managers* template and click the *Apply* button.

7. In the *Permissions for My Resources* grid, **deselect** the *Allow* option for the *Approve Timesheets* permission (**do not** select either the *Allow* or *Deny* permission and simply leave them both unchecked).

8. In the *Global Permissions* grid, select the *Resource Managers* template and then click the *Apply* button.

9. Click the *Save* button to save the new group.

The preceding set of steps allows Resource Manager A to accept timesheets from his resources and give interim approval to timesheets.

Warning: If Resource Manager A is also a member of the Resource Managers group, you must remove this resource from the Resource Managers group. This is because the default permissions in Project Server 2010 allow Resource Managers final approval of timesheets, not interim approval. As a member of the custom *Timesheet Reviewers* group, Resource Manager A can review and give interim approval to Timesheets, but cannot give final approval.

After creating the custom *Timesheet Reviewers* group, you must set up the "chain" of approvals by completing the following steps:

1. Navigate to the *Resource Center* page in Project Web App.

2. Select the option checkboxes for Senior Manager A, Resource Manager A, and Team Member A, and then click the *Edit Details* button.

3. Add Senior Manager A to the *Resource Managers* group and the *Executives* group, and then click the *Save and Continue* button.

4. Set Senior Manager A as the *Timesheet Manager* for Resource Manager A and then click the *Save and Continue* button.

5. Set Resource Manager A as the *Timesheet Manager* for Team Member A and then click the *Save* button.

Adding Senior Manager A to the *Resource Managers* group designates this manager the final timesheet approver for submitted timesheets. Adding Resource Manager A to the new *Timesheet Reviewers* group makes this manager an interim timesheet approver who must submit timesheets to Senior Manager A for final approval. Therefore, using the preceding customization, when Team Member A submits a timesheet for approval, it goes to Resource Manager A. When Resource Manager A approves the timesheet from Team Member A, the timesheet goes to Senior Manager A for final approval.

Module 13

Building the Project Environment

Learning Objectives

After completing this module, you will be able to:

- Import projects and templates into the enterprise
- Change the Owner and Manager of an imported project
- Build an OLAP cube

Inside Module 13

Building the Project Environment..545

Importing Existing Projects and Templates...545

    Publishing an Imported Project...555

    Changing the Project Owner and Status Manager...556

Building the OLAP Cube 562

Building the Project Environment

In previous modules you learned how to configure custom fields, add resources to the enterprise resource pool, set the initial configuration options in Project Server 2010, set up time and task tracking, and configure security using categories and groups. The next steps in setting up your Project Server 2010 system are as follows:

- Import existing production projects and templates into the system.

- Build the OLAP cube with live project data.

I discuss each of these steps individually.

Importing Existing Projects and Templates

If you have existing production projects already in use, you must bring them into the Project Server 2010 database by importing them. I recommend that you always use the *Import Project Wizard*. In order to use this wizard, the first thing you need to do is to expose the button that starts the wizard, as Microsoft neglected to include this button in any of the built-in ribbons. To begin, launch Project Professional 2010 and connect to your Project Web App instance. Click on the *File* tab and select options from the menu. The system displays the *Project Options* page shown in Figure 13 - 1.

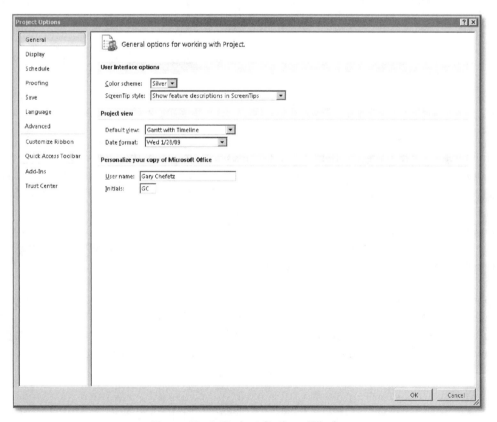

Figure 13 - 1: Project Options Window

Click on the *Quick Access Toolbar* link and the system changes the page display to show the *Customize the Quick Access Toolbar* page shown in Figure 13 - 2 .

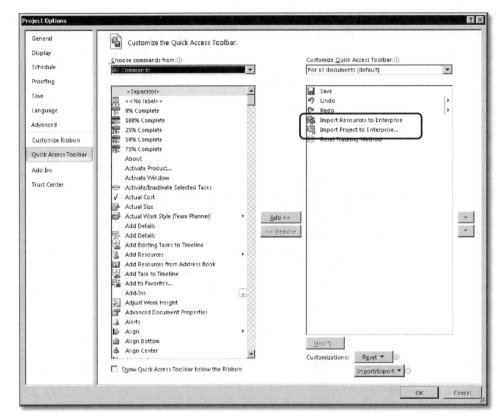

Figure 13 - 2: Customize the Quick Access Toolbar page

In the upper left hand side of the screen, select the *All Commands* option from the *Choose commands from* pick list. Figure 13 - 2 shows that I selected this option. In the list of commands on the left, locate the *Import Project to Enterprise* option and select it, then click on the *Add* button to add it to the list of commands for the *Quick Access Toolbar* on the right. Notice in Figure 13 - 2 that I added both *Import Resources to Enterprise* and *Import Projects to Enterprise* to my *Quick Access Toolbar*, as neither of these appear in the Project 2010 Professional interface by default. You can, however, access *Import Resources to Enterprise* from Project Web App, as I showed you in Module 09. Click the *OK* button on the *Customize the Quick Access Toolbar* page to complete your customization.

Before you import either a project or a template into the system, close any open projects, including the blank numbered project that Microsoft Project 2010 creates by default when you launch the application. If you have a plan open, the system assumes that you want to import the open plan. Click on the *Import Projects to Enterprise* button that you added to your *Quick Access Toolbar*. The system displays the *Open* dialog shown in Figure 13 - 3.

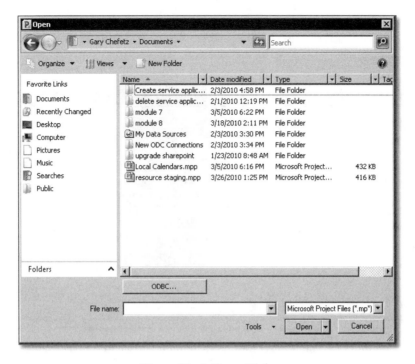

Figure 13 - 3: Open Dialog

Using this dialog, navigate to the folder or network share containing the production project or project template you want to import. Select a project or a template, and then click the *Open* button. Microsoft Project Professional 2010 opens the project or template, and then displays the *Import Project Wizard* sidepane shown in Figure 13 - 4.

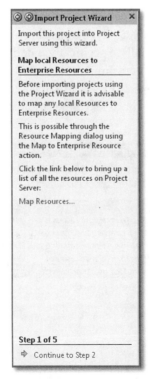

Figure 13 - 4: Import Project Wizard sidepane

The *Import Project Wizard* sidepane assists you in moving non-enterprise projects and templates into the enterprise environment. If your project contains resources, click the *Map Resources* link in the sidepane. The system displays the *Map Project Resources onto Enterprise Resources* dialog shown in Figure 13 - 5.

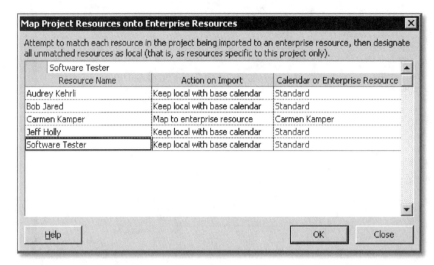

Figure 13 - 5: Map Project Resources onto Enterprise Resources dialog

Use the *Map Project Resources onto Enterprise Resources* dialog to match local resources in the project or template with enterprise resources in your organization's Enterprise Resource Pool. By default, the system automatically matches local resources with same-named enterprise resources. For example, in Figure 13 - 5 notice that the system automatically matched a local resource named Carmen Kamper with the enterprise resource named Carmen Kamper. If the system cannot locate a corresponding enterprise resource to match a local resource, then the system leaves the local resources unmatched.

In order for the system to map a resource automatically, the spelling of both names must be identical. Notice in Figure 13 - 6, that I had to make two mappings manually. Specifically, I had to map Audrey Kerhrli manually because her name is misspelled in the plan that I am importing. Similarly, I had to map Jeff Holly in the local plan to Jeffrey Holly in the enterprise resource pool. When the system does not match a local resource with an enterprise resource, you have the option to map the resource manually or to leave the resource as a local resource.

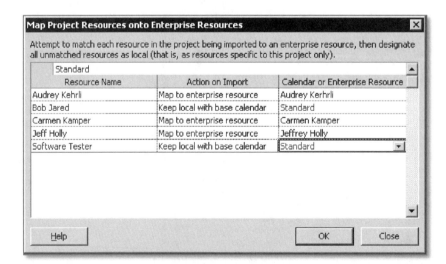

Figure 13 - 6: Map Enterprise Resources manually

To map a local resource to an enterprise resource, click the *Action on Import* pick list for the resource and then select the *Map to enterprise resource* item on the list, as shown in Figure 13 - 6. Click the *Calendar or Enterprise Resource* pick list and select the name of the enterprise resource in the enterprise resource pool. You must repeat this process individually for every local resource that you want to map to an enterprise resource.

Do not rush through the process of matching resources in the Map Project Resources onto Enterprise Resources dialog. Take your time to confirm you match each local resource with the correct enterprise resource. Other than the automatic matching the system performs with same-named resources, there is no fast way to manually match resources.

MSProjectExperts recommends that you spend time to clean up your stand-alone projects and templates before attempting to import them. Because the system allows you to map a resource only once, you should make sure that all resources in your stand-alone plans are consistently named and appear in only one form in each plan.

When you finish mapping local resources with enterprise resources, click the *OK* button to close the *Map Project Resources onto Enterprise Resources* dialog. The system returns control to the *Import Project to Enterprise* wizard sidepane. Click the *Continue to Step 2* link in the sidepane. Project Server 2010 displays the *Confirm Resources* page of the *Import Project to Enterprise wizard* sidepane as shown in Figure 13 - 7. This page lists the number of local (non-enterprise) resources remaining in the project, along with the number of resource errors. An example of what might trigger a resource error is when the Windows User Account information for a resource no longer matches the information on the network or is a duplicate of one already used in the enterprise resource pool.

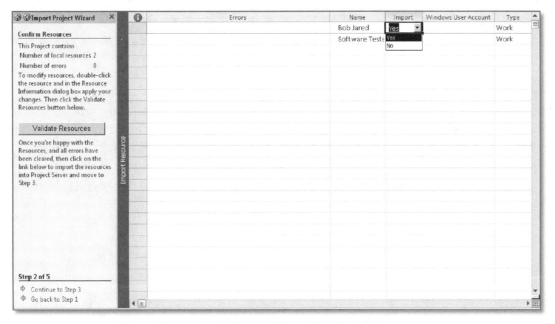

Figure 13 - 7: Import Project Wizard Confirm Resources page

Notice in Figure 13 - 7 that the *Import Project Wizard* shows the Software Tester and Bob Jared as local resources. The *Import* field on this page gives me the option to import this resource as a new enterprise resource, which in this case, I do not want to do. In some cases, however, you might actually need to import a local resource as a new enterprise resource. To do this, set the *Import* field value to *Yes* and continue the import process. If you do not want to import the local resource as a new enterprise resource, make sure you set the *Import* field value to *No*.

Warning: The default functionality in Project Server 2010 is to set a *Yes* value in the *Import* field for each local resource for which you selected *the Keep local with base calendar* option in *the Map Project Resources onto Enterprise Resource* dialog. If you complete the project import process with the Yes value selected, the system automatically imports all of the resources you designated as local resources, and converts them into enterprise resources. Because you are a Project Server administrator, you must manually specify a *No* value in the *Import* field for the resources you want to leave as local resources before you continue to Step 3 in the wizard.

In my particular case, I want to import the Software Tester resource, which I will later convert to a generic resource, and I want to leave Bob Jared as a local resource because he is a part-time contractor who will work on this project only, and is unlikely to be used again; therefore, I set the value in the *Import* field to *No*, using the selector as shown previously in Figure 13 - 7.

Warning: The default behavior of the *Import Project Wizard* in Project Server 2010 is to leave local resources on in-progress tasks (tasks with Actual Work but Remaining Work > 0 hours), even when you match the local resource to an enterprise resource. The Wizard does correctly transfer completed tasks and unstarted tasks to the mapped enterprise resources, however. After importing the project, you must manually replace the local resources with enterprise resources using the *Replace* functionality in the *Assign Resources* dialog.

If you see any resource errors on the *Confirm Resources* page, you must correct any reported errors before you can continue. The resource information on the right side of the window tells you the name of the problematic resource and the nature of the error. After you correct any resource errors, click the *Validate Resources* button in the *Import Project Wizard* sidepane to confirm that you resolved the error successfully. Click the *Continue to Step 3* link in the sidepane when you complete the *Confirm Resources* page. Project Server 2010 displays the *Task Field Mapper* page in the *Import Project Wizard* sidepane shown in Figure 13 - 8.

Figure 13 - 8: Task Field Mapper page

Use the *Task Field Mapper* page to map any local custom task fields in your project with corresponding custom enterprise task fields in your Project Server 2010 system. If the project contains any local custom task fields, click the *Map Task Fields* link in the sidepane. The system displays the *Map Custom Fields* dialog shown in Figure 13 - 9.

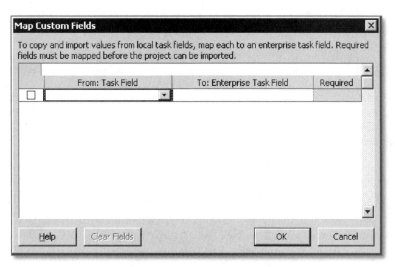

Figure 13 - 9: Map Custom Fields dialog

In the *Map Custom Fields* dialog, click the *From: Task Field* pick list and select a local custom task field. Click the *To: Enterprise Task Field* pick list and select the corresponding custom enterprise task field. Repeat this process for every local custom task field, and then click the *OK* button to complete your mappings.

> If you map custom local task fields with custom enterprise task fields using the *Map Custom Fields* dialog, the system copies the information from the local fields to the corresponding enterprise fields. The system **does not** remove your custom local task fields from your project. After importing your project, you can safely remove your local fields using the *Organizer* dialog or the *Custom Fields* dialog.

The system returns to the *Task Field Mapper* page in the *Import Project Wizard* sidepane. Click the *Continue to Step 4* link in the sidepane. The system displays the *Confirm Tasks* page in the *Import Project Wizard* sidepane shown in Figure 13 - 10.

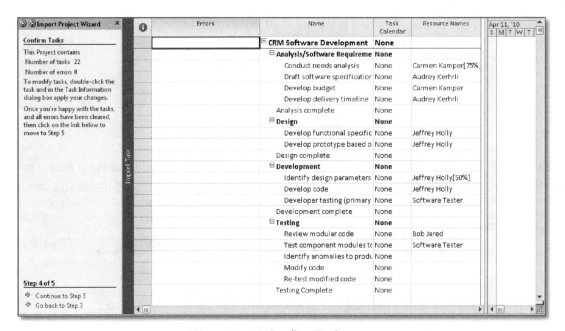

Figure 13 - 10: Confirm Tasks page

If you see task errors in the *Errors* column on the *Confirm Tasks* page, you must correct the errors before the system allows you to continue. The *Task Information* section tells you the nature of the each task error and identifies the tasks causing the errors. Notice in Figure 13 - 10 that the system found no task errors. One way to correct task errors is to double-click the name of any task containing an error. The system displays the *Task Information* dialog for the selected task, shown in Figure 13 - 11.

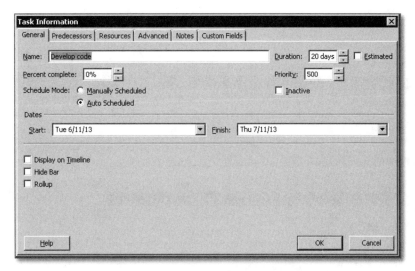

Figure 13 - 11: Task Information dialog

Correct any task errors in the *Task Information* dialog and then click the *OK* button. After you correct the task problems, the system redisplays the *Confirm Tasks* page shown previously in Figure 13 - 10, without any errors listed in the *Errors* column. Click the *Continue to Step 5* link in the sidepane. Project Server 2010 displays the *Save Project to Project Server* page in the *Import Project Wizard* sidepane shown in Figure 13 - 12.

**Figure 13 - 12: Save Project
to Project Server page**

Click the *Save As* link in the *Import Project Wizard* sidepane. The system displays the *Save to Project Server* dialog shown in Figure 13 - 13.

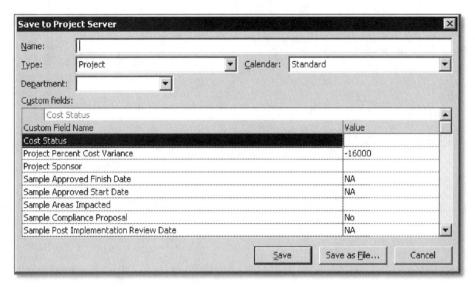

Figure 13 - 13: Save to Project Server dialog

In the *Save to Project Server* dialog, enter the following information:

- Enter a name for the project in the *Name* field according to your organization's naming convention for enterprise projects.

- Click the *Type* pick list and select the type of project (project or a template).

- Click the *Calendar* pick list and select a *Base* calendar to serve as the project calendar for the project, if different from the *Standard* calendar.

- Enter or select values for custom enterprise project fields in the *Custom fields* section.

If you want to import the project as an enterprise project template, remember to click the *Type* pick list and select the *Template* item in the *Save to Project Server* dialog.

Click the *Save* button in the *Save to Project Server* dialog. The system saves the project in the Project Server 2010 database and redisplays the *Import Project Wizard* sidepane with a congratulations message, as shown in Figure 13 - 14.

**Figure 13 - 14: Save Project to Project
Server page with Congratulations message**

In the *Import Project Wizard* sidepane, click the *Close* link to conclude the import process. The system closes the side-pane but leaves the project open for additional action.

Publishing an Imported Project

If the project is already underway, you may need to publish the project to allow team members to begin reporting progress using their *Tasks* and/or *Timehseet* pages in Project Web App. To publish the project, click the *File* tab and select *Publish* from the menu. The system displays the confirmation dialog to save the project shown in Figure 13 - 15.

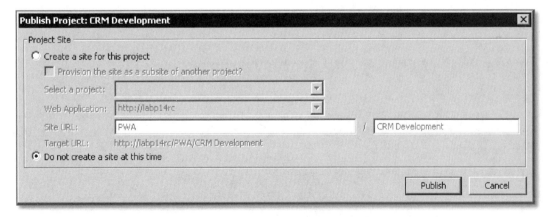

Figure 13 - 15: Publish Project dialog

In the *Publish Project* dialog, you must determine how Project Server 2010 provisions a *Project Site* for the selected project. The default settings create a *Project Site* in the main site. If the system already contains other projects, and the current project is a subproject of another project, you can select the *Provision the site as a subsite of another project* option. When you complete your selections, click the *Publish* button to publish the project and create its Project Workspace.

 During the publishing process, Project Professional 2010 displays the status of the publishing operation in the *Status Bar* at the bottom of the application window. The system reports the percentage of publishing completed, along with an estimate of the time remaining until it completes the operation. When completed, the *Status Bar* displays a *Publish job completed successfully* message.

Click the *File* tab then click *Close* from the menu to close the newly imported and published project. The system displays the confirmation dialog shown in Figure 13 - 16.

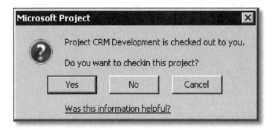

Figure 13 - 16: Confirmation dialog for checking in and closing an imported project

In the confirmation dialog, click the *Yes* button to check in and close the project. At this point, you are ready to import another project or template into the Project Server 2010 database.

 If the project is in the planning stage only, or is planned but not ready to be published, you may omit the publishing operation.

Changing the Project Owner and Status Manager

If you, as the Project Server administrator, import a project into the Project Server database, the system designates you as the *Owner* of the project. If you publish the newly-imported project, the system also designates you as the *Status Manager* for all tasks in the project as well. The *Status Manager* is the person to whom Project Server 2010 sends task updates from team members in the project.

At some point, you will likely need to "hand off" the project to the project manager who must actually own the project and manage assignments in the project. To change the *Owner* of the project, complete the following steps:

1. Log in to Project Web App with administrator permissions.

2. Click the *Project Center* link in the Quick Launch menu. Project Server 2010 displays the *Project Center* page in Project Web App shown in Figure 13 - 17.

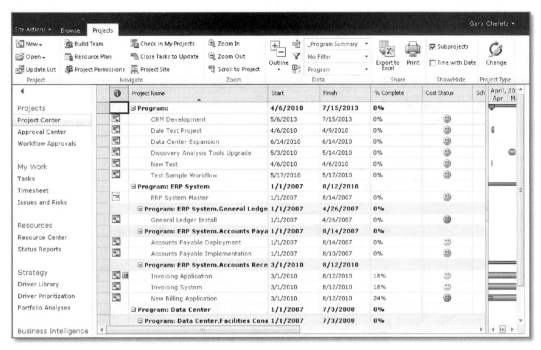

Figure 13 - 17: Project Center page in Project Web App

3. Click the name of your project in the *Project Name* column to select it. The system displays the *Project Schedule* page for the selected project as shown in Figure 13 - 18.

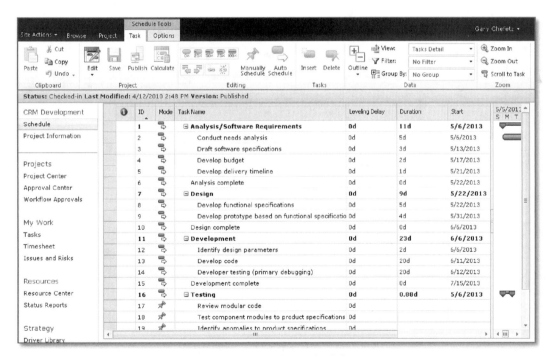

Figure 13 - 18: Project Schedule page

4. Click the *Edit* button pick list and select the *In Project Web App* item. The system opens the project for editing, lighting up the ribbon buttons and options as shown in Figure 13 - 19.

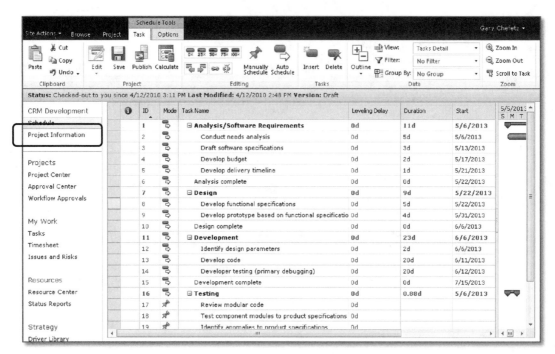

Figure 13 - 19: Project Open for Editing in Project Web App

5. Select the *Project Information* link in the section above the Quick Launch menu. The section begins with the project name. The system displays the *Project Information* page shown in Figure 13 - 20.

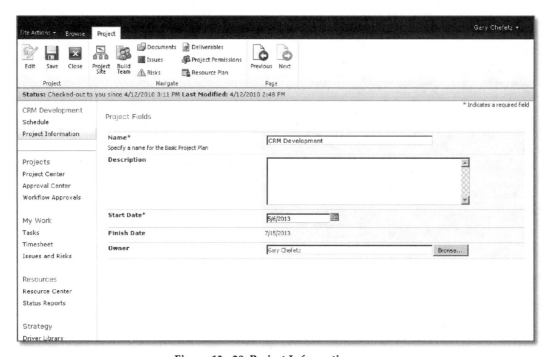

Figure 13 - 20: Project Information page

6. In the *Owner* section, click the *Browse* button to find the new project owner. The system displays the *Pick Resource* dialog shown in Figure 13 - 21.

Figure 13 - 21: Pick Resource dialog

7. Select the new owner for the project from the *Pick Resource* dialog and click the *OK* button to accept your selection. The system closes the *Pick Resource* dialog and returns to the *Project Information* page shown previously in Figure 13 - 20. Click the *Save* button in the *Project* section of the *Project* ribbon. Then click the *Schedule* link in the upper left hand section above the Quick Launch menu to redisplay the *Scheule* page shown in Figure 13 - 22.

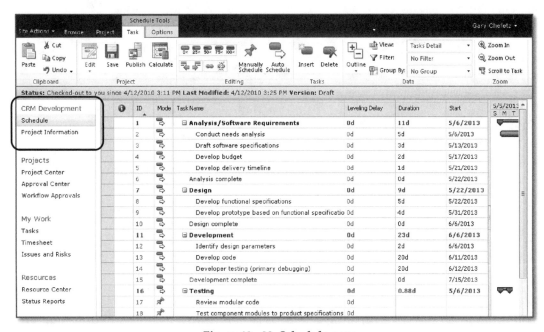

Figure 13 - 22: Schedule page

8. Click on the *Publish* button in the *Project* section of the *Task* ribbon. This publishes the project, including the new owner information. Switch to the *Project* ribbon and click the *Close* button in the *Project* section. The system displays the *Close* dialog shown in Figure 13 - 23. Click the *Yes* button to close and check in the project.

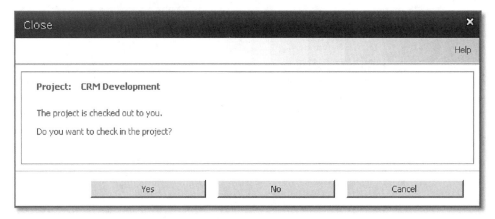

Figure 13 - 23: Close dialog for project

I selected Dale Howard as the new *Owner* of the project. By setting a project manager as the new *Owner* of the project, you give the project manager read/write access to the project in Project Professional 2010. Because Dale is the new *Owner* of the project, Dale must now complete the following steps to take over as the *Manager* of the project as well:

1. Launch Project Professional 2010 and log in to Project Server.

2. Click the *File* tab and select *Open*, and select the newly imported project, and click the *Open* button.

3. Apply any task view, such as the *Gantt Chart* view.

4. Right-click on the column header to the right of the *Task Name* column and select *Insert Column* from the shortcut menu.

5. In the *Column Definition* dialog, click the *Field name* pick list and select the *Status Manager* item from the list, as shown in Figure 13 - 24.

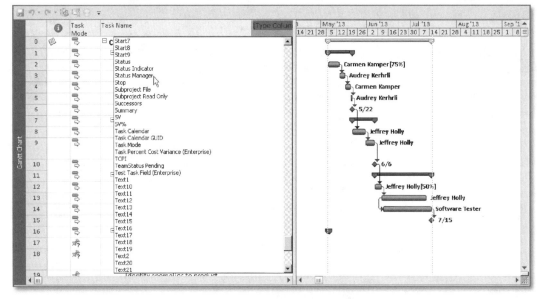

Figure 13 - 24: Field Name Pick list

6. Select the *Status Manager* column to insert the *Status Manager* column to the right of the *Task Name* column, as shown in Figure 13 - 25.

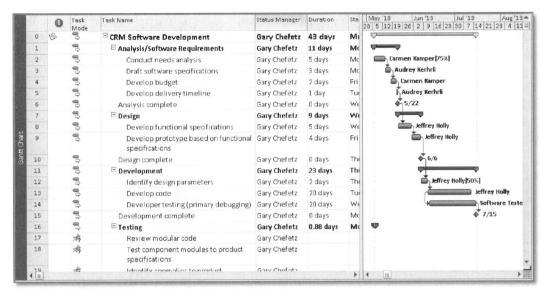

Figure 13 - 25 Status Manager column to the right of the Task Name column

7. For every task in the project, the project manager must select his/her name from the *Status Manager* pick list.

To rapidly change the *Status Manager* value for all tasks in the project, set yourself as *the Status Manager* for the first task. Then use the *Fill Handle* as you do in Microsoft Office Excel to fill the value into successive cells.

8. Click *File* tab and click *Save* to save the project, and then click the *File* tab and select *Publish* to publish the latest changes to the project.

9. Close the project, and when prompted click the *Yes* button to check in the project.

Warning: You, as the Project Server administrator, cannot set the project manager as the *Status Manager* value for tasks in the enterprise project. The project manager must open the enterprise project and specify him/herself as the *Status Manager* for each task.

Given the complexity of changing the *Owner* and *Status Manager* of an imported project, MSProjectExperts recommends that you require each project manager to import his/her own projects into the Project Server 2010 database. This guarantees that the system designates the project manager as both the *Owner* of the project and the *Status Manager* of all the tasks. The Project Server administrator should only import production projects into the system if the original project manager is no longer with the organization.

Building the OLAP Cube

In Module 10, Initial Project Server Configuration, I showed you how to set the options for building the OLAP cube. Until your Project Server database contains published projects, information contained in the OLAP cube is not very useful. Once you have loaded published projects into your Project Server database, it is time to finalize the periodic settings for automatic OLAP cube generation and to launch the OLAP cube build process for the first time.

To begin the process of building the OLAP cube, click the *OLAP Database Management* link from the *Database Administration* section of the *Server Settings* page. Project Server 2010 displays the *OLAP Database Management* page shown in Figure 13 - 26.

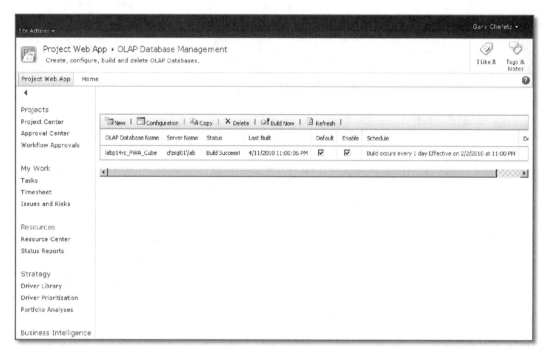

Figure 13 - 26: OLAP Database Management page

Click the name of your OLAP database to finalize the build settings. The system displays the *OLAP Database Build Settings* page for the selected OLAP database, as shown in Figure 13 - 27.

Remember from Module 10, Initial Project Server Configuration, that the options in the *Project Department* section and the *Resource Department* section allow you to restrict the projects and resources shown in the OLAP database. If you need to restrict the list of projects included in the OLAP database, click the *Project Departments* pick list and select one or more departments. If you need to restrict the list of resources included in the OLAP database, click the *Resource Departments* pick list and select one or more departments.

In the *Database Date Range* section, finalize your date range settings. When making your date selections, keep in mind that the broader the date range you select, the more data the system must process and store. This has a profound effect on data storage requirements and processing times.

In the *OLAP Database Update Frequency* section of the page, select the default *Update periodically* option to specify automatic updating using the frequency and time options you set. Set the frequency and schedule for building the OLAP cube in the *Update every*, *Start date*, and *Start time* fields.

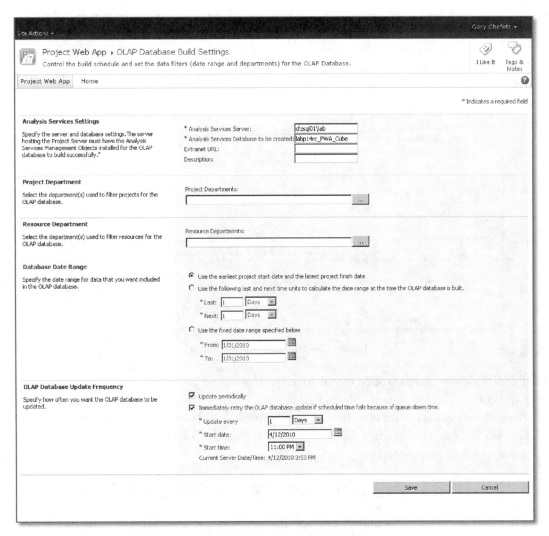

Figure 13 - 27: OLAP Database Build Settings page

When finished, click the *Save* button, and the system redisplays the *OLAP Database Analysis Administration* page. To begin the cube building process for the first time, click the *Build Now* button. The system refreshes the *OLAP Database Management* page and displays a *Processing* value in the *Status* field for the OLAP database. To monitor the progress of the OLAP build process, click the *Processing* value in the *Status* field. Project Server 2010 displays the *Build Status* dialog shown in Figure 13 - 28.

As the system builds the OLAP cube, the *Build Status* dialog refreshes periodically to inform you of the current state of the cube building process. Notice that Figure 13 - 28 shows an interim update about the status of the cube building process. Notice the additional information in the *Build Stages* section and in the *Build Tracking Comments* section.

Warning: When you launch the cube build process, the system should be idle. You should not be running other applications, and users should be off the system. The cube build can consume significant SQL Server resources on the server running Analysis Services. If this is on a production machine serving other applications, it can severely degrade performance for other applications until the cube build process completes.

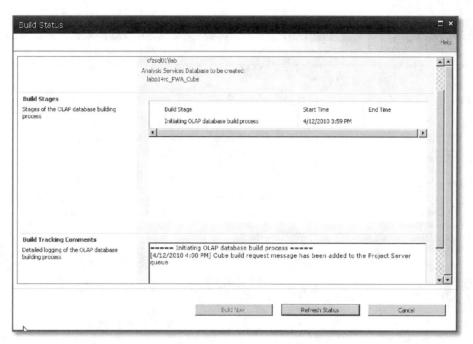

Figure 13 - 28: Build Status dialog

The amount of time the system takes to build the OLAP cube depends on your server specifications and the amount of data it needs to process. When the system finishes building the OLAP cube, the *Build Status* dialog refreshes to show final OLAP cube building status information, as shown in Figure 13 - 29. Notice in the *Build Stages* section that the system shows a *Process Completed* status, while the final line of the *Build Tracking Comments* section shows the *Cube build request completed successfully* message.

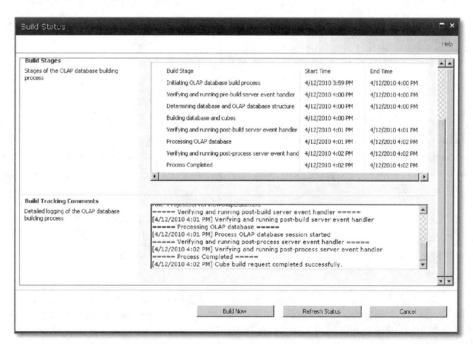

Figure 13 - 29: Build Status dialog shows OLAP cube build success

To close the *Build Status* dialog, click the *Cancel* button.

Module 14

Creating and Managing Views

Learning Objectives

After completing this module, you will be able to:

- Create and manage Gantt Chart formats
- Create and manage Grouping formats
- Create and modify Project Web App views
- Create custom enterprise Task and Resource views in Project Professional 2010

Inside Module 14

Understanding Views 567

Creating Gantt Chart Formats 568

Creating Grouping Formats 572

Managing Project Web App Views 575

    Copying and Modifying Views 577

    Deleting Views 578

Creating Custom Views in Project Web App 579

    Creating a Custom Project View 580

    Creating a Custom Project Center View 585

    Creating a Custom Resource Assignments View 588

    Creating a Custom Resource Center View 592

    Modifying My Work Views 596

    Creating a Custom Resource Plan View 600

    Modifying a Team Tasks View 602

    Creating a Custom Team Builder View 604

    Modifying the Timesheet View 608

    Creating a Portfolio Analyses View 609

Creating a Portfolio Analysis Project Selection View 613

Understanding Enterprise Views in Project Professional 2010 .... **614**

Working with the Enterprise Global File... 615

Adding Custom Views to the Enterprise Global... 616

Removing Pollution from the Enterprise Global.. 617

Using the 4-Step Method to Create a New View **619**

Select or Create a Table.. 620

Select or Create a Filter.. 620

Select or Create a Group.. 620

Create the New Custom View... 620

Creating Useful Enterprise Views **621**

Creating an Enterprise Duration Variance View... 621

Creating an Enterprise Publishing View 631

Creating an Enterprise Resource Sheet View... 634

Understanding Views

In Module 13, Building the Project Environment, you learned how to build and manage the Project Server 2010 project environment, including how to import production projects into the system. With both project data and resource data in the Project Server database, the next step is to create the custom views your system users need. You likely need to create two types of views:

- Views visible in Project Web App

- Views visible in Project Professional 2010

> It is not possible to create a view that is visible in both Project Web App and Project Professional 2010. If you need to display the same information in both applications, you must create two separate views. In this Module, I teach you how to create both types of views.

Project Server 2010 includes eleven types of Project Web App views:

- **Project Center** views are portfolio-level views that display *Project Summary Task* information across the portfolio of projects, with a single line of information for each project.

- **Project** views display information for a single project. You access these by clicking the name of a project in the *Project Center* page. In Project Server 2010, these are not simply views, but also provide editing access to the projects that they display. These are further complemented by *Project Detail Pages* that you learned about in Module 8, which provide read/write access to additional project information.

- **Resource Assignments** views display task assignment information for selected resources across all projects in the Project Server database.

- **Resource Center** views display information about the resources in the enterprise resource pool.

- **My Work** views show project team members their task assignment information on the *Tasks* page and the *Assignment Details* page.

- **Resource Plans** views display *Resource Plan* information for proposals and enterprise projects.

- **Team Tasks** views display tasks assigned to *Team* resources. Accessed from the *Tasks* page by clicking the *Insert Task* button, *Team Tasks* views allow team members to take responsibility for tasks assigned to the *Team* resource.

- **Team Builder** views allow managers to build a team on an enterprise project from Project Web App.

- **Timesheet** views show project team members their assignment or project information on the *Timesheet* page using the *My Timesheet* or *My Work* views.

- **Portfolio Analysis Project Selection** views display workflow information for all projects and display in the project selection process of creating a Portfolio Analysis.

- **Portfolio Analyses** views display during the analysis process when performing a portfolio analysis.

Before you create any of these types of custom views for Project Web App, you may also need to create custom *Gantt Chart* formats and custom *Grouping* formats to apply to your custom views.

Creating Gantt Chart Formats

Before you begin creating Project Web App views, you should be aware of supporting customizations that can greatly enhance the visual appearance of the views you create. You must apply a *Gantt Chart format* to views that contain a Gantt chart, and you can optionally apply a *Grouping* format to most views in the system. For both of these elements you can use an existing format in the system or one that you customize using the built-in tools. Project Server 2010 displays Gantt charts in *Project Center, Project,* and *Assignment* views in Project Web App, along with the *Approval Preview* window available from the *Approvals* page. *Resource Center* views do not include a Gantt chart.

To create or modify *Gantt Chart formats,* log in to Project Web App with administrator permissions and then click the *Server Settings* link in the Quick Launch menu. Click the *Gantt Chart Formats* link in the *Look and Feel* section of the *Server Settings* page. The system displays the *Gantt Chart Formats* page partially shown in Figure 14 - 1.

Figure 14 - 1: Gantt Chart Formats page (partial)

From the *Gantt Chart Formats* page, you can define up to 23 Gantt formats for use in Project Web App views. These formats are as follows:

- Personal Gantt (Tasks)

- Gantt Assign Info 1-4

- Approvals Gantt

- Gantt Chart (Project Center)

- Tracking (Project Center)

- Gantt Chart (Views)

- Detail Gantt (Views)

- Leveling Gantt

- Tracking Gantt

- Gantt 1–11

The *Personal Gantt (Tasks)*, *Approvals Gantt*, and *Gantt Assign Info* 1-4 formats apply to *Assignment* views only. You may apply the remaining Gantt formats to *Project Center* views and *Project* views. The *Personal Gantt (Tasks)*, *Approvals Gantt*, and *Gantt Assign Info 1-4* formats offer graphical symbols for each of the following types of tasks:

- Normal Task

- Delegated Task

- Milestone

- Summary Task

- Group By Summary

- Progress

- Old Task (Approvals Gantt only)

- Old Summary (Approvals Gantt only)

- Old Milestone (Approvals Gantt only)

Project Center views and Project formats offer graphical symbols for the following types of tasks:

- Normal Task

- Critical Task

- External Task

- Milestone

- Summary Task

- Project Summary

- Group By Summary

- Progress

- Summary Progress

- Baseline Task

- Baseline Summary

- Baseline Milestone

- Preleveled Task

- Preleveled Summary

- Preleveled Milestone

- Deadline

- Slippage

- Delay

- Custom Duration 1–10

- Early Schedule

- Late Schedule

- External Milestone

From the preceding list of *Gantt Chart format* symbols, detailed task information does not apply to *Project Center* views. In other words, when you apply a *Gantt Chart format* that includes graphical symbols for detailed task information to a *Project Center* view, the system ignores task-level formatting because *Project Center* views do not display detailed task information.

For each symbol you select in the *Gantt Chart format*, you can determine whether the system displays the element, and if it does, you can select the start and end shapes, the middle bar shape, and the bar color and pattern for each shape. Project Server 2010 provides you a selection of 11 bar patterns, 17 colors, 22 start and end shapes, and 7 middle bar shapes. Using these options, you can create a distinctive look to emphasize specific information.

To create a custom *Gantt Chart format*, click the *Gantt Chart* pick list and select one of the custom *Gantt Chart formats* from the list. For example, notice in Figure 14 - 2 that I am selecting the *Gantt 1* format from the *Gantt Chart* pick list.

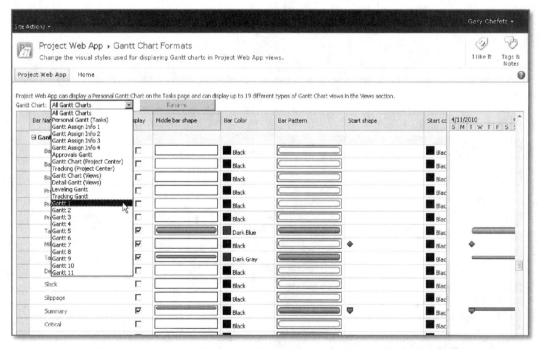

Figure 14 - 2: Select the Gantt 1 format from the Gantt Chart pick list

I want to create a custom *Gantt Chart format* using the Gantt 1 format to show the critical path in detailed project views. In this custom *Gantt Chart format*, I want the system to format critical tasks in red and non-critical tasks in green, and I do not want to display external tasks. To create this custom *Gantt Chart format*, I must complete the following steps:

1. Select the *Gantt 1* format from the *Gantt Chart* pick list, click the *Rename* button and name the format *Critical Path Gantt*, and then click the *OK* button as shown in Figure 14 - 3. After you click the *OK* button, you must reselect the *Gantt Chart Format* by its new name in the pick list.

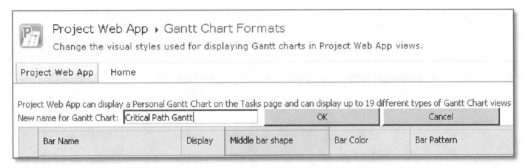

Figure 14 - 3: Renaming Gantt 1 to Critical Path Gantt

2. For the *Task* element, click the *Bar Color* pick list and select the *Green* color from the list. Click the *Bar Pattern* pick list and select the *Medium Fill* bar pattern (fourth item on the list).

3. For the *Critical* element, select the check box in the *Display* column. Click the *Middle Bar* pick list and select the first bar shape. Click the *Bar Color* pick list and select the *Red* color from the list. From the *Bar Pattern* pick list, select the *Medium Fill* bar pattern (fourth item on the list).

4. Deselect the *Display* check box option for the *External Task* element.

5. Click the *Save* button at the bottom of the screen. Project Server 2010 displays the confirmation dialog shown in Figure 14 - 4.

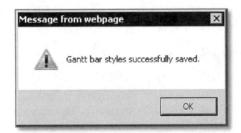

**Figure 14 - 4: Confirmation dialog
for saving new Gantt Chart format**

Figure 14 - 5 shows the completed custom Critical Path Gantt format definition. After you create a new custom *Gantt Chart format*, it becomes an available option for any related custom views you create for Project Web App. Click the *Cancel* button to exit the *Gantt Chart Formats* page to return to the *Server Settings* page.

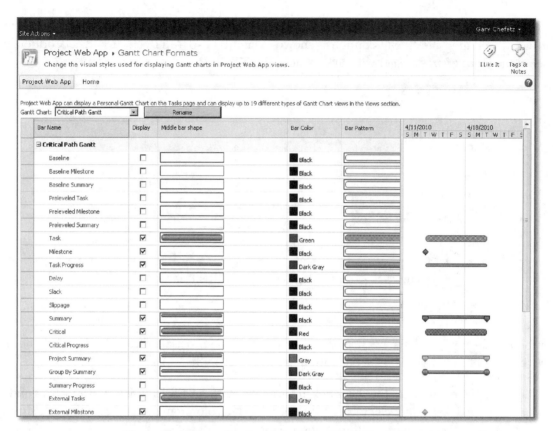

Figure 14 - 5: Completed custom Critical Path Gantt format

Creating Grouping Formats

Project Server allows you to create custom *Grouping formats* that apply colorful formatting to grouping levels in Project Web App views. To create a custom *Grouping format*, click the *Grouping Formats* link in the *Look and Feel* section of the *Server Settings* page. The system displays the *Grouping Formats* page shown in Figure 14 - 6.

Project Server 2010 includes two default *Grouping formats*, the *Timesheet* and *Views* formats, and also includes a *Generic* format plus nine additional *Grouping formats* that you can customize. The twelve available *Grouping formats* are as follows:

- Timesheet

- Views

- Generic

- Grouping 1–9

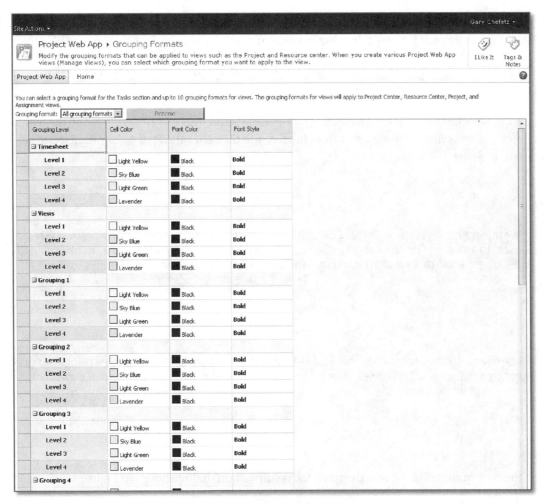

Figure 14 - 6: Grouping Formats page

You may determine the style of each *Grouping format* by selecting the following criteria for each of the four available grouping levels:

- Cell Color

- Font Color

- Font Style

Your color choices for cell colors and font colors for grouping formats are also limited to 16 colors like the *Gantt Chart formats*, however the color assortment introduces lighter colors that are more applicable to use for backgrounds. The ability for you to choose cell pattern styles is no longer available in Project Server 2010, a change from Project Server 2007. Because grouping styles apply to the text as well as cell background formatting for rows in views, you also have the option to select from text font styles Regular, Italic, Bold, and Bold Italic for your custom *Grouping format*.

To create a custom *Grouping format*, click the *Grouping format* pick list and select one of the nine custom formats from the list. For example, I selected the Grouping 1 format because I want to create a custom grouping format using my company's official colors. These colors are primarily blue and yellow with some gray. To create this custom *Grouping format*, complete the following steps:

1. Click the *Rename* button, name the format *Company Colors*, and then click the *OK* button. The system redisplays the *Grouping Formats* page. Reselect your renamed *Grouping format* from the pick list.

2. For the Level 1 grouping, click the *Cell Color* pick list and select the *Light Yellow* color from the list, and then click the *Font Color* pick list and select the *Black* color from the list.

3. For the Level 2 grouping, click the *Cell Color* pick list and select the *Aqua* color from the list, then click the *Font Color* pick list and select the *Black* color from the list.

4. For the Level 3 grouping, click the *Cell Color* pick list and select the *Light Gray* color from the list, click the *Font Color* pick list and select the *Black* color from the list, and then click the *Font Color* pick list and select the *Black* color from the list.

Warning: Although Project Server 2010 allows you to define four levels of grouping, the system allows users to apply only three levels of grouping in Project Web App views. Therefore, there is no point in defining the fourth level of grouping for any custom *Grouping format*.

MSProjectExperts recommends that you use font colors that contrast with the cell colors you select for each grouping level. This makes it easier for users to read the grouping level text in views that use your custom grouping formats.

5. Click the *Save* button. The system displays the confirmation dialog shown in Figure 14 - 7.

Figure 14 - 7: Grouping Format confirmation

6. Click the *OK* button when prompted in the confirmation dialog. Figure 14 - 8 shows my new custom Company Colors custom *Grouping format*.

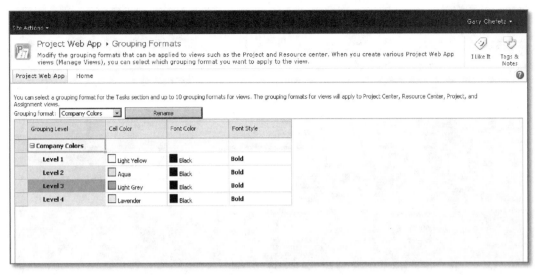

Figure 14 - 8: Company Colors custom Grouping Format

7. Click the *Cancel* button to exit the *Grouping Formats* page and return to the *Server Settings* page.

Managing Project Web App Views

To create or modify Project Web App views, click the *Manage Views* link in the *Look and Feel* section of the *Server Settings* page. The system displays the *Manage Views* page shown in Figure 14 - 9. As you prepare to create custom views in Project Server 2010, the *Manage Views* page shows all default views that ship with the system, grouped by view type. The system offers eleven types of views:

- Project

- Project Center

- Resource Assignments

- Resource Center

- My Work

- Resource Plans

- Team Tasks

- Team Builder

- Timesheet

- Portfolio Analyses

- Portfolio Analysis Project Selection

Figure 14 - 9: Manage Views page

The *Manage Views* page provides three buttons at the top of the page to assist you with managing views: the *New View*, *Copy View*, and *Delete View* buttons. Use the *New View* button to create a new view from scratch. Use the *Copy View* button to create a new view by copying an existing view and then modifying it. Use the *Delete View* button to delete an existing view.

Copying and Modifying Views

Using the *Copy View* button is the fastest way to create a new view, particularly if an existing view is close to what you want. You can also use the *Copy View* button to make a backup of a default view if you need to modify the default view. Backing up the default view allows you to recover the original view configuration if your customization fails to provide the desired results.

To make a copy of an existing view, select anywhere in the *Name* cell or the *Description* cell for the view you want to copy. **Do not** click the name of the view, however, since this action displays the *Edit View* page for the selected view. After selecting the view you want to copy, click the *Copy View* button. Project Server 2010 displays the *Copy View* dialog shown in Figure 14 - 10.

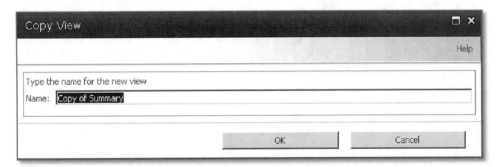

Figure 14 - 10: Copy View dialog

In the *Name* field, enter a new name for the new custom view according to your organization's naming convention as demonstrated in Figure 14 - 11, and then click the *OK* button.

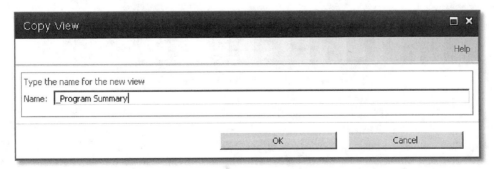

Figure 14 - 11: Copy View dialog with new name

The system adds the new view to the data grid in the *Manage View* page as shown in Figure 14 - 12. Notice in Figure 14 - 12 that I created a new _Program Summary view to use in the *Project Center*. I prefixed the view name with the underscore character (_) to force this view to the top of the *View* pick list on the *Project Center* page.

Project Center	
_Program Summary	Displays basic project information
_Status Summary	Displays basic project information
Cost	Displays cost information
Earned Value	Displays earned value information
Summary	Displays basic project information
Tracking	Displays schedule vs. baseline dates
Work	Displays work information

Figure 14 - 12: Program Summary view added to view list

MSProjectExperts recommends that your organization establish a standard naming convention for all custom views in both Project Web App and Project Professional 2010.

After copying an existing view, you must modify the copied view to create your new view according to your specifications. To modify your newly-copied view, click the name of the view in the data grid. Project Server 2010 displays the *Edit View* page for the selected view, ready for modification. Because the steps used to edit views are nearly identical to the steps used to create new views from scratch, I discuss all of the necessary steps in the next major section of this module.

Deleting Views

To delete an existing view, select the view in the data grid and then click the *Delete View* button. The system displays the confirmation dialog shown in Figure 14 - 13. Click the *OK* button to delete the view or click the *Cancel* button to cancel the deletion.

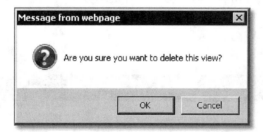

Figure 14 - 13: Deletion confirmation dialog

Warning: If you do not back up the default Project Web App views using the system's *Administrative Backup* tool, and then you delete a default view, there is no way to undo the deletion. Therefore, think twice before you delete any default Project Web App view.

Creating Custom Views in Project Web App

To create a completely new custom view in Project Web App, click the *New View* button at the top of the data grid on the *Manage Views* page. The system displays the *New View* page shown in Figure 14 - 14. Notice that the system selects the *Project Center* value in the *View Type* field by default. This is because I had a Project Center view description selected in the *Manage Views* page before I clicked the *New View* button.

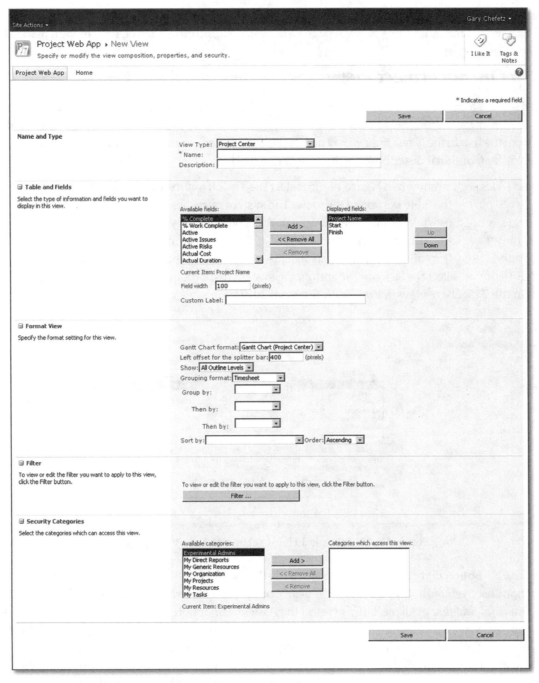

Figure 14 - 14: New View page for a custom Project Center view

If you select the *Name* cell or *Description* cell for any view in the *Manage Views* page and then click the *New View* button, Project Server 2010 automatically sets the *View Type* field value to the type of view currently selected in the data grid.

In the *Name and Type* section of the *New View* page, click the *View Type* pick list and select one of the eleven available *View* types. The system refreshes the *New View* page with options appropriate to the type of view you select.

Creating a Custom Project View

If you defined any custom enterprise task fields in your Project Server 2010 system, project views are the ideal location in which to display these custom fields. To create a custom project view, click the *View Type* pick list and select the *Project* item from the list. In the *Name and Type* section of the page, enter a name for your new project view in the *Name* field and then add an optional description in the *Description* field.

In the *Table and Fields* section shown in Figure 14 - 15, select the *Task, Resource,* or *Assignment* option to determine the type of fields to display in the table portion of the view. The system refreshes the *Available fields* list and the *Displayed fields* list to include only those fields appropriate for the option you select. If you select the *Task* option, Project Server 2010 displays only *Task* fields, such as those shown in the *Gantt Chart* view in Project Professional 2010. If you select the *Resource* option, the system displays only *Resource* fields, such as those shown in the *Resource Sheet* view in Project Professional 2010. If you select the *Assignment* option, the system displays a mix of *Task* and *Resource* fields, such as those shown in the *Task Usage* view in Project Professional 2010.

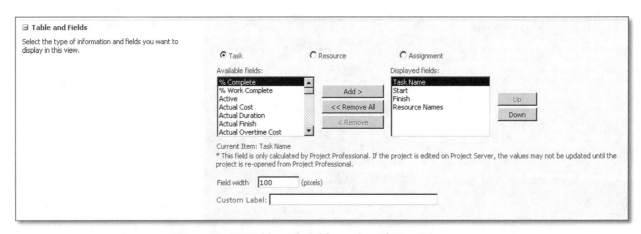

Figure 14 - 15: Table and Fields section of New View page

If you select the *Task* option in this section, the system adds the *Task Name, Start, Finish,* and *Resource Names* fields to the *Displayed fields* list by default. If you select the *Resource* option, the system adds the *Unique ID* and *Resource Name* fields to the *Displayed fields* list by default. If you select the *Assignment* option in this section, the system adds the *Task Name, Start,* and *Finish* fields to the *Displayed fields* list by default. These fields are mandatory in any Project view, and the system does not allow you to remove any of these default fields from the *Displayed fields* list. In the *Available fields* list, select the fields you want to display in your new view, and then click the *Add* button to move the selected fields to the *Displayed fields* list. To move fields up or down in this list, select one or more fields and then click either the *Up* or *Down* button.

Warning: Project Server 2010 does not allow you to select a block of fields and then move the fields as a group. Therefore, you can move fields only one at a time.

There are two options at the bottom of the *Table and Fields* section that control how Project Server 2010 displays the fields in the view. For each field in the *Displayed fields* list, you may select one of two options:

- Select the *Field width _____ (pixels)* option and specify a fixed width in pixels for the column.

- Set the *Custom Label* to change the display title for the field in this particular view. Enter an alternate name for the field in the *Custom Label* column. You can enter a shorter name (or "nickname") for any field that has a long name. For example, you might enter *% W Comp* as a nickname for the *% Work Complete* field.

 You can use the *Field width _____ (pixels)* option to almost hide any default field that you do not want visible in your new view. Set the pixel value to 1 to almost hide a field. This trick does not work as well in Project Server 2010 as it did in in the previous version of the tool.

In the *Format View* section of the *New View* page, select the options to format your custom view display. If you selected the *Task* or *Assignment* option in the *Tables and Fields* section, the *Format View* section includes a *Gantt Chart format* pick list and a *Left offset for the splitter bar* field. When you select the *Resource* option, the system omits both of these fields. Click the *Gantt Chart format* pick list and select one of the available Gantt chart formats. The default *Gantt Chart format* value is *Gantt Chart (Views)*.

 If you customize one of the other nine *Gantt Chart formats*, such as the *Critical Path Gantt* format I created earlier in this module, then you can select the custom format from the *Gantt Chart Format* pick list.

In the *Left offset for the splitter bar* field, specify the number of pixels to offset the vertical split bar from the left side of the page. The default offset value is *400 pixels*. Because this value and the *Field Width* values are difficult to set precisely without being able to see the results immediately, you may need to finish creating the view, and then navigate back and forth between your new custom project view and the *Edit Views* page to fine-tune these values precisely.

 To position the splitter bar on the far right side of the view to hide the Gantt chart portion of the view, set the value in the *Left Offset for the Splitter Bar* field to at least *1200 pixels*.

Click the *Show* pick list and select the number of *Outline Levels* to display. The default setting for this field is *All Outline Levels*. If you want to see all tasks in the view, be sure to select the *All Outline Levels* option. Click the *Grouping format* pick list and select one of the available *Grouping formats*. The default *Grouping format* is the *Timesheet* format.

 If you customize one of the nine *Grouping formats*, such as the Company Colors format I created earlier in this Module, you can select the custom grouping format from the *Grouping format* pick list.

To apply grouping to the fields in your custom view, click the *Group by* pick list and the *Then by* pick lists, and then select the fields that you want the system to use for grouping. Each of these pick lists contains only those fields in the *Displayed fields* list.

To apply sorting to the rows displayed in the custom view, click the *Sort by* pick list and select a field, and then click the *Order* pick list and select either the *Ascending* or *Descending* item from the pick list. The *Sort* pick list contains only those fields in the *Displayed fields* list. By default, Project Server 2010 does not apply grouping or sorting in any custom view.

In the *Filter* section, the system allows you to build a custom filter to apply to the data in your custom view. To build a filter, click the *Filter* button. The system displays the *Custom Filter* dialog shown in Figure 14 - 16.

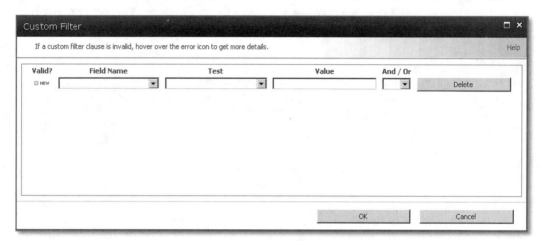

Figure 14 - 16: Custom Filter dialog

Click the *Field Name* pick list and select the first field on which you want to filter. The *Field Name* pick list contains a field set based on your selection of the *Task, Resource,* or *Assignment* option in the *Table and Fields* section of the dialog. Click the *Test* pick list and select the type of test used in the filter. Manually enter a value in the *Value* field. If you want to create a compound filter, click the *And/Or* pick list, select an item from the pick list, and then add additional lines to the test. If you enter invalid test criteria, the system displays a red X character in the *Valid* column as shown in Figure 14 - 17.

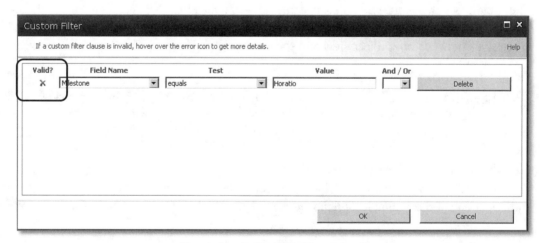

Figure 14 - 17: Invalid Filter Criteria

If your filter contains an error of any type, you see the error indicator in the *Valid* column; when you try to save it, the system will prompt you with the warning dialog shown in Figure 14 - 18.

Figure 14 - 18: Invalid row warning

Figure 14 - 19 shows the *Custom Filter* dialog with the custom filter I created for my project view. I want this filter to display only regular tasks, but not summary tasks or milestones. After you create a valid filter, click the *OK* button to close the *Custom Filter* dialog.

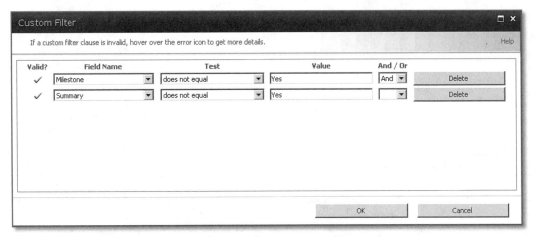

Figure 14 - 19: Custom Filter dialog containing a valid filter

After you create your filter, Project Server 2010 does not display any information about it in the *Filter* section of the *New View* page that indicates that the view contains a filter. To determine whether a view contains a filter, you must always click the *Filter* button and examine the *Custom Filter* dialog.

> To delete the filter criteria line in the *Define Custom Filter* dialog, click the *Delete* button to the right of the criteria line you want to delete.

In the *Security Categories* section, select one or more categories in the *Available Categories* list and click the *Add* button to add them to the *Categories which access this view* list. The categories you select determine which users can see the custom view in Project Web App. For example, if you want the *Executives* group to see the custom view, add the *My Organization* category to the *Categories which access this view* list. If you want the *Project Managers* to see the custom view, then add the *My Projects* category to the *Categories which access this view* list. Click the *Save* button on the *New View* page to save your custom view.

> **Warning:** If you fail to add any categories to the *Categories which access this view* list, **no one** in your organization can see the new custom view, **including you**!

Figure 14 - 20 shows the *Edit View* page for my new custom project view. I created this _Schedule Status view to show both schedule and cost indicators in a project detail view that my project managers can use to quickly identify problems with schedule or cost overruns in the project. To create this custom view, I completed the following steps:

- I added the *Task Schedule Indicator* and *Task Cost Indicator* custom fields to the *Displayed fields* list and then moved the fields into the correct order.

- I applied a *Cost* custom label to the *Task Cost Indicator* custom field and a *Schedule* custom label to the *Task Schedule Indicator* custom field. The system indicates the custom label on the *Task Schedule Indicator* field, for example, using the text string *"Schedule – Task Schedule Indicator"* in the *Displayed Fields* list.

- I set the *Field Width* value to *75 pixels* on the indicator fields to maximize those for the view and changed the width of the *Task Name* field to 200 pixels to accommodate longer task names.

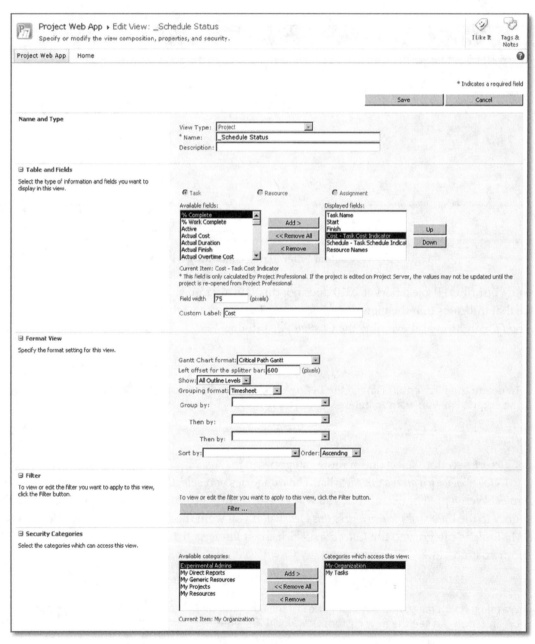

Figure 14 - 20: Edit View page for custom view

- I set the *Left offset for the splitter bar* field value to *600* pixels to move the splitter bar to the right of its default setting.

- In the *Show* pick list, I selected the *All Outline Levels* option.

- I left the default *Timesheet* grouping format because the view does not use grouping.

- I created a filter to display only regular tasks, but not summary tasks or milestones.

- I added the *My Organization* and *My Tasks* categories to the *Categories which access this view* list.

When you finish defining your custom view, click the *Save* button. The system adds the new custom view to the *Project* section of the *Manage Views* page. To access this new project view, users must navigate to the *Project Center* page and click the name of any enterprise project. The system displays the *Project Details* page for the selected project. Users must then select the *Schedule* page and click the *View* pick list and select the custom view. Figure 14 - 21 shows the new custom view applied to an enterprise project on the *Schedule* page.

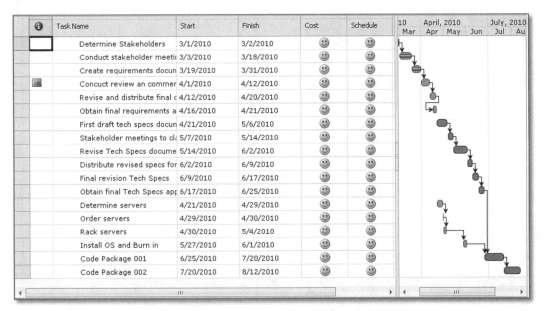

Figure 14 - 21: _Schedule Status custom view applied

Creating a Custom Project Center View

If you defined any custom enterprise project fields in your Project Server 2010 system, *Project Center* views are the ideal location in which to display these custom fields. To create a new *Project Center* view, click the *New View* button on the *Manage Views* page. On the *New View* page, click the *View Type* pick list and select the *Project Center* item from the list. The system refreshes the *New View* page as shown in Figure 14 - 22.

Creating a *Project Center* view is nearly identical to creating a *Project* view, except that this page does not contain the *Task, Resource, and Assignment* options in the *Table and Fields* section. The *Available fields* list contains both standard task fields, along with built-in and custom enterprise project fields. By default, the system includes the *Project Name, Start,* and *Finish* fields in the *Displayed fields* list. Remember that these three fields are default fields that must be included in every *Project Center* view, and you cannot remove them. The system also pre-selects the *Gantt Chart (Project Center)* format in the *Gantt Chart format* pick list, and pre-selects the *Timesheet* format in the *Grouping format* pick list.

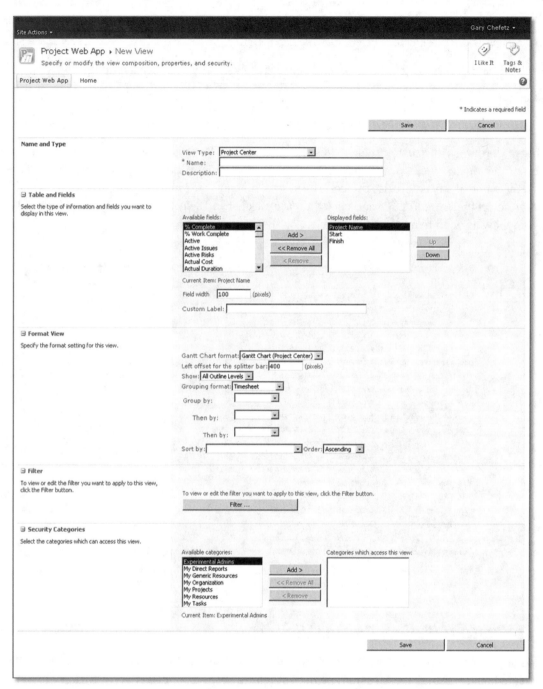

Figure 14 - 22: New View page for a Project Center view

As with *Project* views, create a new *Project Center* view by completing information in each of the five sections. Figure 14 - 23 shows the definition for a custom Project Center view.

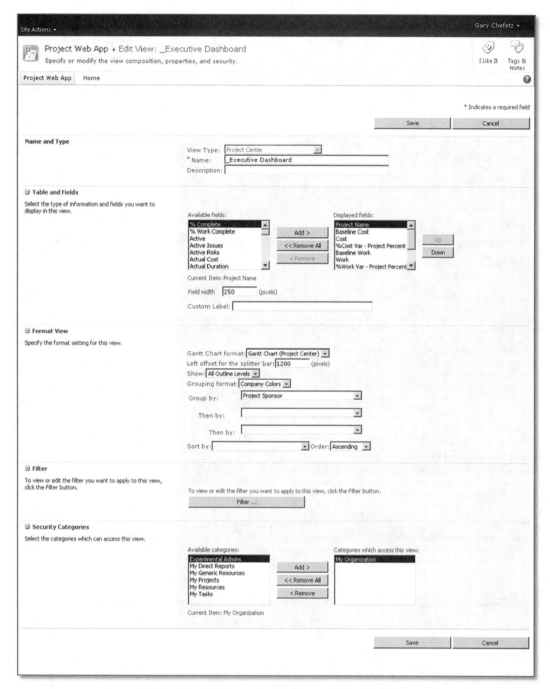

Figure 14 - 23: Executive Dashboard view definition

I created the custom Executive Dashboard view shown in Figure 14 - 23 to give our executives easy access to our company's portfolio of projects so that they can view high-level project information in our custom enterprise project fields. To create this custom *Project Center* view, I completed the following steps:

- I added the *Baseline Cost, Cost, Project Percent Cost Variance, Baseline Work, Work, Project Percent Work Variance, Duration Variance* and *Project Sponsor* fields to the *Displayed fields* list, and then moved these fields into the correct order.

- I applied *Custom Label* values on the fields with long names to display short names for the fields.

- I set the *Field width* value to *1 pixel* for the *Start* field and *Finish* field to limit their appearance in the view.

- I set the *Left offset for the splitter bar* value to *1200* pixels to hide as much of the Gantt chart as possible.

- I selected the *Project Sponsor* field in the *Group by* pick list.

- I added the *My Organization* category to the *Categories which access this view* list.

Click the *Save* button to save your custom *Project Center* view to Project Server. To view the Executive Dashboard view, navigate to the *Project Center* page, click the *View* pick list and select the custom view. Figure 14 - 24 shows the new custom Project Center view.

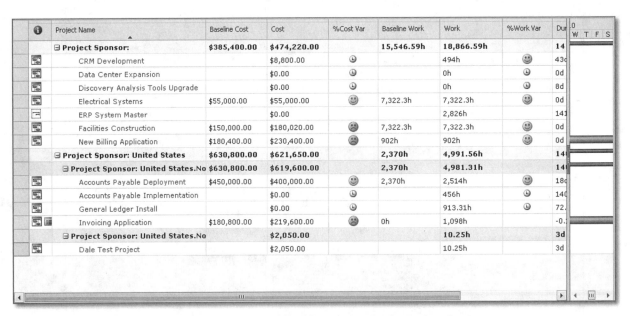

Figure 14 - 24: Executive Dashboard view in the Project Center

Creating a Custom Resource Assignments View

Resource Assignments views help managers to determine the tasks to which selected resources are assigned across all projects in the Project Server 2010 database. To create a new *Resource Assignments* view, click the *New View* button on the *Manage Views* page. Click the *View Type* pick list and then select the *Resource Assignments* option. The system refreshes the *New View* page as shown in Figure 14 - 25.

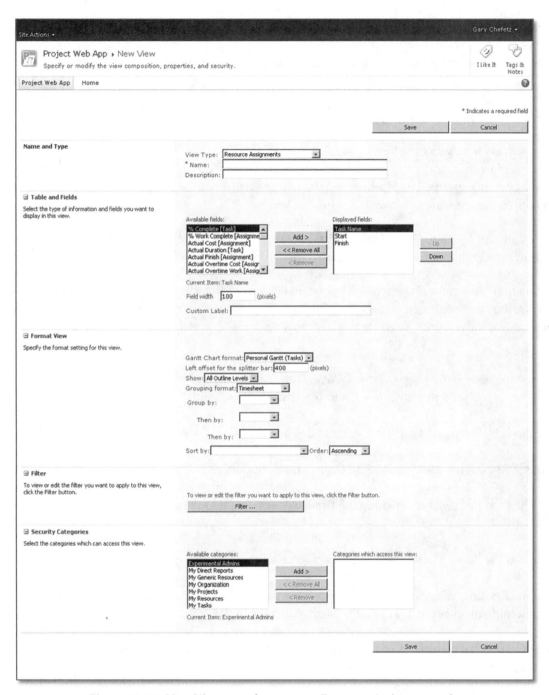

Figure 14 - 25: New View page for a custom Resource Assignments view

Creating a custom *Resource Assignments* view in Project Web App is similar to the process for creating Project and Project Center views. To create a custom *Resource Assignments* view, begin by entering a name for the view in the *Name* field and an optional description in the *Description* field.

In the *Table and Fields* section of the page, the *Available fields* list contains both standard and custom task fields and resource fields. By default, the system includes the *Task Name*, *Start*, and *Finish* fields in the *Displayed fields* list. In addition to the three default fields, you **must** also add the following fields to the *Displayed fields* list:

• Resource Name

- Project Name

Because a *Resource Assignments* view shows task assignments, grouped by resource and then by project, you **must** include the *Project Name*, *Task Name*, and *Resource Name* fields in your custom *Resource Assignments* view. Add any other fields you want to the *Displayed fields* list, and then move the fields into the correct display order. Enter a *Custom Label* value for any field with a long name if you like.

In the *Format View* section, select the items you need in the *Gantt Chart format*, *Show*, and *Grouping format* pick lists. Remember to enter a value greater than 0 in the *Left offset for the splitter bar* field. Because a *Resource Assignments* view shows task assignments, grouped by resource and then by project, you **must** set the *Group by* value to *Resource Name* and set the *Then by* value to *Project Name*.

In the *Security Categories* section, remember to add at least one category to the *Categories which access this view* list. Figure 14 - 26 shows the definition for a custom *Resource Assignments* view.

I created the custom _Assignment Owner view shown in Figure 14 - 26 to display the name of the person who reports task progress on the *Tasks* page for each task assignment, whether the resource him/herself, or a "proxy" who reports progress on behalf of the resource. To create this custom *Resource Assignments* view, I completed the following steps:

- I added the *Assignment Owner, Baseline Work, Work, Actual Work, Remaining Work, Project Name,* and *Resource Name* fields to the *Displayed fields* list, and then moved these fields into the correct order.

- I set the *Left offset for the splitter bar* value to *800* pixels.

- In the *Show* pick list, I selected the *All Outline Levels* option.

- I selected the *Resource Name* field in the *Group by* pick list and selected the *Project Name* field in the *Then by* pick list.

- I selected the *Resource Name* field in the *Sort by* pick list.

- I put the *Resource Name* field and the *Project Name* field at the end of the list and set these to 1 pixel width in order to hide them as much as possible as they display in the grouping.

- I selected the *Task Name* field and increased the pixel width to 400 to better display the name of the task and the values in the grouping fields.

- I added the *My Organization, My Projects,* and *My Resources* categories to the *Categories which access this view* list.

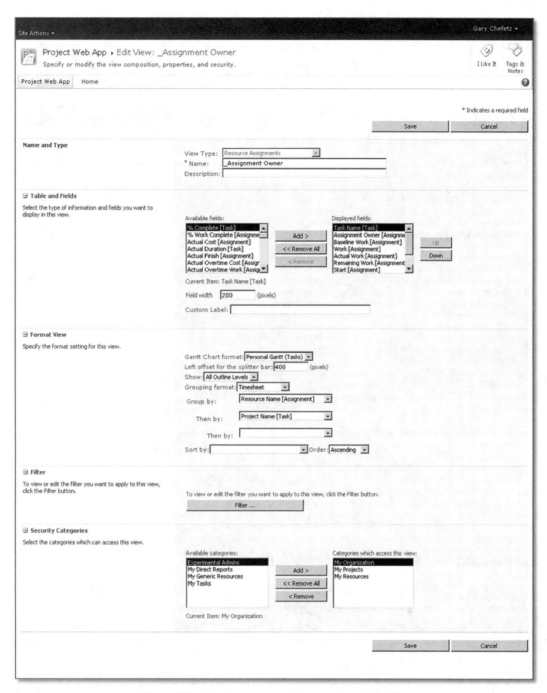

Figure 14 - 26: _Assignment Owner view definition

Click the *Save* button when finished. To access a *Resource Assignments* view, navigate to the *Resource Center* page and select the option checkbox to the left of each resource whose task assignments you want to see. Click the *Resource Assignments* button from the *Navigate* section of the *Resources* ribbon. On the *Resource Assignments* page, click the *View* pick list and select the custom view. Figure 14 - 27 shows the new custom *Resource Assignments* view named _Assignment Owner.

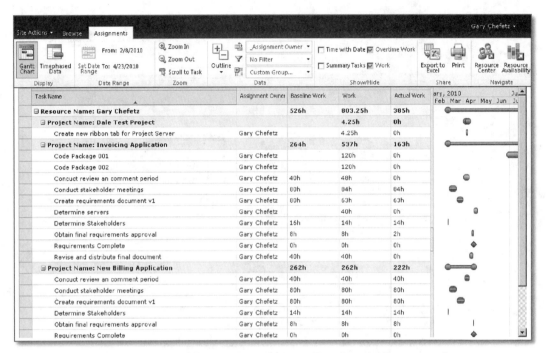

Figure 14 - 27: _Assignment Owner custom Resource Assignments view

Creating a Custom Resource Center View

The *Resource Center* page provides an interface for resource managers and Project Server administrators to manage enterprise resources. If you defined any custom enterprise resource fields in your Project Server 2010 system, then *Resource Center* views are the ideal location in which to display these custom fields. To create a new *Resource Center* view, click the *New View* button on the *Manage Views* page. Click the *View Type* pick list and then select the *Resource Center* option. The system refreshes the *New View* page as shown in Figure 14 - 28.

Creating a custom *Resource Center* view in Project Web App is very similar to creating *Project, Project Center*, and *Resource Assignments* views. To create a custom *Resource Center* view, begin by entering a name for the view in the *Name* field and an optional description in the *Description* field. In the *Table and Fields* section of the page, the *Available fields* list contains both standard and custom resource fields. The only required field in the *Displayed fields* list is the *Resource Name* field. Add additional fields to the *Displayed fields* list and format each field, as needed. Select the options you want in both the *Format View* and *Filter* sections of the page.

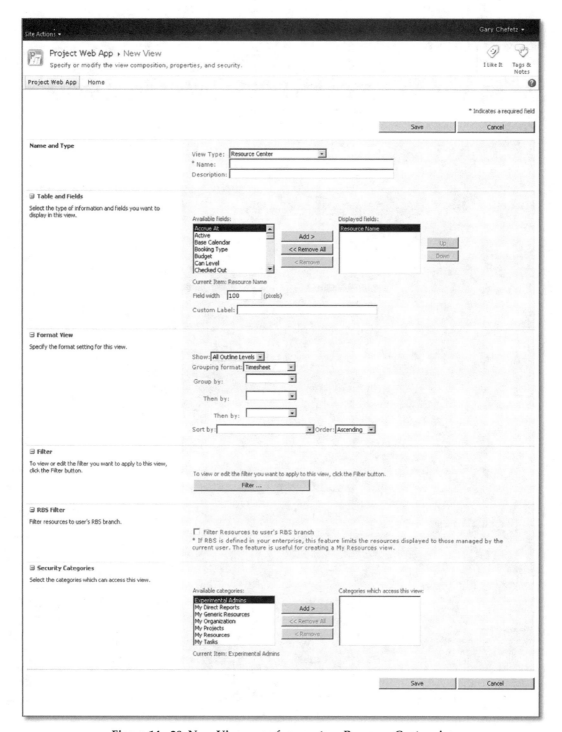

Figure 14 - 28: New View page for a custom Resource Center view

Notice the *RBS Filter* section near the bottom of the *New View* page shown in Figure 14 - 28. In this section, select the *Filter Resources to user's RBS branch* option to limit the resources displayed in the view to only those managed by the current user who is accessing the *Resource Center* view. This option is useful only if you populated the lookup table in the *RBS* field and specified an RBS value for each resource in the enterprise resource pool. In the *Security Categories* section, remember to add at least one category to the *Categories which access this* list. Figure 14 - 29 shows the definition for a custom *Resource Center* view.

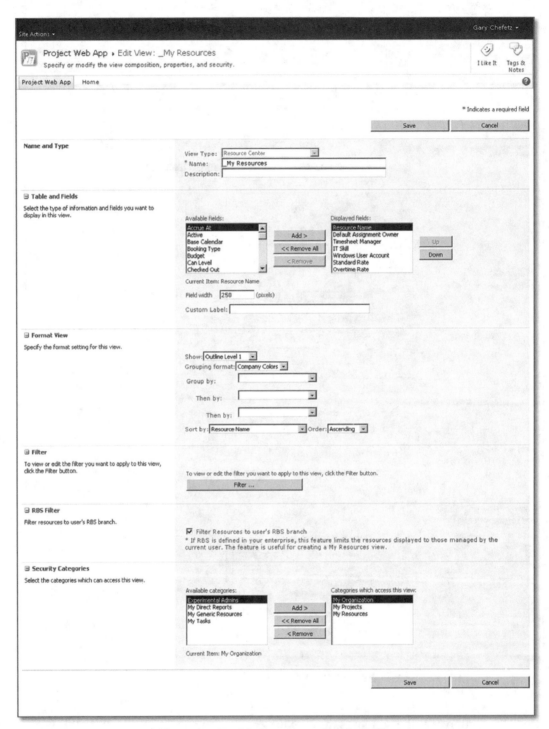

Figure 14 - 29: _My Resources view definition

I created the custom _ My Resources view shown in Figure 14 - 29 for resource managers to display the standard and custom fields for the resources that report to them. To create this custom *Resource Center* view, I did the following:

- I added the *Default Assignment Owner, Timesheet Manager, IT Skill, Windows User Account, Standard Rate,* and *Overtime Rate* fields to the *Displayed fields* list.

- I applied the *Proxy* custom label to the *Default Assignment Owner* to narrow the width of the column.

- I applied *Ascending* sorting on the *Resource Name* field.

- I selected the *Filter Resources to user's RBS branch* option to limit the resources displayed in the view to only those managed by the current user who is accessing the *Resource Center* view.

- I added the *My Organization, My Projects,* and *My Resources* categories to the *Categories which access this view* list.

- I added a filter to show only *Active* resources.

Click the *Save* button when finished. To access a custom *Resource Center* view, navigate to the *Resource Center* page. Click the *View* pick list and select the custom view. Figure 14 - 30 shows the _My Resources custom *Resource Center* view.

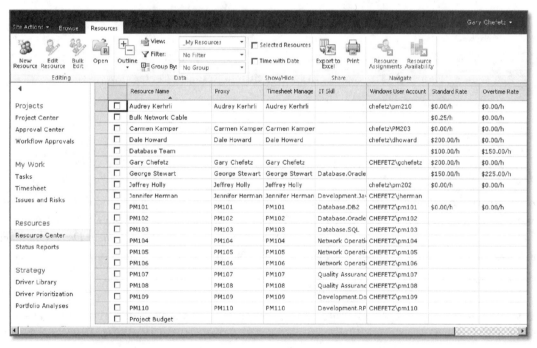

Figure 14 - 30: _My Resources custom Resource Center view

Earlier in this module, I demonstrated how to create a new custom view by copying an existing view. In the following example, I create a custom *Resource Center* view that displays only *Generic* resources. I copied the *All Resources* view in the *Resource Center* section of the *Manage Views* page and renamed it _ Generic Resources. To edit the _ Generic Resources view, I click the name of the view in the *Manage Views* page. The system displays an *Edit View* page that is identical in every way to the *New View* page, except the system locks the *Resource Center* item on the *View Type* pick list. While editing this new view, I remove irrelevant fields from the *Displayed fields* list and add relevant fields, and then create a custom filter that uses the following criteria: **Generic = Yes**. Figure 14 - 31 shows the resulting _Generic Resources view in the *Resource Center* page.

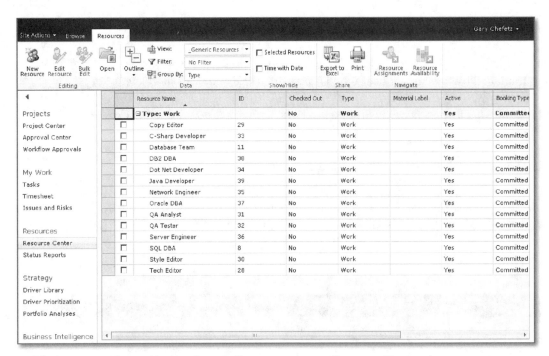

Figure 14 - 31: _Generic Resources custom Resource Center view

Modifying My Work Views

The *My Work* section of the *Manage Views* page lists two default views: *My Assignments* and *Details*. *My Assignments* is the default view when a team member navigates to the *Tasks* page in Project Web App. When a team member clicks the name of a task on the *Tasks* page, the system displays the *Details* view on the *Assignment Details* page. Figure 14 - 32 shows the *Tasks* page for a team member. Figure 14 - 33 shows the *Assignment Details* page after the team member clicks on a task on the *Tasks* page.

Although Project Server 2010 allows you to create additional *My Work* views, I strongly recommend that you **do not** create any additional views of this type. Adding extra views to the *Tasks* page can confuse team members who must remember to select the correct view on this page. Instead, I recommend that you edit the default *My Assignments* view, as I showed you in Module 11, to reflect your organization's method of tracking progress, and edit the *Details* view if your requirements call for it.

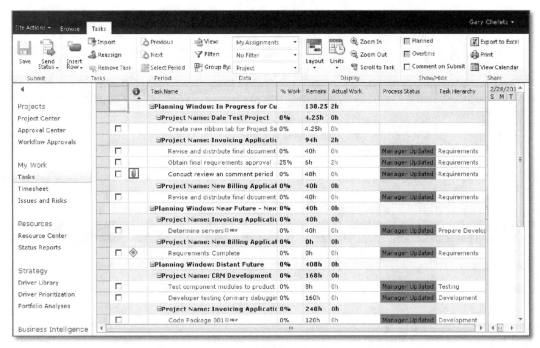

Figure 14 - 32: Tasks page displays the My Assignments view

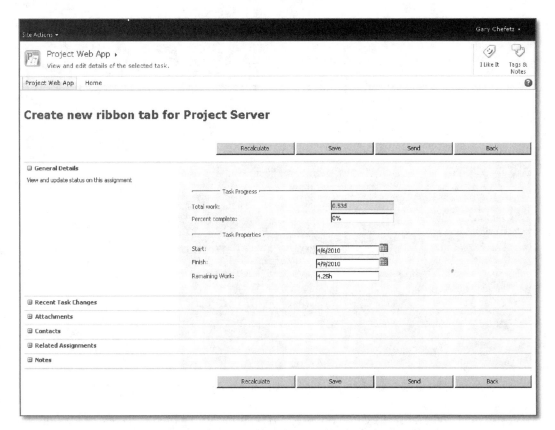

Figure 14 - 33: Assignment Details page displays the Details view

Before you modify the *My Assignments* view, make a backup of the default view and rename it something like *My Assignments Backup*. Modify the backed up view and remove any categories from the view so that the view is no longer visible in Project Web App. Making a backup of *the My Assignments* view allows you to recover the original view if your edits to the original view fail to produce the desired results.

To modify the *My Assignments* view, click the *My Assignments* link in the *My Work* section of the *Manage Views* page. Project Server 2010 displays the *Edit View* page for the *My Assignments* view, shown in Figure 14 - 34.

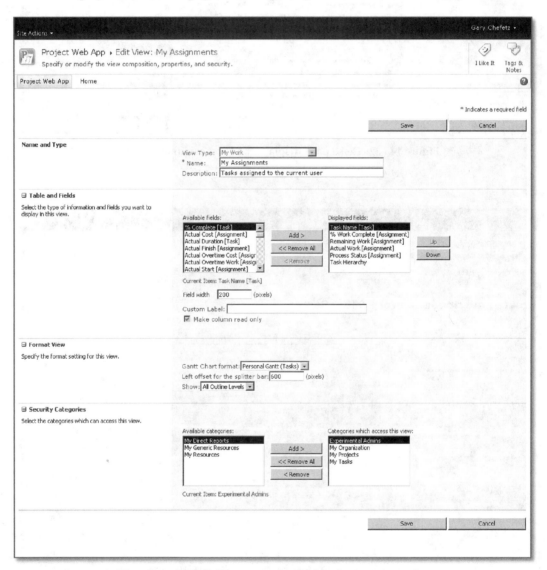

Figure 14 - 34: Edit View page for the My Assignments view

The *Edit View* page for the *My Assignments* view contains four sections with which you are already familiar: the *Name and Type, Table and Fields, Format View,* and *Security Categories* sections. To edit this view, begin by modifying the fields shown in the *Displayed fields* list in the *Table and Fields* section. By default, Project Server 2010 includes the following fields in the *Displayed fields* list: *Task Name [Task], % Work Complete [Assignment], Start [Assignment], Finish [Assign-*

ment], *Remaining Work [Assignment], Actual Work [Assignment], Work [Assignment], Process Status,* and *Resource Name [Assignment].* Remove the fields you do not want to display in the view and then add any other fields you want to display. The fields you select in the *Displayed fields* list should conform to the default method of tracking progress you selected for your Project Server instance.

The *Make column read only* option is a very important feature in the *Table and Fields* section of the page. Use this feature to lock any field so that the user cannot change any values in the field. For example, Project Server 2010 does not lock the *Start* and *Finish* fields by default, which means that users can manually change the start or finish date of their task assignments. If you select the *Start* field and then select the *Make column read only* option, you lock the field and make it read-only for users to prevent them from changing the *Start* date of their task assignments.

Specify a *Column Label* value for any field with a long name. For example, you might enter *% W Comp* in the *Column Label* field to shorten the display name of the *% Work Complete* field. Click the *Save* button when finished.

You may also want to edit the *Details* page to include the same fields used in the *My Assignments* view. Unfortunately, Project Server 2010 does not allow you to copy the *Details* view, so you must modify the original view. To modify the *Details* view, click the *Details* link in the *My Work* section of the *Manage Views* page. Project Server 2010 displays the *Edit View* page for the *Details* view, shown in Figure 14 - 35.

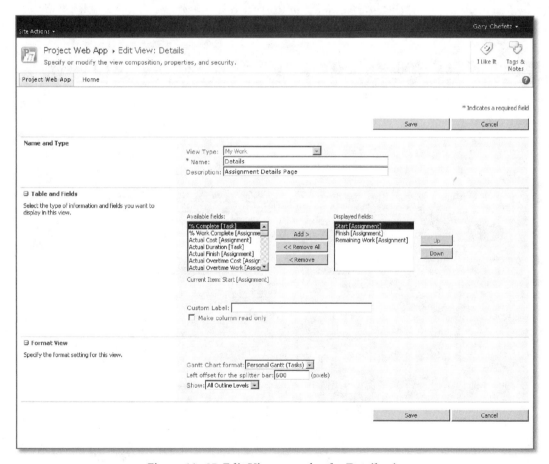

Figure 14 - 35: Edit View page for the Details view

By default, Project Server 2010 includes the following fields in the *Displayed fields* list for the *Details* view: *Start [Assignment], Finish [Assignment],* and *Remaining Work [Assignment].* Remove the fields you do not want to display in the *Details* view and then add the fields you do want to display. Click the *Save* button when finished.

If your organization does not want to allow team members to adjust the *Remaining Work* value, remove the *Remaining Work [Assignment]* field from the *Displayed Felds* list or lock the field by selecting the *Make column read only* option.

Creating a Custom Resource Plan View

Project managers and resource managers use *Resource Plans* to define resource requirements for enterprise projects when the precise resource requirements are not yet known. For example, a project manager creates a *Resource Plan* in a proposed project to show that she needs a specific resource role to work full-time during the first two months and work half-time during the remaining three months of the project. The project manager can then set the *Resource Plan* to create the demand for resources in the system. Using a *Resource Plan* view, the project manager can define these general requirements for each resource role required to execute the project. *Resource Plan* views are an ideal place to feature your custom enterprise resource fields.

To create a new *Resource Plan* view, click the *New View* button on the *Manage Views* page. Click the *View Type* pick list and then select the *Resource Plan* option. The system refreshes the *New View* page as shown in Figure 14 - 36.

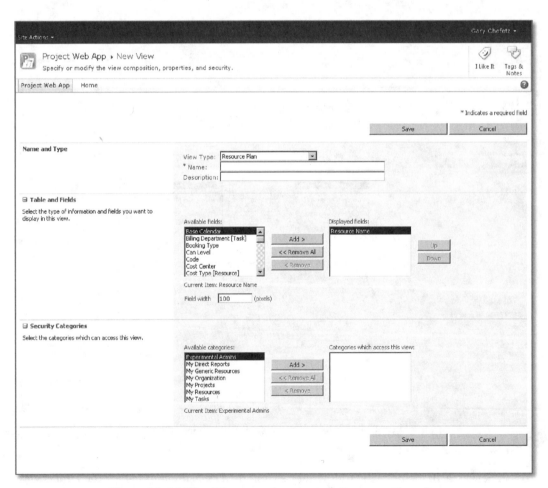

Figure 14 - 36: New View page for a custom Resource Plan view

Creating a custom *Resource Plan* view in Project Web App is very similar to creating *Project, Project Center, Resource Assignments,* and *Resource Center* views. To create a custom *Resource Plan* view, begin by entering a name for the view in the *Name* field and an optional description in the *Description* field. In the *Table and Fields* section of the page, the *Available fields* list contains both standard and custom resource fields, plus built-in and custom enterprise task fields. The only required field in the *Displayed fields* list is the *Resource Name* field. Add additional fields to the *Displayed fields* list as you require. In the *Security Categories* section, remember to add at least one category to the *Categories which access this view* list. Figure 14 - 37 shows the definition for a custom *Resource Plan* view.

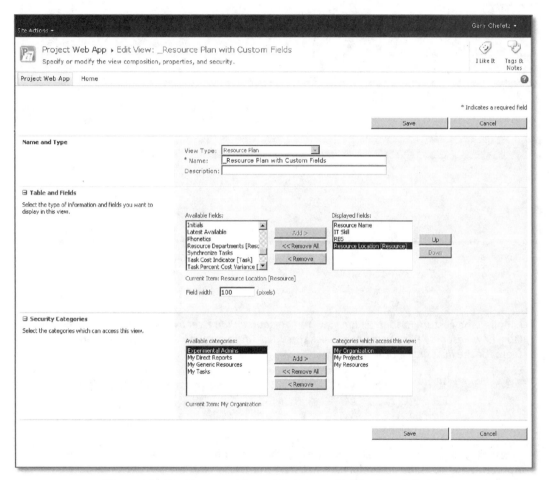

Figure 14 - 37: _Resource Plan with Custom Fields view definition

I created the custom _Resource Plan with Custom Fields view shown in Figure 14 - 37 to display our organization's custom enterprise resource fields to assist a project manager with creating a *Resource Plan* for an enterprise project or proposed project. To create this custom *Resource Plan* view, I did the following:

- I added the IT *Skill, Resource Location,* and *RBS* fields to the *Displayed fields* list.

- I added the *My Organization, My Projects,* and *My Resources* categories to the *Categories which access this view* list.

Click the *Save* button to save your configuration. To access a custom *Resource Plan* view, navigate to the *Project Center* page. Select an enterprise project, and then click the *Resource Plan* button on the *Project* ribbon. The system displays the *Resource Plan* for the selected project. Click the *View* pick list and select the new custom view.

Figure 14 - 38 shows the custom *Resource Plan* view called _Resource Plan with Custom Fields applied to a proposed project. Notice that the custom view shows the *IT Skill, Resource Location,* and *RBS* fields.

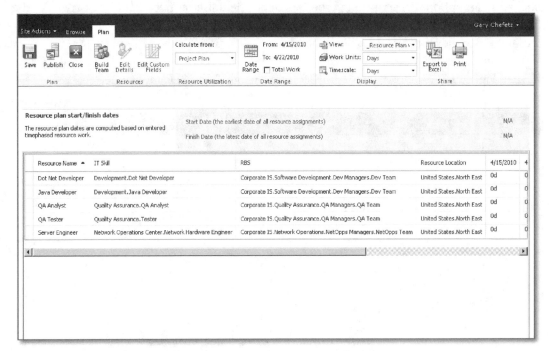

Figure 14 - 38: Custom Resource Plan view

 I applied the custom *Resource Plan* view to a *Resource Plan* already containing resources on the team. On a new *Resource Plan*, users must click the *Build Team* button in the *Resource Plan* page to build the team for the *Resource Plan*.

 Warning: The grid that the *Resource Plan* display uses is not the same as other pages use in Project Web App. This grid does not allow the user to adjust the column widths, it does not respect the column width settings you make while defining the view, and it does not provide tooltips. The consequence of this is a significant amount of horizontal scrolling in the display when you add many fields or fields that contain hierarchical values.

Modifying a Team Tasks View

If you created *Team* resources in your organization's enterprise resource pool, your project managers can use *Team* resources in enterprise projects and proposed projects to assign a group of resources to a task. After the project manager publishes the enterprise project, resources represented by the *Team* resource can view the team assignment pool on the *Team Tasks* page and self-assign these tasks to themselves.

Although Project Server 2010 allows you to create additional *Team Tasks* views, I strongly recommend that you **do not** create any additional views of this type. Adding extra views to the *Team Tasks* page can confuse team members who must remember to select the correct view on this page. Instead, edit the default *Resource Team Assignments* view to include the fields your resources require.

> Before you modify the *Resource Team Assignments* view, make a backup of the default view and rename it something like Resource Team Assignments Backup. Modify the backed up view by removing any categories from the view so that the it is no longer visible in Project Web App. Making a backup of the *Resource Team Assignments* view allows you to restore the original view if your edits fail to produce the desired results.

To modify the *Resource Team Assignments* view, click the *Resource Team Assignments* link in the *Team Tasks* section of the *Manage Views* page. Project Server 2010 displays the *Edit View* page for the *Resource Team Assignments* view, shown in Figure 14 - 39.

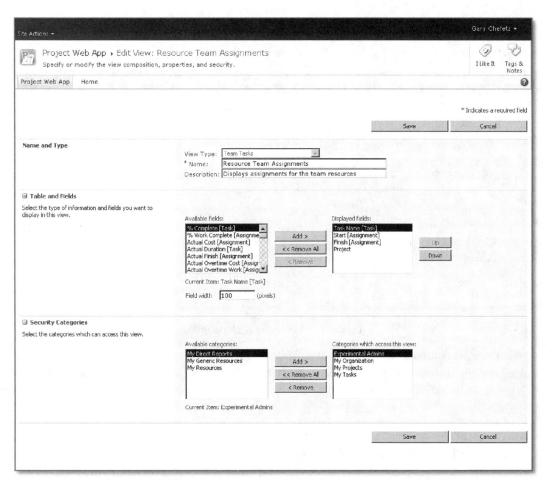

Figure 14 - 39: Edit View page for the Resource Team Assignments view

The *Edit View* page for the *Resource Team Assignments* view contains three sections with which you should already be familiar: the *Name and Type*, *Table and Fields*, and *Security Categories* sections. To edit this view, modify the fields shown in the *Displayed fields* list in the *Table and Fields* section. By default, Project Server 2010 includes only the following fields in the *Displayed fields* list: *Task Name*, *Start*, *Finish*, and *Project*. Remove the fields you do not want to display in the view and then add the fields you do want to display. Move your selected fields into position and click the *Save* button when you complete your configuration.

To access the team assignments, team members must first navigate to the *Tasks* page in Project Web App, click the *Insert Row* pick list button, and then choose the *Insert Team Tasks* item on the pick list as shown in Figure 14 - 40.

Figure 14 - 40: Insert Team Tasks

The system displays the *Team Tasks* page and applies the modified *Resource Team Assignments* view. For example, Figure 14 - 41 shows the *Team Tasks* page for a member of the Team named DBA.

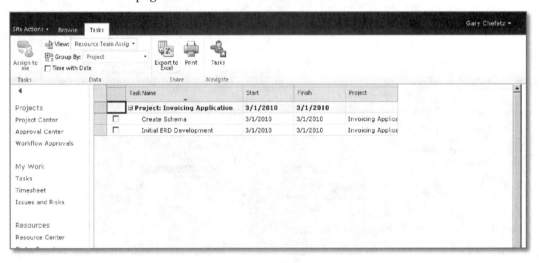

Figure 14 - 41: Team Tasks page

On the *Team Tasks* page, a resource must select the checkbox for one or more *Team* tasks and then click the *Assign to me* button. Project Server 2010 removes the *Team* task from the *Team Tasks* page and moves it to the resource's *Tasks* page. Only one resource can self-assign a *Team* task. Once one resource self-assigns a task, the task is no longer available to the rest of the team.

Creating a Custom Team Builder View

Resource managers who do not use Project Professional 2010 can build a team for enterprise projects using the *Build Team* tool in Project Web App. Project managers or resource managers must also use the *Build Team* tool to build a team in a proposed project. While using the *Build Team* tool, managers can apply *Team Builder* views to help find and select the correct resources for the team. If you defined any custom enterprise resource fields in your Project Server 2010 system, *Team Builder* views are an ideal location in which to display these custom fields. Project Server 2010 ships with four *Team Builder* views: *All Resources, Cost Resources, Work Resources,* and *Material Resources.* You can create new views, or modify the built-in views.

To create a new *Team Builder* view, click the *New View* button on the *Manage Views* page. Click the *View Type* pick list and then select the *Team Builder* option. The system refreshes the *New View* page as shown in Figure 14 - 42.

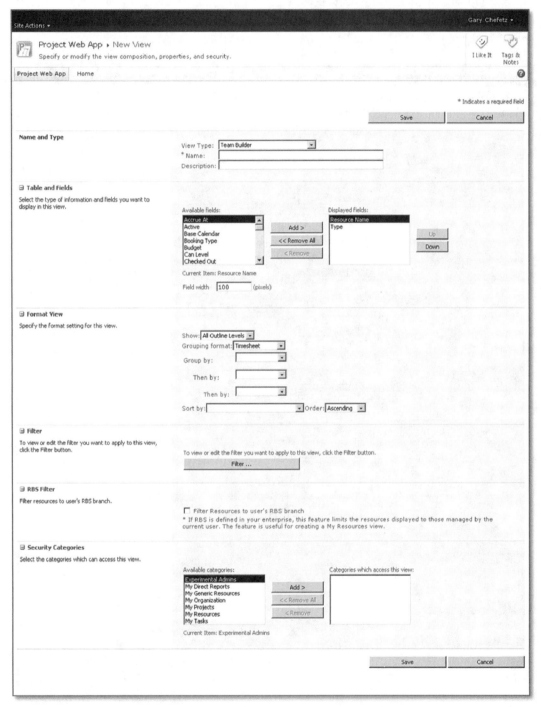

Figure 14 - 42: New View page for a Team Builder view

To create a custom *Team Builder* view, begin by entering a name for the view in the *Name* field and an optional description in the *Description* field. In the *Table and Fields* section of the page, the *Available fields* list contains both standard and custom resource fields. By default, the *Displayed fields* list contains one required field, the *Resource Name* field, and one non-required field, the *Type* field. Add additional fields to the *Displayed fields* list as you require. Select the options you want in both the *Format View* and *Filter* sections of the page.

In the *RBS Filter* section, select the *Filter Resources to user's RBS branch* option to limit the resources displayed in the view to only those managed by the current user accessing the *Team Builder* view. In the *Security Categories* section, remember to add at least one category to the *Categories which access this view* list. Figure 14 - 43 shows the definition for a custom *Team Builder* view.

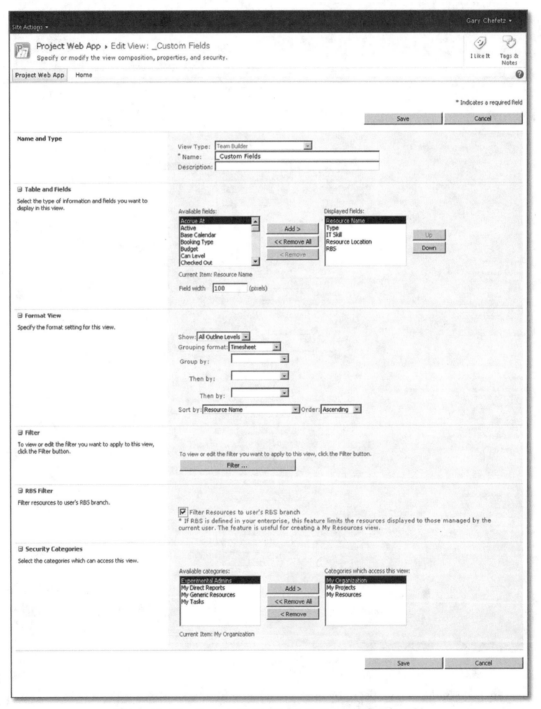

Figure 14 - 43: _Custom Fields Team Builder view definition

I created the custom _Custom Fields view shown in Figure 14 - 43 to display our organization's custom enterprise resource fields to assist a project manager with adding resources to a team in an enterprise project or proposed project. To create this custom *Team Builder* view, I did the following:

- I added the *IT Skill, Resource Location,* and *RBS* fields to the *Displayed fields* list.

- I applied *Ascending* sorting on the *Resource Name* field.

- I selected the *Filter Resources to user's RBS branch* option to limit the resources displayed in the view to only those managed by the current user who is accessing the *Team Builder* view.

- I added the *My Organization, My Projects,* and *My Resources* categories to the *Categories which access this view* list and clicked the *Save* button to finish.

To apply a *Team Builder* view in Project Web App, resource managers and project managers can use either of the following methods:

- To build a team directly on a project, navigate to the *Project Center* page, select an enterprise project or proposed project, and then click the *Build Team* button from the *Navigate* section of the *Projects* ribbon.

- To build a team for a project from a *Resource Plan*, navigate to the *Project Center* page, select an enterprise project or proposed project and click the *Resource Plan* button from the *Navigate* section of the *Projects* menu, and then click the *Build Team* button from the *Resources* section of the *Plan* ribbon to create the *Resource Plan* team.

After accessing the *Build Team* page using any of the preceding methods, click the *View* pick list and select a standard or custom *Team Builder* view. For example, Figure 14 - 44 shows my custom *Team Builder* view on the *Build Team* page.

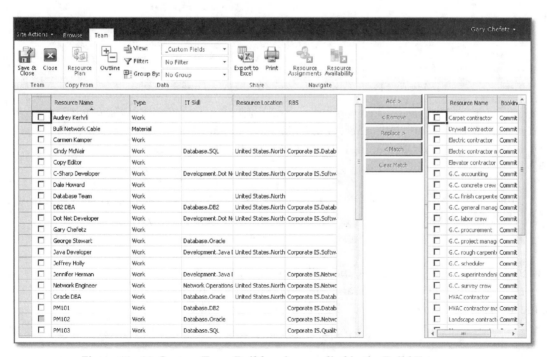

Figure 14 - 44: Custom Team Builder view applied in the Build Team page

Modifying the Timesheet View

If your organization uses the *Timesheet* functionality in Project Server 2010, you may need to modify the *My Timesheet* view. Although Project Server 2010 allows you to create additional *Timesheet* views, I strongly recommend that you **do not** create any additional views of this type. Adding extra views to the *Timesheet* page can confuse resources who must remember to select the correct view on this page. Instead, I recommend that you edit the default view to include the fields required for your organization's timesheet reporting method. Unfortunately, Project Server 2010 does not allow you to copy the *My Timesheet* view to make a backup; therefore, you must modify the original view.

To modify the *My Timesheet* view, click the name of the view in the *Timesheet* section of the *Manage Views* page. The system displays the *Edit View* page for the *My Timesheet* view, shown in Figure 14 - 45.

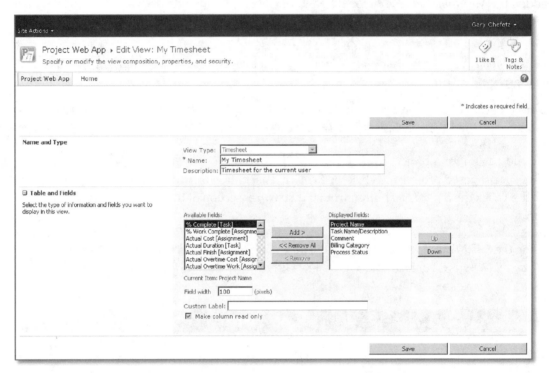

Figure 14 - 45: Edit View page for the My Timesheet view

The *Edit View* page for the *My Timesheet* view offers two sections of information: the *Name and Type* section, and the *Table and Fields* section. By default, Project Server 2010 displays standard task, resource, and assignment fields, plus any custom enterprise task fields containing a lookup table in the *Available Fields* list.

 Project Server 2010 **does not** include custom enterprise Task fields containing a multi-value (MV) Lookup Table in the *Available Fields* list for the *Timesheet* view.

By default, Project Server 2010 displays the following fields in the *Displayed fields* list: *Project Name, Task Name/Description, Comment, Billing Category,* and *Approval Status,* The only required field is *Task Name/Description*. To customize the *My Timesheet* view, you can do any of the following:

- Remove unneeded fields from the *Displayed fields* list.

- Add additional fields to the *Displayed fields* list.

- Move the fields into a display order.

- Set the column width for any field.

- Specify a *Column Label* value for any field.

- Make any field as Read-Only.

When finished, click the *Save* button.

> **Warning:** If you add the *Remaining Work* column to the *Timesheet* view, this column is locked for data entry **unless** your organization uses the *Single Entry Mode* option in Project Server 2010. With this option enabled, users must enter all time and task progress in the *Timesheet* page, and cannot manually enter progress in the *Tasks* page.

Creating a Portfolio Analyses View

A *Portfolio Analyses* view is one of two new types of views in Project Server 2010 that support the Portfolio Analyses features. The system includes one default *Portfolio Analyses* view, the *Summary* view, but you can create other *Portfolio Analyses* views as your organization requires. *Portfolio Analyses* views appear when you select the *Analysis* ribbon when you analyze cost or analyze resources as shown in Figure 14 - 46. You can modify the existing *Summary* view, or you can create additional views for your users.

Figure 14 - 46: Portfolio Analyses view

Portfolio Analyses views are unique in that there are fields that appear in these views that you cannot control from the *Edit View* page, and there are fields that appear in the view based on the selections that users make when they create a new portfolio analysis. Notice in Figure 14 - 46 that the view displays the *Priority* and *Force in/out* fields. These do not

609

 appear in the *Edit View* page for this view shown in Figure 14 - 47. These two fields are default fields for the view and Project Server injects them into the view. This is not user-definable. Notice also the *Sample Proposal Cost* field. This is the cost constraint field that the user selected when creating this particular portfolio analysis. More importantly, notice in Figure 14 - 47 that the only fields defined in the *Edit View* page are *Project Name, Enterprise Project Type,* and *Workflow Stage Name.* You cannot remove the *Project Name* field.

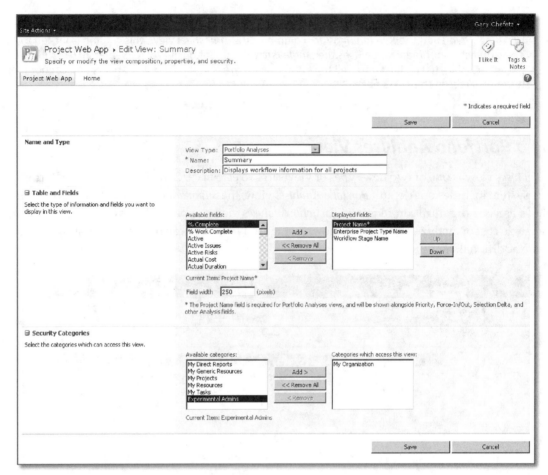

Figure 14 - 47: Edit View page for Portfolio Analyses Summary view

Figure 14 - 48 shows the same *Summary* view in the *Analyze Resources* screen. Notice the addition of the *Original Start, New Start,* and *Has Resource* fields. Project Server injects these fields into the view. The *Original Start* field value is based on the project start date. You use the *New Start* field to move projects within a portfolio analysis exercise, but it does not appear anywhere else in the system as this is a functional field specifically for this purpose.

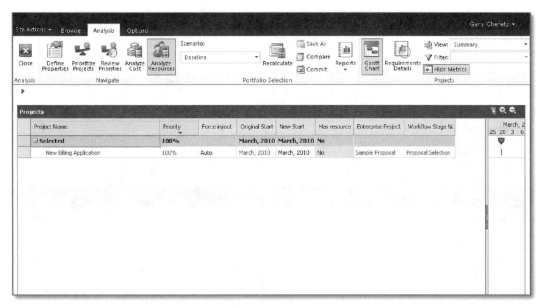

Figure 14 - 48: Portfolio Analyses view Analyze Resources

To create a new *Portfolio Analyses* view, click the *New View* button on the *Manage Views* page. Click the *View Type* pick list and then select the *Portfolio Analyses* option. The system refreshes the *New View* page as shown in Figure 14 - 49.

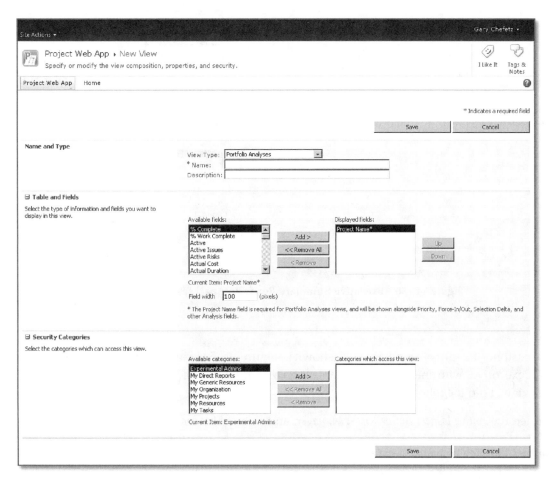

Figure 14 - 49: New View page for a custom Portfolio Analyses view

To create a custom *Portfolio Analyses* view, begin by entering a name for the view in the *Name* field and an optional description in the *Description* field. In the *Table and Fields* section of the page, the *Available fields* list contains both standard and custom project fields, fields reflecting important information in the Project Site for the project (such as the *Active Issues* and *Active Risks* fields), and fields used in the workflow process (such as the *Workflow Stage Name* and *Workflow State* fields). By default, the *Displayed fields* list contains one required field, the *Project Name* field. Add additional fields to the *Displayed fields* list as you require.

In the Security Categories section, remember to add at least one Category to the *Categories which access this view* list. Figure 14 - 50 shows the definition for a custom Portfolio Analyses view.

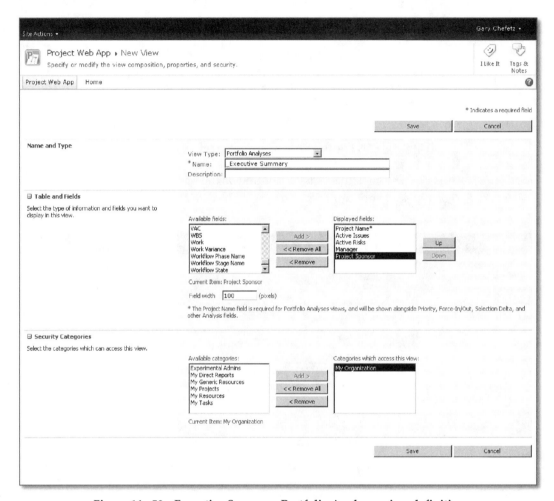

Figure 14 - 50: _Executive Summary Portfolio Analyses view definition

I created the custom _ Executive Summary view shown in Figure 14 - 50 to display the project information fields that can assist our executives with analyzing our organization's portfolio of project requests. To create this custom Portfolio Analyses view, I did the following:

- I added the *Active Issues, Active Risks, Manager,* and *Project Sponsor* fields to the *Displayed fields* list.

- I added the *My Organization* category to the *Categories which access this view* list.

Creating a Portfolio Analysis Project Selection View

A *Portfolio Analysis Project Selection* view is the second type of view specific to the portfolio analyses capabilities in Project Server 2010. The system includes one default *Portfolio Analysis Project Selection* view, the *Summary* view, but you can create other *Portfolio Analysis Project Selection* views that your users may require. *Portfolio Analysis Project Selection* views appear in the *Select Projects* dialog shown in Figure 14 - 51. These views appear in the *Select Projects* dialog that appears when a user clicks the *Selected Projects* button on the *New Portfolio Analysis* page when a user creates a new portfolio analysis, or when a user clicks the *Define Properties* button from an existing analysis and the system displays the *Edit Portfolio Analysis* page.

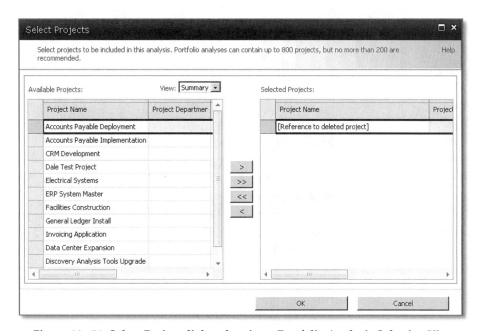

Figure 14 - 51: Select Project dialog showing a Portfolio Analysis Selection View

To create a new *Portfolio Analysis Project Selection* view, click the *New View* button on the *Manage Views* page. Click the *View Type* pick list and then select the *Portfolio Analysis Project Selection* option. The system refreshes the *New View* page as shown in Figure 14 - 52.

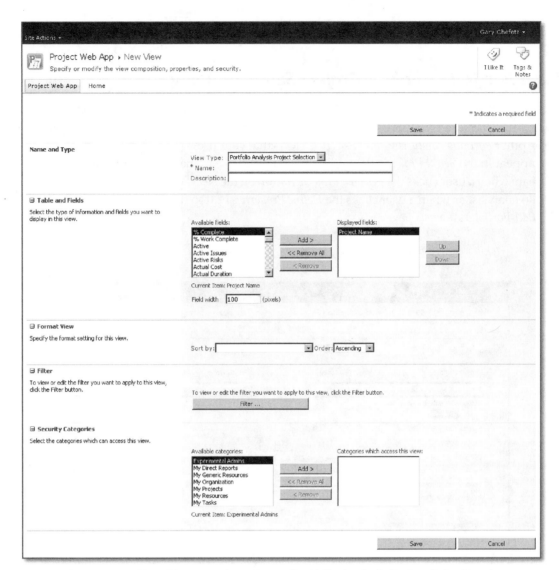

Figure 14 - 52: New View page for a custom Portfolio Analysis Project Selection view

To create a custom Portfolio Analyses view, begin by entering a name for the view in the *Name* field and an optional description in the *Description* field. In the *Table and Fields* section of the page, the *Available fields* list contains both standard and custom project fields, fields used in the Project Site (such as the *Active Issues* and *Active Risks* fields), and fields used in the workflow approval process (such as the *Workflow Stage Name* and *Workflow State* fields). By default, the *Displayed fields* list contains one required field, the *Project Name* field. Add additional fields to the *Displayed fields* list as you require.

Understanding Enterprise Views in Project Professional 2010

Many Project Professional 2010 users define a view as a "way of looking at our project data." In that regard, we are right. However, the software generally defines a view as follows:

View = Table + Filter + Group + Screen

In order to extract meaningful information from projects, you may need to create custom enterprise views so that your project managers can open a project and apply a view which allows them to:

- See the columns of data that they require (the Table).

- See only specific data rows (the Filter).

- See the data grouped by a specific attribute (the Group).

- See their project data using a specific layout (the Screen).

After you create custom enterprise views for your project managers, they can click the *View* menu in Project Professional 2010 and select the custom enterprise view.

The *Screen* option that you select determines what appears on the right side of the view. The screen can display a Gantt chart of some type (such as in the *Gantt Chart* or *Tracking Gantt* views), a timephased grid (such as in the *Task Usage* or *Resource Usage* view), or nothing on the right side of the view (such as in the *Task Sheet* view). The screen you select is very important to the effectiveness of each view you create; therefore, give careful thought to the screen needed by users in each view.

Working with the Enterprise Global File

The *Enterprise Global* file is your organization's "library" of custom enterprise objects, including views, tables, filters, groups, reports, etc. Every time a project manager launches Project Professional 2010 and connects to Project Server, the system opens a copy of the *Enterprise Global* file in the background. This gives your project managers access to all custom objects you create, including custom enterprise views.

Before creating a custom enterprise view, table, filter, or group, most Project Server administrators assume that they must first open the *Enterprise Global* and then create the objects directly in the *Enterprise Global* file. Instead, I strongly recommend that you **do not** open the *Enterprise Global* file before you build your custom view. Instead, use the following approach for creating all custom enterprise objects:

1. Open an existing enterprise project read-only.

To open a project read-only, click the *File* tab and select *Open* from the menu. In the *Open* dialog, select the project, select the *Read Only* option at the bottom of the dialog, and then click the *Open* button.

2. In the enterprise project you opened read-only, create the custom view, table, filter, and group.

3. Test the new custom view in the enterprise project to confirm that the view works as you intended.

4. To open the *Enterprise Global* for editing, click the *File* tab and select the *Info* tab. Click on the *Manage Global Template* button in the *Organize Global Template* section of the backstage and select the *Open Enterprise Global* item from the pick list.

5. Use the organizer tool to copy the new custom enterprise view, table, filter, and group from the enterprise project to the *Enterprise Global* file. To open the *Organizer* tool, repeat the actions in Step 4 above, but select the *Organizer* item from the pick list.

6. Close the enterprise project without saving it.

7. Save and close the *Enterprise Global* file.

8. Exit and re-launch Project Professional 2010 and reconnect to Project Server to gain access to the new custom enterprise view, table, filter, and group.

 MSProjectExperts recommends that you always use the above steps to create custom enterprise views. Using these steps prevents accidental "pollution" of the *Enterprise Global* file caused by the typcial experimentation you tend to do while creating the custom view, table, filter, and group.

Adding Custom Views to the Enterprise Global

After creating and testing your new view in the read-only enterprise project, you are ready to copy the new view and its components to the *Enterprise Global*. To open the *Enterprise Global* file, click the *File* tab and select the *Info* tab in the backstage. Click on the *Manage Global Template* button in the *Organize Global Template* section of the backstage and select the *Open Enterprise Global* item from the pick list. The system opens and checks out the *Enterprise Global* file for editing. To add the new view, table, and filter to the *Enterprise Global* file, you must use the *Organizer* tool. Click the *File* tab and select the *Info* tab in the backstage. Click on the *Manage Global Template* button in the *Organize Global Template* section of the backstage, and select the *Organizer* item from the pick list to display the *Organizer* dialog shown in Figure 14 - 53.

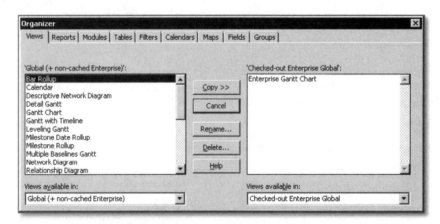

Figure 14 - 53: Organizer dialog

In Microsoft Project Professional 2010, you use the *Organizer* to manage any of the custom enterprise objects that you create. The *Organizer* dialog includes pages for each of the following types of objects: views, tables, filters, groups, reports, forms, calendars, maps, modules, and fields.

 You can use the *Fields* page of the Organizer *dialog* to manage only local task and resource fields. You cannot use this page to manage enterprise fields.

The right side of the dialog lists the enterprise objects currently found in the *Enterprise Global* file. To copy the new custom view from the read-only enterprise project to the *Enterprise Global* file, complete the following steps:

1. Click the *View* tab.

2. In the lower left corner of the *Organizer* dialog, click the *Views available in* pick list and select the read-only enterprise project.

3. In the list of views on the left side of the dialog, select one or more custom views and then click the *Copy* button.

4. Click the *Tables* tab, select one or more custom tables, and then click the *Copy* button.

5. Click the *Filters* tab, select one or more custom filters, and then click the *Copy* button.

6. Click the *Groups* tab, select one or more custom groups, and then click the *Copy* button.

7. Click the *Close* button to close the *Organizer* dialog.

> **Warning:** When you use the *Organizer* to copy a new custom view to the *Enterprise Global* file, **remember** to copy **all** new tables, filters, or groups you created to support your custom view. If you neglect to copy all objects included in the new custom view, Project Professional 2010 displays an error message when a user attempts to apply the new enterprise view to a project.

After copying the new custom views, custom tables, custom filters, and custom groups to the *Enterprise Global* file, save and close the *Enterprise Global* file, and then close the read-only enterprise file as well. Exit Project Professional 2010, then re-launch the software and reconnect to Project Server. You must exit and re-launch Project Professional 2010 to "refresh" your copy of the *Enterprise Global* file and to gain access to the new custom view. In addition, after you add a new view to the *Enterprise Global* file, all of your project managers must exit and re-launch Project Professional 2010 to obtain the new view.

Removing Pollution from the Enterprise Global

A common mistake of many self-taught Project Server administrators is to create custom views, tables, filters, and/or groups while they have the *Enterprise Global* file open. During this process, Project Professional 2010 often copies non-enterprise objects into the *Enterprise Global*. Because the *Enterprise Global* file must contain **only** enterprise objects, the presence of these non-enterprise objects "pollutes" the file. This is why I recommend that you create custom views in a read-only enterprise project, and then copy the views to the *Enterprise Global* file. This process prevents the accidental "pollution" of the *Enterprise Global*.

When the *Enterprise Global* file becomes polluted with non-enterprise objects, the most likely non-enterprise "culprits" are the *Gantt Chart* view and the task *Entry* table. The accidental pollution always happens when you create a new view or table by copying an existing view or table, such as the *Gantt Chart* view or task *Entry* table. The pollution happens when you apply any non-enterprise view while you have the *Enterprise Global* open. For instance, examine

Figure 14 - 53, shown previously. Notice that the only view on the right side, the *Checked-out Enterprise Global,* is the *Enterprise Gantt Chart.* Now look at the *Organizer Dialog* in Figure 14 - 54.

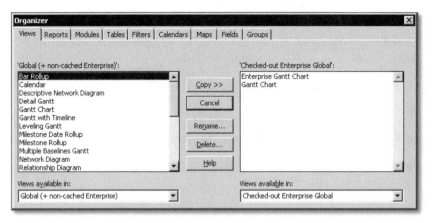

Figure 14 - 54: Enterprise Global containing non-enterprise object

Notice that *Gantt* Chart view is now in the *Checked-out Enterprise Global* file. In order to make this happen, all I did was apply the *Gantt* Chart view in the current project. The system then automatically copied this into the *Enterprise Global* file. This is the way the software behaves. It is treating the *Enterprise Global* file just as it does any other open file. When you apply a view for the first time in a new project, the system copies that view to the current project, and the project then retains that copy of the view until you remove it. That is how the system remembers the formatting you apply to a view. It simply keeps its own copy of it in each project file. When you accidentally pollute the *Enterprise Global* file with non-enterprise objects, the system warns users of Project Professional 2010 about duplicate views or tables in their projects **every time** they open a project. For example, Figure 14 - 55 shows a Microsoft Project warning dialog about a duplicate *Gantt Chart* view in the *Enterprise Global* file. I created this error by saving the *Enterprise Global* file after creating the pollution shown in Figure 14 - 54, shown previously.

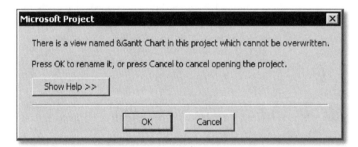

Figure 14 - 55: Warning dialog about a duplicate view

If your users begin to receive warning messages such as the one shown in Figure 14 - 55, it means that your *Enterprise Global* is polluted with non-enterprise objects, and that you must rid the file of any non-enterprise objects. In the example above, the system also complains about the *Entry* table, as that is the table that the *Gantt Chart* view uses, and it gets copied into the *Enterprise Global* file along with the view. The easiest way around this mess is to rename these objects temporarily. When you see the warning dialog shown previously in Figure 14 - 55, click the *OK* button and the system displays the *Rename* dialog shown in Figure 14 - 56.

Figure 14 - 56: Rename Dialog

To clean up the mess, open the *Enterprise Global* and then open the *Organizer*. Make sure that you have an Enterprise view selected before you proceed further. Begin with the *Views* page and look for any view that is a non-enterprise view. Typical non-enterprise views you may see are the *Gantt Chart* and *Resource Sheet* views. To delete a non-enterprise view, select the view from the list on the right side of the dialog and click the *Delete* button. When prompted, click the *Yes* button to confirm the deletion.

After deleting any non-enterprise views, click the *Tables* tab and make sure the *Task* option is selected in the upper left corner of the *Tables* page. Examine the list of task tables shown on the right side of the dialog. Again, look for any non-enterprise tables such as the <u>Entry</u> table. Select and delete any non-enterprise task tables. Select the *Resource* option in the upper left corner of the <u>Tables</u> page to look for non-enterprise resource tables. Select and delete any non-enterprise resource tables.

Click the *Filters* tab. The only non-enterprise filters allowable in the *Enterprise Global* file are the *All Tasks*, *Confirmed*, *Unconfirmed*, and *Update Needed* filters. The system does not allow you to delete the *All Task* filter, but you can delete the other three filters if you wish. If you see any other non-enterprise filters, select them and delete them.

Click the *Groups* tab. The only non-enterprise groups allowable in the *Enterprise Global* file are the *No Group* and *TeamStatus Pending* groups. The system does not allow you to delete the *No Group* group, but you can delete the other group. If you see any other non-enterprise groups, select them and delete them. When finished, click the *Close* button, then save and close the *Enterprise Global*. Exit and re-launch Project Professional 2010.

In addition to copying and deleting enterprise objects in projects and in the *Enterprise Global* file, the *Organizer* dialog allows you to rename objects as well. To rename an object, select it and then click the *Rename* button. Enter a new name for the object and then click the *OK* button.

Using the 4-Step Method to Create a New View

You create a custom enterprise view by following a 4-step method based on the definition of a view detailed previously. These four steps are:

1. Select or create a table.

2. Select or create a filter.

3. Select or create a group (most of the time this step is optional).

4. Create a new view using the desired table, filter, group, and screen.

Select or Create a Table

The first step is to select an existing table or to create a new table if no existing table meets your reporting needs. By definition, a table is a collection of fields or columns. A key question to ask before attempting to create a view is, "What columns of data do users need to see in my new view?" The answer to this question leads you either to select an existing table or to create a new custom table.

> A quick way to create a new table is to copy an existing table and then to modify the copy. MSProjectExperts recommends that you never modify the default tables in Project Professional 2010. Instead, create new tables for your reporting needs.

Select or Create a Filter

The second step is to select an existing filter, or to create a new filter if no existing filter meets your reporting needs. The filter extracts the particular rows of data your users will see.

Select or Create a Group

The third step is to select an existing group, or to create a new group if no existing group meets your reporting needs. In Project Professional 2010, groups are a way of categorizing, sorting, and summarizing the data in a view. Because very few default groups exist in the software, it is very likely that you will need to create a new group as part of creating any new view that has a grouping requirement.

Create the New Custom View

The final step is to create a new custom view by selecting your table, filter, group, and screen for the view. The screen is a very important part of any custom view because it controls how the software arranges the project data. Some of the common screens from which you might choose are the *Gantt Chart*, *Task Sheet*, *Task Usage*, and *Resource Usage* screens.

Notice that the screen choices I just listed are the same as many of the common views contained in Project Professional 2010. When creating a new task view, your screen choice allows you to decide whether to include the Gantt chart on the right of your new view (as with the *Gantt Chart* view), or whether to display the *Task Sheet* without a Gantt chart (as with the *Task Sheet* view).

> **Warning:** Carefully select the *Screen* option before you complete the new view, as you **cannot change** the this selection when editing the view at a later time.

Creating Useful Enterprise Views

Part of your job as the Project Server implementer or administrator is to determine what views your project managers need for communication and reporting in Project Professional 2010. You should meet with your project managers to determine these needs, and then create the necessary custom views. You should also periodically review these requirements to ensure that your system continues to meet your user's needs. It is very likely that your stakeholder requirements demand custom views for reporting project variance, such as cost variance or date variance. You should also consider creating three special views: one to help you administer the system, one to help your project managers publish their projects, and one to help your project managers analyze schedule variance. These useful views in Project Professional 2010 include the following:

- A custom enterprise *Task* view that allows Project Managers to analyze duration variance for each task in a project.

- A create a custom *Enterprise Task Usage* view to allow your project managers better access to important parameters when publishing a project.

- A custom *Enterprise Resource Sheet* view that allows you to edit your organization's custom enterprise resource fields for the resources in your enterprise resource pool.

In the remainder of this module, I teach you how to create each of these types of views. I begin first by creating a variance view used to track task duration variance. Next I show you how to create the *Enterprise Publishing* view in the form of an *Enterprise Task Usage* view. After that I teach you how to create a custom *Enterprise Resource Sheet* view used for editing the enterprise resource pool.

Creating an Enterprise Duration Variance View

Project Professional 2010 allows users to analyze four types of task variance: start and finish variance (date variance), work variance, cost variance, and duration variance. Users can analyze date variance using the *Tracking Gantt* view and the task *Variance* table. Users can analyze work variance using the task work table or analyze cost variance using the task cost table, Oddly enough, Project Professional 2010 **does not** offer any default view or table that allows a user to analyze duration variance.

Duration variance is the difference between the current duration of a task and the original baseline duration of the task, which the system measures in days by default. For example, if the current duration of a task is 8 days, while the baseline duration of the task is 5 days, the duration variance for this task is 3 days (8 days – 5 days). Project managers need to be able to analyze duration variance in their projects, so you should create a custom view for this purpose. You create this view using the four-step process detailed previously.

Remember to open an enterprise project **read-only** before you create the custom view. After you create and test the view in the project, you can open the *Enterprise Global* file and copy the new view from the project to the *Enterprise Global* file.

Select or Create a Table

Before creating a new table, it is always wise to determine if an existing table meets your reporting needs. Because Project Professional 2010 does not include a default duration table, you must create a custom table. The easiest way to create a new table is to copy an existing table, and then modify the copy.

Although the task *Work* table contains work fields, such as work and baseline work, each work field has a corresponding duration field, such as duration and baseline duration. Therefore, you can copy the *Work* table and replace each work field with its corresponding duration field. This makes quick work out of an otherwise tedious process you might go through to determine which duration fields to show in your new *Duration* table.

To create the *Duration* table, apply the *Gantt Chart* view and then select the *View* ribbon and click on the *Tables* button in the *Data* section. Select the *More Tables* item from the pick list, and the system displays the *More Tables* dialog shown in Figure 14 - 57.

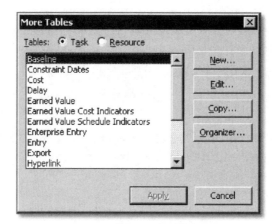

Figure 14 - 57: More Tables dialog

Select the *Work* table and click the *Copy* button. The system displays the *Table Definition* dialog shown in Figure 14 - 58.

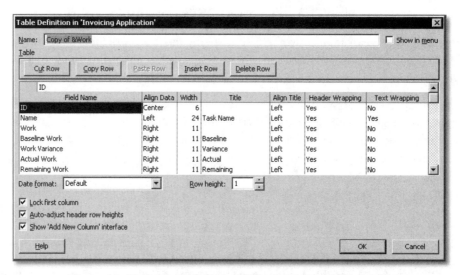

Figure 14 - 58: Table Definition dialog for Copy of Work table

In the *Name* field at the top of the dialog, enter a name for the new table according to your organization's naming convention, and then select the *Show in menu* option. In our organization, we prefix the name of every custom object with

622

"_" to indicate that it is an enterprise object and float it to the top of the menu. Therefore, I enter _ Duration in the *Name* field.

 Prefixing the table name with the underscore character (_) forces it to the top of the list of tables displayed in the *Tables* menu in Project Professional 2010.

After copying the *Work* table to create the _*Duration* table, this new table does not include the *Indicators* field. To insert the *Indicators* field, select the *Name* field and then click the *Insert Row* button. The system adds a new blank row above the *Name* field, as shown in Figure 14 - 59.

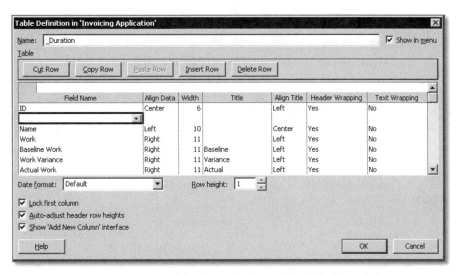

Figure 14 - 59: New blank row in the Table Definition dialog

Click the pick list button in the *Field Name* column for the blank row and select the *Indicators* field from the pick list. For the *Indicators* field, specify the values shown in Table 14 - 1.

Column Name	Value
Align Data	Left
Width	8
Align Title	Left
Header Wrapping	Yes

Table 14 - 1: Settings for the Indicators field

Figure 14 - 60 shows the new _Duration table with the *Indicators* field added to the table.

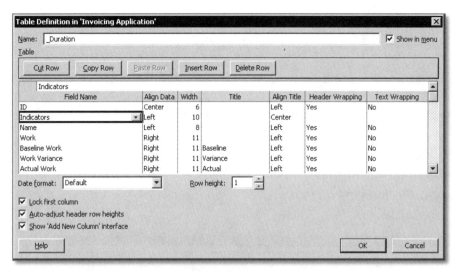

Figure 14 - 60: _Duration table includes the Indicators field

After adding the *Indicators* field to the _Duration table, replace each *Work* field with its corresponding *Duration* field. For example, to replace the *Work* field with the *Duration* field, click the pick list in the *Work* field and select the *Duration* field. Replace each of the *Work* fields with the corresponding *Duration* fields shown in Table 14 - 2.

Work Field	Duration Field
Work	Duration
Baseline Work	Baseline Duration
Work Variance	Duration Variance
Actual Work	Actual Duration
Remaining Work	Remaining Duration
% Work Complete	% Complete

**Table 14 - 2: Replace Work fields
with corresponding Duration fields**

In Table 14 - 2, notice that I replace the *% Work Complete* field with the *% Complete* field. Most people do not realize that the *% Complete* field actually represents the **% Duration Complete** for a task, and shows the percentage of the Duration window "used" over the life of the task.

In the *Table Definition* dialog, remove the value in the *Title* column for every *Duration* field. Click in the *Title* column for each *Duration* field and then press the **Backspace** key to delete the information. **Do not** use the **Delete** key, which removes the entire field.

Because the *Duration Variance* field contains the information most relevant to our project managers, I want to move this field to the immediate right of the *Task Name* field. To move the *Duration Variance* field to a new location, select the field and then click the *Cut Row* button. Select the *Duration* field and then click the *Paste Row* button. Figure 14 - 61 shows the completed definition for the _ *Duration* table in the *Table Definition* dialog.

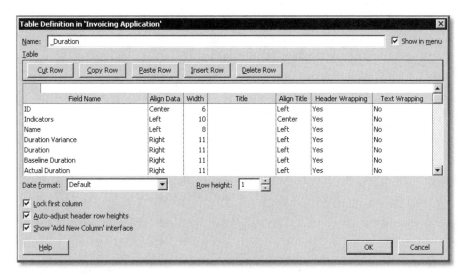

Figure 14 - 61: Completed _Duration definition in the Table Definition dialog

Click the *OK* button. Project Professional 2010 shows the new _*Duration* table at the top of the list in the *More Tables* dialog shown in Figure 14 - 62.

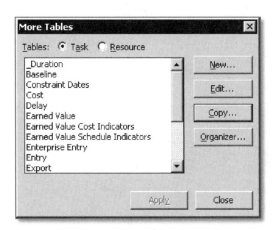

**Figure 14 - 62: More Tables dialog
showing new table**

In the *More Tables* dialog, click the *Close* button. To view and test the new table, click the *Tables* button on the ribbon and select the new _*Duration* table. Pull the split bar to the right to see all of the columns in the new table. Figure 14 - 63 shows the new _*Duration* table for a project that is currently in-progress. Notice that the *Duration Variance* column shows several tasks with *Duration Variance* greater than 0 days, in this case indicating that the duration is taking less time than planned.

	ⓘ	Name	Duration Variance	Duration	Baseline Duration	Actual Duration	Remaining Duration	% Comple
0		⊟ **Invoicing Application**	**-0.14 days?**	**117.57 days?**	**17.71 days?**	**21.01 days**	**96.56 days?**	**18%**
1		⊟ **Requirements**	**-0.29 days?**	**37.43 days?**	**37.71 days?**	**23.74 days**	**13.69 days?**	**63%**
2	✓	Determine Stakeholde	-0.29 days	2 days	2 days	2 days	0 days	100%
3	✓	Conduct stakeholder m	0.57 days	12 days	11.43 days	12 days	0 days	100%
4	✓	Create requirements d	-2.43 days	9 days	11.43 days	9 days	0 days	100%
5	ⅰ	Concuct review an com	1 day	6.86 days	5.71 days	0 days	6.86 days	0%
6	ⅰ	Revise and distribute fi	0 days	5.71 days	5.71 days	0 days	5.71 days	0%
7	ⅰ	Obtain final requireme	0 days?	1.14 days?	1.14 days?	0.29 days	0.86 days?	25%
8	✓	Requirements Complet	0 days	0 days	0 days	0 days	0 days	100%
9		⊟ **Technical Specifications**	**0.14 days**	**45.86 days**	**45.71 days**	**0 days**	**45.86 days**	**0%**
10	ⅰ	First draft tech specs d	0.14 days	11.57 days	11.43 days	0 days	11.57 days	0%
11	ⅰ	Stakeholder meetings to clarify issues	0 days	5.71 days	5.71 days	0 days	5.71 days	0%
12	ⅰ	Revise Tech Specs docu	0 days	11.43 days	11.43 days	0 days	11.43 days	0%
13	ⅰ	Distribute revised spec	0 days	5.71 days	5.71 days	0 days	5.71 days	0%
14	ⅰ	Final revision Tech Spe	0 days	5.71 days	5.71 days	0 days	5.71 days	0%
15	ⅰ	Obtain final Tech Specs	0 days	5.71 days	5.71 days	0 days	5.71 days	0%
16		⊟ **Prepare Development En**	**0 days**	**28.57 days**	**28.57 days**	**0 days**	**28.57 days**	**0%**
17		Determine servers	0 days	5.71 days	5.71 days	0 days	5.71 days	0%
18		Order servers	0 days	1 day	1 day	0 days	1 day	0%
19		Rack servers	0 days	2 days	2 days	0 days	2 days	0%

Figure 14 - 63: _Duration table applied

Select or Create a Filter

After you create your new custom table, you turn your attention to the filter you need for the view. The filter extracts the rows of information your project managers need to see. If an existing filter meets your criteria, you can use the existing filter; otherwise, create a new filter. To see the list of available filters, click on the *Filter* pick list in the *View* ribbon as shown in Figure 14 - 64.

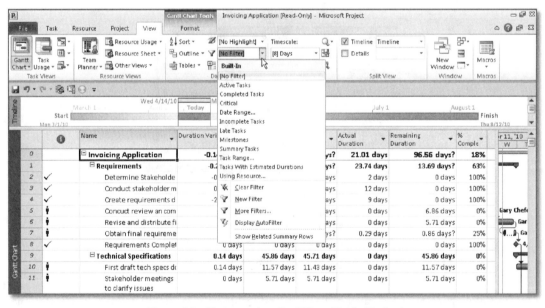

Figure 14 - 64: Accessing the Filters list in Project

Select the *More Filters* item from the pick list. Project Professional 2010 displays the *More Filters* dialog shown in Figure 14 - 65.

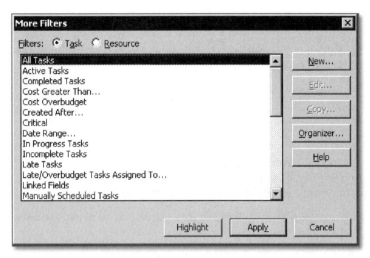

Figure 14 - 65: More Filters dialog

Based on the view requirements, I need to apply a filter that shows tasks with a duration variance greater than 0 days. After examining the list of available filters in Project Professional 2010, I quickly determine that there is no default filter that meets my reporting needs. Therefore, I must create a new custom filter for this purpose. To create a new filter, click the *New* button in the *More Filters* dialog. The system displays the *Filter Definition* dialog shown in Figure 14 - 66.

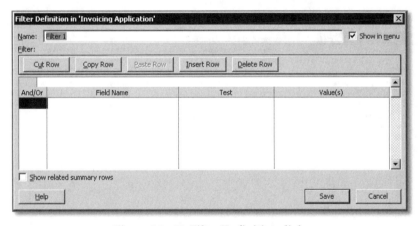

Figure 14 - 66: Filter Definition dialog

In the *Filter Definition* dialog, enter the filter criteria shown in Table 14 - 3.

Name	_Duration Variance > 0d		
Show in menu	Selected		
And/Or	**Field Name**	**Test**	**Value(s)**
	Duration Variance	is greater than	0
Show related summary rows	Selected		

Table 14 - 3: Filter Criteria for the Duration Variance > 0d filter

To create a filter with multiple criteria, add additional criteria on each line in the data grid and select a value in the *And/Or* field for each additional line.

When you select the *Show related summary rows* option in the *Filter Definition* dialog, it guarantees that the filter displays the *Work Breakdown Structure* (WBS) of summary tasks that represent phases and deliverables in your project, even if the summary tasks do not meet the filter criteria.

Click the *Save* button to complete your filter configuration. The system displays the new _Duration Variance > 0d filter at the top of the list in the *More Filters* dialog and selects the new filter. Click the *Apply* button to test the new custom filter.

Figure 14 - 67 shows the project with the custom _ Duration Variance > 0d filter applied. Notice that the filter displays only those tasks with a duration variance value greater than 0 days, indicating all tasks where current duration value is greater than their original *Baseline Duration* value.

	ⓘ	Name	Duration Variance	Duration	Baseline Duration	Actual Duration	Remaining Duration	% Comple	r 11, '10 W T
0		⊟ **Invoicing Application**	**-0.14 days?**	**117.57 days?**	**l7.71 days?**	**21.01 days**	**96.56 days?**	**18%**	
1		⊟ **Requirements**	**-0.29 days?**	**37.43 days?**	**37.71 days?**	**23.74 days**	**13.69 days?**	**63%**	
3	✓	Conduct stakeholder m	0.57 days	12 days	11.43 days	12 days	0 days	100%	
5	ⱼ	Conduct review an com	1 day	6.86 days	5.71 days	0 days	6.86 days	0%	Gary Chefe
9		⊟ **Technical Specifications**	**0.14 days**	**45.86 days**	**45.71 days**	**0 days**	**45.86 days**	**0%**	
10	ⱼ	First draft tech specs d	0.14 days	11.57 days	11.43 days	0 days	11.57 days	0%	
24		⊟ **Database**	**1 day?**	**1 day?**	**0 days?**	**0 days**	**1 day?**	**0%**	
25		Initial ERD Developmer	1 day?	1 day?	0 days?	0 days	1 day?	0%	
26	ⱼ	Create Schema	1 day?	1 day?	0 days?	0 days	1 day?	0%	

Figure 14 - 67: _Duration table with the _ Duration Variance > 0d filter applied

Notice in Figure 14 - 67 that there are two tasks in the Requirements section that show a positive *Duration Variance* values, while the section roll-up is actually -.29 days. This inidicates that although there are late-completing tasks for the Requirements deliverable, this time is made up in other tasks that are ahead of schedule. I could adjust the filter to trap for negative *Duration Variance* values as well as positive ones to capture these tasks as well.

After testing your filter to confirm that it works, press the **F3** function key to reapply the *All Tasks* filter and display all tasks in the project.

Select or Create a Group

Because my organization does not want to apply grouping in the new custom enterprise duration variance view, I do not need to create a new custom group for this view. Later in this module, however, I show you how to create a custom group when you create a custom enterprise *Resource Sheet* view.

Create the New View

Before creating a new task view, it is wise to restore the default *Gantt Chart* view. Therefore, if you have a filter currently applied, press the **F3** function to reapply the *All Tasks* filter. Click the *Tables* pick list from the *Data* section of the *View* ribbon to reapply the default *Entry* table. Once done, you are ready to create a new view.

To create the new enterprise _Duration Variance view, click the *View* pick list from the *Task Views* section of the *Views* ribbon or the *Views* section of the *Task* ribbon and select the *More Views* item. The system displays the *More Views* dialog shown in Figure 14 - 68.

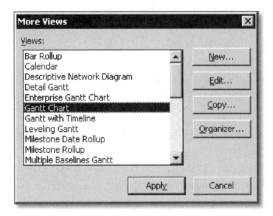

Figure 14 - 68: More Views dialog

In my new _Duration Variance view, I want to include the *Tracking Gantt* chart on the right side of the view. To accomplish this, I copy the existing *Tracking Gantt* view by selecting it and clicking the *Copy* button. The system displays the *View Definition* dialog shown in Figure 14 - 69.

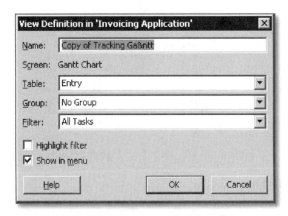

Figure 14 - 69: View Definition dialog

629

In the *View Definition* dialog, name your new view according to your organization's naming convention for custom views. In addition, enter or select the options shown in Table 14 - 4.

Field Name	Value
Name	_Duration Variance
Table	_Duration
Group	No Group
Filter	_Duration Variance > 0d
Highlight filter	Selected
Show in menu	Selected

Table 14 - 4: Options for the new _Duration Variance view

Select the *Highlight Filter* option to apply your selected Filter as a Highlight Filter. When applied, a Highlight Filter displays all tasks, and highlights all tasks that meet the Filter criteria using yellow cell background formatting.

Click the *OK* button to return to the *More Views* dialog, and then click the *Apply* button to apply the new custom view. The system displays the _Duration Variance view, shown in Figure 14 - 70.

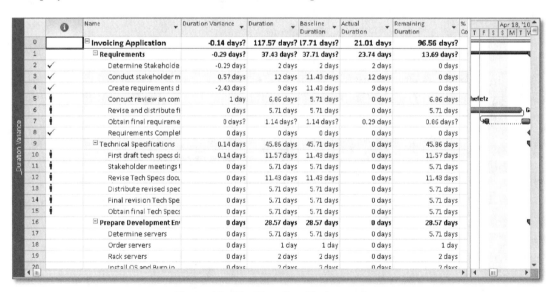

Figure 14 - 70: _Duration Variance view

When you apply a filter as a *Highlight* filter, the system highlights the tasks using the cell background formatting functionality in Project Professional 2010, highlighting the tasks using yellow cell background formatting, which makes the highlighted tasks very visible. After you complete this custom view, open the *Enterprise Global* file and use the *Organizer* tool to copy the new view, filter, and new table to the *Enterprise Global* file.

Creating an Enterprise Publishing View

One very important view you should create for your Project Professional 2010 users is one to assist them with publishing a project. During project publishing, users need to control three factors: the manager of each task, whether to publish each task, and the assignment owner of each task assignment. To create this custom enterprise view, begin by opening any enterprise project read-only. Because you need to be able to see tasks and resource assignments (the resources assigned to each task), initially apply the *Task Usage* view for testing purposes by selecting it from the *Task Views* section of the *View* ribbon. Then follow the four-step method to create the view.

Select or Create a Table

Because no default table contains the columns we need to see in the table, you must create a custom table. The columns that users need to see in the table are as follows:

- ID

- Indicators

- Task Name

- Status Manager

- Publish

- Assignment Owner

Because the task *Entry* table contains three of the required columns, create a new custom table by copying the task *Entry* table. Select the *View* ribbon and click on the *Tables* button in the *Data* section. Select the *More Tables* item from the pick list and the system displays the *More Tables* dialog. In the *More Tables* dialog, select the *Entry* table and click the *Copy* button.

In the *Name* field at the top of the *Table Definition* dialog, enter a name for the new table according to your organization's naming convention and then select the *Show in menu* option. I entered _ Publishing in the *Name* field. Individually select the *Duration*, *Start*, *Finish*, *Predecessors*, and *Resource Names* fields and then click the *Delete Row* button to remove each of these fields.

In the first blank row below the *Name* field, click the pick list button in the *Field Name* column and select the *Status Manager* field from the list. For the *Status Manager* field, specify the following values:

Column Name	Value
Align Data	Left
Width	15
Align Title	Left
Header Wrapping	Yes

In the blank row below the *Status Manager* field, click the pick list button in the *Field Name* column and select the *Publish* field from the list. For the *Publish* field, specify the following values:

Column Name	Value
Align Data	Center
Width	10
Align Title	Center
Header Wrapping	Yes

In the blank row below the *Publish* field, click the pick list button in the *Field Name* column and select the *Assignment Owner* field from the list. For the *Publish* field, specify the following values:

Column Name	Value
Align Data	Left
Width	20
Align Title	Left
Header Wrapping	Yes

When you complete your entries, select the *Show in menu* option and click the *OK* button to close the *Table Definition* dialog. In the *More Tables* dialog, click the *Apply* button to view and test the new custom table. Figure 14 - 71 shows the _Publishing table displayed in the *Task Usage* view in a new enterprise project. Notice that the *Task Usage* view shows each task in the project, as well as the resource assignments for each task.

			Task Name	Status Manager	Publish	Assignment Owner	Details	W	T	F	S
12			⊟ Revise Tech Specs document	Gary Chefetz	Yes	Stephen Sanderlin	Work				
			Stephen Sanderlin			*Stephen Sanderlin*	Work				
13			⊟ Distribute revised specs for review	Gary Chefetz	Yes	Stephen Sanderlin	Work				
			Stephen Sanderlin			*Stephen Sanderlin*	Work				
14			⊟ Final revision Tech Specs	Gary Chefetz	Yes	Stephen Sanderlin	Work				
			Stephen Sanderlin			*Stephen Sanderlin*	Work				
15			⊟ Obtain final Tech Specs approval	Gary Chefetz	Yes	Stephen Sanderlin	Work				
			Stephen Sanderlin			*Stephen Sanderlin*	Work				
16			⊟ **Prepare Development Environment**	**Gary Chefetz**	**No**		Work				
17			⊟ Determine servers	Gary Chefetz	Yes	Gary Chefetz	Work				
			Gary Chefetz			*Gary Chefetz*	Work				
18			Order servers	Gary Chefetz	Yes		Work				
19			Rack servers	Gary Chefetz	Yes		Work				
20			Install OS and Burn in	Gary Chefetz	Yes		Work				
21			⊟ **Development**	**Gary Chefetz**	**No**		Work				
22			⊟ Code Package 001	Gary Chefetz	Yes	Dale Howard,Gary Che	Work				
			Dale Howard			*Dale Howard*	Work				
			Gary Chefetz			*Gary Chefetz*	Work				
23			⊟ Code Package 002	Gary Chefetz	Yes	Dale Howard,Gary Che	Work				
			Dale Howard			*Dale Howard*	Work				
			Gary Chefetz			*Gary Chefetz*	Work				

Figure 14 - 71: _Publishing table applied in the Task Usage view

Notice in Figure 14 - 71 that the system designates my login as the *Status Manager* for every task. This is because I imported and published the project initially. The person named in the *Status Manager* field is the person to whom Project Server 2010 directs task updates from the resource(s) assigned to the task. Project managers can use the *Status Manager* field to take over ownership of selected tasks or an entire project, either temporarily or permanently.

Notice also in Figure 14 - 71 that the system sets the default value in the *Publish* field to *Yes*. The value in this field determines whether Project Server 2010 publishes the information for each task on the *Tasks* page in Project Web App for the assigned resource(s). If a project manager is not ready to publish all tasks in a project, such as when they may have completely planned one phase but the other phases are only in skeleton form, then by setting the *Publish* field value to *Yes* in the first phase, and to *No* for all tasks in the other phases, a project manager can selectively publish only the information ready for public consumption.

Lastly, notice in Figure 14 - 71 shown previously that the system sets each assigned resource as the owner of each resource assignment in the *Assignment Owner* field. The person designated in the *Assignment Owner* field for an assignment is the person who sees the assignment on their *Tasks* page in Project Web App and is the person responsible for submitting task progress on that assignment. If your organization uses a proxy to update task assignments, such as team leads that may have the responsibility to perform this duty, you can specify the team lead in the *Assignment Owner* field for the manager's tasks. As you can clearly see, this custom table becomes extremely valuable to your Project Professional 2010 users in controlling their publishing operations.

Before you can choose any other resource (such as an administrative assistant or team lead serving as a proxy) in the *Assignment Owner* field for an assignment, you must add that resource to the project team using the *Build Team from Enterprise* dialog.

Select or Create a Filter

Because your users need to see all tasks in every project, you do not need to create a custom filter. Instead, use the default *All Tasks* filter in your custom view.

Select or Create a Group

Because your users do not need to apply grouping in this view, you do not need to create a custom group. Instead, use the default *No Group* group in your custom view.

Create the New View

Before creating a new task view, reapply the default *Entry* table by clicking the *Tables* pick list from the *View* ribbon and selecting *Entry* item. To create the new enterprise publishing view, select the *More Views* item from the *Views* pick list. In the *More Views* dialog, click the *New* button and then click the *OK* button in the *Define New View* dialog, leaving the default item, *Single View*, selected.

In the *View Definition* dialog, name your new view according to your organization's naming convention for custom views. In addition, enter or select the following options in this dialog:

Field Name	Value
Name	_Publishing
Screen	Task Usage
Table	_Publishing
Group	No Group
Filter	All Tasks
Highlight filter	Not Selected
Show in menu	Selected

Click the *OK* button to return to the *More Views* dialog. Click the *OK* button in the *More Views* dialog to close this dialog as well. To apply the new custom enterprise view, select it from the *View* pick list. After you complete this custom view, open the *Enterprise Global* file and use the *Organizer* tool to copy the new view and new table to the *Enterprise Global* file.

Creating an Enterprise Resource Sheet View

To simplify your work with managing your organization's resources in the enterprise resource pool, you should create a custom *Resource Sheet* view containing your organization's custom enterprise resource fields. You can use this view to speed up the process of adding new resources or editing the custom information about existing resources in the enterprise resource pool.

Before you create this new custom view, I recommend that you create a temporary blank project by clicking on the *File* tab and selecting the *New* tab, and then double-clicking the *Blank Project* item from the *Home* section in the backstage. In this temporary project, add all or some of the resources in the enterprise resource pool to your project team to create what looks and functions like a temporary resource pool for testing purposes. Apply the *Resources* ribbon and select the *Add Resources* pick list from the *Insert* section, and select the *Build Team from Enterprise* item. Project Professional 2010 displays the *Build Team* dialog, shown in Figure 14 - 72.

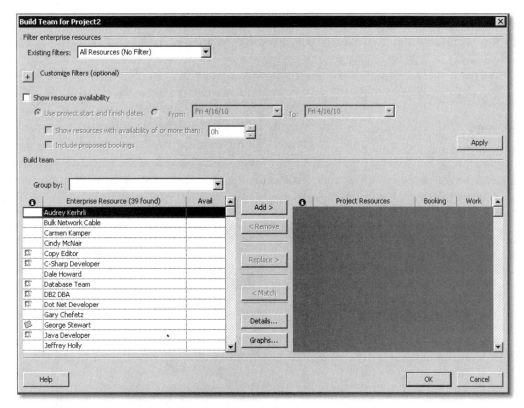

Figure 14 - 72: Build Team dialog for a new blank project

In the *Build Team* dialog, select all of the resources on the left side of the dialog (select the first resource at the top of the list, then scroll to the bottom and press and hold the Shift key and click on the last resource in the list) and then click the *Add* button to add all resources to the project team. Click the *OK* button to complete the team-building operation. Use the *View* pick list to apply the *Resource Sheet* to see the project team in the temporary project, as shown in Figure 14 - 73.

	ⓘ	Resource Name	Type	Material	Initials	Group	Max.	Std. Rate	Ovt. Rate	Cost/Use	Accrue At	Base Ca
1		Audrey Kerhrli	Work		A		100%	$0.00/hr	$0.00/hr	$0.00	Prorated	Standa
2		Bulk Network Cable	Material	Feet	B			$0.25		$0.00	Prorated	
3		Carmen Kamper	Work		C		100%	$0.00/hr	$0.00/hr	$0.00	Prorated	Standa
4		Cindy McNair	Work		C		100%	$0.00/hr	$0.00/hr	$0.00	Prorated	Standa
5	🖫	Copy Editor	Work		C		100%	$100.00/hr	$150.00/hr	$0.00	Prorated	Standa
6	🖫	C-Sharp Developer	Work		C		100%	$100.00/hr	$150.00/hr	$0.00	Prorated	Standa
7		Dale Howard	Work		D		100%	$200.00/hr	$0.00/hr	$0.00	Prorated	Standa
8	🖫	Database Team	Work		D		100%	$100.00/hr	$150.00/hr	$0.00	Prorated	Standa
9	🖫	DB2 DBA	Work		D		100%	$100.00/hr	$150.00/hr	$0.00	Prorated	Standa
10	🖫	Dot Net Developer	Work		D		100%	$100.00/hr	$150.00/hr	$0.00	Prorated	Standa
11		Gary Chefetz	Work		G		100%	$200.00/hr	$0.00/hr	$0.00	Prorated	Standa
12	🖾	George Stewart	Work		GS	dev	100%	$150.00/hr	$225.00/hr	$0.00	Prorated	Standa
13	🖫	Java Developer	Work		J		100%	$100.00/hr	$150.00/hr	$0.00	Prorated	Standa
14		Jeffrey Holly	Work		J		100%	$0.00/hr	$0.00/hr	$0.00	Prorated	Standa
15		Jennifer Herman	Work		J		100%	$0.00/hr	$0.00/hr	$0.00	Prorated	Standa
16	🖫	Network Engineer	Work		N		100%	$100.00/hr	$150.00/hr	$0.00	Prorated	Standa
17	🖫	Oracle DBA	Work		O		100%	$100.00/hr	$150.00/hr	$0.00	Prorated	Standa
18		PM101	Work		P		100%	$0.00/hr	$0.00/hr	$0.00	Prorated	Standa
19		PM102	Work		P		100%	$0.00/hr	$0.00/hr	$0.00	Prorated	Standa
20		PM103	Work		P		100%	$0.00/hr	$0.00/hr	$0.00	Prorated	Standa
21		PM104	Work		P		100%	$0.00/hr	$0.00/hr	$0.00	Prorated	Standa
22		PM105	Work		P		100%	$0.00/hr	$0.00/hr	$0.00	Prorated	Standa

Figure 14 - 73: Resource Sheet view applied to temporary Resource Pool project

635

You use this temporary resource pool project to simulate the "look and feel" of the actual enterprise resource pool displayed in the *Resource Sheet* view. To create the new custom enterprise *Resource Sheet* view, you again use the four-step method.

Select or Create a Table

In Project Professional 2010, no default table contains your organization's custom enterprise resource fields, but the *Entry* table does contain some of the columns your Project Server administrators need to see. Therefore, you should create a new custom enterprise table by copying the *Entry* table. From the *View* ribbon, select the *Tables* pick list and select the *More Tables* item. In the *More Tables* dialog, select the *Resource* option at the top of the dialog and then select the *Entry* table and click the *Copy* button. The system displays the *Table Definition* dialog shown in Figure 14 - 74.

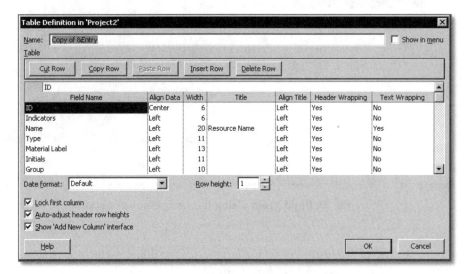

Figure 14 - 74: Table Definition dialog

To manage the custom field values for the resources in the enterprise resource pool, the Project Server administrators in our organization need to see the following fields displayed in the following order:

- ID
- Indicators
- Resource Name
- Type
- Material Label
- IT Skill
- Resource Location
- RBS

In the *Table Definition* dialog, name your custom table according to your organization's naming convention, and then select the *Show in menu* option. I named this table the _Resource Entry table. Using the skills gained in the last three major sections of this module, delete the rows you do not need and add additional rows in the data grid to show all of your organization's custom enterprise resource fields. For each field you add, set your preferred values for the *Align Data, Width, Title, Align Title,* and *Header Wrapping* columns. When you finish, click the *OK* button. In the *More Tables* dialog, click the *Apply* button to view your new Table. Figure 14 - 75 shows the new _Resource Entry table applied in the *Resource Sheet* view.

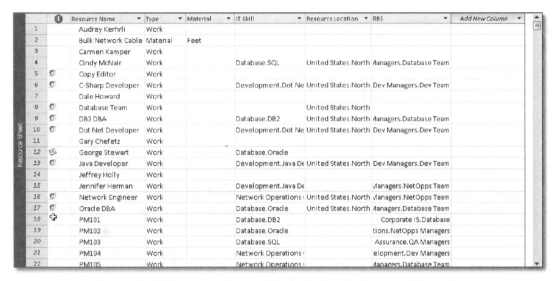

	ⓘ	Resource Name	Type	Material	IT Skill	Resource Location	RBS	Add New Column
1		Audrey Kerhrli	Work					
2		Bulk Network Cable	Material	Feet				
3		Carmen Kamper	Work					
4		Cindy McNair	Work		Database.SQL	United States.North	Managers.Database Team	
5	⚙	Copy Editor	Work					
6	⚙	C-Sharp Developer	Work		Development.Dot Ne	United States.North	Dev Managers.Dev Team	
7		Dale Howard	Work					
8	⚙	Database Team	Work			United States.North		
9	⚙	DB2 DBA	Work		Database.DB2	United States.North	Managers.Database Team	
10	⚙	Dot Net Developer	Work		Development.Dot Ne	United States.North	Dev Managers.Dev Team	
11		Gary Chefetz	Work					
12	✎	George Stewart	Work		Database.Oracle			
13	⚙	Java Developer	Work		Development.Java De	United States.North	Dev Managers.Dev Team	
14		Jeffrey Holly	Work					
15		Jennifer Herman	Work		Development.Java De		Managers.NetOpps Team	
16	⚙	Network Engineer	Work		Network Operations	United States.North	Managers.NetOpps Team	
17	⚙	Oracle DBA	Work		Database.Oracle	United States.North	Managers.Database Team	
18	✛	PM101	Work		Database.DB2		Corporate IS.Database	
19		PM102	Work		Database.Oracle		tions.NetOpps Managers	
20		PM103	Work		Database.SQL		Assurance.QA Managers	
21		PM104	Work		Network Operations		elopment.Dev Managers	
22		PM105	Work		Network Operations		Managers.Database Team	

Figure 14 - 75: Resource Entry table applied in the Resource Sheet view

Select or Create a Filter

Because your users need to see all of the resources in the enterprise resource pool, you do not need to create a custom filter. Instead, use the default *All Resources* filter in your custom view.

Select or Create a Group

Your Project Server administrators want to apply grouping in three different ways: *IT Skills, Resource Location,* or *RBS* value. Project Professional 2010 does not include any default groups that provide the type of grouping you need. Therefore, you must create three different custom groups. In this section of the module, I teach you how to create one of the three groups, and you can use this knowledge to create the other two groups.

To create a custom group, select the *Group by* pick list from the *Data* section of the *View* ribbon and select the *More Groups* item. Project Professional 2010 displays the *More Groups* dialog shown in Figure 14 - 76.

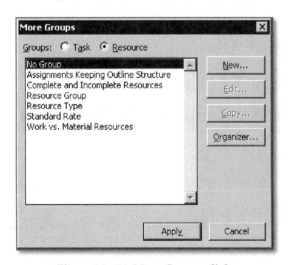

Figure 14 - 76: More Groups dialog

In the *More Groups* dialog, click the *New* button. The system displays the *Group Definition* dialog shown in Figure 14 - 77.

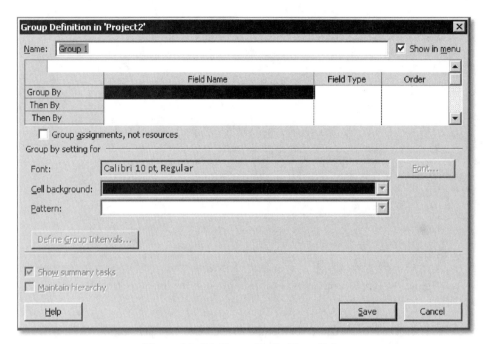

Figure 14 - 77: Group Definition dialog

In the *Group Definition* dialog, name your custom group according to your organization's naming convention and then select the *Show in menu* option. I named this group the *_IT Skill* group. Click the pick list button for the *Group By* line in the *Field Name* column, and select the first field you want to group by. In my case, I selected the *IT Skill* field. Figure 14 - 78 shows the completed *Group Definition* dialog for the *_IT Skill* group.

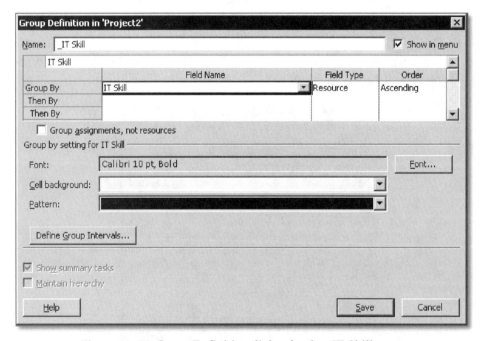

Figure 14 - 78: Group Definition dialog for the _IT Skill group

Notice in the *Group Definition* dialog that Project Professional 2010 allows you to create multiple levels of grouping by selecting other fields on the *Then By* lines in the data grid.

In the *Group Definition* dialog, you can create a group specifically intended for use in the *Resource Usage* view. Select the *Group assignments not resources* option and then select the *Assignment* item in the *Field Type* pick list.

In the *Group Definition* dialog, leave all options set to their default values, and then click the *OK* button. In the *More Groups* dialog, click the *Apply* button to apply the new custom group. Figure 14 - 79 shows the *_IT Skill* group applied to the resources in the temporary resource pool project. Notice how nicely the system groups resources by *IT Skill*.

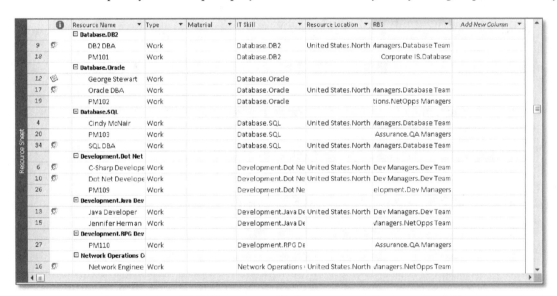

Figure 14 - 79: _IT Skill group applied to temporary Resource Pool file

Notice that the system uses the literal values from the *IT Skill* field as grouping labels. If you enter information in the *Description* field when you setup your lookup table, the system uses these values for the groupling labels instead.

Using the skills you gained in this section of the module, create all other groups required by your Project Server administrators. For my organization, I also created a *_RBS group* and a *_Resource Location* group.

Create the New View

Before creating a new *Resource* view, restore the default *Resource Sheet* view by selecting the *No Group* item from the *Groups* pick list to remove grouping from the list of resources. Select the *Entry* table from the *Tables* pick list as well. To create the new enterprise *Resource Sheet* view, select the *More Views* item from the *Views* pick list. In the *More Views* dialog, click the *New* button and then click the *OK* button in the *Define New View* dialog. In the dialog, name your new view according to your organization's naming convention for custom views. In addition, enter or select the following options in this dialog:

Field Name	Value
Name	_ Resource Sheet
Screen	Resource Sheet
Table	_Resource Entry
Group	_ IT Skill
Filter	All Resources
Highlight filter	Not Selected
Show in menu	Selected

Click the *OK* button to return to the *More Views* dialog. Click the *Apply* button to apply the new view. After you complete and test this custom view, open the *Enterprise Global* file and use the *Organizer* tool to copy the new view, new table, and the new groups from the temporary resource pool file to the *Enterprise Global* file. Close the temporary resource pool file and do not save the changes. Exit Project Professional 2010 and re-launch the software to see and use all of your new views, tables, filters, and groups.

Module 15

Managing Project Sites

Learning Objectives

After completing this module, you will be able to:

- Understand the SharePoint content management model
- Set Project Site provisioning options
- Manage Project Sites and their contents
- Create a new Project Site template

Inside Module 15

Introducing SharePoint **643**

Understanding the SharePoint Model 644

Managing the SharePoint/Project Server Connection **650**

Managing Project Site Provisioning 650

Managing Project Sites.. 653

Bulk Updating Project Sites... 656

Modifying Project Sites **656**

Managing List and Library Metadata 657

Managing Views of List and Library Items.. 674

Managing List and Library Settings.. 692

Creating New Lists and Libraries... 720

Creating and Editing Pages.. 734

Managing Project Site Settings... 744

Introducing SharePoint

SharePoint Foundation and SharePoint Server 2010 are core technologies in Microsoft's EPM solution. While SharePoint Foundation provides the building blocks for the Project Web App interface and *Project Sites* in Project Server 2010, SharePoint Server 2010 provides a collection of enterprise features such as Excel Services and Business Connectivity Services, an extensive library of Web Parts, and expanded searching capabilities.

All pages that users see in Project Web App are SharePoint pages. As demonstrated in Figure 15 - 1, SharePoint Foundation provides the web interface for PWA and the *Project Sites* that include features such as Risks, Issues, Documents, and Deliverables. The Project Server 2010 application builds upon SharePoint Foundation by adding a project and resource scheduling engine, the mechanisms for task updating, and a project and resource reporting engine. SharePoint Server 2010 provides business intelligence and line of business connectivity features, plus many other additional features, such as a large library of web parts.

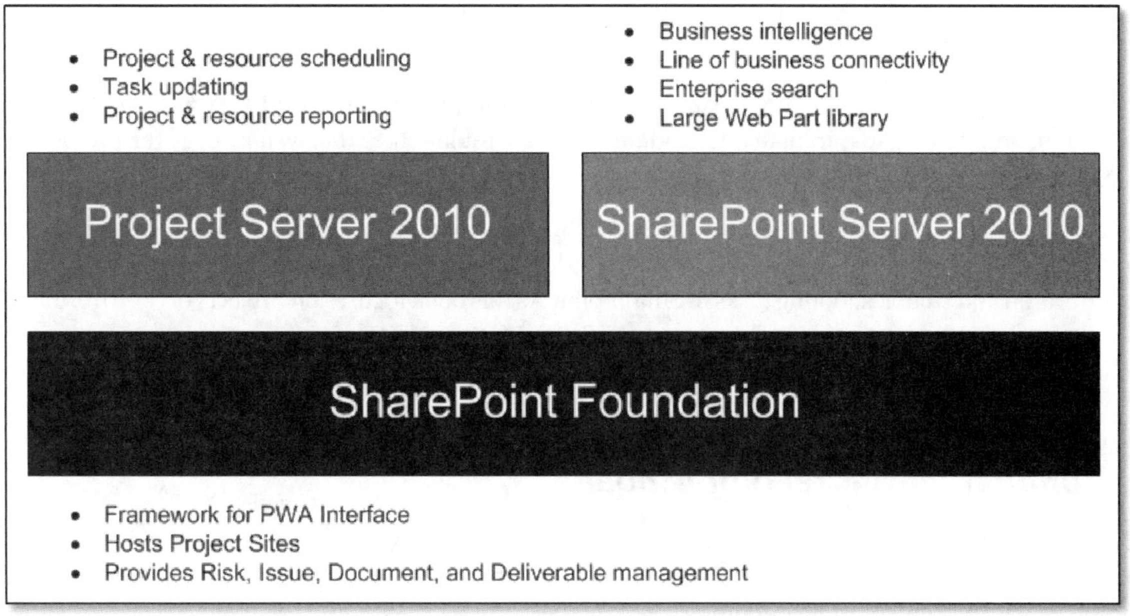

Figure 15 - 1: SharePoint Project Server features

If you configure Project Server to provision *Project Sites* automatically, then the system provisions a new *Project Site* when a project manager publishes a new project for the first time. If you configure Project Server to provision *Project Sites* manually, then the system provisions a new *Project Site* only when the project manager chooses to do so. The *Project Site* provides a central collaboration area for the project team. Figure 15 - 2 represents the publishing and provisioning sequence.

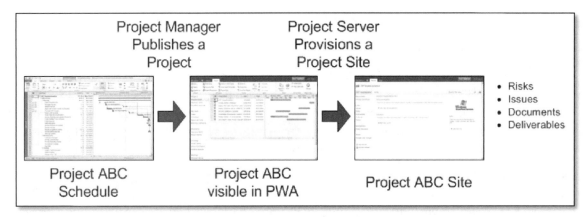

Figure 15 - 2: Publishing and provisioning sequence

Because Project Server 2010 is a SharePoint application, you must be confident working within the SharePoint envelope to be effective as a Project Server administrator. The first topics in this module familiarize you with the basic SharePoint model, including some of the core concepts of collaboration and content management. Next, you must understand how to work with the tools within the PWA interface to control SharePoint provisioning for new *Project Sites* and for managing existing sites.

You should also understand ways that you can modify an existing *Project Site*, the PWA web site (which is also a SharePoint site), and how to manipulate and update the site template that the system uses for provisioning new *Project Sites*.

It is extremely helpful for you to understand general SharePoint administration and to become familiar with the *SharePoint Central Administration* web site. You should understand the SharePoint architecture and how to perform basic configuration and troubleshooting tasks in SharePoint. As this book focuses on Project Server 2010, the following provides "bare bones" knowledge to get you moving in the right direction. To dive deeper into working with SharePoint technologies, you should consider acquiring additional reference materials and training.

Understanding the SharePoint Model

At a high level, SharePoint is a family of tools for creating and managing web sites for teams to collaborate and share many different types of structured and unstructured information or content Table 15 - 1 lists examples of both structured and unstructured content in SharePoint.

Structured Content	Unstructured Content
• Task lists	• Documents
• Risk logs	• Forms
• Issue logs	• Web pages
• Event calendars	• Images
• Discussion forums	• Wiki pages
• Surveys	

Table 15 - 1: Structured and unstructured content examples

Structured content is a collection of data stored and organized in tables, whereas **unstructured content** is stored in files, such as Microsoft Office Word or Excel files. SharePoint stores structured content in SharePoint lists, and unstructured content in SharePoint libraries.

Although SharePoint exists in two distinct flavors, SharePoint Foundation and Microsoft SharePoint Server 2010, many people use the word SharePoint as a generic term to describe the collection of storage and collaboration features offered by this family of products. Figure 15 - 3 illustrates the SharePoint architecture, with SharePoint Foundation serving as a base layer for both Project Server and SharePoint Server.

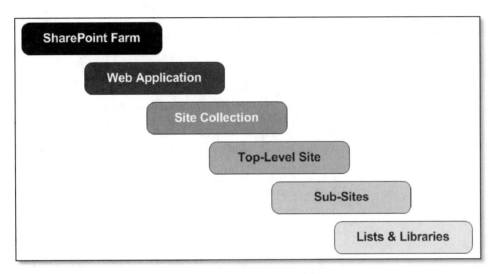

Figure 15 - 3: SharePoint architecture

SharePoint helps to organize data and enables collaboration. Regardless of the type of data, there are several main concepts that recur throughout the system, including the following:

- Storage

- Administration

- Security

- Templates

- Recycle bins

- Metadata

- Version Control

- Alerts

- Workflow

Storage

SharePoint stores and organizes your content according to the nested hierarchical model shown in Figure 15 - 4.

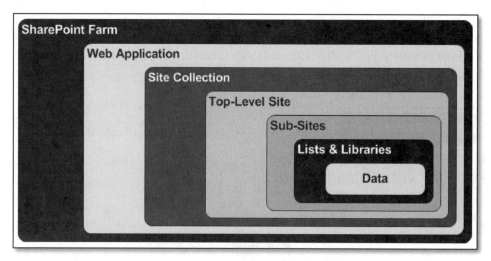

Figure 15 - 4: SharePoint storage hierarchy

SharePoint Farm: A collection of one or more servers that work together to serve SharePoint functionality.

Web Application: An IIS web site extended with SharePoint to host Site Collections.

Site Collection: A collection of SharePoint sites that contains a top-level site and optional child sites, and is the base unit for ownership, security, and recovery.

Top-Level Site: The top-most user-accessible site in a SharePoint Site Collection, which can contain pages, lists, libraries, and child sites.

Sub-Sites: Child sites in a SharePoint Site Collection organized in a hierarchical fashion below a Top-Level site, and can contain pages, lists, libraries, and other child sites.

Lists and Libraries: Containers that hold structured and unstructured data within a SharePoint site.

Each subsequent level within this storage and management structure has an increasing level of granularity for administration, security, and control over the data stored within.

Administration

SharePoint provides an array of administration tools to help you manage the system and the data contained in the system.

SharePoint Central Administration web site: A web-based tool for administering a SharePoint farm, creating and managing web applications, and creating and managing site collections.

STSADM command line tool: A command-line tool that you use to administer a SharePoint farm; you can access many of the administrative functions in the SharePoint Central Administration web site through this tool. STSADM is a carry-over feature from previous versions of SharePoint, and is superseded by the new and more powerful Powershell administrative tool.

PowerShell: A console-style tool that you can use to administer the Windows operating system, similar to the DOS-style command prompt, only much more powerful. SharePoint provides a snap-in component for PowerShell that allows it to interact directly with SharePoint, providing the capability to perform many administrative functions. The snap-in provides hundreds of commands that you can run manually or integrate into automated PowerShell scripts.

Site Collection settings: An administrative area available within the top-level web site in a SharePoint Site Collection that you use to manage configuration settings that cascade down to all of the child sites within the collection. Examples include security settings, navigation, template galleries, and metadata management.

Site settings: An administrative area available within each child site in a SharePoint Site Collection that you use to manage configuration settings that apply to that site only. Examples include site-specific security settings, navigation, and metadata management.

List and Library settings: An administrative area available within each list or library in a SharePoint web site that you use to manage configuration settings within that list or library only. Examples include list-specific security settings, version control, and metadata management.

You learn how to use each of these tools to perform various administrative functions throughout the remainder of this module.

Security

Similar in concept to Project Server and many other systems, you use SharePoint security to manage Users, Groups, and Permissions. A user is an individual who can access the system and use its features. A group is a collection of users who fill a similar role on a team or in the organization. Permissions are specific functions available to users of the system. You grant access to permissions in SharePoint by first adding users to the system, placing them into groups, and then assigning specific permissions to groups of users as illustrated in Table 15 - 2.

Users	Groups	Permissions
Jan Michael	Executives	View Risks View Issues View Documents View Deliverables
Jim Dwight Angela	Managers	Edit Risks Edit Issues Edit Documents Edit Deliverables
Kevin Pam Andy Oscar	Team Members	Edit Risks Edit Issues Edit Documents View Deliverables

Table 15 - 2: Users, groups, and permissions

Project Server manages security for your *Project Sites* through a synchronization process built into the Project Server application. When a project stored in Project Server has a *Project Site* associated with it, the synchronization process runs automatically when the project manager republishes the project to PWA, as shown in Figure 15 - 5. I discuss the specific configuration options for this synchronization process later in this module.

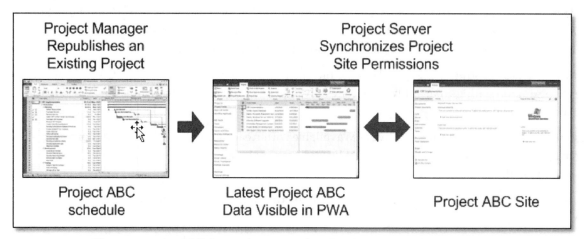

Figure 15 - 5: Republish a project to synchronize the Project Site permissions

Typically, Project Server configures the user, group, and permission settings within a *Project Site* at the site level, and those settings cascade down to each library and list within the site as well as to each data item stored within each library and list. However, if your business processes require it, you can break this security inheritance, allowing you to independently control which users have access to which data within the site. Understand that once you break the inheritance, you must manage security for the site manually.

Templates

SharePoint helps you streamline site and list creation by employing site templates and list templates. The quantity and selection of site and list templates installed in your system depends on the version of SharePoint you deploy. If none of the built-in templates meet your needs, you can create your own custom templates, which you can use to create future sites or lists within your SharePoint environment.

When Project Server provisions a new *Project Site* for a project, it uses a template. As a Project Server administrator, you can create new templates for associating with various *Project Types* in your organization and update the default template, causing all future *Project Sites* to reflect the changes you implement in the new site template. Note that when you update a site template, it does not update sites previously created from the template. Examples of list templates that are included in both versions of SharePoint are:

- Announcements
- Contacts
- Discussion Board
- Links
- Calendar
- Tasks
- Survey

List templates are not necessary for creating new lists within a SharePoint site. Rather, they streamline the process of creating a new list if the type of data that you want to store is similar to one of the existing templates.

Recycle Bins

Similar to a PC desktop, SharePoint offers site-level *Recycle Bin* functionality. Each site has a recycle bin that stores files and list items when you delete them from libraries and lists within that SharePoint site, allowing you to easily restore them to their original locations. SharePoint includes a 2-stage recycle bin process. When a person deletes an item from the site-level recycle bin, the item moves to a site collection administrative recycle bin for a period of time. This second-stage recycle bin is accessible only by a SharePoint administrator.

Metadata

SharePoint stores various types of structured and unstructured content. You can attach additional pieces of descriptive data to classify each item, whether the item is an expense report, a document, a calendar event, or a project issue. This additional data, also known as metadata, can be quite helpful for sorting, grouping, filtering, or searching for the content within the SharePoint content store.

For example, your team members are tracking a list of issues that are impeding the progress of your project. The core data entity is an issue, but you may also want to capture additional data that further classifies each issue, such as the date when you logged the issue, the person who is responsible for following the issue to resolution, and the date by which the issue must be resolved.

Version Control

SharePoint provides automatic version control, a mechanism for tracking updates contributed by members of a team. When you enable this functionality you can track major versions (1.0, 2.0, 3.0, etc.) for each item of structured content in a SharePoint list. Each time you make a change to an item stored in a list, the system automatically increments the version number and stores the previous version of the item for later review and retrieval. You can also track both major and minor versions (1.0, 1.1, 1.2, 2.0, etc.) for each unstructured content item that you store in a SharePoint library. When you enable minor versioning for files in a library, these minor versions are drafts. When you enable versioning for a list or library within a SharePoint site, the system includes all of the content items stored in that list or library.

Alerts

As a SharePoint user, you can use two different notification mechanisms to learn about content changes in a SharePoint list or library. SharePoint provides both email alerts and RSS feeds. Assuming that you configured the email notification functionality by connecting to an SMTP server for sending outbound messages, you can request that the system send an email notification when all or certain items in a list or library are created, changed, or deleted. If you enable RSS feeds in SharePoint, each list or library in a SharePoint site can provide its own feed, which lists any recent alterations including additions, changes, and deletions that users make to its content. Any user with access to the list or library can subscribe to this feed with an RSS reader such as Microsoft Office Outlook 2010, which automatically fetches the feed on a regular basis and displays the updates for the user on their desktop without requiring a site visit.

Workflow

A workflow in SharePoint is an electronic representation of a business process. More specifically, it is a way of attaching business logic to content stored and managed in a SharePoint web site. Whether you want to represent a review and approval process, an issue escalation process, or a project proposal process, you can break down each process into a set of activities or tasks that are then represented, stored, and tracked by the SharePoint workflow engine. Each workflow can automatically perform actions on content stored in a SharePoint list or library, such as update a status field from "Submitted" to "Approved" or move an expense report from one location to another. Workflows can also initiate a request to a person to perform an action on an item, such as review a project issue and assign it to the appropriate team member for resolution. You can use a number of options and tools for creating workflows in SharePoint, including each of the following.

- **Built-in Workflows:** Because Project Server 2010 installs with Microsoft SharePoint Server, the system provides a number of built-in workflows for Project Server Lifecycle Management. You do not need to have custom code development capabilities to use and configure built-in workflows.

- **Microsoft SharePoint Designer:** This Microsoft desktop application has a convenient wizard-style interface for building workflows for non-developers. It allows you to represent sophisticated processes that may have several process steps and can contain conditional logic as well as perform several types of actions on the content stored in a SharePoint list or library. These workflows are limited, in that they can interact within the scope of only a single site.

- **Microsoft Visual Studio:** You can use this developer tool to build much more sophisticated SharePoint workflows, including custom interactive forms, interaction with multiple lists and libraries, and interaction with other applications or Line of Business systems. Leveraging this power and flexibility comes at a price: you must be proficient with the tool and have knowledge of .NET application development and deployment.

- **Third-Party Tools:** There are various third-party tools available for building SharePoint workflows. These tools combine the ease of use provided by SharePoint Designer with the power and flexibility of Visual Studio workflows.

I cover only the built-in workflows in this module. If you are interested in learning more about building workflows with SharePoint Designer, Visual Studio, or third party tools, you should consider acquiring additional reference materials and training.

Managing the SharePoint/Project Server Connection

There are three administration pages within Project Web App that you use to set *Project Site* provisioning settings and to administer existing *Project Sites*. Because Project Web App is a SharePoint application, you can also leverage many SharePoint tools embedded in each PWA page to change the look and feel of your PWA instance and to change the content of pages to tailor them to your organizational requirements. These built-in features provide you with an unprecedented ability to mold your application.

Managing Project Site Provisioning

From the Quick Launch menu in Project Web App, click the *Server Settings* link. On the *Server Settings* page, and then click the *Project Site Provisioning Settings* link in the *Operational Policies* section of the page. Project Server 2010 displays the *Project Site Provisioning Settings* page shown in Figure 15 - 6.

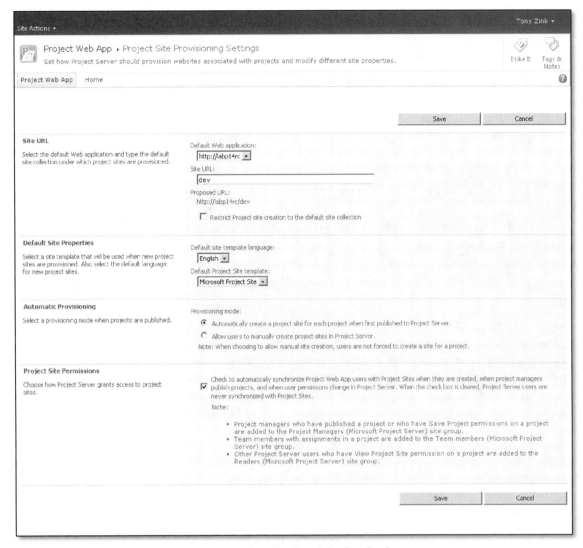

Figure 15 - 6: Project Site Provisioning Settings page

When you first access the *Project Site Provisioning Settings* page, the system displays the default settings for provisioning *Project Sites*. In the *Site URL* section, you can change the default *Web application* under which the system creates your sites, although in most circumstances, you do not need to change this setting. The system derives the values in the *Default Web application* field and the *Site URL* field from the information you supplied during Project Server 2010 installation, or while creating a new Project Server instance.

In the *Default Site Properties* section, you can change the language settings for new site provisioning and change the base template that the system uses to create the sites. The system specifies your language in the *Default site template language* field and selects the built-in *Microsoft Project Site* template in the *Default Project Site template* field.

Warning: You **must** use the *Microsoft Project Site* template, or a template created from this template. This is because the *Microsoft Project Site* template contains specific customizations that support the *Risks, Issues, Documents*, and *Deliverables* features in Project Server 2010.

If you are using *Enterprise Project Types* in Project Server and if any of them are not associated with a specific *Project Site* template, then those *Project Types* will utilize the *Default Project Site template* when creating new *Project Sites*.

In the *Automatic Provisioning* section, the system pre-selects the *Automatically create a project site for each project when first published to Project Server* option to automatically create a *Project Site* when a project manager publishes a project for the first time. Whether you use this automatic provisioning option or set your provisioning mode to "manual" depends on your requirements. In most cases, automatic provisioning makes sense. With automatic provisioning, the system forces the creation of a *Project Site* for every project published in the system.

When does it make sense to use the *Allow users to manually create project sites in Project Server* option? You might choose this setting if most of your projects are rolled up into programs, and you have a need to create the component projects before you create the program's master project. Because Project Server 2010 gives you the choice to create your *Project Site* as a sub-site of another *Project Site*, you can create a program site with individual project sites below it in the hierarchy. Setting your provisioning mode to manual gives you the chance to create a *Project Site* after the project is published. Keep in mind that the collaborative features provided in the *Project Site* are not available to your users until you create a *Project Site*. Another instance when you might select manual provisioning is when you simply do not intend to use *Project Sites*, including the *Risks, Issues, Documents,* and *Deliverables* features in your environment.

In the *Project Site Permissions* section of the *Project Site Provisioning Settings* page, the system pre-selects the option to provision sites with automatic user synchronization. Leave this option selected if you want the system to automatically manage user permissions for you. Notice that the information on the page clearly defines the permissions synchronization that occurs when you select this option. In most cases, selecting this option is appropriate. If you deselect this option, you must manually manage these permissions in the system or provide your own synchronization routine. Click the *Save* button to save any changes you make on this page.

When you set your system to manual, your project managers see the *Publish Project* dialog shown in Figure 15 - 7. Notice that the *Do not create a site at this time* option is the default. This dialog continues to appear during each publish operation until the project manager chooses to provision the *Project Site* or until an administrator provisions one.

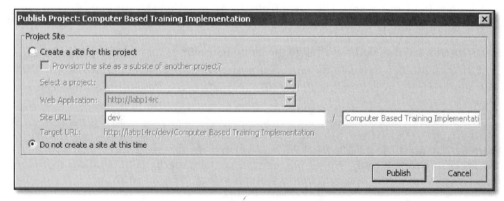

Figure 15 - 7: Publish Project dialog

With the exception of the *Project Site Permissions* option, changes you make on the *Project Site Provisioning Settings* page affect sites created after the change date. In the case of *Project Site Permissions*, any user permissions already synchronized to a site remain unchanged when you turn off automatic synchronization. Deselecting this option stops future synchronization on current sites.

Managing Project Sites

In the *Operational Policies* section of the *Server Settings* page, click the *Project Sites* link to manually provision or delete *Project Sites*, or to manage existing sites. The system displays the *Project Sites* page shown in Figure 15 - 8.

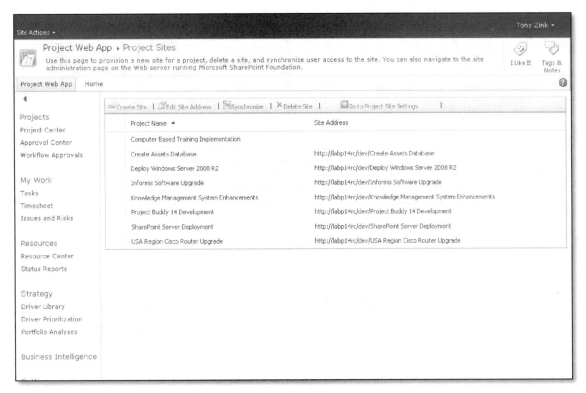

Figure 15 - 8: Project Sites page

Notice that the page contains a data grid with a toolbar running across the top. The system does not activate any of the toolbar buttons until you select a project name or site address in the grid.

The *Site Address* column contains a link to the *Project Site* for the specified project. If you click the link for any project in the *Site Address* column, the system navigates you to the selected *Project Site*. The *Site Address* column should always contain a link for every project when you select the automatic provisioning option, unless the provisioning process fails, which leaves the *Site Address* column blank. This page gives you the ability to recover from a failed automatic provisioning by allowing you to manually provision a site.

The *Project Sites* toolbar offers you five options, which are as follows:

- *Create Site* causes the system to create a site for the selected project. If the project does not have a URL in the *Site Address* column, the *Project Site* does not exist for that project. Click the *Create Site* button to manually provision a *Project Site*. Notice in Figure 15 - 8 that one of the projects in the system does not have a *Project Site*. Select the project for which you want to create a site and click the *Create Site* button. The system displays

653

the *Create Project Site* form shown in Figure 15 - 9. You can both select the web application under which to provision the site and also determine the URL. The URL defaults to the project name, and this is usually the best naming convention to use.

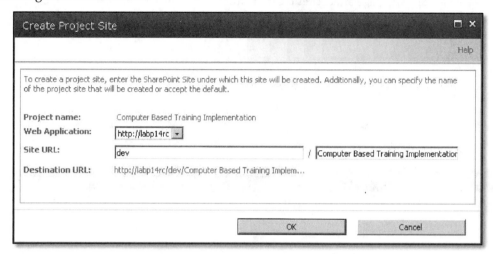

Figure 15 - 9: Create Project Site form

- *Edit Site Address* allows you to change the *Project Site* URL for the project as might be required should an existing site become corrupt, requiring you to move the content to a new site. It also allows you to remove the URL for a *Project Site,* effectively breaking the link between the project and the *Project Site*. When you click the *Edit Site Address* button, the system displays the *Edit Site Address* form shown in Figure 15 - 10. By default, the system selects the *Type a new SharePoint site URL* option. Make sure that you use the *Test URL* button to test the site address before saving your changes. Select the *Remove the URL for the SharePoint site* option to remove the URL from the project's record. Click the *OK* button to complete your action or the *Cancel* button to abort the change.

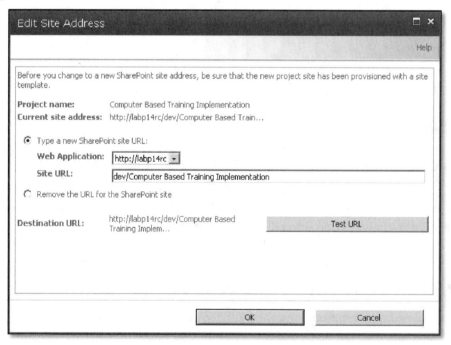

Figure 15 - 10: Edit Site Address form

- *Synchronize* allows you to force a permissions synchronization to occur for the project you select in the grid. The system places a synchronization job in the Project Server Queue when you click this button and redisplays the *Project Sites* page. It does not give you any additional feedback; however, you can verify that the job succeeded through the *Manage Queue Jobs* page covered in Module 17.

- *Delete Site* gives you the ability to completely remove a *Project Site* including all of its content. Use this feature when you archive a project and do not want to retain the *Project Site,* or if you have a need to recreate a site. When you click the *Delete Site* button, the system displays the dialog shown in Figure 15 - 11. Click the *OK* button to continue removing the site and all of its contents. Click the *Cancel* button to exit without deleting the site.

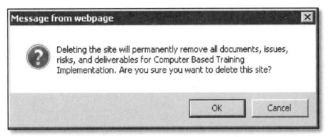

Figure 15 - 11: Delete Project Site warning dialog

 Warning: When you delete a site, the system **does not** place the site or its contents in a Recycle Bin. Therefore, there is no undo available to reverse this action. Use this feature very judiciously.

- *Go to Project Site Settings* takes you directly to the *Site Settings* page for the selected *Project Site.* Figure 15 - 12 shows the *Site Settings* page for a *Project Site.* From the *Site Settings* page, you can manage the look and feel of your *Project Site,* perform site administration, and control several other site features. SharePoint gives you built-in tools to customize the site and add content through its user interface without requiring custom coding.

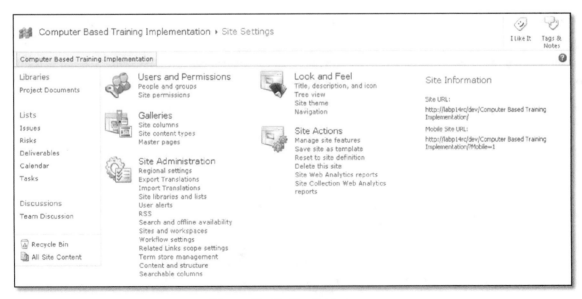

Figure 15 - 12: Site Settings page

Bulk Updating Project Sites

Some situations may require you to update the paths in Project Server to its associated *Project Sites;* for example, you may need to migrate the *Project Sites* from one web application or content database to another, thus breaking the original links between Project Server and the *Project Sites* because the sites have new URLs. In the *Operational Policies* section of the *Server Settings* page, click the *Bulk Update Project Sites* link to make bulk corrections to *Project Site* URLs, content type definitions, and permissions after migrating sites from location to another. The system displays the *Bulk Update Project Sites* page shown in Figure 15 - 13.

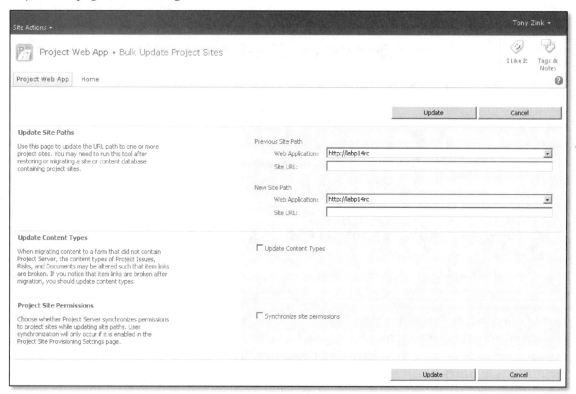

Figure 15 - 13: Bulk Update Project Sites page

In the *Update Site Paths* section of the page, select the previous *Web Application* and enter the previous *Site URL*, then select the new *Web Application* and enter the new *Site URL*.

In the *Update Content Types* section of the page, select the *Update Content Types* option to ensure that the Issues, Risks, and Documents content types are updated in the new location in order to maintain object links.

In the *Project Site Permissions* section of the page, select the *Synchronize site permissions* option to ensure that Project Server users will have access to the data in its new location.

After selecting the appropriate options and entering the appropriate information on the page, click the *Update* button. Project Server updates the information in the system and displays the *Server Settings* page.

Modifying Project Sites

As I mention previously in this module, each *Project Site* that you create for a project is based on the *Microsoft Project Site* template that installs with Project Server 2010. Because every company, department, and team may follow different processes and therefore operate with different requirements, the features included in the built-in *Project Site* template may not meet all of your business process needs.

Fortunately, you can modify each *Project Site* to better map it to your existing business processes. You can also customize the site template that the system uses to generate new *Project Sites*, saving you the effort required to manually modify each newly provisioned *Project Site*. I describe how to customize a *Project Site* template later in this module.

Managing List and Library Metadata

SharePoint stores both structured content and unstructured content; SharePoint lists act as containers for structured content, and SharePoint libraries act as containers for unstructured content. A SharePoint list stores a collection of structured data items similar to a bulleted list of values, and a SharePoint library stores a collection of unstructured items in the form of files. Because the functionality and configuration options are so similar for lists and libraries, I primarily present instructions and examples for lists in this module, but the information I present typically applies to libraries as well, with only minor differences.

Regardless of whether it is in a list or library, each item stored in SharePoint has descriptive metadata to help classify the items for sorting, grouping, filtering, or otherwise locating specific items of interest. This is especially helpful when lists or libraries contain hundreds or thousands of items. SharePoint *columns* are the pieces of descriptive metadata that you can use to classify items in lists and libraries.

SharePoint columns are a fundamental building block for lists and libraries. In the event that your business process requires you to capture additional metadata to describe or categorize the items in a list or library, the system allows you to modify existing columns or create new custom columns in the *Project Site* for a selected project. Although Microsoft uses the word *column* to describe this feature, it is very similar to a custom *field* in Project Server.

Figure 15 - 14 displays a form for editing or logging a new project issue; you can see in this form that there are several metadata columns (Title, Owner, Assigned To, Status, etc.) that describe and classify the issue being logged in the *Issues* list:

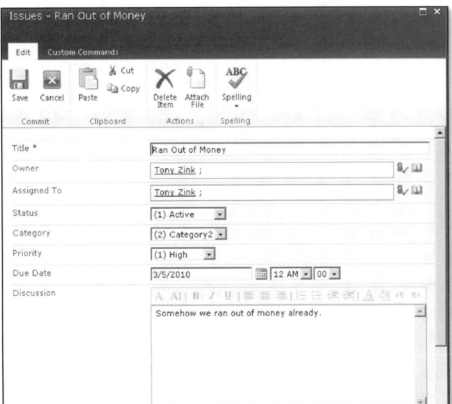

Figure 15 - 14: Issue Form with several metadata columns

Creating a New Column

To create a new column within a SharePoint list, navigate to the list, click the *List* ribbon tab, then click the *Create Column* button in the *Manage Views* section of the ribbon menu, as shown in Figure 15 - 15.

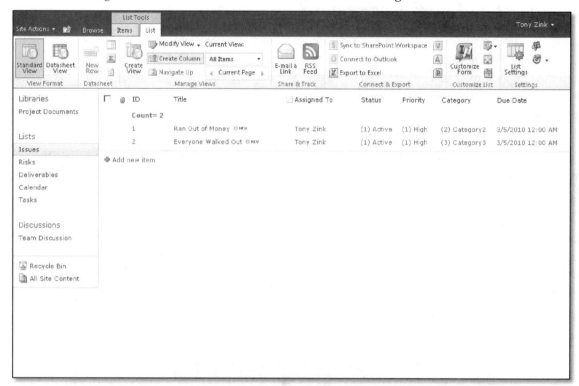

Figure 15 - 15: Selecting the Create Column Button on the Issues page

The system displays the *Create Column* form as shown in Figure 15 - 16.

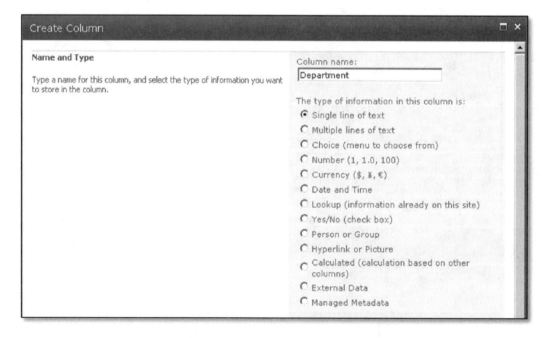

Figure 15 - 16: Create Column dialog for the Issues list

To create the new custom column, enter a descriptive name for the column in the *Column name* field, then select an option that describes the data type for the information to be entered into the column. The system offers a number of data types, including each of the following:

- Single line of text

- Multiple lines of text

- Choice (menu to choose from)

- Number (1, 1.0, 100)

- Currency ($, ¥, €)

- Date and Time

- Lookup (information already on this site)

- Yes/No (check box)

- Person or Group

- Hyperlink or Picture

- Calculated (calculation based on other columns)

- External Data

- Managed Metadata

When you select an option for the column data type, the system redraws the *Additional Column Settings* section of the form for the type of data you select. For example, Figure 15 - 17 shows the *Additional Column Settings* section after selecting the *Choice (menu to choose from)* option.

In the *Additional Column Settings* section of the form, select your options for the new custom column. For example, when using the *Choice* data type for the column, you must do the following:

- Enter an optional description for the column.

- Specify whether the field is required.

- Specify whether unique values should be enforced.

- Enter the list of choices.

- Determine how the system displays the choices (as a pick list menu, as radio buttons, or as checkboxes).

- Determine whether to allow a user to append the list with additional choices.

- Specify a default value in the column.

- Determine whether to add the column to the default view.

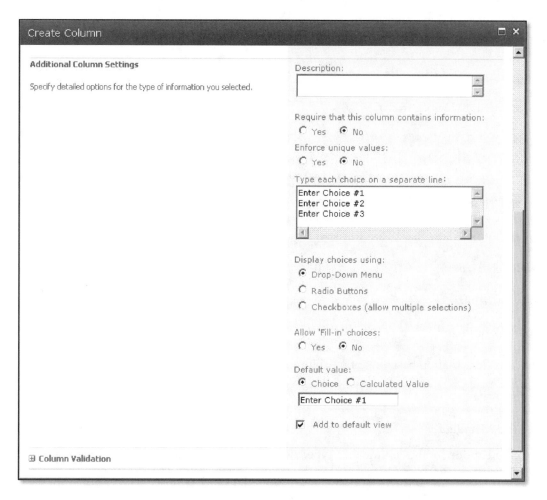

Figure 15 - 17: Additional Column Settings section for the Choice data type

Finally, there is an optional *Column Validation* section at the end of the *Create Column* form; you need to click the heading to expand this section. As shown in Figure 15 - 18, you may enter a validation formula which prevents people from entering incorrect data into the column when it comes time for them to add or edit items in the list. To enter a validation rule for data entered into this column, enter an expression into the *Formula* text box using similar syntax as is used for SharePoint calculated columns, which is based on Microsoft Excel formulas.

If data entered into the column does not comply with the validation rule that you enter, SharePoint does not save the item and an alert message appears for the user. To enter a custom alert message, enter the message into the *User message* text box.

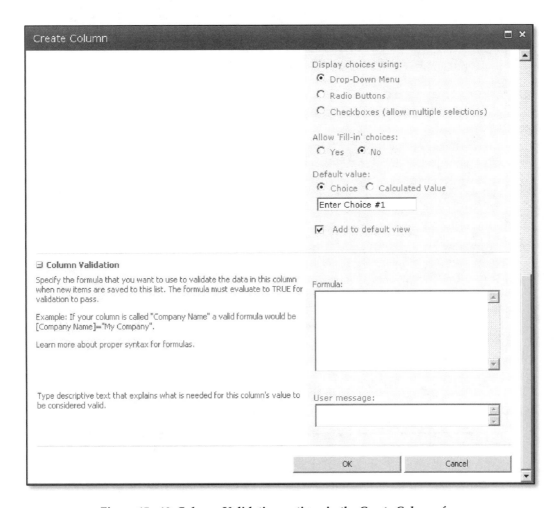

Figure 15 - 18: Column Validation options in the Create Column form

For example, one of your business process requirements may state that the customer number for any item entered into the list must start with the text "Cust-". The validation formula for this scenario is:

=LEFT([Customer],5)="Cust-"

This formula states that the left 5 characters of the data entered into the *Customer* column must equal "Cust-". The user alert message for this scenario is:

You must begin the customer number with the text "Cust-".

Figure 15 - 19 shows a case in which column validation fails; the user alert message appears below the *Customer* column:

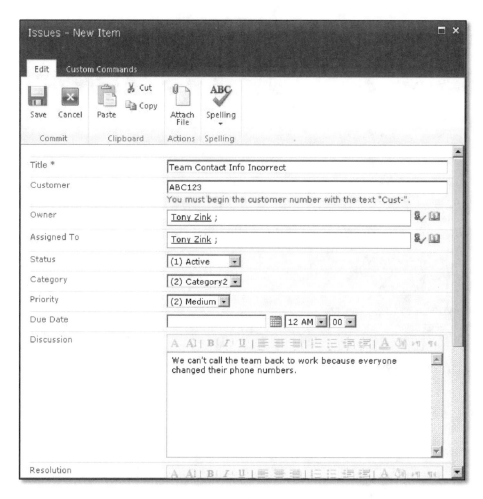

Figure 15 - 19: Column Validation failure

A column validation formula cannot refer to any columns other than itself. For example, you cannot enter a column validation formula for the *Due Date* column that compares it against the *Created* column. This can, however, be accomplished through list validation settings, which I cover later in this module.

Warning: Multiple columns within the same list can have unique column validation rules; be careful not to enter rules that conflict with one another, preventing people from entering any new items into the list.

After you configure all of the settings for the new custom column, click the *Save* button at the top of the form or the *OK* button at the bottom of the form. If you selected the *Add to default view* option, SharePoint adds the new custom column on the far right side of the default view for the selected list, the issues list in this example, as shown on the *Issues* page in Figure 15 - 20.

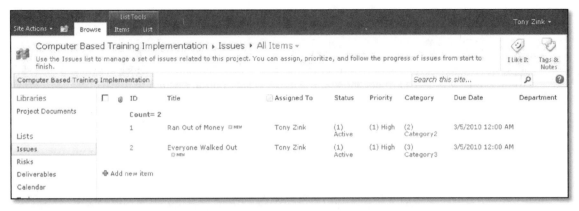

Figure 15 - 20: Department column added to the Issues page

If the new column requires data entry, rather than the system calculating data, then you must edit each of the items in the list to populate that new piece of metadata. For example, Figure 15 - 21 shows the new field at the bottom of the Issues edit form, along with the values available on the choice list.

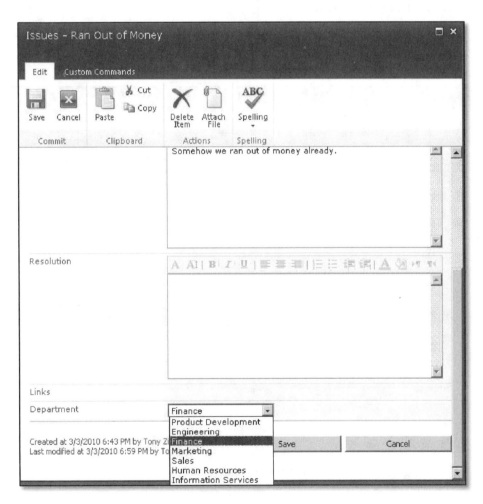

Figure 15 - 21: Department column at bottom of Issue form

A column that you create within a SharePoint list or library is available *only* to the list or library in which you create it. Later in this module, you learn how to create a *Site Column*, which allows you to create a column centrally within a Project Site and use it in any list or library within that site.

MSProjectExperts recommends that if you have a generalized need for *Project Site* customizations such as new or modified columns, you modify the base template for *Project Sites*. If you are using the *Enterprise Project Types* feature in Project Server, each project type can utilize its own *Project Site* template that has unique customizations for that *Project Type*.

Modifying or Deleting an Existing Column

To modify or delete an existing column within a SharePoint list, navigate to the list, click the *List* ribbon tab, then click the *List Settings* button in the *Settings* section of the ribbon menu, as shown in Figure 15 - 22.

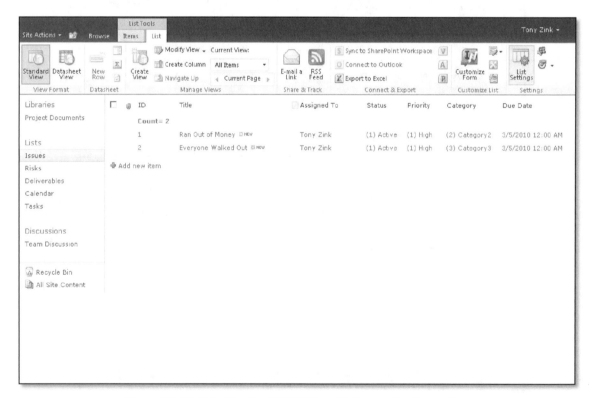

Figure 15 - 22: Selecting the List Settings Button on the Issues Page

The system displays the *List Settings* page as shown in Figure 15 - 23, which contains links to all of the administrative configuration options for the list.

664

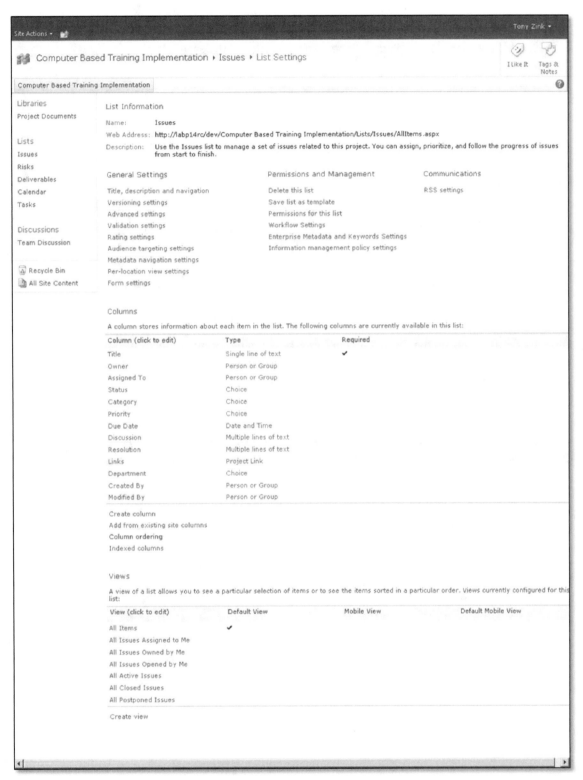

Figure 15 - 23: List Settings page for the Issues list

You may also create a new column by visiting the *List Settings* page, then clicking the *Create column* link, located below the list of columns in the *Columns* section of the page.

The *Columns* section of the *List Settings* page displays the entire list of columns for the selected list; to modify one of the existing columns, click on the name of the column in the list.

MSProjectExperts recommends that you modify the built-in *Category* column and enter choice values that are relevant to your organization's business processes.

The system displays the *Change Column* page as shown in Figure 15 - 24, which contains the same column configuration options that are available on the *Create Column* form shown in the previous section. When you finish modifying the behavior of the column, as shown in Figure 15 - 24 where I change the *Category* choice values, click the *OK* button at the bottom of the page. If you need to delete the column from the list, click the *Delete* button at the bottom of the page.

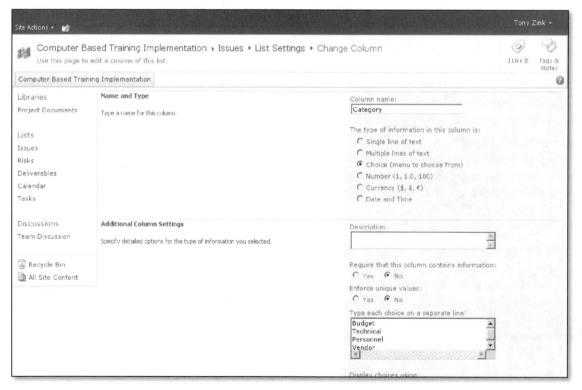

Figure 15 - 24: Modifying the Category column in the Issues list

Warning: Do not delete any built-in columns from the *Risks, Issues, Deliverables* lists, or from the *Project Documents* library. Doing so will prevent Project Server from synchronizing properly with the Project Site.

Creating a New Site Column

You may find that you need to add the same column to multiple lists and libraries within a *Project Site*; if you find yourself in this situation, then you can create a *site column* centrally that acts as a reusable column throughout the entire site. You can then easily add this site column to any list to capture metadata for classifying items within the site.

To create a new site column, click the *Site Actions* menu from any page within the *Project Site*, then select *Site Settings*, as shown in Figure 15 - 25.

Figure 15 - 25: Opening the Site Actions menu

The system displays the *Site Settings* page as shown in Figure 15 - 26, which contains links to all of the administrative configuration options for the *Project Site*. On the *Site Settings* page, click the *Site columns* link, located below the *Galleries* heading.

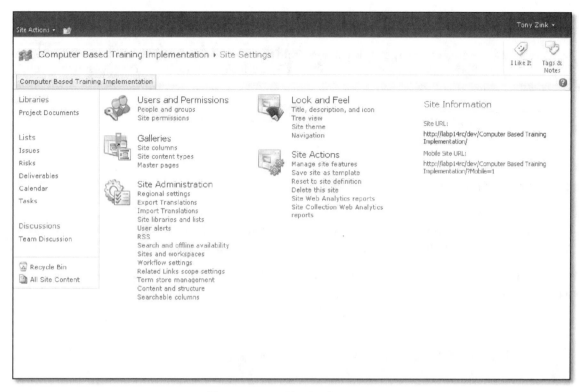

Figure 15 - 26: Site Settings page

The system displays the *Site Columns* page as shown in Figure 15 - 27, which displays all of the site columns for the *Project Site*. Click the *Create* link, located near the top of the page, to create a new site column.

Figure 15 - 27: Site Columns page

On the *New Site Column* page, you see options very similar to those presented when you create a new custom column for a list, as shown in Figure 15 - 28. The main difference is the addition of the *Group* section of the page, which allows you to place your new site column into a group when it appears on the *Site Columns* page. You may select from an existing group or create your own group as shown in the figure. When finished specifying all of the options for the new site column, click the *OK* button at the bottom of the page.

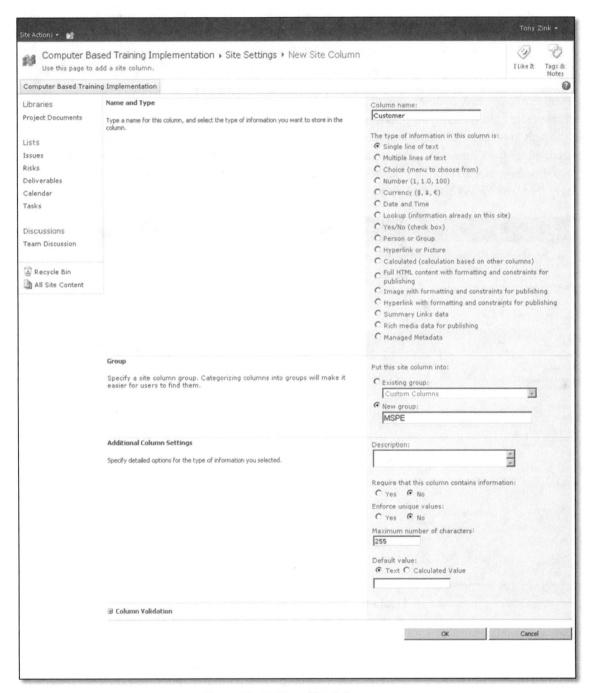

Figure 15 - 28: New Site Column page

MSProjectExperts recommends that you create a new group to categorize any new site columns that you create in a Project Site. This will make it easier to separate and find your custom site columns in the future.

The system displays the *Site Columns* page again, and you can scroll the page to find your new site column listed in the group that you specified.

Modifying or Deleting an Existing Site Column

Although you cannot modify or delete any of the built-in site columns from a *Project Site*, you may need to modify or delete a custom site column that you previously created. To do so, visit the *Site Columns* page in the *Project Site* as shown in the previous section, locate the site column in the list that you need to modify or delete, then click its name. The system displays the *Change Site Column* page as shown in Figure 15 - 29, allowing you to make any modifications necessary to the selected site column. Click the *OK* button at the bottom of the page, or if you need to delete the column entirely from the *Project Site*, click the *Delete* button at the bottom of the page.

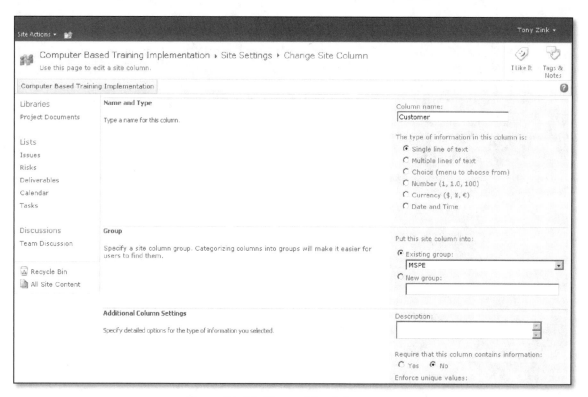

Figure 15 - 29: Change Site Column page

Deleting a "parent" site column from a *Project Site* will not remove any associated "child" columns from lists or libraries within the site. However, all "child" instances of the column will become "orphaned," and they will function independently of one another.

Adding a Site Column to a List

Once you create a new custom site column for a *Project Site*, you can add that site column to one or more lists or libraries within that site. To add a site column to a list, navigate to the list, click the *List* tab, then click the *List Settings* button in the *Settings* section of the ribbon menu. On the *List Settings* page, scroll to the *Columns* section and click the *Add from existing site columns* link, located below the column listing. The system displays the *Add Columns from Site Columns* page, as shown in Figure 15 - 30.

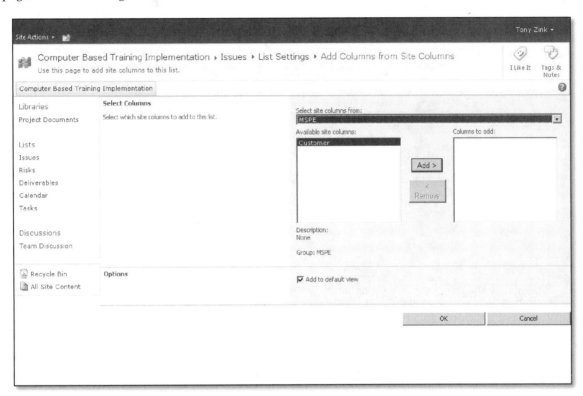

Figure 15 - 30: Add Columns from Site Columns page

The *Add Columns from Site Columns* page allows you to select your custom site columns to add to the current list. The *Select site columns from* pick list displays *All Groups*; therefore all site columns from all groups appear in the *Available site columns* list. If you created a site column and placed it into a new custom group, select the group from the *Select site columns from* drop-down. Your custom site column appears in the *Available site columns* list, as shown in Figure 15 - 30. Select the desired site column and click the *Add* button. To add the site column to the default view for the list, select the *Add to default view* option, then click the *OK* button at the bottom of the page. The system returns to the *List Settings* page and displays the newly added site column in the *Columns* section of the page. If you selected the *Add to default view* option, return to the list and view the site column in the default view.

Removing a Site Column from a List

Removing a site column from a list is similar to deleting a standard column. Navigate to the list, click the *List* tab, then click the *List Settings* button in the *Settings* section of the ribbon menu. On the *List Settings* page, scroll to the *Columns* section and click the name of the site column that you need to remove.

The *List Settings* page does not indicate which columns were created from site columns.

On the *Change Column* page, click the *Delete* button at the bottom of the page. A warning message appears, as shown in Figure 15 - 31; click the *OK* button to acknowledge the message and continue with the removal of the column.

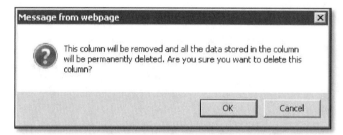

Figure 15 - 31: Delete column warning message

Deleting a site column from a list or library will not delete the site column entirely from the *Project Site*. It will remain in any other lists or libraries that are using it.

Controlling Column Ordering in Forms

When you create new columns in a list or add columns from existing site columns, the new columns are added at the bottom of the new and edit forms, as shown previously in this module. Depending upon your business process requirements, you may need to change the order of the columns in these forms. To control column ordering in list and library forms, navigate to the list, click the *List* tab, then click the *List Settings* button in the *Settings* section of the ribbon menu. On the *List Settings* page, scroll to the *Columns* section and click the *Column ordering* link, located below the collection of columns. The system displays the *Change Field Order* page, as shown in Figure 15 - 32.

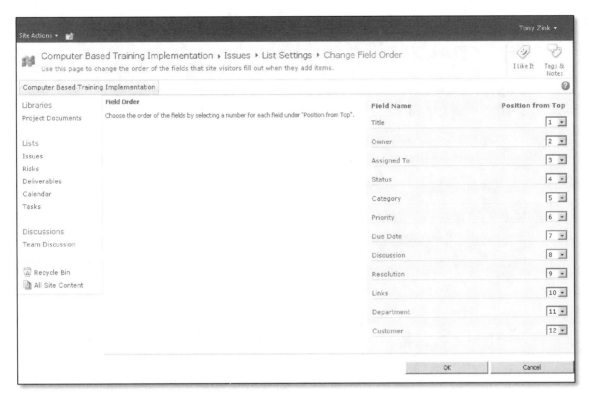

Figure 15 - 32: Change Field Order page

 Don't be confused here! Even though this page refers to "*fields,*" you are working with SharePoint *columns* within the selected list or library.

The *Change Field Order* page displays all of the columns associated with the list, as well as the order that they are displayed in new or edit forms. To change their order in the forms, select the appropriate numeric value next to each column; the system re-arranges the columns automatically to show the current order. Click the *OK* button at the bottom of the page to accept the column ordering.

Notice in Figure 15 - 33 that the columns displayed on the *New Item* form now reflect the new ordering selected on the *Change Field Order* page.

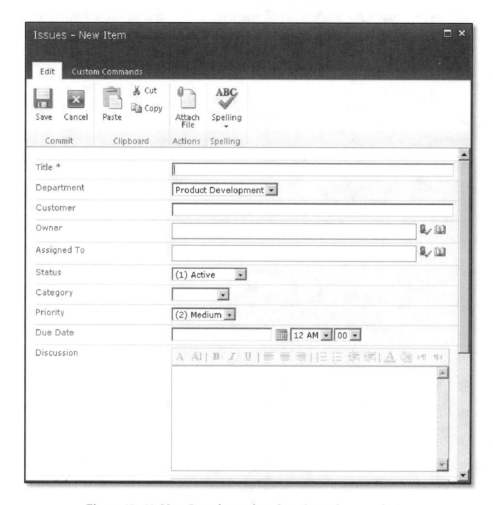

Figure 15 - 33: New Item form after changing column ordering

Managing Views of List and Library Items

After people enter structured and unstructured content into a *Project Site*, SharePoint can display those content items in many ways, allowing project team members and stakeholders to review, analyze, and interact with the data. A *view* of a SharePoint list or library is an interactive report that provides the functionality for reviewing, analyzing, and interacting with the items stored there.

As I mention previously in this module, each new *Project Site* is created automatically from a site template; this site template includes not only several lists and libraries in which to store project data, deliverables, and artifacts, but it also includes several built-in views for each list and library. In the event that your business process requires you to interact with the data differently, the system allows you to modify existing views or create new custom views in the *Project Site* for a selected project.

Figure 15 - 34 displays a view of the *Issues* list for a project; notice that the view displays a listing of issue items in table format, including a collection of columns that hold additional information describing each issue item.

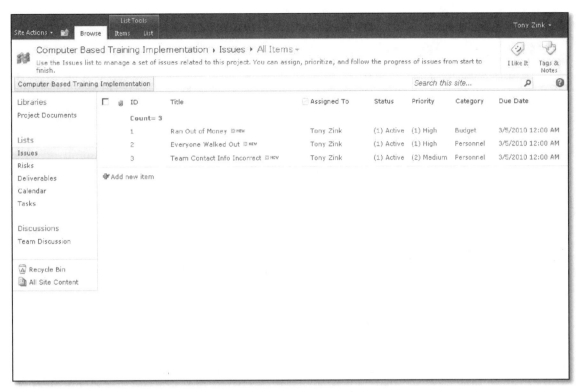

Figure 15 - 34: View of the Issues list

When customizing an existing view or creating a new view for a SharePoint list or library, following are a few questions you need to ask:

- Which items do the people need to see? Should they see all items in the list or library, or only specific items of interest?

- When displaying items in a view, which columns of metadata do people need to see for each item, and in which order should the view display them?

- When displaying items in a view, should the view sort the rows into a specific order?

- When displaying items in a view, should the view create groupings of similar items?

The answers to these questions are useful when you define list and library views in a *Project Site*.

Modifying or Deleting an Existing View

To modify an existing view in a list, navigate to the list, click the *List* tab, select the desired view from the *Current View* pick list, and then click the *Modify View* button in the *Manage Views* section of the ribbon menu. The system displays the *Edit View* page, as shown in Figure 15 - 35. Select the appropriate options as described below and then click the *OK* button.

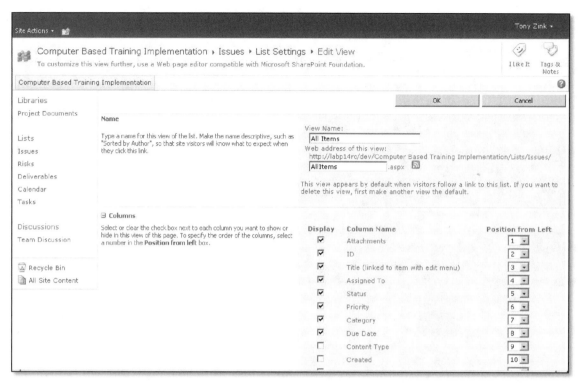

Figure 15 - 35: Edit View page

 You can also access the *Edit View* page by navigating to the list or library, clicking the *List* tab, and clicking the *List Settings* button in the *Settings* section of the ribbon menu. Once on the *List Settings* page, scroll to the *Views* section of the page and click on the name of the view.

In the *Name* section of the page as shown in Figure 15 - 36, rename the view or change the unique URL of the view as necessary. Enter a new name into the *View Name* text box, or enter a new URL ending into the *Web address of this view* text box.

Figure 15 - 36: Name section of the Edit View page

In the *Columns* section of the page shown in Figure 15 - 37, change which columns appear in the view and the ordering of those columns. Select your desired columns by selecting the *Display* option next to each and then adjust the ordering of the selected columns by adjusting the *Position from Left* values next to each.

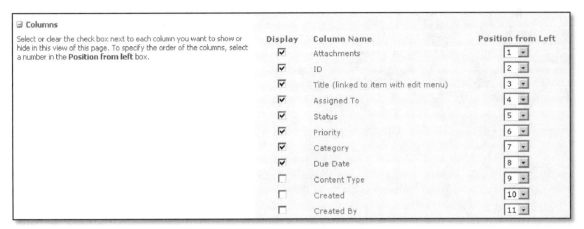

Figure 15 - 37: Columns section of the Edit View page

In the *Sort* section of the page as shown in Figure 15 - 38, change the sort order of the item rows in the view. Select a column to use for sorting from the *First sort by the column* pick list, then select whether the rows sort in ascending or descending order, based on the values in that column. To sort the rows based on multiple columns, select a second column using the *Then sort by the column* pick list and pick a sort order.

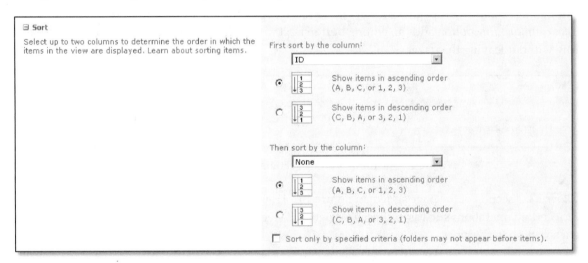

Figure 15 - 38: Sort section of the Edit View page

In the *Filter* section of the page as shown in Figure 15 - 39, display only specific items of interest in the view, rather than all of the items in the list. Select the *Show items only when the following is true* option and then configure one or more conditions that each item must meet before appearing in the view. To configure a conditional test, select a column from the first pick list, select a test from the second pick list, and enter a value in the text box.

For example, to show items that belong to the Human Resources Department, you may create a condition such as:

Column	Test	Value
Department	is equal to	Human Resources

To configure multiple conditional tests, select the appropriate *And / Or* option after the first conditional test, then configure a second conditional test using the second set of options in the *Filter* section. To configure more than two conditional tests, click the *Show More Columns* link.

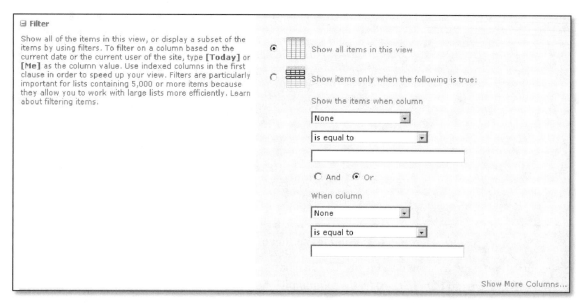

Figure 15 - 39: Filter section of the Edit View page

In the *Inline Editing* section of the page shown in Figure 15 - 40, you can enable quick inline editing in the view. Selecting the *Allow inline editing* option adds an editing button next to each row in the view and allows editing of the item on that row without leaving the page.

Figure 15 - 40: Inline Editing section of the Edit View page

In the *Tabular View* section of the page shown in Figure 15 - 41, you can allow people to select multiple item rows in the view for certain operations such as multi-item deletion. Select the *Allow individual item checkboxes* option to allow multi-item selection in the view.

Figure 15 - 41: Tabular View section of the Edit View page

In the *Group By* section of the page shown in Figure 15 - 42, you can rearrange the rows in the view to group similar items together under common headings. Select a column from the *First group by the column* pick list, then select whether the group headings sort in ascending or descending order. To create a second level of nested groupings within the first level of groupings, select another column using the *Then group by the column* pick list, then select whether the nested group headings sort in ascending or descending order. Select whether the groupings appear collapsed or expanded by selecting the appropriate option for *By default, show groupings*. Finally, enter a value for *Number of groups to display per page* in the text box. If there is more than the specified number of groupings in the view, SharePoint displays links to navigate between multiple pages of items.

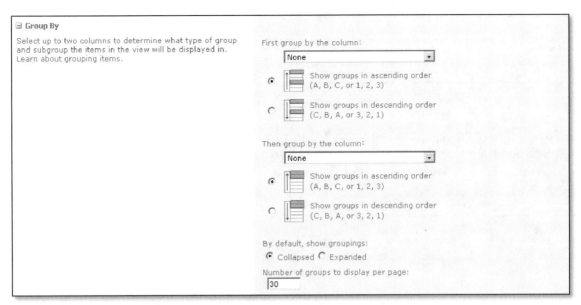

Figure 15 - 42: Group By section of the Edit View page

In the *Totals* section of the page shown in Figure 15 - 43, you can display totals at the bottom of any column in the view. The page displays a listing of all of the columns selected to appear in the view, as well as the option to display a total for each column. Select the appropriate option for each listed column.

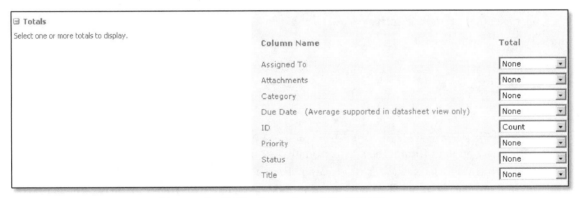

Figure 15 - 43: Totals section of the Edit View page

In the *Style* section of the page shown in Figure 15 - 44, you control the formatting of the items displayed in the view. Select the desired formatting option from the *View Style* pick list.

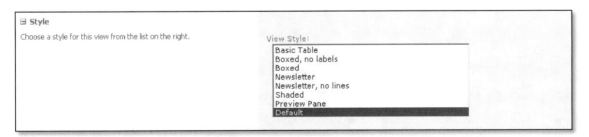

Figure 15 - 44: Style section of the Edit View page

In the *Folders* section of the page shown in Figure 15 - 45, you control whether folders appear in the view. Select the *Show items inside folders* option or the *Show all items without folders* option, depending upon your requirements.

Figure 15 - 45: Folders section of the Edit View page

In the *Item Limit* section of the page shown in Figure 15 - 46, you control how many item rows appear on each page in the view. Enter a number into the *Number of items to display* text box, then select the *Display items in batches of the specified size* option or the *Limit the total number of items returned to the specified amount* option, depending upon your requirements.

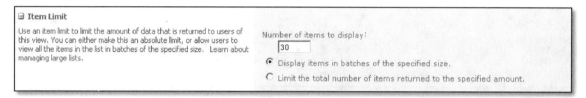

Figure 15 - 46: Item Limit section of the Edit View page

 A large number of items displayed in a view could have adverse effects on system performance.

In the *Mobile* section of the page shown in Figure 15 - 47, you can control mobile options for the view. Select the *Enable this view for mobile access* option to format the view optimally for mobile devices with small screens such as PDAs or mobile phones. Select the *Make this view the default view for mobile access* option to configure the view as the default mobile view. To limit the number of items displayed in the mobile view, enter a number in the *Number of items to display in list view web part for this view* text box.

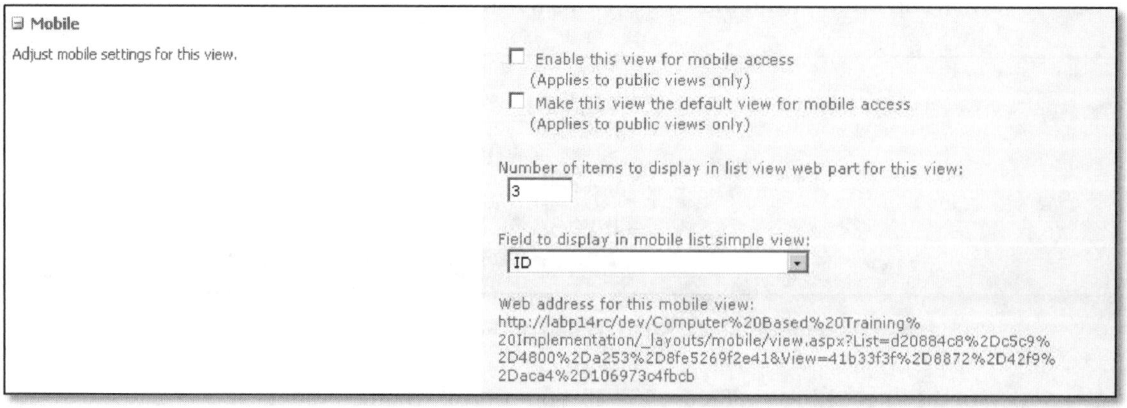

Figure 15 - 47: Mobile section of the Edit View page

MSProjectExperts recommends that if you have a generalized need for *Project Site* customizations such as new or modified views, you modify the base template for *Project Sites*. If you are using the *Enterprise Project Types* feature in Project Server, each project type can utilize its own *Project Site* template that has unique customizations for that Project Type.

Creating a New Standard View

A standard view is a basic SharePoint list view that displays items in table format with rows and columns. Figure 15 - 48 shows an example of a standard view.

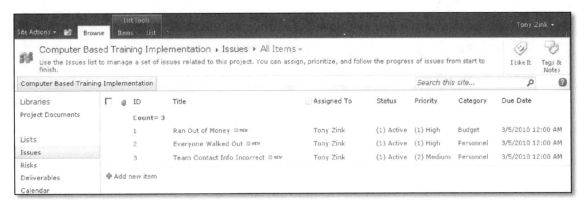

Figure 15 - 48: Example of a Standard view

To create a new standard view for a list, navigate to the list, click the *List* tab, then click the *Create View* button in the *Manage Views* section of the ribbon menu. In the *Choose a view format* section of the *Create View* page shown in Figure 15 - 49, click the *Standard View* option.

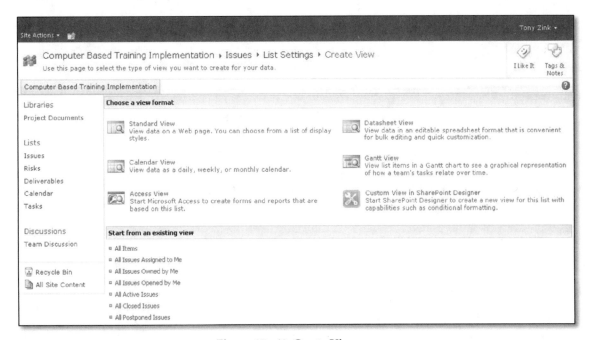

Figure 15 - 49: Create View page

The system displays the *Create View* page shown in Figure 15 - 50, which is very similar to the *Edit View* page shown previously. Enter a name for the new view in the *View Name* text box, and then select the *Make this the default view* option if you want this view to be the default view for everyone who visits the list. Next select the *View Audience* for the new view; to create a view that is visible only to you, select the *Create a Personal View* option, or to create a view that is visible to everyone, select the *Create a Public View* option. Select the other options on the page as described in the previous section, then click the *OK* button.

You can set only a Public View as the default view for a list or library.

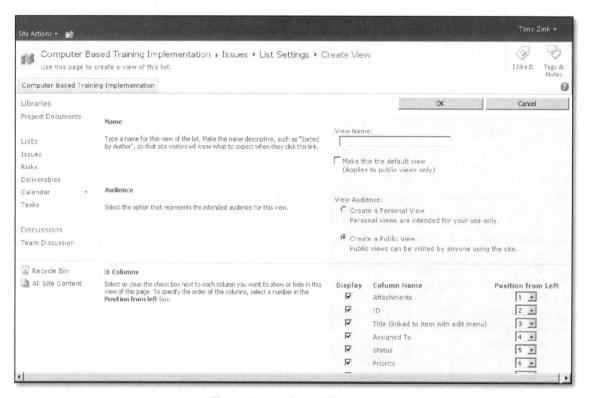

Figure 15 - 50: Create View page

You can also access the *Create View* page by navigating to the list or library, clicking the *List* or *Library* tab, and clicking the *List* or *Library Settings* button in the *Settings* section of the ribbon menu. Once on the *List* or *Library Settings* page, scroll to the *Views* section of the page and click the *Create view* link.

Creating a New Calendar View

A calendar view is a SharePoint list view that displays items in monthly, weekly, or daily calendar format. Figure 15 - 51 shows an example of a calendar view.

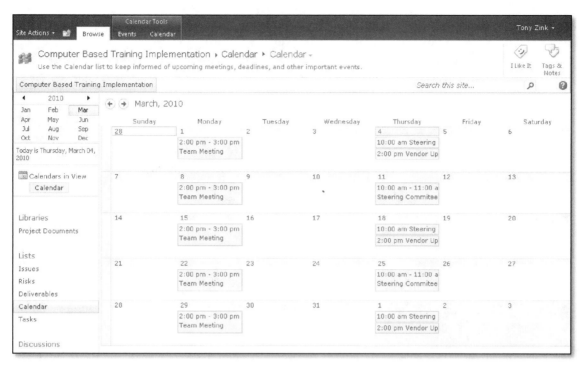

Figure 15 - 51: Example of a Calendar view

Calendar views are most useful for viewing lists of tasks, events, or other date-driven items.

To create a new calendar view for a list, navigate to the list, click the *List* tab, then click the *Create View* button in the *Manage Views* section of the ribbon menu. In the *Choose a view format* section of the *Create View* page, click the *Calendar View* option. The system displays the *Create Calendar View* page, shown in Figure 15 - 52. Select the appropriate options as described below and then click the *OK* button.

Figure 15 - 52: Create Calendar View page

The *Create Calendar View* page has several sections and options; some are similar to those for creating a standard view as described previously, and some are unique to calendar views. To control when each item begins and ends on the timeline, scroll to the *Time Interval* section of the *Create Calendar View* page shown in Figure 15 - 53. Select the column that contains the begin date for each item from the *Begin* pick list, and select the column that contains the end date for each item from the *End* pick list.

Figure 15 - 53: Time Interval section of the Create Calendar View page

 You **must** select a column in both the *Begin* and *End* pick lists. The system uses the dates in the selected columns to display items graphically on the calendar. Only columns that contain date information will appear in the *Begin* and *End* pick lists.

To control which columns of data appear for each item in the calendar view, scroll to the *Calendar Columns* section of the *Create Calendar View* page shown in Figure 15 - 54. Because a calendar view can be displayed in daily, weekly, or monthly format, you can configure a different column to appear as the title for each item in each of these types of views. To specify the title that appears for each item in the monthly calendar view, select the appropriate column from the *Month View Title* pick list. To specify the title that appears for each item in the weekly calendar view, select the appropriate column from the *Week View Title* pick list. To specify the title that appears for each item in the daily calendar view, select the appropriate column from the *Day View Title* pick list. Optionally, select a sub-heading to appear for each item in the weekly calendar view or the daily calendar view by selecting the appropriate column in the *Week View Sub Heading* pick list and the *Day View Sub Heading* pick list.

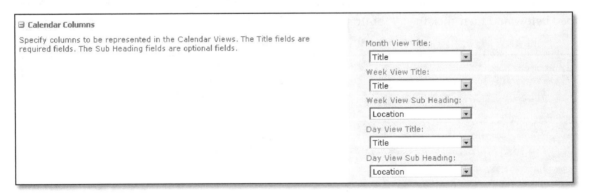

Figure 15 - 54: Calendar Columns section of the Create Calendar View page

To control whether the default calendar view is displayed in daily, weekly, or monthly calendar format, scroll to the *Default Scope* section of the *Create Calendar View* page shown in Figure 15 - 55 and select the appropriate *Default scope* option.

Figure 15 - 55: Default Scope section of the Create Calendar View page

Creating a New Access View

An Access view allows you to create a report or an interactive form in Microsoft Access by creating a local Access database on your PC that is connected to the SharePoint list; you can then create custom reports or forms that draw data from the local database. Any changes that you make to the local data are also transferred to the original SharePoint list in the *Project Site*. Figure 15 - 56 shows an example of a report originated through an *Access* view, and Figure 15 - 57 shows an example of a data entry form originated through an *Access* view.

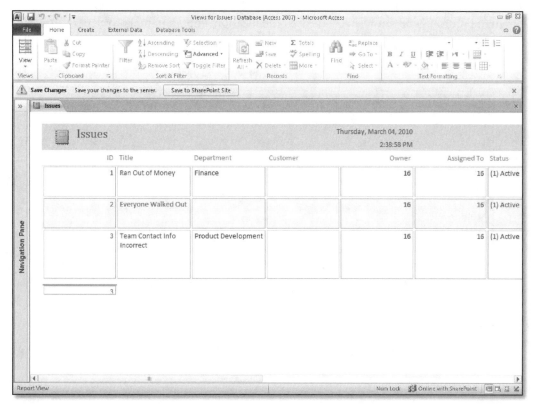

Figure 15 - 56: Example of an Access report

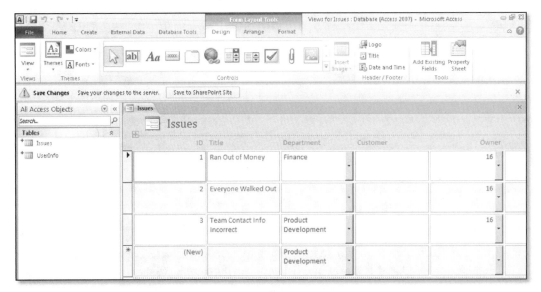

Figure 15 - 57: Example of an Access data entry form

To create a new *Access* view for a list, navigate to the list, click the *List* tab, then click the *Create View* button in the *Manage Views* section of the ribbon menu. In the *Choose a view format* section of the *Create View* page, click the *Access View* option. The system launches Microsoft Access on your desktop, which offers to create and save a new local database file, as shown in Figure 15 - 58; browse to a desired file location, enter a name for the new Access database file, and click the *Save* button.

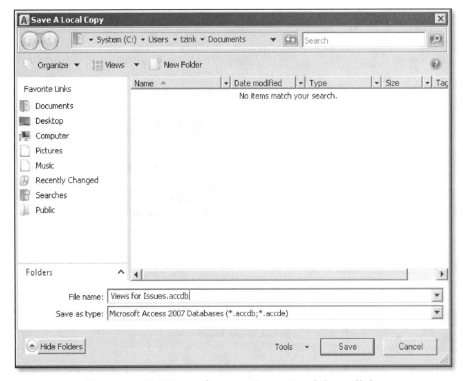

Figure 15 - 58: Microsoft Access Save a Local Copy dialog

You must have Microsoft Access 2010 installed on your computer in order to create an *Access* view.

Microsoft Access displays the *Create Access View* dialog shown in Figure 15 - 59 that presents options for creating a new report or interactive form based on the data from the *Project Site*. To create a new report, select the *Report* option, then click the *OK* button.

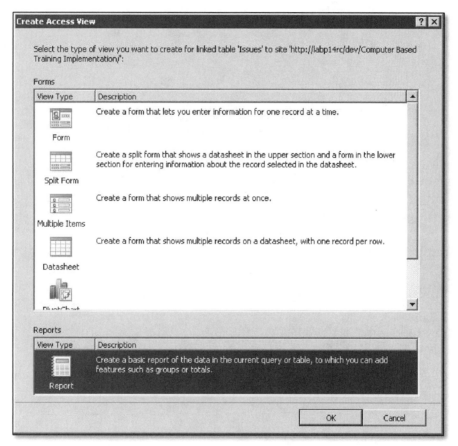

Figure 15 - 59: Microsoft Access Create Access View dialog

Microsoft Access displays the report designer, including live data from the *Project Site* that was copied to the local database file, as shown in Figure 15 - 60.

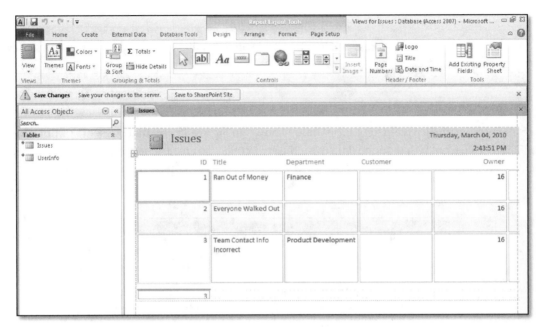

Figure 15 - 60: Microsoft Access report designer with live data

To create a new interactive form instead of a report, select one of the *Form* options in the *Create Access View* dialog, then click the *OK* button. Figure 15 - 61 shows a split form created in Microsoft Access, including live data from the *Project Site* that was copied to the local database file. Any data changes that you make locally through the form are also transferred to the original SharePoint list in the *Project Site*.

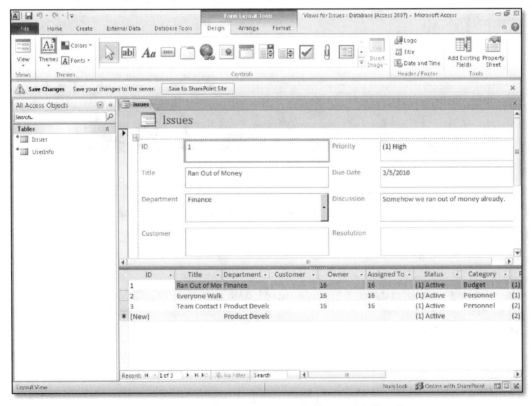

Figure 15 - 61: Microsoft Access split form with live data

Creating a New Datasheet View

A datasheet view is an interactive SharePoint view that displays items in table format with rows and columns and allows in-page editing of the data, including adding and deleting of items, as if you are working in an embedded spreadsheet. Figure 15 - 62 shows an example of a datasheet view.

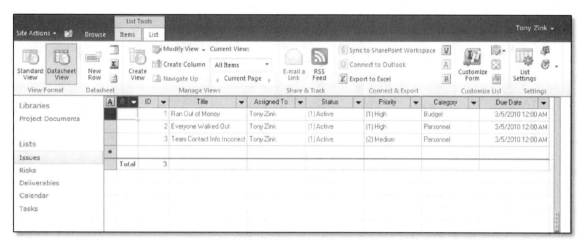

Figure 15 - 62: Example of a Datasheet view

To create a new datasheet view for a list, navigate to the list, click the *List* tab, then click the *Create View* button in the *Manage Views* section of the ribbon menu. In the *Choose a view format* section of the *Create View* page, click the *Datasheet View* option. The system displays the *Create Datasheet View* page, as shown in Figure 15 - 63. The sections and options available to configure the view are nearly identical to those available for creating a standard view described previously. Select the appropriate options for the view and then click the *OK* button.

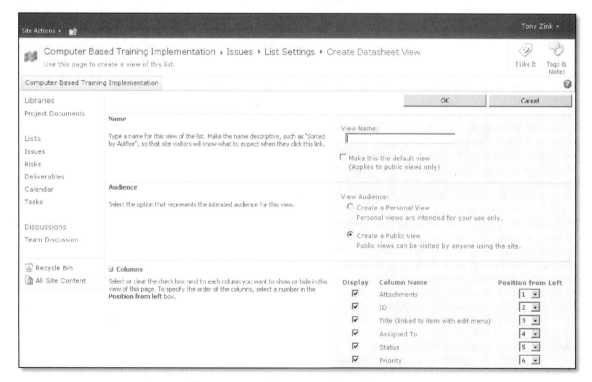

Figure 15 - 63: Create Datasheet View page

Creating a New Gantt View

A Gantt view is a SharePoint list view that displays items in Gantt chart format. Figure 15 - 64 shows an example of a Gantt view.

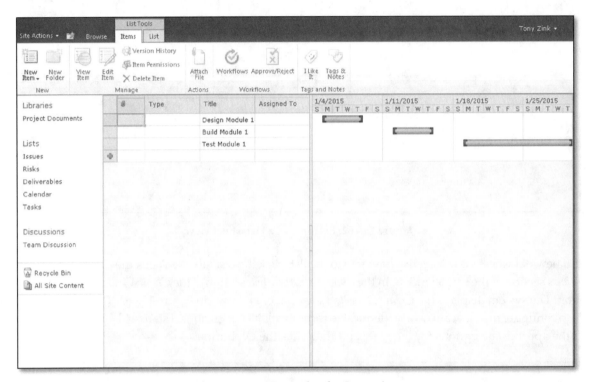

Figure 15 - 64: Example of a Gantt view

 Gantt views are most useful for viewing lists of tasks, events, or other date-driven items.

To create a new Gantt view for a list, navigate to the list, click the *List* tab, then click the *Create View* button in the *Manage Views* section of the ribbon menu. In the *Choose a view format* section of the *Create View* page, click the *Gantt View* option. The system displays the *Create Gantt View* page, as shown in Figure 15 - 65. Select the appropriate options as described below and then click the *OK* button.

Figure 15 - 65: Create Gantt View page

The *Create Gantt View* page has several sections and options; some are similar to those for creating a standard view as described previously, and some are unique to Gantt views. To control which columns represent the title for each Gantt bar, the date when each item begins and ends on the timeline, as well as the progress and predecessors for each Gantt bar, scroll to the *Gantt Columns* section of the *Create Gantt View* page shown in Figure 15 - 66. Select the column that contains the title for each Gantt bar from the *Title* pick list, select the column that contains the begin date for each item from the *Start Date* pick list, and select the column that contains the end date for each item from the *Due Date* pick list. Optionally select the column that contains the progress value for each Gantt bar from the *Percent Complete* pick list, and optionally select the column that contains the predecessor information for each Gantt bar from the *Predecessors* pick list.

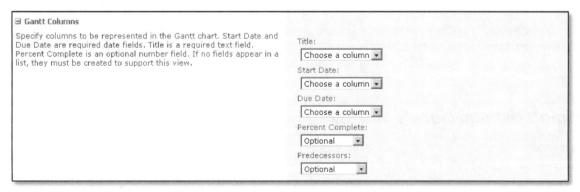

Figure 15 - 66: Gantt Columns section of the Create Gantt View page

You **must** select a column in both the *Start Date* and *Due Date* pick lists. The system uses the dates in the selected columns to display items graphically on the Gantt chart. Only columns that contain date information will appear in the *Start Date* and *Due Date* pick lists.

Creating a New View Based on an Existing View

Perhaps the easiest way to create a new view for a SharePoint list is by making a copy of an existing view, then making slight adjustments to achieve a view that meets your business requirements. To create a new view based on an existing one, navigate to the list, click the *List* tab, then click the *Create View* button in the *Manage Views* section of the ribbon menu. In the *Start from an existing view* section of the *Create View* page, click the name of the existing view upon which you want to base the new view. The system displays the *Create View* page, shown in Figure 15 - 67. Notice that if you scroll through the various sections of the page, the options are configured to match the existing view that you copied. Enter a name for the new view and select or adjust the appropriate options depending upon the type of view, then click the *OK* button.

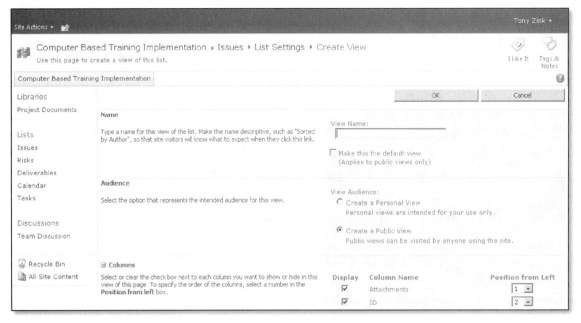

Figure 15 - 67: Create View page

Managing List and Library Settings

As I mentioned previously in this module, SharePoint organizes structured and unstructured content into list and library containers within a *Project Site*. There are several ways to control the behavior of these containers, which affects all of the items that are stored within them. To view and adjust the configuration settings for an entire list, navigate to the list, click the *List* tab, then click the *List Settings* button in the *Settings* section of the ribbon menu. As shown previously, the *List Settings* page provides options to configure columns and views for the list, as well as several other general settings and behaviors that I describe in the following sections.

Specifying List Title, Description, and Navigation Settings

To change the name or description for a list or to control whether the list is easily accessible from the Quick Launch navigation menu, click the *Title, description and navigation* link on the *List Settings* page, located below the *General Settings* heading. The system displays the *General Settings* page as shown in Figure 15 - 68.

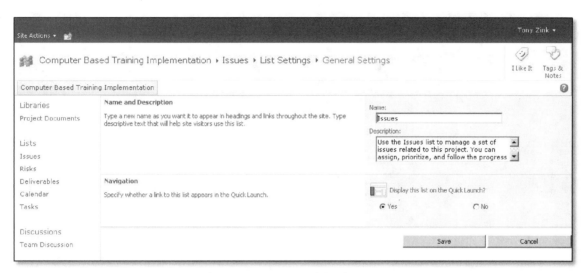

Figure 15 - 68: General Settings page

To change the name of the list, update the contents of the *Name* text box. To change the description of the list, update the contents of the *Description* text box. To control the Quick Launch navigation to the list, select the appropriate option for *Display this list on the Quick Launch*. Select the *Yes* option to display the list on the Quick Launch navigation menu, or select the *No* option to prevent the list from appearing on the menu.

Removing the Quick Launch navigation to a list **does not** remove the list itself from the Project Site; there are more indirect ways to navigate to a list if it does not appear on the Quick Launch menu.

MSProjectExperts recommends that you rename the *Calendar* and *Tasks* lists that are available in the default *Project Site*, as these names can imply to some people that they contain project task information. Consider renaming the *Calendar* list to *Event Calendar* or similar, and consider renaming the *Tasks* list to *Action Items* or similar.

Specifying List Versioning Settings

To change the content approval or item versioning behavior for a list, click the *Versioning Settings* link on the *List Settings* page, located below the *General Settings* heading. The system displays the *Versioning Settings* page as shown in Figure 15 - 69.

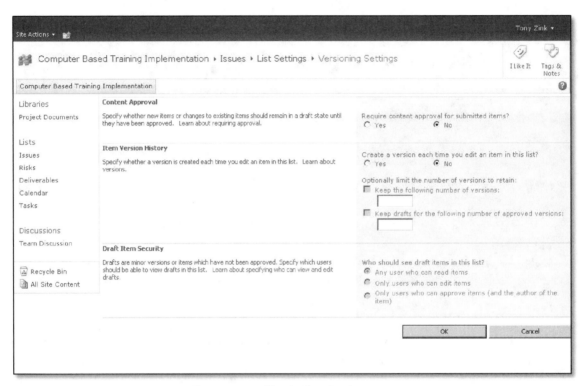

Figure 15 - 69: Versioning Settings page

In the *Content Approval* section of the page, select whether content approval is enabled in the list. Enabling content approval places a hold on all item submissions until someone with the appropriate permissions approves them. Submitted content items are not visible to the rest of the project team until they are approved. Select the *Yes* option to enable content approval for the list, or select the *No* option to disable content approval.

In the *Item Version History* section of the page, select whether item version control is enabled in the list. Enabling item versioning creates a new copy of an item each time someone with appropriate permissions edits the item. With item versioning enabled, you may also limit the number of versions that are retained for each item in the list. Select the *Yes* option to enable item versioning for the list, or select the *No* option to disable versioning. To limit the number of versions retained when versioning, select the *Keep the following number of versions* option and then enter a number of versions into the text box.

In the *Draft Item Security* section of the page, the options are inactive unless you enable content approval for the list. If you enable content approval, select which group of people should have access to unapproved draft items in the list.

MSProjectExperts recommends that you **do not** enable content approval in most cases for lists and libraries; doing so can impose an unnecessary process bottleneck, since project team members will not be able to see items such as new risks, issues, and project documents until they are approved.

MSProjectExperts recommends that you enable item version control in lists and libraries; doing so can provide valuable historical information for artifacts stored in a Project Site.

Specifying List Advanced Settings

To change several other behaviors for items stored in the list, such as item-level permissions, attachments, and search visibility, click the *Advanced Settings* link on the *List Settings* page, located below the *General Settings* heading. The system displays the *Advanced Settings* page shown in Figure 15 - 70.

Figure 15 - 70: Advanced Settings page

In the *Item-level Permissions* section of the page previously shown in Figure 15 - 70, select the options to control which items can be read and which items can be edited in the list. For *Read access*, there are two available options to control

695

which items people are allowed to read: *Read all items* or *Read items that were created by the user*. For *Create and Edit access*, there are three available options to control which items people are allowed to edit: *Create and edit all items*, *Create items and edit items that were created by the user*, or *None*.

MSProjectExperts recommends that you select *Read all items* for *Read access* and *Create and edit all items* for *Create and Edit access*.

In the *Attachments* section of the page, select whether people should have the ability to attach files to items stored in the list. Select the *Enabled* option to enable file attachments, or select the *Disabled* option to prevent file attachments. In the *Folders* section of the page, select whether people have the ability to create folders in the list for organizing items. Select the *Yes* option to display the *New Folder* command in the list and enable creation of folders, or select the *No* option to prevent folder usage.

MSProjectExperts recommends that you prevent people from organizing list items into folders. Attaching metadata columns to a list is a much better way to classify, organize, and locate items stored in a list.

In the *Search* section of the page shown in Figure 15 - 70 select whether the SharePoint search engine indexes content items in the list and makes them visible in search results. Select the *Yes* option to allow items in the list to appear in search results, or select the *No* option to prevent the items from appearing in search results.

Unless you have a specific reason to exclude items from appearing in search results, MSProjectExperts recommends that you enable searching within a list.

In the *Offline Client Availability* section of the page, select whether the items in the list should be downloadable to offline client programs such as Microsoft Office. Select the *Yes* option to allow offline client access, or select the *No* option to prevent offline client access. In the *Datasheet* section of the page, select whether datasheet views are enabled for the list. Datasheet views allow people to perform bulk editing of multiple items in a spreadsheet-like interface. Select the *Yes* option to enable datasheet views for the list, or select the *No* option to prevent datasheet views.

Datasheet views in SharePoint require that the proper Micrsoft Office components are installed on the desktop PC and that the appropriate ActiveX security permissions are enabled in the web browser. If your company has restrictions in these areas, then you may want to disable datasheet functionality.

In the *Dialogs* section of the page, select whether new, edit, and display item forms are launched in a dialog. If dialogs are not used, the system navigates to an entirely separate page each time people create new items, edit existing items, or display existing items in the list. Select the *Yes* option to enable form dialog functionality, or select the *No* option to disable dialog functionality.

Specifying List Validation Settings

To enforce certain business rules when people enter new items or edit existing data in a list, click the *Validation settings* link on the *List Settings* page, located below the *General Settings* heading. The system displays the *Validation Settings* page as shown in Figure 15 - 71.

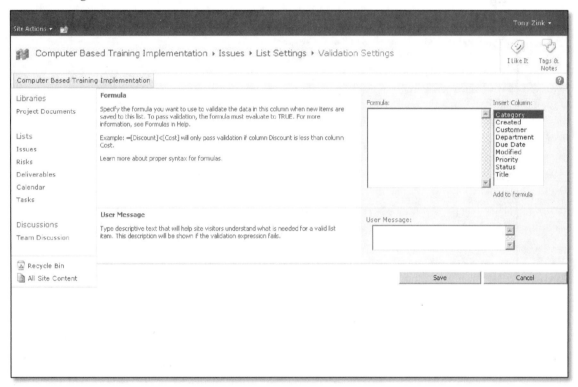

Figure 15 - 71: Validation Settings page

As with SharePoint column validation described previously in this module, you may enter a validation formula which prevents people from entering incorrect data when they add or edit items in the list. To enter a validation rule for the list, enter an expression into the *Formula* text box using similar syntax as is used for SharePoint calculated columns, which is based on Microsoft Excel formulas. To insert a reference to an existing column in the list, select the column in the *Insert Column* list, then click the *Add to formula* link below the column listing.

If data entered into the list does not comply with the validation rule that you enter, SharePoint does not save the item and an alert message appears for the user. To enter a custom alert message, enter the message into the *User message* text box.

For example, one of your business process requirements may state that the due date for any item entered into the list must be later than the date identified. The validation formula for this scenario is:

=[Due Date]>[Identified]

This formula states that the contents of the *Due Date* column must be greater than the contents of the *Identified* column. The user alert message for this scenario is:

You must enter a due date that is later than the identified date.

697

Figure 15 - 72 shows a case in which validation fails and the user alert message appears near the top of the form:

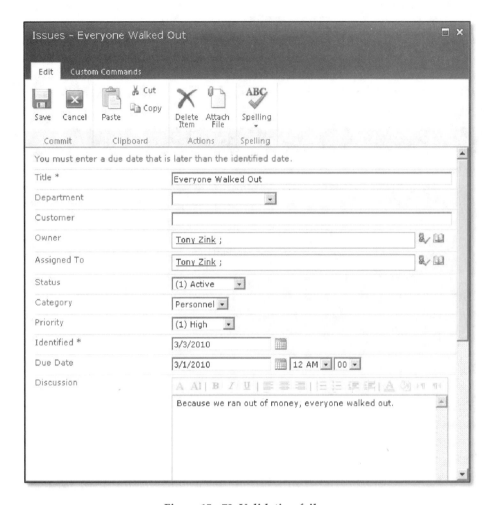

Figure 15 - 72: Validation failure

 Unlike SharePoint column validation described previously in this module, a list validation formula **can** refer to other columns in the list.

 You can enter only one list validation rule on the *Validation Settings* page; if you have multiple business rules to enforce on a list, you may need to use column validation, since each column in a list can have a unique validation rule.

Specifying List Rating Settings

To enable 5-star content item ratings in the list, click the *Validation settings* link on the *List Settings* page, located below the *General Settings* heading. The system displays the *Rating Settings* page shown in Figure 15 - 73.

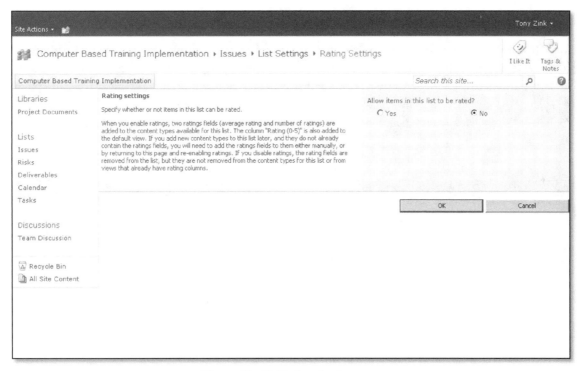

Figure 15 - 73: Rating Settings page

As Figure 15 - 74 shows, if you enable ratings in the list, the system adds two columns to the list, *Rating (0-5)* and *Number of Ratings*, as displayed on the *List Settings* page. SharePoint uses these two columns to store the average rating for each item in the list and the number of people who have rated each item.

Figure 15 - 74: Rating (0-5) and Number of Ratings columns on the List Settings page

If you enable ratings in the list, the system also adds the *Rating (0-5)* column to the default list view, as shown in Figure 15 - 75.

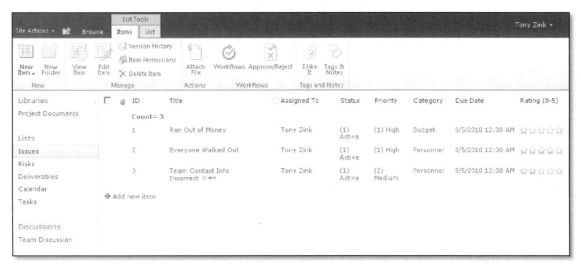

Figure 15 - 75: Issues list with Rating (0-5) column

Specifying List Audience Targeting Settings

SharePoint 2010 allows targeting of individual list items to specific audiences within the system; in other words, you may need to add to the *Issues* list an item that only a specific group of people can view, rather than the entire project team. To enable audience targeting in the list, click the *Audience targeting settings* link on the *List Settings* page, located below the *General Settings* heading. The system displays the *Modify List Audience Targeting Settings* page shown in Figure 15 - 76. Select the *Enable audience targeting* option to enable the feature, and then click the *OK* button.

Figure 15 - 76: Modify List Audience Targeting Settings page

With list audience targeting enabled, the system adds the *Target Audiences* column to the list and displays the column at the bottom of the new item and edit item forms, as shown in Figure 15 - 77. If you enter an audience into the *Target Audiences* column for an item, only the members of that audience can view the item.

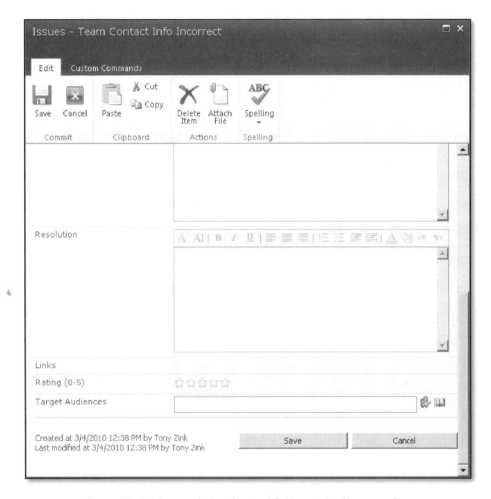

Figure 15 - 77: Issue editing form with Target Audiences column

To fully leverage the SharePoint audiences feature, you will need to create audiences and add people to those audiences in the SharePoint 2010 Central Administration web site for the farm.

Specifying List Metadata Navigation Settings

SharePoint 2010 has expanded metadata features compared to previous versions, including the ability to provide metadata-based navigation for filtering and locating items in large lists. To enable metadata-based navigation in the list, click the *Metadata navigation settings* link on the *List Settings* page, located below the *General Settings* heading. The system displays the *Metadata Navigation Settings* page shown in Figure 15 - 78. The page displays three groups of options: *Configure Navigation Hierarchies*, *Configure Key Filters*, and *Configure automatic column indexing for this list*.

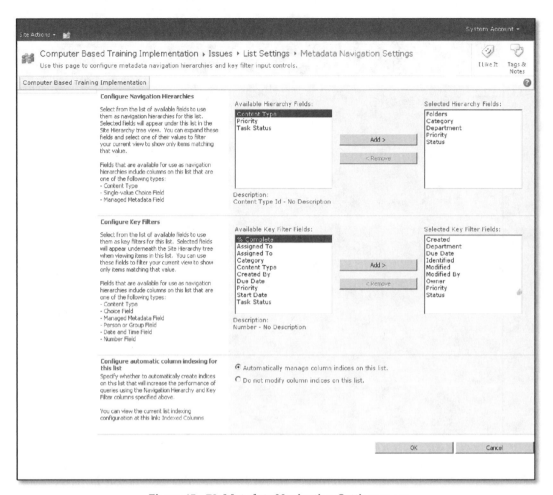

Figure 15 - 78: Metadata Navigation Settings page

In the *Configure Navigation Hierarchies* section of the page, select columns or fields in the *Available Hierarchy Fields* pick list, then click the *Add* button to add them to the *Selected Hierarchy Fields* listing. The terms in the *Selected Hierarchy Fields* list appear in a hierarchical metadata navigation pane that appears in the lower portion of the Quick Launch menu for the list.

In the *Configure Key Filters* section of the page, select columns or fields in the *Available Key Filter Fields* pick list, then click the *Add* button to add them to the *Selected Key Filter Fields* listing. The terms in the *Selected Key Filter Fields* list appear in a *Key Filters* metadata navigation pane that appears in the lower portion of the Quick Launch menu for the list.

In the *Configure automatic column indexing for this list* section of the page, select whether automatic column indexing is enabled for faster performance while using the metadata navigation pane. Select the *Automatically manage column indices on this list* option to enable the feature for the list, or select the *Do not modify column indices on this list* option to disable the feature.

With hierarchical metadata-based navigation enabled, the system adds the hierarchical metadata navigation pane to the list below the Quick Launch menu, shown in Figure 15 - 79. If you browse through the metadata hierarchy in the pane and click on a term, the system filters the list of items to show only those items that match your selection.

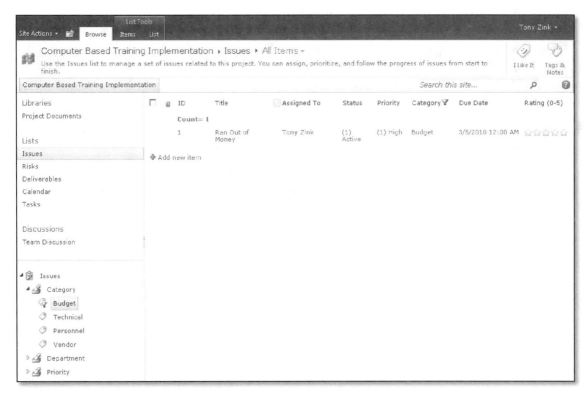

Figure 15 - 79: Issues list with hierarchical metadata navigation enabled

With *Key Filter* navigation enabled, the system adds the *Key Filter* navigation pane to the list below the Quick Launch menu, as shown in Figure 15 - 80. If you select or enter values for one or more terms in the pane and click the *Apply* button, the system filters the list of items to show only those items that match your selection.

Figure 15 - 80: Issues list with Key Filters metadata navigation enabled

Specifying Per-Location View Settings

Building on the expanded metadata and navigation features, SharePoint allows you to control which views are available under certain conditions; more specifically, you can attach views to metadata terms or content types and display those views only when people are accessing specific types of items in the list. For example, you may create a specially tailored view to be used only when working with budget issues in the *Issues* list.

To configure this selective view access feature, click the *Per-Location view settings* link on the *List Settings* page, located below the *General Settings* heading. The system displays the *Per-Location View Settings* page shown in Figure 15 - 81.

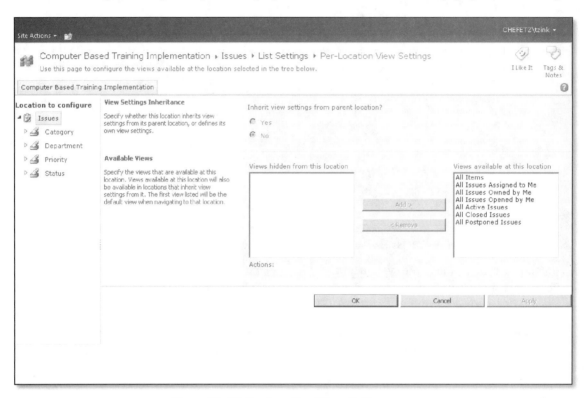

Figure 15 - 81: Per-Location View Settings page

 To fully leverage the *Per-Location View Settings* feature, you will need to associate multiple content types with a list or enable metadata navigation for the list.

The *Per-Location View Settings* page contains three sections: the *Location to configure* panel, the *View Settings Inheritance* section, and the *Available Views* section. To configure which views are available for the overall list, select the list name in the *Location to configure* panel, then add or remove views for this "location" in the *Available Views* section of the page. To hide a view from this location, select the view name in the *Views available at this location* pick list and click the *Remove* button. To make a view available for use in this location, select the view name in the *Views hidden from this location* pick list and click the *Add* button.

For example, to hide the *Budget Issues* custom view from the overall *Issues* list shown in Figure 15 - 81, shown previously, I select the *Budget Issues* view in the *Views available at this location* pick list, click the *Remove* button, and click the *Apply* button. When I navigate back to the *Issues* list, you see that the *Budget Issues* view no longer appears in the *Current View* pick list, as shown in Figure 15 - 82.

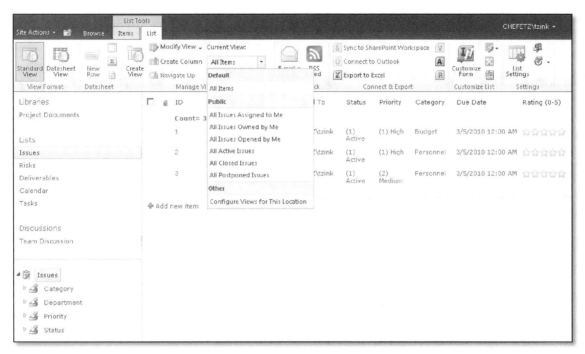

Figure 15 - 82: Issues list with Budget Issues view hidden

Continuing the example, to make the *Budget Issues* view available when people view budgetary issues in the list, I return to the *Per-Location View Settings* page, browse into the metadata hierarchy in the *Location to configure* panel, and click the *Budget* term, as shown in Figure 15 - 83. The terms shown are modifications from the built-in category column values from the *Project Site* template. The page refreshes and the *View Settings Inheritance* section of the page activates, allowing selection of either the *Yes* or the *No* option. I then select the *No* option to break view inheritance from the parent list, then I add the *Budget Issues* to the *Views available at this location* pick list and click the *Apply* button.

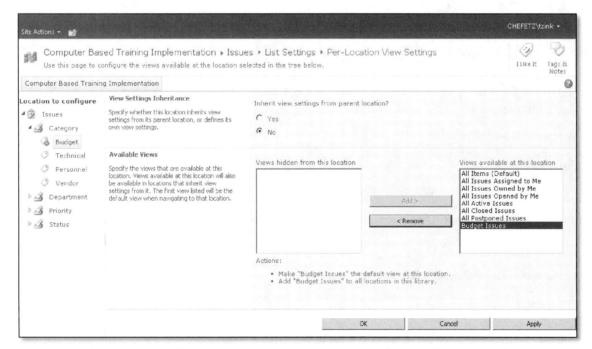

Figure 15 - 83: Adding the Budget Issues view for the budget term in the hierarchy

When I navigate back to the *Issues* list and select the *Budget* category in the hierarchical metadata navigation, you see that the *Budget Issues* view now appears in the *Current View* pick list, as shown in Figure 15 - 84.

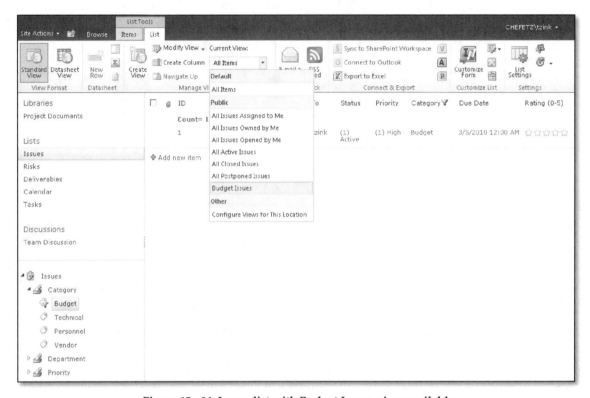

Figure 15 - 84: Issues list with Budget Issues view available

Adding Content Types to a List

A SharePoint content type is a type of information stored in the system that has a collection of configuration settings describing the entity, including the following:

- A collection of metadata columns for classifying the information.

- A file template, if it is a file content type.

- A retention and expiration policy.

- An auditing policy.

- One or more automated electronic workflows.

A common example of a content type is a *Trip Expense Report*, which may have the following attributes:

- Metadata columns such as *Trip Start*, *Trip End*, *Date Submitted*, *Trip Purpose*, and *Customer*.

- A Microsoft Excel spreadsheet file template.

- A three-year retention policy.

- An expense submission and approval electronic workflow.

Each *Project Site* has several built-in *Site Content Types* that you can associate with a list, and you can create custom content types based on your business requirements. To associate an existing content type with a list, you must first enable the usage of content types with the list. To enable content types for the list, click the *Advanced settings* link on the *List Settings* page, located below the *General Settings* heading. On the *Advanced Settings* page as described previously in this module, select the *Yes* option for *Allow management of content types* and click the OK button. The system displays the *List Settings* page again, and the *Content Types* section appears on the page as shown in Figure 15 - 85.

Figure 15 - 85: Content Types section of the List Settings page

To associate another content type with the list, click the *Add from existing site content types* link in the *Content Types* section of the page. The system displays the *Add Content Types* page shown in Figure 15 - 86. Select a group from the *Select site content types from* pick list to filter the *Available Site Content Types* pick list. Select one or more existing content types from the *Available Site Content Types* pick list, click the *Add* button to move them to the *Content types to add* list, then click the *OK* button.

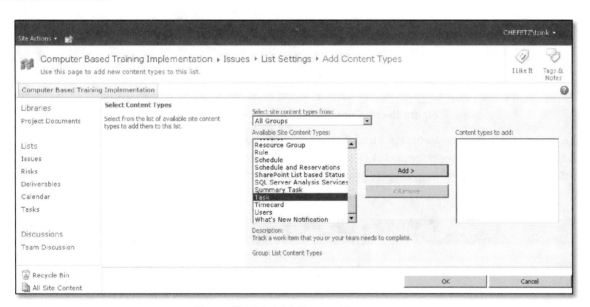

Figure 15 - 86: Add Content Types page

The system re-displays the *List Settings* page. Notice that the system now displays the newly added content type in the *Content Types* section of the page, as shown in Figure 15 - 87.

Figure 15 - 87: Content Type added to the Content Types section of the List Settings page

The system also displays the newly added content type under the *New* button for the list, as shown in Figure 15 - 88, and project team members can now add new items in the list using the new content type.

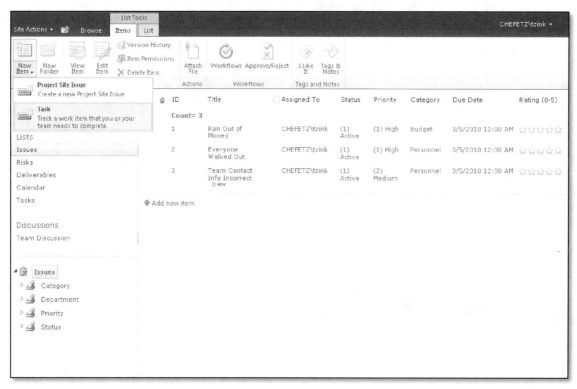

Figure 15 - 88: Content Type added to the New button

To change the ordering of the content types under the *New* button, as well as the default content type associated with the list, return to the *List Settings* page and click the *Change new button order and default content type* link in the *Content Types* section of the page; the system displays the *Change New Button Order and Default Content Type* page shown in Figure 15 - 89.

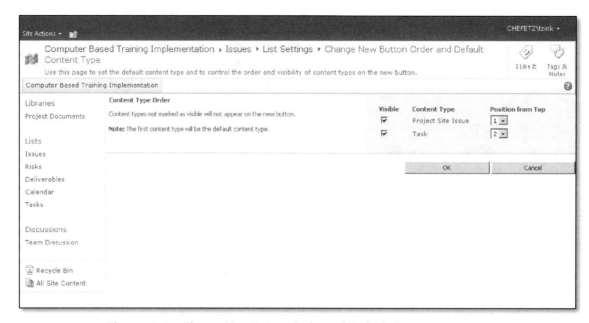

Figure 15 - 89: Change New Button Order and Default Content Type page

To change the order of the content types as they appear under the *New* button, select the appropriate position numbers next to each listed content type; the first listed content type also becomes the default content type associated with the list. To hide a content type from the *New* button entirely, deselect the *Visible* option next to the content type. When finished making adjustments, click the *OK* button.

Deleting a List

To delete a list entirely from the *Project Site*, click the *Delete this list* link on the *List Settings* page, located below the *Permissions and Management* heading. The system displays the confirmation dialog shown in Figure 15 - 90.

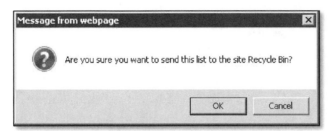

Figure 15 - 90: Warning dialog when deleting a list

Click the *OK* button to confirm the list deletion. The system then deletes the list, places it into the site recycle bin, and displays the *All Site Content* page.

Saving a List as a Template

SharePoint allows you to modify a list and save it as a template that you and others can use to create future lists. To save a list as a template, click the *Save list as template* link on the *List Settings* page, located below the *Permissions and Management* heading. The system displays the *Save as Template* page shown in Figure 15 - 91.

Figure 15 - 91: Save as Template page

In the *File Name* section of the page, enter a name, without a file extension, into the *File name* text box. In the *Name and Description* section of the page, enter a name for the template into the *Template name* text box and a brief description of the template into the *Template description* text box. In the *Include Content* section of the page, select the *Include Content* option to save all of the existing list items as part of the template. When finished entering the appropriate information, click the *OK* button. The system saves the list as a template and displays the *Operation Completed Successfully* message shown in Figure 15 - 92. Click the *OK* button to return to the *List Settings* page.

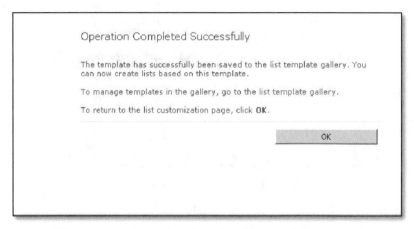

Operation Completed Successfully

The template has successfully been saved to the list template gallery. You can now create lists based on this template.

To manage templates in the gallery, go to the list template gallery.

To return to the list customization page, click **OK**.

OK

Figure 15 - 92: Operation Completed Successfully message

Warning: Although including content from the list in the template can be convenient for pre-populating new lists with data, doing so increases the size of the template file.

Specifying List Workflow Settings

An electronic workflow provides automation for business processes that your team follows; it can do many things, but a workflow generally routes information to the appropriate people and asks them to review or act upon that information. SharePoint typically tracks human interactions with an electronic workflow process by assigning workflow tasks to people; when those people complete their assigned workflow tasks, such as reviewing a document or approving a project proposal, the workflow can proceed to the next defined step or stage in the process.

To configure an electronic workflow that interacts with the items in a list, click the *Workflow Settings* link on the *List Settings* page, located below the *Permissions and Management* heading. The system displays the *Add a Workflow* page shown in Figure 15 - 93. If you already have a workflow installed on the list, the system displays an additional *Workflow Settings* page that lists your current workflows. From this page, click the *Add a Workflow* link.

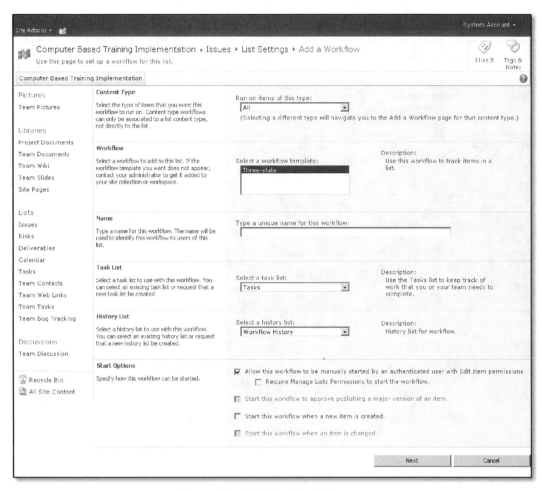

Figure 15 - 93: Add a Workflow page

In the *Content Type* section of the page, select whether the workflow should act upon all items in the list or on only certain content types that may exist there. If there are multiple content types associated with the list, they are available for selection from the *Run on items of this type* pick list. In the *Workflow* section of the page, select a workflow template to create the workflow. In a default installation of Project Server, only the *Three-state* workflow template appears in the *Select a workflow template* pick list. Using the *Three-state* template creates a three-stage workflow consisting of initial submission, first level approval, and final approval. If your organization needs additional workflows, you must create them with a tool such as Microsoft SharePoint Designer, Visual Studio, or another third party workflow tool.

In the *Name* section of the page, enter a name for the workflow in the *Type a unique name for this workflow* text box. In the *Task List* section of the page, select the task list that the system uses to track any workflow tasks generated by the system. By default, a single task list appears in the *Select a task list* pick list; this is the task list that is included in the default *Project Site* template. To create a new task list for tracking workflow tasks, select the *Tasks (new)* option from the pick list.

In the *History List* section of the page, select the workflow history list that they system uses to track historical workflow tasks. By default, there is no workflow history list included in the *Project Site* template; select the *Workflow History (new)* option from the *Select a history list* pick list. In the *Start Options* section of the page, select the appropriate options to control when the workflow is initiated for an item in the list. For example, to initiate a workflow automatically when a new item is added to the list, select the *Start this workflow when a new item is created* option. Click the *Next* button to proceed to the next step in the workflow configuration process. The system displays the *Customize* page for the selected workflow, shown in Figure 15 - 94.

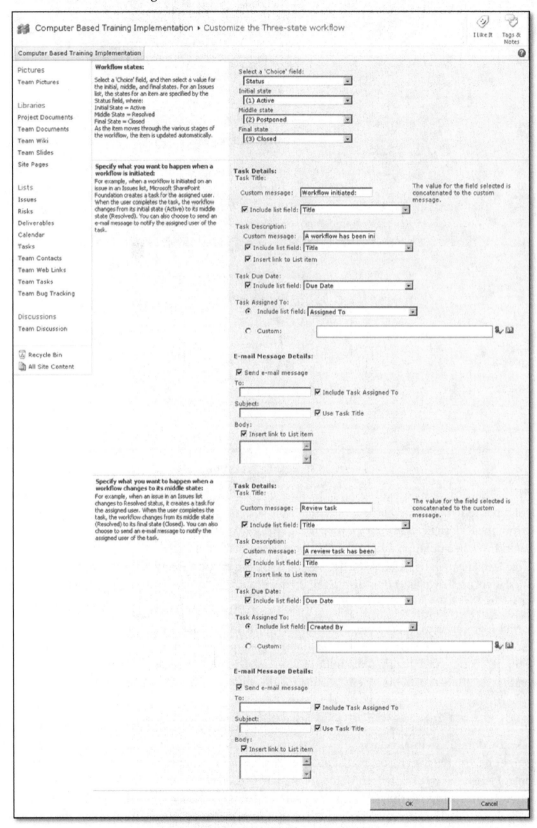

Figure 15 - 94: Customize workflow page

In the *Workflow states* section of the page, select the appropriate list column from the *Select a 'Choice' field* pick list that contains the three stages that the workflow manages. Notice that the pick list contains only *choice* columns. If you need to create a custom column that contains the three workflow stages, you need to create the column before proceeding through this workflow configuration process. Notice also that the *Initial state*, the *Middle state*, and the *Final state* pick lists are pre-populated with values from the selected choice column. This indicates to the system which value represents each stage in the workflow process. As the item moves through each stage of the process, the system assigns a workflow task that requires attention from a person. When the assigned person completes the assigned workflow task, the system automatically changes the column value to the next state and proceeds to the next stage. Make adjustments as necessary by selecting the appropriate values in each pick list.

In the *Specify what you want to happen when a workflow is initiated* section of the page shown in **Error! Reference source not found.**, select the appropriate options to control the workflow task that the system generates during the initiation stage and whether the system should also send a notification email message to the person assigned. There are several options that control the *Task Title*, the *Task Description*, the *Task Due Date*, and the *Task Assigned To.* Review the options and select them accordingly for your situation.

In the *Task Details* subsection, specify the values used to generate the title of the workflow task. In the *Custom message* field, enter a text string that forms the beginning of the *Task* name. By default, the system selects the *Include list field* option and selects the *Title* field on the accompanying pick list. The information in the *Title* field forms the second half of the *Task* name.

Use the next three options to generate the description for the new workflow task. In the *Custom message* field, enter a text string that forms the beginning of the task description. By default, the system selects the *Include list field* option and selects the *Title* field on the accompanying pick list. The information in the *Title* field forms the second half of the task description. Select the *Insert link to List item* option to create a hyperlink to the new list item in the workflow task description.

The next option in the *Task Details* subsection allows you to specify how SharePoint generates the Task Due Date. By default, the system selects the *Include list field* option and pre-selects the *Due Date* field. Use the final options in this subsection to control which person the system assigns to the workflow task. By default, the system selects the *Include list field* option and selects the *Assigned To* field on the accompanying pick list. If you want to assign the workflow task to a particular user, select the *Custom* option and enter the name of the user in the accompanying field.

In the *E-mail Message Details* subsection, select the default *Send e-mail message* option to force SharePoint to send an e-mail message to the person assigned to the new task. In the *To* field, enter an optional e-mail address for a person other than the one who is assigned to the workflow task. For example, you might enter the e-mail address of the PMO Director. If you select the default *Include Task Assigned To* option, the system automatically sends the message to the person assigned to the task. In the *Subject* field, enter an optional subject for the e-mail message. If you select the default *Include Task Title* option, the system automatically includes the name of the workflow task in the e-mail description section. In the *Body* field, enter the body of the e-mail message. If you select the default *Insert link to List item* option, the system adds a hyperlink to the new list item in the body of the e-mail message.

In the *Specify what you want to happen when a workflow changes to its middle state* section of the page, select the appropriate options to control the workflow task that the system generates during the middle stage and whether the system should also send a notification email message to the person assigned. As described for the previous section, there are several options that allow you to control the *Task Title*, the *Task Description*, the *Task Due Date*, and the *Task Assigned To* options. Review the options and select them according to your requirements. When finished configuring all of the workflow options, click the *OK* button.

To view the workflows previously created for the list, click the *Workflow Settings* link on the *List Settings* page; the system displays the *Workflow Settings* page. In addition to displaying workflows attached to the list, the page also displays whether the workflows have any instances in progress.

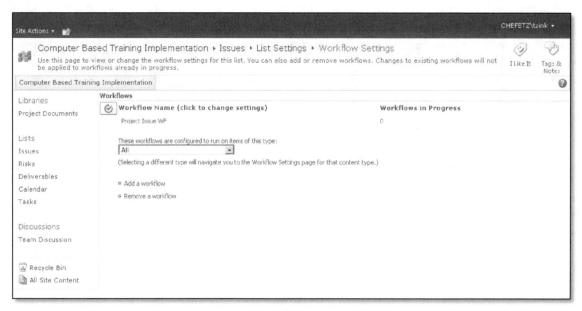

Figure 15 - 95: Workflow Settings page

To add another electronic workflow to the list, click the *Add a workflow* link on the *Workflow Settings* page; the system displays the *Add a Workflow* page and proceeds through the configuration process described previously.

To remove a workflow from the list, click the *Remove a workflow* link on the *Workflow Settings* page; the system displays the *Remove Workflows* page shown in Figure 15 - 96. To prevent a new instance of the workflow from running on any additional items in the list while allowing existing workflows to complete, select the *No New Instances* option; to remove a workflow entirely from the list, select the *Remove* option, then click the *OK* button.

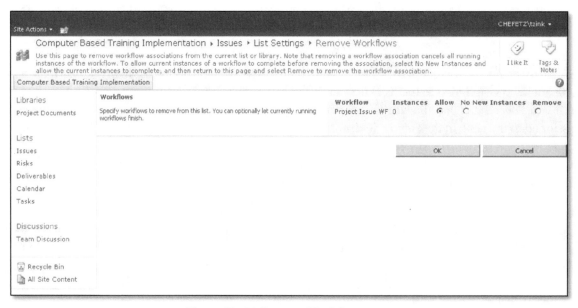

Figure 15 - 96: Remove Workflows page

Warning: Be careful not to remove a workflow that may have instances in-progress, as this may confuse people and be disruptive to the business process. It is better to first select the *No New Instances* option for a workflow for a certain period of time to allow any currently running instances the opportunity to complete before you remove the workflow entirely.

Specifying Information Management Policy Settings

In some organizations, modifying, deleting, and printing electronic information can have regulatory and legal ramifications. SharePoint offers tools for enforcing data retention, auditing, and printing policies in these environments through the *Information Management Policy* feature.

To configure the data retention, auditing, and printing policy settings for a list, click the *Information management policy settings* link on the *List Settings* page, located below the *Permissions and Management* heading. The system displays the *Information Management Policy Settings* page shown in Figure 15 - 97. Notice that the page displays a listing of the content types associated with the list, as well as information about any policies that are configured for each. For example, the *Information Management Policy Settings* page for the *Issues* list shows the *Project Site Issue* and the *Folder* content types. The *Project Site Issue* content type is the primary content type for the list.

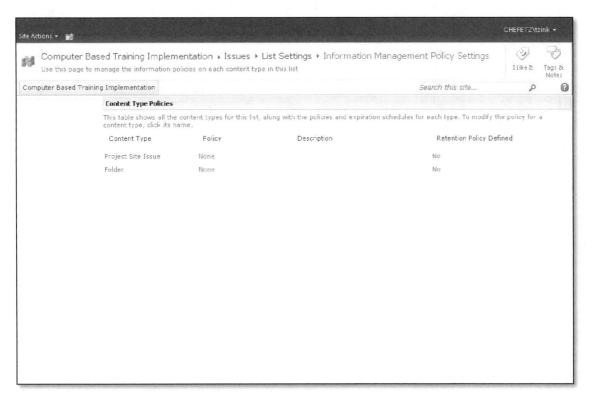

Figure 15 - 97: Information Management Policy Settings page

To configure the policy settings for a content type, click on the content type name. The system displays the *Edit Policy* page, shown in Figure 15 - 98. The *Edit Policy* page contains several sections: *Name and Administrative Description*, *Policy Statement*, *Retention*, *Auditing*, *Barcodes*, and *Labels*.

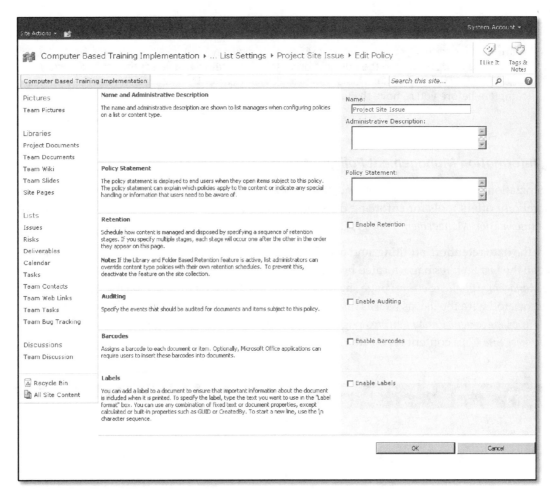

Figure 15 - 98: Edit Policy page

In the *Name and Administrative Description* section of the page enter a description of the policy into the *Administrative Description* text box. The *Administrative Description* appears on the *Information Management Policy Settings* page for the selected content type. In the *Policy Statement* section of the page, enter a statement into the *Policy Statement* text box. The *Policy Statement* appears when people view items in the list that the policy applies to.

In the *Retention* section of the page, select the *Enable Retention* option to configure a retention policy for the selected content type. For example, your regulatory guidelines may state that project issues be retained for five years, then they are automatically deleted.

After clicking the *Enable Retention* option, the *Add a retention stage* link appears; click the link to configure a retention stage. The system displays the *Stage Properties* dialog, shown in Figure 15 - 99. In the *Stage Properties* dialog, select the column from the *Time Period* pick list that contains the date that the system uses to begin the retention timeframe. Next enter the number and time units to designate the length of the retention period. Finally select an action from the *When this stage is triggered, perform this action* pick list, then click the *OK* button. In Figure 15 - 99, I indicate that the retention period begins at the item creation date and spans five years, then at the end of the time period the system moves the item to the recycle bin.

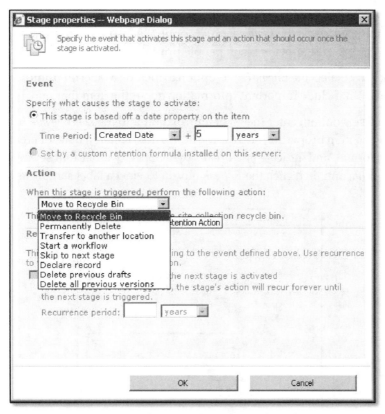

Figure 15 - 99: Auditing section of the Edit Policy page

The system displays the retention information in the *Retention* section of the *Edit Policy* page shown in Figure 15 - 100. To edit or delete an existing retention policy stage, click on the link for the listed policy. To add a new retention stage, click the *Add a retention stage* link and repeat the process.

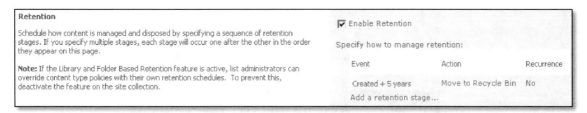

Figure 15 - 100: Retention section of the Edit Policy page

In the *Auditing* section of the page shown previously in Figure 15 - 98, select the *Enable Auditing* option to instruct the system to track specific types of item-related events for the content type. After clicking the *Enable Auditing* option, the following events become available for auditing:

- Opening or downloading documents, viewing items in lists, or viewing item properties

- Editing items

- Checking out or checking in items

- Moving or copying items to another location in the site

- Deleting or restoring items

Select the events that meet your auditing needs. The system tracks the selected events in a log when they occur.

In the *Barcodes* section of the page, select the *Enable Barcodes* option to instruct the system to assign a barcode for each item of the content type. The barcode appears when people print the item.

In the *Labels* section of the page, select the *Enable Labels* option to include a label on printouts when people print items of this content type. Labels can include important information about the item that may not normally be printed.

After selecting the *Enable Labels* option, enter the label information into the *Label format* text box. You can enter any combination of static text and item properties, such as the item's title, creation date, or creator. Enter item properties using the **{column name}** format, and indicate line breaks by **\n**. Specify other font settings such as *Font*, *Size*, *Style*, *Justification*, *Height*, and *Width*, and then click the *Refresh* button to view a label sample as shown in Figure 15 - 101.

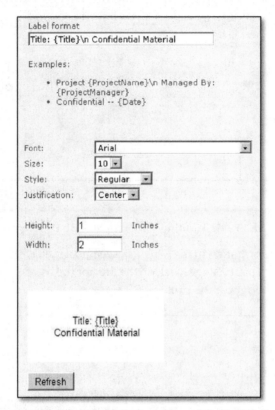

Figure 15 - 101: Expanded Labels section of the Edit Policy page

Specifying List RSS Settings

All SharePoint lists are capable of generating an RSS feed, which is an XML-based data feed that people or other systems can subscribe to and consume. An RSS feed for a SharePoint list contains the latest items added to that list.

To configure the RSS settings for a list, click the *RSS settings* link on the *List Settings* page, located below the *Communications* heading. The system displays the *Modify RSS Settings* page shown in Figure 15 - 102. The *Modify RSS Settings* page contains four sections: *List RSS*, *RSS Channel Information*, *Columns*, and *Item Limit*.

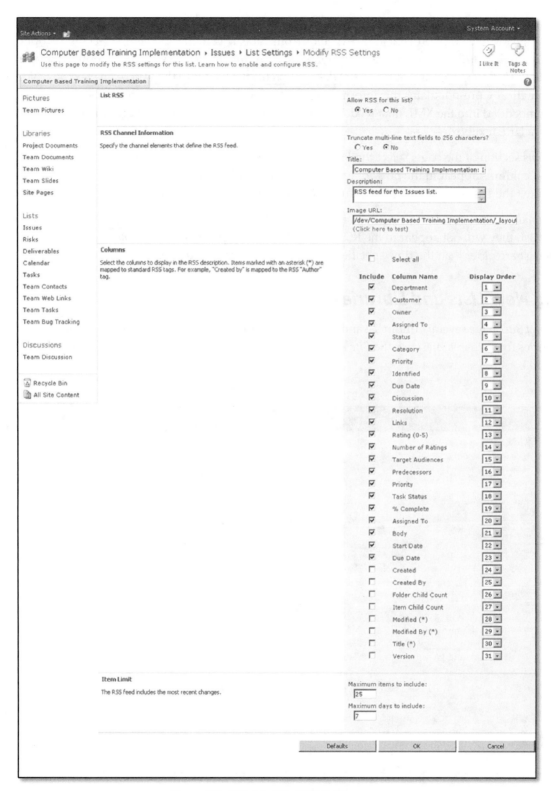

Figure 15 - 102: Modify RSS Settings page

In the *List RSS* section of the page, select whether the system should generate an RSS data feed for the list. Select the *Yes* option to enable the RSS feed, or select the *No* option to disable the RSS feed.

In the *RSS Channel Information* section of the page, specify general information about the list that the system embeds in the header of the XML feed. To prevent long text fields from appearing in the RSS feed, select the *Yes* option for *Truncate multi-line text fields to 256 characters?*; to allow long text fields into the feed, select the *No* option. Enter a title for the RSS feed into the *Title* text box, and enter a brief description for the feed into the *Description* text box. Notice that the system automatically pre-populates this information. Each RSS feed can contain an image, such as a company logo, that is also embedded into the XML data feed. To specify a location for a custom image, enter the URL of the image into the *Image URL* text box.

In the *Columns* section of the page, select the *Include* option for each column of data to appear in the RSS data feed. Any selected columns appear in the body of each item in the RSS feed. To control the display order for the selected columns, adjust the *Display Order* pick list value next to each selected column that will appear in the feed.

In the *Item Limit* section of the page, enter an item limit in the *Maximum items to include* text box; if there are more items in the list, they will not appear in the RSS feed. Enter a time limit into the *Maximum days to include* text box; if items in the list are older than the time specified, they will not appear in the feed.

Creating New Lists and Libraries

Default *Project Sites* have several built-in list and library repositories for project team collaboration. To view a listing of the repositories for a *Project Site*, click the *Site Actions* menu and select the *View All Site Content* option, as shown in Figure 15 - 103.

Figure 15 - 103: Selecting View All Site Content from the Site Actions menu

The system displays the *All Site Content* page shown in Figure 15 - 104.

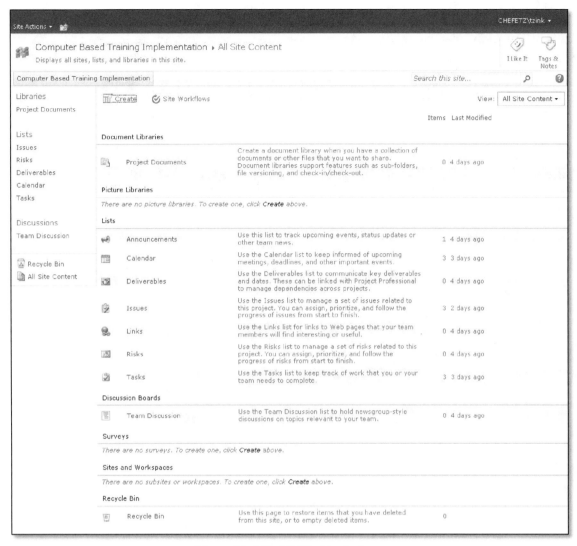

Figure 15 - 104: All Site Content page

The default *Project Site* includes the following content repositories:

- Project Documents

- Announcements

- Calendar

- Deliverables

- Issues

- Links

- Risks

- Tasks

- Team Discussion

Although *Project Sites* have several built-in lists and libraries for project team collaboration, you may need to add a new repository in an individual *Project Site,* or you may need to add a new repository to a *Project Site* template that the system uses to generate future *Project Sites.*

In the following sections I describe how to create some of the more common types of list and library repositories in a *Project Site.* To create a new repository in a *Project Site,* click the *Create* link on the *All Site Content* page. The system displays the *Create* page shown in Figure 15 - 105 where you select the type of repository to create.

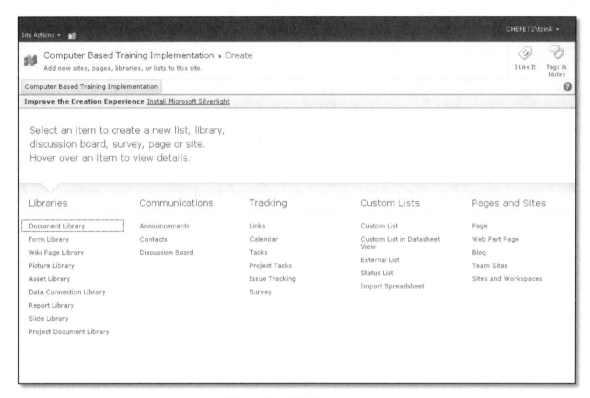

Figure 15 - 105: Create page

 As a shortcut to the *Create* page, you may also select *More Options* from the SharePoint *Site Actions* menu.

Creating a New Document Library

A SharePoint document library is a repository for storing documents and other types of files to share with the Project Team. To create a new document library in a *Project Site,* navigate to the *Create* page in the *Project Site* as described previously, and click the *Document Library* link, located below the *Libraries* heading. The system displays the *New* page shown in Figure 15 - 106.

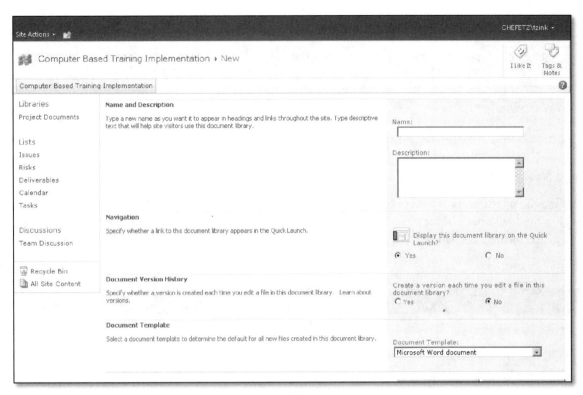

Figure 15 - 106: New document library page

The *New* page contains four sections: *Name and Description*, *Navigation*, *Document Version History*, and *Document Template*. In the *Name and Description* section of the page, enter a name for the new document library into the *Name* text box, and enter a brief description for the new library into the *Description* text box. In the *Navigation* section of the page, select whether the new library will appear in the *Project Site* Quick Launch navigation menu. Select the *Yes* option to display a link to the new library in the Quick Launch menu, or select the *No* option to hide the library from the menu.

In the *Document Version History* section of the page, select whether to enable version control in the new library. Select the *Yes* option to enable versioning in the new library, or select the *No* option to disable versioning. In the *Document Template* section of the page, select a default file type that the system uses when people click the *New* button. Select one of the types from the *Document Template* pick list and click the *Create* button. Figure 15 - 107 shows a newly-created document library with documents added.

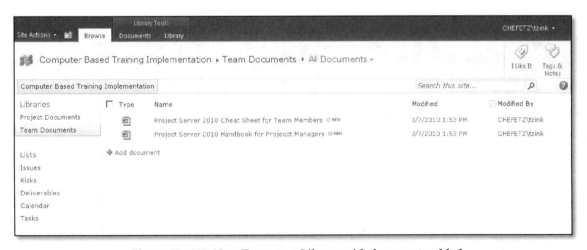

Figure 15 - 107: New Document Library with documents added

MSProjectExperts recommends that you visit the *Library Settings* page and review the configuration of the new library and make adjustments based on your business requirements.

Creating a New Wiki Page Library

A SharePoint wiki page library is a set of connected and easily editable web pages that the project team can contribute to. To create a new wiki page library in a *Project Site*, navigate to the *Create* page in the *Project Site* and click the *Wiki Page Library* link, located below the *Libraries* heading. The system displays the *New* page shown in Figure 15 - 108.

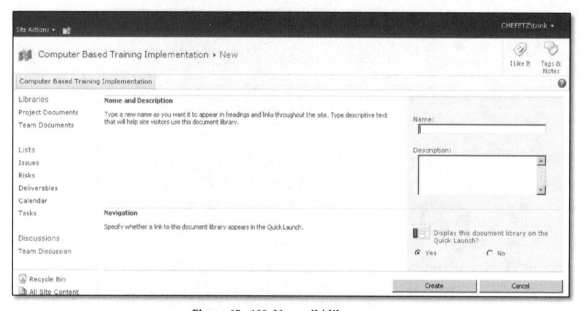

Figure 15 - 108: New wiki library page

In the *Name and Description* section of the page, enter a name for the new library into the *Name* text box, and enter a brief description for the new library into the *Description* text box. In the *Navigation* section of the page, select whether the new library appears in the *Project Site* Quick Launch navigation menu. Select the *Yes* option to display a link to the new library in the Quick Launch menu, or select the *No* option to hide the library from the menu. Figure 15 - 109 shows a newly-created wiki library home page.

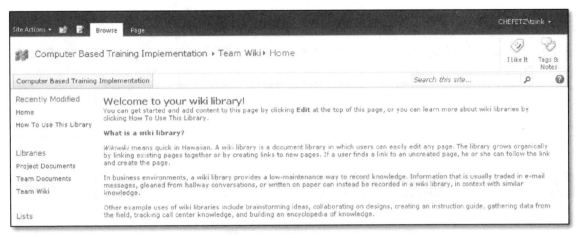

Figure 15 - 109: New Wiki Library home page

 MSProjectExperts recommends that you visit the *Library Settings* page and review the configuration of the new library and make adjustments based on your business requirements.

Creating a New Picture Library

A SharePoint picture library is a repository for storing pictures and other types of images to share with the Project Team. To create a new picture library in a *Project Site*, navigate to the *Create* page in the *Project Site* and click the *Picture Library* link, located below the *Libraries* heading. The system displays the *New* page shown in Figure 15 - 110.

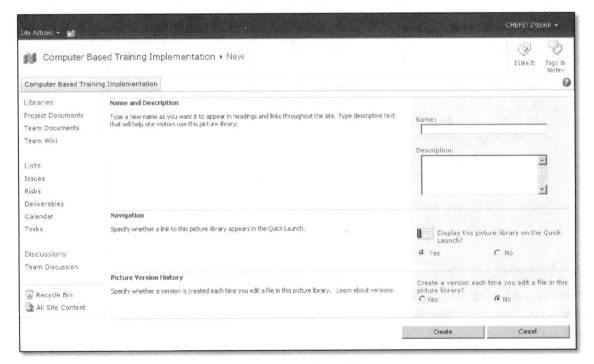

Figure 15 - 110: New picture library page

In the *Name and Description* section of the page, enter a name for the new library into the *Name* text box, and enter a brief description for the new library into the *Description* text box. In the *Navigation* section of the page, select whether the new library appears in the *Project Site* Quick Launch navigation menu. Select the *Yes* option to display a link to the new library in the Quick Launch menu, or select the *No* option to hide the library from the menu. In the *Picture Version History* section of the page, select whether to enable version control in the new library. Select the *Yes* option to enable versioning in the new library, or select the *No* option to disable versioning. Figure 15 - 111 shows a newly created picture library with pictures added.

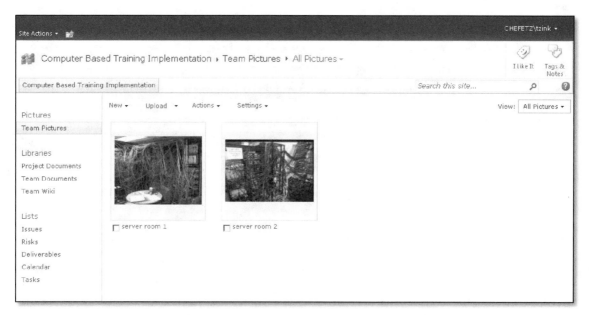

Figure 15 - 111: New picture library with pictures added

 MSProjectExperts recommends that you visit the *Library Settings* page and review the configuration of the new library and make adjustments based on your business requirements.

Creating a New Slide Library

A SharePoint slide library is a repository for storing Microsoft PowerPoint slides to share with the Project Team. To create a new slide library in a *Project Site*, navigate to the *Create* page in the *Project Site* and click the *Slide Library* link, located below the *Libraries* heading. The system displays the *New* page shown in Figure 15 - 112.

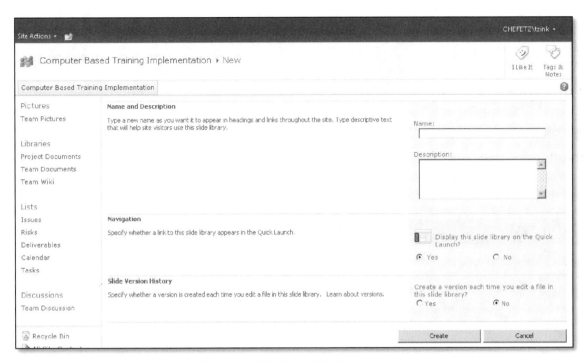

Figure 15 - 112: New slide library page

In the *Name and Description* section of the page, enter a name for the new library into the *Name* text box, and enter a brief description for the new library into the *Description* text box. In the *Navigation* section of the page, select whether the new library appears in the *Project Site* Quick Launch navigation menu. Select the *Yes* option to display a link to the new library in the Quick Launch menu, or select the *No* option to hide the library from the menu. In the *Slide Version History* section of the page, select whether to enable version control in the new library. Select the *Yes* option to enable versioning in the new library, or select the *No* option to disable versioning. Figure 15 - 113 shows a newly created slide library with Microsoft PowerPoint slides added.

Figure 15 - 113: New slide library with Microsoft PowerPoint slides added

MSProjectExperts recommends that you visit the *Library Settings* page and review the configuration of the new library and make adjustments based on your business requirements.

Creating a New Contacts List

A SharePoint contacts list is a repository for storing contact information to share with the Project Team. To create a new contacts list in a *Project Site*, navigate to the *Create* page in the *Project Site* and click the *Contacts* link, located below the *Communications* heading. The system displays the *New* page shown in Figure 15 - 114.

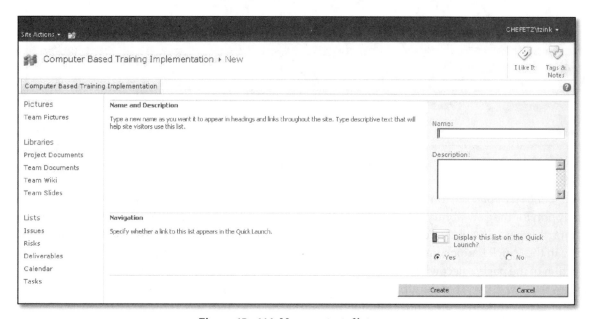

Figure 15 - 114: New contacts list page

In the *Name and Description* section of the page, enter a name for the new list into the *Name* text box, and enter a brief description for the new list into the *Description* text box. In the *Navigation* section of the page, select whether the new list appears in the *Project Site* Quick Launch navigation menu. Select the *Yes* option to display a link to the new list in the Quick Launch menu, or select the *No* option to hide the list from the menu. Figure 15 - 115 shows a newly created contacts list with contacts added.

Figure 15 - 115: New contacts list with contacts added

MSProjectExperts recommends that you visit the *List Settings* page and review the configuration of the new list and make adjustments based on your business requirements.

Creating a New Links List

A SharePoint links list is a repository for storing web links to share with the Project Team. To create a new links list in a *Project Site*, navigate to the *Create* page in the *Project Site* as described previously and click the *Links* link, located below the *Tracking* heading. The system displays the *New* page shown in Figure 15 - 116.

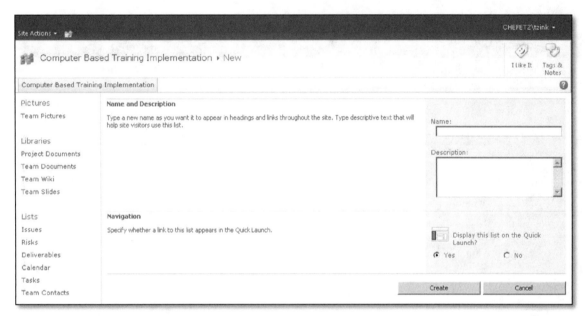

Figure 15 - 116: New links list page

In the *Name and Description* section of the page, enter a name for the new list into the *Name* text box, and enter a brief description for the new list into the *Description* text box. In the *Navigation* section of the page, select whether the new list appears in the *Project Site* Quick Launch navigation menu. Select the *Yes* option to display a link to the new list in the Quick Launch menu, or select the *No* option to hide the list from the menu. Figure 15 - 117 shows a newly created links list with web links added.

Figure 15 - 117: New links list with web links added

MSProjectExperts recommends that you visit the *List Settings* page and review the configuration of the new list and make adjustments based on your business requirements.

Creating a New Project Tasks List

A SharePoint project tasks list is a repository for storing tasks and displaying them in Gantt Chart format to share with the Project Team. To create a new project tasks list in a *Project Site*, navigate to the *Create* page in the *Project Site* and click the *Links* link, located below the *Tracking* heading. The system displays the *New* page shown in Figure 15 - 118.

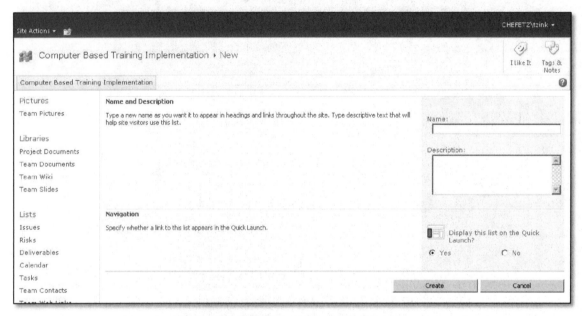

Figure 15 - 118: New project tasks list page

In the *Name and Description* section of the page, enter a name for the new list into the *Name* text box, and enter a brief description for the new list into the *Description* text box. In the *Navigation* section of the page, select whether the new list appears in the *Project Site* Quick Launch navigation menu. Select the *Yes* option to display a link to the new list in the Quick Launch menu, or select the *No* option to hide the list from the menu. Figure 15 - 119 shows a newly created project tasks list with a Gantt view and tasks added.

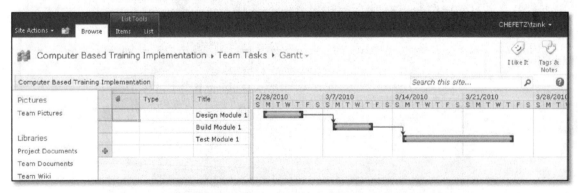

Figure 15 - 119: New project tasks list Gantt view with tasks added

MSProjectExperts recommends that you visit the *List Settings* page and review the configuration of the new list and make adjustments based on your business requirements.

As with a standard SharePoint tasks list, a project tasks list is not intended to track work that is managed by Microsoft Project Server. Use tasks lists and project tasks lists to track and manage action items, punch list items, and other items that are too small in scope or schedule to track in a Microsoft Project schedule.

Creating a New Custom List

At times you may need to create a custom repository in a *Project Site* that does not fit into any of the provided template categories. For example, a project team may need a list for tracking directional decisions that may impede project progress if not addressed in a timely manner, or the team may need a list for tracking bugs discovered in a new software product under development.

To manually create a new custom list in a *Project Site*, navigate to the *Create* page in the *Project Site* and click the *Custom List* link, located below the *Custom Lists* heading. The system displays the *New* page shown in Figure 15 - 120.

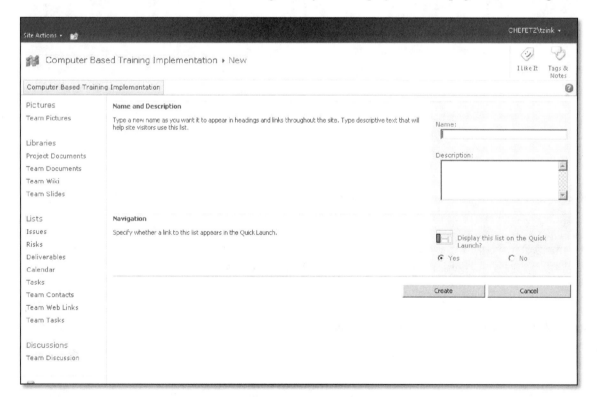

Figure 15 - 120: New custom list page

In the *Name and Description* section of the page, enter a name for the new list into the *Name* text box, and enter a brief description for the new list into the *Description* text box. In the *Navigation* section of the page, select whether the new list appears in the *Project Site* Quick Launch navigation menu. Select the *Yes* option to display a link to the new list in the Quick Launch menu, or select the *No* option to hide the list from the menu.

Figure 15 - 121 shows a newly created custom list. Depending upon your list requirements, you may need to add columns, enable version control, create views, and so forth. Click the *List Settings* button to navigate to the *List Settings* page and further configure the new custom list.

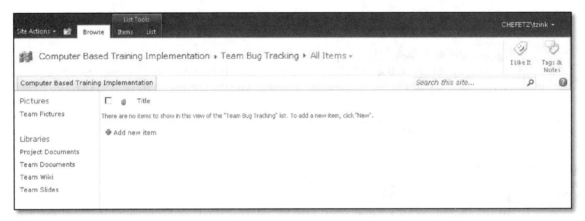

Figure 15 - 121: New Custom List

Figure 15 - 122 shows an example of a fully-configured custom list for tracking software bugs discovered during the product development process.

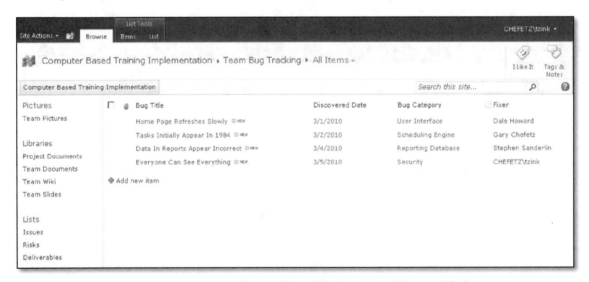

Figure 15 - 122: New Custom List with columns and items added

Creating a New Custom List by Importing a Spreadsheet

At times you may need to convert a Microsoft Excel spreadsheet into a SharePoint list in a *Project Site* to share the data with members of the project team.

To create a new custom list in a *Project Site* by importing a spreadsheet, navigate to the *Create* page in the *Project Site* and click the *Import Spreadsheet* link, located below the *Custom Lists* heading. The system displays the *New* page shown in Figure 15 - 123.

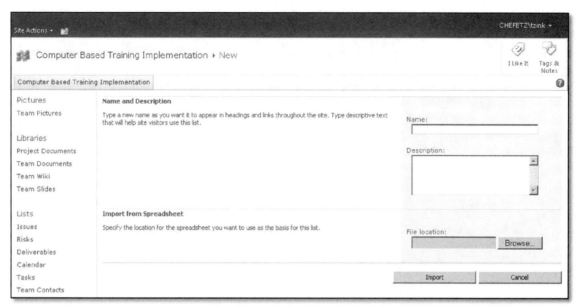

Figure 15 - 123: Create list from spreadsheet page

In the *Name and Description* section of the page, enter a name for the new list into the *Name* text box, and enter a brief description for the new list into the *Description* text box. In the *Import from Spreadsheet* section of the page, click the *Browse* button to browse for the Microsoft Excel spreadsheet on your local hard drive. The system displays the *Import* dialog, shown in Figure 15 - 124. Select the appropriate options in the dialog to select the data from the spreadsheet, and click the *Import* button.

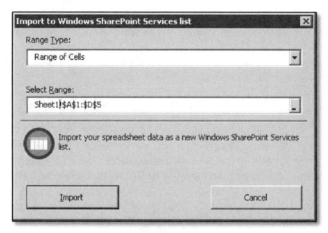

Figure 15 - 124: Import dialog

 Warning: The selected data from the spreadsheet needs to include a header row, because SharePoint uses this information to create new columns in the list to hold the imported data.

The system creates a new custom list and imports the data from the spreadsheet into the list as new items, as shown in Figure 15 - 125.

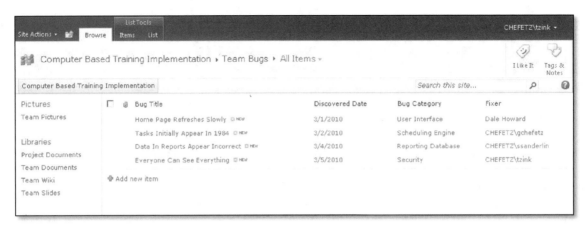

Figure 15 - 125: New custom list with columns and items added

MSProjectExperts recommends that you visit the *Library Settings* page and review the configuration of the new library and make adjustments based on your business requirements.

Warning: Although SharePoint automatically creates new columns in the list to hold the imported data, you should visit the *List Settings* page, inspect the newly created columns, and verify that they are configured correctly.

Warning: When using this method to create a custom SharePoint list, the system **does not** automatically create a link to the new list on the Quick Launch navigation menu. To access the new list, you may visit the *All Site Content* page. You may then navigate to *List Settings* page and add a link to the Quick Launch menu.

Creating and Editing Pages

In addition to the list and library repositories that the system creates for storing and managing content within a *Project Site*, SharePoint also provides *pages* for presenting that content in an organized and meaningful manner to *Project Site* visitors. Each *Project Site* contains a single *Home* page that can act as a central landing page or dashboard, and you can create additional pages based on your business process needs.

SharePoint provides a user-friendly web browser-based interface for creating and editing pages, and new pages reside in libraries, much like other types of unstructured SharePoint content. The exception is the *Home* page, which does not reside in a library.

Editing the Project Site Home Page

The *Project Site Home* page is a web part page, which allows placement of one or more web parts onto the page, organized into one or more web part zones. A web part is a page component that allows you to add content or functionality to a page; a web part zone is an area on the page where you may place one or more web parts. To edit the *Project Site Home* page in order to manipulate the web parts on the page, select *Edit Page* from the *Site Actions* menu, as shown in Figure 15 - 126.

Figure 15 - 126: Selecting Edit Page from the Site Actions menu

 You can also switch the page into editing mode by clicking the *Page* tab on the ribbon menu, then clicking the *Edit Page* button.

The system displays the *Home* page in editing mode as shown in Figure 15 - 127, allowing you to manipulate the contents of the page in any of the following ways:

- Add a web part to a web part zone

- Reposition a web part within a web part zone

- Move a web part to a different web part zone

- Remove a web part from the page

Notice that the *Home* page contains six web parts by default:

- The *Welcome to your site* web part, located in the *Left* web part zone, which displays a welcome message and general site use instructions

- The *Deliverables* web part, located in the *Left* web part zone, which displays items in the *Deliverables* list

- The *Issues* web part, located in the *Left* web part zone, which displays items in the *Issues* list

- The *Risks* web part, located in the *Left* web part zone, which displays items in the *Risks* list

- The *Site Image* web part, located in the *Right* web part zone, which displays a predefined image

- The *Links* web part, located in the *Right* web part zone, which displays items in the *Links* list

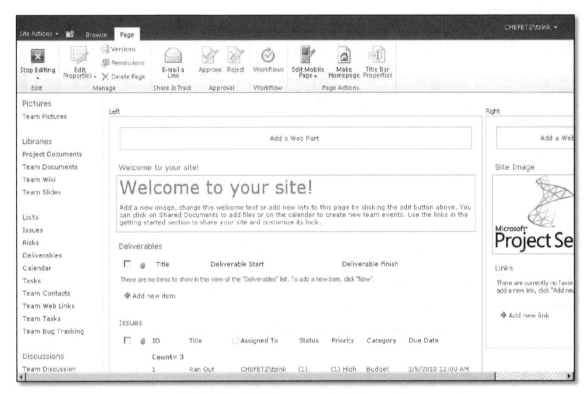

Figure 15 - 127: Home page in editing mode

To add a web part to the *Home* page, click the *Add a Web Part* link near the top of both the *Left* web part zone and the *Right* web part zone. The system displays a panel below the ribbon menu that lists web parts available to add to the page, as shown in Figure 15 - 128.

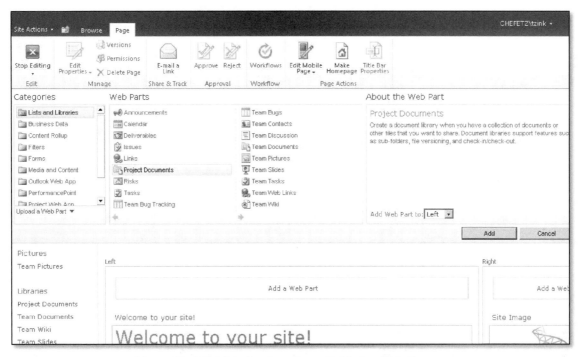

Figure 15 - 128: List of web parts available to add to the page

Select a web part type from the *Categories* listing, then select a web part from the *Web Parts* listing, then click the *Add* button. The system adds the web part to the top of the selected web part zone, as illustrated in Figure 15 - 129.

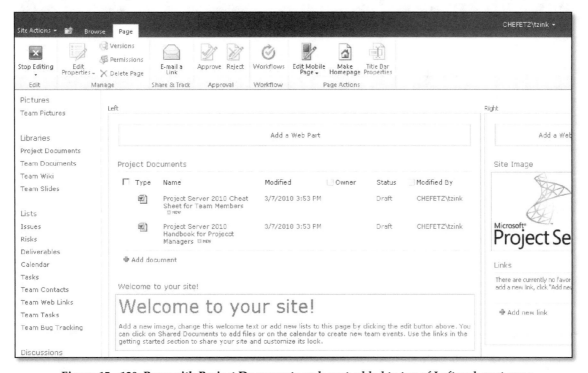

Figure 15 - 129: Page with Project Documents web part added to top of Left web part zone

To reposition a web part within a web part zone or to move it to a different zone, click the title bar of the web part and drag it into the desired position on the page, as shown in Figure 15 - 130. Notice that a blue bar indicates positions where you may drop the web part on the page.

Figure 15 - 130: Repositioning the Welcome web part on the page

The system displays the repositioned web part on the page, as shown in Figure 15 - 131.

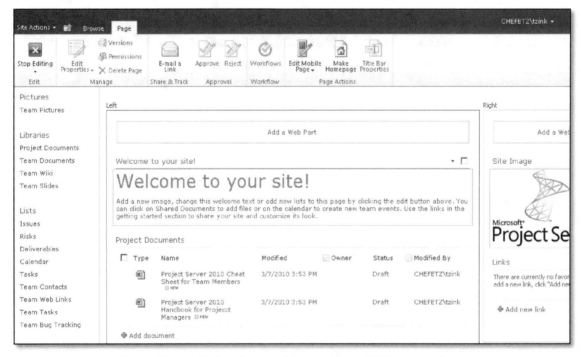

Figure 15 - 131: Updated page with repositioned Welcome web part

To remove a web part from the page, float the mouse cursor over the web part title bar to activate the web part menu, indicated by a tiny downward-pointing arrow in the upper right corner of the web part. Click the arrow to open the web part menu and select the *Delete* option, as shown in Figure 15 - 132.

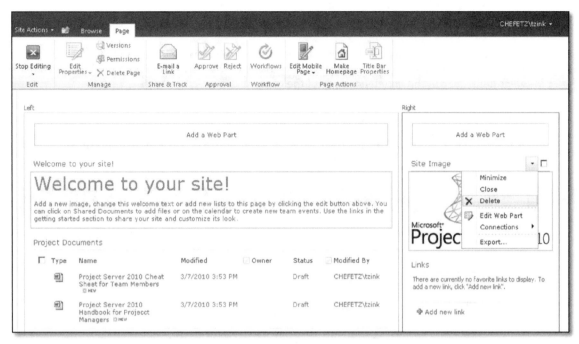

Figure 15 - 132: Deleting the Site Image web part via the web part menu

The system displays the warning dialog shown in Figure 15 - 133; click the *OK* button to acknowledge the message and proceed with the web part deletion.

Figure 15 - 133: Web part deletion warning dialog

The system displays the updated web part page with the web part removed, as shown in Figure 15 - 134.

Figure 15 - 134: Updated web part page with Site Image web part removed

Warning: *Deleting* a web part removes it **completely** from the page. Selecting the *Close* option from the web part menu or clicking the **X** in the upper right corner of the web part *hides* it on the page, but it still remains embedded in the underlying code of the page.

To stop editing the page, click the *Stop Editing* button on the ribbon menu. The system displays the final version of the page in viewing mode as shown in Figure 15 - 135.

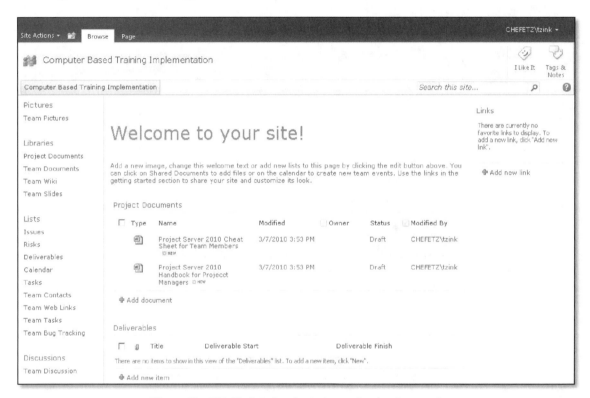

Figure 15 - 135: Updated web part page in viewing mode

Depending upon your last page editing action, you may need to click the *Page* tab on the ribbon menu to display the *Stop Editing* button.

Creating a New Web Part Page

To create a new web part page in the *Project Site* to display information for the project team, navigate to the *Create* page by selecting *More Options* from the *Site Actions* menu. On the *Create* page, select *Web Part Page*, located below the *Pages and Sites* heading. The system displays the *New Web Part Page* page, shown in Figure 15 - 136.

In the *Name* section of the page, enter a name for the new web part page. The system uses this name to create the file name for the page, and it also displays this name on the page when people visit the *Project Site*. In the *Layout* section of the page, select an item from the *Choose a Layout Template* pick list to specify how many web part zones will appear on the page, as well as how to arrange them. In the *Save Location* section of the page, select the *Document Library* where the new web part page will reside. Click the *Create* button to complete the process and instruct the system to create the new web part page.

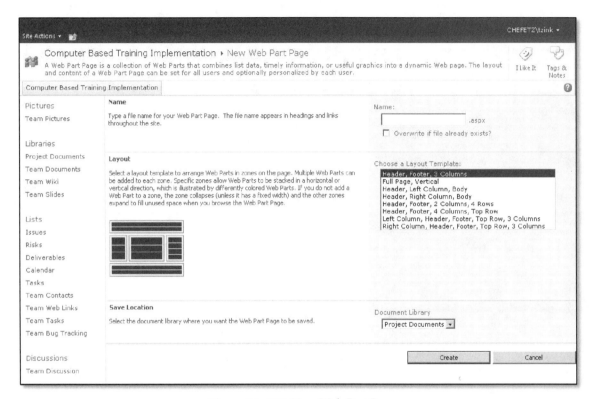

Figure 15 - 136: New Web Part Page

You **must** specify where the new web part page will reside by selecting from the listing of **existing** document libraries. If you need to create a new library to contain the new web part page, then you should first manually create that library before proceeding through this process.

MSProjectExperts recommends that you create a library in the *Project Site* to contain any web part pages that may be created in that site; name the library *Web Part Pages* or similar, and select *Web Part page* as the default *Document Template*.

The system displays the new empty web part page in editing mode, as shown in Figure 15 - 137. You may add to, re-arrange, or otherwise edit and manipulate web parts on the page as described previously in this module. To stop editing the page, click the *Stop Editing* button on the ribbon menu.

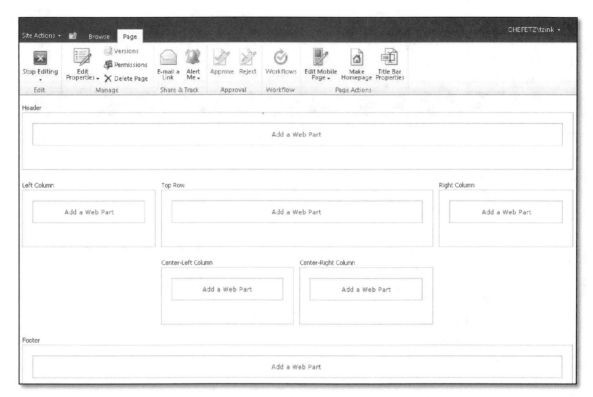

Figure 15 - 137: New Web Part Page in editing mode

Creating a New Content Page

A SharePoint content page is similar to a web part page, except that you can also easily add formatted text, images, and other types of content in addition to web parts. Content pages function similarly to wiki pages, and therefore they reside in a wiki library that the system creates specifically for storing content pages.

To create a new content page in the *Project Site*, navigate to the *Create* page by selecting *More Options* from the *Site Actions* menu. On the *Create* page, select *Page*, located below the *Pages and Sites* heading. The system displays the *Create Default Wiki Libraries* dialog, shown in Figure 15 - 138. Click the *Create* button to instruct the system to create a wiki library to house this and future content pages in the *Project Site*.

Figure 15 - 138: Create Default Wiki Libraries dialog

The system also creates a *Site Assets* library to contain images, videos, and other types of content that you may upload to the site and insert into content pages.

The system displays the *New Page* dialog, shown in Figure 15 - 139. Enter a name for the new content page into the *New page name* text box, then click the *Create* button.

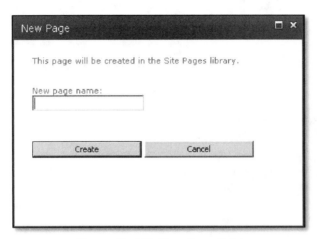

Figure 15 - 139: New Page dialog

The system displays a new empty content page in editing mode shown in Figure 15 - 140. Use the various text formatting, image, layout, and other tools on the ribbon menu to add and format content in the new page, then click the *Save* button on the ribbon menu to save your changes and stop editing the page.

Depending upon your last page editing action, you may need to click the *Page* tab on the ribbon menu to display the *Save* button.

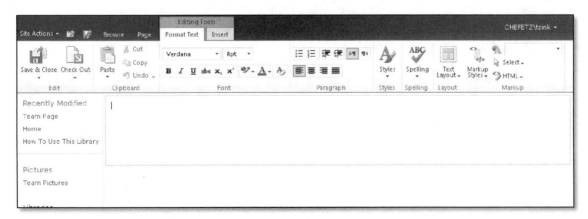

Figure 15 - 140: New Content Page in editing mode

Figure 15 - 141 shows an example of a content page with formatted text, an image, and a web part.

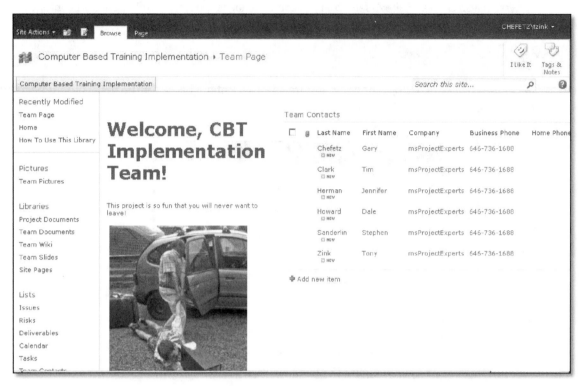

Figure 15 - 141: New Content Page with various types of content inserted

Managing Project Site Settings

As I described previously in this module, the SharePoint administration model provides the ability to manage list and library settings as well as overall site settings for an entire *Project Site*. List and library settings control the behavior of each individual repository within the site, but site settings control the behavior of the entire site and all repositories contained within it.

To view and adjust the configuration settings for an entire *Project Site*, select *Site Settings* from the *Site Actions* menu. The system displays the *Site Settings* page shown in Figure 15 - 142. The *Site Settings* page provides options to configure many aspects and behaviors of the *Project Site* that I describe in the following sections.

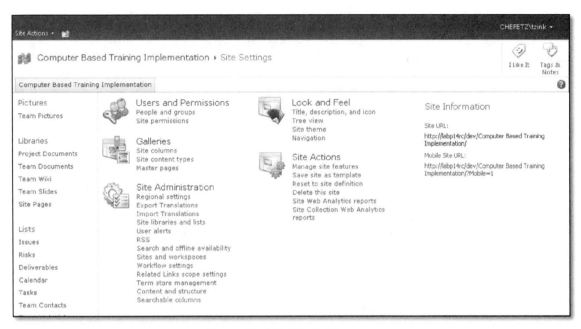

Figure 15 - 142: Site Settings page

Specifying Title, Description, and Icon Settings

To change the overall title or description of the *Project Site*, as well as the icon that appears in the upper left corner of each page next to the site name, navigate to the *Site Settings* page and click on *Title, description, and icon*, located below the *Look and Feel* heading. The system displays the *Title, Description, and Icon* page shown in Figure 15 - 143.

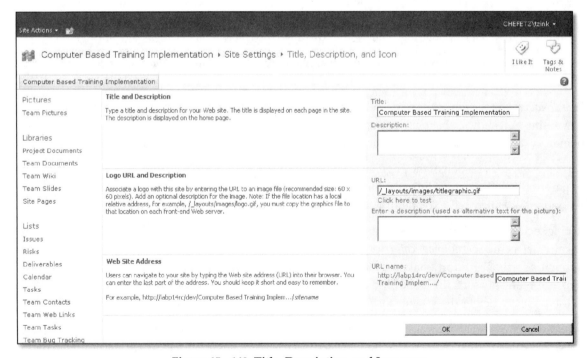

Figure 15 - 143: Title, Description, and Icon page

The *Title and Description* section of the page displays the current name and description for the *Project Site*. To change the overall name of the site, update the contents of the *Title* text box. To change the overall description of the site, update the contents of the *Description* text box.

Warning: Changing the Project Site *Title* is not recommended, as this may confuse the members of the project team.

The *Logo URL and Description* section of the page displays the URL for the current icon that each page displays in the upper left corner next to the *Project Site* name. To use a different image for the site icon, update the contents of the *URL* text box. You can also enter an optional brief description into the *Enter a description* text box. This description appears in place of the icon if the system cannot display the icon for any reason.

The *Web Site Address* section of the page displays the current URL of the *Project Site*. To change the end of the URL, update the contents of the *URL* name text box.

Warning: Changing the URL of the *Project Site* is not recommended, as this will break the connection between the *Project Site* and Project Server. If you need to change the URL of a *Project Site*, you will also need to update the URL on the Project Server *Project Sites* page.

Specifying Site Navigation and Menu Settings

To change the global navigation tabs across the top of each *Project Site* page, as well as the links that appear in the Quick Launch navigation menu on the left side of each page, navigate to the *Site Settings* page and click on *Navigation*, located below the *Look and Feel* heading. The system displays the *Navigation Settings* page shown in Figure 15 - 144.

The Site *Navigation Settings* page contains five sections: *Global Navigation, Current Navigation, Sorting, Navigation Editing and Sorting,* and *Show and Hide Ribbon.* Each individual section is described separately below.

In the *Global Navigation* section of the page, select whether the *Project Site* inherits the global navigation tabs from the parent PWA site, or it shows tabs for site or page destinations below the *Project Site*. The provided options are fairly self-explanatory. Select from the appropriate options provided in this section of the page.

In the *Current Navigation* section of the page, select whether the *Project Site* inherits the Quick Launch navigation links from the parent PWA site, shows links for the current site pages and subsites, or shows links only for subsites. The provided options are fairly self-explanatory. Select from the appropriate options provided in this section of the page.

In the *Sorting* section of the page, select whether the system sorts navigation links automatically or manually. To sort automatically, select the *Sort automatically* option. To sort manually, select the *Sort manually* option. Notice that if you select automatic sorting, an additional *Automatic Sorting* section appears on the page, allowing you to determine how the system automatically sorts the global and current navigation links. Select the appropriate option from the *Sort by* pick list, then select whether the system sorts the items *in ascending order* or *in descending order*.

In the *Navigation Editing and Sorting* section of the page, add, remove, and re-order the global and current navigation links as necessary. Notice that if you select the *Display the navigation items below the current site* option in the *Global Navigation* section of the page, global navigation links appear in this section for editing.

In the *Show and Hide Ribbon* section of the page, select whether people have the ability to show and hide the ribbon menu within the *Project Site*. To allow the show / hide functionality, select the *Yes* option, or to prevent the functionality, select the *No* option.

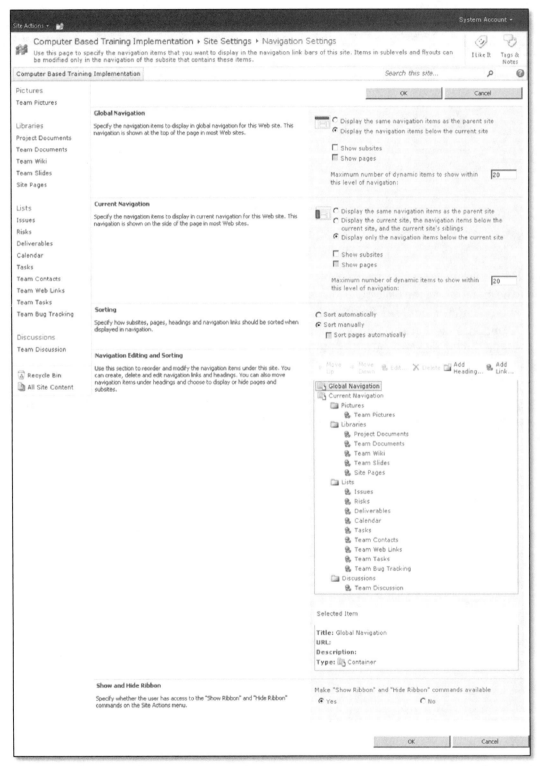

Figure 15 - 144: Site Navigation Settings page

To change whether the Quick Launch navigation menu is visible in the *Project Site* and whether the system displays a tree-style version of the menu, navigate to the *Site Settings* page and click on *Tree view*, located below the *Look and Feel* heading. The system displays the *Tree view* page shown in Figure 15 - 145.

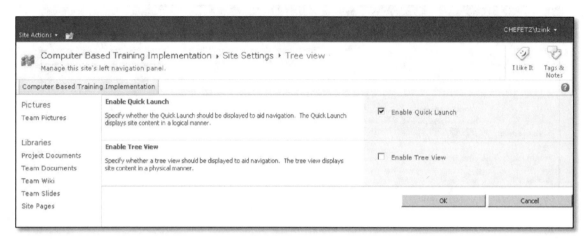

Figure 15 - 145: Tree view page

The *Enable Quick Launch* section of the page enables the standard Quick Launch navigation menu within the *Project Site*. To enable the menu, select the *Enable Quick Launch* option. The *Enable Tree View* section of the page enables a hierarchical tree-style version of the Quick Launch menu within the *Project Site*. To enable the tree-style menu, select the *Enable Tree View* option. Note that selecting both options displays **both** versions of the Quick Launch menu on the left side of pages within the *Project Site*. Figure 15 - 146 shows the *Project Site* with the standard Quick Launch menu disabled and the tree-style Quick Launch enabled.

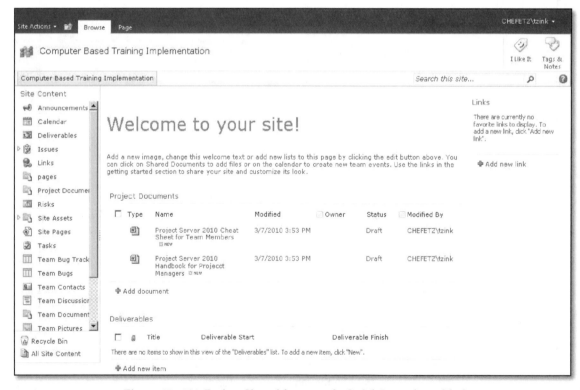

Figure 15 - 146: Project Site with tree style Quick Launch enabled

Warning: Select the standard Quick Launch menu or the tree-style menu, but do not select both, as this would confuse people who use the Project Site.

Specifying Site Theme Settings

To select or modify the color scheme of the *Project Site,* navigate to the *Site Settings* page and click on *Site theme,* located below the *Look and Feel* heading. The system displays the *Site Theme* page shown in Figure 15 - 147.

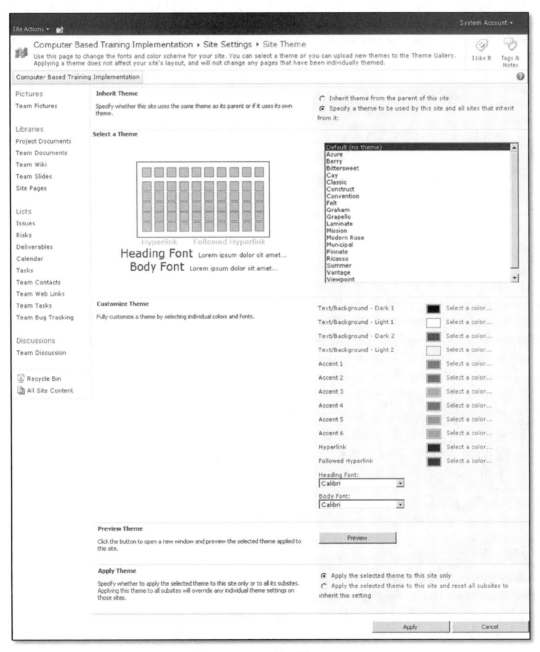

Figure 15 - 147: Site Theme page

The *Site Theme* page contains five sections: *Inherit Theme, Select a Theme, Customize Theme, Preview Theme,* and *Apply Theme.* I describe each individual section below.

In the *Inherit Theme* section of the page, select whether the *Project Site* inherits its theme from the parent PWA site. To inherit the theme, select the *Inherit theme from the parent of this site* option. To specify a unique theme for the *Project Site*, select the *Specify a theme to be used by this site and all sites that inherit from it* option.

In the *Select a Theme* section of the page, select a built-in site theme from the pick list. Notice that a preview color palette and some formatted text examples appear to the left of the pick list when you select a theme.

In the *Customize Theme* section of the page, select custom colors for each element of the color scheme. To select a different color for any type of item, click the *Select a color* link next to the item; the *Colors* dialog appears, as shown in Figure 15 - 148, allowing you to select a different color or enter of a 6-character hexadecimal color code. When you are finished selecting or entering a new color, click the *OK* button. To change the font style that the selected theme uses, select new values in the *Heading Font* and the *Body Font* pick lists.

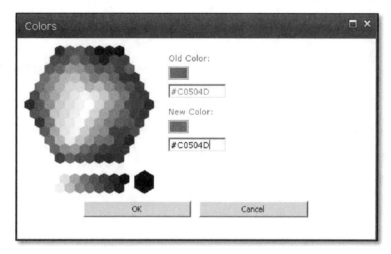

Figure 15 - 148: Colors dialog

In the *Preview Theme* section of the page, click the *Preview* button to launch the *Project Site* in a separate web browser session to preview the new theme. In the *Apply Theme* section of the page shown in **Error! Reference source not found.**, select whether to apply the new theme only to the current *Project Site* or whether it also applies to any subsites. To apply the theme to the current *Project Site* only, select the *Apply the selected theme to this site only* option, or to apply the theme to all subsites as well, select the *Apply the selected theme to this site and reset all subsites to inherit this setting* option.

Specifying Regional Settings

Regional settings control how the system formats and displays certain types of text, number, and date information throughout the *Project Site*. To specify regional settings for the *Project Site*, such as language, time zone, and calendar formats, navigate to the *Site Settings* page and click on *Regional settings*, located below the *Site Administration* heading. The system displays the *Regional Settings* page shown in Figure 15 - 149.

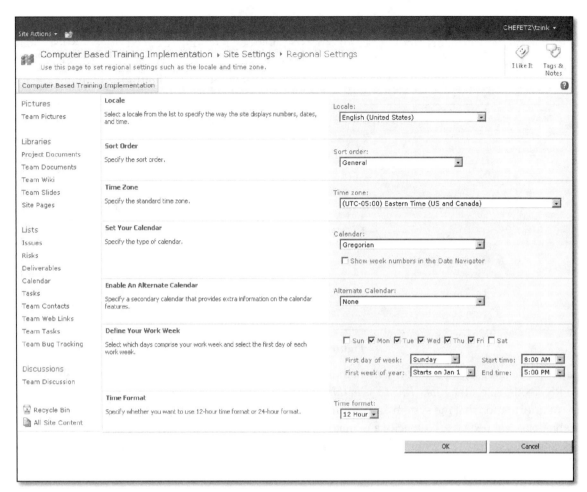

Figure 15 - 149: Regional Settings page

In many cases you do not need to modify any of the settings on this page, as they are configured automatically during the installation process. However, it is still wise to verify that they are set appropriately.

In the *Locale* section of the page, select a value from the *Locale* pick list to instruct the system how to display number, date, and time information in the *Project Site*. In the *Sort Order* section of the page, select a value from the *Sort order* pick list to instruct the system how to sort items displayed in the *Project Site*. In the *Time Zone* section of the page, select a value from the *Time zone* pick list which best describes your local time zone. In the *Set Your Calendar* section of the page, select a value from the *Calendar* pick list which best describes the type of calendar that you follow. In the *Enable An Alternate Calendar* section of the page, select a value from the *Alternate Calendar* pick list if multiple calendar formats are required in the *Project Site*. In the *Define Your Work Week* section of the page, select the week days which represent typical work days at your company, select the first day of the week that will be displayed in calendar views, select when the first week of a new year begins, and select start and end times for a typical work day at your company. In the *Time Format* section of the page, select the appropriate *12 Hour* or *24 Hour* format from the *Time format* pick list to instruct the system how to display times in the *Project Site*.

Specifying Site RSS Settings

As I showed you previously in this module, SharePoint is capable of generating RSS feeds for every list and library in a *Project Site*. To specify RSS settings for the *Project Site*, navigate to the *Site Settings* page and click on *RSS*, located below the *Site Administration* heading. The system displays the *RSS* page shown in Figure 15 - 150.

Figure 15 - 150: RSS page

In the *Enable RSS* section of the page, specify whether the *Project Site* generates RSS data feeds for its lists and libraries. To enable RSS feeds, select the *Allow RSS feeds in this site* option. In the *Advanced Settings* section of the page, specify key pieces of information that the system embeds in all RSS data feeds. To specify copyright information for the site, populate the *Copyright* text box. To specify a managing editor for the site, populate the *Managing Editor* text box. To specify a webmaster for the site, populate the *Webmaster* text box. To specify how often RSS feeds in the site are refreshed with newly added data, adjust the *Time To Live (minutes)* text box value.

Specifying Search and Offline Availability Settings

SharePoint utilizes a powerful search engine to index the content in *Project Sites* and make it available through search results. SharePoint also provides rich interaction between *Project Sites* and offline client programs such as Microsoft Office. To specify search engine and offline client availability settings for the *Project Site*, navigate to the *Site Settings* page and click on *Search and offline availability*, located below the *Site Administration* heading. The system displays the *Search and Offline Availability* page shown in Figure 15 - 151.

Figure 15 - 151: Search and Offline Availability page

In the *Indexing Site Content* section of the page, specify whether the SharePoint search engine will index the content stored in the *Project Site* and present the content in search results. To allow searching of content in the site, select the *Yes* option, or to prevent searching, select the *No* option.

In the *Indexing ASPX Page Content* section of the page, specify whether the SharePoint search engine will index web part pages or content pages containing web parts within the site. If you configure the site with fine-grained item-level permissions and want to prevent certain sensitive content from inadvertently appearing in search results for the wrong people, even if it is visible to other people through web part pages, select the *Do not index Web Parts if this site contains fine-grained permissions* option. If the search engine should always index the contents of pages and make it available in search results, select the *Always index all Web Parts on this site* option. If the search engine should never index the content that is exposed through web part pages, select the *Never index any Web Parts on this site* option.

In the *Offline Client Availability* section of the page, select whether offline programs such as Microsoft Office can connect to lists and libraries in the *Project Site* and access the data contained there. To allow offline client access, select the *Yes* option, or to prevent access, select the *No* option.

Deleting the Project Site

To delete a *Project Site* completely from the system, navigate to the *Site Settings* page and click on *Delete this site*, located below the *Site Actions* heading. The system displays the *Delete This Site* page shown in Figure 15 - 152.

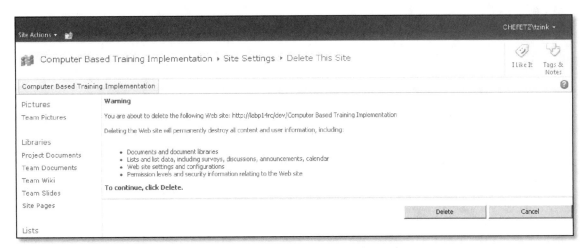

Figure 15 - 152: Delete This Site page

Warning: Use caution when deleting a Project Site. This action **cannot** be reversed!

You can also delete a Project Site by visiting the *Project Sites* page in PWA.

To delete the *Project Site*, click the *Delete* button. The system displays a final warning dialog shown in Figure 15 - 153.

Figure 15 - 153: Project Site Deletion warning dialog

To confirm the deletion of the *Project Site*, click the *OK* button. The system displays a confirmation dialog, as shown in Figure 15 - 154.

Figure 15 - 154: Project Site deletion confirmation dialog

Click the *Go back to site* link in the confirmation dialog to return to the PWA site.

Creating a New Project Site Template

Every *Project Site* generates from a default site template that installs with Project Server 2010. Your business processes may require you to modify *Project Sites* to add or remove features to better tailor the sites to the needs of the project team. Examples of custom business requirements include:

- Force documents to be checked out of the *Project Documents* library when people edit them.

- Enable version control on the *Project Documents* library to track document revision history.

- Modify the *Category* choices in the *Risks* and *Issues* lists.

- Enable version control on the *Risks* and *Issues* lists to track item history.

- Add columns to the *Project Documents*, *Risks*, or *Issues* repositories to capture additional metadata.

- Add or modify views in the *Project Documents*, *Risks*, or *Issues* repositories.

- Modify the *Project Site Home* page by rearranging, adding, or removing web parts.

- Rename the *Tasks* list to avoid people confusing this list with project tasks tracked by Project Server.

- Create a *Decisions* list for tracking important decisions during the project lifecycle.

You can make each of these modifications quite easily within a *Project Site*, but if you want to make numerous modifications that apply to every new *Project Site*, it can become tedious to do this on a project-by-project basis. When you try to manually implement these changes, you introduce a chance for human error and lack of standardization across projects. Rather than manually making these changes to each *Project Site*, you can include them into a new site template for generating future *Project Sites*.

> If you are using *Enterprise Project Types* in Project Server, MSProjectExperts recommends that you create a custom *Project Site* template for each *Project Type*, since each project type can utilize its own *Project Site* template that has unique customizations.

To create a new *Project Site* template for all future projects or for a specific project type, follow these main steps:

- Create a new blank site using the Microsoft *Project Site* template.

- Customize the new site based on your business process requirements.

- Save the updated site as a template.

- Activate the new site template for use with Project Server.

To create a new blank site using the Microsoft *Project Site* template, visit the PWA web site and select *New Site* from the *Site Actions* menu, as shown in Figure 15 - 155.

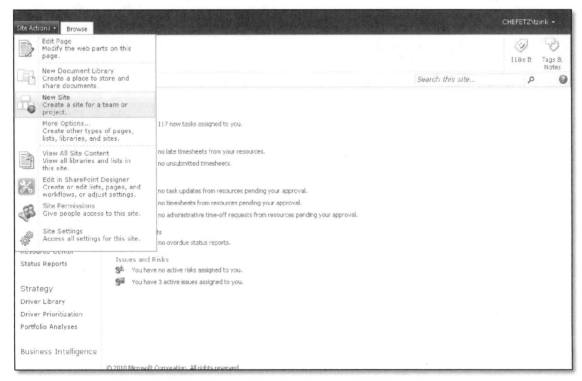

Figure 15 - 155: Selecting New Site from the PWA Site Actions menu

The system displays the *New SharePoint Site* page, as shown in Figure 15 - 156.

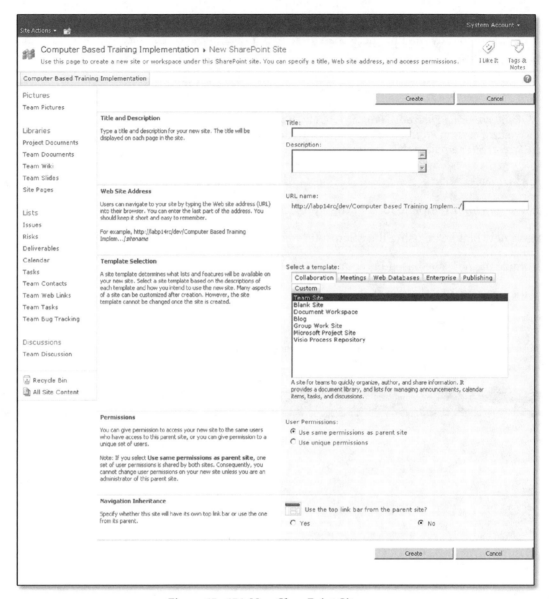

Figure 15 - 156: New SharePoint Site page

The *New SharePoint Site* page contains five sections: *Title and Description, Web Site Address, Template Selection, Permissions*, and *Navigation Inheritance*. Because of the length of the *New SharePoint Site* page, Figure 15 - 156 shows only the first two sections of the page. I describe each individual section separately. In the *Title and Description* section of the page, enter a name for the new site into the *Title* text box, and enter a brief description for the new site into the *Description* text box. In the *Web Site Address* section, enter a URL ending for the new site into the *URL name* text box. In the *Template Selection* section of the page shown previously in **Error! Reference source not found.**, select *Microsoft Project Site* from the *Select a template* pick list.

Warning: You **must** select the *Microsoft Project Site* template or the process will fail.

In the *Permissions* section of the page, select the *Use unique permissions* option. In the *Navigation Inheritance* section of the page, under *Use the top link bar from the parent site?* select the *No* option.

MSProjectExperts recommends that you enter or select the following options on the *New SharePoint Site* page:

Title: Project Site Template 01 (if creating templates for project types, use the project type name)

Description: Project Site Template

URL Name: projectsitetemplate01

Tempate: Microsoft Project Site

User Permissions: Use unique permissions

Navigation Inheritance: No

Click the *Create* button to create the new SharePoint site. The system displays the *Set Up Groups for this Site* page shown in Figure 15 - 157. In the *Visitors to this Site* section of the page, select the *Create a new group* option if it is not already selected. In the *Members of this Site* section of the page, select the *Create a new group* option if it is not already selected, and enter your UserID into the text box if it is not already present. In the *Owners of this Site* section of the page, select the *Create a new group* option if it is not already selected, and enter your UserID into the text box if it is not already present. Click the *OK* button to proceed.

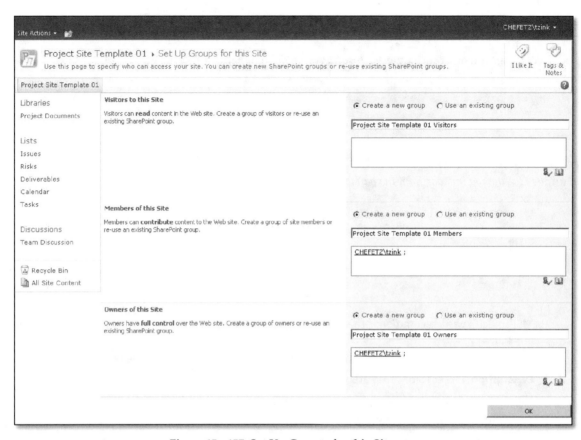

Figure 15 - 157: Set Up Groups for this Site page

The system creates a new *Project Site* and displays its *Home* page shown in Figure 15 - 158.

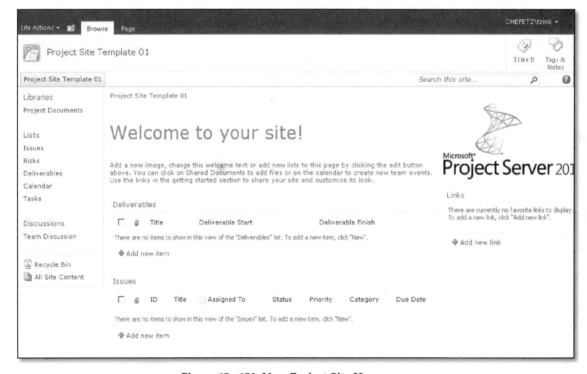

Figure 15 - 158: New Project Site Home page

Customize the site based on your business process requirements. Figure 15 - 159 shows an example of a customized site with updated list configurations, an updated home page, and an updated site theme.

Figure 15 - 159: Customized Project Site example

To save the newly customized *Project Site* as a template, visit the *Site Settings* page within the site and click on *Save site as template*, located below the *Site Actions* heading. The system displays the *Save as Template* page shown in Figure 15 - 160.

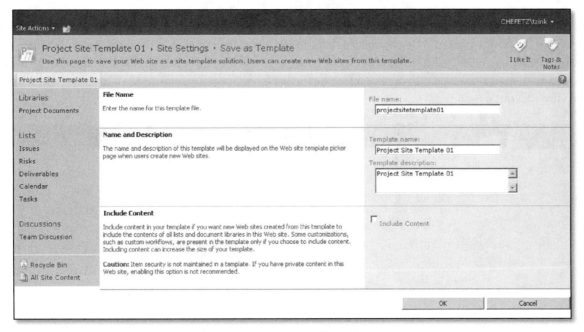

Figure 15 - 160: Save as Template page

MSProjectExperts recommends that you visit the *Library Settings* page and review the configuration of the new library and make adjustments based on your business requirements.

Creating a New Contacts List

A SharePoint contacts list is a repository for storing contact information to share with the Project Team. To create a new contacts list in a *Project Site*, navigate to the *Create* page in the *Project Site* and click the *Contacts* link, located below the *Communications* heading. The system displays the *New* page shown in Figure 15 - 114.

Figure 15 - 114: New contacts list page

In the *Name and Description* section of the page, enter a name for the new list into the *Name* text box, and enter a brief description for the new list into the *Description* text box. In the *Navigation* section of the page, select whether the new list appears in the *Project Site* Quick Launch navigation menu. Select the *Yes* option to display a link to the new list in the Quick Launch menu, or select the *No* option to hide the list from the menu. Figure 15 - 115 shows a newly created contacts list with contacts added.

Figure 15 - 115: New contacts list with contacts added

If you choose to visit the *Solution Gallery* immediately after creating a new *Project Site* template, the system displays the *Solutions* page shown in Figure 15 - 162. To navigate to the *Solution Gallery* from another location in the system, visit the PWA *Site Settings* page by selecting *Site Settings* from the *Site Actions* menu, then click on *Solutions*, located below the *Galleries* heading on the *Site Settings* page.

The *Solution Gallery* is a SharePoint tool for importing, exporting, and managing custom solutions within the system. When you create a new *Project Site* template, the system stores it in this gallery as a solution and activates it automatically. Using the tools in the *Solution Gallery*, you can import, export, activate, deactivate, and delete solutions in the system.

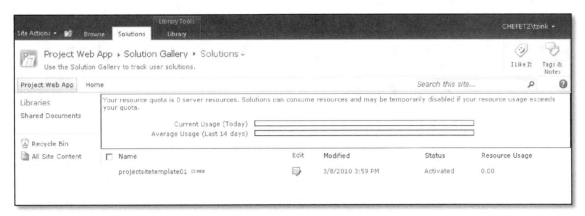

Figure 15 - 162: Solutions page with new Project Site template

The name that you see in the solution listing is the *FIle name* that you enter when you create a *Project Site* template.

Notice that the new *Project Site* template is listed on the *Solutions* page and that the *Status* is *Activated*. To use the new *Project Site* template to create new future *Project Sites* in Project Server, navigate to the *Project Site Provisioning Settings* page as shown in Figure 15 - 163, select the new *Project Site* template from the *Default Project Site template* pick list in the *Default Site Properties* section, and click the *Save* button. To use the new *Project Site* template as the default template for an *Enterprise Project Type*, please refer to Module 08, Configuring Lifecycle Management.

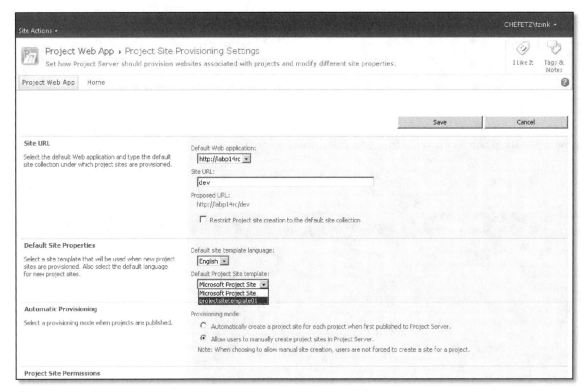

Figure 15 - 163: Selecting the new Project Site template on the Project Site Provisioning Settings page

Changing the default *Project Site* template does not affect any existing *Project Sites* in the system.

Module 16

Configuring Business Intelligence and Reporting

Learning Objectives

After completing this module, you will be able to:

- Understand Business Intelligence concepts and apply them to Project Server

- Understand the Business Intelligence Center and the Project Server reporting architecture

- Use the built-in Microsoft Excel assets for Project Server reporting

- Build custom Microsoft Excel reports using the built-in Excel assets

- Build dashboard pages for aggregating various types of reporting content

- Control access to the Business Intelligence Center

Inside Module 16

Reporting and Business Intelligence Overview..765
Reporting Architecture Overview...768
   Relational Database Overview..768
   OLAP Database Overview 769
Business Intelligence Center Overview 774
   Understanding the Business Intelligence Center Site 774
   Built-In Microsoft Excel Reports Overview 779
   Business Intelligence Center Security Overview..779
Microsoft SharePoint Excel Services Overview 780
Working With the Built-In Microsoft Excel Reports..782
   Excel Sample Reports Overview...782
   Excel Report Templates Overview 784
   Excel Data Connection Files Overview..785
   Viewing the Sample Excel Reports in Your Web Browser..789
   Opening the Sample Excel Reports with Microsoft Excel 794
   Creating a Custom Excel Report by Modifying a Sample Report..796
   Creating a Custom Excel Report Based on a Template 798

Common Methods of Modifying an Excel Pivot Report 800

Creating a Custom Excel Report Using a Data Connection File.. 813

Working with SharePoint Dashboards...**821**

Creating a Dashboard Page... 821

Embedding Excel Data into a Dashboard Page 823

Adding Non-Project Server Users as Report Viewers..**827**

Reporting and Business Intelligence Overview

Business Intelligence (BI) is a set of processes, tools, and techniques for gathering, organizing, and analyzing large volumes of complex data in an effort to develop an accurate understanding of business dynamics, and it is used to improve strategic and tactical business decision-making. In other words, the purpose of BI is to capture large amounts of data, make some sense out of it, and use it to make sound business decisions. The ultimate goal is to develop the ability to spot problems and trends, and to make informed decisions to mitigate risks, improve efficiencies, and identify opportunities.

Organizations spend time and money implementing Project Server to capture work data, make sense out of it, and use it to make decisions such as:

- Spotting problems and trends - Is the project running late or over budget?

- Mitigating risks - What can we do to avoid missing our launch deadline?

- Improving efficiencies - Who is the best-qualified person to perform the work?

- Identifying opportunities - What if we design the database and the user interface at the same time?

A well-designed BI system should do the following:

- Extract large amounts of complex data from one or more sources, such as CRM, supply chain management, ERP, and EPM systems

- Centralize, organize, and standardize information in repositories such as data warehouses or data marts

- Provide analytical tools through multiple delivery methods that allow business and technical specialists to run queries against the data and to perform analyses to uncover patterns and diagnose problems

- Present the right information, at the right time, in the right format in order to make the right decisions and take the right actions to achieve the right performance

Project Server helps to do these things already. It aggregates different types of complex work data from different locations into a central set of databases and OLAP cubes, or BI Data Store, such as those shown in Figure 16 - 1:

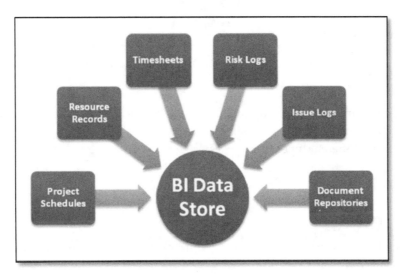

Figure 16 - 1: Aggregating Project Server Data into the BI Data Store

Module 16

Project Server, when used in conjunction with SharePoint Server, also provides a set of rich analytical tools to build reports and visuals for analysis of that data, such as listed below and represented in Figure 16 - 2:

- Project Center Reports
- Project Detail Reports
- Project Professional Reports
- Microsoft Visio Diagrams
- Microsoft Excel Tabular and Pivot-Style Reports
- Key Performance Indicators
- Balanced Scorecards
- Interactive Dashboards

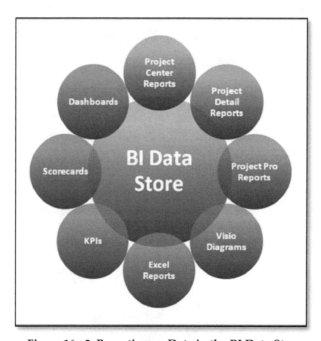

Figure 16 - 2: Reporting on Data in the BI Data Store

Business Intelligence is much more than operational and status reporting, such as a extracting work hours for billing purposes, issues logs for fire-fighting, or simply determining "what is my team working on today?" BI tools assist you in performing different types of analyses:

- Historical analyses, such as what, when, who, and how much
- Predictive analyses, such as forecasting, profiling, trend analysis of why and what-if scenarios

Historical analyses provide a look at what happened, while predictive analyses provide a look at what might happen, as illustrated in Figure 16 - 3.

766

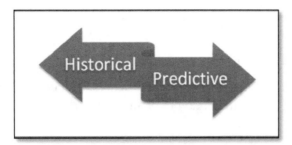

Figure 16 - 3: Historical vs. Predictive Reporting

A few examples of analyses that people typically perform with a BI system might include demographic trends, product line profitability, group or office profitability, profit margins, billing volumes, utilization, billing lags, payment lags, product trends, measurement of goals, cross-departmental data. A few examples of questions that work analyses in Project Server might answer include:

- Which departments have availability to work on IT projects?

- How much time have Project Managers spent performing administrative work?

- Have we been spending more time on operational work or project work?

- What types of projects have more risks or issues, and what are the types of risks or issues?

- If we hire more engineers, can we complete more projects this year?

- Can we improve deliverable quality if people work less?

Designing the tools to help answer these questions is the job of the Business Analyst. That person must ask the right questions, capture the right requirements, and design the right solution for managing and analyzing the organization's work with Project Server. As illustrated in Figure 16 - 4, BI in Project Server can deliver the following:

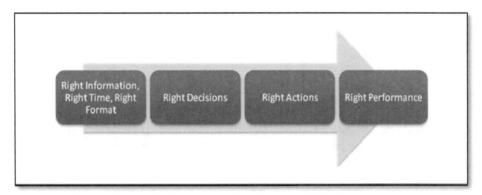

Figure 16 - 4: Right Decisions, Right Actions, and Right Performance

- **Correct information**: Actual work, actual work billable, actual work non-billable, or actual overtime work. Is the data accurate, consistent, and complete? High-level or detailed?

- **At the right time**: Is the data too old? Is the data too far into the future? Are we making decisions based on last month's data?

- **In the right format**: Pivot tables? Pivot charts? Tables? Lists? Gantt charts? Online?

- **Make the right decisions**: How do we bring project ABC back on track? Crash? Fast-track? De-scope?

- **Take the right actions**: Are there any resources with the right skills and availability? How should we re-allocate our resources?

- **For the right performance**: What is the work variance, cost variance, schedule variance of project ABC?

In any organization, many different groups of people, or audiences, may use the same BI tools to extract different types of information in order to perform different types of analyses and make different types of decisions:

- Purchasing Department

- Finance Department

- Information Services Department

- Engineering Department

- Executive team and senior-level management

- Project Management Office

- Resource or functional managers

- Project team members

Therefore, a well-designed BI solution should be flexible, powerful, and secure enough to accommodate everyone's needs, allowing people to access the targeted information that they need without giving them the keys to the castle. The BI reporting tools included with Project Server allow users to extract the appropriate data from the appropriate areas of the BI Data Store while securing that data so that only specific people can access it.

Reporting Architecture Overview

The reports and dashboards that you build in Project Server extract their data primarily from two areas in Project Server's BI Data Store:

- Project Server Reporting Database (RDB)

- OLAP databases

Relational Database Overview

The Project Server RDB contains project, resource, timesheet, issue, and risk data stored in a set of *Tables* and *Views*, each of which consists of a set of rows and columns of data, similar to tabular data in a spreadsheet. Database tables typically contain normalized data, as illustrated in Figure 16 - 5.

ID	Name	Start	Finish
1	Design	2010-02-03	2010-02-19
2	Build	2010-02-03	2010-02-19
3	Test	2010-02-03	2010-02-19
4	Implement	2010-02-03	2010-02-19

Database Table

Figure 16 - 5: Example of a database Table

Views combine data from one or more tables and organize it into a format that is user-friendly for reporting as shown in Figure 16 - 6. View data can come from many tables in the database.

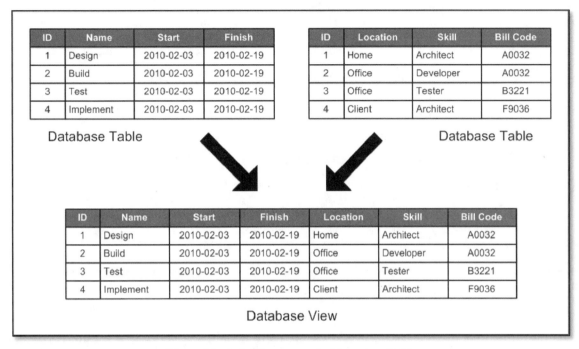

Figure 16 - 6: A View generated from two Tables

OLAP Database Overview

An OLAP, or On Line Analytical Processing, database differs from a traditional database in several ways. Fundamentally, traditional database tables store data in a flat two-dimensional format. In order to derive data totals from a relational database, such as **sales for the month**, users must execute a query. OLAP databases, on the other hand, consist of data cubes that store pre-processed data in a multi-dimensional format, allowing users to work with factual data that has already been totaled along various business dimensions for detailed data mining and analytics.

What Is OLAP?

The On Line Analytical Processing (OLAP) technology relies on a multidimensional view of project, resource, and task data. The relational database structure that underpins most transactional applications is two-dimensional. OLAP leverages data cubes based on relational fact sources, which contain preprocessed three-dimensional data, typically time-phased and aggregated by business dimension. The advantages of employing OLAP technologies for business analytics include the performance advantages of using preprocessed data and, more important, the transparent enforcement of standardized analytical formulas.

It is important to note the flow and the timing of data through Project Server's BI Data Store. The source data for all projects originates in the Project Server *Draft* database. The system copies the data to the Project Server *Published* database when Project Managers publish their schedules. As a part of the publishing process, the system also re-organizes the project data and copies it to the Project Server *Reporting* database, making it immediately available for reporting in the form of tables and views. Finally, on a schedule specified by the Project Server administrator (usually daily or weekly), the system ships the data to SQL Server Analysis Services, which then re-organizes the data, tallies it by business dimensions, and stores it in an OLAP database, making it available for reporting in the form of OLAP Cubes as shown in Figure 16 - 7.

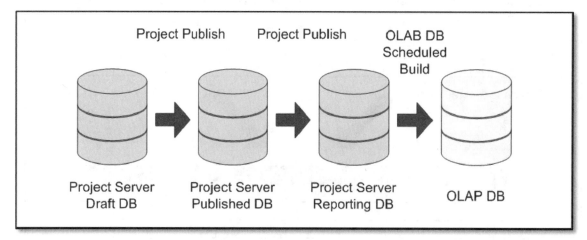

Figure 16 - 7: Data flow through Project Server BI Data Store

OLAP cubes contain analytical data that you can use to create PivotTables, PivotCharts, and PivotDiagrams, allowing the breakdown of data across business dimensions. OLAP data includes total-field information, such as various types of work and costs, for all projects, tasks, and resources in the system. The data also includes information stored in *Project Sites* relating to project *Deliverables, Risks, Issues,* and *Documents.* As an example of how OLAP data can be used to generate reports for detailed multi-dimensional analysis, consider the following reporting requirements for an organization:

- The organization must track the total amount of work for all projects in a portfolio of projects.

- The organization must track the work by year for 2010, 2011, and 2012.

- The organization must separate the work for its eastern and western regions.

- The organization must capitalize certain types of work while expensing other types of work.

The time dimension (2010, 2011, 2012) is inherent to the system, but to help meet these reporting needs, the Project Server administrator must create two custom fields: An *Enterprise Project* field called Region, and an *Enterprise* Task field called Expense Type, which become dimensions in the OLAP cube. The Region field includes a *Lookup Table* with the eastern and western regions listed. The Expense Type field contains a *Lookup Table* with the Capital and Expense items listed. The Project Server administrator must add these fields to the OLAP database configuration.

After the system ships its data to SQL Server Analysis Services and rebuilds the OLAP database with the current data for all projects, users can "slice and dice" the project work data according to their reporting needs. To illustrate this conceptually, Figure 16 - 8 shows the OLAP cube with work data, revealing 87,000 hours of total work across all projects in the Project Server database.

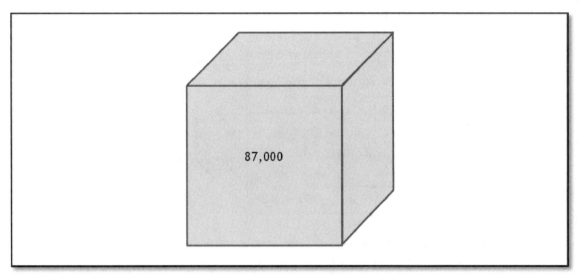

Figure 16 - 8: OLAP Cube shows Total Work for all projects

Figure 16 - 9 shows the OLAP cube with the total project work broken down by year for 2010, 2011, and 2012.

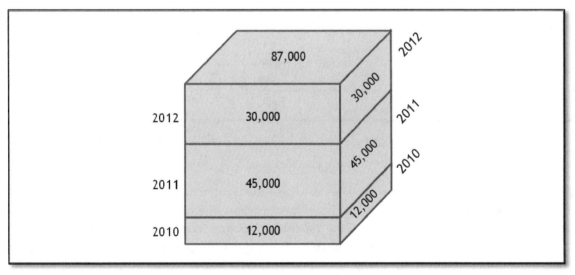

Figure 16 - 9: OLAP Cube shows Total Work by Year

Figure 16 - 10 shows the OLAP cube with the total project work, broken down by both year and by region.

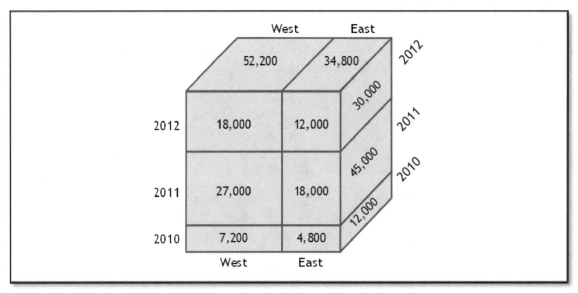

Figure 16 - 10: OLAP Cube shows Total Work by Year and by Region

Figure 16 - 11 shows the OLAP cube with the total work broken down by year, by region, and amortization type.

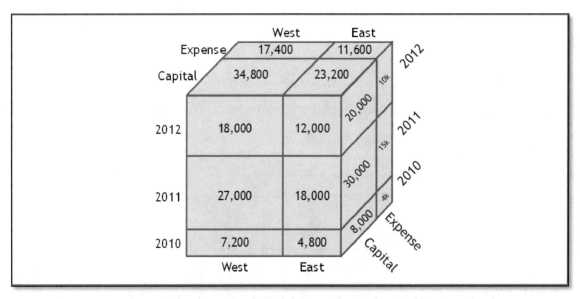

Figure 16 - 11: OLAP Cube shows Total Work by Year, by Region, and by Amortization type

OLAP cubes contain data classifiable into two main categories:

- **Totals, Measures, or Sum Values:** You can use these terms interchangeably. They describe lump sums of data, such as total work or total cost, that you can break down and analyze along various business dimensions. You may see references to the *Totals* and *Measures* terms in OLAP or Analysis Services tools and documentation, and you may see references to the *Sum Values* term in Excel PivotTable or PivotChart tools and documentation. In the previous example, the *Work* field falls into this category.

- **Dimensions, Column Labels, or Row Labels:** You can use these terms interchangeably. They describe various ways that *Totals, Measures,* or *Sum Values* can be broken down for analysis. You may see references to the *Dimensions* term in OLAP or Analysis Services tools and documentation, and you may see references to the *Column Labels* or *Row Labels* terms in Excel PivotTable or PivotChart tools and documentation. In the previous example, the *Year*, *Region*, and *Expense Type* fields fall into this category.

You configure the system to generate one or more OLAP databases and configure each cube with custom measures and dimensions, as you learned in Module 10. Each OLAP database consists of 14 OLAP cubes:

- Assignment Non Timephased
- Assignment Timephased
- Deliverables
- EPM Timesheet
- Issues
- MSP_Portfolio_Analyzer
- MSP_Project_SharePoint
- MSP_Project_Timesheet
- Project Non Timephased
- Resource Non Timephased
- Resource Timephased
- Risks
- Task Non Timephased
- Timesheet

As you create reports that draw data from the various OLAP cubes, it is very important that you know exactly what type of data each OLAP cube contains. Using the OLAP Cube Dimensions and Total Fields.xls workbook and the OLAP Cube Search Tool.xls workbook, you can easily locate an OLAP cube that contains the data fields you need for your report. You find these two Excel workbooks, each available in Excel 2007 and Excel 2010 formats, in the download that accompanies this book. If you have not already downloaded this package, see the front-matter section of the book for the download URL.

As I stated previously in this module, a well-designed BI solution should be flexible, powerful, and secure enough to accommodate everyone's needs, regardless of their group or level within the organization. Not only is data stored in different locations and formats in the Project Server BI Data Store, but you can provide different sets of filtered data for different audiences by configuring the system to create multiple OLAP databases. You can filter each OLAP database based on:

- Project and Resource Departments
- Date Range
- Selected Project, Task, Resource, and Assignment custom field data
- Selected Cost, Work, Earned Value, and Baseline data

If your Finance Department needs reports that contain work and cost data for the entire organization, but not earned value or baseline data, then you can create a finance-specific OLAP database that contains only the data elements that your Finance Department requires. If your Engineering group should see only their own projects and resources and no cost data, you can also easily accommodate that requirement by creating an OLAP database containing only the data that your engineers need.

Business Intelligence Center Overview

Different people in the organization also need different report delivery methods. Some may want their data delivered in the form of Microsoft Excel-based reports that allow for easy manipulation and sharing, and others may need only web-based reports in the form of tables, charts, or interactive dashboards. SharePoint, Project Server, and Microsoft Office offer tools for visualizing the data that you extract from the various data stores:

- **Microsoft Excel:** A desktop application for creating and managing spreadsheets containing static data or data connected to external systems

- **Microsoft Visio:** A desktop application for creating and managing diagrams containing static or data-driven images

- **Microsoft SharePoint Excel Services:** A component of SharePoint 2010 that allows publishing of interactive spreadsheets to the web

- **Microsoft SharePoint Visio Services:** A component of SharePoint 2010 that allows publishing of interactive Visio diagrams to the web

- **Microsoft SharePoint Dashboards:** A feature of SharePoint 2010 that allows aggregation and visualization of multiple types of data in a central location

- **Microsoft SharePoint Chart Web Parts:** Components of SharePoint 2010 that allow easy charting of data on the web

- **Microsoft SharePoint PerformancePoint Services:** A component of SharePoint 2010 that provides tools for visualizing data through Key Performance Indicators (KPIs), scorecards, and interactive dashboards

Understanding the Business Intelligence Center Site

The *Business Intelligence Center*, a sub-site of your PWA site in the SharePoint hierarchy, organizes and provides immediate access to all of these report delivery tools in a single location. This site, evolved from the Microsoft Office SharePoint Server 2007 Reporting Center, ties all of the BI tools together and provides a starting point for a Project Server BI portal.

To visit the *Business Intelligence Center*, click the *Business Intelligence* link in the Quick Launch menu. The system displays the *Business Intelligence Center* home page shown in Figure 16 - 12. To navigate back to the PWA site, click the *Project Web App* tab located above the Quick Launch menu in the upper left corner of the page.

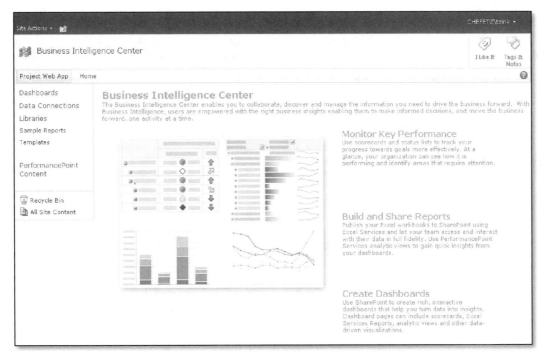

Figure 16 - 12: Business Intelligence Center home page

The *Business Intelligence Center* home page displays several tools for creating visual status indicators, reports, dashboards, and other BI tools. The page displays information and links categorized into three main areas:

- Monitor Key Performance

- Build and Share Reports

- Create Dashboards

To view information and links contained in the *Monitor Key Performance* section, float your mouse pointer over the *Monitor Key Performance* heading on the right side of the page. The system displays tools and help for visual status indicators and scorecards, as shown in Figure 16 - 13.

Figure 16 - 13: Business Intelligence Center home page, Monitor Key Performance selected

A key performance indicator, or KPI, is a business metric for tracking progress toward a specific defined goal. To view an example dashboard containing KPIs, click the *View SharePoint samples* link under the *Start Keeping Track with SharePoint Status Lists* heading on the *Business Intelligence Center* home page. The system displays a SharePoint dashboard page with sample indicators shown in Figure 16 - 14.

Figure 16 - 14: Sample dashboard with status indicators

PerformancePoint Services can integrate several individual KPIs into a scorecard that displays an overall view of your organization's performance. To learn how to use PerformancePoint Services to build a scorecard, click the *Start using PerformancePoint Services* link under the *Create Scorecards with PerformancePoint Services* heading on the *Business Intelligence Center* home page. The system displays a page with a button to launch the PerformancePoint *Dashboard Designer,* as well as additional information and help about PerformancePoint Services, shown in Figure 16 - 15.

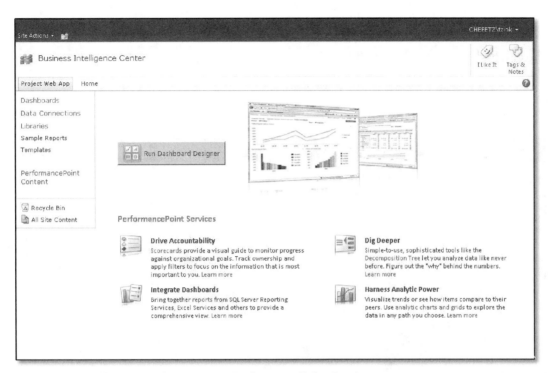

Figure 16 - 15: PerformancePoint Services page

To view information and links contained in the *Build and Share Reports* section, float your mouse pointer over the *Build and Share Reports* heading on the right side of the page. The system displays tools and help for Excel Services and related visualizations, shown in Figure 16 - 16.

Figure 16 - 16: Business Intelligence Center home page, Build and Share Reports

Excel Services is a feature of SharePoint that allows you to publish data contained in Microsoft Excel 2007 or Excel 2010 workbooks to the web as static or interactive online reports. To view an example dashboard containing an Excel Services workbook, click the *View Excel Services samples* link under the *Analyze and Share with Excel Services* heading on the *Business Intelligence Center* home page. The system displays a SharePoint dashboard page with an embedded Excel workbook shown in Figure 16 - 17.

Figure 16 - 17: Sample dashboard page with embedded Excel data

PerformancePoint Services can embed Excel Services workbooks into a dashboard page and visualize Excel data in the form of a hierarchical decomposition tree. To learn to use PerformancePoint Services to build a dashboard with these components, click the *Start using PerformancePoint Services* link under the *Explore Your Data with Visualizations* heading on the *Business Intelligence Center* home page. The system displays a page with a button to launch the PerformancePoint *Dashboard Designer*, as well as additional information and help about PerformancePoint Services, as shown previously in Figure 16 - 15.

To view information and links contained in the *Create Dashboards* section, float your mouse pointer over the *Create Dashboards* heading on the right side of the page. The system displays tools and help for creating interactive dashboards, as shown in Figure 16 - 18.

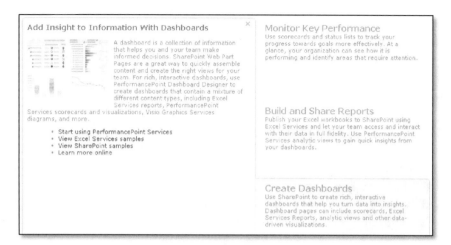

Figure 16 - 18: Business Intelligence Center home page, Create Dashboards selected

As I stated previously in this module, a dashboard is a feature of SharePoint 2010 that allows aggregation and visualization of multiple types of data in a central location for reporting and analysis. To view information and tools for using PerformancePoint Services, as well as dashboard examples, follow the links shown below the *Add Insight to Information With Dashboards* heading.

Built-In Microsoft Excel Reports Overview

In addition to these reporting tools, the *Business Intelligence Center* arrives pre-populated with Microsoft Excel-based reporting tools for quickly creating reports based on data from Project Server:

- 10 sample reports

- 7 templates for creating new reports based on data from the Project Server Reporting Database

- 14 templates for creating new reports based on data from each OLAP Database

- 13 shared Office Data Connection (ODC) files for connecting to the Project Server Reporting Database

- 14 shared Office Data Connection (ODC) files for connecting to each OLAP cube. The system creates these for every OLAP database you create

These sample reports, templates, and ODC files save you a considerable amount of effort, while creating the various types of Business Intelligence reports that your organization requires. I provide detailed information about using these tools in subsequent sections of this module.

Business Intelligence Center Security Overview

The *Business Intelligence Center* site does not adhere to the same security model as Project Server. It utilizes the SharePoint security model to grant people access to the site and all of its contents, and it utilizes the Secure Store Service to grant people access to the data in Project Server BI Data Store. You can secure each report individually using the techniques I demonstrated in Module 5.

Although a SharePoint sub-site typically inherits its security settings from its parent site (the PWA site, in this case), you can break the security inheritance and manage it separately using the SharePoint security model. If you must control access to specific items within the *Business Intelligence Center* site, such as specific report folders or individual reports within a folder, you can easily customize the SharePoint security permissions through the web interface. Having separate security also allows you to delegate *Business Intelligence Center* administrative duties to another person who is quite possibly not a Project Server user.

Microsoft SharePoint Excel Services Overview

Microsoft SharePoint Excel Services is a feature of SharePoint Server 2010 that allows you to publish Microsoft Excel 2007 or Excel 2010 workbooks to the web to create read-only or interactive online reports, rather than forcing people to download an Excel workbook to the desktop and open it locally with Microsoft Excel. A major benefit of using Microsoft Excel with Excel Services as a Project Server reporting tool is that it provides a familiar tool to build, view, and interact with reports, with familiar manipulation features such as sorting, filtering, and grouping, and familiar visualization features such as charting, key performance indicators (KPIs), and conditional formatting.

Your workbooks can contain static data that you update manually, or they can contain dynamic data from external data sources. A report author can connect an Excel workbook to a data source such as a database, extract data, and display the report online without giving viewers direct access to the data source, as illustrated in Figure 16 - 19.

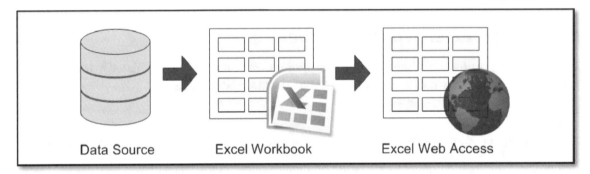

Figure 16 - 19: Excel workbook fetching data from a data source and publishing to the web

In addition to publishing a workbook for online viewing, a report author can control which data within the workbook the viewers can access when they view it online. For instance, you can display the results of a calculation without exposing the underlying formula, or you can display a summary chart without exposing the underlying data, as illustrated in Figure 16 - 20.

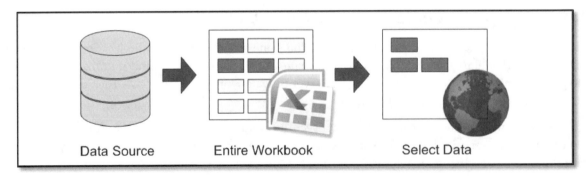

Figure 16 - 20: Exposing only select Excel data via the web

When you publish an Excel workbook to the web for online viewing, you can display the workbook using two methods:

1. Display the workbook on its own page using the Excel Services web viewer.
2. Embed selected sections of the workbook in a SharePoint dashboard page.

Figure 16 - 21 shows a workbook as a web page using Excel Services.

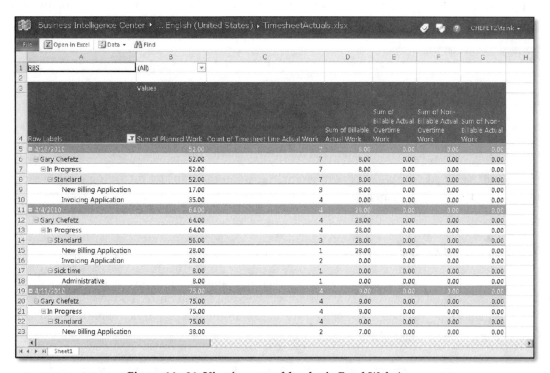

Figure 16 - 21: Viewing a workbook via Excel Web Access

Figure 16 - 22 shows a workbook as part of a SharePoint dashboard page.

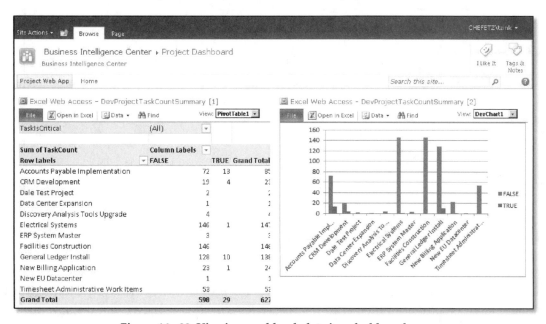

Figure 16 - 22: Viewing workbook data in a dashboard page

Working With the Built-In Microsoft Excel Reports

As stated previously in this module, when you publish an Excel workbook to the web, it can contain static data or it can extract its data from one or more external data sources. In the case of Project Server reports, Excel extracts its data from the Project Server Reporting database or one of possibly several OLAP databases.

To manually create an Excel report based on Project Server data, you must perform the following manual steps:

1. Create an Office Data Connection (ODC) file connecting to the RDB or an OLAP database, and write an SQL query to extract the data.

2. Open Microsoft Excel and create a new workbook.

3. Connect the workbook to your ODC file.

4. Format your data and create visualizations.

5. Save the Excel workbook file to a trusted file location in SharePoint.

Fortunately, Microsoft saves you the effort of performing these manual steps by providing sample reports, report templates, and pre-built ODC files connected to Project Server data. You access these assets from the *Business Intelligence Center* site.

Excel Sample Reports Overview

Project Server 2010 provides sample Microsoft Excel reports that are pre-connected to the Project Server Reporting Database through ODC files saved in the Project Server BI Data Store. To view these reports, visit the *Business Intelligence Center* site and click the *Sample Reports* link in the Quick Launch menu. The system displays the *Sample Reports* page shown in Figure 16 - 23.

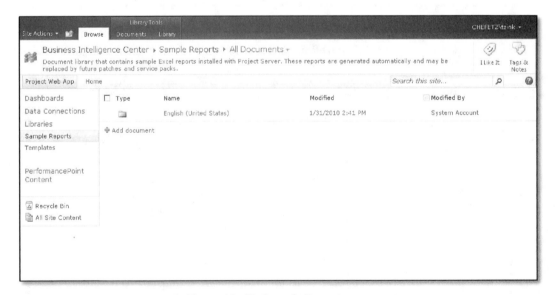

Figure 16 - 23: Sample Reports page

The *Business Intelligence Center* supports multi-language reporting, and the *Sample Reports* library contains a separate folder for each language pack that you configure for Project Server. To view the English language reports, click the *English (United States)* folder in the *Sample Reports* library. The system displays the contents of the *English (United States)* folder as shown in Figure 16 - 24.

782

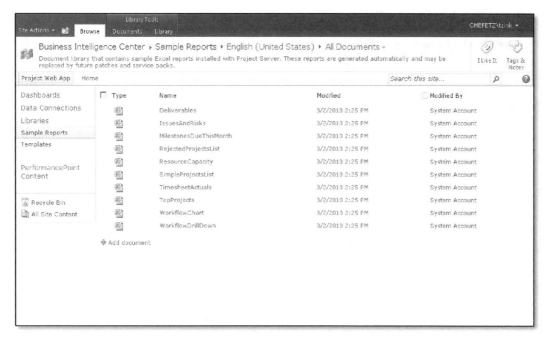

Figure 16 - 24: English language folder contents in the Sample Reports library

Notice in Figure 16 - 24 that the Sample Reports library contains the following sample reports:

- Deliverables (Deliverables.xlsx)

- Issues and Risks (IssuesAndRisks.xlsx)

- Milestones Due This Month (MilestonesDueThisMonth.xlsx)

- Rejected Projects (RejectedProjectsLists.xlsx)

- Resource Capacity (ResourceCapacity.xlsx)

- Simple Projects List (SimpleProjectsList.xlsx)

- Timesheet Actuals (TimesheetActuals.xlsx)

- Top Projects (TopProjects.xlsx)

- Workflow Chart (WorkflowChart.xlsx)

- Workflow Drilldown (WorkflowDrillDown.xlsx)

Excel Report Templates Overview

Project Server also provides you with Microsoft Excel report templates that use the pre-connected ODC files. To view these report templates, from the *Business Intelligence Center* click the *Templates* link in the Quick Launch menu. The system displays the *Templates* page shown in Figure 16 - 25.

Figure 16 - 25: Templates page

The *Business Intelligence Center* supports multi-language reporting, and the *Templates* library contains a separate folder for each language pack that you provision for your Project Server. To view the English language reports, click the *English (United States)* folder in the *Templates* library. The system displays the contents of the *English (United States)* folder as shown in Figure 16 - 26.

Figure 16 - 26: English language folder contents in the Templates library

The Excel report templates help you build new reports quickly. You can use these as-is, or you can use them as starting points to develop your own custom reports. The English language folder contains seven report templates that arrive pre-connected to the Project Server Reporting Database including:

- Dependent Projects (DependentProjects.xltx)

- Issues (Issues.xltx)

- Projects and Assignments (ProjectsAndAssignments.xltx)

- Projects and Tasks (ProjectsAndTasks.xltx)

- Resources (Resources.xltx)

- Risks (Risks.xltx)

- Timesheet (Timesheet.xltx)

Every time you create a new OLAP database, the system automatically creates another folder in the *Templates* library containing an additional 14 report templates for that new OLAP database. Each folder contains 14 templates pre-connected to each of the 14 OLAP cubes in each OLAP database as follows:

- OLAP Assignment Non-Timephased (OlapAssignmentNonTimephased.xltx)

- OLAP Assignment Timephased (OlapAssignmentTimephased.xltx)

- OLAP Deliverables (OlapDeliverables.xltx)

- OLAP EPM Timesheet (OlapEpmTimesheet.xltx)

- OLAP Issues (OlapIssues.xltx)

- OLAP Portfolio Analyzer (OlapPortfolioAnalyzer.xltx)

- OLAP Project Non-Timephased (OlapProjectNonTimephased.xltx)

- OLAP Project SharePoint (OlapProjectSharePoint.xltx)

- OLAP Project Timesheet (OlapProjectTimesheet.xltx)

- OLAP Resource Non-Timephased (OlapResourceNonTimephased.xltx)

- OLAP Resource Timephased (OlapResourceTimephased.xltx)

- OLAP Risks (OlapRisks.xltx)

- OLAP Task Non-Timephased (OlapTaskNonTimephased.xltx)

- OLAP Timesheet (OlapTimesheet.xltx)

 Note that the file extension for the Excel report templates is *.xltx*, rather than *.xlsx*, indicating that they are Excel template files.

Excel Data Connection Files Overview

As I stated previously, the sample Excel reports and report templates in the *Business Intelligence Center* are pre-connected to their respective data sources in the Project Server BI Data Store. Although each of these Excel files could have their data connection information embedded directly in each workbook, instead the *Business*

Intelligence Center manages these data connections centrally in the *Data Connections* library. This library contains 13 shared Office Data Connection (ODC) files for connecting to the Project Server Reporting Database, and it contains 14 shared Office Data Connection (ODC) files for connecting reports to each OLAP Database. Each data connection file is essentially an XML file that contains three key pieces of information describing the connection to the data source:

- The data source connection information, such as the database server name and the database name

- The specific description of the retrieved data, such as a SQL query or OLAP cube name

- The authentication information, such as the user credentials or Secure Store Service ID (SSID)

The benefits of separating the data connection files from the workbook files include:

- Eliminates the need for report authors to know detailed technical information such as server names, database names, or SQL syntax.

- Many reports can share a small common set of data connection files.

- If you need to update the data connections, such as when you move a database to a different server, you can change the connection information in one place and the system updates all of your connected report files automatically.

- You can secure your Data connection files separately.

To view these data connection files, navigate to the *Business Intelligence Center* and click the *Data Connections* link in the Quick Launch menu. The system displays the *Data Connections* page shown in Figure 16 - 27.

Figure 16 - 27: Data Connections page

To view the English language data connection files, click the *English (United States)* folder in the *Data Connections* library. The system displays the *English (United States)* folder partially shown in Figure 16 - 28.

786

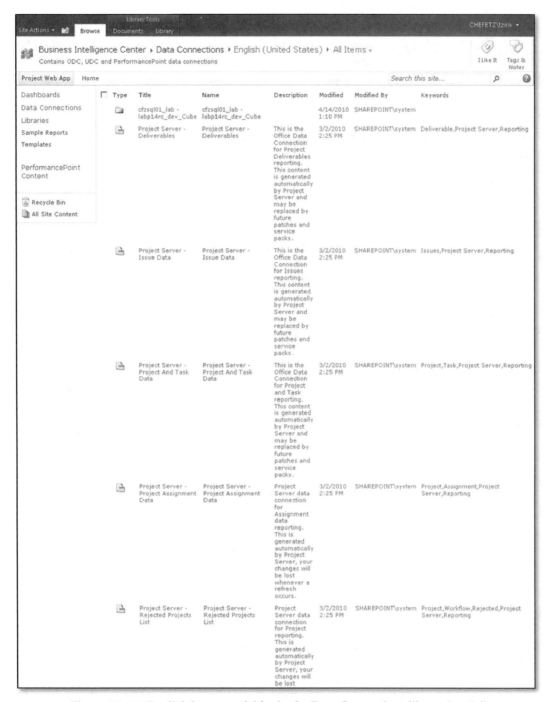

Figure 16 - 28: English language folder in the Data Connections library (partial)

The English language folder contains 13 data connection files for connecting reports to the Project Server Reporting database:

- Project Server - Deliverables (Project Server - Deliverables.odc)

- Project Server - Issue Data (Project Server - Issue Data.odc)

- Project Server - Project And Task Data (Project Server - Project And Task Data.odc)

- Project Server - Project Assignment Data (Project Server - Project Assignment Data.odc)

- Project Server - Rejected Projects List (Project Server - Rejected Projects List.odc)

- Project Server - Resource Capacity (Project Server - Resource Capacity.odc)

- Project Server - Resource Data (Project Server - Resource Data.odc)

- Project Server - Risk Data (Project Server - Risk Data.odc)

- Project Server - Simple Projects List (Project Server - Simple Projects List.odc)

- Project Server - Timesheet Data (Project Server - Timesheet Data.odc)

- Project Server - Top Projects Data (Project Server - Top Projects Data.odc)

- Project Server - Workflow Chart Data (Project Server - Workflow Chart Data.odc)

- Project Server - Workflow Drilldown Data (Project Server - Workflow Drilldown Data.odc)

The English language folder also contains a sub-folder for each OLAP database, each containing 14 data connection files for connecting reports to each of the 14 OLAP cubes in the OLAP database:

- OLAP Assignment Non Timephased (OlapAssignmentNonTimephased.odc)

- OLAP Assignment Timephased (OlapAssignmentTimephased.odc)

- OLAP Deliverables (OlapDeliverables.odc)

- OLAP EPM Timesheet (OlapEpmTimesheet.odc)

- OLAP Issues (OlapIssues.odc)

- OLAP Portfolio Analyzer (OlapPortfolioAnalyzer.odc)

- OLAP Project Non Timephased (OlapProjectNonTimephased.odc)

- OLAP Project SharePoint (OlapMSProjectSharePoint.odc)

- OLAP Project Timesheet (OlapProjectTimesheet.odc)

- OLAP Resource Non Timephased (OlapResourceNonTimephased.odc)

- OLAP Resource Timephased (OlapResourceTimephased.odc)

- OLAP Risks (OlapRisks.odc)

- OLAP Task Non Timephased (OlapTaskNonTimephased.odc)

- OLAP Timesheet (OlapTimesheet.odc)

Note that the file extension for the data connection files is *.odc*, rather than *.xlsx or *.xltx*, indicating that they are Office Data Connection files.

Viewing the Sample Excel Reports in Your Web Browser

To view any of the sample Excel reports via the web, click the name of the report in the *Sample Reports* library. The system uses Excel Services to open and render the report in your web browser without downloading it to your desktop. I provide a brief description of each sample Excel report as the system presents it via the web.

Deliverables Report

The *Deliverables* report extracts a listing of all Project Server 2010 deliverables from the Project Server *Reporting* database and displays the data in Excel PivotTable format in your web browser, as shown in Figure 16 - 29.

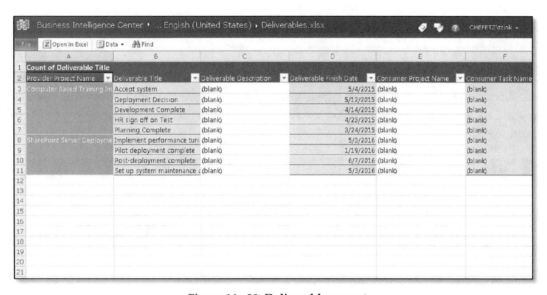

Figure 16 - 29: Deliverables report

Issues and Risks Report

The *Issues and Risks* report extracts a listing of all Project Server issues and risks from the Project Server RDB and displays the data in Excel PivotTable format in your web browser, as shown in Figure 16 - 30 and Figure 16 - 31.

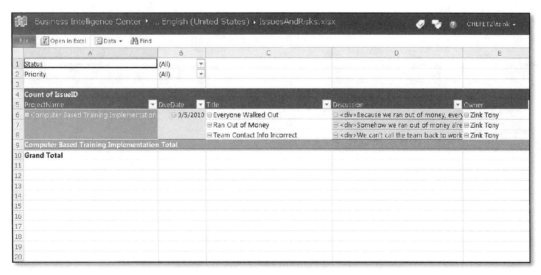

Figure 16 - 30: Issues and Risks report, Issues tab

Figure 16 - 31: Issues and Risks report, Risks tab

Milestones Due This Month Report

The *Milestones Due This Month* report extracts a listing of all Project Server milestones that are scheduled to complete during the current month and displays the data in Excel PivotTable format in your web browser, as shown in Figure 16 - 32.

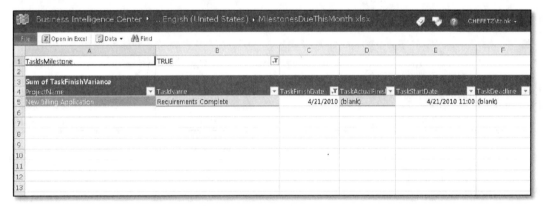

Figure 16 - 32: Milestones Due This Month report

Rejected Projects Report

The *Rejected Projects* report extracts a listing of all rejected Project Server projects and displays the data in Excel PivotTable format in your web browser, as shown in Figure 16 - 33.

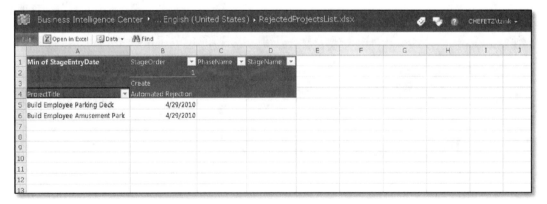

Figure 16 - 33: Rejected Projects report

Resource Capacity Report

The *Resource Capacity* report extracts a listing of all Project Server resource capacities and displays the data in Excel PivotTable and PivotChart format in your web browser, as shown in Figure 16 - 34 and Figure 16 - 35.

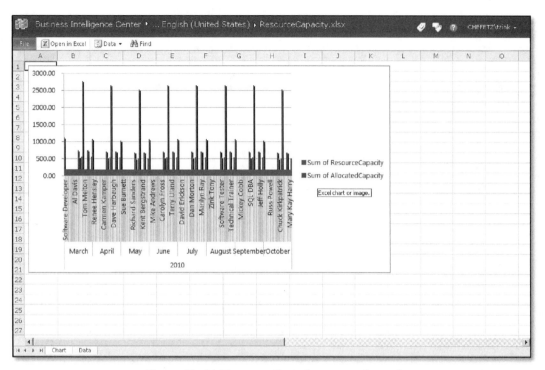

Figure 16 - 34: Resource Capacity report, chart tab

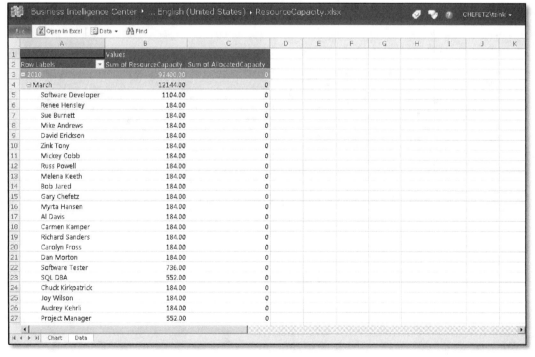

Figure 16 - 35: Resource Capacity report, data tab

791

Simple Projects List Report

The *Simple Projects List* report extracts a listing of all Project Server projects from the Project Server RDB and displays the data in Excel PivotTable format in your web browser, as shown in Figure 16 - 36.

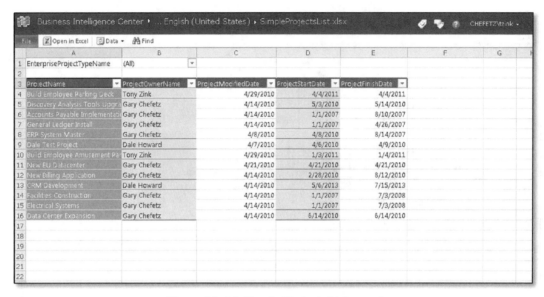

Figure 16 - 36: Simple Projects List report

Timesheet Actuals Report

The *Timesheet Actuals* report extracts a listing of all Project Server timesheet work hours from the Project Server RDB and displays the data in Excel PivotTable format in your web browser, as shown in Figure 16 - 37.

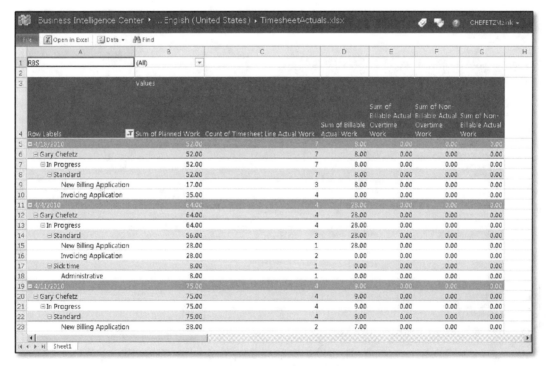

Figure 16 - 37: Timesheet Actuals report

Top Projects Report

The *Top Projects* report extracts a listing of top proposals and costs from the Project Server Reporting Database and displays the data in Excel PivotTable and PivotChart format in your web browser, as shown in Figure 16 - 38.

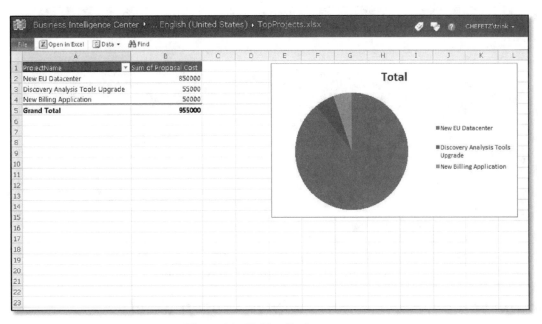

Figure 16 - 38: Top Projects report

Workflow Chart Report

The *Workflow Chart* report displays a count of all projects by system workflow stage from the Project Server RDB and displays the data in Excel PivotTable and PivotChart format in your web browser, as shown in Figure 16 - 39.

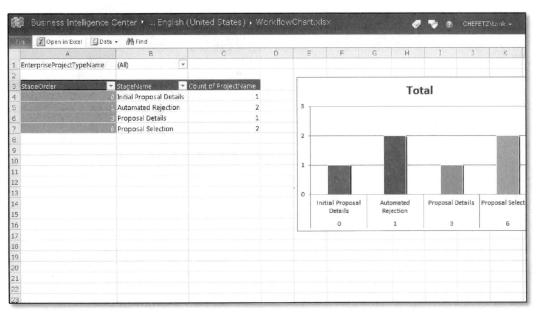

Figure 16 - 39: Workflow Chart report

Workflow Drilldown Report

The *Workflow Drilldown* report extracts a listing of detailed workflow stage status information from the Project Server RDB and displays the data in Excel PivotTable format in your web browser, as shown in Figure 16 - 40.

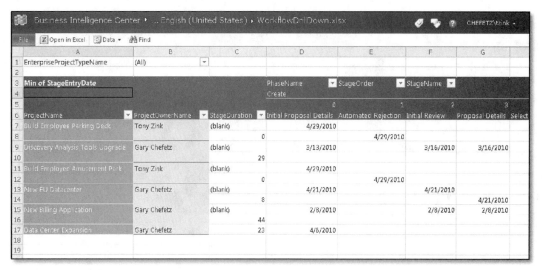

Figure 16 - 40: Workflow Drilldown report

Opening the Sample Excel Reports with Microsoft Excel

To open any of the sample reports in Microsoft Excel for editing, printing, or copying information into another desktop application, navigate to the *Sample Reports* library and float your mouse pointer over the name of the report to reveal the pick list that appears to the right of the file name, and select the *Edit in Microsoft Excel* option.

The system launches Microsoft Excel if it is not already running, and depending upon the security settings within Excel, the tool may display a *Protected View* alert in a yellow message bar near the top of the window when it opens the workbook from the server, as shown in Figure 16 - 41.

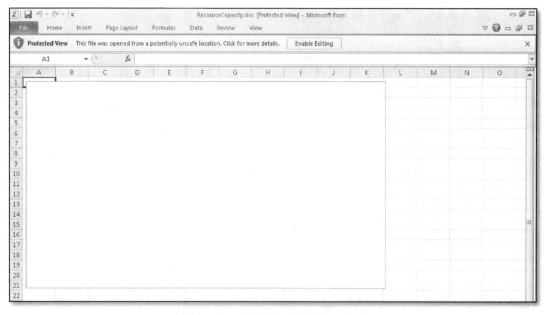

Figure 16 - 41: Protected View alert

You may either click the *Enable Editing* button in the yellow message bar or select the *Click for more details* link in the yellow message bar. If you click the *Enable Editing* button, the security settings in Excel remain unchanged and it continues to prompt you with the same alert each time you choose to open an Excel report for editing. If you click the *Click for more details* link, Excel displays the Backstage and displays options for changing the *Protected View* settings, as shown in Figure 16 - 42.

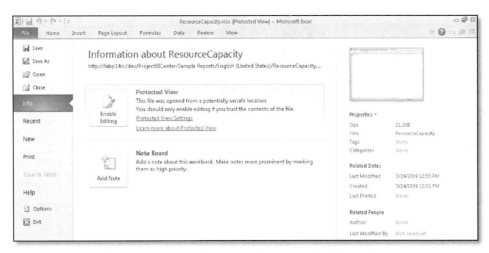

Figure 16 - 42: Backstage with Protected View options

To change the *Protected View* settings in Excel, click the *Protected View Settings* link in the *Protected View* section of the Backstage. Excel displays the *Protected View* page in the *Trust Center* dialog shown in Figure 16 - 43.

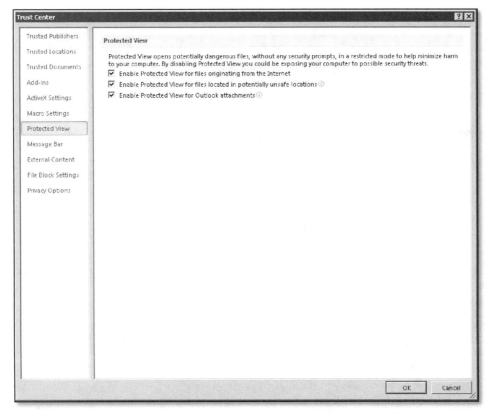

Figure 16 - 43: Protected View page in the Trust Center dialog

795

Select the appropriate options in the *Trust Center* dialog according to your organization's security policies and click the *OK* button to close the dialog, and then click the *File* tab again to exit the Backstage. Microsoft Excel opens and displays the report as shown in Figure 16 - 44.

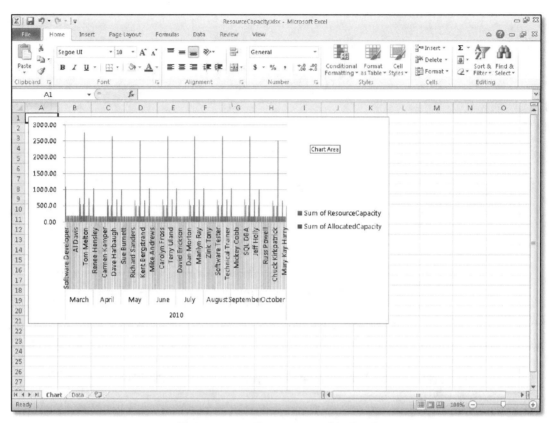

Figure 16 - 44: Report opened in Excel

Warning: Per Microsoft's recommendation, do not save changes to any of the built-in sample reports, report templates, or data connection files. When Microsoft releases patches and service packs in the future, they may recreate the default items, overwriting any changes that you may have made to them.

Creating a Custom Excel Report by Modifying a Sample Report

You can use the 10 sample Excel reports as-is, or you can use them as a starting point to build custom reports to meet the needs of your organization. To create a new custom report based on one of the sample Excel reports, visit the *Sample Reports* library in the Project Server *Business Intelligence Center* and float your mouse pointer over the name of the report, click the pick list arrow that appears to the right of the file name, and select the *Edit in Microsoft Excel* option from the pick list. Microsoft Excel launches and displays the report..

With the sample report open in editing mode, you may make changes to the report to meet your organization's business needs, such as adding or removing fields of data, changing the formatting of the data, adding a chart, or changing the formatting of a chart as necessary. I describe common methods of modifying a Microsoft Excel PivotTable or PivotChart report in a subsequent section in this module.

I do not show many of the possibilities available for editing a PivotTable or PivotChart, but rather a few of the most common ways to customize a report. For more information on working with Excel PivotTables and PivotCharts, seek additional guidance or training.

After making your desired modifications to the sample report, click the *File* tab in the Excel ribbon and select the *Save As* option in the *Backstage* menu. Excel displays the *Save As* dialog shown in Figure 16 - 45.

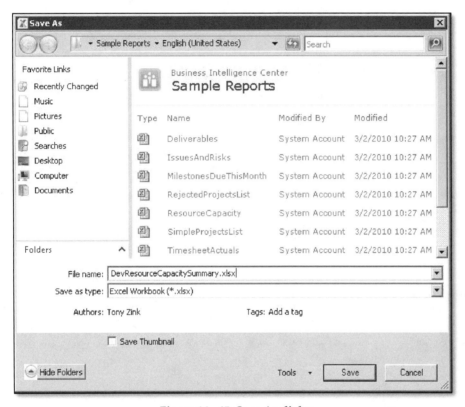

Figure 16 - 45: Save As dialog

In the *Save As* dialog, browse to a report storage library such as the *Sample Reports* library in the Project Server *Business Intelligence Center* site, enter a new report file name into the *File name* field, then click the *Save* button. The new Excel report becomes available for online viewing in the report library, as shown in Figure 16 - 46.

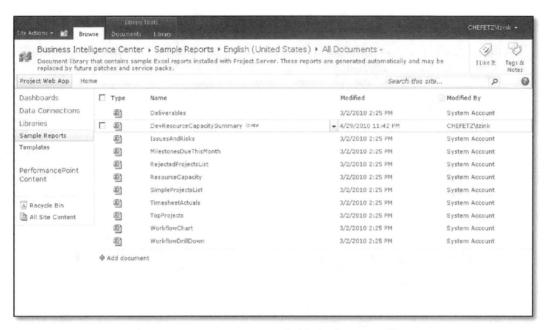

Figure 16 - 46: New report available in the report library

You may create a custom report storage library by simply creating a new document library in the *Business Intelligence Center* site. Remember that in order for people to view the reports in the web browser using Excel Services, you must add your new library as an Excel Services trusted file location via the SharePoint *Central Administration web* site, using the methods you learned in Module 5.

Warning: Per Microsoft's recommendation, do not save changes to any of the built-in sample reports, report templates, or data connection files. When Microsoft releases patches and service packs in the future, they may recreate the default items, overwriting any changes that you may have made to them.

Creating a Custom Excel Report Based on a Template

Unlike the 10 sample Excel reports that are available in the *Business Intelligence Center Sample Reports* library, the Excel report templates available in the *Templates* library are not intended to be used as-is. Because they are Excel template files (*.xltx), they are configured to open directly in Microsoft Excel for you to use as a basis for creating new reports. To create a new custom report based on one of the Excel report templates, from the *Templates* library in the Project Server *Business Intelligence Center*, click the name of the template you want to use. Microsoft Excel launches and displays the template.

With the report template open in editing mode, you may make changes to the report to meet your organization's business needs, such as adding or removing fields of data, changing the formatting of the data, adding a chart, or changing the formatting of a chart as necessary. I describe common methods of modifying a Microsoft Excel PivotTable or PivotChart report later in this module.

Note that unlike the sample Excel reports, the Excel report templates do not contain any pre-built PivotTables or PivotCharts. Although the templates contain an empty PivotTable area to begin your work, you need to add any data fields and formatting that are required based on your organization's reporting requirements.

After making the desired modifications to customize a Microsoft Excel report, click the *File* tab in the Excel ribbon and select the *Save As* option in the *Backstage* menu. Excel displays the *Save As* dialog as shown in Figure 16 - 47.

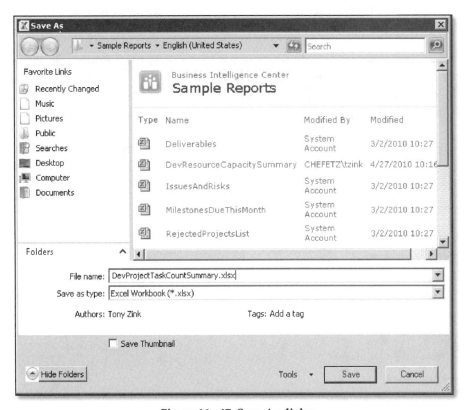

Figure 16 - 47: Save As dialog

In the *Save As* dialog, browse to a report storage library such as the *Sample Reports* library in the Project Server *Business Intelligence Center* site, enter a new report file name into the *File name* field, select *Excel Workbook (*.xlsx)* from the *Save as type* pick list, then click the *Save* button. The new Excel report becomes available for online viewing in the selected report library.

 Warning: It is important that you do not forget to select the Excel workbook (*.xlsx) file type, otherwise Excel will save the file as a template, rather than a report that is viewable in the web browser.

Common Methods of Modifying an Excel Pivot Report

Exploring all of the possibilities available for editing a PivotTable or PivotChart report are beyond the scope of this book, but the following are several common methods of modifying an Excel report to meet your organization's business needs. To learn more about working with Microsoft Excel, consider additional books or training.

Adding or Removing Data Fields in a PivotTable Report

To add a data field to an Excel PivotTable report, select any cell in the PivotTable to display the *PivotTable Field List* sidepane, locate your desired field in the *Choose fields to add to report* list in the side panel, and select the checkbox next to the field name. Excel adds the selected field to the PivotTable as shown in Figure 16 - 48.

To re-open a closed *PivotTable Field List* side panel, select any cell in the PivotTable, select the *Options* tab in the *PivotTable Tools* section of the ribbon menu, and click the *Field List* button in the *Show* section of the ribbon.

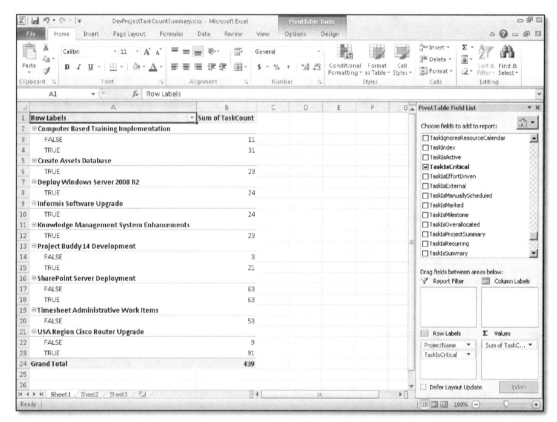

Figure 16 - 48: Adding a field to a PivotTable

The *PivotTable Field List* shows the only data fields available for this report, which is a select subset of all available fields in the RDB. To build a report that includes more fields, you need to base the report on a different sample report, base it on one of the included report templates, or you can create a new ODC file with a modified SQL query to support your reporting needs.

To remove a data field from an Excel PivotTable style report, select any cell in the PivotTable to display the *PivotTable Field List* side panel, locate the field in the *Choose fields to add to report* list in the side panel, and deselect the checkbox next to the field name. Excel removes the deselected field from the PivotTable.

Reorganizing Data Fields in a PivotTable Report

When Excel displays a data field in a PivotTable report, that field can appear in any of four areas of the PivotTable, as shown in Figure 16 - 49:

- It can appear as a *Sum Value*, located in the main body of the report. This is a field of data that you want to break down various ways for analysis.

- It can appear as a *Column Label*, located at the top of the main body of the report. This is a field that you use to break down Sum Values horizontally for analysis.

- It can appear as a *Row Label*, located on the left side of the main body of the report. This is a field that you use to break down Sum Values vertically for analysis.

- It can appear as a *Report Filter*, located in the upper left corner of the report. This is a field that you use to show only the individual Sum Values of interest, while hiding the rest.

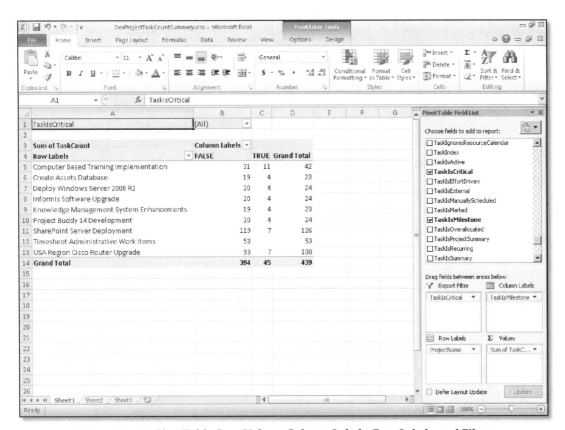

Figure 16 - 49: PivotTable Sum Values, Column Labels, Row Labels, and Filters

When adding a data field to an Excel PivotTable report, Excel automatically places the field into one of the *Sum Value, Column Label*, or *Row Label* areas in the PivotTable, based on the nature of the data field. To move a data field from one PivotTable area to another, select any cell in the PivotTable to display the *PivotTable Field List* side panel. In the lower portion of the side panel, locate the desired field, click the pick list arrow located to the right

801

of the field name, and select the appropriate option to move the data field to another area of the PivotTable, as shown in Figure 16 - 50.

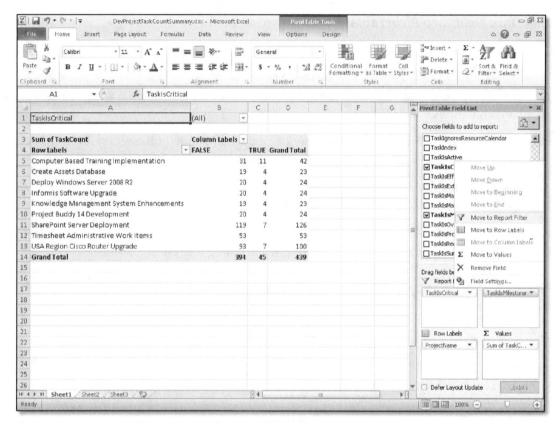

Figure 16 - 50: Moving a field to another PivotTable area

Excel displays the data field in its new location and updates the rest of the PivotTable data accordingly.

 You can also move a PivotTable data field to another area by dragging the field name between the *Sum Values*, *Column Labels*, *Row Labels*, and *Report Filter* sections of the *PivotTable Field List* side pane.

Adding a Calculated Data Field to a PivotTable Report

You may want to add a calculated data field to an Excel PivotTable report that is not available in the PivotTable Field List. To add a calculated data field to an Excel PivotTable style report, select any cell in the PivotTable, select the *Options* tab in the *PivotTable Tools* section of the ribbon, and select *Calculated Field* from the *Fields, Items, & Sets* pick list in the *Calculations* section of the ribbon. Excel displays the *Insert Calculated Field* dialog shown in Figure 16 - 51.

Configuring Business Intelligence and Reporting

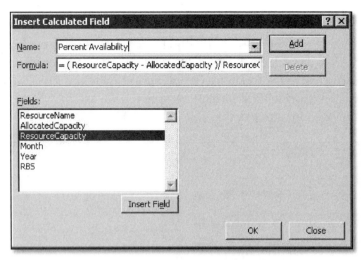

Figure 16 - 51: Insert Calculated Field dialog

You must manually type or build an expression based on existing fields in the *Insert Calculated Field* dialog. For example, to add a *Percent Availability* calculated field to the *Resource Capacity* report, enter the following information into the dialog, then click the *OK* button:

- **Name:** Percent Availability

- **Formula:** = (ResourceCapacity - AllocatedCapacity) / ResourceCapacity

Enter fields into the formula by manually typing their names into the *Formula* field, or by selecting them from the *Fields* list and clicking the *Insert Field* button in the dialog. Excel creates the new calculated field and adds it to the PivotTable in the report, as shown in Figure 16 - 52.

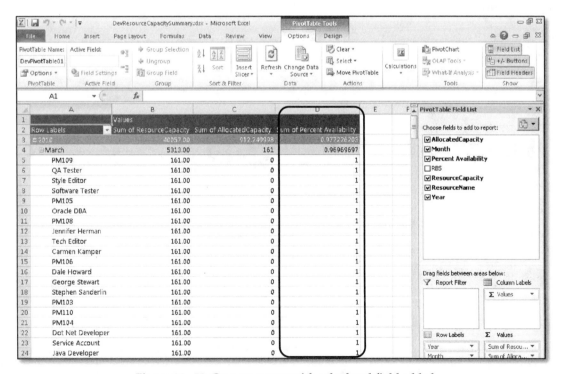

Figure 16 - 52: Custom report with calculated field added

803

Changing Number Formatting in a PivotTable Report

Numerical data in a report sometimes requires reformatting, such as to display currencies, dates, or percentages. In the previous example, the calculated *Percent Availability* field displays as a decimal number, but should appear formatted as a percentage. To change the formatting of numerical data in a PivotTable, select the desired data, click the *Home* tab in the ribbon, then select a formatting option from the pick list in the *Number* section of the ribbon. The pick list offers several formatting options, as shown in Figure 16 - 53.

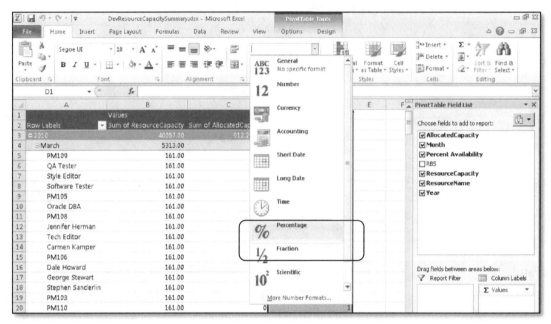

Figure 16 - 53: Selecting a number format

Excel changes the formatting of the selected numerical data, a shown in Figure 16 - 54.

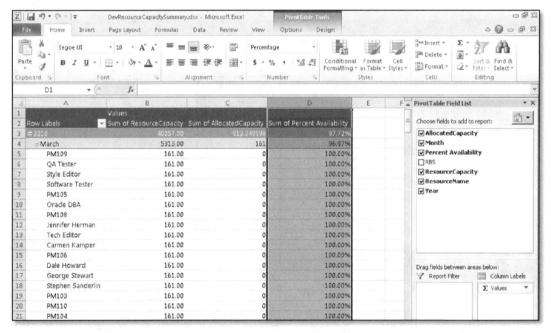

Figure 16 - 54: Custom report with numerical data formatted as percentages

Adding Conditional Formatting and Indicators to a PivotTable Report

Excel conditional formatting is a feature that allows you to add graphical indicators to the data in a PivotTable for data visualization. To add conditional formatting to an Excel PivotTable report, select a range of cells to display the conditional formatting, select the *Home* tab on the ribbon, then select your formatting option from the *Conditional Formatting* pick list, shown in Figure 16 - 55.

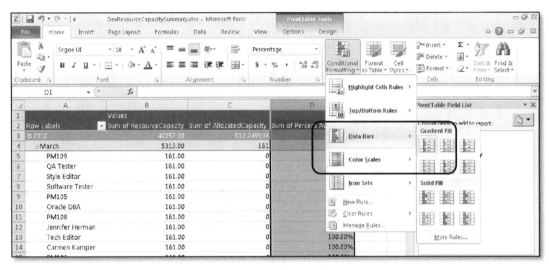

Figure 16 - 55: Applying gradient fill data bar formatting to a PivotTable

Excel formats the selected range of cells using the selected conditional formatting scheme as shown in Figure 16 - 56.

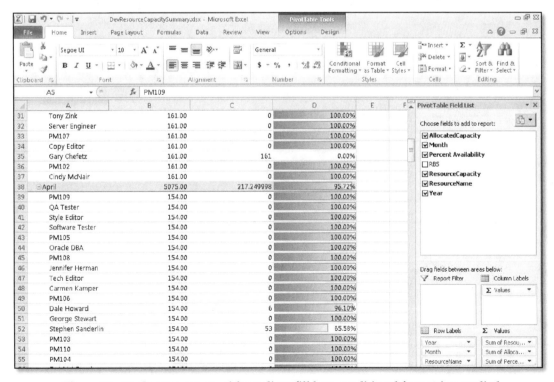

Figure 16 - 56: Custom report with gradient fill bars conditional formatting applied

To apply multiple conditional formatting schemes to the same range of data values, select another option from the *Conditional Formatting* pick list, such as an icon set, as shown in Figure 16 - 57.

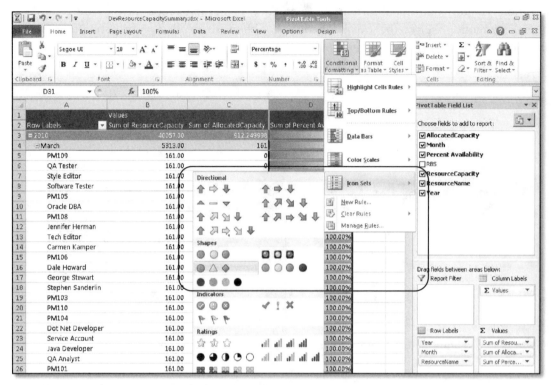

Figure 16 - 57: Applying conditional icon set formatting to a PivotTable

Excel superimposes the multiple conditional formatting rules over the same range of data values, as shown in Figure 16 - 58.

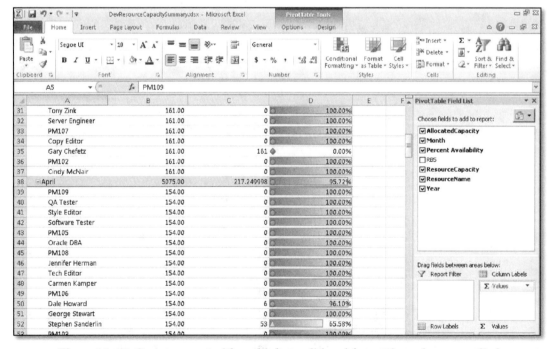

Figure 16 - 58: Custom report with multiple conditional formatting schemes applied

To modify the rules or thresholds that Excel uses to apply conditional formatting to a range of data values, select the range of cells and select the *Manage Rules* option from the *Conditional Formatting* pick list on the *Home* ribbon. Excel displays the *Conditional Formatting Rules Manager* dialog as shown in Figure 16 - 59 and provides tools for creating new, deleting, editing, and reordering sets of conditional formatting rules.

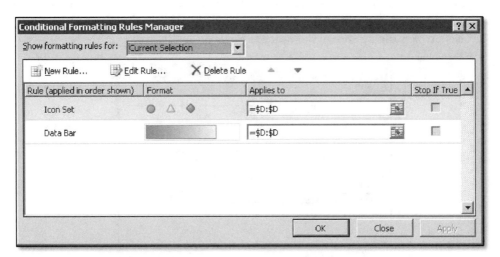

Figure 16 - 59: Conditional Formatting Rules Manager dialog

For example, to modify the thresholds that Excel uses for an icon set, select the *Icon Set* rule in the dialog and click the *Edit Rule* button. Excel displays the *Edit Formatting Rule* dialog and provides tools for modifying the behavior of the icon set, such as icon styles and threshold values, as shown in Figure 16 - 60.

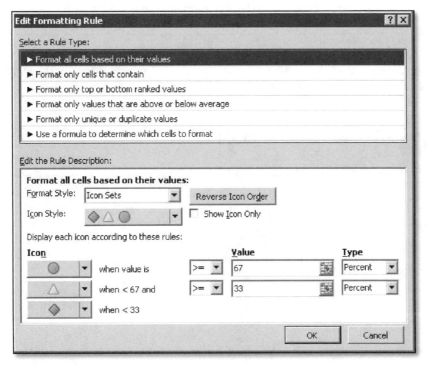

Figure 16 - 60: Edit Formatting Rule dialog

Renaming Data Fields in a PivotTable Report

When Excel displays a data field in a PivotTable report, it uses the field's literal name as it appears in the Project Server RDB or OLAP database. That literal name may not be user-friendly, or it may be too long to make the best use of space in the report. To change a field's display name in an Excel PivotTable, select any cell in the PivotTable to display the *PivotTable Field List* side panel. In the lower portion of the side panel, locate the field, click the pick list arrow located to the right of the field name, and select the *Value Field Settings* option. Excel displays the *Value Field Settings* dialog shown in Figure 16 - 61.

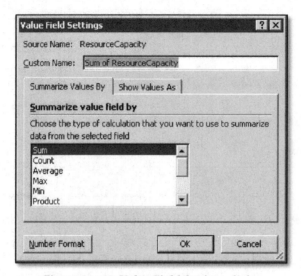

Figure 16 - 61: Value Field Settings dialog

In the *Value Field Settings* dialog, change the display name by entering a new name into the *Custom Name* field, then click the *OK* button. Excel updates the field's display name in the PivotTable, as shown in Figure 16 - 62.

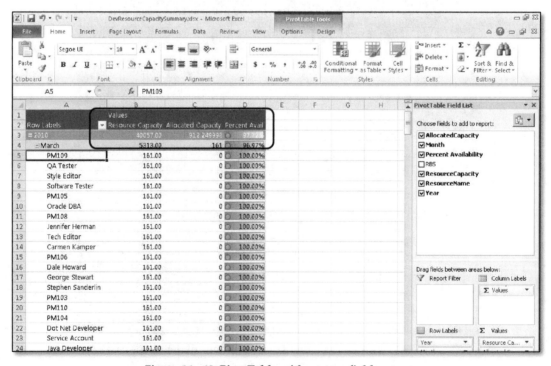

Figure 16 - 62: PivotTable with custom field names

Changing or Assigning a PivotTable Name in a Report

Excel Services is capable of publishing an entire Microsoft Excel workbook for online viewing, or only the portions of the workbook that you choose to make visible via the web. By assigning a name to an Excel PivotTable, you enable Excel Services to publish that named object to the web, while hiding the remainder of the data in the workbook.

To change or assign an Excel PivotTable name, select any cell in the PivotTable, then select the *Options* tab in the *PivotTable Tools* section of the ribbon. In the *PivotTable* section at the left end of the ribbon, enter a name into the *PivotTable Name* field as shown in Figure 16 - 63.

Figure 16 - 63: Changing or assigning a PivotTable name

 Pressing the *Enter* key on your computer keyboard or clicking in another area of the Excel workbook will force Excel to accept the name change.

 Assigning a name to an Excel PivotTable will allow embedding of the table in a dashboard page, as described later in this module.

 Not all PivotTable reports lend themselves nicely to charting. In general, a PivotTable should have counts or sums in order to generate a useful PivotChart.

 You can add a PivotChart to a separate worksheet tab in the Excel workbook file, or you can add it to an existing worksheet tab. If you add a PivotChart to an existing worksheet tab, position it such that it does not hide any existing data in the worksheet, as online viewers cannot reposition the PivotChart.

Adding a PivotChart to a Report

Several of the sample reports do not include an accompanying PivotChart to help viewers visualize the data in the report. To add a PivotChart to an Excel report, select any cell in the PivotTable, click the *Insert* tab on the ribbon, then click the chart type you want to use from the *Charts* section of the ribbon. Excel inserts a new PivotChart into the current worksheet, as shown in Figure 16 - 64.

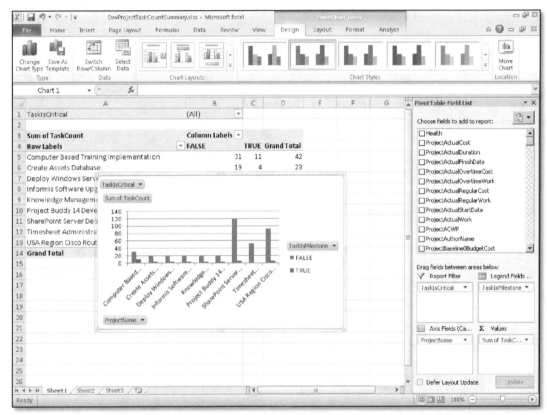

Figure 16 - 64: New PivotChart added to worksheet

At this point, you may reposition or reformat the PivotChart in the same worksheet, or you may create a new worksheet tab and move the PivotChart to the new worksheet by cutting and pasting the chart into its new location.

Changing a PivotChart Type in a Report

In an Excel report that contains a PivotChart, you may want to change the chart type. To change the chart type for an Excel PivotChart, select the chart and then select the *Design* tab in the *PivotChart Tools* section of the ribbon, and click the *Change Chart Type* button in the *Type* section of the ribbon. Excel displays the *Change Chart Type* dialog shown in Figure 16 - 65.

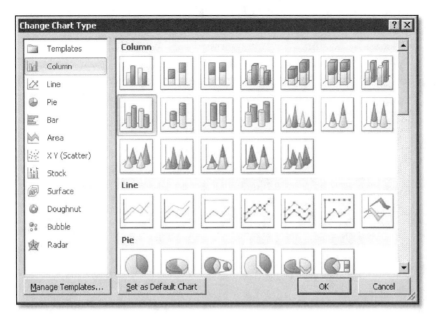

Figure 16 - 65: Change Chart Type dialog

Microsoft Excel provides several categories of charts for visualizing the data in a report, with each category containing several types:

- **Column:** 19 types

- **Line:** 7 types

- **Pie:** 6 types

- **Bar:** 15 types

- **Area:** 6 types

- **X Y (Scatter):** 5 types

- **Stock:** 4 types

- **Surface:** 4 types

- **Doughnut:** 2 types

- **Bubble:** 2 types

- **Radar:** 3 types

Select the chart type you want to use in the *Change Chart Type* dialog, and click the *OK* button to apply the change. Excel updates the PivotChart to reflect the selected type, as shown in Figure 16 - 66.

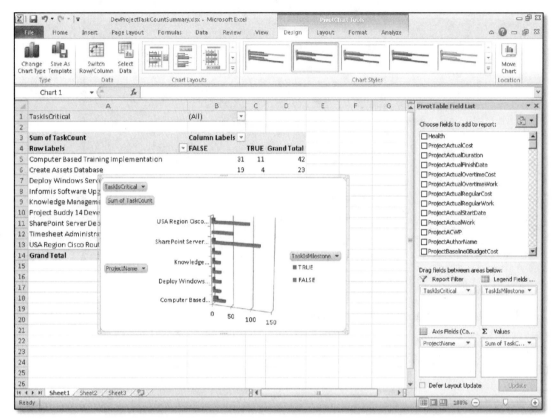

Figure 16 - 66: New chart type applied to PivotChart

Changing or Assigning a PivotChart Name in a Report

Excel Services is capable of publishing an entire Microsoft Excel workbook for online viewing, or only the portions of the workbook that you choose to make visible via the web. By assigning a name to an Excel PivotChart, you enable Excel Services to publish that named object to the web while hiding the remainder of the data in the workbook.

To change or assign an Excel PivotChart name, select the PivotChart, and then select the *Layout* tab in the *PivotChart Tools* section of the ribbon. In the *Properties* section at the right side of the ribbon, enter a name into the *Chart Name* field, as shown in Figure 16 - 67.

Figure 16 - 67: Changing or assigning a PivotChart name

Hitting the *Enter* key on your computer keyboard or clicking in another area of the Excel workbook will force Excel to accept the name change.

 Assigning a name to an Excel PivotChart will allow embedding of the chart in a dashboard page, as described later in this module.

Creating a Custom Excel Report Using a Data Connection File

When none of the sample reports or report templates meets your organization's reporting requirements, you can create a custom Excel report by starting with a blank workbook and connecting to the appropriate data source with one of the supplied data connection files. To create a custom Excel report using one of the supplied data connection files, launch Microsoft Excel and create a new blank workbook, click the *Data* tab in the ribbon, then click the *Connections* button in the *Connections* section of the ribbon. Excel displays the *Workbook Connections* dialog, as shown in Figure 16 - 68.

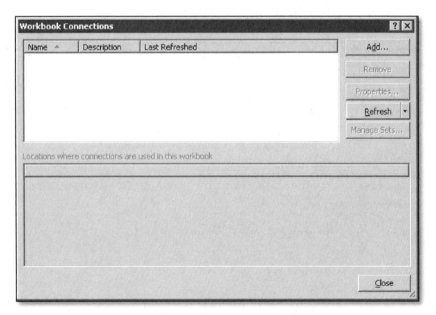

Figure 16 - 68: Workbook Connections dialog

In the *Workbook Connections* dialog, click the *Add* button. Excel displays the *Existing Connections* dialog shown in Figure 16 - 69.

Figure 16 - 69: Existing Connections dialog

In the *Existing Connections* dialog, click the *Browse for More* button located in the lower left corner of the dialog. Excel displays the *Select Data Source* dialog as shown in Figure 16 - 70.

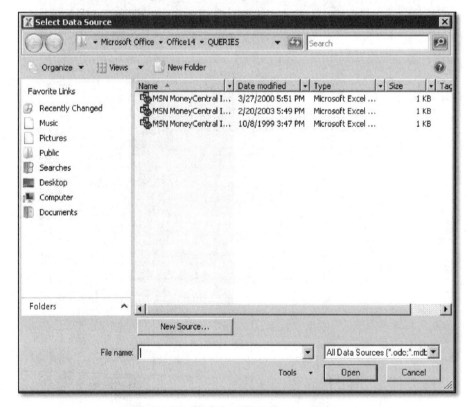

Figure 16 - 70: Select Data Source dialog

In the *Select Data Source* dialog, click your mouse cursor in the right end of the folder path area, located at the top of the dialog, to enable manual entry of a file location. Enter the *Business Intelligence Center* site URL as shown in Figure 16 - 71, and hit the *Enter* key on your computer keyboard:

http://<Server Name>/<PWA Name>/ProjectBICenter

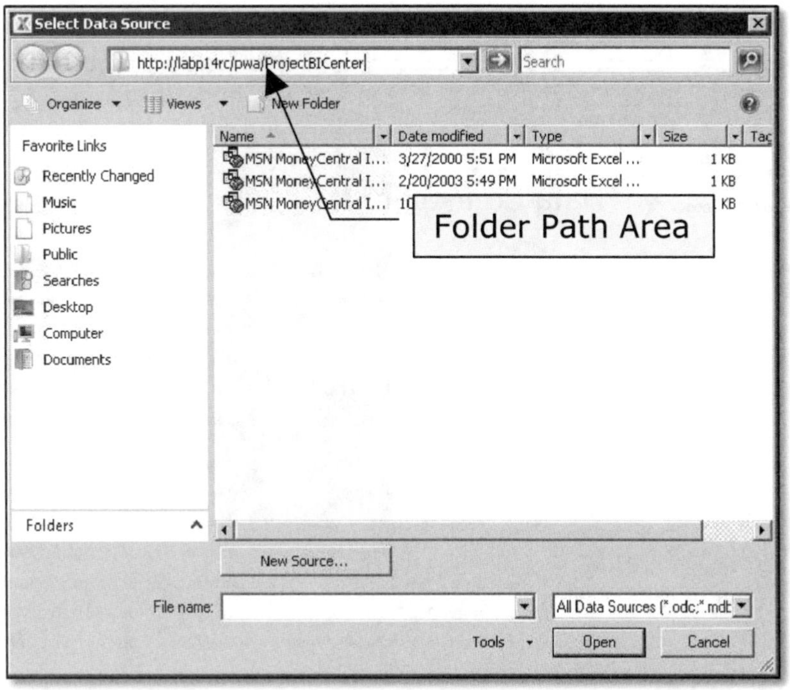

Figure 16 - 71: Entering the Business Intelligence Center URL

The dialog displays a listing of libraries in the *Business Intelligence Center* site, as shown in Figure 16 - 72.

Figure 16 - 72: Business Intelligence Center libraries

Double-click the *Data Connections* library in the list, and then double-click the *English (United States)* folder that appears in the library. The dialog displays a listing of data connection files in the *Data Connections* library, as shown in Figure 16 - 73.

Figure 16 - 73: Data connection files

Locate the appropriate data connection file for your report, select the name of the file in the listing, then click the *Open* button. The *Select Data Source* dialog closes, returning control to the *Workbook Connections* dialog, where your selected data connection file appears. Click the *Close* button to close the *Workbook Connections* dialog.

Now that the Excel workbook contains a connection to a data source, click the *Data* tab on the ribbon and click the *Existing Connections* button in the *Get External Data* section of the ribbon. Excel displays the *Existing Connections* dialog shown in Figure 16 - 74, displaying your selected data connection in the connection list.

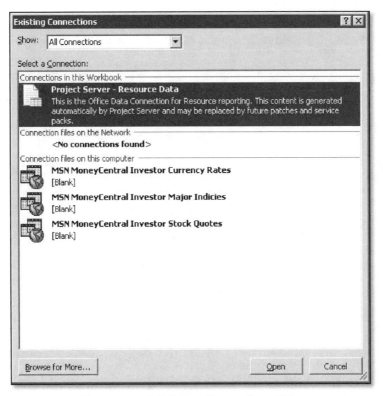

Figure 16 - 74: Existing Connections dialog

In the *Existing Connections* dialog, select the connection and click the *Open* button. Excel displays the *Import Data* dialog as shown in Figure 16 - 75.

Figure 16 - 75: Import Data dialog

The *Import Data* dialog offers three options for adding the external data to the Excel workbook:

- Table

- PivotTable Report

- PivotChart and PivotTable Report

Select the appropriate option to display the imported data in the workbook, and then click the *OK* button. If you select the *Table* option, the Excel adds the data in tabular format, as shown in Figure 16 - 76.

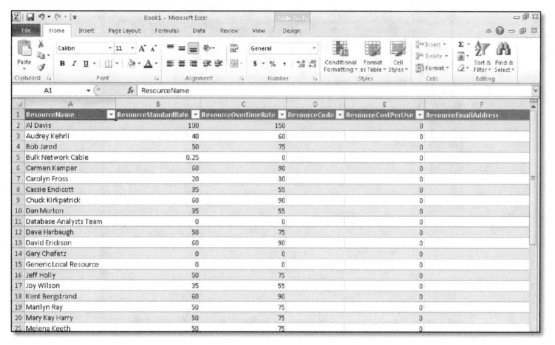

Figure 16 - 76: Adding data to the workbook in tabular format

If you select the *PivotTable Report* option, Excel adds an empty PivotTable area and displays the *PivotTable Field List* side panel as shown in Figure 16 - 77, allowing you to build a custom PivotTable report.

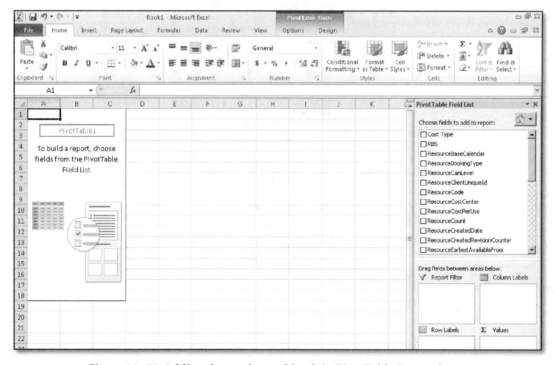

Figure 16 - 77: Adding data to the workbook in PivotTable Report format

If you select the *PivotChart and PivotTable Report* option, Excel adds an empty PivotTable area and an empty PivotChart area, and displays the *PivotTable Field List* side panel as shown in Figure 16 - 78, allowing you to build a custom PivotTable and PivotChart report.

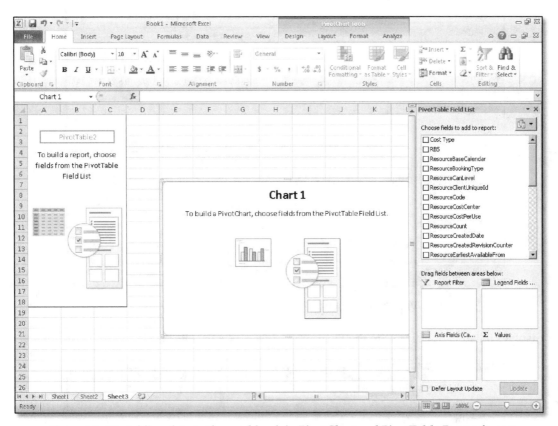

Figure 16 - 78: Adding data to the workbook in PivotChart and PivotTable Report format

After you build your custom report, click the *File* tab on the ribbon to enter the Backstage, then select the *Save As* option in the Backstage menu. Excel displays the *Save As* dialog.

If the *Business Intelligence Center* destination library you want to use does not appear in the *Save As* dialog, click into the right end of the folder path area, located at the top of the dialog, to enable manual entry of a file location. Enter the *Business Intelligence Center* site URL as shown in Figure 16 - 79 and hit the *Enter* key on your computer keyboard:

http://<Server Name>/<PWA Name>/ProjectBICenter

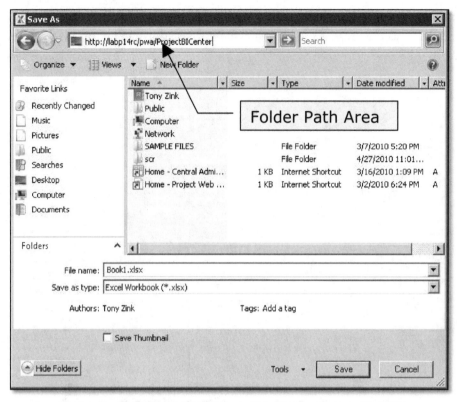

Figure 16 - 79: Entering the Business Intelligence Center site URL

The dialog displays a listing of libraries in the *Business Intelligence Center* site, as shown in Figure 16 - 80.

Figure 16 - 80: Business Intelligence Center libraries

Double-click the destination library and then optionally double-click a language folder in the library, such as the *English (United States)* folder. Enter a name for the new report in the *File name* field and click the *Save* button. The new Excel report becomes available for online viewing in the selected report library.

> Be sure to save the new report in the proper format by selecting the *Excel Workbook (*.xlsx)* option from the *Save as type* pick list.

Working with SharePoint Dashboards

SharePoint dashboards allow you to aggregate and visualize multiple types of data in a central location for reporting and analysis. More specifically, you can easily build a dashboard by creating a SharePoint web part page and adding various web parts to display the types of data that your organization needs for analysis and decision-making. The Project Server *Business Intelligence Center* includes a *Dashboards* library where you can create and store these dashboard pages.

Creating a Dashboard Page

To create a new SharePoint dashboard page, from the *Business Intelligence Center* site click the *Dashboards* link in the Quick Launch menu. The system displays the *Dashboards* library shown in Figure 16 - 81.

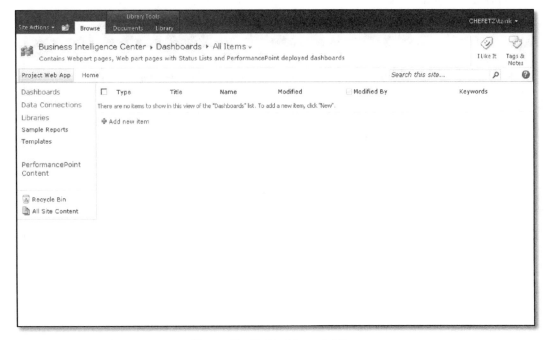

Figure 16 - 81: Dashboards library

Click the *Documents* tab in the SharePoint ribbon, open the *New Document* pick list in the *New* section of the ribbon, and select the *Web Part Page* option from the pick list. The system displays the *New Web Part Page* page shown in Figure 16 - 82.

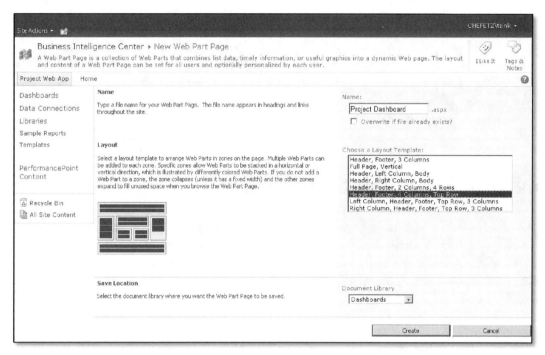

Figure 16 - 82: New Web Part Page page

In the *Name* section of the page, enter a name for the new dashboard page. In the *Layout* section of the page, select a web part page layout template that allows you to position the web parts on the page based on your requirements, and then click the *Create* button. The system creates a new dashboard page and displays the page in editing mode, as shown in Figure 16 - 83.

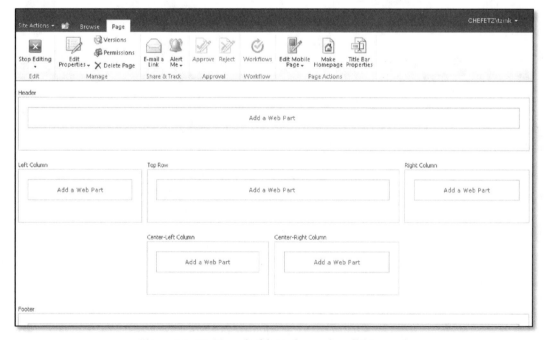

Figure 16 - 83: New dashboard page in editing mode

The new dashboard page is now capable of accepting web parts to display various types of data.

Embedding Excel Data into a Dashboard Page

Although the system can display individual Excel reports as shown previously in this module, in a dashboard you typically want to display related sets of data from multiple published Excel workbooks to provide a broader view of the data in the system, usually at a high level. The Excel Services component of SharePoint allows online viewing of an Excel workbook, as well as embedding selected sections of a workbook in a dashboard page. To that end, SharePoint includes an Excel Web Access web part that you can add to any dashboard page to display a named object from a published Excel workbook file.

Warning: In order to include components of an Excel workbook file in a dashboard page, it is important that you publish the Excel workbook file into a library that Excel Services recognizes as a trusted file location. To set a library as a trusted file location, follow the direction I provide in Module 5.

Warning: It is imporant that you name the tables and charts in your Excel workbooks, otherwise the Excel Web Access web part cannot identify and display the contents of the workbooks.

To add a named object from an Excel report to a dashboard, such as a PivotTable or PivotChart, browse to an existing SharePoint dashboard page, select the *Page* tab from the SharePoint ribbon, and then click the *Edit Page* button in the *Edit* section of the ribbon to switch the page into editing mode. With the page in editing mode, select a web part zone and click the *Add a Web Part* link located at the top of the zone. The system displays a panel at the top of the page for selecting a web part, as shown in Figure 16 - 84.

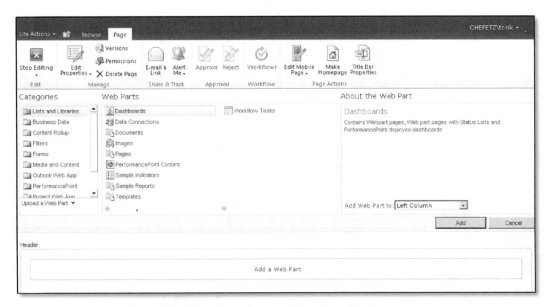

Figure 16 - 84: Web part page with web part selection panel

In the *Categories* section of the web part panel, select the *Business Data* category. The *Web Parts* list displays a list of Business Data web parts. Select the *Excel Web Access* web part from the *Web Parts* list and click the *Add* button. The system adds the Excel Web Access web part to the selected web part zone, as shown in Figure 16 - 85.

Figure 16 - 85: Web part page with Excel Web Access web part added

In the Excel Web Access web part, click the *Click here to open the tool pane* link. The system displays the *Excel Web Access* web part tool pane on the right side of the page, shown in Figure 16 - 86.

Figure 16 - 86: Web part page with Excel Web Access web part tool pane

In the *Workbook Display* section of the tool pane, click the selector button located to the right of the *Workbook* field. The system displays the *Select an Asset* dialog, shown in Figure 16 - 87.

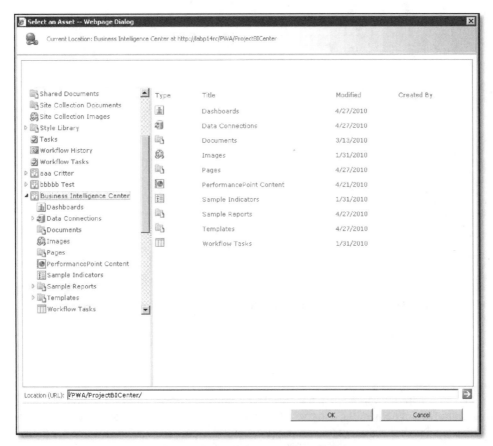

Figure 16 - 87: Select an Asset dialog

In the right pane of the *Select an Asset* dialog, double-click the name of the library containing your target Excel workbook file. If the library contains folders for organizing the workbook files, such as the English language library, then click to navigate through the folder structure until you locate the workbook. Click the name of the workbook file and click the *OK* button. The system closes the *Select an Asset* dialog.

In the *Workbook Display* section of the web part tool pane, type the name of the table or chart into the *Named Item* field, then scroll to the bottom of the tool pane and click the *OK* button. The system fetches the table or chart from the originating Excel workbook file and displays it in the Excel Web Access web part, as shown in Figure 16 - 88.

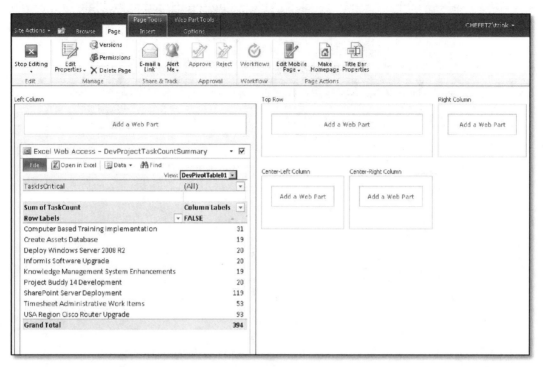

Figure 16 - 88: Dashboard page with PivotTable displayed in Excel Web Access web part

Warning: Although the *Named Item* field displays a selector button, this button does not allow you to browse through the named items in the selected Excel workbook. You must manually type the name of the item into the field. If you do not know which named items are available in the workbook, then you must open the workbook file with Microsoft Excel to retrieve them.

Warning: If you did not name the desired table or chart in the Excel workbook file, then you must open the Excel file and name the item as I described previously in this module.

To add multiple objects from one or more published Excel workbooks to the dashboard page, repeat the steps described in this section. When you complete your additions, select the *Page* tab in the ribbon and click the *Stop Editing* button in the *Edit* section of the ribbon. Figure 16 - 89 shows an example of a dashboard page with a table and a chart originating from published Excel workbook files in the *Business Intelligence Center*.

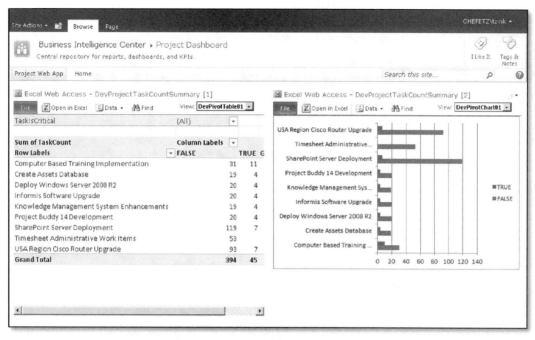

Figure 16 - 89: Dashboard page with a table and a chart

Adding Non-Project Server Users as Report Viewers

You can manage the security model in the *Business Intelligence Center* site separately from the Project Server security model, providing the ability to grant non-Project Server users such as executives, clients, or partners read-only access to the information stored in the site. Assuming that you created a report viewers group in Active Directory that you learned about in Module 05, it is an easy task to grant those group members access to the *Business Intelligence Center* site.

To grant the members of your Report Viewers group access to the *Business Intelligence Center* site, select the *Site Permissions* option from the *Site Actions* menu. The system displays the *Permissions* page as shown in Figure 16 - 90.

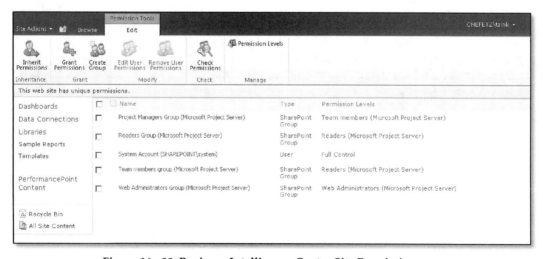

Figure 16 - 90: Business Intelligence Center Site Permissions page

On the *Permissions* page, click the *Readers Group (Microsoft Project Server)* group. The system displays the *Readers Group (Microsoft Project Server)* page, as shown in Figure 16 - 91.

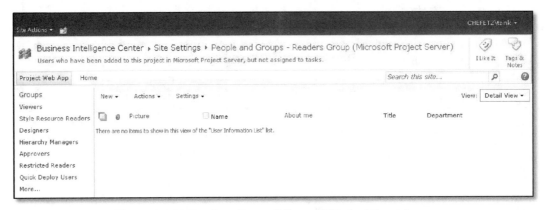

Figure 16 - 91: Readers Group (Microsoft Project Server) page

On the *Readers Group (Microsoft Project Server)* page, click the *New* button. The system displays the *Grant Permissions* dialog as shown in Figure 16 - 92.

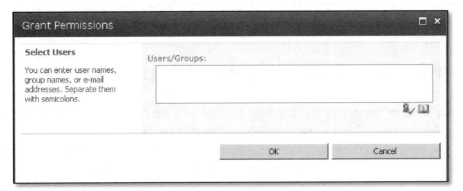

Figure 16 - 92: Grant Permissions dialog

In the *Grant Permissions* dialog, enter the name of the Active Directory group that you created for report viewers, in the format DOMAIN\GROUP NAME. If you are unsure of the exact spelling of the group name, click the *Check Names* button to verify the group name spelling, or click the *Browse* button to search for the group name in Active Directory. After entering the correct group name, click the *OK* button. The system displays the *Readers Group (Microsoft Project Server)* page with the new group name added, as shown in Figure 16 - 93.

Figure 16 - 93: Readers Group page with new Active Directory group added

Module 17

Managing Project Server Day to Day

Learning Objectives

After completing this module, you will be able to:

- Check in enterprise objects such as projects and resources
- Clean up the Project Server database
- Backup and restore a single project
- Configure and manage the Queue
- Monitor Project Server licenses
- Monitor server health
- Set up and schedule a SQL Server Database Maintenance Plan
- Run a SQL Server Database Maintenance Plan

Inside Module 17

Supporting Project Server 831

Performing Database Management through PWA 831

Checking in Enterprise Objects 831

Deleting Enterprise Objects 833

    Deleting Enterprise Projects 834

    Deleting Resources and Users 837

    Deleting Status Report Responses 841

    Deleting Timesheets 842

    Deleting User Delegates 843

Working with Administrative Backups 844

    Setting an Automatic Daily Backup Schedule 845

    Backing Up Enterprise Objects Manually 846

    Restoring Backed-up Objects 847

Changing or Restarting Workflows..**849**

Configuring and Managing the Queue **852**

   Understanding the Queue Process...853

   Understanding Job States 854

   Working with the Manage Queue Jobs Page 856

   Troubleshooting the Queue..860

   Configuring the Queue 861

Monitoring Project Server Licenses...**864**

Monitoring and Troubleshooting Project Server..**865**

   Working with Unified Logging Service (ULS) files 866

   Using the Reliability and Performance Monitor...871

Configuring a SQL Server 2008 Maintenance Plan **872**

Supporting Project Server

Now that you know how to configure your server, load it with projects and resources, and can create useful views and reports for your user community, it is time to explore the nitty-gritty world of everyday Project Server management. By far, Project Server 2010 provides more management tools than most of its predecessors did, but it also gives you a whole lot more to manage. Moreover, you have the added complexity of managing Windows SharePoint Foundation and Windows SharePoint Server Enterprise.

I begin with a wrap-up of the more mundane tasks, including simple backups and forcing enterprise object check-ins, and then move on to a rowdy exploration of Queue Management and the wonderful world of ULS logs. Let the support mode begin!

Performing Database Management through PWA

Project Server provides a friendly user interface for basic database management tasks that is very approachable for the non-technical user. Keep in mind that these tasks do not replace the need for database and database server management. Rather, they provide non-technical users access to managing some of the most common tasks. Your database administration role can include any of the following tasks:

- You check in enterprise objects, such as enterprise projects "stuck" in checked out mode.

- You delete enterprise objects, such as completed enterprise projects.

- You back up enterprise objects, either manually or automatically, such as backing up the latest version of each enterprise project.

- You restore enterprise objects, such as restoring an enterprise project to a previous version.

I discuss each of these topics individually.

Checking in Enterprise Objects

When a project manager opens an enterprise project in Project Professional 2010 or Project Web App, the system marks the project as "checked out" in the Project Server database. When the project manager checks in the project, the system marks the project as "checked-in." If a technical problem, such as a system crash, forces Project Professional 2010 to shut down without closing the project, the project can remain in a checked-out state in the database. This prevents the project manager from opening the project in read/write mode to work on it. Although project managers in your environment may have permission to force check-in their own projects, there may be times when a user with Administrator permissions must intervene.

Project Server 2010 manages a number of enterprise objects through the check-out and check-in process. These objects include:

- Enterprise Projects

- Enterprise Resources

- Enterprise Custom Fields

- Enterprise Lookup Tables for Enterprise Custom Fields

- Enterprise Calendars

- Resource Plans

To force check-in any of the above enterprise objects, click the *Force Check-in Enterprise Objects* link in *the Database Administration* section on the *Server Settings* page. The system displays the *Force Check-in Enterprise Objects* page shown in Figure 17 - 1.

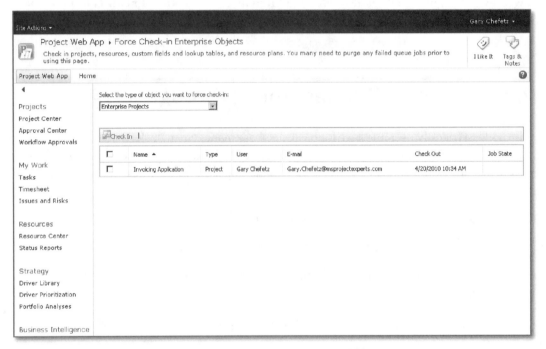

Figure 17 - 1: Force Check-in Enterprise Objects page

Notice in Figure 17 - 1 that one project appears in the grid in a checked out state. Notice also the *Select the type of object you want to force check-in* pick list in the upper left corner of the page. Click this pick list to select the object type you want to check in. By default, the system initially selects the *Enterprise Projects* item on the *Select the type of object you want to force check-in* pick list.

To check in a single object or multiple objects, select the checkbox for each object you want to check in and then click the *Check In* button. The system warns you with the dialog shown in Figure 17 - 2.

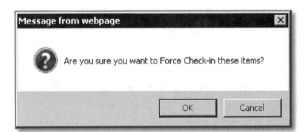

Figure 17 - 2: Check In Warning dialog

If you force check-in an enterprise project that someone is currently working with, you prevent that person from saving any changes to the project. Therefore, make sure that you verify your action with the person who has the item checked out before taking this action. Click the *OK* button to check in the object. Note that the project may or may not disappear from the system immediately. When you force check-in an enterprise object, you send a job to the queue, and that job does the work once the system processes it. Notice that the *Job State* field changes to "Waiting To Be Processed" after you submit the job.

Forcing check-in for the other types of enterprise objects functions the same as it does for forcing a check-in on an enterprise project. The only difference is that the fields displayed in the grid contextually change for the type of object you select.

> Project Server 2010 allows project managers to force check-in their own projects using the *Check In My Projects* button from the *Navigate* section of the *Projects* ribbon menu in the *Project Center* page. Teaching your users to check in their own projects can save you time and save them frustration!

Deleting Enterprise Objects

During your tenure as a Project Server administrator, expect to have a relatively frequent need to delete enterprise objects. Besides cleaning up accidental resource additions and saved projects, you may need to delete projects in order to restore other versions to recover from errors or file corruption.

Like the force check-in interface, the *Delete Enterprise Objects* page provides one-stop shopping for deleting all types of enterprise objects, including each of the following:

- Projects

- Resources and Users

- Status Report Responses

- Timesheets

- User Delegates

To delete any of the above enterprise objects, click the *Delete Enterprise Objects* link in the *Database Administration* section on the *Server Settings* page. The system displays the *Delete Enterprise Objects* page shown in Figure 17 - 3.

Figure 17 - 3: Delete Enterprise Objects page

Notice in Figure 17 - 3 that Project Server 2010 sets the *What do you want to delete from Project Server?* option to the *Projects* value by default. Notice also that the page contains a sub-section for the *Delete the selected project(s)* option that allows you to control to which databases to apply the deletion. When you select enterprise objects other than projects, the system removes the sub-option section.

Deleting Enterprise Projects

Before you delete an enterprise project, you must first decide which deletion option to use in the *Delete the selected project(s)* section of the page. Your options consist of the following:

- *Delete projects from Draft and Published databases* – Select this option to remove the project from both the *Draft* and *Published* databases. Selecting this option does not remove the project from the *Archive* database if an archived copy exists. Removing a project from the *Published* database removes it from the *Reporting* database as well.

- *Delete projects only from Published database* – Select this option to remove a project from the *Published* and *Reporting* databases, without removing the latest version from the *Draft* database. Use this option to "unpublish" a project in its entirety, and to allow the project manager to publish it again at a later date. This option is very helpful when a project manager accidentally publishes a project, or your organization cancels a project prior to reaching planning or execution.

- *Delete projects only from Archived database* – Select this option to remove archived projects from the *Archive* database. Use this option to remove old files from the archive store.

In the *Delete the selected project(s)* section of the page, notice the *Delete the associated Microsoft SharePoint Foundation sites?* option immediately below the three deletion options. Select this option to delete any associated Project Site along with the project deletion. If you do not select this option, the associated Project Sites for the deleted projects remain active in the system. When you click each of the three deletion options, the screen refreshes as the system retrieves the list of projects in the database(s) you selected.

Warning: If you select the *Delete projects only from Published database* option to un-publish a project, you should also select the *Delete the associated Microsoft SharePoint Foundation sites* option to delete the Project Site as well. If you select only the first of these two options when un-publishing a project, the system may prevent the project manager from publishing the project, and will display an error message indicating the Project Site already exists if you use automatic site provisioning.

Once you determine the database(s) from which you want to delete an enterprise project, select a single one or more projects in the grid. After making your selections, click the *Delete* button to complete your deletion. The system displays the confirmation dialog shown in Figure 17 - 4.

Figure 17 - 4: Deletion confirmation dialog

Click the *OK* button to confirm the deletion. The system refreshes the *Delete Enterprise Objects* page as shown in Figure 17 - 5. Notice that the system displays a *Processing* value in the *Job State* field for each deleted project, and displays the following message at the top of the page:

> **The selected Projects have been scheduled for deletion. This deletion happens through a queue, and you may continue to see the Projects on this page while the deletions are being processed.**

Notice also in Figure 17 - 5 that the system checks out the project before placing the job in the Queue, indicated by a *Yes* value in the *Checked Out* field. The page does not automatically redisplay when the job state changes; you must refresh the page using the browser *Refresh* button. When the job completes, it no longer displays on the page.

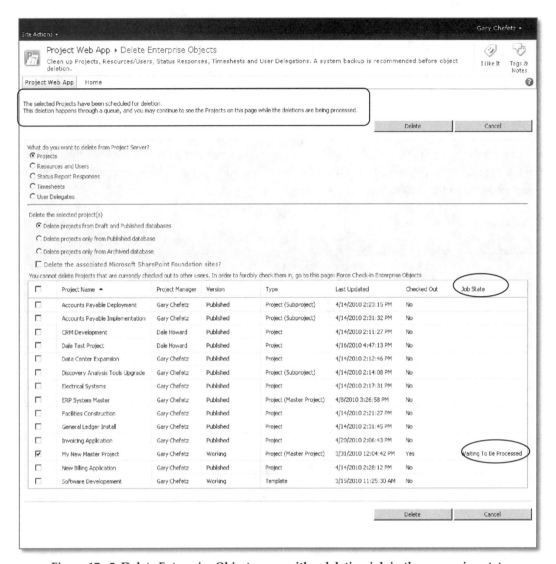

Figure 17 - 5: Delete Enterprise Objects page with a deletion job in the processing state

Warning: There is no undo process to reverse the deletion of an enterprise project. If you manually or automatically backed up enterprise projects, you can restore an individual project from the Archive database. Otherwise, you must retrieve the project from the last SQL Server database backup. I discuss how to back up enterprise projects in the next section of this Module.

If you attempt to delete an enterprise project that is checked out to another user, the system prevents the deletion and warns you with a message at the top of the page, as shown in Figure 17 - 6.

Figure 17 - 6: Deletion warning about deleting a checked-out project

If the user is actually working on the checked-out project, you cannot delete the project until the user closes the project and checks in the project. If, on the other hand, the project is "stuck" in a checked-out condition, you can quickly navigate from the *Delete Enterprise Objects* page by clicking the *Force Check-In Enterprise Objects* link on the right side of the *Delete the Selected Project(s)* section. The system displays the *Force Check-In Enterprise Objects* page, where you can force check-in the project that is "stuck" in a checked-out state. When finished, return to the *Delete Enterprise Objects* page to delete the project in question.

Warning: Although Project Server 2010 does not allow you to delete a project checked out to another user, the system **does** allow you to delete a project currently **checked out to you**. In fact, if you attempt to delete a project while it is checked out to you, the system performs the deletion **without warning you**.

Deleting Resources and Users

It is only appropriate to delete a resource or user when the person is no longer available for project work, such as when an employee leaves the company, and when the resource has no uncompleted task assignments in active projects. Further, the resource's historical data in the system should be beyond its retention date as determined by your organization's data retention policies. To delete a resource or user permanently, select the *Resources and Users* option at the top of the page. The system displays the *Delete Enterprise Objects* page as shown in Figure 17 - 7.

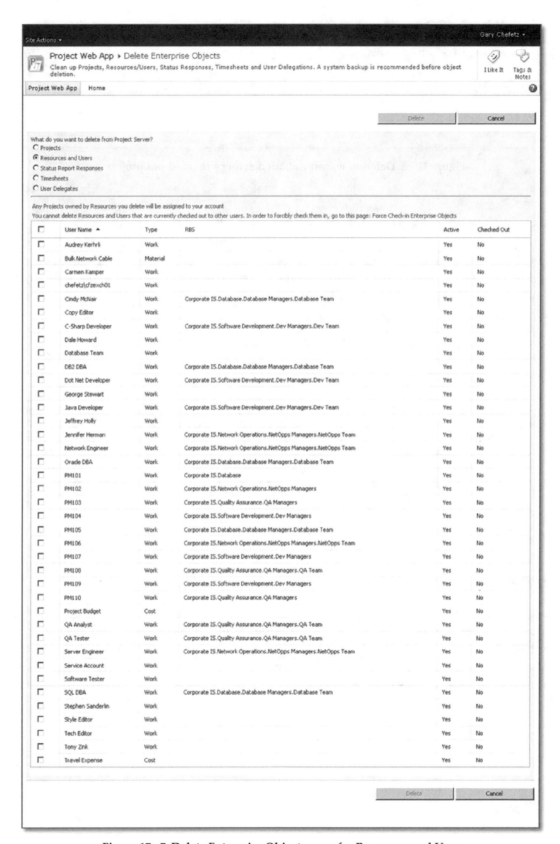

Figure 17 - 7: Delete Enterprise Objects page for Resources and Users

In the data grid, select the option checkbox for each resource you want to delete. Click the *Delete* button and the system displays the confirmation dialog shown previously in Figure 17 - 4. Click the *OK* button in the confirmation dialog to complete the deletion of the resource. The system deletes the resources immediately and then refreshes the page with a confirmation message at the top of the page, as shown in Figure 17 - 8.

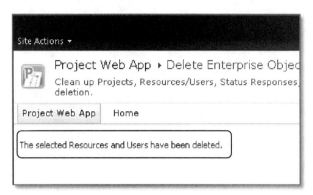

**Figure 17 - 8: Delete Enterprise Objects page
confirmation for resource deletion**

As with enterprise projects, Project Server 2010 does not allow you to delete resources that are checked out to other users, but it does allow you to delete resources that are checked out to you. If you attempt to delete a resource that is checked out by another user, the system prevents the deletion and warns you with a message at the top of the page, as shown in Figure 17 - 9. Therefore, you must check in the resource before you can delete it.

Figure 17 - 9: Warning about Deleting a Checked Out Resource

Deleting a resource in this manner does not completely remove the resource from the Project Server database. Instead, the deletion has the following consequences:

- The system removes deleted resources from their current and future assignments and replaces them with local resources. The local resource carries the same name as the deleted resource.

- The system completely removes deleted resources from the Enterprise Resource Pool.

- The system completely removes the user accounts for deleted resources in Project Web App.

- If you delete a resource that is the owner of any projects, the system will designate you as the owner of the projects.

When you delete a resource that is active in any enterprise project, the next time the project manager opens a project containing the resource, the system displays the warning shown in Figure 17 - 10.

Figure 17 - 10: Warning dialog about resources deleted from Enterprise Resource Pool

Figure 17 - 11 shows the *Resource Sheet* view in the project containing a deleted resource, Audrey Kerhrli. Notice that the system converted this deleted enterprise resource to a same-named local resource.

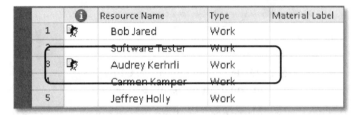

Figure 17 - 11: Resource Sheet view
shows deleted resources as Local resources

Before deleting enterprise resources, you should assess whether they have any remaining work in the system. You can easily accomplish this using the *Resource Assignments* page reached from the *Resource Center*. You should determine the effect on active projects, which is also something for which you can use the *Resource Assignments* page. Before deleting resources, take the necessary action to resolve open assignments.

MSProjectExperts recommends that you contact all project managers with enterprise projects containing resources that are candidates for deletion, and alert them to the change. Make sure that they reassign all uncompleted work on active assignments to alternate resources.

Warning: There is no undo process to reverse the deletion of a resource. If you manually or automatically backed up the Enterprise Resource Pool, you can restore the entire enterprise resource pool from the *Archive* database. I discuss how to back up the Enterprise Resource Pool in the next section of this Module.

When Project Server 2010 converts the resource to a local resource in the enterprise project, it maintains the resource's name, along with other standard and custom resource information, such as the Windows user account, e-mail address, group, standard rate, etc. If you add the resource back to the Enterprise Resource Pool, the system does not automatically replace each local resource with the same-named enterprise resource in each enterprise project. In other words, you cannot simply press a button and convert them back to enterprise resources in every plan. Instead, your

Deleting Status Report Responses

To delete *Status Report Responses*, select the *Status Report Responses* option on the *Delete Enterprise Objects* page. The system displays the *Delete Enterprise Objects* page with the *Delete all status report responses, for all users, with a period end date earlier than* option, as shown in Figure 17 - 12.

Notice that this feature is for deleting old data, and does not provide much in the way of selectable options. It simply provides a time horizon that you can set in days, weeks, months, or years. For example, using this feature, you might delete all *Status Report* responses earlier than 1 year back from today.

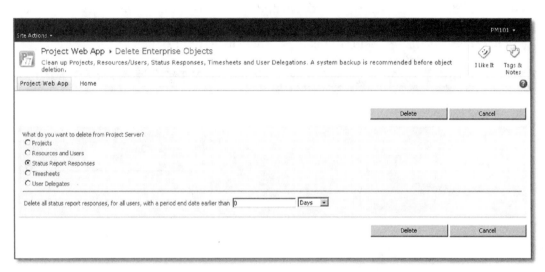

Figure 17 - 12: Delete Enterprise Objects page for Status Report Responses

Select your time horizon parameters and click the *Delete* button to delete all *Status Report Responses* that occur before your horizon date. The system displays the confirmation dialog shown previously in Figure 17 - 4. Click the *OK* button in the confirmation dialog to complete the deletion of the *Status Report Responses*.

The system redisplays the *Delete Enterprise Objects* page with a "The selected Status Report Responses have been deleted" message at the top of the page, as shown in Figure 17 - 13. Keep in mind that the system gives you little real feedback or control over the deletion process. The message simply indicates that no system errors occurred because of the deletion request. It does not even indicate whether any status reports were subject to deletion. In my case, there were none in the system to delete.

Figure 17 - 13: Status Report Responses deletion confirmation

To delete a *Status Report* request, the manager who created the *Status Report* must delete it through the *Request a Status Report* page. The Project Server administrator **cannot** delete a *Status Report* request through the Project Server *Delete Enterprise Objects page*.

Deleting Timesheets

To delete *Timesheets* created by users, select the *Timesheets* option on the *Delete Enterprise Objects* page. The system displays the *Delete Enterprise Objects* page with the *Delete all Timesheets for all users where the time reporting period end date is* section and with the *From* and *Through* fields enabled, as shown in Figure 17 - 14.

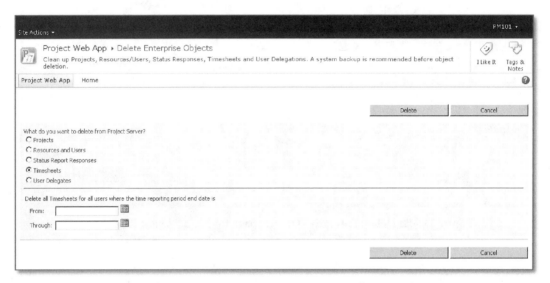

Figure 17 - 14: Delete Enterprise Objects page for Timesheets

Select a date range for the ending date of each *Timesheet* in the *From* and *Through* fields and then click the *Delete* button. The system displays the confirmation dialog shown previously in Figure 17 - 4. Click the *OK* button in the confirmation dialog to complete the deletion of the Timesheets. The system redisplays the *Delete Enterprise Objects* page with a "The selected Timesheets have been scheduled for deletion" message at the top of the page, as shown in Figure 17 - 15.

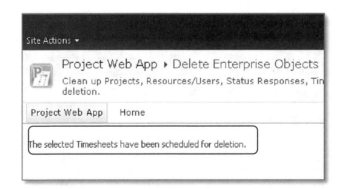

Figure 17 - 15: Timesheet deletion confirmation

When you delete *Timesheets*, the system resets the *Status* field value to *Not Yet Created* for each user's *Timesheet* during the selected time period on the *Timesheets* page. On the *Timesheet* page, if a user clicks the *Click to Create* link to create a

Timesheet for a period that the Project Server administrator previously deleted, the user **does not** see a completely blank *Timesheet*. Instead, the user sees all Administrative time categories reset to blank, but the *Timesheet* retains any actual work entered for project tasks during the selected period.

Deleting User Delegates

To delete *User Delegates*, select the *User Delegates* option on the *Delete Enterprise Objects* page. The system displays the *Delete Enterprise Objects* page with the *Delete all Delegates, for all users, with an end date earlier than* option, as shown in Figure 17 - 16.

As with *Status Report Responses*, notice that this feature is for deleting old data, and does not provide much in the way of selectable options. It simply provides a time horizon that you can set in days, weeks, months, or years. For example, using this feature, you might delete all *User Delegates* earlier than 1 year from today.

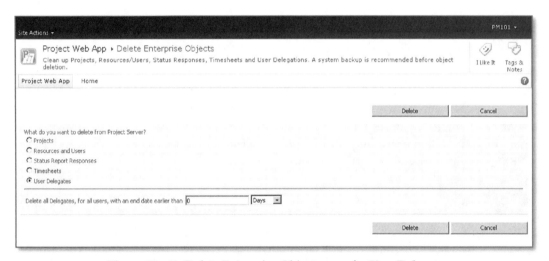

Figure 17 - 16: Delete Enterprise Objects page for User Delegates

The system allows you to select from *Days, Weeks, Months,* or *Years* from the pick list. Select your time horizon parameters and click the *Delete* button to delete all *User Delegates* that occur before your horizon date. The system displays the confirmation dialog shown in Figure 17 - 17. Click the *OK* button in the confirmation dialog to complete the deletion of the *User Delegates*.

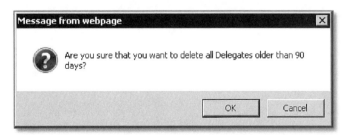

Figure 17 - 17: Confirmation dialog to delete User Delegates

The system redisplays the *Delete Enterprise Objects* page with a "The selected User Delegates have been deleted" message at the top of the page, as shown in Figure 17 - 18. Keep in mind that the system gives you little real feedback or control over the deletion process. The message simply indicates that no system errors occurred because of the deletion request.

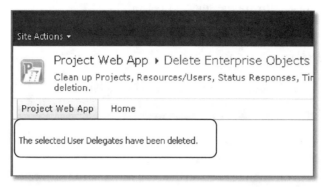

Figure 17 - 18: User Delegates deletion confirmation

Working with Administrative Backups

Project Server 2010 allows you to use the *Archive* database as a user-friendly backup and restore source. This functionality provides a first-line backup tool that non-technical application administrators can use to preserve and recover data for enterprise objects without the assistance of a Database Administrator. As with any enterprise database system, a SQL Server DBA, and/or other responsible parties who manage system and data backup, must schedule the backup program for your system based on your organizational standards for data retention and preservation and your specific EPM requirements.

Warning: The *Administrative Backup, Daily Schedule Backup*, and *Administrative Restore* tools do not substitute for system-level and data-level backup and solid disaster recovery plans.

Project Server 2010 allows you to set up automated daily backups or to manually back up objects, and then restore them at any time. Using this feature supports item-level restore. You can back up and restore the following enterprise objects:

- Projects

- Enterprise Resource Pool and Calendars

- Enterprise Custom Fields

- Enterprise Global

- View Definitions

- System Settings

- Category and Group Settings

Project Server 2010 backs up all objects to the *Archive* database, regardless of whether you schedule automatic daily backups or manually back up the objects.

Setting an Automatic Daily Backup Schedule

To schedule the automatic daily backup of individual objects, click the *Daily Schedule Backup* link in the *Database Administration* section of the *Server Settings* page. The system displays the *Daily Backup Schedule* page shown in Figure 17 - 19.

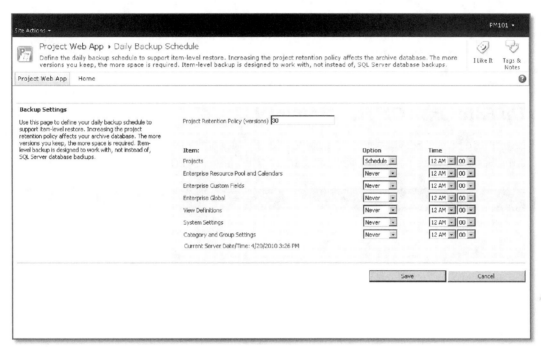

Figure 17 - 19: Daily Backup Schedule page

On the *Daily Backup Schedule* page, set the *Project Retention Policy (versions)* field value to the number of versions you wish to keep for projects that you back up. This setting applies to Projects only and not to other types of enterprise objects. For each of the other types of objects, the system maintains only the most recent version of the backup. The *Project Retention Policy (versions)* field applies to all *Administrative Backups* whether they occur because of a scheduled event or a manual event. The retention count includes both types of backups cumulatively.

Determining the optimum project backup retention setting requires some thought. Work with your user community to determine how many days of history for which they need easy restore access. In other words, if your users require that you restore projects from previous states for 30 days, then you need to set the retention number to 30. Remember that the more project versions you keep, the larger the Archive database becomes. For each object that you want to back up, click the *Option* pick list and select the *Schedule* item from the pick list. For each selected object, specify a *Time* value for the backup and then click the *Save* button after you complete your entries.

When you archive projects automatically, the system archives only projects that have changed since the last backup. Consider the following example:

- On Monday, your Project Server 2010 instance contains 100 projects.

- On Monday, you schedule automatic backups of projects for the first time, beginning tonight (Monday) at 10:00 PM.

- Monday night at 10:00 PM, the system backs up all 100 projects.

- On Tuesday, your project managers make changes to only 17 projects.

- Tuesday night at 10:00 PM, the system backs up only the 17 changed projects.

- On Wednesday, your project managers make changes to 4 of the 17 projects.

- Wednesday night at 10:00 PM, the system backs up only the 4 changed projects.

- The Archive database now contains three Versions of 4 projects, two Versions of 17 projects, and only one Version of the remaining 83 projects.

Backing Up Enterprise Objects Manually

To back up one or more Project Server object manually, click the *Administrative Backup* link in the *Database Administration* section of the *Server Settings* page. The system displays the *Administrative Backup* page shown in Figure 17 - 20.

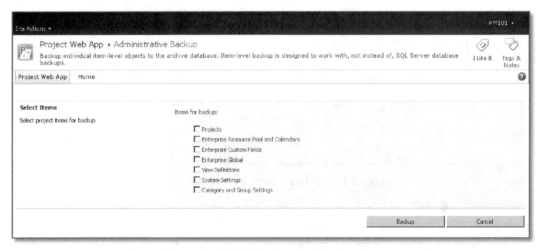

Figure 17 - 20: Administrative Backup page

In the *Items for backup* list, select the checkboxes for the objects you want to back up, and then click the *Backup* button. Project Server 2010 places the backup job in the Queue and displays the confirmation shown in Figure 17 - 21.

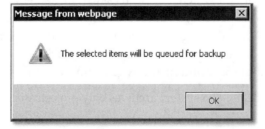

Figure 17 - 21: Backup Confirmation dialog

Although the backup appears to be instantaneous, like all Project Server 2010 operations the backup jobs enter the Queue for processing. To verify that a backup job was successful, you can check for failures on the *Manage Queue Jobs* page. When you select to back up any object type other than projects, the system backs up all objects of that type. This means that you cannot selectively back up specific items only.

When you manually back up projects for the first time, the system backs up all projects. When you back up projects again at a later date, the system backs up only those projects that have changed since the last backup. I documented this behavior in the previous section with using the automatic daily backup functionality of Project Server 2010.

Restoring Backed-up Objects

To use the *Administrative Restore* feature, click the *Administrative Restore* link in *the Database Administration* section of the *Server Settings* page. The system displays the *Administrative Restore* page shown in Figure 17 - 22. Notice in Figure 17 - 22 that the *Administrative Restore* page contains an *Item* pick list, a display grid, and two buttons below the display grid. Naturally, the *Item* pick list contains the same restore choices that you have to back up. By default, the item pick list shows the *Projects* option, so the page contains a list of project backups, and the version date.

Notice in the figure that this page contains numerous project backups occurring on different dates. This is the result of a nightly backup running for all projects since April 9, 2010, with a retention policy of 30 days in effect. You can easily see the effect that project changes have on the backup schedule. You can also see by the timestamps on the backup records that my nightly backup is set to begin at midnight, as each backup has a timestamp shortly after midnight.

When you restore a project, Project Server 2010 restores the project to only the *Draft* database. If the restored project is a published project, the system does not restore the project to the *Published* or *Reporting* databases. This means that the project manager must publish the project to communicate the latest project schedule information to the *Published* and *Reporting* databases.

Figure 17 - 22: Administrative Restore page

When you click the *Item* pick list and select an enterprise object other than projects, the resulting display page does not include a data grid because the administrative backup system retains only one version of each of the other objects. Figure 17 - 23 shows the *Administrative Restore* page with the *Enterprise Resource Pool and Calendars* value selected on the *Item* pick list.

Figure 17 - 23: Administrative Restore page with Enterprise Resource Pool and Calendars selected

If you want to restore an enterprise project, select the specific project and version you want to restore, and click the *Restore* button. To restore any other enterprise object, select the object type from the *Item* pick list and then click the *Restore* button. Project Server 2010 displays the confirmation dialog shown in Figure 17 - 24.

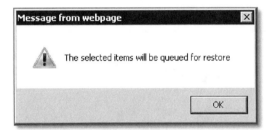

Figure 17 - 24: Item queued for restore dialog

Changing or Restarting Workflows

After people begin using Project Server 2010, at some point you may need to manage in-progress workflows by changing or restarting them. To manage in-progress workflows, click the *Change or Restart Workflows* link in the *Workflow and Project Detail Pages* section of the *Server Settings* page. The system displays the *Change or Restart Workflow and Skip to Workflow Stage* page shown in Figure 17 - 25 and Figure 17 - 26.

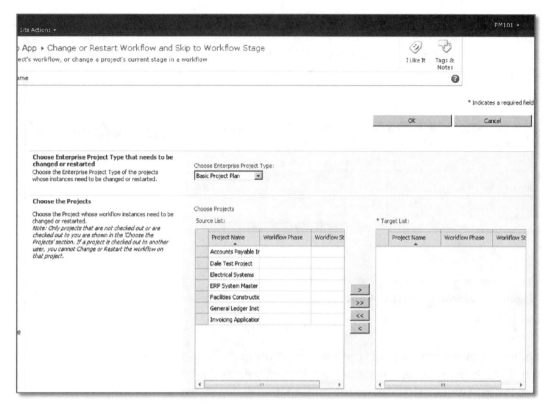

Figure 17 - 25: Change or Restart Workflow and Skip to Workflow Stage top of page

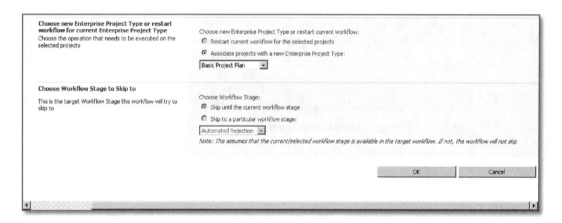

Figure 17 - 26: Change or Restart Workflow and Skip to Workflow Stage bottom of page

To begin the process of managing in-progress workflows, click the *Choose Enterprise Project Type* pick list and select a default or custom *Enterprise Project Type*. The system refreshes the *Choose the Projects* section to show all in-progress workflows for the selected *Enterprise Project Type*. For example, notice in Figure 17 - 27 that with *Sample Proposal* selected on the *Choose Enterprise Project Type pick* list, the system displays three in-progress project proposals, one currently in the *Create* stage and two in the *Select* stage.

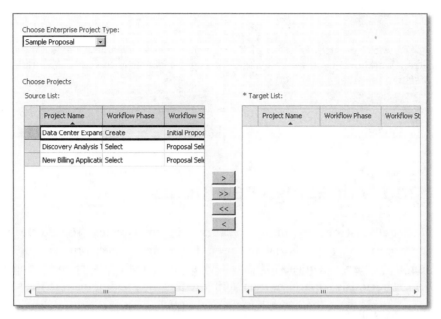

Figure 17 - 27: Change or Restart Workflow page, Sample Proposal selected

In the *Choose Projects* section, you must select either the project(s) you want to restart completely or the project(s) whose current *Stage* you need to change. Select at least one project in the *Source List* section and then click the **>** button (*Move* button). To select all of the projects in the *Choose Projects* section, click the (**>>**) button (*Move All* button). The system moves the selected project(s) to the *Target List* section.

After you move at least one project to the *Target List* section, Project Server 2010 offers you a number of options for every project in the *Target List* section. These options include:

- Restart the Workflow process from the beginning.

- Associate the project Proposal(s) with a different Enterprise Project Type.

- Skip until the current Stage.

- Skip to a different Stage.

The *Choose new Enterprise Project Type or restart workflow for current Enterprise Project Type* section of the page offers you the first two options. To restart the workflow process from the beginning, select the *Restart current workflow for the selected projects* option. To associate the project proposal with a different *Enterprise Project Type*, select the *Associate projects with a new Enterprise Project Type* option, click the associated pick list, and then select a different *Enterprise Project Type* from the pick list.

When you select the *Restart current workflow for the selected projects* option, you must then choose the appropriate option in the *Choose Workflow Stage to Skip to* section of the page, which allows you to simply restart the workflow and advance it to its current workflow stage, or to change the workflow stage for the projects to a specific stage that you select from the *Skip to a particular workflow stage* pick list. To simply restart the workflow and return it to the current stage, select the *Skip until the current stage* option. To skip to a different stage in the workflow, select the *Skip to a particular stage* option, click the associated pick list, and select a different stage from the list.

851

Warning: The *Skip to a particular stage* pick list includes every available stage, even those not available in the current workflow. If you select a stage that is not available in the current workflow, the workflow does not skip to the stage you select.

Click the *OK* button when finished.

Configuring and Managing the Queue

Every time you stand in line at a fast food restaurant, you are waiting in a "queue." The Queue in Project Server 2010 provides a pipeline for job processing requests that manages, and to some degree optimizes, job request traffic hitting the server. When the number of service requests to the system is greater than the system serving capacity, the Project Server 2010 Queue Service graciously supervises the waiting requests, ushering them to the server as it is ready to handle them.

Some common situations that drive the need for a queuing system within Project Server 2010 are as follows:

- Just before quitting time Friday afternoon, all team members submit time and task progress on their *Timesheet* page and *Tasks* page in Project Web App.

- Every Monday morning, all project managers receive, review, and update project progress for the projects they manage.

- Every Monday morning, resource managers receive, review, and approve timesheets for the resources they manage.

All of the previous examples involve system crunch-time use. Project Server 2010 uses the Microsoft Project Server Queue Service to handle these spikes in demand in an orderly manner. The Queue receives all the user input, records an entry for each request in the SQL Server database, and then processes the data on a first-come, first-served basis. The system handles nearly all critical operations using the Queue. Some of these operations include the following:

- Saving and publishing a project

- Saving and submitting a timesheet

- Backing up or restoring Project Server data

- Using the Report Data Service

- Using the Cube Building Service

- Server-side Scheduling

There are two Queues operating within the system. The **Timesheet Queue** handles the submission of timesheet information and status reports. The **Project Queue** handles all other types of processes, such as saving a project or building the OLAP cube. The reason Microsoft employed two Queue services in the architecture is that the Timesheet Queue operates in the published database, while the Project Queue operates in the draft database. This allows the system to distribute jobs to the Queue services in the database that affect performance efficiency the most.

You can manage the settings for each Queue separately, allowing you to fine-tune your platform to serve your usage patterns best. For instance, if you do not intend to implement timesheets and status reports, you can set the Timesheet

Queue to function less aggressively, thereby preserving resources for the Project Queue. To manage and control either Queue service, you can use any of the following four avenues:

- The **Queue Settings** page allows administrators to specify many Queue service parameters, such as polling frequency, retry intervals, and SQL timeout, to name a few.

- The **Manage Queue Jobs** page allows administrators to view and assess the completion or failure states of all Queue Jobs in the system.

- The **My Queued Jobs** page allows each user to see the status of their personal Queue Jobs in the system.

- The **Project Services Interface (PSI)** allows developers to place jobs in the Queue, detect job status, and access corrective actions available in the Queue.

Understanding the Queue Process

In a sense, the Project Queue Service functions like a distribution center, receiving and managing job requests much like a trucking distribution center receives and manages shipments. Figure 17 - 28 illustrates the Queue Process cycle..

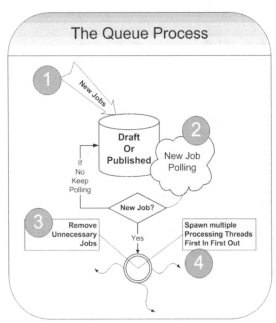

Figure 17 - 28: Queue Process

In the interest of simplification, I reduce this complicated process to four key states: job listening, job detection, job optimization, and job execution, each state corresponding with the numbers in the Figure 17 - 28. The Queue Process works as follows:

1. Upon starting, the Queue Service sets up a listening thread that periodically looks for new job requests within the database.

2. When it detects a new job, it places the job into processing based on the concurrent processing limits and other parameters that you set as the application administrator.

3. As it stacks and holds requests for processing, it organizes the requests into correlation groups and removes unnecessary processing steps within the correlation group to optimize it. It also manages the group to preserve data integrity.

4. It executes the job threads and monitors them through success or failure, blocking correlated transactions, if necessary, and reporting the results back to the database.

It is easy to conceive and understand the notion that the software listens for incoming jobs and takes an action to process the job and manages the process. The correlation process embedded in the Queue Service logic takes more explanation. To understand what is going on "under the hood," consider the following sequence of actions:

1. Project Manager <u>changes</u> Project Plan A.

2. Project Manager <u>saves</u> Project Plan A.

3. Project Manager <u>publishes</u> Project Plan A.

4. Project Manager <u>changes</u> Project Plan A.

5. Project Manager <u>saves</u> Project Plan A.

6. Project Manager <u>publishes</u> Project Plan A.

7. Project Manager <u>changes</u> Project Plan A.

8. Project Manager <u>saves</u> Project Plan A.

9. Project Manager <u>publishes</u> Project Plan A.

Depending on your server platform, during a low-load period, the system may process each of these requests sequentially, executing all of them almost instantaneously. In this case, the system does not optimize the requests because they do not dwell in the Queue. During a high system load, however, these requests may remain in the Queue. At this time, the Queue Service management logic kicks in.

Logic tells the Queue Service that if three change/save events occur sequentially, then each incremental change/save must succeed in order to process its successor. Processing the save event in Step 8 without first processing the save events in Steps 2 and 5 compromises data integrity. To prevent this from happening, the Queue Service orchestrates this series into a correlation group and manages the transactional integrity at the group, individual request, and sub-job levels. If the first change/save event fails in the correlation, the Queue Service logic prevents or "blocks" the successor job requests from processing. Note that the high-level job requests in the example in turn spawn sub-jobs that the Queue system also manages. It manages dependencies across parent/child relationships as well.

In the preceding correlation, the system skips the first two publishing events because its logic tells it that one publishing event, after completing all incremental saves, is all that is necessary in this case. Understanding that the system correlates and optimizes jobs is important to understanding Queue management, as you must have some recognition of various failure states to take effective action when jobs fail.

Understanding Job States

Error! Reference source not found. shows the possible job states in the order that they should happen in the Queue. Microsoft does not document the first state, "Getting Queued." Based on that, I assume that nobody anticipated a failure in this state, but these failures do occur, unfortunately.

Job State	Description	Next Possible State
Getting Queued	The Queue Service is currently handling the request.	• Processing • Cancelled • Waiting to be Processed
Waiting to be Processed Waiting to be Processed (On Hold) Waiting to be Processed (Ready for Launch) Waiting to be Processed (Sleeping)	The Queue Service is aware of the job and managing the request.	• Processing • Cancelled • Blocked • Skipped for optimization
Processing	The Queue Service is currently processing the job.	• Success • Failed and Not Blocking Correlation • Failed and Blocking Correlation • Cancelled
Success	The Queue Service succeeded in processing the job.	• End
Blocked Due to a Failed Job	The Queue Service blocked processing on the job because another job in its correlation group failed to process. The system holds the job to retry until someone cancels the job.	• Processing • Cancelled

Job State	Description	Next Possible State
Failed But Not Blocking Correlation	Job processing failed, but the failure is not blocking any other jobs in its correlation group.	• End
Failed and Blocking Correlation	Job has failed and may be blocking one or more dependent jobs.	• Cancelled • Processing
Skipped For Optimization	The system optimized correlation by skipping multiple jobs of the same type (such as multiple publishing operations on the same project).	• Blocked (due to a failed job) • Cancelled • Success • Failed and Not Blocking Correlation • Failed and Blocking Correlation • Processing
Cancelled	The Project Server administrator cancelled the job.	• None

Table 17 - 1: Queue Job States

Working with the Manage Queue Jobs Page

If you configured your server correctly, it is very rare that the Queue encounters a problem. Normally, individual jobs encounter problems, not the entire Queue Service. The *Manage Queue Jobs* page provides the tools you need to view current, waiting, and recently processed jobs, as well as the ability to cancel or retry them. You access the *Manage Queue Jobs page* by clicking the *Manage Queue Jobs* link in the *Queue* section of the *Server Settings* page. The system displays the *Manage Queue Jobs* page shown in Figure 17 - 29 and Figure 17 - 30.

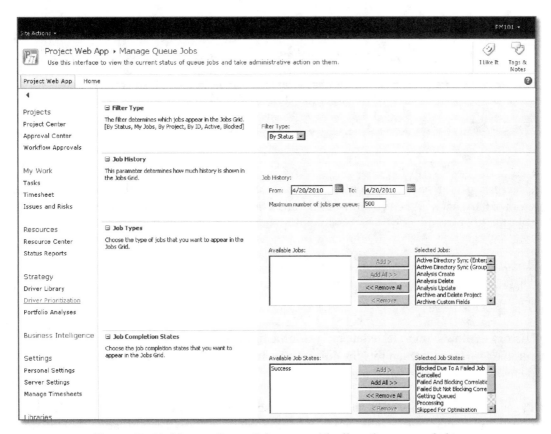

Figure 17 - 29: Manage Queue Jobs page with all sections expanded top

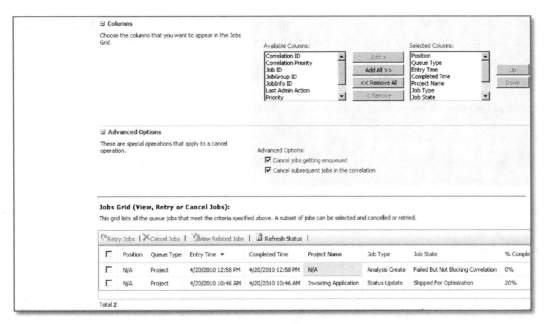

Figure 17 - 30: Manage Queue Jobs page with all sections expanded bottom

> For the sake of simplicity, the preceding figures show the *Manage Queue Jobs* page with all sections expanded. When you apply the page, however, the system collapses the *Job History, Job Types, Job Completion States, Columns*, and *Advanced Options* sections by default. You can click the *Expand/Collapse* indicator (+) for any section to view its contents.

The *Manage Queue Jobs* page gives you six control sections that allow you to narrow the results displayed in the *Jobs Grid* at the bottom of the display. When you must find transactions in a very active system, the following controls help you in your search:

- **Filter Type** – Allows you to filter the results using the values in a pick list. The *Filter Type* pick list contains the following filters: *By Status, My Jobs, By Project, By ID, Active,* and *Blocked*. The *By Status* filter is the default value on the *Filter Type* pick list.

- **Job History** – Allows you to set a date range for the results and restrict the results set to a specific count. By default, the *Job History* section sets the current date in the *From* and *To* fields, and specifies *500* jobs in the *Maximum number of jobs per queue* field.

- **Job Types** – Allows you to display all job types or restrict the display to specific job types. By default, the system selects and displays all job types. By viewing the entire *Job Types* list, you can see the full set of job types that the system processes.

- **Job Completion States** – Allows you to display all completion states or restrict the display to specific completion states. By default, the system excludes only the *Success* completion state from the results, logically assuming that administrators are more concerned about exceptions than successes.

- **Columns** – Allows you to determine which data columns to include in the *Jobs Grid* section of the page.

- **Advanced Options** – Offers you two options that allow you to cancel jobs in the Queue. By default, the system selects both options in this section, giving you full control to cancel one or more Queue jobs as needed.

- **Jobs Grid** – Displays the result set based on the selections you make in the sections above.

When you click the *Filter Type* pick list and choose any filter other than the default *By Status* filter, the system refreshes the page to include the sections and the options needed for the selected filter. For example, Figure 17 - 31 shows the *Manage Queue Jobs* page with the *By Project* filter selected. Notice the system included all of the default sections on the *Manage Queue Jobs* page, but also added a *Projects* section, and then selected all projects in the *Selected Projects* list. Select only those projects whose Queue jobs you want to see and then click the *Refresh Status* button.

Figure 17 - 32 shows the *Manage Queue Jobs* page with the *By ID* filter selected. Notice the system included only three of the default sections on the *Manage Queue Jobs* page, but also added a *Job/Job Group IDs* section. In the *Job/Job Group IDs* section, select either the *Job ID* option or the *Job Group ID* option, and then enter the ID number of the Job or Job Group on which you want to filter. Click the *Refresh Status* button to view the Queue jobs you want to see.

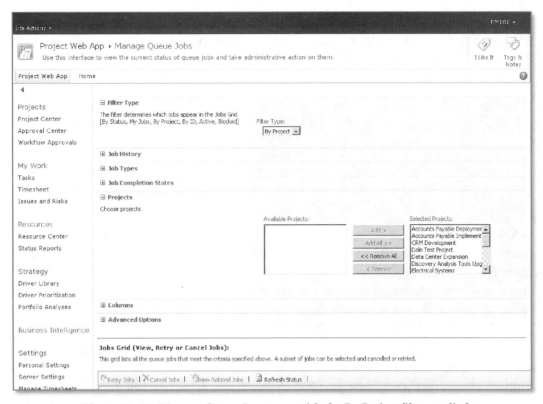

Figure 17 - 31: Manage Queue Jogs page with the By Project filter applied

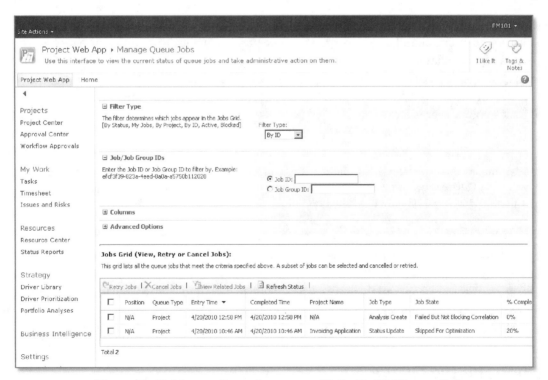

Figure 17 - 32: Manage Queue Jogs page with the By ID filter applied

When any job in the Queue fails, you should resolve the issue that is causing the failure and possibly blocking successor jobs. For instance, if a project is stuck in the "Getting Queued" state, a good first step is always to retry the Queue job by selecting the checkbox to the left of the job name and clicking the *Retry Jobs* button. If this fails, you may need to cancel the job by selecting the checkbox to the left of the job name and clicking the *Cancel Jobs* button. After cancelling the Queue job, you should review the project to determine whether there is an underlying problem before resubmitting it.

To find the root cause of a Queue job failure, you may need to review the history of Queue jobs and look for the blocking job. Expand the *Job History* section and enter a date earlier than today in the *From* field. Expand the *Job Completion States* section and select blocking jobs in the *Queue Job States* list, such as the *Failed and Blocking Correlation* job state. Click the *Refresh Status* button to view the Queue jobs you want to see. If this does not reveal the blocking job(s), set an even earlier date in the *From* field and then click the *Refresh Status* button again.

When searching for blocking jobs, keep in mind that the system deletes successful Queue jobs by default every 24 hours, while it deletes non-successful jobs once a week. If a failure happens and more than a week passes, the job will no longer be in the Queue history unless you made changes to the Queue retention settings. If a failure happens and less than a week has passed, you should be able to find the reporting job that failed. If you have many jobs in your Queue, that job may be several pages down in the results list. If you cannot find a record of a transaction that should be in the Queue, it may be that the reporting job that writes the record failed. In this case, you should see evidence of the failure in the Application Event log on the server.

Because all reporting jobs go through the Queue, whether or not the underlying transaction processed successfully, you should verify that the reporting job associated with the Queue jobs you are concerned about has processed successfully before you try to locate it in the Queue. Keep in mind that because reporting jobs tend to run long, they are set to a lower priority than other jobs in the system, with the exception of Cube Building, which carries the lowest priority by default. This means that even if a Project Save job enters the Queue after a Reporting job, the Project Save job runs first.

If the Queue processes most jobs without a problem and only a few projects seem to fail, then you should turn your attention to the projects in question. This behavior indicates a problem in the data rather than a problem in the Queue, particularly when other similar jobs process without problems. Restarting the Queue can bump things forward, because when the Queue starts, it detects incomplete processing jobs and deals with them. This is a failsafe measure only, however. Your best practice is to knowingly deal with your stuck Queue jobs as I describe above. This way, you are aware of the issues your server is facing.

Warning: If you restart the Queue Service, this can lead to unknown data loss. If you take this action while the Queue is receiving a new job, the Queue may not be able to receive the job completely. Consider taking this action only at times when you are certain nobody is using the system.

While managing Queue jobs you may encounter jobs whose *Job Completion State* value is the *Waiting to Be Processed (Sleeping)* state. You should never do anything to a *Sleeping* job. Remember the old adage, "Let sleeping jobs lie!" Jobs put themselves to sleep for a reason, and there is no way for you to determine the reason. Essentially the job is waiting for another event to occur or to complete. If a project remains in this state for a prolonged time, it indicates that a predecessor job is blocked or failed. You should determine the cause before risking the consequences of killing the job.

Troubleshooting the Queue

When your Queue log indicates problems, there are actions you can take to investigate why the Queue is not processing jobs for a particular project, including any of the following:

- Determine whether the Queue is running properly. If it continues to process jobs other than the ones for the projects that are "blocked," it is likely that the Queue Service is behaving correctly.

- Use the *Manage Queue Jobs* page to look at correlations, using the *CorrelationUID* column to aggregate jobs and determine why the system blocked a correlation group. Use the *By Project* filter for looking at the Queue job history for specific projects. If you cannot see any problems, and your Queue is still working, then your filters on the *Manage Queue Jobs* page may need adjusting, especially the *Job History* section.

- Look for jobs in the Failed and Blocking Correlation state. These jobs block others in the same correlation. You can retry these jobs if the error looks like something recoverable, such as the loss of network connectivity. Your other option is to cancel these jobs. Canceling with the default settings cancels the entire correlation, so make sure you know what data you lose in the process.

- When you see jobs stuck in the Getting Queued state, the user may have closed Project 2010 before the new job fully passed from the local cache to the Queue Service. When this is the case, ask the user to open Project 2010 to determine whether Project 2010 can continue sending the project. If that does not work, then you must cancel the job. Cancelling the job effectively means that the save operation never happened in the system, and the user must save the data again. Fortunately, the most recent version of the project should still be in the project manager's local cache, and they can try to save again. Cancelling the job causes the same type of data loss that restarting the Queue Service causes; but, in this case, you know what data you are losing.

- Look at the *Error* column to determine why the failure occurred. Sometimes you can correct the problem and re-save/re-submit your job.

> When you click the *Click to View Error Details* link in the *Error* column for any Queue job, the system displays a *Queue Job Error Details* dialog. If you find it difficult to read and decipher the information shown in the dialog, click the *Copy to Clipboard* button in the dialog and then paste the Clipboard data into Microsoft Word.

- Compare your server Event Logs to what you find in the *Manage Queue Jobs* page. Look for errors that occur at nearly the same time as failed jobs in the Queue. This helps you determine whether there may be underlying system failures contributing to your Queue Process failures.

- Compare the SharePoint ULS Logs to what you find in the *Manage Queue Jobs* page. Similar to reviewing the server Event Logs, you should look for errors that occur at nearly the same time as failed jobs in the Queue. Corresponding errors may indicate issues in SharePoint services or SharePoint configuration contributing to the problems.

Configuring the Queue

Queue settings are configurable from the *Server Settings* page. You must have the *Manage Queue* permission to see the *Queue Settings* link on the *Server Settings* page. Be very careful when editing Queue settings, as some of the settings can have a large impact on the throughput and efficiency of the server. If you do not fully understand any of the settings before editing them, do not make the change until you understand its potential impact.

To configure the Queue, click the *Queue Settings* link in the *Queue* section of the *Server Settings* page. The system displays the *Queue Settings* page shown in Figure 17 - 33 and Figure 17 - 34. Because of the length of the *Queue Settings* page, I break this into two separate figures.

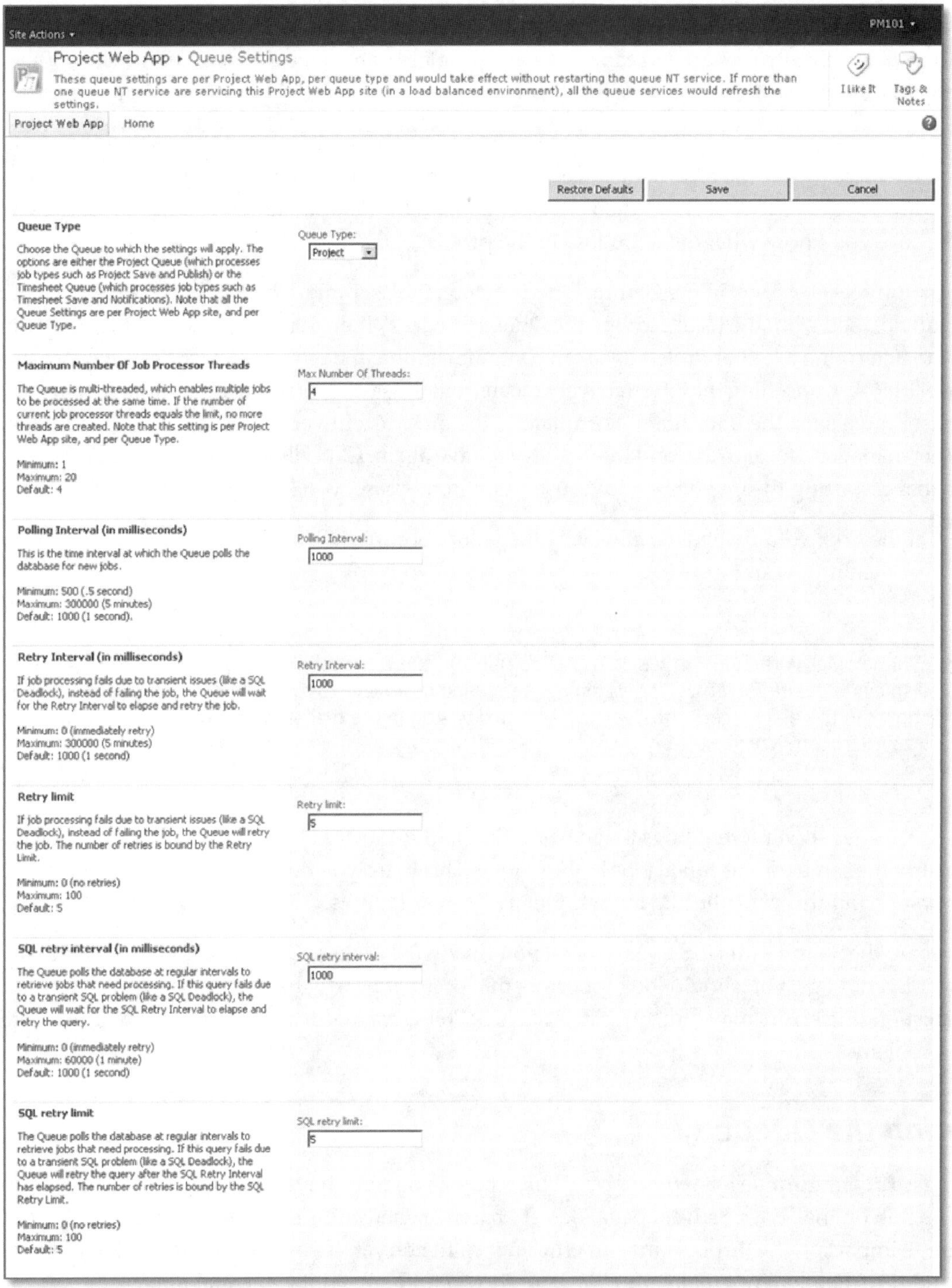

Figure 17 - 33: Queue Settings page top of the page

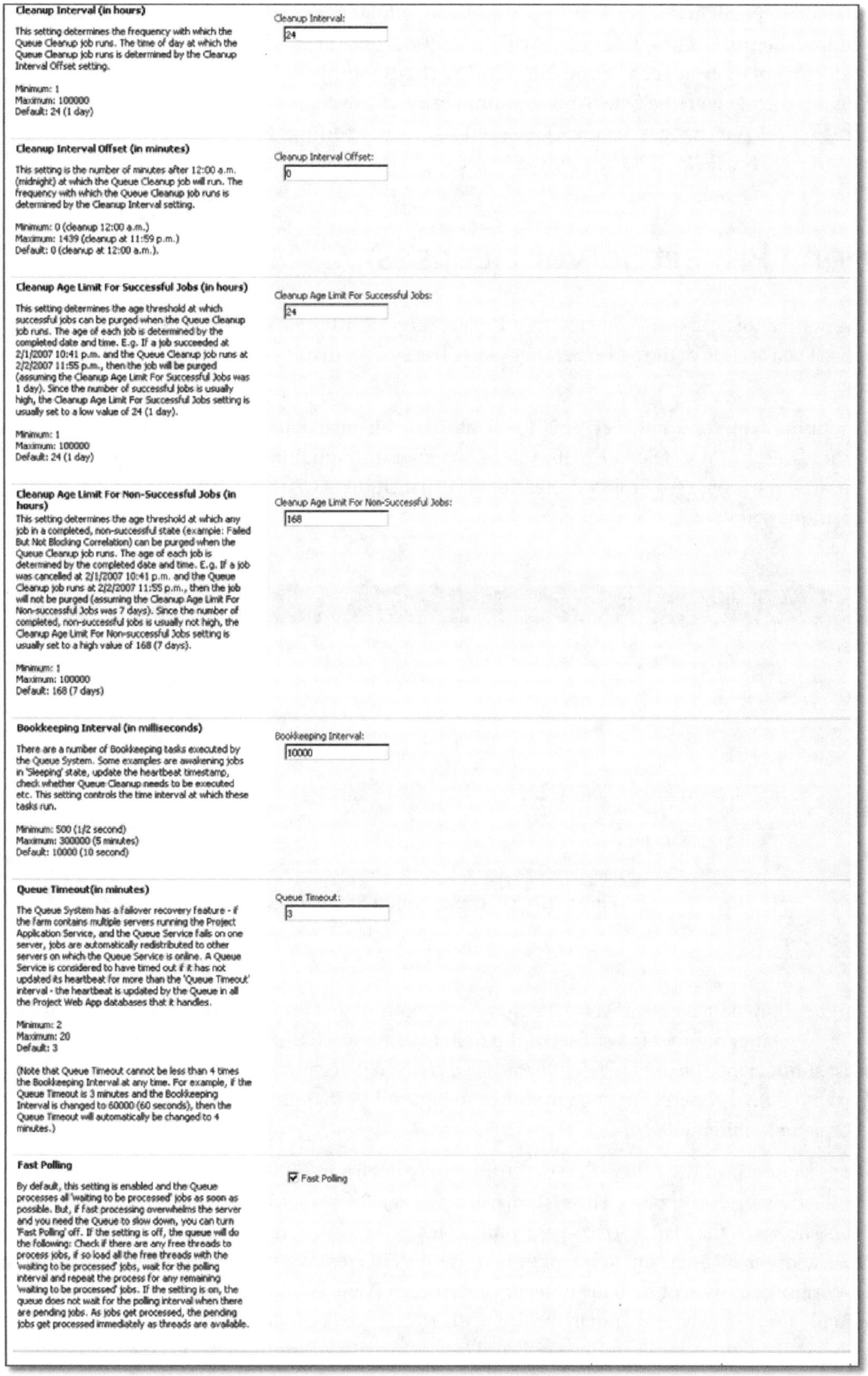

Cleanup Interval (in hours)

This setting determines the frequency with which the Queue Cleanup job runs. The time of day at which the Queue Cleanup job runs is determined by the Cleanup Interval Offset setting.

Minimum: 1
Maximum: 100000
Default: 24 (1 day)

Cleanup Interval:
`24`

Cleanup Interval Offset (in minutes)

This setting is the number of minutes after 12:00 a.m. (midnight) at which the Queue Cleanup job will run. The frequency with which the Queue Cleanup job runs is determined by the Cleanup Interval setting.

Minimum: 0 (cleanup 12:00 a.m.)
Maximum: 1439 (cleanup at 11:59 p.m.)
Default: 0 (cleanup at 12:00 a.m.).

Cleanup Interval Offset:
`0`

Cleanup Age Limit For Successful Jobs (in hours)

This setting determines the age threshold at which successful jobs can be purged when the Queue Cleanup job runs. The age of each job is determined by the completed date and time. E.g. If a job succeeded at 2/1/2007 10:41 p.m. and the Queue Cleanup job runs at 2/2/2007 11:55 p.m., then the job will be purged (assuming the Cleanup Age Limit For Successful Jobs was 1 day). Since the number of successful jobs is usually high, the Cleanup Age Limit For Successful Jobs setting is usually set to a low value of 24 (1 day).

Minimum: 1
Maximum: 100000
Default: 24 (1 day)

Cleanup Age Limit For Successful Jobs:
`24`

Cleanup Age Limit For Non-Successful Jobs (in hours)

This setting determines the age threshold at which any job in a completed, non-successful state (example: Failed But Not Blocking Correlation) can be purged when the Queue Cleanup job runs. The age of each job is determined by the completed date and time. E.g. If a job was cancelled at 2/1/2007 10:41 p.m. and the Queue Cleanup job runs at 2/2/2007 11:55 p.m., then the job will not be purged (assuming the Cleanup Age Limit For Non-successful Jobs was 7 days). Since the number of completed, non-successful jobs is usually not high, the Cleanup Age Limit For Non-successful Jobs setting is usually set to a high value of 168 (7 days).

Minimum: 1
Maximum: 100000
Default: 168 (7 days)

Cleanup Age Limit For Non-Successful Jobs:
`168`

Bookkeeping Interval (in milliseconds)

There are a number of Bookkeeping tasks executed by the Queue System. Some examples are awakening jobs in 'Sleeping' state, update the heartbeat timestamp, check whether Queue Cleanup needs to be executed etc. This setting controls the time interval at which these tasks run.

Minimum: 500 (1/2 second)
Maximum: 300000 (5 minutes)
Default: 10000 (10 second)

Bookkeeping Interval:
`10000`

Queue Timeout (in minutes)

The Queue System has a failover recovery feature - if the farm contains multiple servers running the Project Application Service, and the Queue Service fails on one server, jobs are automatically redistributed to other servers on which the Queue Service is online. A Queue Service is considered to have timed out if it has not updated its heartbeat for more than the 'Queue Timeout' interval - the heartbeat is updated by the Queue in all the Project Web App databases that it handles.

Minimum: 2
Maximum: 20
Default: 3

(Note that Queue Timeout cannot be less than 4 times the Bookkeeping Interval at any time. For example, if the Queue Timeout is 3 minutes and the Bookkeeping Interval is changed to 60000 (60 seconds), then the Queue Timeout will automatically be changed to 4 minutes.)

Queue Timeout:
`3`

Fast Polling

By default, this setting is enabled and the Queue processes all 'waiting to be processed' jobs as soon as possible. But, if fast processing overwhelms the server and you need the Queue to slow down, you can turn 'Fast Polling' off. If the setting is off, the queue will do the following: Check if there are any free threads to process jobs, if so load all the free threads with the 'waiting to be processed' jobs, wait for the polling interval and repeat the process for any remaining 'waiting to be processed' jobs. If the setting is on, the queue does not wait for the polling interval when there are pending jobs. As jobs get processed, the pending jobs get processed immediately as threads are available.

☑ Fast Polling

Figure 17 - 34: Queue Settings page bottom of the page

Unlike nearly all other pages in Project Web App, the *Queue Settings* page includes complete descriptive information about every setting. Because of this, I do not provide additional documentation on these settings. You should study the Microsoft documentation on TechNet, and developers should study the information in the Project Server SDK for information on interacting with the Queue programmatically. If you change any of the default Queue settings, click the *Save* button to save your changes. If your Queue settings do not perform to your expectations, return to the *Queue Settings* page and click the *Restore Defaults* button to return to the system defaults.

Monitoring Project Server Licenses

To monitor the number of licenses needed for your Project Server 2010 environment, click the *About Project Server* link in the Enterprise Data section of the *Server Settings* page. The system displays the *About Project Server* page shown in Figure 17 - 35.

The licensing requirements for Project Server 2010 dictate that you must obtain a web Client Access License (CAL) for each user that accesses the Project Server 2010 system, whether through Project Web App or through Project Professional 2010. Because the license for Project Professional 2010 includes a CAL, you do not need to purchase a separate CAL for users of this software.

Figure 17 - 35: About Project Server page

Notice in the figure that the system indicates the number of both Active Project Server Users (19) and Project Professional Users (7). The latter number is a subset of the first. In other words, of the total *Active Number of Project Server Users*, you must subtract the *Number of Project Professional Users* to determine your Web CAL requirements. Using the information from the *About Project Server* page shown in Figure 17 - 35, I must own 12 CALs (19 – 7) to comply with Microsoft's licensing requirements.

Perhaps you are wondering how Project Server 2010 actually determines the number of users in the two categories shown on the *About Project Server* page. The system calculates the *Number of Active Project Server Users* value from the number of users shown on the *Manage Users* page minus one, as the system does not count the service account used to install the Project Server 2010 system. Remember that the system creates a user account automatically for every resource with a Windows user account in the Enterprise Resource Pool. As you already know, you can also create user accounts manually for people who are not in the Enterprise Resource Pool, such as for executives or customers. If you create a resource in the Enterprise Resource Pool, and do not specify a Windows user account for that resource, the system **does not** create a corresponding Project Web App user account. This means that the user cannot access the Project Server 2010 system, and thus does not need a CAL.

The system calculates the *Number of Project Professional Users* value by counting the number of users that have the *Log on to Project Server from Project Professional* permission set to Allowed. By default, the system sets this permission to Allowed for members of the Administrators, Portfolio Managers, Project Managers, and Resource Managers groups.

Monitoring and Troubleshooting Project Server

The most important monitoring you can do for your Project Server 2010 system is to review the server event logs regularly. Checking on the machine(s) that are running your farm can reveal application errors that indicate problems on the server. Right-click the *Computer* button on your server Start menu and then click the *Manage* item from the shortcut menu. In the *Server Manager* dialog, expand the *Event Viewer* section as shown in Figure 17 - 36.

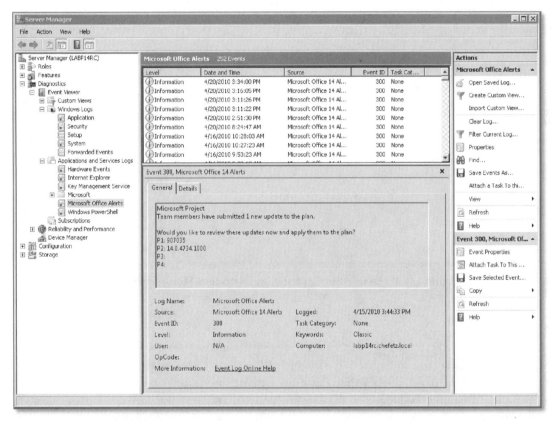

Figure 17 - 36: Server Manager Event Viewer expanded

Notice in Figure 17 - 36 the standard Windows Server logs in the *Windows Logs* section. Notice also the *Microsoft Office Alerts* log in the *Microsoft* section of the tree. Because this is a lab server I use for writing, I also have the Office 2010 client applications installed, and therefore this log appears on a server, where you wouldn't normally expect to find it. I point this out as this is a useful tool for helping you troubleshoot user issues.

Use the *Application* log to find systemic errors occurring with applications running on your server. Use the *Security* log to help investigate authentication issues. Use the *Microsoft Office Alerts* log to help you troubleshoot issues on end-user systems. These are particularly good for tracing the users' actions through the software.

Working with Unified Logging Service (ULS) files

The most important server logs in diagnosing issues with SharePoint and Project Server are the *Unified Logging Service (ULS)* logs. You control server logging settings for these through SharePoint Central Administration. From you Share-Point Central Administration home page, select the *Monitoring* item. The system displays the *Monitoring* page shown in Figure 17 - 37.

Figure 17 - 37: SharePoint Central Administration Monitoring page

From the *Monitoring* page, select the *Configure diagnostic logging* item from the *Reporting* section. The system displays the *Diagnostic Logging* page shown in Figure 17 - 38, which allows you to control how your system logs events. The *Event Throttling* section of the page allows you to fine-tune logging operations on your server so that specific events cause more or less information to be logged by the system. Notice that within this section, you see entries for all of the service applications and services that use the *ULS* logs within the SharePoint envelope. The techniques I discuss here are equally applicable to troubleshooting issues with other SharePoint service applications as well as Project Server.

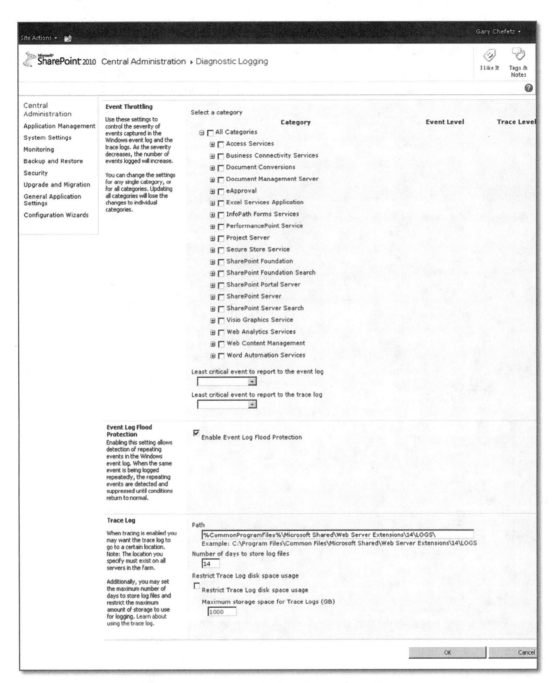

Figure 17 - 38: Diagnostic Logging configuration page

To see the detail level that you can control for Project Server, you must expand the *Project Server* item in the *Category* list. Figure 17 - 39 shows the *Project Server* category section expanded.

☐ Project Server		
☐ Active Cache Enterprise Resource Load	Information	Medium
☐ Active Cache Load	Information	Medium
☐ Active Cache operations	Information	Medium
☐ Active Cache Save	Information	Medium
☐ Active Directory Synchronization	Information	Medium
☐ Administration	Information	Medium
☐ Analysis Cube Building	Information	Medium
☐ Archive, Restore	Information	Medium
☐ Calendars	Information	Medium
☐ Database	Information	Medium
☐ Exchange Sync	Information	Medium
☐ General	Information	Medium
☐ Global	Information	Medium
☐ Logging Correlation Data	Information	Medium
☐ Notifications	Information	Medium
☐ Portfolio Management	Information	Medium
☐ Portfolio Strategy Drivers and Prioritizations	Information	Medium
☐ Portfolio Strategy Optimizer	Information	Medium
☐ Portfolio Strategy Planner	Information	Medium
☐ Project Server Cache	Information	Medium
☐ Project Server Shared	Information	Medium
☐ Project Server Workflow	Information	Medium
☐ Project Web App	Information	Medium
☐ Provisioning	Information	Medium
☐ Queue	Information	Medium
☐ Reporting	Information	Medium
☐ Reports	Information	Medium
☐ Resource	Information	Medium
☐ Security	Information	Medium
☐ Server-Side Events	Information	Medium
☐ Server-side Project Operations	Information	Medium
☐ Shared Services	Information	Medium
☐ Sharepoint Integration	Information	Medium
☐ SQM	Information	Medium
☐ Status Reports	Information	Medium
☐ Summary Resource Assignments	Information	Medium
☐ Task Statusing and Updates	Information	Medium
☐ Timesheet	Information	Medium
☐ Unified Logging Service	Information	Medium

Figure 17 - 39: Project Server Category section expanded

Notice the granularity of the events that generate log entries into the *ULS*, and that, by default, the *Trace Level* for each event category is set to medium. Hypothetically, if you were trying to determine the cause of issues users are reporting to you related to *Timesheets,* one strategy you might try is to increase the logging detail for the *Timesheet* category. To do this, you select the *Timesheet* check box and adjust the logging level as shown in Figure 17 - 40. Notice that the system provides two pick lists, one for *Least critical event to report to the event log,* which allows you to control the verbosity of logging to the Windows *Application Event* log, and the second, *Least critical event to report to the trace log,* which allows you to control the verbosity of the logging for the *ULS*.

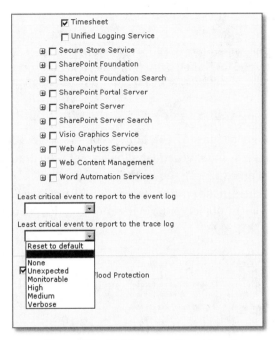

Figure 17 - 40: Changing Trace Level

Your options for the two logging systems are slightly different. For the *Application Event* log, choose from the following:

- None

- Critical

- Error

- Warning

- Information

- Verbose

For the *ULS* logs:

- None

- Unexpected

- Monitorable

- High

- Medium

- Verbose

Warning: Increasing logging verbosity can cause log files to grow very quickly on an active system. Use this technique judiciously and for limited periods of time, and during troubleshooting sessions only. As a rule, using *Medium* trace level logging is adequate for normal system monitoring.

The *Trace Log* section of the page, shown in Figure 17 - 41, allows you to set a location for your *ULS* log files, and to set certain retention restrictions including days to save, and it allows you to constrain log retention based on disk space usage by setting a limit in gigabits. Figure 17 - 41 shows the system default for *ULS* storage. Each server in your SharePoint farm, by default, stores its logs in the path shown under the *Program Files* folder, usually located on the C: drive. You may want to change this for a multi-server farm in order to collect all of the logs on one server or network file share for easier retrieval.

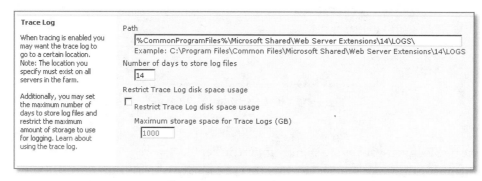

Figure 17 - 41: Trace log section

Figure 17 - 42 shows my *ULS* directory in a *Windows Explorer* view.

Name	Date modified	Type	Size	Tags
LABP14RC-20100421-0449.log	4/21/2010 5:19 AM	Text Document	696 KB	
LABP14RC-20100421-0419.log	4/21/2010 4:49 AM	Text Document	686 KB	
LABP14RC-20100421-0349.log	4/21/2010 4:19 AM	Text Document	698 KB	
LABP14RC-20100421-0319.log	4/21/2010 3:49 AM	Text Document	674 KB	
LABP14RC-20100421-0249.log	4/21/2010 3:19 AM	Text Document	874 KB	
LABP14RC-20100421-0219.log	4/21/2010 2:49 AM	Text Document	1,309 KB	
LABP14RC-20100421-0149.log	4/21/2010 2:19 AM	Text Document	1,346 KB	
LABP14RC-20100421-0119.log	4/21/2010 1:49 AM	Text Document	1,330 KB	
LABP14RC-20100421-0049.log	4/21/2010 1:19 AM	Text Document	1,473 KB	
LABP14RC-20100421-0019.log	4/21/2010 12:49 AM	Text Document	1,349 KB	
LABP14RC-20100420-2349.log	4/21/2010 12:19 AM	Text Document	1,933 KB	
LABP14RC-20100420-2319.log	4/20/2010 11:49 PM	Text Document	1,324 KB	
LABP14RC-20100420-2249.log	4/20/2010 11:19 PM	Text Document	1,384 KB	
LABP14RC-20100420-2219.log	4/20/2010 10:49 PM	Text Document	1,303 KB	
LABP14RC-20100420-2149.log	4/20/2010 10:19 PM	Text Document	1,320 KB	
LABP14RC-20100420-2119.log	4/20/2010 9:49 PM	Text Document	1,301 KB	
LABP14RC-20100420-2049.log	4/20/2010 9:19 PM	Text Document	1,312 KB	
LABP14RC-20100420-2019.log	4/20/2010 8:49 PM	Text Document	1,297 KB	
LABP14RC-20100420-1949.log	4/20/2010 8:19 PM	Text Document	1,317 KB	
LABP14RC-20100420-1919.log	4/20/2010 7:49 PM	Text Document	1,299 KB	
LABP14RC-20100420-1849.log	4/20/2010 7:19 PM	Text Document	1,318 KB	
LABP14RC-20100420-1819.log	4/20/2010 6:49 PM	Text Document	1,272 KB	
LABP14RC-20100420-1749.log	4/20/2010 6:19 PM	Text Document	1,306 KB	
LABP14RC-20100420-1719.log	4/20/2010 5:49 PM	Text Document	1,297 KB	
LABP14RC-20100420-1649.log	4/20/2010 5:19 PM	Text Document	1,358 KB	
LABP14RC-20100420-1619.log	4/20/2010 4:49 PM	Text Document	1,365 KB	

Figure 17 - 42: ULS files in Windows Explorer view

You can open one of these log files using Microsoft Excel by forcing Excel to import the file the same way it does for other tab-delimited files. The advantage to opening these in Excel is apparent in Figure 17 - 43, which shows a log file open in Microsoft Excel. By using Excel, you can use all of its built in data-mining tools to help you locate the specific data you need to find.

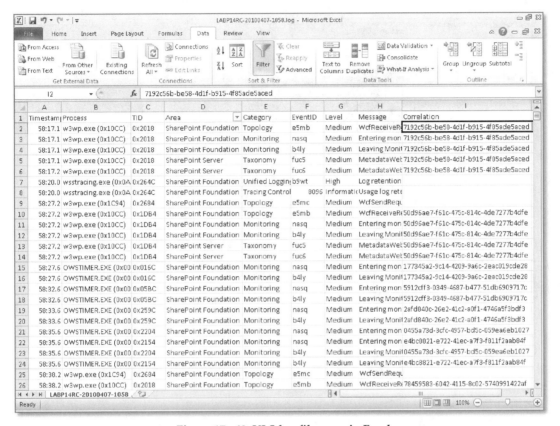

Figure 17 - 43: ULS log file open in Excel

Notice in Figure 17 - 43 the far-right column of data visible is the *Correlation* id, a system-generated unique identifier for the particular logged event. These *Correlation* id numbers also appear in error messages that surface to the user and in other places in the system, such as the *Cube Build Status* page and in the *Queue Management* page. By harvesting these numbers from local sources, you can cross-reference them in the *ULS* logs by using Excel to search in the *Correlation* column after locating the log file with the correct time stamp range.

You can also deploy third-party *ULS* log viewers. There is at least one solution available in the Codeplex gallery, and you should also look for starter solutions that might become available in the MSDN code gallery.

Using the Reliability and Performance Monitor

You can also use the *Reliability and Performance Monitor* tool to set up monitors for your system and to review these periodically. To access the *Reliability and Performance Monitor*, select the *Reliability and Performance Monitor* item from the *Administrative Tools* menu to open the tool shown in Figure 17 - 44. Refer to the Windows Server 2008 Help files for more information on using the System Monitor to configure *Data Collector* sets for your system. You also use this tool to monitor your system and application processes currently running on your system. You use this tool as an investigative aid when tracking down performance issues. This can help eliminate hardware issues and indicate what operations cause system resource slowdowns.

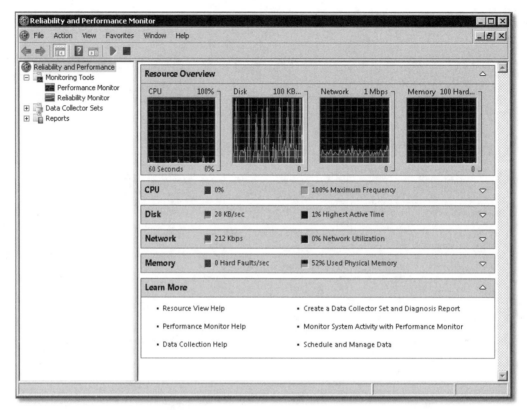

Figure 17 - 44: Reliability and Performance Monitor

Configuring a SQL Server 2008 Maintenance Plan

The *Administrative Backup and Restore* features in Project Server do not provide complete backups of your system, and you cannot use them to provide backup records outside of the database. Further, SQL maintenance plans can perform additional database maintenance tasks that you must provide for in maintaining your system. In order to provide true system backup and restore capabilities, you must implement a SQL Server maintenance plan or third-party database recovery tool, and provide for disaster recovery by considering such things as off-premises backup. Before you determine your disaster recovery plans, download the Project Server 2010 Disaster Recovery Guide from Microsoft. This information is available on TechNet. Before you start using your Project Server 2010 instance, use the following procedures to set up a *Database Maintenance Plan* for your Project Server databases and the SharePoint Configuration, Content and Project Site Content databases. You must back up all of these in order to recover from a disaster. This assumes that you already have a maintenance plan for other SQL Server objects such as your master database.

The easiest way to configure a Database Maintenance Plan for your Project Server database is to use the SQL Server Maintenance Plan Wizard. Launch your SQL Server 2008 Management Studio and connect to the Database Engine. The system displays the *SQL Server Management Studio* interface shown in Figure 17 - 45.

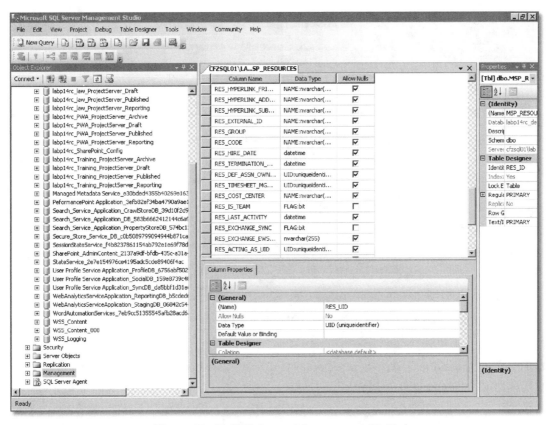

Figure 17 - 45: SQL Server Management Studio

Before you can create a SQL Server Maintenance Plan, you may need to enable the SQL Server Agent service, which handles scheduled jobs. Notice in the figure the *SQL Server Agent* item in the *Object Explorer* pane on the left. If this is not showing a green arrow indicating that it is running, right-click on the item and select the *Start* item from the shortcut menu. The system starts the service for you. If you do not enable the SQL Server Agent and you attempt to define a Maintenance Plan, SQL Server throws the error. Once you verify that the SQL Server Agent service is active, expand the *Management* folder in the *Object Explorer* pane and right-click on the *Maintenance Plans* folder as shown in Figure 17 - 46.

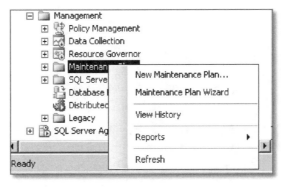

Figure 17 - 46: Management folder expanded

Notice in Figure 17 - 46 that after I right-clicked on the *Maintenance Plans* folder, the system displayed a shortcut menu. Select the *Maintenance Plan Wizard* option from the menu. The system displays the *SQL Server Maintenance Plan Wizard* dialog shown in Figure 17 - 47.

873

Figure 17 - 47: SQL Server Maintenance Plan Wizard dialog

Click the *Next* button to continue. The system redisplays the *Select Plan Properties* page shown in Figure 17 - 48. Provide a name for your new maintenance plan.

Figure 17 - 48: Select Plan Properties page

In the *Description* field, enter descriptive information about your new Maintenance Plan. Click the *Change* button in the *Schedule* section of the page to setup a schedule for your new maintenance plan. The system displays the *Job Schedule Properties* page shown in Figure 17 - 49.

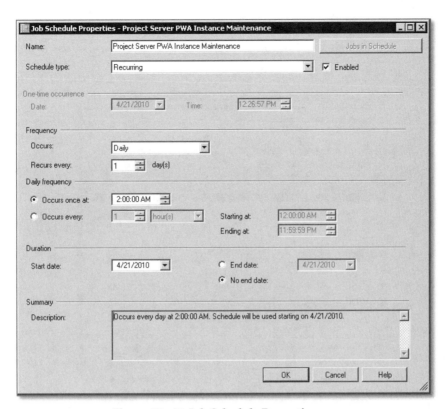

Figure 17 - 49: Job Schedule Properties page

Notice in the figure that I selected to schedule the job on a daily basis and run the plan at 2:00 a.m. When you complete your entries, click the *OK* button to continue. The system returns you to the *Select Plan Properties* page shown previously in Figure 17 - 48. Click the *Next* button to continue. The system displays the *Select Maintenance Tasks* page shown in Figure 17 - 50.

Figure 17 - 50: Select Maintenance Tasks page

Notice on this page that I select the checkboxes for *Backup Database (Full)* and the *Backup Database (Transaction Log)* options. In addition, I selected the *Update Statistics* item. You can choose the tasks that you need to run in your plan.

Click the *Next* button when you complete your selections. The system displays the *Select Maintenance Task Order* page shown in Figure 17 - 51.

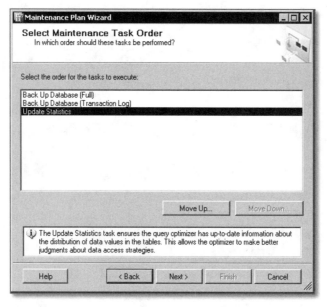

Figure 17 - 51: Select Maintenance Task Order page

Use the *Move Up* and *Move Down* buttons to place your maintenance tasks in the order you want them to process. Notice that I ordered the tasks so that a full backup of the database is followed by a backup of the Transaction Log and then followed by the Update Statistics task. When you have completed the ordering of your maintenance plan tasks, click the *Next* button to continue. The system displays the *Define Back Up Database (Full) Task* page shown in Figure 17 - 52 following the order you selected for processing.

Backing up the Transactions Log is a very important part of your maintenance plan, as the transaction logs for your Project Server 2010 databases tend to grow very rapidly and can fill your available disk space if you do not manage them.

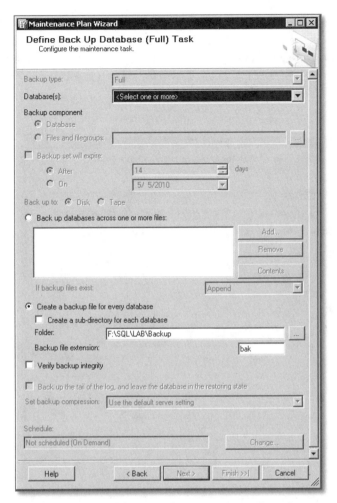

Figure 17 - 52: Define Back Up Database (Full) Task page

From the *Databases* pick list, select your Project Server databases from the list as shown in Figure 17 - 53.

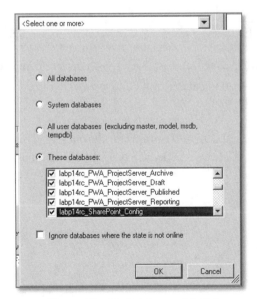

Figure 17 - 53: Database pick list

Once you select your databases from the list, the system redisplays the *Define Back Up Database (Full)* page with the additional options available to set. Select a destination for your backup files and select the *Verify backup integrity* option if you want the system to perform an integrity check on the backup. Click the *Next* button to continue. The wizard displays the *Define Back Up Database (Transaction Log) Task* page shown in Figure 17 - 54.

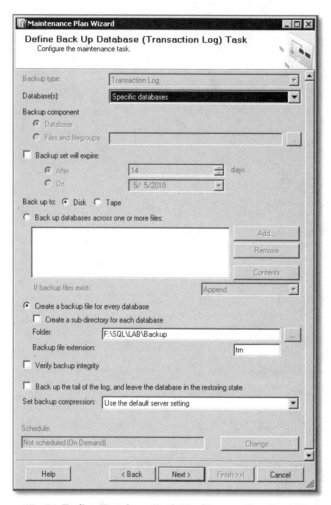

Figure 17 - 54: Define Database Back Up (Transaction Log) Task page

Notice in the figure that I selected the databases and options for the backup. This page functions exactly the same way as the previous page functions. Use the *Databases* pick list to select your databases and click the *Next* button to continue. The system displays the *Define Update Statistics Task* page shown in Figure 17 - 55.

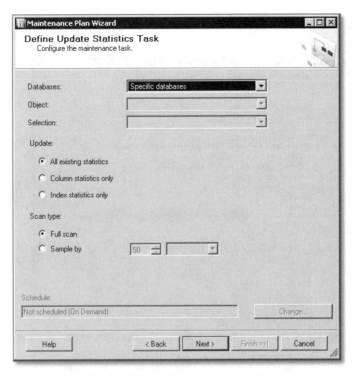

Figure 17 - 55: Define Update Statistics Task page

Once again you need to select your Project Server databases from the *Databases* pick list and set your options on the page, and then click the *Next* button to continue. The system continues to display a task page for each maintenance item you selected for your plan, allowing you to configure each step in the plan process. If this is the last item on your list, then the system displays the *Select Report Options* page when you click the *Next* button, as shown in Figure 17 - 56.

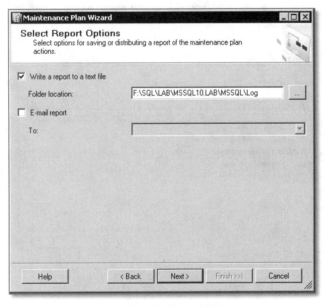

Figure 17 - 56: Select Report Options page

The *Select Report Options* page allows you to select whether to write a results report to disk and/or email the report to a system operator. You must first define operators before you can use the e-mail option. Click the *Next* button to continue.

The wizard displays the *Complete the Wizard* page shown in Figure 17 - 57.

Figure 17 - 57: Complete the Wizard page

Review your selections on the *Complete the Wizard* page. If you need to make any changes, use the *Back* button to navigate to the page requiring the change. Otherwise, click the *Finish* button to complete the wizard. The system creates your new maintenance plan based on the inputs you provided and displays the *Maintenance Plan Wizard Progress* page to display the plan creation progress. When you achieve full success with each item, you can optionally view a report or click the *Close* button to complete the wizard.

Figure 17 - 58: Maintenance Plan Wizard Progress page

You can view your new maintenance plan by expanding the *Management* folder and then expanding the *Maintenance Plan* folder. Double click on the name of your new plan to view it in SQL Server Management Studio.

Index

Active Directory Synchronization 382–84, 534–37

   with security Groups 534–37

   with the Enterprise Resource Pool 382–84

Administrative Time, configuring 450–52

Alerts and Reminders, configuring 418–19

Assignment Details View, modifying in Project Web App 596–600

Backing Up and Restoring Enterprise Objects 844–50

   enabling automatic backup 845–46

   performing a manual backup 846–47

   restoring a backup 847–50

Business Drivers 214, 304–6

   creating 304–6

   introducing 214

Business Intelligence Center ....*See* Reporting

Categories 499–508, 518–30

   creating a new Category 527–29

   deleting a Category 530

   managing Categories 518–27

   overview of Category and Group interaction 499–508

   understanding the built-in Categories 506–8

Compatibility Mode 407

Cost resources, creating 363–65

Cost Type lookup table 222–23

Creating an Additional Project Server 2010 Instance 171–80

Currency settings 409–10

Deleting Enterprise Objects 833–44

   deleting enterprise projects 834–37

   deleting enterprise resources and users 837

   deleting Status Report responses 841–42

   deleting timesheets 842–43

   deleting User Delegates 843–44

Demand Management ....*See* Lifecycle Management

Departments... 211–13, 240–42, 373–74

   modifying the Project Departments field 240–42

   modifying the Resource Departments field 240–42

   setting the Resource Department value for enterprise resources..373–74

   understanding 211–13

Deploying Project Server 2010..39–70

   following a deployment process 46–70

      1. Managing the Discovery phase..46–53

      2. Managing the Definition phase 53–62

      3. Managing the Design phase 62–67

      4. Managing the Deployment phase 67–68

      5. Managing the Pilot phase...68–69

      6. Managing the Rollout phase 69–70

   understanding the deployment process 39–46

      defining the deployment team 39–46

Dynamic Workflow Solution Starter, deploying and configuring..329–35

Enterprise Calendars 270–81

   creating a new enterprise Base calendar...278–79

   importing a Base calendar from a project..280–81

   modifying the enterprise Standard calendar 270–78

Enterprise Fields and Lookup Tables 211–70

   built-in fields and lookup tables 215–28

      modifying..218–28

      understanding 215–18

   creating a custom enterprise field...233–70

      creating a custom enterprise field with a formula..243–57

      creating a custom enterprise field with a Lookup Table 237–42

      creating a custom enterprsie field with Graphical Indicators...259–67

      creating a free entry custom field...234–37

      importing a local custom field as an enterprise custom field 257–59

      making a custom enterprise field Required 236–37

      planning for matching Generic resources with human resources..268–70

   creating a new Lookup Table 226–27, 228–33

   deleting a custom enterprise field...267–68

   deleting a custom enterprise Lookup Table 267–68

   Departments 211–13

   field types..215

   metadata changes in Project Server 2010 ....211–70 overview of fields and lookup tables 214–15

Project Types...213

Enterprise Global, managing Project Professional 2010 custom views **615–19**

Enterprise Project Templates...**312–19, 545–55**

creating manually 312–19

importing using the Import Project Wizard 545–55

Enterprise Resource Pool...........................**8, 339–402, 415–16, 415–16, 491–92, 499**

creating enterprise resources using Active Directory Synchronization 382–84

creating enterprise resources using Project Professional 2010...346–66

creating Cost resources...363–65

creating Generic resources..362–63

creating Material resources..362

creating Team resources..365–66

creating Work resources..348–62

creating enterprise resources using Project Web App 369–76, 415–16

setting Exchange synchronization options with enterprise resources.................373, 415–16

setting the Resource Department value for enterprise resources.............................373–74

deactivating an enterprise resource..400–402, 499

defined...8

editing enterprise resources in Project Professional 2010...367–69

editing enterprise resources using Project Web App 376–81

importing enterprise resources from an external source...384–99

creating a local resource pool file..384–97

importing enterprise resources from a local resource pool file 384–97

overview..8, 339–402

resource types...339–41

understanding users vs. resources...491–92

using the Resource Center page to manage resources...341–46

Enterprise Resources ....*See* **Enterprise Resource Pool**

Event Handlers, configuring...**428–31**

Excel Services...**123–36, 174–75, 780–81, 823**

configuring..125–27

configuring Global Settings 129–31

configuring Trusted Data Connection libraries 131–32

creating an Excel Services Application for a new Project Server 2010 instance 174–75

embedding Excel data into a SharePoint Dashboard page 823

harvesting URLs for Trusted Data Connection libraries and Report libraries 127–29

overview for Business Intelligence reporting...780–81

preparing to configure...123–25

working with Microsoft Excel reports..782–821

   creating a custom Microsoft Excel report 796–99, 813–21

   modifying a custom Microsoft Excel report 800–813

   overview of built-in Microsoft Excel report templates 779

   overview of built-in Microsoft Excel reports...779

   overview of Excel Data Connection files 785–88

   viewing built-in Microsoft Excel reports 789–96

Fields .... *See* **Enterprise Fields and Lookup Tables**

Financial Periods, creating **439–42**

Fiscal Periods .... *See* **Financial Periods or Time and Task Tracking**

Gantt Chart Formats, creating for use in Project Web App views.......................................**568–72**

Generic resources, creating **362–63**

Grouping Formats, creating for use in Project Web App views..**572–75**

Groups **499–508, 511–18**

   creating a new Group...516–17

   deleting a Group 517–18

   managing Groups 511–16

   overview of Group and Category interaction..499–508

   understanding the built-in Groups...506

Health lookup table..**223–24**

Import Project Wizard..**545–55**

Importing Projects and Templates **545–61**

   changing the Owner of an imported project 556–61

   changing the Status Manager of an imported project...556–61

   importing a project or template using the Import Project Wizard.......................................545–61

   publishing an imported project...555–56

Installing Project Server 2010 ....**73–119**

   creating a Service Application manually 117–19

   creating the Project Web App instance 112–17

   installing the application software 90–112

      configuring the SharePoint farm...106–12

      installing pre-requisite software using the SharePoint Server 2010 Preparation Tool 90–93

      installing the Project Server 2010 software 97–100

      installing the SharePoint Server 2010 software..94–97

      running the SharePoint Products Configuration Wizard 100–106

   overview of the installation process 73

preparing to install SharePoint Server and Project Server 2010 73–90

    creating the service accounts 75–77

    meeting hardware and software requirements 74–75

    preparing SQL Server Analysis Services for Project Server 2010 86–89

    preparing SQL Server for Project Server 2010 77–86

    preparing the server for Project Server 2010 89–90

Lifecycle Management **285–335**

    configuration process overview 288–89

    configuring Lifecycle Management elements 289–329

        configuring Project Workflow Settings 328–29

        configuring workflow Phases 306–7

        configuring workflow Stages 307–11

        creating and editing Project Detail Pages 296–304

        creating and modifying Project Types 314–19

        creating Business Drivers 304–6

        creating enterprise project templates 312–19

        demonstration of Project Detail Pages functionality 289–96

        Dynamic Workflow Solution Starter, deploying and configuring 329–35

        Sample Workflow, adapting and working with 319–28

        using Project Detail Pages 300–304

    Decision Management described 285

    Demand Management described 285

    overview 285–89

    Phases and Stages described 287–88

    Project Detail pages (PDP) described 288

    Project Types in the LifeCycle Management process 286–87

Line Classifications, creating for Timesheets **446**

Local Base Calendars, allowing in Project Server 2010 ....**408**

Lookup Tables .... *See* **Enterprise Fields and Lookup Tables**

Managing Project Server 2010 ....**831–81**

    backing up and restoring enterprise objects 844–50

        enabling automatic backup 845–46

        performing a manual backup 846–47

        restoring a backup 847–50

    checking in enterprise objects 831–33

    deleting enterprise objects 833–44

        deleting enterprise projects 834–37

        deleting enterprise resources and users 837

deleting Status Report responses 841–42

deleting timesheets 842–43

deleting User Delegates 843–44

managing the Queue 853–65

configuring the Queue..862–65

troubleshooting Queue problems 857–62

understanding the Queue 853–57

using the Manage Queue Jobs page 857–61

monitoring Project Server 2010 for problems

using the Reliability and Performance Monitor...872

using ULS files...867–72

monitoring Project Server 2010 for problems..866–73

monitoring Project Server licenses..865–66

restarting or changing Workflows...850–53

setting up a SQL maintenance plan...873–81

Master Projects, allowing in Project Server 2010 ....**408**

Material resources, creating **362**

Metadata **211–14, 240–42, 286–87, 304–6**

Business Drivers...214, 304–6

creating 304–6

introducing...214

Departments 211–13, 240–42

modifying the Project Departments field..240–42

modifying the Resource Departments field...240–42

understanding 211–13

introducing metadata changes in Project Server 2010 211–14

Project Types...213, 286–87, 314–19

creating and modifying..314–19

interaction with the Lifecycle Management process 286–87

introducing..213

Microsoft Exchange **373, 411, 412–18**

configuring Exchange Server for synchronization with Project Server 2010.............................412–13

configuring Project Server 2010 for synchronization with Exchange Server.............................413–15

enabling Exchange Server synchronization on the Additional Server Settings page................411

setting synchronization options with enterprise resources...373, 415–16

understanding how Exchange synchronization works 416–18

My Assignments View, modifying in Project Web App **596–600**

Near Future Planning Window, defining..**462–63**

OLAP Cube **420–27, 562–64, 769–74**

building the OLAP cube 562–64

configuring the default OLAP database 420–23

configuring the OLAP cubes 423–27

deleting an OLAP database 427

OLAP Database for Business Intelligence reporting 769–74

Organizational Permissions, setting on the Project Web Access Permissions page **477–91**

Owner, changing the Owner of an imported project **556–61**

PDP ....*See* **Project Detail Pages**

Post-Installation Steps After Installing Project Server 2010 ....**123–80**

configuring SharePoint Service Applications 123–41

configuring the Secure Store Service 136–41

configuring Trusted File Locations 132–36

Excel Services 123–36

configuring 125–27

configuring Global Settings 129–31

configuring Trusted Data Connection libraries 131–32

harvesting URLs for Trusted Data Connection libraries and Report libraries 127–29

preparing to configure 123–25

configuring the Cube Building Service 141–51

creating a SQL login for the Service Account running Analysis Services 149–51

downloading the SQL Server Feature Pack components 141–42

installing the SQL Server Management Objects Collection 146–48

installing the SQL Server Native Client 142–45

creating an additional instance of Project Server 2010 171–80

configuring the new Project Server 2010 instance 173–74

creating an Excel Services Application for a new Project Server 2010 instance 174–75

pointing Data Connections to the new Secure Store Target Application for the new instance 176–80

setting optional SQL Server performance enhancements 151–52

testing Project Server functionality 153–71

creating a Project Server login account in Project Professional 2010 154–57

testing OLAP cube building 165–68

testing Project Professional with Project Server 2010 158–64

testing Project Web App connectivity 153

testing reporting functionality in the Business Intelligence Center 168–71

Preparing to Implement Project Server 2010 ....**21–36**

planning strategies for implementation success 27–36

understanding formulas for implementation disaster ....24–27 understanding the role of Project Management in an implementation..21–24

Project Center Views, creating in Project Web App..**585–88**

Project Detail Pages..**288, 289–306**

    creating and editing...296–304

    demonstration of Project Detail Pages functionality...289–96

    understanding..288

    using Project Detail Pages...300–304

Project Professional Versions, setting...**407–8**

Project Server 2010 Overview...**3–18**

    databases used in Project Server 2010...13

    EPM platform stack..9–10

    EPM platform tools..6–7

    installation types...11–12

    project communication life cycle...13–18

    what's new in Project Server 2010..3–6

Project Server Security..**477–541, 827–28**

    Active Directory Synchronization with security Groups...534–37

    adding non-Project Server users to Business Intelligence Center reports.....................................827–28

    Categories...499–508, 518–30

        creating a new Category...527–29

        deleting a Category...530

        managing Categories...518–27

        overview of Group and Category interaction...499–508

        understanding the built-in Categories..506–8

    Groups..499–508, 511–18

        creating a new Group..516–17

        deleting a Group..517–18

        managing Groups...511–16

        overview of Group and Category interaction...499–508

        understanding the built-in Groups..506

    overview...477

    Security Templates..530–34

        creating a new Security Template...531–33

        deleting a Security Template...534

        managing Security Templates..530–31

    setting organization permissions on the Project Web Access Permissions page............................477–91

    understanding permissions (Denied, Allowed, Not Allowed)..509–11

    understanding users vs. resources..491–92

User accounts...492–99

    creating a new User account..493–98

    deactivating a User account...499

    managing User accounts...492–93

Project Templates...*See* **Enterprise Project Templates**

Project Types..**213, 286–87, 314–19**

    creating and modifying...314–19

    interaction with the LifeCycle Management process...286–87

    introducing...213

Project Views, creating in Project Web App..**580–85**

Project Web Access...*See* **Project Web App**

Project Web App...**183–207**

    data grids, working with and manipulating..197–201

    logging into from another user's workstation..186

    Server Settings page..202–7

    understanding the user interface...183–86

    using Ribbon menus...188–97

    using the Administrator interface...202–7

    using the Quick Launch Menu..186

Project Workflow Settings, configuring...**328–29**

Publish a Project...**555**

Queue...**853–65**

    configuring the Queue...862–65

    troubleshooting Queue problems..857–62

    understanding..853–57

    using the Manage Queue Jobs page...857–61

Quick Launch menu...*See* **Project Web App**

Quick Launch menu, customizing...**431–36**

RBS lookup table...**224–26**

Reporting...**765–828**

    adding non-Project Server users to Business Intelligence Center reports.............827–28

    Business Intelligence Center overview...774–80

    Business Intelligence overview...765–68

    Excel Services overview for Business Intelligence reporting...................................780–81

    reporting architecture overview...768–74

        OLAP Database overview..769–74

        Reporting Database overview..768–69

SharePoint Dashboards 821–27

    creating a new SharePoint Dashboard page 821–27

    embedding Excel data into a SharePoint Dashboard page 823

  working with Microsoft Excel reports 782–821

    creating a custom Microsoft Excel report 796–99, 813–21

    modifying a custom Microsoft Excel report 800–813

    overview of built-in Microsoft Excel report templates 779

    overview of built-in Microsoft Excel reports 779

    overview of Excel Data Connection files 785–88

    viewing built-in Microsoft Excel reports 789–96

Resource Assignments Views, creating in Project Web App **588–92**

Resource Capacity settings **410**

Resource Center Views, creating in Project Web App **592–96**

Resource Plan Work Day settings **410–11**

Resources ....*See* **Enterprise Resource Pool**

Sample Workflow, adapting and working with **319–28**

Secure Store Service, configuring **136–41**

Security Templates **530–34**

  creating a new Security Template 531–33

  deleting a Security Template 534

  managing Security Templates 530–31

Server Settings page in Project Web App **202–7**

SharePoint **643–762**

  managing the SharePoint/Project Server 2010 connection 650–56

  overview of SharePoint functionality 643–50

  Project Sites 650–56

    bulk updating Project Sites 656

    Content Types, adding to a List 706–9

    creating a new Project Site Template 754–62

    creating and editing Project Site pages 734–44

    creating new Lists and Libraries 720–34

    creating, editing, and deleting SharePoint columns 657–74

    creating, editing, and deleting SharePoint views 674–92

    deleting a List 709

    deleting a Project Site 753–54

    Information Management Policy settings 715–18

    List Per Location View settings 704–6

List Targeting settings 700–701

List Validation settings 697–98

List Versioning settings 693–94

List Workflow settings 710–15

managing List and Library settings 692–720

managing Project Site provisioning 650–53

managing Project Sites 653–55

managing Site Settings 744–54

modifying Project Sites 656–762

saving a List as a template 709–10

SharePoint Model, understanding 644–50

SharePoint Dashboards, creating **821–27**

SharePoint Products Configuration Wizard, using **100–106**

SharePoint Server 2010 Preparation Tool, using **90–93**

Single Entry Mode, setting **449–50**

SQL Maintenance Plan **873–81**

SQL Server **74–75, 77–89, 123–25, 141–51**

creating a SQL login account for Excel Services 123–25

creating a SQL login for the Service Account running Analysis Services 149–51

downloading the SQL Server Feature Pack components 141–42

installing the SQL Server Management Objects Collection 146–48

installing the SQL Server Native Client 142–45

preparing SQL Server Analysis Services for Project Server 2010 86–89

preparing SQL Server for Project Server 2010 77–86

requirements for Project Server 2010 74–75

setting optional SQL Server performance enhancements 151–52

Status Manager, changing the Status Manager of an imported project **556–61**

Task Mode settings **411**

Task Progress Tracking Method, setting **454–63**

Tasks Page, customizing **466–72**

Team resources, creating **365–66**

Time and Task Tracking **439–73**

configuring Administrative Time 450–52

creating Line Classifications for Timesheets 446

customizing the Tasks page for your method of tracking progress 466–72

defining the Near Future Planning Window 462–63

defining Time Reporting Periods ....442–45 defininging Financial Periods 439–42

disabling the Timesheet functionality 452–54

overview 439

overview of task tracking methods 454–56

selecting the method for tracking task progress 454–63

setting Single Entry Mode 449–50

setting up the Timesheet page 463–66

specifying Timesheet Settings 447–50

tips for tracking progress 472–73

Time Reporting Periods, defining **442–45**

Timesheet Page, setting up **463–66**

Timesheet Periods .... *See* **Time Reporting Periods or Time and Task Tracking**

Timesheet Settings, specifying **447–50**

User Accounts **492–99**

creating a new User account 493–98

deactivating a User account 499

managing 492–93

Views **567–640, 674–92**

overview 567–68

Project Professional 2010 views 614–40

creating custom views in Project Professional 2010 619–40

overview 614–15

working with the Enterprise Global file 615–19

Project Web App views 567–614

creating custom Project Web App views 579–614

creating a custom Portfolio Analyses view 609–12

creating a custom Portfolio Analysis Project Selection view 613–14

creating a Project Center view 585–88

creating a Project View 580–85

creating a Resource Assignments view 588–92

creating a Resource Center view 592–96

modifying the Assignment Details view 596–600

modifying the My Assignments view 596–600

modifying the Timesheet view 608–9

creating Gantt Chart Formats 568–72

creating Grouping formats 572–75

managing, copying, editing, and deleting PWA views 575–78

SharePoint views .... 674–92 creating, editing, and deleting views in Project Sites..674–92

Work resources, creating 348–62

Workflow management ....*See* **Lifecycle Management**

Workflow Phases, configuring..306–7

Workflow Stages, configuring..307–11

Workflows, restarting or changing..850–53

You may also need these books!

Buy direct from our website or your favorite bookseller

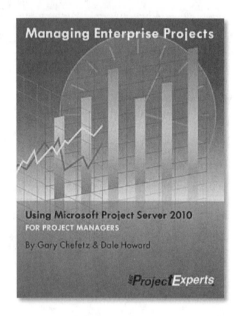

Managing Enterprise Projects Using Microsoft Project Server 2010

ISBN 978-1-934240-11-3

This is an unprecedented learning guide and reference for project managers who use the Microsoft EPM platform. Our goal in writing this training/reference manual is to help you build on your knowledge of the stand-alone tool by mastering the enterprise project management environment. Follow our best practices to success and heed our warnings to avoid the pitfalls.

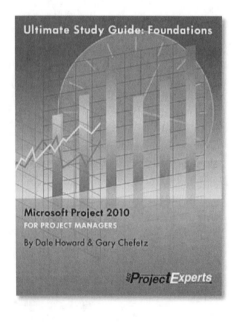

Ultimate Study Guide: Foundations Microsoft Project 2010

ISBN 978-1-934240-13-7

A comprehensive learning system for Microsoft Project 2010. The latest from the authoring team of Gary L. Chefetz and Dale A. Howard, is based on MSProjectExperts successful courseware series. Ultimate Study Guide combines a field-tested learning approach with in-depth reference to deliver the most comprehensive combined leaning/reference manual ever published for Microsoft Project.

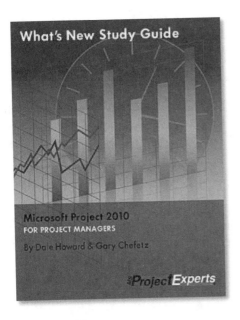

What's New Study Guide Microsoft Project 2010

ISBN 978-1-934240-16-8

A learning guide to get you up to speed with the revolutionary new features in Microsoft Office Project 2010. Learn how to use manually scheduled tasks, the team planner, and the new user interface. The content of this book derives from the Ultimate Study Guide: Foundations, Microsoft Project 2010.

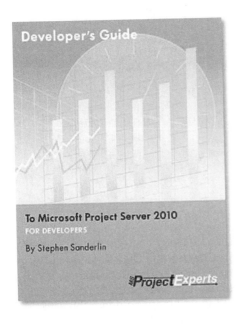

Developer's Guide To Microsoft Project Server 2010

ISBN 978-1-934240-08-3

The first book covering development for Project Server. A complete guide to the PSI, including sample code that you can use to build your own solutions.

msProjectExperts provides a complete line of Microsoft Project and Project Server courseware covering every role in the enterprise. Each book has its own Instructor documentation and file downloads to support classroom training or self-study. Contact us at (646) 736-1688 for more information or visit our website at:

http://www.msprojectexperts.com

CONSULTING

TRAINING

BOOKS AND COURSEWARE

SUPPORT

You deserve the best, do not settle for less! MSProjectExperts is a Microsoft Certified Partner specializing in Microsoft Office Project Server since its first release. This is not something we "also do," it's all we do. Microsoft recognizes our consultants as being among the world's top experts with three Microsoft Project MVPs on staff.

MSProjectExperts

90 John Street, Suite 404

New York, NY 10038

(646) 736-1688

To learn more about MSProjectExperts:

http://www.msprojectexperts.com

For the best Project and Project Server training available:

http://www.projectservertraining.com

To learn more about our books:

http://www.projectserverbooks.com

For FAQs and other free support:

http://www.projectserverexperts.com